Communications in Computer and Information Science 709

Commenced Publication in 2007
Founding and Former Series Editors:
Alfredo Cuzzocrea, Dominik Ślęzak, and Xiaokang Yang

K.C. Santosh · Mallikarjun Hangarge
Vitoantonio Bevilacqua · Atul Negi (Eds.)

Recent Trends in Image Processing and Pattern Recognition

First International Conference, RTIP2R 2016
Bidar, India, December 16–17, 2016
Revised Selected Papers

 Springer

Editors
K.C. Santosh
The University of South Dakota
Vermillion, SD 57069
USA

Mallikarjun Hangarge
Karnatak Arts, Science and Commerce
 College
Bidar
India

Vitoantonio Bevilacqua
Polytecnico di Bari
Bari
Italy

Atul Negi
University of Hyderabad
Hyderabad
India

ISSN 1865-0929   ISSN 1865-0937 (electronic)
Communications in Computer and Information Science
ISBN 978-981-10-4858-6   ISBN 978-981-10-4859-3   (eBook)
DOI 10.1007/978-981-10-4859-3

Library of Congress Control Number: 2017939716

Printed on acid-free paper

This Springer imprint is published by Springer Nature
The registered company is Springer Nature Singapore Pte Ltd.
The registered company address is: 152 Beach Road, #21-01/04 Gateway East, Singapore 189721, Singapore

Preface

It is our great pleasure to introduce the collection of research papers in the *Communication in Computer and Information Science* (CCIS) Springer series from the first International Conference on Recent Trends in Image Processing and Pattern Recognition (RTIP2R). The RTIP2R conference event took place at the Karnatak Arts, Science and Commerce College, Bidar, Karnataka, India, during December 16–17, 2016. The conference was sponsored by Karnatak Arts, Science and Commerce College, Bidar, Karnataka, India, and in part by INNS, India Regional Chapter.

As announced in the call for paper, RTIP2R attracted current and/or recent research on image processing, pattern recognition, and computer vision with several different applications such as document understanding, biometrics, and medical imaging. Altogether, we have received 99 submissions and accepted 39 papers based on our thorough review reports. We followed a double-blind submission policy and therefore the review process was extremely solid. We also made the authors aware of plagiarism, and we rejected a few papers even after making review reports (with acceptance in the first phase). With 39 papers at the conference, this event was found to be a great platform bringing research scientists, academics, and industry practitioners throughout the world (not just limited to India). We categorized the papers into five different tracks: (a) document analysis, (b) pattern analysis and machine learning, (c) image processing, (d) biomedical image analysis, and (e) biometrics. In addition to regular submissions, to enhance the proceedings quality, nine papers were invited from established and well-known research scientists and professors in the research community. Not surprisingly, as for regular submissions, we made thorough review reports for invited articles to make sure of the quality of the work. Therefore, not considering the invited research papers, our acceptance rate is 33.31%.

We also selected the best papers based on the review reports, review scores, and presentation at the conference, and provided authors an opportunity to publish their extended works in the *International Journal of Computer Vision and Image Processing* (IJCVIP), IGI global.

The conference event was full of new ideas including keynote speeches. We were honored and pleased to have five keynote speeches that were focused on health-care informatics (medical image analysis), document understanding, bioinformatics, and machine learning.

March 2017

K.C. Santosh
Mallikarjun Hangarge
Vitoantonio Bevilacqua
Atul Negi

Organization

Executive Committee

Chief Patron

Basawaraj G. Patil	KRE Society, India
S.R. Niranjana	Gulbarga University, India
A.H. Rajasab	Tumkur University, India
K. Chidananda Gowda	Kuvempu University, India

Patron

B.G. Shetkar	KRE Society, India
Basawaraj Jabshetty	KRE Society, India
Basavaraj Patil	KRE Society, India

Co-patron

B.S. Biradar	KASCC, India
S.V. Juja	KASCC, India

Honorary Chairs

P. Nagabhushan	University of Mysore, India
B.B. Chaudhuri	ISI Kolkata, India
Rajkumar Buyya	University of Melbourne, Australia

Advisory Committee

Rangchar Kasturi	University of South Florida, USA
Ishwar K. Sethi	Oakland University, USA
Sargur N. Srihari	CEDAR, USA
K.R. Rao	University of Texas at Arlington, Texas
Umapada Pal	ISI Kolkata, India
Arun Agarwal	University of Hyderabad, India
P.S. Hiremath	Gulbarga University, India
Suryakanth Gangashetty	IIIT Hyderabad, India
Deepak Garg	Thapar University, Punjab
B.M. Mehtre	IRDBT Hyderabad, India
Karbhari Kale	BAMU, India
Abdulkadir Sengur	Firat University, Turkey
Suresha	University of Mysore, India

Program Committee

General Chairs

Jean-Marc Ogier	Université de La Rochelle, France
Laurent Wendling	Université Paris Descartes, France
B.V. Dhandra	Gulbarga University, India
G. Hemantha Kumar	University of Mysore, India
D.S. Guru	University of Mysore, India

Program Chairs

K.C. Santosh	University of South Dakota, USA
Mallikarjun Hangarge	Karnatak College, India
Vitoantonio Bevilacqua	Polytechnic of Bari, Italy
Atul Negi	University of Hyderabad, India

Publicity Chairs

Manjunath M.S.	Central University of Kerala, India
V.T. Humbe	SRTMU, India
S.S. Showhan	SRTMU, India
Shivanand Rumma	Gulbarga University, India
Ravindran Hegadi	Solapur University, India
Shivanand Gornale	RCU, India
M.A. Jabbar	Muffakham Jha College of Engineering and Technology, India

Publicity Chairs (International)

Szilard Vajda	Central Washington University, USA
P. Shivakumara	University of Malaya, Malaysia
Bunyarit Uyyanonvara	Thammasat University, Thailand

Local Support

Srikanth Doddamani	Karnatak College, India
Rajmohan Pardeshi	Karnatak College India

Additional Reviewers

S. Agarwal	V. Bevilacqua	S. Chowhan
S. Angadi	V. Bhateja	M. Coustaty
K.V. Arya	U. Bhattacharya	N. Das
B.H. Shekar	K. Biswas	A. Desai
V.K. Banga	E. Borovikov	N. Dey
P. Bannerjee	M.R. Bouguelia	B. Dhandra
S. Barrat	A. Choudhary	T.H. Do

A. Ekbal
U. Garain
S. Gornale
D.S. Guru
M. Hangarge
M. Hasegawa
R. Hegadi
P. Hiremath
V. Humbe
K. Kale
V. Kamat
A. Khare
R. Kumar
M.M. Luqman
V. Mankar
R. Manza
A. Martin
J. Meerja
B. M. Mehtre
I. Methasate
G. Mukarambi

H. Mukherjee
P. Mukherji
S. Naik
N. Nain
A. Negi
A. Nigam
S. Pal
P.B. Pati
J. Peters
S. Phadikar
G. Rajput
K. Roy
P.P. Roy
S. Manjunath
J.-P. Salmon
K.C. Santosh
P. Shivakumara
Md O. Sk
J.H.S. Azuela
G. Subrahmanyam
B.N. Subudhi

T. Thasleema
S. Vajda
J. Peters
J. Humberto
B. Uyyanonvara
H. Cecotti
A. Danti
B.N. Subudhi
S. Agarwal
K. Vijayakumar
A.J.S. Azad
D. Gopal
S. Shivashankar
I. Humanabad
C.J. Prabhakar
J. Pujari
S.S. Patil
A. Agrawal
S. Prakash
K.V. Arya
R. Rajesh

Contents

Pattern Analysis and Machine Learning

Image Analysis

Biomedical Image Analysis

Document Analysis

Complex and Composite Graphical Symbol Recognition and Retrieval: A Quick Review

K.C. Santosh[(✉)]

Department of Computer Science, The University of South Dakota,
414 E Clark Street, Vermillion, SD 57069, USA
santosh.kc@usd.edu

Abstract. One of the key difficulties in graphics recognition domain is to work on complex and composite symbol recognition, retrieval and spotting. This paper covers a quick view on complex and composite symbol recognition, which is inspired by real-world industrial problem. Considering it as a pattern recognition problem, three different approaches: statistical, structural and syntactic are taken into account. It includes fundamental concepts or techniques and research standpoints or directions derived by a real-world application.

Keywords: Symbol recognition · Complex and composite symbols · Statistical · Structural and syntactic approaches · Document processing

1 Introduction

1.1 Overview

This paper substantially covers contributions made by the author (PhD thesis, 2011 at the INRIA Nancy Grand Est, Université de Lorraine [52]). Starting with the lineal and/or obvious isolated symbol, the paper reaches the research standpoints that were contributed by focussing on Fresh FP-6 Strep European project. Therefore, this view may not cover the whole literature, we have in graphics recognition community. At this moment, a thorough review can be found in [37, 63, 64].

1.2 What Are Graphical Symbols?

Graphical symbols are referred to as visual images or designs, interpreting information about the context. They are generally 2D-graphical shapes, including their composition in the highest level of conceptual information. Overall, it plays a crucial role in a variety of applications such as automatic interpretation and recognition of circuit diagrams [22, 44], engineering drawings and architectural drawings [16, 20, 35, 79], line drawings [81], musical notations [46], maps [51], mathematical expressions [6], and optical characters [28, 59, 60, 84]. To avoid possible confusions, in this paper, other works – in the framework of graphics recognition – such as logo detection/spotting and music scores are not taken in this study.

© Springer Nature Singapore Pte Ltd. 2017
K.C. Santosh et al. (Eds.): RTIP2R 2016, CCIS 709, pp. 3–15, 2017.
DOI: 10.1007/978-981-10-4859-3_1

1.3   Organization of the Paper

The remainder of the paper is organized as follows. Section 2 deals with the position of graphical symbol recognition in framework of document processing. It also includes regular contests (primarily organized together with the international workshops) and the real-world issues whether they have covered. Section 3 reviews research standpoints by categorizing them into three different approaches: statistical, structural and syntactic, and personal views based on more than a decade of experience. It also includes possible use of hybrid approaches (taking two or more approaches to develop) for graphics recognition. Section 4 concludes the paper by highlighting remarks.

2   Document Image Processing (DIP)

2.1   Graphical Symbol Recognition: Where Does It Lie in DIP?

Document analysis or processing is mainly related to texts and graphics. It includes text and or graphics separation, localization and recognition [24]. According to [42], document analysis is related to document image analysis (DIA) since both research works have been concerned with document image interpretation. In a similar manner, Kasturi et al. [31] categorize document image analysis into two domains:

(1) textual processing and
(2) graphics processing.

In both articles [31,42], the basic tasks are image segmentation, layout understanding and graphics recognition. Graphical symbol recognition, in particular, has a long history since the 70's, and it is considered as the core part of graphical document image analysis and recognition systems. In 1998 [70,71], a prominent researcher has made a statement: 'none of these methods works' in general. Since then, it has been actively extended [17,36,71,73,74]. Very recently, the importance and the usage of graphics recognition have been reported [17,37,63,64].

Graphics are often combined with text, illustration, and color. Therefore, in document image processing, graphical symbols, for instance, convey crucial cues about the context in comparison to texts. Beside generic approaches, text recognition is distinct from symbol recognition, even though their boundaries are not obvious. Thus, their solutions complement each other [7,24].

The recognition of graphical symbols or any meaningful shapes has been the subject of numerous reviewed research articles [7,18,29,30,35,38,40]. Most of these proposed systems are roughly described using the following two major units: (1) data acquisition and preprocessing; and (2) data representation and recognition. The techniques used in data acquisition and preprocessing vary since they are problem dependent. Text/graphics separation aims at segmenting document into two layers so that one can focus on regions-of-interest, where graphical symbols lie. The usefulness of text/graphics separation can be found in [67]. Graphical symbols are represented either in the form of feature vectors by estimating the overall shape or in more structured forms (i.e., graphs) by using meaningful primitives that are extracted from the whole symbol. Again, primitive selection tools are application dependent. As a consequence, matching techniques follow the way we represent symbols, to be used in the decision process. In general, a good data representation is assumed to be compact and discriminant, and minimizes the intra-class distance and maximizes the inter-class distance [36]. Existing approaches, specifically those based on feature based matching, can mainly be split into three different categories: statistical, structural and syntactic (see Sect. 3).

2.2 Do Regular Contests Hit Real-World Issues?

This section aims to include how far regular contests cover real-world issues (or problems). Since 1915, international association of pattern recognition (IAPR) sponsored graphics recognition (GREC) workshops, supported by technical committee 10 (TC-10: http://iapr-tc10.univ-lr.fr/) have been organized together with several contests: graphical symbol recognition, retrieval and spotting. The primary objective of the GREC contests is to evaluate the state-of-the-art of graphics recognition techniques and to generate performance evaluation tools and datasets for future research [13–15,48]. Figure 1 shows a few model symbols [26,78]. Beside several other contests, in recent years, researchers figured out the significance of 'end-to-end document analysis benchmarking' and 'open resource sharing repository' to advance as well as to facilitate fair comparison [33,34].

Considering a real-world problem, symbol recognition is not straightforward as shown in Fig. 1. In general, common applications are recognition and localization (in some cases, we call it - spotting) of graphical symbols in electronic documents, in architectural floor plans (see Fig. 2), wiring diagrams and network drawings [15,36,52]. More specifically, in this paper, a challenging problem has been addressed (see Fig. 3), where the dataset is composed of a variety of symbols such as lineal, complex and composite. These samples (entitled as FRESH dataset) are taken from [76]. The symbols may look either very similar in shape – and only differ by slight details – or completely different from a visual point of view [25,50,75]. Symbols may also be composed of other known and significant symbols and need

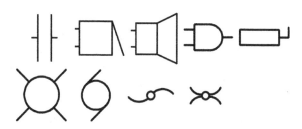

Fig. 1. Graphical symbols. An example illustrating lineal and fully isolated symbols [26].

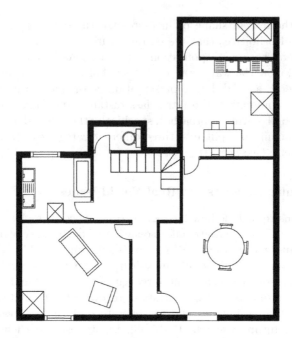

Fig. 2. Several different graphical symbols, appearing in the floor plans [15]. An example of how one can go for symbol spotting.

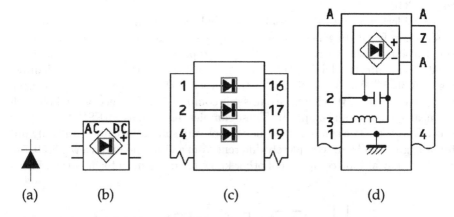

Fig. 3. An example of (a) a query and (b–d) graphical symbol/element spotting. This also illustrates the complexity of the FRESH dataset [52,76], starting with an isolated graphical symbol (moving from left to right). This example shows how the known and significant part can be spotted based on the applied query.

not necessarily be connected. For such complex and composite symbols, as before, an isolated query symbol is applied not only to recognize similar symbols from the dataset, but also to detect known and significant parts (graphical elements) which are associated with the query symbol. Therefore, we are not just limited to symbol recognition problem. We also need to spot the visual elements (i.e., meaningful parts or regions). Besides, it is expected to see how two different symbols are similar to what extent. In the literature, the latter issue has been considered as the most challenging problem. On the whole, we refer to this task as either the parts or the whole graphical symbol recognition [15, 36, 39, 43, 49, 52]. Such a problem requires strong knowledge about how we can represent graphical symbols and recognize, detect or spot them.

3   Research Standpoints

In general, the whole symbol recognition process is based on either

(1) matching features between a query and dataset symbols or
(2) comparing decomposed parts (or meaningful regions/primitives) such as lines and arcs as well as the relations between them.

These are commonly categorized into three different approaches: statistical, structural and syntactic. In most of the cases, methods are particularly suited for isolated line symbols, not for composite symbols connected to a complex environment [10, 11, 35, 36].

3.1   Statistical Approaches

The techniques used in statistical approaches fairly computes the differences between two feature vectors [10, 41]. An overview of the performance of the most commonly used shape descriptors (refer to the statistical approaches) for symbol representation is provided in [80]. Global shape representation is widely used because of its implementation simplicity since it does not require extra pre-processing and segmentation, in contrast to local pattern representation [1, 85]. For more details about shape and symbol recognition, we refer to the works presented in [10, 11, 69], where usefulness of the shape descriptors for document analysis and a collection of techniques employed for graphical symbols recognition have been reported. Most methods are particularly suited for isolated line symbols, not for composed symbols connected to a complex environment [11, 36]. In statistical approaches, global signal-based descriptors [4, 32, 66, 84–86] are usually quite fault tolerant to image distortions, since they tend to filter out small change in details.

For a thorough shape analysis, in [82], authors computed a histogram for every pixel to figure out the distribution of constraints among the other pixels. These histograms are then statistically integrated to form a feature vector. In [87], authors proposed a similarity assessment of graphical symbols based on Kullback-Leibler divergence, where symbols are represented as 2D kernel densities. In a similar way, in [21], the authors deal with the changes in appearance (i.e., shape) from which these types of symbols differ. In [3], authors describe another framework to learn a model of shape variability in a set of patterns. Further, the Radon transform (RT) has also been widely used to globally describe the shape of any pattern [12,66]. Motivated by this, the histogram of the RT has been used instead of compressing them (i.e., profiles) into a single vector [65], assuming that the studied patterns are equal in size. We remind the readers that the RTs are essentially a set of parametrized histograms. Therefore, in contrast to [65], in [54,57], authors used dynamic time warping (DTW) to align every histogram for each projecting angle to absorb varying histogram sizes resulting from image signal variations. In a recent PhD thesis [27], author developed the bridge between the literature of sparse representation and the visual vocabulary construction by apply the learned dictionary algorithm for learning a visual vocabulary based on local descriptors of symbols. These technique are, unfortunately, inappropriate in case where symbols are composed of other known and significant symbols (need not necessarily be connected) as well as texts (see Fig. 3).

3.2   Structural Approaches and Possible Integration with Statistical Features

Structural approaches are particularly used when symbols are decomposed into several meaningful graphical elements [20,47,52], for instance. Their interpretations, however, depend on the studied application as well as on their specific local context. Therefore, primitive extraction and symbol recognition, on the whole, are the key steps toward understanding and interpreting content within a document. They mainly include embedded graph based classification problems like attributed relational graphs (ARG) [39], region adjacency graphs (RAG) [35] and constraint networks [2], in general. Structural techniques are able to handle all types of symbols (e.g., isolated, composite), and have a powerful relational representation. However, they suffer from intense computational complexity due to the general NP-hard problem of sub-graph matching resulting from the variation of graph structure with the level of noise, occlusion, distortion *etc.*

In case of composite documents (wiring diagram, a real-world industrial problem, see Fig. 3) that contain textual and graphical elements, one needs to be able to extract and formalize the links that exist between the images and the surrounding text, in order to exploit the information embedded in those documents. Therefore, correct extraction, representation of both visual data, textual and graphical structures, and organization are the first steps towards further automated knowledge, information discovery and information retrieval or data mining on more complex data than just text. Within this context, we primarily focus on three main items:

(1) the extraction of visual elements (vocabulary) that compose an image [47];
(2) the expression of visual relations between the elements;
(3) knowledge discovery, formal learning techniques and classification using the vocabulary and relations mentioned above, including vocabulary shape analysis.

Having the aforementioned framework, we have tested the use spatial relational signatures between the possible pairs of labeled vocabulary types such as *circles* and *corners*. These are basically used as a basis for building an attributed relational graph (ARG) that fully describes the symbol [56, 61]. Thanks to our labeling of attribute types, corresponding relation alignments are possible between the two graphs while avoiding the general NP-hard graph matching problem. Further, very recently, we have introduced a new concept named bag-of-relations (BoRs) for symbol recognition, retrieval and spotting [62]. The key characteristic of the technique is to use topological relation information to categorize them in terms of bags and to guide directional relations. The method has been extended to a variety of datasets (symbols) in the domain. Further, usefulness of the method for symbol spotting and for user-friendly symbol retrieval applications has been attested.

Again, recognizing isolated symbols does not solve the real-world problem (wiring diagram, for instance), since symbols may appear either very similar in shape – and only differ by slight details – or completely different from a visual point of view [25, 50, 75]. In such a case, statistical signatures using shape descriptors, for instance, do not perform well because they take global appearance into account, and on the other side, usability of structural approaches may be limited due to intense computational complexity. In such a context, addressing the interest of integrating two different worlds would be a new scope of the work. Considering both approaches: structural and statistical, we have addressed the use of their best possible efficient combinations [52, 58], which has been highlighted in the GREC-2010 workshop [74]:

> '... the recurring wish for methods capable of efficiently combining structural and statistical methods' and 'the very structural and spatial nature of the information we work with makes structural methods quite natural in the community.'

In [56], the method is primarily based on the spatio-structural description of visual 'vocabulary'. But, it lacks the information about their shape features. Therefore, keeping the ARG based symbol description as reported in [56], shape signatures are integrated in two different ways to improve the performance. First, shape signatures are for labeling vertices [55]. Second, shape features are applied only to the vocabulary which show significant shape variations, and are grouped them via unsupervised clustering [58]. In both cases, major set of well-known state-of-the-shape descriptors are integrated with spatial relations. Overall, we bring an attention to the use of a hybrid approach in symbol recognition, and try to avoid the shortcomings of each of them: structural and statistical.

The problem can further be extended to symbol spotting, but one can view this as a kind of retrieval [15, 45, 49, 62, 68], which is guided by user queries. Additionally, the recognition/retrieval process can be made with the help of local descriptors like scale invariant feature transform (SIFT) and with the use of techniques like bag-of-features so that either primitive or region extraction (segmentation) can be avoided. The question always remains the same, 'what approach does what (i.e., performance) in which context?'.

3.3   Syntactic Approaches

The techniques based on graph grammar will be more suitable to search symbols in technical documents where information is close to a feature vector description that follows composition rules of primitives [8,9,19,23,53,77,83].

In the earlier framework (see Sect. 3.2 in second paragraph), very interestingly, we have presented the use of formal learning techniques to automatically learn non-trivial descriptions of symbols [53]. It means that we have transformed the vocabulary sets and their possible relations that exist between them into a first-order logic (FOL) description for a complete image. This representation is then used as an input to an inductive logic programming (ILP) solver, in order to deduce non obvious characteristics that may lead to a more semantic related recognition process. Considering the experience we have so far, the idea is appropriate for classifying a set of symbols (images) characterizing common behavior with respect to another set of symbols (images) or counter samples. But by definition, even though the reported concept in [53] can be extended to any image synthesis problem (for different application domain). It, however, is challenging to transform statistical signatures (quantified values) to the closer semantics.

4   Remarks

No doubt, graphics recognition has an extremely rich state-of-the-art literature in symbol recognition and localization [5,11,17,36]. They are limited to solve specific problems, motivated by the limited posed by industrial partners. This means that major state-of-the-art methods for symbol recognition, do not conclude on the existence of a set of generic methods that can yield the best results, even though they are easy to implement (with fewer parameters) and are reproducible. This has been seen on three different approaches: statistical, structural and syntactic. Besides, very similar statement has been reported in [74], where the author pointed out: '*which features distinguish graphics recognition from general pattern recognition problems?*'. Therefore, there still exists growing interest in graphics recognition domain.

References

1. Adam, S., Ogier, J.M., Cariou, C., Mullot, R., Labiche, J., Gardes, J.: Symbol and character recognition: application to engineering drawings. Int. J. Doc. Anal. Recogn. **3**(2), 89–101 (2000)
2. Ah-Soon, C., Tombre, K.: Architectural symbol recognition using a network of constraints. Pattern Recogn. Lett. **22**(2), 231–248 (2001)
3. Almazán, J., Fornés, A., Valveny, E.: A non-rigid appearance model for shape description and recognition. Pattern Recogn. **45**(9), 3105–3113 (2012)
4. Belongie, S., Malik, J., Puzicha, J.: Shape matching and object recognition using shape contexts. IEEE Trans. Pattern Anal. Mach. Intell. **24**(4), 509–522 (2002)
5. Bunke, H., Wang, P.S.P. (eds.): Handbook of Character Recognition and Document Image Analysis. World Scientific, Singapore (1997)

6. Chaudhuri, B.B., Garain, U.: An approach for recognition and interpretation of mathematical expressions in printed document. Pattern Anal. Appl. **3**(2), 120–131 (2000)
7. Chhabra, A.K.: Graphic symbol recognition: an overview. In: Proceedings of 2nd International Workshop on Graphics Recognition, Nancy, France, pp. 244–252, August 1997
8. Claus, V., Ehrig, H., Rozenberg, G. (eds.): Graph-Grammars and Their Applications to Computer Science and Biology. LNCS, vol. 73. Springer, Heidelberg (1979)
9. Cordella, L.P., Foggia, P., Genna, R., Vento, M.: Prototyping structural descriptions: an inductive learning approach. In: Amin, A., Dori, D., Pudil, P., Freeman, H. (eds.) SSPR /SPR 1998. LNCS, vol. 1451, pp. 339–348. Springer, Heidelberg (1998). doi:10.1007/BFb0033252
10. Cordella, L.P., Vento, M.: Symbol and shape recognition. In: Proceedings of 3rd International Workshop on Graphics Recognition, Jaipur, India, pp. 179–186, September 1999
11. Cordella, L.P., Vento, M.: Symbol recognition in documents: a collection of techniques? Int. J. Doc. Anal. Recogn. **3**(2), 73–88 (2000)
12. Deans, S.R.: Applications of the Radon Transform. Wiley Interscience Publications, New York (1983)
13. Delalandre, M., Ramel, J.-Y., Sidere, N.: A semi-automatic groundtruthing framework for performance evaluation of symbol recognition and spotting systems. In: Kwon, Y.-B., Ogier, J.-M. (eds.) GREC 2011. LNCS, vol. 7423, pp. 163–172. Springer, Heidelberg (2013). doi:10.1007/978-3-642-36824-0_16
14. Delalandre, M., Valveny, E., Lladós, J.: Performance evaluation of symbol recognition and spotting systems: an overview. In: Kise, K., Sako, H. (eds.) Proceedings of International Workshop on Document Analysis Systems, pp. 497–505. IEEE Computer Society (2008)
15. Delalandre, M., Valveny, E., Pridmore, T., Karatzas, D.: Generation of synthetic documents for performance evaluation of symbol recognition and spotting systems. Int. J. Doc. Anal. Recogn. **13**(3), 187–207 (2010)
16. Devaux, P.M., Lysak, D.B., Kasturi, R.: A complete system for the intelligent interpretation of engineering drawings. Int. J. Doc. Anal. Recogn. **2**(2/3), 120–131 (1999)
17. Doermann, D., Tombre, K.: Handbook of Document Image Processing and Recognition. Springer, London (2014)
18. Doermann, D.S.: An introduction to vectorization and segmentation. In: Tombre, K., Chhabra, A.K. (eds.) GREC 1997. LNCS, vol. 1389, pp. 1–8. Springer, Heidelberg (1998). doi:10.1007/3-540-64381-8_34
19. Dori, D., Pnueli, A.: The grammar of dimensions in machine drawings. Computer Vision, Graphics and Image Processing **42**, 1–18 (1988)
20. Dosch, P., Tombre, K., Ah-Soon, C., Masini, G.: A complete system for analysis of architectural drawings. Int. J. Doc. Anal. Recogn. **3**(2), 102–116 (2000)
21. Escalera, S., Fornés, A., Pujol, O., Lladós, J., Radeva, P.: Circular blurred shape model for multiclass symbol recognition. IEEE Trans. Syst. Man Cybern. Part B Cybern. **41**(2), 497–506 (2011)
22. Feng, G., Viard-Gaudin, C., Sun, Z.: On-line hand-drawn electric circuit diagram recognition using 2D dynamic programming. Pattern Recogn. **42**(12), 3215–3223 (2009)
23. Flasiński, M.: Characteristics of edNLC-graph grammar for syntactic pattern recognition. Comput. Vis. Graph. Image Process. **47**, 1–21 (1989)

24. Fletcher, L.A., Kasturi, R.: A robust algorithm for text string separation from mixed text/graphics images. IEEE Trans. Pattern Anal. Mach. Intell. **10**(6), 910–918 (1988)
25. FRESH: Final report on symbol recognition with evaluation of performances. http://www.aero-scratch.net/fresh.html. Deliverable 2.4.2.-FP6-516059
26. GREC: International symbol recognition contest at GREC2003 (2003). http://www.cvc.uab.es/grec2003/SymRecContest/
27. Ha, D.T.: Sparse representation over learned dictionary for document analysis. Ph.D. thesis, LORIA, Université de Lorraine, France (2014)
28. Heutte, L., Nosary, A., Paquet, T.: A multiple agent architecture for handwritten text recognition. Pattern Recogn. **37**(4), 665–674 (2004)
29. Jain, A.K., Duin, R.P.W., Mao, J.: Statistical pattern recognition: a review. IEEE Trans. Pattern Anal. Mach. Intell. **22**(1), 4–37 (2000)
30. Kasturi, R., Raman, R., Chennubhotla, C., O'Gorman, L.: document image analysis: an overview of techniques for graphics recognition. In: Pre-proceedings of IAPR Workshop on Syntactic and Structural Pattern Recognition, Murray Hill, NJ (USA), pp. 192–230 (1990)
31. Kasturi, R., O'Gorman, L., Govindaraju, V.: Document image analysis: a primer. Charact. Recogn. **27**(1), 3–22 (2002)
32. Kim, W.Y., Kim, Y.S.: A region-based shape descriptor using Zernike moments. Sig. Process. Image Commun. **16**(1–2), 95–102 (2000)
33. Lamiroy, B., Lopresti, D.P.: An open architecture for end-to-end document analysis benchmarking. In: International Conference on Document Analysis and Recognition, pp. 42–47 (2011)
34. Lamiroy, B., Lopresti, D.P., Korth, H.F., Heflin, J.: How carefully designed open resource sharing can help and expand document analysis research. In: Document Recognition and Retrieval XVIII, Part of the IS&T-SPIE Electronic Imaging Symposium
35. Lladós, J., Martí, E., Villanueva, J.J.: Symbol recognition by error-tolerant subgraph matching between region adjacency graphs. IEEE Trans. Pattern Anal. Mach. Intell. **23**(10), 1137–1143 (2001)
36. Lladós, J., Valveny, E., Sánchez, G., Martí, E.: Symbol recognition: current advances and perspectives. In: Blostein, D., Kwon, Y.-B. (eds.) GREC 2001. LNCS, vol. 2390, pp. 104–128. Springer, Heidelberg (2002). doi:10.1007/3-540-45868-9_9
37. Lladós, J., Rusiñol, M.: Graphics Recognition Techniques, pp. 489–521. Springer, London (2014)
38. Loncaric, S.: A survey of shape analysis techniques. Pattern Recogn. **31**(8), 983–1001 (1998)
39. Luqman, M.M.: fuzzy multilevel graph embedding for recognition, indexing and retrieval of graphic document images. Ph.D. thesis, Francois Rabelais University of Tours France and Autonoma University of Barcelona Spain (2012)
40. Marshall, S.: Review of shape coding techniques. Image Vision Comput. **7**(4), 281–294 (1989)
41. Müller, S., Rigoll, G.: Engineering drawing database retrieval using statistical pattern spotting techniques. In: Proceedings of 3rd International Workshop on Graphics Recognition, Jaipur, India, pp. 219–226, September 1999
42. Nagy, G.: Twenty years of document image analysis in PAMI. IEEE Trans. Pattern Anal. Mach. Intell. **22**(1), 38–62 (2000)
43. Nayef, N.: Geomatric-based symbol spotting and retrieval in technical line drawings. Ph.D. thesis, University of Kaiserslautern, Germany (2012)

44. Okazaki, A., Kondo, T., Mori, K., Tsunekawa, S., Kawamoto, E.: An automatic circuit diagram reader with loop-structure-based symbol recognition. IEEE Trans. Pattern Anal. Mach. Intell. **10**(3), 331–341 (1988)
45. Qureshi, R.J., Ramel, J.-Y., Barret, D., Cardot, H.: Spotting symbols in line drawing images using graph representations. In: Liu, W., Lladós, J., Ogier, J.-M. (eds.) GREC 2007. LNCS, vol. 5046, pp. 91–103. Springer, Heidelberg (2008). doi:10.1007/978-3-540-88188-9_10
46. Rebelo, A., Capela, G., Cardoso, J.S.: Optical recognition of music symbols: a comparative study. Int. J. Doc. Anal. Recogn. **13**(1), 19–31 (2010)
47. Rendek, J., Masini, G., Dosch, P., Tombre, K.: The search for genericity in graphics recognition applications: design issues of the Qgar software system. In: Marinai, S., Dengel, A.R. (eds.) DAS 2004. LNCS, vol. 3163, pp. 366–377. Springer, Heidelberg (2004). doi:10.1007/978-3-540-28640-0_35
48. Rusiñol, M., Lladós, J.: A performance evaluation protocol for symbol spotting systems in terms of recognition and location indices. Int. J. Doc. Anal. Recogn. **12**(2), 83–96 (2009)
49. Rusiñol, M., Lladós, J.: Symbol Spotting in Digital Libraries: Focused Retrieval over Graphic-rich Document Collections. Springer, London (2010)
50. Salmon, J.P.: Reconnaissance de Symboles Complexes. Ph.D. thesis, Institut National Polytechnique de Lorraine (2008)
51. Samet, H., Soffer, A.: MARCO: map retrieval by content. IEEE Trans. Pattern Anal. Mach. Intell. **18**(8), 783–798 (1996)
52. Santosh, K.C.: Graphics recognition using spatial relations and shape analysis. Ph.D. thesis, INRIA - Institut National Polytechnique de Lorraine, Université de Lorraine, November 2011
53. Santosh, K.C., Lamiroy, B., Ropers, J.P.: Inductive logic programming for symbol recognition. In: Proceedings of International Conference on Document Analysis and Recognition, pp. 1330–1334. IEEE Computer Society (2009)
54. K.C., S., Lamiroy, B., Wendling, L.: DTW for matching radon features: a pattern recognition and retrieval method. In: Blanc-Talon, J., Kleihorst, R., Philips, W., Popescu, D., Scheunders, P. (eds.) ACIVS 2011. LNCS, vol. 6915, pp. 249–260. Springer, Heidelberg (2011). doi:10.1007/978-3-642-23687-7_23
55. Santosh, K.C., Lamiroy, B., Wendling, L.: Spatio-structural symbol description with statistical feature add-on. In: Kwon, Y.-B., Ogier, J.-M. (eds.) GREC 2011. LNCS, vol. 7423, pp. 228–237. Springer, Heidelberg (2013). doi:10.1007/978-3-642-36824-0_22
56. Santosh, K.C., Lamiroy, B., Wendling, L.: Symbol recognition using spatial relations. Pattern Recog. Lett. **33**(3), 331–341 (2012)
57. Santosh, K.C., Lamiroy, B., Wendling, L.: DTW-radon-based shape descriptor for pattern recognition. Int. J. Pattern Recogn. Artif. Intell. **27**(3), 1350008 (2013)
58. Santosh, K.C., Lamiroy, B., Wendling, L.: Integrating vocabulary clustering with spatial relations for symbol recognition. Int. J. Doc. Anal. Recogn. **17**(1), 61–78 (2014)
59. Santosh, K.C., Nattee, C., Lamiroy, B.: Relative positioning of stroke-based clustering: a new approach to online handwritten Devanagari character recognition. Int. J. Image Graph. **12**(2), 25 (2012)
60. Santosh, K.C., Wendling, L.: Character recognition based on non-linear multi-projection profiles measure. Front. Comput. Sci. **9**(5), 678–690 (2015)
61. Santosh, K.C., Wendling, L., Lamiroy, B.: Using spatial relations for graphical symbol description. In: Proceedings of the IAPR International Conference on Pattern Recognition, pp. 2041–2044. IEEE Computer Society (2010)

62. Santosh, K.C., Wendling, L., Lamiroy, B.: BoR: Bag-of-Relations for symbol retrieval. Int. J. Pattern Recogn. Artif. Intell. **28**(06), 1450017 (2014)
63. Santosh, K., Wendling, L.: Graphical Symbol Recognition, pp. 1–22. Wiley, New York (2015)
64. Tabbone, S., Terrades, O.R.: An Overview of Symbol Recognition, pp. 523–551. Springer, London (2014)
65. Tabbone, S., Terrades, O.R., Barrat, S.: Histogram of radon transform. A useful descriptor for shape retrieval. In: Proceedings of the IAPR International Conference on Pattern Recognition, pp. 1–4 (2008)
66. Tabbone, S., Wendling, L., Salmon, J.P.: A new shape descriptor defined on the radon transform. Comput. Vis. Image Underst. **102**(1), 42–51 (2006)
67. Tabbone, S., Wendling, L., Tombre, K.: Matching of graphical symbols in line-drawing images using angular signature information. Int. J. Doc. Anal. Recogn. **6**(2), 115–125 (2003)
68. Tabbone, S., Wendling, L., Zuwala, D.: A hybrid approach to detect graphical symbols in documents. In: Marinai, S., Dengel, A.R. (eds.) DAS 2004. LNCS, vol. 3163, pp. 342–353. Springer, Heidelberg (2004). doi:10.1007/978-3-540-28640-0_33
69. Terrades, O.R., Tabbone, S., Valveny, E.: A review of shape descriptors for document analysis. In: Proceedings of International Conference on Document Analysis and Recognition, pp. 227–231 (2007)
70. Tombre, K.: Analysis of engineering drawings: state of the art and challenges. In: Tombre, K., Chhabra, A.K. (eds.) GREC 1997. LNCS, vol. 1389, pp. 257–264. Springer, Heidelberg (1998). doi:10.1007/3-540-64381-8_54
71. Tombre, K.: Ten years of research in the analysis of graphics documents: achievements and open problems. In: Proceedings of 10th Portuguese Conference on Pattern Recognition, Lisbon, Portugal, pp. 11–17, March 1998
72. Tombre, K., Chhabra, A.K. (eds.): GREC 1997. LNCS, vol. 1389. Springer, Heidelberg (1998). doi:10.1007/3-540-64381-8
73. Tombre, K.: Graphics recognition: the last ten years and the next ten years. In: Proceedings of 6th IAPR International Workshop on Graphics Recognition, Hong Kong, pp. 422–426 (2005)
74. Tombre, K.: Graphics recognition - what else? In: Ogier, J.M., Liu, W., Lladós, J. (eds.) Graphics Recognition. Achievements, Challenges, and Evolution. LNCS, vol. 6020, pp. 272–277. Springer, Heidelberg (2010). doi:10.1007/978-3-642-13728-0_25
75. Tombre, K., Lamiroy, B.: Pattern recognition methods for querying and browsing technical documentation. In: Progress in Pattern Recognition, Image Analysis and Applications, 13th Iberoamerican Congress on Pattern Recognition, pp. 504–518 (2008)
76. Tooley, M., Wyatt, D.: Aircraft electrical and electronic systems: principles, operation and maintenance. Butterworth-Heinemann, Oxford (2008). Aircraft engineering principles and practice
77. Tsai, W.H., Fu, K.S.: Attributed grammar: a tool for combining syntactic and statistical approaches to pattern recognition. IEEE Trans. Syst. Man Cybern. **10**(12), 873–885 (1980)
78. Valveny, E., Dosch, P.: Symbol recognition contest: a synthesis. In: Lladós, J., Kwon, Y.-B. (eds.) GREC 2003. LNCS, vol. 3088, pp. 368–385. Springer, Heidelberg (2004). doi:10.1007/978-3-540-25977-0_34
79. Valveny, E., Martí, E.: A model for image generation and symbol recognition through the deformation of lineal shapes. Pattern Recogn. Lett. **24**(15), 2857–2867 (2003)

80. Valveny, E., Tabbone, S., Ramos, O., Philippot, E.: Performance characterization of shape descriptors for symbol representation. In: Liu, W., Lladós, J., Ogier, J.-M. (eds.) GREC 2007. LNCS, vol. 5046, pp. 278–287. Springer, Heidelberg (2008). doi:10.1007/978-3-540-88188-9_26
81. Wendling, L., Tabbone, S.: A new way to detect arrows in line drawings. IEEE Trans. Pattern Anal. Mach. Intell. **26**(7), 935–941 (2004)
82. Yang, S.: Symbol recognition via statistical integration of pixel-level constraint histograms: a new descriptor. IEEE Trans. Pattern Anal. Mach. Intell. **27**(2), 278–281 (2005)
83. You, K.C., Fu, K.S.: Distorted shape recognition using attributed grammars and error-correcting techniques. Comput. Vis. Graph. Image Process. **13**, 1–16 (1980)
84. Yuen, P.C., Feng, G.C., Tang, Y.Y.: Printed chinese character similarity measurement using ring projection and distance transform. Int. J. Pattern Recogn. Artif. Intell. **12**(2), 209–221 (1998)
85. Zhang, D., Lu, G.: Review of shape representation and description techniques. Pattern Recogn. **37**(1), 1–19 (2004)
86. Zhang, D., Lu, G.: Shape-based image retrieval using generic fourier descriptor. Sig. Process. Image Commun. **17**(10), 825–848 (2002)
87. Zhang, W., Wenyin, L., Zhang, K.: Symbol recognition with kernel density matching. IEEE Trans. Pattern Anal. Mach. Intell. **28**(12), 2020–2024 (2006)

Word-Level Thirteen Official Indic Languages Database for Script Identification in Multi-script Documents

Sk Md Obaidullah[1]([⊠]), K.C. Santosh[2], Chayan Halder[3], Nibaran Das[4],
and Kaushik Roy[3]

[1] Department of Computer Science and Engineering,
Aliah University Kolkata, West Bengal, India
sk.obaidullah@gmail.com
[2] Department of Computer Science, The University of South Dakota,
Vermillion, SD 57069, USA
santosh.kc@usd.edu
[3] Department of Computer Science and Engineering,
Jadavpur University, Kolkata, India
chayan.halderz@gmail.com, kaushik.mrg@gmail.com
[4] Department of Computer Science, West Bengal State University, Kolkata, India
nibaran@gmail.com

Abstract. Without a publicly available database, we cannot advance research nor can we make a fair comparison with the state-of-the-art methods. To bridge this gap, we present a database of eleven Indic scripts from thirteen official languages for the purpose of script identification in multi-script document images. Our database is composed of 39K words that are equally distributed (i.e., 3K words per language). At the same time, we also study three different pertinent features: spatial energy (SE), wavelet energy (WE) and the Radon transform (RT), including their possible combinations, by using three different classifiers: multilayer perceptron (MLP), fuzzy unordered rule induction algorithm (FURIA) and random forest (RF). In our test, using all features, MLP is found to be the best performer showing the bi-script accuracy of 99.24% (keeping Roman common), 98.38% (keeping Devanagari common) and tri-script accuracy of 98.19% (keeping both Devanagari and Roman common).

Keywords: Multi-script documents · Official indic script database · Script identification

1 Introduction

Researches on multi-script document processing have real impact for a country like India, where 23 different languages (including English) and 13 different scripts (including Roman) exist. In general, OCRs are script specific, and processing documents having more than one scripts is not easy. Therefore,

© Springer Nature Singapore Pte Ltd. 2017
K.C. Santosh et al. (Eds.): RTIP2R 2016, CCIS 709, pp. 16–27, 2017.
DOI: 10.1007/978-981-10-4859-3_2

one of the common/suggested solutions is to develop a script identification system (SIS), so that we can take it as a precursor to the specific OCR. To highlight this issue, in this paper, we present a database that is composed of 13 different languages under 11 different scripts (having fairly large amount words in it) for an automatic script identification in multi-script documents.

Until today, few works have been reported on Indic script identification. Pati et al. [1] reported 11 different scripts in their study, which is found to be the maximum number of scripts in the literature. They used a database from 11 different languages, where two languages: Kashmiri and Dogri originating from Northern part of India were not considered. To represent the scripts, Gabor filter and directional cosine transform (DCT) based frequency domain techniques were used. Based on these features, their reported performances are 98% for bi-Script and tri-Script, and 89% for eleven-scripts by using three different classifiers: nearest neighbor, linear discriminative and support vector machine (SVM). Since then, this can be considered as a benchmark work on printed script identification (PSI) at word level. Among other available popular PSI works on Indic and Non-Indic scripts, Hochberg et al. [2] proposed a technique to identify six different scripts: Arabic, Armenian, Devanagari, Chinese, Cyrillic, and Burmese, using some textual features. Pal et al. [3] proposed a line level script identification technique considering five different scripts: Bangla, Devnagari, Chinese, Arabic and Roman. Jahawar et al. [4] proposed a headline and contextual information based technique to identify Devnagari and Telugu scripts using principal component analysis (PCA) and SVM. Chanda et al. [5] proposed a word level script identification technique considering six different scripts: Bangla, Devnagari, Roman, Malayalam, Gujarati and Telugu. Joshi et al. [6] proposed a Gabor energy based paragraph level technique to identify ten different Indic scripts using k-nearest neighbor (k-NN) classifier. Dhanya et al. [7] proposed a script identification technique using Gabor filter based directional feature and SVM classifier considering Tamil and Roman scripts. Chaudhury et al. [8] proposed script identification techniques by combining trainable classifiers for six different scripts: Devnagari, Telugu, Roman, Malayalam, Bangla and Urdu. In the script identification review paper [9], authors pointed out the unavailability issue of benchmark works by considering all official Indic scripts. Following this review, we are, indeed, motivated to publish a benchmark database and results considering all 13 official Indic scripts.

The remainder of the paper is organized as follows. In Sect. 2, we explain our database. We then describe our method in Sect. 3. It includes pre-processing, feature extraction, and script identification. In Sect. 4, we provide experimental test results and analysis. We conclude the paper in Sect. 5.

2   Database

As shown in Fig. 1 our database of thirteen different official Indic languages: (1) Bangla (BEN), (2) Devnagari (DEV), (3) Dogri (DOG), (4) Gujarati (GUJ), (5) Gurumukhi (GUR), (6) Kannada (KAN), (7) Kashmiri (KAS), (8) Malayalam (MAL), (9) Oriya (ORY), (10) Roman (ROM), (11) Tamil (TAM), (12)

1) Bangla
2) Devanagari
3) Dogri
4) Gujarati
5) Gurumukhi
6) Kannada
7) Kashmiri
8) Malayalam
9) Oriya
10) Roman
11) Tamil
12) Telugu
13) Urdu

Fig. 1. Sample word images of 13 different official Indic languages, i.e. 11 different scripts

Telugu (TEL), (13) Urdu (URD) with 3K words per languages. Altogether, we have collected 39K words. The sources of data collection were newspaper, articles and books. For example, Bangla words were collected from scanned copy of different Tagores books, novels, poems and newspaper. As a consequence, the collected samples vary writing style, thickness of the characters and resolution. Document image scanning was carried out using HP flatbed scanner, resolution 300 dpi and stored at 8-bit gray level jpeg format. The word dimension is found in the range of 150 × 50 pixels. Note that the word images are extracted by an automated process, as explained in [10,11].

The database is created for public use but, limited to research purpose. A part of the database is available on-line, and will be provided upon the request.

3   Script Identification

Our study is not an exception, we start with pre-processing, and then extract features for script identification purpose. In our study, we study three different features: (1) spatial energy (SE), (2) wavelet energy (WE) and (3) the Radon transform (RT), including their possible combinations, by using three different classifiers: (1) multilayer perceptron (MLP), (2) fuzzy unordered rule induction algorithm (FURIA) and (3) random forest (RF). Again, Our idea is not only to check what features but also to check what classifiers can consistently provide optimal performance.

3.1   Pre-processing

The word images are binarized by using the following steps. (1) In grayscale word image, region-of-interests (ROIs) are generated using a local window-based algorithm. Run length smoothing algorithm is applied to overcome the presence of stray/hollow regions generated due to window size. Connected component labelling is applied and the ROIs are mapped to the original grayscale images. (2) A global thresholding technique is then applied on ROIs.

3.2   Features

As said before, we propose to study three different features: spatial energy (SE), wavelet energy (WE) and the Radon transform (RT).

Spatial Energy (SE). SE distribution varies in accordance with the change in textural information, and therefore, it is important in our study. SE distribution was observed by computing entropy on the grayscale images. It can be represented by

$$Entropy = -\sum p(i,j)log(p(i,j)).$$

In general, entropy is complement of energy. Therefore, for any non-uniform or aperiodic gray level distribution, there exists high entropy.

Another measure is the standard deviation of binary images of different scripts. Standard deviation is a measure of the variability of the image pixels. It can be represented by

$$\sigma_x = \sqrt{\frac{1}{n}\left\{\sum_{i=1}^{n}x_i^2 - \frac{1}{n}\left(\sum_{i=1}^{n}x_i\right)^2\right\}},$$

where, $x_1, x_2, ..., x_n$ be n observations of a random variable X, which is representation of an arbitrary image pixel.

Wavelet Energy (WE). For present work, wavelet packets has been generated using DWT or discrete wavelet transform which uses sub-band coding on images with respect to spatial and frequency components and allows analysis the images from coarse to fine level [15]. Here Daubechies wavelets dbN where $N = 1, 2, 3$ are chosen to generate sub-band images with approximation coefficients cA, cH, cV and cD. Their advantage includes computational ease with minimum resource and time requirements. These orthogonal wavelets are characterized by maximum number of vanishing moments for some given support. Here a signal (for present work it is an word image) is decomposed into different frequencies with different resolutions for further analysis. In general the family of Daubechies wavelet is denoted as dbN, where the family is denoted by the term db and the number of vanishing moments is represented by N.

To study the applicability of wavelet analysis in our work, we studied that an image can be represented by the combinations of different coefficients i.e. constant, linear, quadratic etc. Daubechies *db1* represent the constant coefficient of the image component, *db2* represent the linear and *db3* can represent quadratic coefficients. So here, wavelet decomposition at level 1 has been made using *db1*, *db2* and *db3* which are capable enough to capture the constant, linear and quadratic coefficients of an image component. Four coefficients namely approximation coefficients (cA), horizontal coefficients (cH), vertical coefficients (cV), and diagonal coefficients (cD) has been generated.

To measure the WE or wavelet energy feature we have computed wavelet entropy on these approximation coefficients for each of the sub-band images.

Suppose ws is the word level image signal and $(ws_i)_i$ the coefficients of ws in an orthonormal basis. Then the normalized shanon entropy is defined as:

$$SE(ws_i) = (ws_i^2)log(ws_i^2).$$

$$\text{So, } SE(ws_i) = -\sum (ws_i^2)log(ws_i^2).$$

It produces a feature vector of dimension of size 15.

The Radon Transform (RT). Motivated by the presence of the strokes at different orientations in the word images, we propose to use the RT. The RT consists of a collection of projections of a pattern at different angles [16], as illustrated in Fig. 2. In other words, the radon transform of a pattern $f(x, y)$ and for a given set of angles can be thought of as the projection of all non-zero points. This resulting projection is the sum of the non-zero points for the pattern in each direction, thus forming a matrix. The matrix elements are related to the

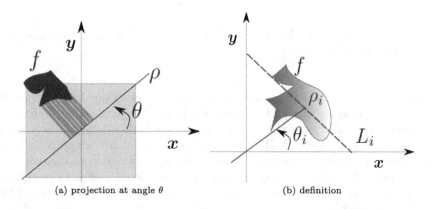

(a) projection at angle θ (b) definition

Fig. 2. Illustrating the Radon transform theory (source: Ref. [17]).

integral of f over a line $L(\rho, \theta)$ defined by $\rho = x \cos \theta + y \sin \theta$ and can formally be expressed as,

$$R(\rho, \theta) = \int_{-\infty}^{\infty} \int_{-\infty}^{\infty} f(x, y) \delta(x \cos \theta + y \sin \theta - \rho) dx dy$$

where $\delta(.)$ is the Dirac delta function, $\delta(x) = 1$, if $x = 0$ and 0 otherwise. Also, $\theta \in [0, \pi)$ and $\rho \in]-\infty, \infty[$. For the RT, L_i be in normal form (ρ_i, θ_i).

Such a description is useful for scripts such as Bangla and Devanagari, where there exists horizontal line, known by the name 'matra' or 'shirorekha'. These clear lines can be exploited by computing 0° projection. Similarly, scripts like Tamil and Roman have many vertical lines which can be represented by 90°. However, to exploit meaningful information, we do not require all possible orientations, and therefore, we study the RT at an interval of 15°.

To compute RT based feature vector we applied the Radon transform on each of the binary word images. Additionally RT spectrum of each of the sub band images is also obtained from Daubechies multi-resolution analysis using db1, db2 and db3 at level 1. Then statistical textural features are computed from the generated Radon spectrum. This step results a sixty five dimensional RT feature vector.

3.3   Script Classification

In our study, three different classifiers are used to train and to identify the words. They are MLP, FURIA and RF, which are briefly explained in the following.

Multilayer Perceptron (MLP). It consists of multiple layers with number of neurons in each layer represented as a directed graph [12]. MLP uses back propagation algorithm to train the network. In our experiment, we choose the configuration of the NN as 84-hl-13 (i.e., 84 number of attributes while taking SE+WE+RT and 13 output classes). We empirically designed the number of neurons in the hidden layer, hl.

Fuzzy Unordered Rule Induction Algorithm (FURIA). It is a fuzzy-rule-based classifier which learns from fuzzy rules and unordered rule sets [13]. It is an extension of the well-known rule learner RIPPER algorithm which is a state-of-the-art rule learner technique. Its preserves its advantages, such as simple and comprehensible rule sets for the learning. Along with that, RIPPER also includes a number of positive modifications and extensions. In particular, FURIA learns fuzzy rules instead of conventional rules and unordered rule sets instead of lists of rules. Moreover, to deal with uncovered examples, it makes use of an efficient rule stretching method. Experimental results show that FURIA significantly outperforms the original RIPPER in terms of classification accuracy.

Random Forest (RF). It is an ensemble learning method for classification, regression and other tasks. RF operates by constructing a multitude of decision trees at training time and providing the output class, which is the mode of the classes (classification) or mean prediction (regression) of the individual trees. RF corrects for decision trees' habit of over fitting to their training set [14].

4 Experiments

4.1 Evaluation Metrics

To measure the performance of the system, we use the following metric,

$$Identification\_rate = \frac{\#correctly\_classified\_words}{\#total\_words} \times 100\%.$$

Very specifically, we have computed the features (*cf.* Sect. 3.2), their possible combinations, and classifiers (*cf.* Sect. 3.3) separately.

4.2 Set up

In our study, from 13 different languages from 11 different scripts, we have considered two different test categories: (1) bi-script and (2) tri-script. In general, there are $^{13}C_2$ and $^{13}C_3$ possible combinations of bi-script and tri-script categories. But, considering the nature of the multi-script documents, these straightforward combinations may not hold true in the real-world (e.g. postal documents and application forms). We have also observed that, Devanagari and Roman exist in most of the documents. This means that any bi-script or tri-script document in general contains either or both Devanagari and/or Roman in addition to their local script. Considering such a context, we have formed two different script sub-categories for bi-script: case 1 and case 2. Bi-script case 1 contains twelve script combinations with Devanagari common. Bi-script case 2 contains Roman as common script, for all remaining 12 scripts. For tri-script category, we have a total number of 11 combinations where both Devanagari and Roman are kept as common with other local scripts.

Also, note that, we have divided the database into training and test sets as 2:1 ratio.

4.3 Results and Analysis

Again, our experimental test framework can be summarized as follows. As said before, in this work, our idea is not only to check what features but also to check what classifiers can consistently provide optimal performance. Therefore, we have seven different tests in accordance with the use of individual features and their possible combinations: SE, WE, RT, SE+WE, SE+RT, WE+RT and SE+WE+RT. These are tested by using three different classifiers: MLP, FURIA and RF.

Table 1. Bi-Script case 1 (Devnagari common): average performance scores (in %) for different feature combinations.

Feature type (dimension)	Classifier		
	MLP	FURIA	RF
SE (4)	81.93	80.30	86.28
WE (15)	91.10	89.30	92.35
RT (65)	96.93	95.31	95.84
SE+WE (19)	94.83	93	94.98
SE+RT (69)	97.86	97.09	97.03
WE+RT (80)	97.80	96.36	96.48
SE+WE+RT (84)	**98.38**	97.42	97.35

Table 2. Bi-Script case 1 (Devnagari common): average performance (in %) scores for 12 different combinations when all features (SE, WE, RT) are combined.

Bi-script combinations case 1	Classifier		
	MLP	FURIA	RF
DEV-BEN	94.70	95.00	94.20
DEV-DOG	99.70	99.00	98.30
DEV-GUJ	99.40	98.70	98.30
DEV-GUR	90.90	89.50	91.60
DEV-KAN	99.20	97.90	97.90
DEV-KAS	99.90	99.30	99.00
DEV-MAL	99.70	98.80	98.30
DEV-ORY	99.90	99.50	99.60
DEV-ROM	99.30	97.60	97.50
DEV-TAM	98.40	95.90	96.10
DEV-TEL	99.90	98.80	98.60
DEV-URD	99.60	99.00	98.80
Average	**98.38**	97.42	97.35

In Table 1, average performance scores for different feature combinations are provided. The results are provided for bi-script case 1. One of the scores in this table is computed by making 12 number of runs as shown in Table 2. Altogether, we have 12(bi-script combinations) × 3(classifers) = 36 runs, for just a single feature type. In Table 1, MLP provides the best performance (i.e., 98.38%) when all features are combined, which, however, does not provide a significant difference other classifiers. In a similar fashion, bi-script case 2 has been tested, where Roman is common. Results are provided in Tables 3 and 4 for bi-script case 2 (follow Tables 1 and 2). In the latter case (i.e., Table 3),

Table 3. Bi-Script case 2 (Roman common): average performance scores (in %) for different feature combinations.

Feature type (dimension)	Classifier		
	MLP	FURIA	RF
SE (4)	80.94	79.93	81.90
WE (15)	92.56	91.2	93.50
RT (65)	98.01	96.67	96.66
SE+WE (19)	95.06	94.07	95.60
SE+RT (69)	98.96	97.68	97.68
WE+RT (80)	99.07	97.58	97.62
SE+WE+RT (84)	**99.24**	97.91	98.11

Table 4. Bi-Script case 2 (Roman common): average performance (in %) scores for 12 different combinations when all features (SE, WE, RT) are combined.

Bi-script combinations case 2	Classifier		
	MLP	FURIA	RF
ROM-BEN	99.00	96.60	97.50
ROM-DEV	99.30	97.60	97.50
ROM-DOG	99.30	97.80	98.00
ROM-GUJ	98.20	94.90	95.40
ROM-GUR	99.30	99.20	98.80
ROM-KAN	99.30	99.00	98.40
ROM-KAS	99.50	99.20	99.40
ROM-MAL	99.10	97.40	98.60
ROM-ORY	99.70	98.90	99.20
ROM-TAM	99.30	97.40	97.10
ROM-TEL	99.50	98.60	99.00
ROM-URD	99.40	98.30	98.4.0
Average	**99.24**	97.91	98.11

the highest possible accuracy is 99.24%. Like before, MLP provides better results when all features are combined – even for tri-script combinations. In Table 5, average performance scores are provided for tri-script combinations, where the highest possible identification rate is 98.19%. In this test, we have submitted 11(tri-script combinations) × 3(classifers) = 33 runs, for just a single feature type. Again, for a comparison (between the classifiers) purpose, their average scores are provided in Table 6, where we found MLP> RF≥FURIA, even though there exists no significant difference between them. In this comparison table, one can also note that higher the script combination, lower the performance of classifiers – which is obvious because it increases number of classes to be classified.

Table 5. Tri-Script (Devnagari & Roman common): average performance (in %) scores for 11 different combinations when all features (SE, WE, RT) are combined.

Tri-script combinations	Classifier		
	MLP	FURIA	RF
DEV-ROM-BEN	96.20	93.40	90.70
DEV-ROM-DOG	99.20	96.90	98.00
DEV-ROM-GUJ	97.80	95.60	94.00
DEV-ROM-GUR	94.00	89.00	84.70
DEV-ROM-KAN	98.90	96.70	96.50
DEV-ROM-KAS	99.60	97.00	96.70
DEV-ROM-MAL	98.70	96.00	95.50
DEV-ROM-ORY	99.50	97.60	98.00
DEV-ROM-TAM	97.90	94.40	94.00
DEV-ROM-TEL	99.30	97.70	97.90
DEV-ROM-URD	99.00	96.70	96.00
Average	**98.19**	95.55	94.73

Table 6. Comparison of classifiers when all features are combined. Average scores are reported.

Test category (combinations)	Classifier		
	MLP	FURIA	RF
Bi-script case 1 (12)	98.38	97.42	97.35
Bi-script case 2 (12)	99.24	97.91	98.11
Tri-script (11)	98.19	95.55	94.73

4.4 Previous Relevant Work – Analogy

Prior to this study, Pati et al. [1] proposed a word-level script identification by using 11 Indic languages, where Gabor and DCT based features are taken. They have compared their performances using three different classifiers namely neural network (NN), linear discriminant analysis (LDA) and support vector machine (SVM). Their performance scores are approximately 98% from both bi-script and tri-script combinations.

In contrast, our work is composed of all 13 official languages under 11 different scripts, with 39k dataset. Three type of features are used: spatial energy, wavelet energy and radon transform. Performances of three different classifiers namely MLP, FURIA, and RF have been compared, and MLP is found to be better performer. In our comprehensive tests, we have script identification rate of 98.38% (keeping Devanagari common) and 99.24% (keeping Roman common) for bi-script combination, and identification rate of 98.19% for tri-script combination. For better understanding a comparative chart is shown by Table 7.

Table 7. Analogy with the previous work.

Method	Database	Identification rate (in %)
Pati et al. [1]	11 languages	98.00 (bi-script)
		98.00 (tri-script)
Proposed work	13 languages	99.24 (bi-script)
		98.38 (bi-script)
		98.19 (tri-script)

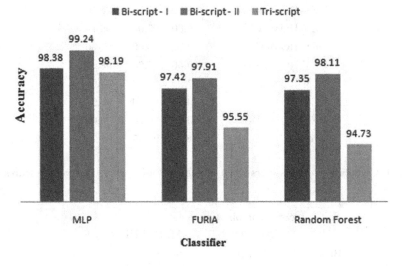

Fig. 3. Performance comparison of different classifiers.

The graphical representation of the performance comparison of different classifiers is illustrated in Fig. 3.

5   Conclusions and Plan

No doubt, script identification has been taken as the well studied problem since several years but, we do not have fairly large database for research, and therefore, one can make fair comparison. Motivated by this, in this paper, we have presented a script identification database, which is composed of 13 official Indic languages for research purpose. Our database is composed of 39K words that are equally distributed (i.e., 3K words per language). We have also studied MLP, FURIA and RF classifiers by using three different features that are derived from spatial energy, wavelet energy and the Radon transform. In our test, using all features, MLP is found to be the best performer showing the bi-script accuracy of 99.24% (keeping Roman common), 98.38% (keeping Devanagari common) and tri-script accuracy of 98.19% (keeping both Devanagari and Roman common).

In our plan, we are in the process to investigate those few misclassification samples (i.e., from Kashmiri-Urdu, Devnagari-Gurumukhi combinations) so that we can come up with new features to achieve the expected performance. Also, integrating classifiers in an immediate step.

References

1. Pati, P.B., Ramakrishnan, A.G.: Word-level multi-script identification. Pattern Recog. Lett. **29**(9), 1218–1229 (2008)
2. Hochberg, J., Kelly, P., Thomas, T., Kerns, L.: Automatic script identification from document images using cluster-based templates. IEEE Trans. Pattern Anal. Mach. Intell. **19**, 176–181 (1997)
3. Pal, U., Chaudhuri, B.B.: Identification of different script lines from multi-script documents. Image Vis. Comput. **20**(13/14), 945–954 (2002)
4. Jawahar, C.V., Kumar, M., Kiran, S.S.R.: A bilingual OCR for Hindi-Telugu documents and its applications. In: Proceedings of International Conference Document Analysis and Recognition, pp. 408–412 (2003)
5. Chanda, S., Sinha, S., Pal, U.: Word-wise English Devnagari and Oriya script identification. In: Speech and Language Systems for Human Communication, pp. 244–248 (2004)
6. Joshi, G.D., Garg, S., Sivaswamy, J.: Script identification from Indian documents. In: 7th International Association of Pattern Recognition Workshop on Document Analysis Systems, pp. 255–267 (2006)
7. Dhanya, D., Ramakrishna, A.G., Pati, P.B.: Script identification in printed bilingual documents. Sadhana **27**(1), 73–82 (2002)
8. Chaudhury, S., Harit, G., Madnani, S., Shet, R.B.: Identification of scripts of Indian languages by combining trainable classifiers. In: Indian Conference on Computer Vision Graphics and Image Processing (2000)
9. Ghosh, D., Dube, T., Shivprasad, S.P.: Script recognition-a review. IEEE Trans. Pattern Anal. Mach. Intell. **32**(12), 2142–2161 (2010)
10. Hangarge, M., Santosh, K.C., Pardeshi, R.: Directional discrete cosine transform for handwritten script identification. In: Proceedings of the International Conference on Document Analysis and Recognition, pp. 344–348 (2013)
11. Pardeshi, R., Chaudhuri, B.B., Hangarge, M., Santosh, K.C.: Automatic handwritten Indian scripts identification. In: 14th International Conference on Frontiers in Handwriting Recognition, pp. 375–380 (2014)
12. Obaidullah, S.M., Mondal, A., Das, N., Roy, K.: Script identification from printed Indian document images and performance evaluation using different classifiers. Appl. Comput. Intell. Soft Comput. **22**, 12 (2014)
13. Huhn, J., Hullermeier, E.: FURIA: an algorithm for unordered fuzzy rule induction. Data Min. Knowl. Discov. **19**(3), 293–319 (2009)
14. Breiman, L.: Random forests. Mach. Learn. **45**(1), 5–32 (2001)
15. Mallat, S.G.: A theory for multiresolution signal decomposition: the wavelet representation. IEEE Trans. Pattern Anal. Mach. Intell. **11**(7), 674–693 (1989)
16. Deans, S.R.: Applications of the Radon Transform. Wiley Interscience Publications, New York (1983)
17. Santosh, K.C., Lamiroy, B., Wendling, B.: DTW for matching radon features: a pattern recognition and retrieval method. In: 13th International Conference on Advances Concepts for Intelligent Vision Systems, pp. 249–260 (2011)

Skew Detection and Correction of Devanagari Script Using Interval Halving Method

Trupti A. Jundale[(⊠)] and Ravindra S. Hegadi

Department of Computer Science, Solapur University, Solapur 413255, India
truptijundale@gmail.com, rshegadi@gmail.com

Abstract. We proposed a method for skew detection and correction of handwritten and printed Devanagari script which is based on pixels of axes parallel rectangle and interval halving also called bisection method. The proposed approach works for skewed word, uniform skewed angle of line and paragraph. The method uses tangential pixels of axes parallel rectangle. By finding these pixels, area of a rectangle which is axes parallel is calculated. Then using numerical bisection method, pixels of this rectangle box are rotated and again area of the rectangle using new rotated pixels is calculated and the calculated area is compared with the previously calculated area. This process continues till we cant get the least area of axes parallel rectangle. The angle with the least area of a rectangle is the skew angle. This technique achieves a good result as compared with other techniques in the literature with the accuracy rate of 95%. The manual trained dataset is used for testing purpose to calculate the accuracy.

Keywords: Pre-processing · Axes-parallel rectangle · Interval halving method · Skew detection · Skew correction

1 Introduction

In the image processing world, OCR is a general technique of digitizing images of handwritten or printed manuscript so that they can be electronically edited, searched, and stored more efficiently and compactly. The aim of an OCR technique is recognition of text in images. As OCR is the most important area in the recognition field, it contains many stages to digitize the document. Skew detection is one of the important stages in the OCR. Without skew detection, OCR system cannot recognize data successfully. So to success the OCR system, skew detection is important. As OCR is applied for both online or offline mode data which is either printed or handwritten, skew detection is also used for the same. Skew detection of handwritten data is quite difficult as compared to detection of skew of printed data. Obviously, because of the variety of handwriting approach and unusual nature of handwritings, the difficulty of offline handwritten recognition is the most demanding problem in OCR and it usually requires language-specific methods. On the other hand, OCR of printed documents is

© Springer Nature Singapore Pte Ltd. 2017
K.C. Santosh et al. (Eds.): RTIP2R 2016, CCIS 709, pp. 28–38, 2017.
DOI: 10.1007/978-981-10-4859-3_3

very much in demand for practical applications such as historical document analysis, official letter and document processing, and vehicle plate recognition. So indirectly skew detection techniques gives applications for the same.

In literature lot of work is done on skew detection for various scripts, but very less work is done in the skew detection of Devanagari script as compared to other script and especially for handwritten data. Skew is the distortion that is often introduced during scanning or copying of a document and it is unavoidable [1]. The angle that departs from x-axis is the skew angle. Generally skew varies in global skew, multiple skew, and non-uniform skew. Global skew contains same angle skew of all text lines of a document. Usually, this is the case of skewed printed scanned or captured document. Multiple skews contain lines of different skew angle within a document and non-uniform skew is the orientation changes within a line. Literature review said that the most of the work that has been done is for detection of skew of scanned document images instead of skewed handwritten text. The successful skew detection and correction turns further stages of OCR like analysis of data, recognition of data to be accurate. In this paper, we proposed an approach for skew detection of handwritten and printed data of Devanagari script.

Devanagari script is a script of a Brahmic family used in countries of India and Nepal. Hindi which has a Devanagari script is a national language of India, so it is widely used in India for an official and commercial purpose. Other languages like Marathi (State language of Maharashtra), Nepali (National language of Nepal), Sanskrit, Kashmiri, Bhojpuri, Maithili, Dogri, Bodo has Devanagari script. The difference of writing style of Devanagari script makes difficult to detect the skew of text as compared to other script.

2   Devanagari Script

Devanagari script is one of the main parts of Brahmic family, which is belonging from Indo-Aryan languages. Devanagari script languages are written from left to right. Unlike Latin script, the concept of upper/lower case is absent in Devanagari script. It consists of 14 vowels and 33 consonants [1]. Shirorekha is the most important feature of Devanagari script languages, usually drawn on a group of

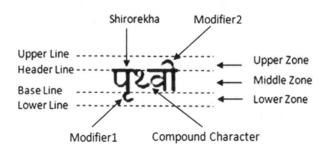

Fig. 1. Devanagari script word

characters which is considered as one word. Vowels that can be written as separate characters or by using diacritic marks on below, upper, before or after
consonants are called modifiers. In Devanagari script, two or three consonants
can be written as a single character, which is known as compound character [2].
Figure 1 shows different features of Devanagari script.

The main characters of word are written in middle zone. Upper zone and
lower zone are for modifiers and Shirorekha is drawn at header line. In Fig. 1
two characters are combined to form a new shape of single character known as
compound character.

3   Literature Survey

Various methods for detection of skew are broadly classified into Hough transform method, projection profile methods, clustering methods, Fourier transform
methods. Other than these methods various other methods are used in the literature for skew detection of scanned document images or for typed or printed
data. Our literature review said that the work is mostly done for scanned document skew detection or for printed data skew as compared to skew detection of
handwritten data. [1] uses tangential pixels of axes parallel rectangle and linear
regression method to calculate the skew of word/line of Devanagari script. The
Shirorekha, which is a feature of Devanagari script, is used for skew detection of
handwritten Devanagari scripts using Hough transform in [2]. Various methods
used for skew detection of Devanagari script are surveyed in [3]. To correct the
skew of QR code, [4] combines Harris corner detection with convex hull algorithm to get the outline of the outer quadrilateral of the QR code, then finds the
four apexes of the QR code image borrowing the geometric algorithm, and finally
corrects the QR code image by perspective collineation. [5] proposed a technique
for global skew estimation which is applied on binary document images of maga-
zine pages. In this skew is estimated by determining the angle between the x-axis
and the first eigenvector of the data covariance matrix. The method based on
interline cross correlation in the scanned images instead of finding the correlation between the entire image is proposed in [6] for document skew detection. [7]
proposed a Rectangular Active Contour Model (RAC Model) for content region
detection and skew angle calculation by imposing a rectangular shape constraint
on the zero-level set in Chain-Vese Model (CV Model) according to the rectangular feature of content regions in document images. Two algorithms, one for
single skew and other for multi-skew for accurate skew detection and correction
of textual documents are presented in [8]. They depend on finding a horizontal RLSA image of the skewed document. The average skew of selected black
connected components in the RLSA image is considered as the skew angle for
the whole document which is finally rotated in the opposite direction by that
amount to obtain the final corrected image.

4   Proposed Methodology

The proposed methodology for skew detection and correction of Devanagari script using Interval halving method is illustrated in this section. The input for the proposed method is a skewed word or line or paragraph of uniform skew. The dataset used for proposed method is manual trained data, means the images contained in the dataset are originally at zero degree. All these images are rotated manually at different angle to make it skewed image. The proposed methodology is applied on these skewed input images and the output of the method is skew corrected image. To calculate the accuracy, the detected skew angle means θ angle is compared with the original rotated angle in the trained dataset. Section 4.1 describes the Preprocessing stage. The description of pixels of axes parallel rectangle is in Sect. 4.2. Bisection methodology is described in Sect. 4.3. Skew detection and skew correction is described in Sects. 4.4 and 4.5 respectively and last Sect. 4.6 describes the algorithm of proposed method.

4.1   Pre-processing

The input to the system is a word or a line or a paragraph of a uniform skew of handwritten Devanagari script which is scanned by a scanner or captured by the camera. Acquired image is preprocessed for removing noise. Firstly the input image is converted into gray scale image and then thresholding is applied over for converting given image into a binary image containing only black and white pixels. In this binarized image, white pixels represent background and black pixels represent foreground. Figure 2 shows the sample result of preprocessed image.

4.2   Border Detection

After getting preprocessed image, peripheral pixels of an input image are calculated by finding the minimum row, maximum row, minimum column and maximum column of foreground pixels of an input image. These outer tangential pixels of an

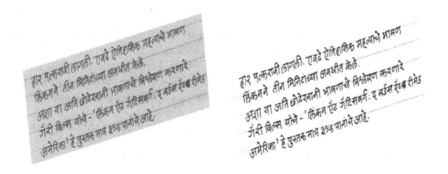

Fig. 2. Left: original image. Right: preprocessed image.

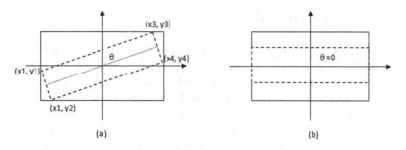

Fig. 3. (a) Skewed rectangle fitted in an axes-parallel rectangle (b) rectangle with zero skew.

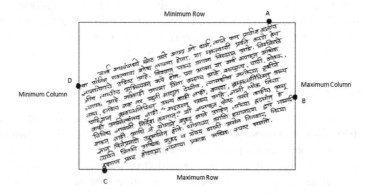

Fig. 4. Pixel detection of rectangle

input word/line are used to form an axes-parallel rectangle. Figure 3 shows tangential pixels of skewed one are embedded into an axes-parallel rectangle. Figure 4 shows the example that shows the tangential pixels of an input image as a minimum row, maximum row, minimum column and maximum column.

4.3   Interval Halving or Bisection Method

The interval halving or bisection method is the most simplest and robust mathematical method used for finding the root of an equation. The Bisection process involves finding a root or solution, of an equation of the form $f(x) = 0$. The algorithm successively divides the interval in half, keeping the solution within its limits, until it reaches the desired level of accuracy. The Bisection method is based on the intermediate value theorem. It works on the following assumption,

1. Start with an initial interval $[a, b]$, in which we know a priori that the solution exists.
2. Calculate the midpoint of the interval using following equation,

$$xmid = (a + b)/2 \qquad (1)$$

3. If $f(xmid) = 0$ then $xmid$ is the solution otherwise use intermediate value theorem to decide whether the solution lies in the interval $[a, xmid]$ or in the interval $[xmid, b]$.

   - If

$$f(a).f(xmid) < 0 \tag{2}$$

   then the function changes sign in the interval $[a, xmid]$ and the solution lies in this interval, set $b = xmid$, so next iteration again lies in the interval $[a, b]$.

   - If

$$f(a).f(xmid) > 0 \tag{3}$$

   then the function changes sign in the interval $[xmid, b]$ and solution lies in this interval, set $a = xmid$, so next iteration again lies in the interval $[a, b]$.

4. Repeat the process until the interval $(b - a)$ becomes smaller or equal to the required accuracy. The graphical representation for above assumption is shown in Fig. 5,

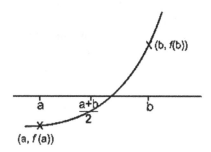

Fig. 5. Graphical representation of the bisection assumption

4.4   Skew Detection

Firstly the text border is detected simply by scanning the document row by row to detect the first and last pixels in each row. From this point forward just use the text border pixels as a representative of the document. After that, four corner pixels of a document are used, which represent a minimum row, maximum row, minimum column and maximum column. These four corner pixels are used to calculate the area of axes parallel rectangle using the mathematical equation of area of rectangle as,

$$Area\_of\_Rectangle = Height * width \tag{4}$$

Here height is calculated by getting the difference of maximum column and minimum column and same for width, which is calculated by getting a difference of maximum row and minimum row. At which direction the rectangle is rotated is decided by rotating border pixels at $\pm 1°$. If an area of a rectangle by incrementing border pixels by $1°$ is less than the area of the original rectangle, then the rotation direction is positive and if an area of a rectangle by decrementing border pixels by $1°$ is less than the area of the original rectangle then rotation direction is negative. Initially skew angle is set to zero when original area of rectangle is calculated. Then area of rectangle is monitored by rotating the image in a loop, while rotating rectangle skew angle is incremented or decremented by rotation direction accordingly. The Bisection method is used to find the angle which gives the minimum area. To verify the calculated θ means the skew angle is correct, it is compared with the original rotated angle. How Bisection method is used for skew detection is detailed in an algorithm.

4.5   Skew Correction

Various methods are used in the literature for skew correction. Skew is corrected by simply rotating pixels at the skew detected angle. The methods used in the literature are direct rotation method, indirect method, contour-oriented method, projection-profile based method etc. The corresponding pixels of input image will be transferred to new location using a rotation transformation is the direct method for skew correction and this uses following matrix for skew correction,

$$\begin{pmatrix} x' \\ y' \end{pmatrix} = \begin{pmatrix} cos(-\theta) & -sin(-\theta) \\ sin(-\theta) & cos(-\theta) \end{pmatrix} \begin{pmatrix} x \\ y \end{pmatrix} \tag{5}$$

Where (x', y') are the co-ordinates for skew correction and (x, y) are the co-ordinates of detected skew and the matrix is the rotation transformation. The following matrix is used for skew correction using indirect method,

$$\begin{pmatrix} x' \\ y' \end{pmatrix} = \begin{pmatrix} cos(\theta) & sin(\theta) \\ -sins(\theta) & cos(\theta) \end{pmatrix} \begin{pmatrix} x \\ y \end{pmatrix} \tag{6}$$

Where (x, y) are the input co-ordinates that will be rotated at detected angle and stored in (x', y') as a output co-ordinates. In this approach, the direct method is used for rotation to correct the skew which is detected by using Bisection method.

4.6   Algorithm

1. Pre-processing- Firstly image is preprocessed to remove noise and to get a binarized image. Also, apply border elimination techniques to prepare the image for skew detection.
2. Border detection- Detect the first and last pixels in each row by simply scanning the document row by row to detect the border. From this point forward just use the text border pixels as a representative of the document.

3. Corner pixel detection-

   $Minimum_{Row}$: Find pixels with the minimum row number. Among them, the pixel with the minimum column number is a pixel of a minimum row, the point A in Fig. 4.

   $Maximum_{Row}$: Find pixels with the maximum row number. Among them, the pixel with maximum column number is a pixel of a maximum row, the point C in Fig. 4.

   $Maximum_{Column}$: Find pixels with the maximum column number. Among them, the pixel with minimum row number is a pixel of maximum column, the point B in Fig. 4.

   $Minimum_{Column}$: Find the pixels with the minimum column. Among them, the pixel with maximum row number is a pixel of minimum column, the point D in Fig. 4.

4. Calculate the area of a rectangle parallel to axes using Eq. 4,

$$Area = (Max_{Column} - Min_{Column}) * (Max_{Row} - Min_{Row}) \qquad (7)$$

$$Area = (B - D) * (C - A) \qquad (8)$$

5. Direction of rotation is decided by rotating border pixels at $\pm 1°$, if an area of a rectangle by incrementing border pixels by $1°$ is less than the area of an original rectangle, then direction of rotation is positive. If an area of a rectangle by decrementing border pixels by $1°$ is less than the original area of a rectangle then the direction is negative, otherwise there is no direction.

6. Rotate the picture $1°$ in a loop in the direction found in step 5 and monitor area of the rectangle If $A(Current) \geq A(Previous)$

       then $\theta = \theta(Previous)$

   where A is area of rectangle and θ is the orientation angle of the rectangle. If $A = A(previous)$ then

       exit the loop

7. To find the angle which gives minimum area using interval halving method, rotate tangential pixels in given positive and negative rotation steps and calculate the area, return the θ value that gives minimum area between the rotation steps with steps of 0.5: Set $\delta = 4$ where δ is the size of rotation step While $\delta \geq 0.125$

       $\delta = \delta/2$

   Rotate original border pixels.

       $A = min(A, A + stepsizeo, A - stepsizeo)$.

   Set θ to the corresponding angle of A which is skew angle of document.

8. θ is the skew angle. Rotate the original image by $-\theta$ using the direct method of rotation to correct the skew angle of the text.

5   Experimental Results

The experimental result gives 95% accuracy for skew correction of handwritten Devanagari script which contains dataset of words/lines/documents of a uniform skew angle of Marathi and Hindi language. The proposed algorithm does

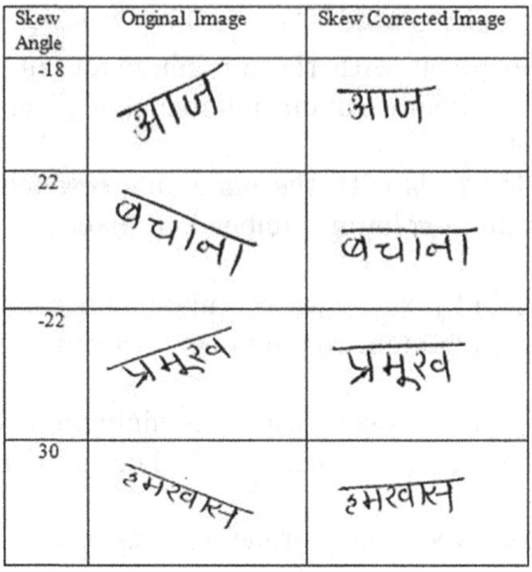

Skew Angle	Original Image	Skew Corrected Image
-18	आज	आज
22	वचाना	वचाना
-22	प्रमूख	प्रमूख
30	हमरवास्त	हमरवास्त

Fig. 6. Sample result of skew corrected words

not only work for handwritten data but also it works for typed or printed data. The algorithm is tested on 200 words, 100 lines and 100 paragraphs of uniform skew angle which containing handwritten and printed Devanagari script data. The dataset is used for proposed algorithm is trained dataset, means the images contained in dataset are originally at zero degree angle. Then each image is skewed manually at different angles for testing purpose. Later algorithm is applied on these manually skewed images and calculated skew angle is compared with their original manually rotated skewed angle. By mathematical formulation, 95% images in the dataset got correct result. In this way, the 95% accuracy of the proposed algorithm is calculated. On the basis of this manual testing process of detecting skew angle, accuracy is calculated. Figure 6 shows the some samples of result for word which shows skewed image and skew corrected image.

Table 1. Sample results of skewed line

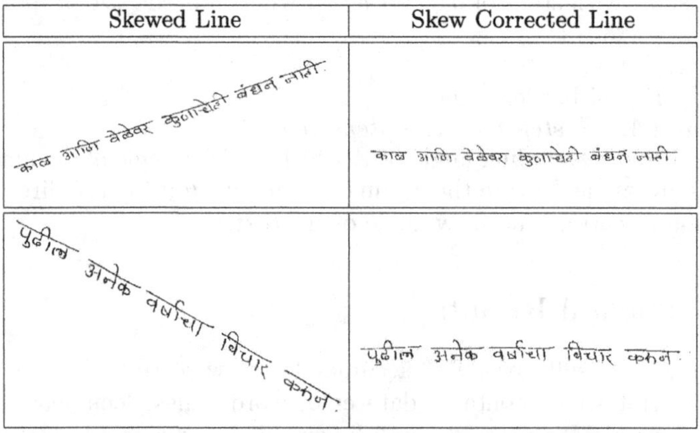

Skewed Line	Skew Corrected Line
काच आणि वेळेवर कुठासेही बंधन जयाती	काच आणि वेळेवर कुठासेही बंधन जयाती
पूर्वील अनेक वर्षांचा विचार करून	पूर्वील अनेक वर्षांचा विचार करून

Table 1 shows the sample results of lines with skew detection of positive and negative angle and skew correction of all these.

Table 2 shows the sample result of skew correction of uniform skew angle of paragraph. .

Table 2. Result for skewed paragraph

Skewed Paragraph	Skew Corrected Paragraph
इतिहासाची ठेवा आठवण एकवटुनी घडवू मीपण घ्या धडका पहाडावरती कोलमडती मला शिखरे दिसती	इतिहासाची ठेवा आठवण एकवटुनी घडवू मीपण घ्या धडका पहाडावरती कोलमडती मला शिखरे दिसती

This algorithm is also work if existance of graphical picture, tables, charts etc. Because the algorithm detects the only outer peripheral pixels to calculate the skew, so it does not matter in calculation of the skew. The only limitation for this case is, the picture or table or chart must be present in between the image. Figure 7 shows the result of skew detection of image containing existance of graphical image.

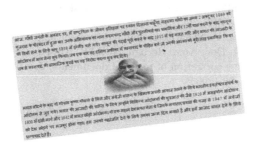

Fig. 7. Upper: skewed image with graphical picture, lower: skew corrected image

6   Conclusion

A new technique for skew detection and correction of handwritten word/line/document of Devanagari script language is presented here. This technique is based on peripheral pixels of an axes-parallel bounding box and bisection method. The dataset used for this experimental result is a primary dataset contains single words, lines and images of uniform skew of different angles of Hindi and Marathi languages (Devanagari script), which is made by collecting from various writers. This method gives 95% accuracy which is very good as compared to other methods. The proposed approach can be modified for future work for skew detection of documents contain multiple or non-uniform skew text.

References

1. Jundale, T.A., Hegadi, R.S.: Skew detection of Devanagari script using pixels of axes-parallel rectangle and linear regression. In: International Conference on Energy Systems and Applications, pp. 480–484. IEEE (2016)
2. Jundale, T.A., Hegadi, R.S.: Skew detection and correction of Devanagari script using Hough transform. Procedia Comput. Sci. **45**, 305–311 (2015)
3. Jundale, T., Hegadi, R.: Research survey on skew detection of Devanagari script. Int. J. Comput. Appl. **30**, 41–44 (2015)
4. Suran, K.: QR code image correction based on corner detection and convex hull algorithm. J. Multimedia **8**(6), 662–668 (2013)
5. Okun, O., Pietikainen, M., Sauvola, J.: Document skew estimation without angle range restriction. Int. J. Doc. Anal. Recogn. 132–144 (1999)
6. Chaudhuri, A., Chaudhuri, S.: Robust detection of skew in document images. IEEE Trans. Image Process. **6**(2), 344–349 (1997)
7. Fan, H., Zhu, L., Tang, Y.: Skew detection in document images based on rectangular active contour. Int. J. Doc. Anal. Recogn. (IJDAR) **13**(4), 261–269 (2010)
8. Abuhaiba, I.S.I.: Skew correction of textural documents. J. King Saud Univ. Comput. Inf. Sci. **15**, 73–93 (2003)

Eigen Value Based Features for Offline Handwritten Signature Verification Using Neural Network Approach

Amruta B. Jagtap$^{(\boxtimes)}$ and Ravindra S. Hegadi

Department of Computer Science, Solapur University, Solapur 413255, India
amrutaj88@gmail.com, rshegadi@gmail.com

Abstract. Handwritten Signature is primary means for authentication and identification process. In this paper, we have extracted the features based on Eigen values techniques. Eigen values are computed from upper and lower envelope, envelopes represents the contours of the signature. In proposed work we are using GPDS Synthetic Signature Corpus database. Significant features are extracted from signatures which consist of large and small Eigen values computed from upper envelope and lower envelope and its union values. Both the envelopes are fused by performing union operation and their covariance is computed. The difference and ratios of high and low points of both the envelopes are computed. Lastly average values of both the envelopes are obtained. These features set are coupled with neural network pattern recognition classifier that lead to 98.1% of accuracy and FAR 1.9%.

Keywords: Upper envelope · Lower envelope · Large Eigen values · Small Eigen values · Neural network classifier

1 Introduction

In the era of growing technology, biometric technique is used for the purpose of security in which the major concern is to avoid forgeries. Techniques are mainly used for personal identification, recognition and access control or for identifying individuals who are under surveillance due to their involvement in criminal activity. Signature verification is one among many of the biometric authentication systems. Basically there are two categories of biometric identifiers: (i) Physiological and (ii) Behavioral. Signature is one of the behavioral biometric identifier. Many other biometric traits are used to authenticate a person for his/her identity by using features such as signature, fingerprint, face etc. Because signature is the primary mechanism for both authentication and authorization in many legal transactions, the need for efficient automated solutions for signature recognition has increased [1]. Identification data such as PIN, Password or key cards, which can be lost, stolen, forgotten, but the handwritten signature are unique to an every person which is impossible to duplicate. In Present century huge number of transactions linked with financial and businesses are being

© Springer Nature Singapore Pte Ltd. 2017
K.C. Santosh et al. (Eds.): RTIP2R 2016, CCIS 709, pp. 39–48, 2017.
DOI: 10.1007/978-981-10-4859-3_4

authorized via signatures only. Hence there is a need for robust technique for automatic handwritten signature recognition.

There are basically two acquisition modes of Signature: (i) Online and (ii) Offline. Online Signature is also known as dynamic signature; it uses an electronic tablet that provides dynamic information usually available at high resolution. When the signature is produced, it captures the flux of the stylus that includes acceleration, velocity, and pen-pressure. Offline signature is also known as static signature that is scanned from paper document. Some times there is variation in the signatures due to sickness, old age, emotional states etc. To overcome these problems there is a need to develop robust signature identification system. Signature forgery is a crime and the act of replicating another person's signature for making fake document. In signature forgery cases, criminals use different methods, practice it and try to sign like original signatures. Though any forged individual tries to make signature like original signatures, still their will be some difference between original and forged signature. Depending on the forgery done by the individual they can be classified as:

(i) Random: The individual that do not recognize the shape of original signature.
(ii) Simple: The individual that can recognize the shape of the original signature.
(iii) Skilled: The individual that can recognize the shape, with much practice of the signature.

The proposed work mainly focuses on whether given signature is genuine or forged. Main task of proposed work is to achieve maximum efficiency and accuracy rate, and reduced false acceptance rate and false rejection rate.

2   Literature Survey

Many researcher's have proposed different techniques on handwritten signature recognition but still it remains challenging problem in image processing. Successive signatures by the same person will differ in their scale and orientation. To improve the efficiency of the signature recognition systems, different methods with various approaches have been developed. Srikanta Pal et al. proposed new encoding techniques which consist of Gabor filter based features with SURF (G-SURF). Implementation is done by using GPDS database and features obtained are applied to SVM which yeild to 97.05% of accuracy [3]. Mujahed Jarad et al. proposed ANN algorithm to detect forgeries, to recognize the system Back-propagation algorithm is used. The system is divided into two stage, training and testing, training is performed on 900 signatures and for testing 400 signatures. System is tested in three stages, at each stage different FAR, FRR values are obtained and average value of FAR 0.10, FRR 0.04 [2]. Mustafa B.Y. et al. developed new approach on combination of HOG and LBP features. To divide the signatures into zones, Cartesian and polar coordinate systems is used. Classification is done by fusion of classifier that is global and user-dependent SVM's. In user dependent svm each user is trained separately, and global svm is trained with all user's signatures. Proposed system achieved 15.41% EER [5]. Vahid Kiani et al. developed a new method using local Radon Transform. The objective of using local radon transform locally is to detect the line segment and also for feature extraction that gives relevant and more detailed information. Implementation is done on two datasets Persian and English datasets which leads to good results. These obtained results were compared with other two methods, which yeild FAR 2% and FRR 19%. Obtained results is best as compared to other two [4]. Poornima G. Patil and Ravindra S. Hegadi have developed a work based on wavelet packets and level based scoring for classification. The Classification result were having FAR 12% and FRR 8% [6]. They further proposed system based on wavelet technique that implemented on standard GPDS database and to train the system they used SVM classifier with linear and non-linear kernel. The results achieved using linear kernel was having FAR of 13% and FRR of 10%, where as for nonlinear kernel FAR of 15% and FRR of 12% were reported [7]. Md. Asraful Haque and Tofik Ali proposed a method based on parallel computing. They partitioned image into some blocks and features are applied on each block. Each block consist of features such as number of pixels, block center and distance from image center. The proposed method obtained 92.82% of accuracy which eliminates simple and random forgeries and reduces skilled forgery [8]. Muhammad Reza Pourshahabi et al. proposed a work based on Contourlet transform. It is most effective tool for image representation. Significant features are derived from images such as localization, directionality, Multiresolution etc. Feature vectors of Persian and English signatures are compared using Euclidean distance as a classifier. For skilled persian they achieved 14.50% of FAR and 12.50% of FRR and for skilled english 22.72% of FAR and 23.18% of FRR [10].

3   Methodology

There are four major steps in implementation of proposed technique for signature recognition. They are as follows:

3.1   Signature Acquisition

In proposed work, we are using GPDS synthetic Signature database. Different modeled pens were used to generate the signatures. We have used 1000 signature's which contain genuine and forged signatures.

3.2   Preprocessing

To improve the efficiency, accuracy and to reduce computational needs preprocessing is very important step. To get good quality results, the signature recognition method requires noise free image as input image. Input image is converted to binary by using gray thresh as shown in Fig. 1. Global threshold is used to convert an intensity image to a binary image, where intensity value will be either 0 or 1. To reduce the intra-class variance of the black and white pixels we used gray thresh function which uses Otsu's method. After binarization, image is resized to standard value and than morphological thinning operation is performed. Thinning is the process that reduces the width of edges, lines and curves in the image to single pixel thickness. Lastly bounding box is applied over the image to remove unwanted region.

3.3   Feature Extraction

Features are image information which are significant to solve the computational task in image processing. Feature extraction is the key process of extracting meaningful or unique information from image. Different features extracted from preprocessed image for the proposed signature recognition are upper and lower envelope, Large and small Eigen values of both envelope, combination of both upper and lower envelope shown in Fig. 3. It is well known fact that the small Eigen value characterizes the linear property of a set of pixels. The smaller the Eigen value of the covariance matrix of connected pixels, the stronger is the evidence that those connected pixels form a linear segment [9].

Upper and Lower Envelope: Upper envelope is a curve connecting uppermost pixels of the signature. Likewise, lower envelope is a curve connecting lower most pixels. Figure 2 depicts the upper and lower envelopes extracted from signatures. To extract upper envelope, each column of the image is traversed from top to bottom. The location of the first white pixel in each column came across is marked as a point of the upper envelope. In the same way for lower envelope, each column of the image is traversed from bottom to top recording the first white pixel of the lower envelope.

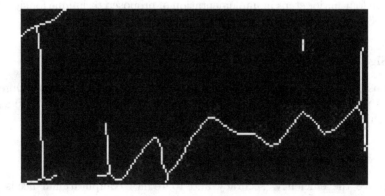

Fig. 1. Input signature

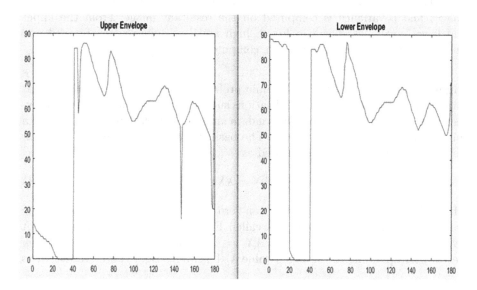

Fig. 2. Upper and lower envelope of input signature

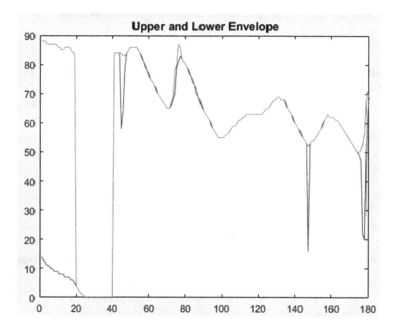

Fig. 3. Fusion of upper and lower envelope

Both these images were fused by applying union operation among these images and covariance is computed on the resultant image. From the upper and lower envelopes shown in Fig. 2, high and low points were obtained and further their difference and ratio are computed.

Eigen Values: In real world dynamic problem, Eigen values have their great importance and used in many applications such as linear algebra, spectral analysis which is important part of Modern data analysis, correlation analysis for data mining and statistical analysis etc. The basic Mathematical equation for computation of Eigen Values is expressed as:

$$AX = \lambda X \tag{1}$$

where $A = n \times n$ matrix, X is a non-zero $n \times 1$ vector, λ is a Scalar value (can be real or complex), which is called Eigen Value of $n \times n$ matrix A. A significant solution exists as X of $AX = \lambda X$. Such an X is called as Eigen Vector corresponding to the Eigen value λ. The above Eq. 1 can be rewritten as

$$A \times X - \lambda \times X = 0 \tag{2}$$

$$A \times X - \lambda \times I \times X = 0 \tag{3}$$

$$(A - \lambda \times I)X = 0 \tag{4}$$

Here I is identity matrix. If X is non-zero then equation becomes

$$\det(A\lambda \times I) = 0 \tag{5}$$

This is called Characteristic Equation of A. For each Eigen value there will be an eigenvector for which the Eigen value equation is true. For calculating large and small Eigen values of both the envelope, firstly we need to calculate covariance of both envelope and then we can compute large and small Eigen values by using following formulae:

$$\lambda_L = \frac{1}{2} \left[C_{11} + C_{22} + \sqrt{(C_{11} - C_{22})^2 + 4C_{12}^2} \right] \tag{6}$$

$$\lambda_S = \frac{1}{2} \left[C_{11} + C_{22} - \sqrt{(C_{11} - C_{22})^2 + 4C_{12}^2} \right] \tag{7}$$

Where, $\begin{bmatrix} C_{11} & C_{12} \\ C_{21} & C_{22} \end{bmatrix}$ is the covariance matrix of λ_L and λ_S. Later we computed union of large and small Eigen values of upper and lower envelopes.

3.4   Neural Network Based Classification

In pattern recognition neural network based classifier is used in various research area like handwritten numeral recognition [11], face recognition and biometrics. All above features extracted from signatures are fed to neural network pattern recognition classifier. Feature matrix with target class labels are passed to neural network for classification purpose. Neural network is trained with scaled conjugate gradient backpropagation, by using 50 hidden layers. Feature matrix is divided into three categories as training 90%, validation 5% and for testing purpose 5% samples are used. The goal is to minimize the cross entropy results along with error percentage. The number of epoch are 1000 but the best performance with gradient $= 0.00048015$ and validation checks $= 6$ is at 49 iterations. The proposed network classifies the vector arbitrarily which is a two-layer feed-forward network with sigmoid hidden and softmax output neurons (Fig. 4).

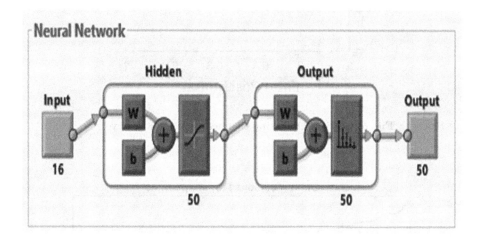

Fig. 4. Two layer feed-forward network.

3.5   Experimental Results

The proposed methodology has been implemented on the data set of 1000 images which contain both genuine and forged signature samples. All the techniques have been implemented by using MATLAB (R2016a) version and relevant output depicted below. All ROC plot shows the result of Training roc, Validation roc and Testing roc (Fig. 5).

The accuracy obtained after implementation of proposed method is 98.1% and False Acceptance rate is 1.9%. Due to accidental change in the shape of character there are some failure in recognition (Fig. 6).

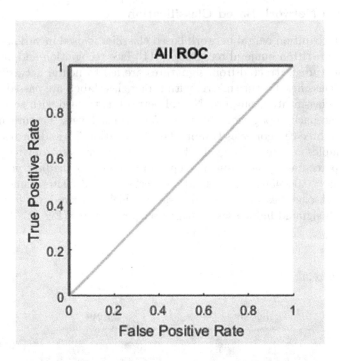

Fig. 5. Receiver Operating Characteristic (ROC) curve.

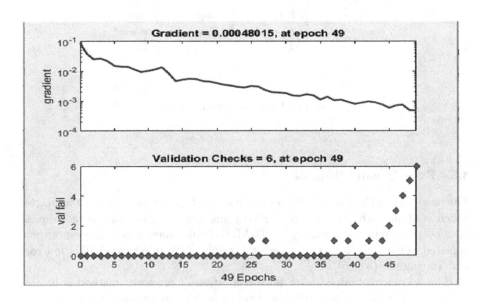

Fig. 6. Gradient and validation checks

4   Conclusion

In this paper, we have presented a neural network based classification technique to recognize the handwritten signatures. Neural network can be trained to solve problem that are difficult for conventional computers. Neural network have provided state-of-art for many applications such as aerospace, automotive, industrial, robotics etc. The proposed method can be used as effective signature verification system to improve the performance, efficiency and accuracy. The area of handwritten signature verification has broadly researched but still today it remains an open research problem. Verification is carried out on the basis of features that extracted from signatures. The overall performance of the proposed system with accuracy is 98.1% and FAR is 1.9%.

Acknowledgments. The first author extends his sincere gratitude to Department of Electronics and Information Technology (DeitY), New Delhi for granting Visvesvaraya PhD fellowship to her through file no. PhD-MLA\4(34)\201-1 Dated: 05/11/2015.

References

1. Prasad, A.G., Amaresh, V.M.: An offline signature verification system. In: IEEE International Conference on Signal and Image Processing Applications, pp. 59–64, 7–9 November 2009
2. Jarad, M., Al-Najdawi, N., Tedmori, S.: Offline handwritten signature verification system using a supervised neural network approach. In: IEEE International Conference on Computer Science and Information Technology, pp. 189–195, 26–27 March 2014
3. Pal, S., Chanda, S., Pal, U., Franke, K., Blumenstein, M.: Off-line signature verification using G-SURF. In: International Conference on Intelligent Systems Design and Applications, 27–29 November 2012
4. Kiani, V., Pourreza-Shahri, R., Pourreza, H.R.: Offline signature verification using local radon transform and support vector machines. Int. J. Image Process. (IJIP) 3(5), 184–194 (2009)
5. Mustafa, B.Y., Berrin, Y., Alisher, K., Caglar, T.: Offline signature verification using classifier combination of HOG and LBP features. In: International Joint Conference on Biometrics (IJCB), 11–13 October 2011
6. Patil, P.G., Hegadi, R.S.: Offline handwritten signatures classification using wavelets and support vector machines. Int. J. Eng. Sci. Innov. Technol. (IJESIT) 2(4), 573–578 (2013)
7. Patil, P.G., Hegadi, R.S.: Offline handwritten signatures classification using wavelet packets and level similarity based scoring. Int. J. Eng. Technol. 5(1), 421–426 (2013)
8. Asraful Haque, M., Ali, T.: Improved offline signature verification method using parallel block analysis. In: International Conference on Recent Advances in Computing and Software Systems, April 2012
9. Guru, D.S., Shekar, B.H., Nagabhushan, P.: A simple and robust line detection algorithm based on small Eigen value analysis. Pattern Recogn. Lett. 25, 1–13 (2003)

10. Pourshahabi, M.R., Pourreza, H.R.: Offline handwritten signature identification and verification using Contourlet transform. In: International Conference of Soft Computing and Pattern Recognition, 7 December 2009
11. Hegadi, R.S., Kamble, P.M.: Recognition of Marathi handwritten numerals using multi-layer feed-forward neural network. In: World Congress on Computing and Communication Technologies (WCCCT), pp. 21–24. IEEE (2014)

An Approach for Logo Detection and Retrieval in Documents

Y.H. Sharath Kumar$^{(\boxtimes)}$ and K.C. Ranjith

Department of Information Science and Engineering,
Maharaja Institute of Technology,
Belawadi, Sri-rangapatna Tq, Mandya, Karnataka, India
sharathyhk@gmail.com, ranjithkc01@gmail.com

Abstract. Detection and Retrieval of logos in document images has become a fundamental concept in the Document Image Analysis and Recognition (DIAR). In this work, we propose a system to identify logos from a given document. The approach initially eliminates the text and later the logos are extracted from the remaining contents through proposed logo detection algorithm using central moments. For detected logos, the scale invariant feature transforms are extracted and the extracted features are reduced using principle component analysis (PCA). For effective retrieval of logos, an indexing mechanism called k-d tree is used. In order to substantiate the efficacy of the proposed model experimentation is conducted based on a dataset over 500 various samples such as conference certificates, degree certificates, attendance certificates, etc. Further, to study the efficiency of the proposed method we have compared the obtained results with the results provided by five human experts and the results are more encouraging.

Keywords: Logo detection · Central moments · Human experts · SIFT · PCA

1 Introduction

Logos are the brand ambassadors of each and every organization whether it is a business or a government, it promotes their ideas or products with the help of the logo by investing millions of rupees on it. In every government and business document in the world has a logo which plays an important role in providing the source information of the document and in identifying the particular organization. Logo detection and recognition has become a hot topic in the Document Image Analysis and Recognition (DIAR) and pattern recognition. Computer vision methodologies and pattern recognition techniques are used in the process of automatic logo recognition and computer aided techniques makes it much easier. Logos in the document convey a lot of information like, to which organization does the document etc. Often logos come in different shapes, forms; dimensions and other complexities like, few are made of only text, graphics and in the combination of both text and graphics. These features of the logo help to

K.C. Santosh et al. (Eds.): RTIP2R 2016, CCIS 709, pp. 49–58, 2017.
DOI: 10.1007/978-981-10-4859-3_5

differentiate from other content in the body of the document. Features of logo contribute in logo detection, retrieval and matching in document.

2   Literature Survey

Here we review the papers that related to logo detection and retrieval. Viet et al. [1] have presented methodology for digital document categorization based on logo spotting. The logos are recognized using key point matching. Initially, the logos are segmented using spatial density-based clustering. Stefan et al. [2] have proposed a highly effective and scalable framework for recognizing logos in images. Alireza et al. [3] proposed a coarse-to-fine logo detection scheme for document images. The content of a document image is pruned by utilizing a decision tree. The Nearest Neighbour (NN) classifier is used for the purpose of classification. Divya and Padmalatha [4] have proposed a technique which can recognize different instances logos. Here the logo classification is depends on the description of a Context Dependent Similarity (CDS) kernel. Baiying et al. [5] have worked on the classification of merchandise logos with the combination of local edge-based Descriptor, spatial histogram and salient region detection. Guangyu et al. [6] presented a automatic retrieval system for document images. SIFT features with Kd-tree indexing algorithm is used for efficient logo retrieval. Rajiv et al. [7] have developed a retrieval system for logo in document images. SURF features with indexing algorithm are used for efficient logo retrieval. Guangyu et al. [8] has proposed an automatic technique to identify logos from documents. Initially, the logos are segmented using boosting algorithm. The SIFT features are extracted from the detected logos. The KD-tree indexing algorithm is used for efficient logo retrieval. Shridevi and Dhandra [9] developed a model for automatic detection and recognition of logos. Marcal et al. [10] have proposed a method which classifies the documents such as receipts or bills using bag-of-words features. Hongye et al. [11] proposed an algorithm for logo detection based on boundaries of the logos. The detected logos are classified using decision tree classifier. Marcal et al. [12] proposed two models for logo detection and classification system. The first method deals with bag-of-visual-words and second with sliding-window technique. The extracted features are fed into support vector machine (SVM) classifier. Marcal et al. [13] designed an approach for grouping and indexing digital logo libraries which are similar to the trademark and patent offices. A queried-by-example retrieval system is proposed, which is able to fetch logos from dataset based on similarity of images. Kuo-Wei et al. [14] presented a logo classification system which extracts features like histograms of oriented gradient (HOGE) and scale invariant feature transform (ASIFT). The extracted features are fed into support vector machine (SVM) classifier. Xiaobing et al. [15] developed a method that focuses on collecting representative logo images automatically without human labeling or the seed images from the internet. Nishanth et al. [16] designed a technique for classifying the logos based on Context-Dependent Similarity (CDS) kernel. Souvik [17] studied shape based feature values of logo images. Mohammadreza et al. [18] discussed the various types of algorithms and their result on retrieval of document images and proposed a framework for classifying the retrieval approaches of document images. Stefan et al. [19] proposed a system for identify the logos in images using local features and spatial structure which is composition of triangles and edges. David et al. [20] proposed a method for recognizing logo with the help of multi-level staged approach which is combination of global and local fine invariants. Aya et al. [21] have described an approach for logo representation based on positive and negative shape features. The organization of paper is as follows. In Sect. 3 the proposed method is explained with neat block diagram along with brief introduction to log detection and central moments. Feature extraction method in Sect. 3.3. In Sect. 3.4, brief description of feature reduction using PCA. The experimental results are discussed in Sect. 5 and paper is concluded in Sect. 6.

3 Proposed Work

The proposed method contains Logo detection, Feature Extraction, Dimensionality Reduction and Experimentation for both detection and Retrieval. The following subsection gives the brief description of each method.

3.1 Proposed Logo Detection Method

The proposed method for detection of logos in a given document is done in three different stages. In the first stage outer boundary and background are eliminated. The second stage detects lines in the document. In final stage the logos are detected using central moment variations. After logos extraction an evaluation process is performed on detection of logos, we asked five human experts identify the logos in documents by drawing rectangular box. Later we match the co-ordinates between the logos identified by proposed method and human experts. The block diagram in Fig. 1 shows computational process involved in the proposed methodology.

Detection. Normally, majority of documents are made up with outer boundary, logo, back-ground, text area etc. Initially for a given document we compute the edges using canny edge detection method [23]. In document, the area of logo and characters with bigger font are the largest part in a document. The unwanted components, which are reasonably smaller in size, are eliminated using morphological opening and closing operations [11]. Figure 2(a) shows a document with background art and logo. Figure 2(b) shows result of document image after eliminating smaller components. Once the smaller components are eliminated from the given document, the remaining part consists of larger components of logo and bigger printed words. The next subsection describes the detection of logo area based on component variations using central moments.

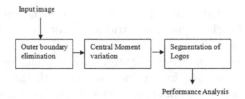

Fig. 1. Shows computational process involved in the proposed methodology.

Fig. 2. (a) Shows a document with background art and logo. (b) Shows result of document image after eliminating smaller components.

3.2   Central Moments

The input documents under consideration like birth/death certificates, degrees and conference certificates have less moment variations for logo regions. Image moments and their functions have been utilized as features in many image processing applications like object classification, target identification and shape analysis [22]. Moments of an image are treated as region based shape descriptors. In this direction we have attempted to identify lines in a document using image moments like Geometric moments [21,22], Zernike moments [21] and Central moments [23]. Out of these central moments are found to be more suitable for line detection. The central moments are one of the image moments that are invariant for both scale and translation and is well suited to describe the shape features of the object. The use of moments for image analysis is straight forward if a binary or grey level image segment is considered as a two-dimensional density distribution function. The invariant features can be achieved using central moments, and the computation of central moments for two dimensional discrete function is defined [23] as,

$$\mu pq = \Sigma_{x=1}^{m} \Sigma_{y=1}^{n} (x - \bar{x})^p (p - \bar{y})^q f(x, y) \tag{1}$$

Where $\bar{x}$ and $\bar{y}$ are the centroid of the image of size m × n, p and q are the order of moments in x and y direction respectively, f(x, y) is the intensity value at given (x, y) coordinates. The logo regions have less moment variations in the document, the moment variations in the document are identified using central moments.

$$\mu 30 = \Sigma_{x=1}^{n} (x - \bar{x})^p f(x, y) \tag{2}$$

For each component of an image, h values of $\mu 30$ are obtained from Eq. (2), where h being the height of the corresponding component. Similar repeated high central moment values indicate the presence of logos in the documents. If μ_{30}^k is the central moment value for kth component, then > threshold describes a in the kth component. High central moment's values for each component are decided based on a threshold value. The threshold value for a component is obtained by assuming an imaginary line for each component and the central moment for the imaginary line is computed. Threshold for the component is fixed as 50 of central moment of imaginary line in that component. The components containing logos are identified and labeled as shown in Fig. 3.

3.3   Scale Invariant Feature Transform (SIFT)

Scale Invariant Feature Transform (SIFT) Descriptors SIFT is one of the most widely used local approaches. It finds local structures that are present in different views of an image. It also provides a description of these structures reasonably invariant to image variations such as translation, rotation, scale, illumination and affine transformations. Moreover, several studies have shown that the SIFT descriptor performs better than others. The SIFT algorithm has four major phases (a) Extrema Detection, (b) Key point Localization, (c) Orientation Assignment, (d) Key point Descriptor Generation.

Fig. 3. Shows a input image and components containing logos are identified using central moments.

3.4   Principal Component Analysis

Principal component analysis [19] is used to reduce the extracted features. The algorithm of PCA is provided below.

Algorithm
Phase-1: Apply PCA to Reduce the Dimension of Data Set
Step 1: Organize the dataset in a matrix X.
Step 2: Normalize the data set using Z-score.
Step 3: Calculate the singular value decomposition of the data matrix. X = UDVT
Step 4: Calculate the variance using the diagonal elements of D.
Step 5: Sort variances in decreasing order.
Step 6: Choose the p principal components from V with largest variances.
Step 7: Form the transformation matrix W consisting of those PCs.
Step 8: Find the reduced projected dataset Y in a new coordinate axis by applying W to X.

4 Dataset

In this work we have created our own database despite an existence of other database. The data set consists of 500 real document images. The samples include conference certificates, attendance certificates, degree certificates, transfer certificates, etc. The copies were scanned using an hp flat-bed scanner to produce bitmap images at 300 dpi. Figure 4 shows some of the samples of logos collected and Fig. 5 shows the samples of document images.

Fig. 4. Samples of logos that are used in the proposed work

5 Experimentation

In this section, we present the results of the experiments conducted to demonstrate the effectiveness of the proposed model on Tobacco-800 dataset. This database has 500 document images.

5.1 Detection Experimentation

During experimentation we asked five human experts to draw manually a minimum rectangular box on logo part of the document for creating ground truth for our experimentation. Figure 6 shows some samples of documents with a minimum bounding rectangular box fixed by the proposed logo detection method. Figure 7 presents some examples of document images with detected logo parts by the proposed method and the corresponding ground truth marked by the five experts HE1, HE2, HE3 HE4 and HE5. The results of the proposed method are compared against each ground truth and percentage of overlapping area (matched area) is calculated as a measure of goodness of the proposed method. The numbers shown below each of the ground truth in Fig. 6 are the calculated matching scores. It shall be noted that the matching scores obtained are of acceptable level, indicating that the logo part detected by the proposed method is almost same as that of the logo part marked by the experts. The overall matching score of the proposed logo detection method due to all 500 images of documents against each expert are shown in Fig. 8. Figure 8; demonstrate that the proposed whorl detection method is more consistent with HE2 and HE4 and less consistent with the other two experts.

Fig. 5. Samples of document images collected

Fig. 6. Shows some samples of documents with a minimum bounding rectangular box fixed by the proposed logo detection method.

Fig. 7. The overall matching score of the proposed logo detection method due to all 500 images of documents against each expert

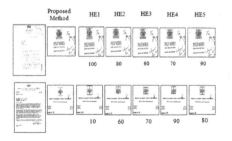

Fig. 8. Presents some examples of document images with detected logo parts by the proposed method and the corresponding ground truth marked by the five experts HE1, HE2, HE3 HE4 and HE5 with the calculated matching scores

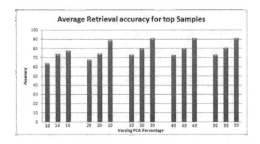

Fig. 9. Retrieval accuracy for top 5 to top 30 samples

5.2 Indexing Experimentation

A general approach to efficiently support drawing retrieval from large databases has not been developed so far. The majority of current approaches are designed to handle a large dataset. Our approach takes the size of databases in consideration. Thus, to accomplish the speed of the retrieval system and to make the retrieval system available to retrieve from the huge dataset, to make this possible and indexing method is used as the part of the whole retrieval system. The kd-tree (k-dimensional) indexing schema lies its efficient from the point of search time. The proposed indexing method reduces time for search, with good pruning. Figure 9 shows the result of the retrieval accuracy for varying PCA from 10 to 50 and also training percentage (30%, 50% and 70%). To evaluate the efficiency of the proposed method the experimentation is conducted by varying the samples from top 5 to top 30. From the experimentation we have got the 91.3% result in retrieving the logo from the database using our proposed method. We have got this result when we kept the PCA to 50% and in retrieving the top 20 samples. This shows the efficiency of the proposed method.

6   Conclusion

In this paper, we have proposed a novel method to identify the logos using Central moments. We have conducted experimentation on our own dataset. To corroborate the efficiency of the proposed method we have created ground truth where five human experts have identified the logos by drawing rectangular bounding box manually. Later we matched the bounding box drawn by the proposed method with bounding box of human experts to study the error analysis. For detected logos, the SIFT features are extracted and reduced using PCA. K-d tree is used to for logo retrieval.

References

1. Le, V.P., Nayef, N., Visani, M., Ogier, J.-M., De Tran, C.: Document retrieval based on logo spotting using key-point matching. In: 22nd International Conference on Pattern Recognition (ICPR), pp. 3056–3061 (2014)

2. Romberg, S., Pueyo, L.G., Lienhart, R., van Zwol, R.: Scalable logo recognition in real-world images. In: ACM International Conference on Multimedia Retrieval (ICMR 2011), Trento, April 2011
3. Alaei, A., Delalandre, M., Girard, N.: Logo detection using painting based representation and probability features. In: Proceedings of 12th International Conference on Document Analysis and Recognition (ICDAR 2013), pp. 1267–1271. IEEE Computer Society (2013)
4. Divya Susmitha, C., Padmalatha, L.: Context dependent logo detection and recognition based on context dependent similarity kernel. Int. J. Comput. Appl. $106(11)$, November 2014. (0975–8887)
5. Lei, B., Thing, V.L.L., Chen, Y., Lim, W.-Y.: Logo classification with edge-based DAISY descriptor. In: 2012 IEEE International Symposium on Multimedia (ISM), pp. 222–228, 10–12 December 2012
6. Zhu, G., Doermann, D.: Logo matching for document image retrieval. In: 10th International Conference on Document Analysis and Recognition (2009)
7. Jain, R., Doermann, D.: Logo retrieval in document images. In: Proceedings of the 2012 10th IAPR International Workshop on Document Analysis Systems, DAS 2012, pp. 135–139 (2012)
8. Zhu, G., Doremann, D.: Automatic document logo detection. In: ICDAR, pp. 864–868 (2007)
9. Soma, S., Dhandra, B.V.: Automatic logo recognition system from the complex document using shape and moment invariant features. Int. J. Adv. Comput. Sci. Technol. (IJACST) $4(2)$, 06–13 (2015)
10. Rusinol, M., Llados, J.: Logo spotting by a bag-of-words approach for document categorization. In: ICDAR, pp. 111–115 (2009)
11. Wang, H., Chen, Y.: Logo detection in document images based on boundary extension of feature rectangles. In: ICDAR, pp. 1335–1339 (2009)
12. Rusinol, M., D'Andecy, V.P., Karatzas, D., Llados, J.: Classification of administrative document images by logo identification. In: Proceedings of the 9th ICGR (2011). doi:10.1007/978-3-642-36824-0_5
13. Rusiñol, M., Lladós, J.: Efficient logo retrieval through hashing shape context descriptors. In: DAS 2010, Boston, MA, USA, 9–11 June 2010
14. Li, K.-W., Chen, S.-Y., Su, S., Duh, D.-J., Zhang, H., Li, S.: Logo Detection with Extendibility and Discrimination. Springer Science+Business Media, New York (2013)
15. Liu, X., Zhang, B.: Automatic collecting representative logo images from the internet. Tsinghua Sci. Technol. $18(6)$, 606–617 (2013)
16. Nishanth, T.R., Simon, J.: Logo Matching, recognition with interest points using context-dependent similarity. In: International Conference on Humming Bird, March 2014. International Journal of Engineering Research, Applications (IJERA), ISSN 2248–9622
17. Datta, S.: Dissertation on logo recognition using moment invariants. Thesis for Master in Multimedia Development (2013)
18. Keyvanpour, M., Tavoli, R.: Document image retrieval: algorithms, analysis and promising directions. Int. J. Softw. Eng. Appl. $7(1)$, 93–106 (2013)
19. Romberg, S., Pueyo, L.G., Lienhart, R., van Zwol, R.: Scalable logo recognition in real-world images. In: Proceedings of ACM International Conference on Multimedia Retrieval. ACM (2011)
20. Doermann, D.S., Rivlin, E., Weiss, I.: Logo recognition using geometric in-variants, pp. 894–897. IEEE (1993)

21. Soffer, A., Samet, H.: Using negative shape features for logo similarity matching. In: 14th International Conference on Pattern Recognition, Brisbane, Australia (1998)
22. Folkers, A., Samet, H.: Content-based image retrieval using Fourier descriptors on a logo database. In: Proceedings of the 16th International Conference on Pattern Recognition, Quebec City, Canada, Vol. III, pp. 521–524, August 2002
23. Canny. J.: A computational approach to edge detection. IEEE Trans. Pattern Anal. Mach. Intell. 8(6), 679–698 (1986)

Spotting Symbol over Graphical Documents Via Sparsity in Visual Vocabulary

Do Thanh Ha[1(✉)], Salvatore Tabbone[2(✉)], and Oriol Ramos Terrades[3(✉)]

[1] Faculty of Mathematics - Mechanics - Informatics,
VNU - Hanoi University of Science, Hanoi, Vietnam
hadt_tct@vnu.edu.vn

[2] Université de Lorraine - LORIA, Vandœuvre-lès-Nancy Cedex, France
tabbone@loria.fr

[3] Universitat Autònoma de Barcelona - Computer Vision Center, Bellaterra, Spain
oriolrt@cvc.uab.cat

Abstract. This paper proposes a new approach to localize symbol in the graphical documents using sparse representations of local descriptors over learning dictionary. More specifically, a training database, being local descriptors extracted from documents, is used to build the learned dictionary. Then, the candidate regions into documents are defined following the similarity property between sparse representations of local descriptors. A vector model for candidate regions and for a query symbol is constructed based on the sparsity in a visual vocabulary where the visual words are columns in the learned dictionary. The matching process is performed by comparing the similarity between vector models. The first evaluation on SESYD database demonstrates that the proposed method is promising.

Keywords: Spotting graphical symbols · Sparsity · Learned dictionary · Shape context · Interested points

1 Introduction

Among the graphics recognition community, a lot of efforts have been devoted in the last years to deal with the problem of identifying regions likely to contain a certain symbol within graphics-rich documents. One of the first approaches was the retrieval of engineering drawings based on the use of a stochastic models [13]. The main advantage of this method is that it works well even where the query symbol is embedded in, for example, is connected to other parts in the drawing. However, this performance is not good for the complex queries having several elements with spatial relationship between them.

Other techniques [2,3,9,12,17] rely on the structural information inherent in graphical symbols such as points, lines, junctions, regions etc. In that methods, graphical entities are encoded as attributed graphs and then the stage of localization symbols in documents is done using subgraph isomorphism algorithms. In general, the subgraph matching algorithms suffer from a huge computational

© Springer Nature Singapore Pte Ltd. 2017
K.C. Santosh et al. (Eds.): RTIP2R 2016, CCIS 709, pp. 59–70, 2017.
DOI: 10.1007/978-981-10-4859-3_6

burden, although particular cases of subgraph isomorphism can be solved in polynomial time [8]. Thus, these approaches are insufficient when working with the larger collection of data. In [6,23], some indexing strategies are proposed to reduce the retrieval time and to increase the potential applications of these approaches.

Some of the methods [17,22] work with low-level pixel features on regions of interest of the documents. After ad-hoc segmentation, global pixel-based descriptors of regions [14] are computed and compared with the query symbols. A distance metric is used to decide the retrieval ranks and to check whether the retrievals are relevant or not. However, the limitation of these methods is one-to-one feature matching and they only work for a limited set of symbols.

Like the methods based on low-level pixel features, the methods as in [18,24] also works with ad-hoc segmentation. However, these methods compute the vectorial signatures instead of pixel feature. The disadvantage of these method is that they do not work well in the real-world applications since symbols are effected by noisy images. In addition, the assumptions the symbol always fall into interest region can compute the vectorial signature inside those regions are other limitation of these methods.

In this paper we propose a new two-stage method for symbol localization in graphical documents. In the first stage, the training database, being the local descriptors computed on interest points of documents, is used to learn the visual dictionary. In the second stage, we define the *similarity* property between two descriptors to localize some candidate regions over documents. In addition, to keep only the candidate regions where the query symbol actually is, we propose to use the visual vocabulary to construct the vector model of region. Then, the regions contains the request symbols over documents are found out by comparing vector models.

The organize of this paper as follow: Sects. 2 and 3 describe how to calculate the local descriptor adapted to the graphical document, and how to learn a visual vocabulary from the training set being the local descriptors. The details of the symbol localization process is addressed in Sect. 4. The first evaluations of proposed approach is dedicated in Sect. 5. Finally, we conclude and discuss the future work in Sect. 6.

2   Local Descriptor for Document

Like the shape context, the shape context of interest points (SCIP) [15] also presents the relationship between points of object, but instead of the relationship between contour points, it describes the relationship between the key-points and the contour points, which not only reduces the size of the descriptor but also remains the invariance to scaling and rotation thanks to the information about the dominant orientation of interest points. In addition, the local descriptor as SCIP and the learned dictionary are used to increase the performance of recognition system [5].

This paper also focus on the use of sparse representation over learned dictionary for spotting symbols in graphical documents. When working on the whole document, the symbols have not been segmented, and using interest points, the contour points being far from them provide less useful information to discriminate objects. Therefore, the SCIP cannot be applied at document level. Instead we define the neighborhood region for each reference interest point as in [4,14]. This region needs to ensure the invariance of SCIP computed inside it, thus it cannot be fix a prior. This difficulty is overcome by using the scale on which the interest point detected. More details, with each interest point, the neighborhood region associated with it is an ellipse that is defined with the centre at this point, and the semi-major axis, the semi-minor axis are decided depending on the scale in which this interest point is detected.

This extension of SCIP descriptor for a document level is called ESCIP descriptor from now on. In fact, ESCIP for the neighborhood region corresponding to one interest point in the document is the SCIPs calculated on this neighborhood region.

3   Visual Vocabulary of ESCIP

Visual vocabulary of ESCIP is the learned dictionary in which visual words are columns in this dictionary. This section describes how to build the learned dictionary of ESCIP descriptors and illustrates how one signal is presented over this dictionary. In general, the learned dictionary of ESCIP is the dictionary constructed from the training dataset $\mathcal{H} = \{\mathcal{H}_1, ..., \mathcal{H}_n\}$ being the ESCIP descriptors extracted from n documents. By applying one of the learned algorithms, we learn the dictionary $A \in \mathbb{R}^{L \times M}$ satisfying that each ESCIP descriptor $h_j \in \mathcal{H}$ in training dataset has an optimally sparse approximation $\bar{x}_j$ in this dictionary satisfying $\|A\bar{x}_j - h_j\|_2 \leq \epsilon$ or finding:

$$\min_{A, x_j} \sum_j \|x_j\|_0 \text{ subject to } \|h_j - Ax_j\|_2 \leq \epsilon, \text{ for all } h_j \in \mathcal{H} \qquad (1)$$

This dictionary can be obtained by the learning process. This process iteratively adjusts A via two main stages: *sparse coding stage* and *update dictionary stage*. In the sparse coding stage, all sparse representation x_j of $h_j \in \mathcal{H}$ are found by solving Eq. (2) on the condition that A is fixed.

$$\min_{x_j} \|x_j\|_0 \text{ subject to } \|Ax_j - h_j\|_2 \leq \epsilon \text{ for all } h_j \in \mathcal{H} \qquad (2)$$

The Eq. (2) can be solved by the greedy techniques or relaxation one. By comparing greedy algorithms, we notice that orthogonal matching pursuit (OMP) algorithm [16] does not provide a better approximation to the solution, but its computing cost time is lower. Moreover, the OMP can be used to find the approximate solutions instead of exact ones by changing its stopping rule as accumulating nonzero elements in the solution vector until the reconstruction error is less than ϵ. Therefore, we decide to use OMP algorithm in this paper.

In the update dictionary stage, an updating rule is applied to optimize the sparse representation $\mathcal{X} = \{x_j\}$ of all $h_j \in \mathcal{H}$. To the best of our knowledge, there

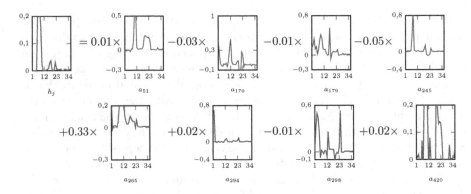

Fig. 1. The presentation of ESCIP descriptor as linear combination of columns in the dictionary A

are 4 well-known learning algorithms named K-SVD [1], MOD [7], ODL [11], and RLS-DLA [20]. The way of updating the dictionary is different from each learning algorithm to others. For example, the K-SVD algorithm makes a modification in the dictionary's columns; the MOD algorithm makes the mean of the set of norm residuals as small as possible. In this paper we use K-SVD algorithm as suggested in [16].

In the K-SVD algorithm, each column a_{j_0} of A is updated sequentially such that the residual error defined in (3) is minimized, where $\mathcal{X}$ and other columns of A are fixed:

$$\|\mathcal{H} - A\mathcal{X}\|_F^2 = \|(\mathcal{H} - \sum_{j \neq j_0} a_j x_j^T) - a_{j_0} x_{j_0}^T\|_F^2 \tag{3}$$

In Eq. (3), the value $(\mathcal{H} - \sum_{j \neq j_0} a_j x_j^T)$ is fixed, therefore the minimum error $\|\mathcal{H} - A\mathcal{X}\|_F^2$ depends only on the optimal a_{j_0} and $x_{j_0}^T$. These optimal solutions $\bar{a}_{j_0}$ and $\bar{x}_{j_0}^T$ can be given by calculating SVD (*Singular Value Decomposition*) over the error matrix defined only on relevant samples. More details about the K-SVD algorithm can be found in [1].

The output of K-SVD algorithm is all optimal sparse representation $\bar{x}_j$ of $h_j \in \mathcal{H}$ and the learned dictionary A, it means each local descriptor h_j can be expressed as a sparse linear combination of the columns in $A = \{a_1, ..., a_M\} \in \mathbb{R}^{L \times M}$, and therefore the sparse vector $\bar{x}_j$ is the new representation for h_j. Figure 1 illustrates the presentation of one local descriptor h_j as linear combination of 8 columns in the dictionary A being $a_{51}, a_{170}, a_{179}, a_{245}, a_{265}, a_{294}, a_{298}, a_{420}$.

4   Spotting Symbols in Graphical Documents

4.1   Document Indexing

Generally, the processes of searching and matching local descriptors computed from interest points usually waste the computing time and the memory. Therefore, some techniques are proposed to overcome this difficulty such as clustering similar descriptors to define visual words being the centroids of clusters. However, the performance of these methods depends directly on the applied clustering algorithm and the characteristic of data. Very recently, Do *et al.* [5] proposed an approach that uses sparse representations of local descriptors. The performance of this approach is good and promising for symbol recognition. However, to apply this method on document level, beside of finding candidate regions that are considered as the segment symbols (in Sect. 4.2), we also need an effectual way to index the content that helps to match candidate regions in each document.

To index the content, an inverted file structure is built based on the learning dictionary of local descriptors. Particularly, the sparse representation of each local descriptor over A gives information about columns of learning dictionary A used to describe this. If we consider each column of A as one visual word then A becomes the visual dictionary and therefore the group of visual words used to describe this descriptor is known. For example, without loss of generality, let h_i^s being the ESCIP number i-*th* in the document D_s and $\bar{x}_i^s = \{\alpha_1^s, 0, ..., 0, \alpha_k^s, 0, ..., 0, \alpha_t^s, 0, ..., 0, \alpha_l^s, 0, ..., 0\}$ being the sparse representation of h_i^s over A, then h_i^s can be expressed as following:

$$h_i^s = \alpha_1^s \times a_1 + \alpha_k^s \times a_k + \alpha_1^t \times a_t + \alpha_1^l \times a_l \qquad (4)$$

Therefore, h_i^s is assigned to the group of visual words $W_i^s = \{a_1, a_k, a_t, a_l\}$ and coefficients $\Delta_i^s = \{\alpha_1^s, \alpha_k^s, \alpha_t^s, \alpha_l^s\}$.

Once the document is described by visual words over visual vocabulary A, we construct an inverted file including two elements: the visual vocabulary and the occurrences. The visual vocabulary is A, and for each visual word in A we store: (1) a list of interest points that its corresponding ESCIP has this word in their sparse representation over dictionary A, (2) the corresponding documents, (3) the group of visual words as well as the coefficients in the representation of these ESCIP (see Fig. 2).

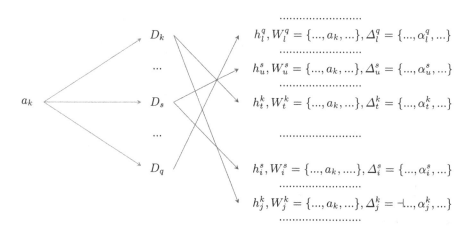

Fig. 2. The inverted file structure

4.2   Location Symbols in Graphical Documents

This section describes our main contribution that includes two steps. The first step is to define candidate regions on documents based on the property of interest points and the similarity in sparse representations of their corresponding local descriptors. In the second step, each candidate region is transformed to the vector by using weight visual words.

Interest Regions over Documents. The interest regions are defined from the interest points of query symbol and the interest points of documents. More specifically, given $q = \{x_q, y_q, \delta_q, \theta_q\}$ and $p = \{x_p, y_p, \delta_p, \theta_p\}$ are two interest points, one from query symbol and one from the document, respectively. The center coordinates (x_r, y_r) of the interest region are defined by the affine transform of the coordinates of q:

$$\begin{pmatrix} x_r \\ y_r \end{pmatrix} = \frac{\delta_p}{\delta_q} G_{\theta_p - \theta_q} \begin{pmatrix} x_c - x_q \\ y_c - y_q \end{pmatrix} + \begin{pmatrix} x_p \\ y_p \end{pmatrix} \quad (5)$$

where $G_{\theta_p - \theta_q}$ is the rotation matrix, (x_c, y_c) is the centre coordinates of the query symbol, and the width w_r, the height h_r and the orientation θ_r of the region are given by:

$$h_r = h \times \frac{\delta_p}{\delta_q}; \quad w_r = w \times \frac{\delta_p}{\delta_q}; \quad \theta_r = \theta_q - \theta_p \quad (6)$$

where h and w are the height and the width of the query symbol. Figure 3 presents an example of how to locate an interested region over the document.

For a particular symbol query, the number of the interest points like p, q is large, therefore the possible regions of interest constructed from two equations

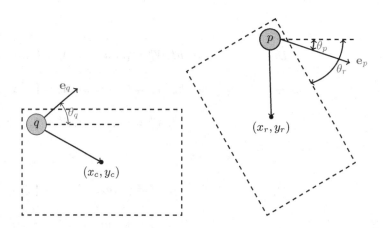

Fig. 3. Example about how to locate an interest region in the document (right) being corresponding to the request symbol (left)

above are large. To select only those where the query symbol may appear we introduce the notion of *similarity* property between pairs of interest points at level c and we select only those regions satisfying this property. We recall that W_p is the set of visual words describing the descriptor h_p computed on p.

Definition 1 (Similarity Property). *Two interest points p and q holds the similarity property at level $c \in (0, 1]$ if the following inequality is satisfied:*

$$c \times |W_q| \leq |W_p \cap W_q| \leq |W_q| \tag{7}$$

Intuitively, we use the similarity property to compare interested points p and q in terms of the visual words used to describe descriptors h_p and h_q. In fact, the value of $c \in (0, 1]$ controls the overlapping degree of W_p and W_q. Moreover, by setting $c = 1$ we force all the visual words used in the representation of h_q appear in the representation of h_p.

Vector Construction for Candidate Region. The *similarity* property permits us to reject regions of document where we can ensure that the query symbol is not found with high confidence degree. However, using only this similarity measure, we will retrieve many false positive instances. Thus, to keep the regions of interest where the query symbol actually is, we propose to construct the vector model for each candidate region and then compare it to the vector model of query symbol.

For each interest point p in $\mathcal{R}$, its descriptor $h_p^{\mathcal{R}}$ is the shape context of interest point calculated in regions $\mathcal{R}$. The optimal sparse representation $\bar{x}_p^{\mathcal{R}}$ of $h_p^{\mathcal{R}}$ is the solution of the Eq. (8) where A is learned dictionary build for training dataset being ESCIP descriptors over graphical documents.

$$\bar{x}_p^{\mathcal{R}} = \min_{x_p^{\mathcal{R}}} \|x_p^{\mathcal{R}}\|_0 \text{ subject to } \|Ax_p^{\mathcal{R}} - h_p^{\mathcal{R}}\|_2 \leq \epsilon \tag{8}$$

The columns of the learned dictionary A play the role of words in a visual word framework and the coefficients play the role of the degree of confidence for visual words. With the purpose of keeping information not only on what visual words in the dictionary are used, but also on the coefficients in the sparse representation, we use the optimal sparse representation $\bar{x}_p^{\mathcal{R}}$ of $h_p^{\mathcal{R}}$ as its characteristic vector and compute the tf and idf factors to build the vector model associated to the candidate region $\mathcal{R}$. On the one hand, we compute the k-th word frequency $tf_k^{\mathcal{R}}$ as:

$$tf_k^{\mathcal{R}} = \frac{\sum_{p \in \mathcal{I}} \bar{x}_p^{\mathcal{R}}(k)}{\sum_{j=1}^{K} \sum_{p \in \mathcal{I}} \bar{x}_p^{\mathcal{R}}(j)} \tag{9}$$

where $\mathcal{I}$ is the set of interest points in $\mathcal{R}$.

On the other hand, the idf factor indicates the importance of the word k for the discrimination between regions. To compute this value, the number of instances of a word k in the whole document have to be computed. However,

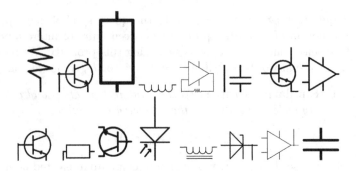

Fig. 4. Some isolated segmented symbols in the reference database.

because of some candidate regions still are false positive instances, thus computing this value on all candidate regions will reduce the precision in discriminating between regions. To overcome this problem, we propose to compute the *idf* factor from an alternative dataset composed of samples of segmented symbols. Figure 4 presents some symbols in the reference database including 1859 segmented symbols. More details, *idf* is calculated as in Algorithm 1:

Algorithm 1. Calculate *idf* factor

1: For each symbol in a reference database: (1a.) Calculate the ESCIP descriptors of this symbol

       (1b.) Calculate all sparse representations of descriptors over the learning dictionary A using OMP algorithm

       (1c.) The sparse representations give the information of what visual word is used to describe this symbol

2: Let l_k be the number of symbols in which the word k appears and N is the number of symbols in reference database, then $idf_k = \log(\frac{N}{1+l_k})$

Therefore, the vector model of candidate region $\mathcal{R}$ is defined as following:

$$v_{\mathcal{R},k} = tf_k^{\mathcal{R}} \times idf_k \tag{10}$$

4.3   Matching Process

For each query symbol, its vector model v_q is calculated as the same way we calculate the vector model of candidate regions $\mathcal{R}$. Next, the vector model of the query symbol and the vector model of candidate regions, $v_{\mathcal{R}}$ is compared using the cosine distance:

$$\text{distance}(v_q, v_{\mathcal{R}}) = \frac{\langle v_q, v_{\mathcal{R}} \rangle}{|v_q| \times |v_{\mathcal{R}}|} \tag{11}$$

Finally, candidate regions with low cosine distance are discarded and the others are ranked in descend order as being the regions containing the requested symbol.

5   Experiment

The goal of the experiments carried out in this paper is to evaluate if the performance of symbol spotting method will be improved when sparse representations are used. The preliminary experiment is performed on subset of the SESYD dataset[1] which is a collection of 15 images and 6 different classes as queries are tested (see Fig. 1). This subset is also used in [4] however in this paper beside of verifying the precision of proposed method, we will also present the computing time for spotting symbols.

The training database in the learned dictionary algorithm is local descriptors ESCIP computed on graphical documents. To provide more weight to the region close to the detected interest points in the direction of the interest point orientation and to increase in such way the discrimination capacity of the local descriptor, ESCIP is computed over the ellipse that is defined using information of orientation and scale of interest point. Particularly, if the scale of the interest point is σ, then the value of the semi-minor and the semi-major axes are $\frac{3}{2}\sigma$, 3σ (set by the experience), respectively. The visual vocabulary A is built using the K-SVD algorithm with the number of columns in A to 512, the number of iterations to 350, and the approximation error to $\epsilon = 0.4$.

In fact, there are numerous works have been proposed to deal with the problem of spotting symbols in the graphical documents [10,19,21]. However, to the best of our knowledge there is no complete evaluation for the existing approaches on the same database.

Thus, we decide to compare proposed approach to the method of Nguyen *et al.* [14] since this method is also based on a local descriptors and use inverted files for document indexing. The main difference between them are: firstly, in the proposed approach sparsity technique is used to build a visual vocabulary, while in [14] a visual vocabulary is the set of centroids of clusters obtained using k-means algorithm. Secondly, in our approach, we first define candidate regions based on the number of shared visual words and then we build and comparing

Table 1. The query classes

| Class1 | Class2 | Class3 | Class4 | Class5 | Class6 |

---

[1] http://mathieu.delalandre.free.fr/projects/sesyd/index.html.

vector models of candidate regions to filter out some false positive instance and therefore improve the precision rate.

Both methods are compared using the widespread precision and recall measures for retrieval tasks. The precision measure is the ratio between the number of relevant retrieved items and the number of retrieved items. On the one hand, precision rate equals to 1 means that all retrieved examples correspond to the queried symbol. That is, there is not false positives samples in the retrieved

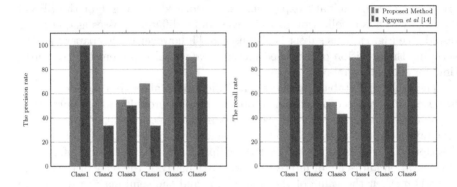

Fig. 5. Spotting results for 6 classes of query in the Table 1

Table 2. The computing time (seconds) that corresponds to each query.

Documents	Classes					
	1	2	3	4	5	6
Document 1	8.6534	11.4800	12.8461	2.6261	21.4594	4.9100
Document 2	8.6961	11.3504	12.8563	2.5374	21.3855	4.8034
Document 3	8.6377	11.4096	12.8259	2.6336	20.7571	4.8560
Document 4	8.7181	11.3959	12.8552	2.6078	20.9517	4.7784
Document 5	8.6534	11.4260	12.8515	2.5890	20.7913	4.8589
Document 6	8.7157	11.3998	12.8658	2.6142	20.9933	4.8065
Document 7	8.6566	11.3706	12.8402	2.6295	20.9692	4.8377
Document 8	8.7488	11.4102	12.8510	2.6098	21.0592	4.7998
Document 9	8.6646	11.3915	12.8696	2.6343	20.9809	4.8657
Document 10	8.7111	11.3695	12.8404	2.5645	20.9928	4.8055
Document 11	8.6586	11.4164	12.8500	2.6580	21.0074	4.8675
Document 12	8.7442	11.3737	12.8369	2.6196	21.2620	4.8178
Document 13	8.6554	11.4137	12.8398	2.6101	20.8022	4.8580
Document 14	8.7265	11.3629	12.8730	2.6024	21.0608	4.8028
Document 15	8.6317	11.4065	12.8353	2.6136	20.5692	4.8669
Average	8.6848	11.3984	12.8558	2.610	20.9361	4.8357

documents and location. Conversely, a lower precision rate, a higher non-relevant (false positive) items included in the results are. On the other hand, the recall rate is the number of relevant items in the collection. It measures the effectiveness of the system in retrieving the relevant items, and it equals 1 in case all the items considered as retrievals are relevant. Indeed, a low recall rate means that relevant items have been missed.

In the Fig. 5 we see that precision and recall rates increase in most cases. Table 2 presents the computing time that corresponds to each query.

6   Conclusion

This paper presents a new approach for symbol spotting systems that uses the visual dictionary being the dictionary constructed from local descriptors. By using learning techniques, the obtained visual vocabulary can be adapted better to the intrinsic properties of the documents datasets. In addition, the proposed approach improves the computing time in the retrieving process by combining sparsity with indexing techniques and therefore only regions in which the queried symbol may appear is considered in the matching phase. First experiments on a subset of benchmark dataset for a symbol spotting application are promising. In the future, we would like to examine the robustness and scalability of this method on other datasets.

References

1. Aharon, M., Elad, M., Bruckstein, A.: K-SVD: an algorithm for designing overcomplete dictionaries for sparse representation. Sig. Process. **54**(11), 4311–4322 (2006)
2. Barbu, E., Héroux, P., Adam, S., Trupin, É.: Using bags of symbols for automatic indexing of graphical document image databases. In: Liu, W., Lladós, J. (eds.) GREC 2005. LNCS, vol. 3926, pp. 195–205. Springer, Heidelberg (2006). doi:10.1007/11767978_18
3. Bodic, P.L., Heroux, P., Adam, S., Lecourtier, Y.: An interger linear program for substitution-tolerant subgraph isomorphism and its use for symbol spotting in technical drawings. Pattern Recogn. **45**(12), 4214–4224 (2012)
4. Do, T.H., Tabbone, S., Terrades, O.R.: Spotting symbol using sparsity over learned dictionary of local descriptors. In: Proceeding of the International Conference on Document Analysis and Recognition, pp. 156–160 (2014)
5. Do, T.H., Tabbone, S., Terrades, O.R.: Sparse representation over learned dictionary for symbol recognition. Sig. Process. **125**, 36–47 (2016)
6. Dutta, A., Llados, J., Pal, U.: A symbol spotting approach in graphical documents by hasing serialized graphs. Pattern Recogn. **43**(3), 752–768 (2013)
7. Engan, K., Aase, S.O., Husoy, J.H.: Frame based signal compression using method of optimal directions (MOD). Proc. Int. Conf. Acoust. Speech Sig. Process. **4**, 1–4 (1999)
8. Eppstein, D.: Subgraph isomorphism in planar graphs and related problems. Graph Algorithms Appl. **3**(3), 1–27 (1999)

9. Llados, J., Marti, E., Villanueva, J.: Symbol recognition by error-tolerant subgraph matching between region adjacency graphs. Pattern Anal. Mach. Intell. **23**(10), 1137–1143 (2001)

10. Lladós, J., Valveny, E., Sánchez, G., Martí, E.: Symbol recognition: current advances and perspectives. In: Blostein, D., Kwon, Y.-B. (eds.) GREC 2001. LNCS, vol. 2390, pp. 104–128. Springer, Heidelberg (2002). doi:10.1007/3-540-45868-9_9

11. Marial, J., Bach, F., Ponce, J., Sapiro, G.: Online dictionary learning for sparse coding. In: Proceeding of the 26th Annual International Conference on Machine Learning, pp. 689–696 (2009)

12. Messmer, B.T., Bunke, H.: Automatic learning and recognition of graphical symbols in engineering drawings. In: Kasturi, R., Tombre, K. (eds.) GREC 1995. LNCS, vol. 1072, pp. 123–134. Springer, Heidelberg (1996). doi:10.1007/3-540-61226-2_11

13. Muller, S., Rigoll, G.: Engineering drawing database retrieval using statistical pattern spotting techniques. In: The Proceeding of GREC 09 Selected Papers from the Thrid International Workshop on Graphics Recognition, Recent Advances, pp. 246–255 (1999)

14. Nguyen, T.-O., Tabbone, S., Boucher, A.: A symbol spotting approach based on the vector model and a visual vocabulary. In: Proceeding of the 10th International Conference on Document Analysis and Recognition, pp. 708–712 (2009)

15. Nguyen, T.-O., Tabbone, S., Terrades, O.R.: Symbol descriptor based on shape context and vector model of information retrieval. In: Proceeding of the 8th the International Workshop on Document Analysis System (2008)

16. Pati, Y., Rezaiifar, R., Krishnaprasad, P.: Orthogonal matching pursuit: recursive function approximation with applications to wavelet decomposition. In: Proceeding of the 27th Annual Asilomar Conference on Signals, Systems, and Computers, pp. 40–44 (1993)

17. Qureshi, R., Ramel, J.-Y., Barret, D., Cardot, H.: Spotting symbols in line drawing images using graph representations. Graph. Recogn. Recent Adv. New Opportunities **5046**, 91–103 (2008)

18. Rusiñol, M., Lladós, J.: Symbol spotting in technical drawings using vectorial signatures. In: Liu, W., Lladós, J. (eds.) GREC 2005. LNCS, vol. 3926, pp. 35–46. Springer, Heidelberg (2006). doi:10.1007/11767978_4

19. Santosh, K.C., Wendling, L.: Graphical symbol recognition. Wiley Encyclopedia of Electrical and Electronics Engineering (2015)

20. Skretting, K., Engan, K.: Recursive least squares dictionary learning algorithm. Sig. Process. **58**(4), 2121–2130 (2010)

21. Tabbone, S., Terrades, O.R.: An overview of symbol recognition. In: Handbook of Document Image Processing and Recognition, pp. 523–551 (2014)

22. Tabbone, S., Wendling, L., Tombre, K.: Matching of graphical symbols in line-drawing images using angular signature information. Int. J. Doc. Anal. Recogn. **6**(2), 115–125 (2003)

23. Tabbone, S., Zuwala, D.: An indexing method for graphical documents. In: Proceeding of the 9th International Conference on Document Analysis and Recognition, pp. 789–793 (2007)

24. Zhang, W., Wenying, L.: A new vectorial signature for quick symbol indexing, filtering and recognition. In: Proceeding of the 9th International Conference on Document Analysis and Recognition, vol. 1, pp. 536–540 (2007)

Word Retrieval from Kannada Document Images Using HOG and Morphological Features

Mallikarjun Hangarge[1], C. Veershetty[1(✉)], P. Rajmohan[1],
and Gururaj Mukarambi[2]

[1] P.G. Department of Computer Science, Karnatak College, Bidar, India
vshetty1180@gmail.com
[2] Department of Computer Science, Gulbarga University, Kalaburagi, India

Abstract. This paper presents a method to retrieve words from Kannada documents. It works on Histogram of Oriented Gradients (HOG) and Morphological filters. A large dataset of 50000 words is created using 250 document pages belongs to different categories. A preprocessed document image is segmented using simple morphological filters. The histogram channels are designed over four-sided cells (i.e. R-HOG) to compute gradients of a word image. In parallel, morphological erosion, opening, top and bottom hat transformations are applied on each word. The densities of the resultant images are estimated. Later on, HOG and morphological features are fused. Then, the cosine distance is used to measure the similarity between two words i.e., query and candidate word, based on it, the relevance of the word is estimated by generating distance ranks. Then correctly matched words are selected at threshold 98%. The experimental results confirm the efficiency of our proposed method in terms of the average precision rate 91.23%, and average recall rate 84.78% as well as average F-measure 89.47%.

Keywords: Word retrieval · Cosine distance · Digital image processing (DIP) · Image retrieval (IR)

1 Introduction

Putting away documents in electronic libraries has turned into a continuous assignment in these days. Retrieving the required documents from this huge repository is a challenging task. Therefore, the document image retrieval (DIR) has picked up consideration as digital libraries started to become popular. The key research of DIR is word spotting, that is finding the frequency of the existing query word in the document image. Word spotting is an alternative way for OCR (Optical Character Recognition). The state-of-the-art techniques for Optical Character Recognition (OCR) is working good when associated with printed text, and poor in handwritten and historical document images. However, OCRs of European languages are robust but not efficient in case of corrupted/degraded document images. Consequently, different scientists are moved towards DIR procedures for information retrieval without changing over the entire document

© Springer Nature Singapore Pte Ltd. 2017
K.C. Santosh et al. (Eds.): RTIP2R 2016, CCIS 709, pp. 71–79, 2017.
DOI: 10.1007/978-981-10-4859-3_7

image into editable text. The process of word spotting can be achieved in two ways: (a) with segmentation (b) without segmentation. In the first approach, the time required to segment the words from a document is an augment to the total time complexity of the retrieval system. But, this is not in the case of second approach. However, most of the reported works indicated that segmentation based method has performed well as compared to segmentation free method. In fact, achieving high accuracy is the ultimate goal of any research. Therefore, this paper focus on word spotting with segmentation. This paper is organized as follows: Sect. 2 presents related work, in the Sect. 3 word retrieval system, further, Sect. 4 presents experimental results of the proposed method, Sect. 5 presents comparative analysis and finally conclusion is drawn in Section 6.

2   Related Work

The word spotting was initially proposed for speech processing and later it was adopted for word spotting. Word spotting is the way towards detecting the word or an expression in the archived image, which was first reported in [2] for printed documents, and later in [3] for handwritten documents. Most of the work done on word spotting (matching and retrieval) is in two unique approaches i.e. with segmentation and without segmentation. Several works [10,11] have been reported to locate keywords and retrieve document images directly without OCR. In [13] a novel word spotting method is proposed based on Recurrent Neural Networks with CTC Token Passing algorithm. Then, DTW technique is used to measure similarity between the words. Recently in [17] authors proposed a method for retrieval of Hindi words based on BLSTM neural networks, these networks are considered to take contextual information into account, for word images that cannot be segmented into individual characters. In [18], the word retrieval technique is proposed for Devanagari, Bangla and Gurumukhi script by considering primitive shape codes. It uses (i) zonal information of extreme points, (ii) vertical shapes, (iii) crossing count, (iv) loop shape and position and (v) background information. Then, an exact string matching technique is used to measure the similarity between the words. Most recently in [19] authors proposed method using Gabor wavelets for retrieval of Kannada words. Gabor features are extracted on each word of the database and query word. Then similarity is measured using cosine distance metric. In [15] authors have proposed HOG features for word spotting, HOG is a gradient distribution based feature with overlapping normalization and redundant expression. They divide the image into smaller rectangular areas called cells. Then, fixed the number of bins into each cell of the image. After reviewing these methods, we understand that still lot of work yet to perform for word retrieval. In this paper, we focus to build efficient model to describe the shape of the word for better retrieval. In this aspect, we have proposed a hybrid system that involves HOG and morphological features. We choose this combination based on the characters' shape of Kannada/Hindi language. To extract the visual attributes of a word such as holes, directional edges, upper and lower cavities, the combination of HOG and morphological features are revealed as best choice.

3   Word Retrieval System

The main steps of a word retrieval system are: (a) data collection and word segmentation (b) feature extraction and (c) matching and ranking. In this Section, we define the process of word retrieval. Figure 1 is the bird view of the proposed method.

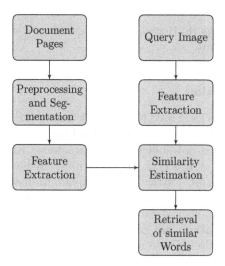

Fig. 1. Bird view of the proposed method.

3.1   Data Collection and Word Segmentation

There is no openly accessible benchmark of Kannada document images at current. Therefore, we have collected 250 document pages belongs to the different fields such as medical science, history, literature etc. Then the documents are scanned at 300 dpi resolution using an HP scanner. The Otsu's universal thresholding technique is applied to change over gray scale image to two-tone image. Otsu's technique picks the edge to minimize the interclass change of the edge high contrast pixels [1]. The two-tone images are then transformed over into 0–1 symbols where the 1 speaks to the object and 0 speaks to the base of the object. The smaller objects like, single or double quotation marks, hyphens and periods, etc. are removed using morphological opening. A dataset of 50000 words segmented from 250 pages using morphological filters. The process of segmentation consist two stages. In the first stage, horizontal and vertical dilation is applied to make a word image as a single component. In the second stage, bounding box is fixed on each word image, then cropped and stored in a library. This dataset includes expressions of various text dimension, style, length and thickness (pixel thickness). The complete process of words extraction from Kannada document can be visualized in Fig. 2.

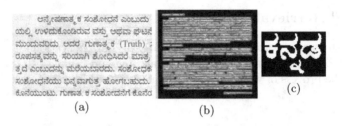

(a)   (b)

(c)

Fig. 2. (a) Document page (b) Horizontal dilation to form a word as connected component (c) Segmented word.

3.2   Feature Extraction

The HOG features are widely used for object detection [12] and document image retrieval. The HOG features are strong in describing edge information. However, only edge information is not sufficient to characterize Kannada/Hindi words. As characters of Indian scripts contains curvatures, cavities such as w-formation and inverse w-formation etc. Particularly, to explain Kannada/Hindi words, need to capture cavity, hole and directional edge information. Therefore, we combined HOG with morphological features to capture these potential properties. Exhaustive experimentations are carried out to show the outstanding performance of this combination. These methods are applied on each word independently to extract features. The computation of HOG and morphological features are explained below. The concept beyond the HOG descriptors is that local object appearance and shape within an image can be labeled by the distribution of intensity gradients or edge directions. HOG divides an image into small rectangular cells, and calculates a histogram of oriented gradients for each cell, further it normalizes the result using a block-wise pattern, and returns a descriptor for each cell by computing a histogram of gradient directions; histograms are also normalized based on their energy (regularized L2 norm). Combination of these histograms represents the descriptor of an underlying image. Let I(x, y) be an input word image, with a sliding window of size 3×3, we can generate a histogram of 9 bins per cell to accommodate the weighted vote of the gradient vector $(0°-180°$ for unsigned gradient) in the cell. To get the vertical and horizontal components of image gradient, Sobel kernel is used. The magnitude M(x, y) and direction D(x, y) of the image is computed as follows:

$$M(x, y) = [G_x + G_y]^{\frac{1}{2}} \tag{1}$$

$$D(x, y) = \tan^{-1}(\frac{G_x}{G_y}) \tag{2}$$

$$G_x = I_s * \begin{bmatrix} -1\ 0\ +1 \\ -2\ 0\ +2 \\ -1\ 0\ +1 \end{bmatrix} \tag{3}$$

$$G_y = I_s * \begin{bmatrix} +1 & +2 & +1 \\ 0 & 0 & 0 \\ -1 & -2 & -1 \end{bmatrix} \quad (4)$$

where I_s is the smoothed image. Then, histogram of every block of the cell is clustered to get the desired feature vector.

Each word image is eroded in four directions viz. $0°$, $90°$, $180°$ and $-45°$. On a word, the opening, top and bottom hat transformations are also applied in vertical and horizontal directions. In addition, background to foreground ratio of a word is computed after hole filling. To perform these operations, basically two images are required, one is input image and another is structuring element. For the experiment, we constructed structuring element based on the average height of characters of a word [6]. As an example, the effect of erosion is illustrated in the following Fig. 3.

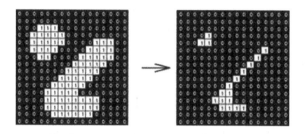

Fig. 3. Effect of erosion using a 3×3 square structuring element.

A pre-processed input image $I(x, y)$ is directly used for erosion, opening, top and bottom hat transformations and an output image $I'(x, y)$ is obtained. The arithmetic means of $I'(x, y)$ is defined as

$$Density(\eta) = \frac{\sum\limits_{i=1}^{R} \sum\limits_{j=1}^{C} I'(x, y)}{R * C} \quad (5)$$

where, R and C stands for number of rows and columns of an image.

Beside, hole fill operation is performed on $I(x, y)$ and obtained hole filled image $I'(x, y)$. Then, its density is computed using Eq. 5. Thus, 11 features are obtained (erode image density-04, opening, top and bottom hat each-02 and foreground and background information after hole filling) and to make the features independent of font size; they were normalized by dividing them with the size of an image. Further, we upend these 11 features to 81 HOG features and yields a feature vector of size 92×1.

3.3 Similarity

Words in the database are ranked on the basis of the similarities between the query and target word (database). In this paper, similarity between the words is measured by two distinct metrics, they are:

Cosine Similarity: cosine similarity is a measure of similarity between two non zero vectors of an inner product space that measures the cosine of the angle between them. The cosine of $0°$ is 1 and it is less than 1 for any other angle. Mathematical expression of the cosine similarity is defined below:

$$Similarity(x, y) = \cos\theta = \frac{x.y}{||x|| * ||y||} \tag{6}$$

where x and y are feature vectors.

Euclidean Similarity: Euclidean distance is the distance between two points, say p and q are the two points in the Euclidean space. The Euclidean distance between p and q is the length of the line segment connecting them and defined below

$$I(p, q) = I(q, p) = \sqrt{(p_1 - q_1^2) + (q_2 - p_2)^2} \tag{7}$$

$$I(p, q) = I(q, p) = \sum_{i=1}^{n}(q_i - p_i)^2 \tag{8}$$

where p and q are the Euclidean vectors.

4   Experimental Results and Discussion

In this Section, we discuss the results obtained for retrieving the relevant words from the document images. The performance of the proposed algorithm is evaluated on two large dataset namely Kannada and Hindi. The Hindi language dataset is publicly available [14]. However, Kannada language dataset is generated using 250 pages to yield 50000 words. The proposed method performance is evaluated through precision, recall and f-measure as described below.

$$Precision = \frac{(RetrievedWords \cap RelevantWords)}{RetrievedWords} \tag{9}$$

$$Recall = \frac{(RetrievedWords \cap RelevantWords)}{RelevantWords} \tag{10}$$

$$F\text{-}measure = \frac{2*(RetrievedWords * RelevantWords)}{(RetrievedWords + RelevantWords)} \tag{11}$$

For experimentation Kannada and Hindi languages datasets are used. The query words of different font style and size are selected from both the dataset. The exhaustive experimentations are performed on both dataset. The experimental results are summarized in Tables 1 and 2. Table 1 illustrates the accuracy of the Kannada word retrieval. It has highest precession, recall and F-measure as 96.96%, 94.11% and 95.11% respectively when the word length is of 5 characters. These parameters speak that the occurrences of word length 5 is high in Kannada language. In case of Hindi, the occurrence of words of length 3 is more. We have made an observation manually by taking a page (consist 175 words) from a dataset and observed that the occurrences of a word of length 5 characters are more. Therefore, the algorithm indicates high precision with the words of length 5 and 3 characters in Kannada and Hindi respectively. To apprehend the performance of the proposed method, experimentation extended to Hindi words retrieval. Table 2 presents the results of Hindi word retrieval. The Hindi words (20000) are taken from IISC (Indian Institute of Science) database. This database was used for script identification [16]. Five query words are selected from the database which are different in size and font style. Table 3 describes the overall performance of the proposed algorithm with different distance measures. The comprehensive statistical analysis of the purposed method is well represented in Table 3 in terms of precision, recall and F-measure.

Table 1. Results of Kannada word retrieval

Length of the query word	Precision (%)	Recall (%)	F-measure (%)
3	91.66	84.61	87.99
4	90.90	88.23	89.54
5	96.96	94.11	95.51
6	90.62	87.87	84.49
7	86.04	84.09	85.05
Average	91.23	87.78	89.47

Table 2. Results of Hindi word retrieval

Length of the query word	Precision (%)	Recall (%)	F-measure (%)
2	88.23	90.90	89.54
3	94.11	96.96	95.51
4	87.87	90.62	84.49
5	84.09	86.04	85.05
6	86.04	84.09	85.05
Average	91.23	87.78	89.47

5 Comparative Analysis

The comparative analysis is made with [17]. Jawahar et al. has worked on Hindi word retrieval and reported the Mean Average Precision (MAP) as 71.82 with Euclidean distance. But, our algorithm showed a remarkable mean average precision as 84.90 against the same script. The cosine distance is also used for experimentation to investigate the performance of the algorithm and found 89.37 as mean average precession. These results are reported in Table 4. Figure 4, highlights word retrieval precision and recall with different word sizes.

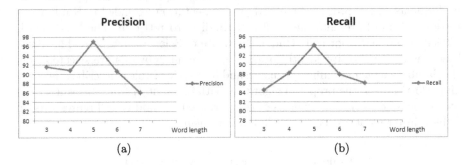

Fig. 4. (a) Word retrieval precision with different word sizes (b) Recall with different word sizes

Table 3. Overall performance of the proposed method

Dataset	Distance	Precision (%)	Recall (%)	F-measure (%)
Kannada (50000)	Euclidean	86.32	89.67	87.34
	Cosine	87.78	91.23	89.47
Hindi (20000)	Euclidean	80.81	89.79	84.90
	Cosine	87.38	91.51	89.37

Table 4. Comparative analysis of the proposed method

Work	Statistics	Euclidean	Cosine
[17]	MAP	71.82	NR
Proposed	MAP	84.90	89.37

6   Conclusion

This paper presents the problem of word retrieval from two major Indian languages namely Kannada and Hindi. The use of HOG features in combination with basic morphological filters exhibited outstanding performance as compared to the performance of the reported works. The proposed method is validated on a large dataset of 70000 words (Kannada-50000, Hindi-20000). To realize the genericness of this method, in future we are extending this work to other Indian scripts.

References

1. Otsu, N.: A threshold selection method from gray-level histograms. Pattern Anal. Mach. Intell. **9**(1), 62–66 (1979)
2. Rath, T.M., Manmatha, R.: Features for word spotting in historical manuscripts, document analysis and recognition. Int. J. Doc. Anal. Recogn. **1**, 218–222 (2003)
3. Konidaris, T., Gatos, B., Ntzios, K.: Keyword-guided word spotting in historical printed documents using synthetic data and user feedback. Int. J. Doc. Anal. Recogn. **9**, 167–177 (2007)
4. Lu, S., Li, L., Tan, C.L.: Document image retrieval through word shape coding. IEEE Trans. Pattern Anal. Mach. Intell. **30**(11), 1913–1918 (2008)
5. Bai, S., Li, L., Tan, C.L.: Keyword spotting in document images through word shape coding. In: Document Analysis and Recognition, pp. 331–335 (2009)
6. Hangarge, M., Dhandra, B.V.: Script identification in indian document images based on directional morphological filters. Int. J. Recent Trends Eng. **2**, 124–126 (2009)
7. Rabaev, I., Biller, O., El-Sana, J., Kedem, K., Dinstein, I.: Case study in Hebrew character searching. In: International Conference on Document Analysis and Recognition, pp. 1080–1084 (2011)
8. Abidi, A., Siddiqi, I., Khurshid, K.: Towards searchable digital Urdu libraries-a word spotting based retrieval approach. In: International Conference on Document Analysis and Recognition, pp. 1344–1348 (2011)
9. Yat, M., Lam, L., Suen, C.Y.: Arabic handwritten word spotting using language models, pp. 43–48 (2012)
10. Doermann, D.: The indexing and retrieval of document images: a survey. Comput. Vis. Image Underst. **70**(3), 287–298 (1998)
11. Lu, S., Chen, B.M., Ko, C.C.: A partition approach for the restoration of camera images of planar and curled document. In: Image and Vision Computing, pp. 837–848 (2006)
12. Dalal, N., Triggs, B.: Histograms of oriented gradients for human detection. In: IEEE Conference on Computer Vision and Pattern Recognition (2005)
13. Frinken, V., Fischer, A., Manmatha, R., Bunke, H.: A novel word spotting method based on recurrent neural networks. IEEE Trans. Pattern Anal. Mach. Intell. **34**(2), 211–224 (2012)
14. www.ee.iisc.ernet.in/new/people/student/phd/pati (2005)
15. Tarasawa, K., Tanaka, Y.: Slit style HOG feature for document image word spotting. In: ICDAR (2009)
16. Pati, P.B., Ramakrishnan, A.G.: Word level multi-script identification. Pattern Recogn. Lett. **29**, 1218–1229 (2008)
17. Jain, R., Frinken, V., Jawahar, C.V., Manmatha, R.: BLSTM neural network based word retrieval for Hindi documents. In: 2011 International Conference on Document Analysis and Recognition, pp. 83–87 (2011)
18. Tarafdar, A., Mondal, R., Pal, S., Pal, U., Kimura, F.: Shape code based word-image matching for retrieval of Indian multi-lingual documents. In: International Conference on Pattern Recognition (2010)
19. Hangarage, M., Veershetty, C., Rajmohan, P., Dhandra, B.V.: Gabor wavelets based word retrieval from Kannada documents. Procedia Comput. Sci. **79**, 441–448 (2016). International Conference on Communication, Computing and Visualization

Hand-Drawn Symbol Recognition in Immersive Virtual Reality Using Deep Extreme Learning Machines

Hubert Cecotti$^{(\boxtimes)}$, Cyrus Boumedine, and Michael Callaghan

Faculty of Computing and Engineering, Ulster University, Magee Campus,
Northland Road, Derry, Londonderry BT48 7JL, Northern Ireland, UK
h.cecotti@ulster.ac.uk

Abstract. Typical character and symbol recognition systems are based on images that are drawn on paper or on a tablet with actual physical contact between the pen and the surface. In this study, we investigate the recognition of symbols that are written while the user is immersed inside a room scale virtual reality experience using a consumer grade head-mounted display and related peripherals. A novel educational simulation was developed consisting of a virtual classroom with whiteboard where users can draw symbols. A database of 30 classes of hand-drawn symbols created from test subjects using this environment is presented. The performance of the symbol recognition system was evaluated with deep extreme learning machine classifiers, with accuracy rates of 94.88% with a single classifier and 95.95% with a multiple classifier approach. Further analysis of the results obtained support the conclusion that there are a number of challenges and difficulties related to drawing in this type of environment given the unique constraints and limitations imposed by virtual reality and in particular the lack of physical contact and haptic feedback between the controller and virtual space. Addressing the issues raised for these types of interfaces opens new challenges for both human-computer interaction and symbol recognition. Finally, the approach proposed in this paper creates a new avenue of research in the field of document analysis and recognition by exploring how texts and symbols can be analyzed and automatically recognized in virtual scenes of this type.

Keywords: Virtual reality · Symbol recognition · Extreme learning machine · Multiple classifier systems

1 Introduction

Virtual reality (VR) extends and augments computer-generated 3D environments providing users with a means to enter, interact with and become immersed in alternate worlds [11]. Access to low cost, efficient, fully immersive and usable consumer grade VR systems with head mounted displays (HMD) and high quality graphics has become a reality for VR enthusiasts with the release of the

© Springer Nature Singapore Pte Ltd. 2017
K.C. Santosh et al. (Eds.): RTIP2R 2016, CCIS 709, pp. 80–92, 2017.
DOI: 10.1007/978-981-10-4859-3_8

Oculus Rift, HTC Vive and similar devices. In addition, the use of 360° motion tracked handheld wireless controllers with accompanying base stations allows the user to directly create, interact with and manipulate elements that are present in the virtual world with a high level of granularity and accuracy. In this context, we have proposed and created an educational simulation consisting of a virtual classroom with whiteboard where users can draw symbols on the screen. The symbols are automatically recognized and identified by the system.

The recognition of symbols is a central pillar of graphical image analysis and recognition systems identifying graphical entities that are present in technical documents (e.g., architectural diagrams, engineering drawings, technical maps) where the main tasks include image segmentation, layout understanding and graphics recognition [9,28]. Graphics recognition has a long history of intensive research in the pattern recognition and document analysis community, and it is considered as a core part of graphical document image analysis and recognition systems. The recognition of single handwritten character and symbols is an old field of research in image processing and pattern recognition [13,20–22,25]. While accuracy remains below 100% for some problems, advances in machine learning and features extraction methods have created systems that reach almost human performance in some visual tasks. However, there are still some challenges remaining, i.e., documents with noisy characters or symbols, and particular scripts [6], which cannot be recognized with commercial optical character recognition technologies [3]. Symbol recognition is typically used in industries with a rich heritage of hand-drawn documents, and where there is a need to extract and understand the content and the logical structure of documents. Symbol recognition is therefore a key aspect of automatic image analysis systems and processes using a number of different approaches (e.g., statistical, structural and syntactic [10]). While in today's society documents are usually created on computers and there is a decline in the use of handwritten and hand-drawn content there are some situations where it is still easier, more convenient and intuitive for the user, to rapidly draw or sketch a symbol instead of searching for it using a menu driven approach [4].

In this paper, we present an application of symbol recognition using symbols created in and captured from a fully immersive virtual reality environment. In [27], a 3D sketch recognition framework for interaction within non-immersive virtual environments was presented, which allowed the user to draw symbols that would trigger subsequent commands or actions. Our approach takes advantage of new consumer-level virtual reality devices (e.g., HTC Vive) to create a room scale virtual reality experience that includes a white board that can be drawn on using the handheld Vive controller represented as a pen in the virtual scene. In contrast to other symbol recognition applications where the variation across examples is largely due to the quality of the input document (e.g., noise in the image) hand-drawn symbols of this type offer similar challenges as are found in handwritten character recognition applications. In addition, the shapes of the symbols created are usually more complex than the shapes of single characters or digits necessitating the use of advanced techniques such as Bayesian Networks and Hidden Markov Models for processing [31,32]. In order to recognize the hand-drawn symbols captured from the virtual reality environment, we propose to use deep extreme learning machines as this type of approach has shown a high level performance and accuracy in state-of-the-art single handwritten digit recognition in different scripts [5].

The remaining parts of the paper are organized as follows. Section 2 describes the Extreme Learning Machine framework and the classifiers used. Section 3 describes the virtual environment and the database of hand-drawn symbols created. The classification results are given in Sect. 4 and finally discussed in Sect. 5.

2   Methods

2.1   Random-Vector Functional Links

Random Vector Functional-Link (RVFL) and Extreme Learning Machine (ELM) networks are a particular type of artificial feedforward neural networks that contain a single hidden layer [14,15,35]. This type of network can be used for both classification and regression [2,24,30]. It corresponds to a linear combination of non-linear representations of the input data (e.g., using a sigmoid function). The main characteristic of this system is the way in which the parameters (i.e., the weights) are assigned. The input weights and biases are set randomly and do not change over time. While this step is simple and it may seem inefficient due to the lack of training, RVFLs have the capability of universal approximation if the dimension of the input representation is large enough [17]. The parameters of a RVFL network can be obtained with linear regression methods using only matrix inversions and multiplications. It is worth noting that these operations are particularly well adapted for distributed learning [29]. Finally, RVFL networks can be estimated with a lead-square approach for learning the weights in the last layer.

Let us first consider a regression problem with one-dimensional scalar outputs $y \in \mathbb{R}$. A Functional Link Artificial Neural Network (FLANN) with a single output neuron is defined as a weighted sum of B non-linear transformations of the input $\mathbf{x}$ [24]:

$$f(\mathbf{x}) = \sum_{m=1}^{B} \beta_m h_m(\mathbf{x}; \mathbf{w}_m) = \beta^T h(\mathbf{x}; \mathbf{w}_1, \ldots, \mathbf{w}_B) \qquad (1)$$

where the mth transformation is obtained with the parameters $\mathbf{w}_m$, and $\mathbf{x} \in \mathbb{R}^d$. Each functional link h_m maps the input data to a real number. The non-linearity is obtained with the sigmoid function, such as the multilayer perceptron:

$$h_m(\mathbf{x}; \mathbf{w}_m; b) = \frac{1}{1 + \exp^{\sigma}} \qquad (2)$$

where $\sigma = -\mathbf{w}^T \mathbf{x} + b$. The set of parameters $\mathbf{w}_m$, $1 \leq m \leq B$, is chosen before the learning process and without any prior assumptions about the data. Moreover, the parameters are set randomly, in relation to a predefined probability distribution [30]. After the estimation of the set of parameters, the weights β must be estimated. We consider a dataset $\mathcal{X}_{Train} = \{(\mathbf{x}_i, y_i)\}$ of N couples that contain an example $\mathbf{x}_i$ and the expected output y_i, $1 \leq i \leq N$. We denote by $\mathbf{H}$ the matrix containing the B representations of the N examples.

$$H = \begin{pmatrix} h_1(\mathbf{x}_1) & \ldots & h_B(\mathbf{x}_1) \\ \vdots & \ddots & \vdots \\ h_1(\mathbf{x}_N) & \ldots & h_B(\mathbf{x}_N) \end{pmatrix} \tag{3}$$

where each function h_m includes the corresponding set of parameters $\mathbf{w}_m$. The estimation of $\beta = [\beta_1, \ldots, \beta_B]^T$ can be obtained through a regularized least-square problem:

$$\beta = \arg \min_{\beta \in \mathbb{R}^B} \frac{1}{2} \|\mathbf{H}\beta - \mathbf{Y}\|_2^2 + \frac{\lambda}{2} \|\beta\|_2^2 \tag{4}$$

where the vector $\mathbf{Y} = [y_1, \ldots, y_N]^T$ is the ground truth of $\mathcal{X}_{Train}$. As the problem is convex, an estimation of $\hat{\beta}$ can be obtained by:

$$\hat{\beta} = \left(\mathbf{H}^T\mathbf{H} + \lambda\mathbf{I} \right)^{-1} \mathbf{H}^T\mathbf{Y} \tag{5}$$

where I is the identity matrix of size $B \times B$. For multiclass classification with M classes, $M \geq 2$, the ground truth $\mathbf{Y}$ is a matrix of size $N \times M$. $\mathbf{Y}(i, j) = 1$ if $\mathbf{x}_i$ belongs to the class j, $1 \leq j \leq M$, $\mathbf{Y}(i, j) = 0$ otherwise.

2.2 Multi-layer RVFL/ELM

Different variations of RVFL and ELM networks have been successfully used in a range of diverse but popular classification problems [16], and have been inspired by other techniques [7,8]. Furthermore, ELM can be extended for deep learning architectures (ML-ELM) [18,33]. The learning approach performs layer-by-layer unsupervised learning by using ELM auto-encoder (ELM-AE), which represents features based on singular values. With an ELM-AE model, the output $\mathbf{Y}$ is similar to the input $\mathbf{X} = [\mathbf{x}_1, \ldots, \mathbf{x}_N]$. The decoder, i.e., the function that maps the input representation $h_1(x), \ldots, h_B(x)$ of the input x to itself, corresponds to the parameters $\hat{\beta}$ that are estimated. In addition, a key function for setting the value of the weights is to constraint the set of random weights in each layer to be orthogonal [18]. To create the coder afterward, $\hat{\beta}^T$ is used to map x to the representation that was obtained. Then, ML-ELM stacks on top of ELM-AE to create a multilayer neural network similar to other deep network architectures. ML-ELM is a greedy approach, and it doesn't require fine-tuning after estimating the weights of the last layer. In a RVFL network with a single hidden layer, we denote by $\hat{\beta}^1$ the estimation of the weights for the first hidden layer. In the same way, we denote $\hat{\beta}^l$ as the estimation of the weights for the layer l, $1 \leq l \leq L$, for ML-ELM of L hidden-layers. An ELM-AE is set for each layer l, and the

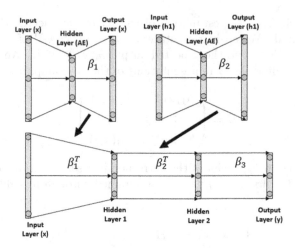

Fig. 1. A deep RVFL/ELM with two hidden layers.

extracted weights of an ELM-AE l are used subsequently to generate the inputs of the ELM-AE at the next layer $l+1$. An example of deep ELM with two hidden layers is presented in Fig. 1

As the generation of the RVFL/ELM classifiers is based on random weights, we assume it is possible to enhance the performance of the overall decision by combining the decisions of different classifiers [26]. We therefore propose to evaluate the performance by combining the decision scores resulting from 10 runs. Three functions are evaluated: the mean (the average score from each run is used before selecting the maximum), the maximum rules (the maximum score in each class and each run), and majority voting (the decision is based on the class that is chosen in most of the runs).

2.3   Performance Evaluation

In the subsequent sections, we evaluate two types of architectures. The first type includes a single hidden layer (the number of neurons is set to: 100, 500, 1000, 10000). The second type includes two hidden layers, the number of neurons in the first hidden layer is set to: 400, 600, or 800, and the number of neurons in the second hidden layer is set to: 6000, 8000, 10000. For each architecture, 10 runs are evaluated.

3   System Overview

3.1   VR Scene

The room scale virtual scene containing the white board is depicted in Fig. 2. The virtual environment was developed with the Unity game engine on an Alienware

X51 desktop (I5-6600k, 16 GB RAM, Nvidia GTX 970 graphics card). The HTC Vive and accompanying base stations facilitate highly accurate 360° motion tracking where virtual representations of the physical handheld wireless controllers, used to navigate and interact with the virtual environment, are visible to the user inside the virtual scene. The HTC Vive wireless handheld controllers offer six degrees of freedom, and are tracked using the Lighthouse technology [1]. Each controller features several customizable buttons that can be tailored to a range of functions required in the application (e.g., a button to validate an image and draw a new image). A trackpad on the face of the controller is also available which is accessible with the users thumb and can be used to erase the content of the white screen.

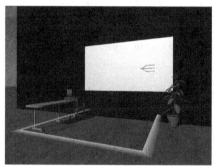

Fig. 2. Room scale virtual environment with the virtual white board: **left:** the virtual scene created (the lines on the ground represent the boundaries area of the simulation where the user can move safely using the Vive Chaperone system), **right:** a user wearing the HTC Vive headset and drawing in the virtual scene.

3.2   Controller Choice

In order to write or draw on a virtual screen in a virtual environment without any physical contact between the controller and the virtual surface we used two main approaches. In the first approach (C1), the points that are drawn on the virtual screen correspond to the intersection between the virtual white board and a line coming from the orientation of the controller. In the second approach (C2), the points that are drawn on the screen are based on the intersection between the plane containing the virtual white board and a tangent to this plane passing by the position of the controller, i.e., parallel to the plane of the ground. In both cases, the representation of the pen in the virtual environment does not need to touch the virtual screen i.e., it is the equivalent of drawing with a pointer. The two approaches were tested before the creation of the database. From this it was found that better results were obtained using first approach, which is based on the orientation of the controller. However, the first approach proved

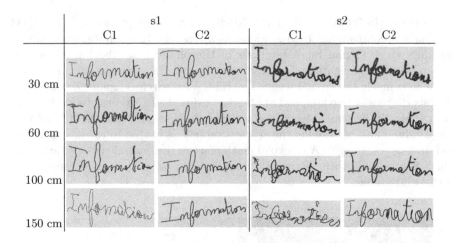

Fig. 3. Effect of the control mode on the style.

more difficult for the user and the level of difficulty increased depending on the distance between the user and the screen as a slight change in orientation of the controller will have a greater impact on the position of what is drawn on the white board. To illustrate the impact of the two different approaches used on the writing style, different examples of the word "Information" have been acquired from two participants, and at different distances (0.3 m, 0.6 m, 1 m, and 1.5 m). Figure 3 depicts the large variability that occurs when a word is written based on controller orientation. The largest variations occur at a distance of 1.5 m where the curves of the letters have many deformations.

3.3 Image Acquisition

Data was recorded from 18 able-bodied participants (age $= 22.8 \pm 3.5$, 3 females). Each participant had to write a series of symbols taken from a subset of 30 symbols that were used during the International Symbol Recognition Contest GREC'2011[1] [12,34]. The distance between users and the screen varied between participants. Each user had to reproduce a version of the symbol that was depicted on the right hand side of the screen. Each model of symbol was presented with eight different orientations (from 0 to 2π, with steps of $\pi/4$). An example of the scene in use is given in Fig. 4. There were no time constraints imposed on participants when drawing the symbols. The total number of acquired images is 3059, with 170 ± 112 examples per person (min $= 23$, max $= 354$).

Each acquired image is in effect a screenshot (1024×768 pixels) of the virtual white screen in the virtual world and as a result the image background contains a number of artefacts related to the lighting effects used in the scene.

---

[1] TC-10: http://iapr-tc10.univ-lr.fr/.

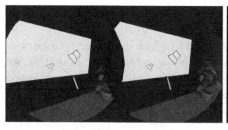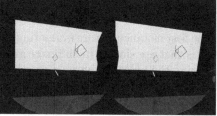

Fig. 4. Experimental paradigm in the virtual scene. The user has to draw the symbol on the left side of the white board following the template or model displayed on the right.

Each image was pre-processed using the following approach: the image is binarized using the Otsu method to separate the background from the drawing [23]. The background of the image is then set to white while the drawing remains in gray scale. The image is then cropped and centered using its center of gravity and the white border around the image removed. The image is resized to 60×60, and a border of 2 white pixels was added around the image to provide a total image size of 64×64. Images drawn based on a particular orientation of the model used were normalized in relation to the orientation of the model in order to keep all the images with the same orientation. In the following section, we only consider symbols from the database with a minimum of 96 examples and limit the number of examples to 96 for each symbol. A representative image of each class is depicted in Fig. 5. For classification purposes, a 8-fold cross validation procedure is performed where for each class 84 examples are used for training and 12 examples are used for the test. In addition, we also consider an extended database where each image is rotated by $\{-15, -10, -5, 5, 10, 15\}$ degrees increasing the total number of images by a factor of 7. We denote this by using DB_0 and DB_1 for the original and the extended databases respectively.

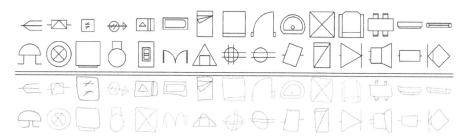

Fig. 5. Representation of the 30 symbols (rows 1 and 2: models, rows 3 and 4: representative examples of hand-drawn symbols acquired in virtual reality).

4   Results

In the first instance, we are evaluating the extent to which it is possible to retrieve images that are similar to an image given as an input or template. To do this, we are using the inner-distance approach that takes into consideration complicated shapes and part structures such as handwritten symbols [19]. The method is evaluated using DB_0 by estimating the bull's eye test where the number of relevant images is summed and divided by the maximum number of relevant images. The best performance is achieved with 1 image at 66% (see Fig. 6).

The results corresponding to image classifications are given in Tables 1, 2, and 3. For each classifier architecture the number of functional links is given for each layer. As the analysis was performed with a 8-fold cross validation and 10 random initializations of the ELM classifiers, all the results correspond to the average accuracy (in %) across 80 runs. The best performance, by using a single classifier, for both DB_0 and DB_1 was obtained with architectures using two hidden layers. For DB_0, the best accuracy, 91.43% was obtained with the most complex architecture $(800, 10000)$. It is worth mentioning that the standard deviation across runs is about 0.01%. For DB_1, the highest level of accuracy was reached using the architecture $(600, 10000)$ with a performance of 94.88%. When the decisions of 10 classifiers are combined, the performance reaches 93.06% and 95.95% for DB_0 and DB_1, respectively, by using the "mean" rule. The performance using the "max" combination rule increases but the impact of this combined approach on the accuracy is lower than with the "mean" rule. The results between the "mean" rule and majority voting are relatively similar. These results suggest that the different random initializations of the ELM classifiers can be exploited to create multi-classifier systems that improve the overall accuracy. By considering results from the top 5 best answers in each example, the accuracy reaches 99%. The accuracy corresponding to the top 5 shows the accuracy when the correct model is detected within the 5 top answers. In these cases, this performance can be used with the controller where the user can directly select one of the best answers with a button click. Finally, the evaluation was performed on

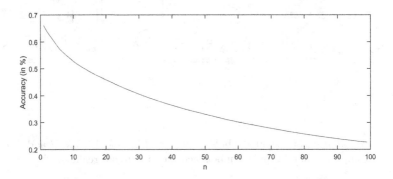

Fig. 6. Bull's eye test with the inner-distance on DB_0, in relation to n selected images.

Table 1. Accuracy (in %) with ELM using a single hidden layer.

	DB_0					DB_1				
	Acc.	Acc. (top5)	Mean	Max	Maj	Acc.	Acc. (top5)	Mean	Max	Maj
(100)	66.50	90.50	76.67	72.33	74.44	64.30	90.51	75.53	70.10	73.35
(500)	75.08	92.52	82.43	79.90	80.69	75.60	93.36	80.84	79.07	80.75
(1000)	71.14	89.92	81.74	78.99	80.83	76.48	93.23	81.54	79.64	81.05
(5000)	70.08	88.43	75.76	73.33	74.79	73.57	91.03	81.07	78.72	80.06
(10000)	73.00	89.81	74.51	73.40	73.61	59.18	83.48	81.88	73.27	78.73

Table 2. Performance with ELM using two hidden layers with DB_0 (time in second, accuracy in %).

	$Time_{train}$	$Time_{test}$	Acc.	Acc. (top5)	Mean	Max	Maj
(400, 6000)	7.55	0.08	90.49	97.96	93.06	91.94	92.71
(400, 8000)	7.84	0.09	90.72	98.04	92.50	91.46	92.15
(400, 10000)	9.17	0.11	90.96	97.94	92.43	92.01	92.36
(600, 6000)	13.04	0.10	90.76	98.15	92.99	91.74	92.85
(600, 8000)	13.17	0.12	91.16	98.13	92.71	91.88	92.78
(600, 10000)	14.73	0.14	91.28	98.24	92.57	92.08	92.29
(800, 6000)	19.21	0.11	90.85	98.06	92.43	91.94	92.64
(800, 8000)	20.63	0.13	91.23	98.32	92.29	92.08	92.22
(800, 10000)	22.40	0.16	91.43	98.28	92.64	91.67	92.36

a desktop with an Intel®Core^{TM}i7-3770 running Matlab 2015b with 16 GB of memory, which resulted in a training time of about 20 s for DB_0 and about one minute for DB_1. The results indicate that the addition of hidden layers in the ELM classifier, the inclusion of the rotated images into the database, and the combination of decisions from several classifiers improve the overall performance.

5 Discussion and Conclusion

The ability to draw with a high level of granularity and accuracy in a fully immersive virtual environment opens new possibilities for a large number of application areas ranging from entertainment (e.g., video games) to professional (e.g., education) and clinical. The types of elements that can be drawn in virtual reality depend on the layout and composition of the virtual environment, the relationships between the devices in the real world and limitations on what can be rendered in the virtual world. The major challenges of using these types of drawing capabilities effectively are related to both the areas of human-computer interaction and pattern recognition i.e., shapes can be drawn in both 2D as in this study, but also in 3D. However, although virtual reality offers key advantages for managing and interacting with technical documents in this way, there are

Table 3. Performance with ELM using two hidden layers with DB_1 (time in second, accuracy in %).

	Time$_{train}$	Time$_{test}$	Acc.	Acc. (top5)	Mean	Max	Maj
$(400, 6000)$	27.37	0.50	94.77	98.99	95.47	95.12	95.59
$(400, 8000)$	35.14	0.70	94.87	99.03	95.46	95.18	95.48
$(400, 10000)$	37.56	0.79	94.83	99.00	95.53	95.33	95.58
$(600, 6000)$	42.19	0.57	94.57	98.85	95.68	95.13	95.46
$(600, 8000)$	48.90	0.76	94.83	98.92	95.66	95.03	95.72
$(600, 10000)$	50.34	0.86	94.88	98.95	95.75	95.36	95.68
$(800, 6000)$	61.91	0.64	94.26	98.69	95.66	95.01	95.66
$(800, 8000)$	71.80	0.95	94.43	98.71	95.95	95.35	95.79
$(800, 10000)$	78.02	1.11	94.41	98.67	95.93	95.17	95.95

challenges related to motion sickness in virtual reality, particularly where the user is immersed for long sessions (none of the 18 participants reported motion sickness). In this paper, we have presented a system based in virtual reality that allows a user to draw on a white screen to create and acquire symbols, which are automatically recognized and categorised. We have shown that it is possible to reliably detect and categorise drawings using a deep extreme learning machine approach taking inputs at pixel level with low number of images per class. By further manipulations (rotating images) to the image database, we greatly increased the sample size and performance of the system with scope for additional performance increases by using more geometric deformations.

The current study uses a virtual white board metaphor to represent a typical class room scenario. The accurate detection of the symbols created on the virtual whiteboard could be used to quickly sketch technical documents and to automate the process of producing documents with a logical structure (i.e., with recognized elements). This type of system could be used in an educational setting where the student or lecturer could quickly draw technical documents or designs using symbols that can be automatically recognized and replaced by their actual models, which are easier to read. The current system only allows the recognition of single symbols however it is possible to draw symbols in sequence and validate each symbol with a button press. In this scenario, the user can do this quickly without the need to search through a long list of symbols. Further research will extend the system to include the online recognition of a range of multi-oriented symbols within the virtual reality environment.

References

1. HTC Vive - Lighthouse Tracking Technology (2016). https://github.com/ValveSoftware/openvr, http://doc-ok.org/?p=1478
2. Alhamdoosh, M., Wang, D.: Fast decorrelated neural network ensembles with random weights. Inf. Sci. **264**, 104–117 (2014)

3. Arica, N., Yarman-Vural, F.T.: An overview of character recognition focused on off-line handwriting. IEEE Trans. Syst. Man Cybern. Part C Appl. Rev. **31**(2), 216–233 (2001)

4. Assenmacher, I., Hentschel, B., Cheng, N., Kuhlen, T., Christian, B.: Interactive data annotation in virtual environments. In: Proceedings of the Eurographics Symposium on Virtual Environments, pp. 119–126. ACM SIGGRAPH (2006)

5. Cecotti, H.: Deep random vector functional link network for handwritten character recognition. In: Proceedings of the International Joint Conference on Neural Networks (IJCNN), pp. 1–6 (2016)

6. Cecotti, H.: Hierarchical k-nearest neighbor with GPUs and a high performance cluster: application to handwritten character recognition. Int. J. Pattern Recogn. Artif. Intell. **31**(2), 1–24 (2017)

7. Chen, C.L.P.: A rapid supervised learning neural network for function interpolation and approximation. IEEE Trans. Neural Netw. **7**(5), 1220–1230 (1996)

8. Chen, C.L.P., Wan, J.Z.: A rapid learning and dynamic stepwise updating algorithm for flat neural networks and the application to time-series prediction. IEEE Trans. Syst. Man Cybern. Part B **29**(1), 62–72 (1999)

9. Chhabra, A.K.: Graphic symbol recognition: an overview. In: Tombre, K., Chhabra, A.K. (eds.) GREC 1997. LNCS, vol. 1389, pp. 68–79. Springer, Heidelberg (1998). doi:10.1007/3-540-64381-8_40

10. Cordella, L.P., Vento, M.: Symbol recognition in documents: a collection of techniques? IJDAR **3**(2), 73–88 (2000)

11. Craig, A.B., Sherman, W.R.: Understanding Virtual Reality: Interface, Application, and Design. Morgan Kaufmann, San Francisco (2002)

12. Dosch, P., Valveny, E.: Report on the second symbol recognition contest. In: Liu, W., Lladós, J. (eds.) GREC 2005. LNCS, vol. 3926, pp. 381–397. Springer, Heidelberg (2006). doi:10.1007/11767978_35

13. Ghosh, D., Dube, T., Shivaprasad, A.: Script recognition: a review. IEEE Trans. Pattern Anal. Mac. Intell. **32**(12), 2142–2161 (2010)

14. Huang, G.B., Saratchandran, P., Sundararajan, N.: A generalized growing and pruning RBF (GGAP-RBF) neural network for function approximation. IEEE Trans. Neural Netw. **16**(1), 57–67 (2005)

15. Huang, G.B., Siew, C.K.: Extreme learning machine with randomly assigned RBF kernels. Int. J. Inf. Technol. **11**(1), 16–24 (2005)

16. Huang, G.B., Zhu, Q.Y., Siew, C.K.: Extreme learning machine: a new learning scheme of feedforward neural networks. In: Proceedings of the IEEE International Joint Conference on Neural Networks, vol. 2, pp. 985–990 (2004)

17. Igelnik, B., Pao, Y.H.: Stochastic choice of basis functions in adaptive function approximation and the functional-link net. IEEE Trans. Neural Netw. **6**(6), 1320–1329 (1995)

18. Kasun, L.L.C., Zhou, H., Huang, G.B., Vong, C.M.: Representational learning with extreme learning machine for big data. IEEE Intell. Syst. **28**(6), 31–34 (2013)

19. Ling, H., Jacobs, D.W.: Shape classification using the inner-distance. IEEE Trans. PAMI **29**(2), 286–299 (2007)

20. Liu, C., Nakashima, K., Sako, H., Fujisawa, H.: Handwritten digit recognition: benchmarking of state-of-the-art techniques. Pattern Recogn. **36**(10), 2271–2285 (2003)

21. Nagy, G.: At the frontiers of OCR. Proc. of IEEE **80**, 1093–1100 (1992)

22. Nagy, N.: Twenty years of document image analysis in PAMI. IEEE Trans. Pattern Anal. Mach. Intell. **22**(1), 38–62 (2000)

23. Otsu, N.: A threshold selection method from gray-level histograms. IEEE Trans. Syst. Man. Cybern. **9**(1), 62–66 (1979)
24. Pao, Y.H., Takefuji, Y.: Functional-link net computing: theory, system architecture, and functionalities. Computer **25**(5), 76–79 (1992)
25. Plamondon, R., Srihari, N.S.: On-line and off-line handwritten recognition: a comprehensive survey. IEEE Trans. Pattern Anal. Mac. Intell. **22**(1), 63–84 (2000)
26. Rahman, A., Fairhurst, M.: Multiple classifier decision combination strategies for character recognition: a review. Int. J. Doc. Anal. Recogn. (IJDAR) **5**(4), 166–194 (2003)
27. Rausch, D., Assenmacher, I., Kuhlen, T.: 3D sketch recognition for interaction in virtual environments. In: Workshop in Virtual Reality Interactions and Physical Simulation (VRIPHYS). The Eurographics Association (2010)
28. Santosh, K.C., Wendling, L.: Graphical Symbol Recognition. Wiley, Hoboken (2015)
29. Scardapane, S., Wang, D., Panella, M., Uncini, A.: Distributed learning for random vector functional-link networks. Inf. Sci. **301**, 271–284 (2015)
30. Schmidt, W.F., Kraaijveld, M.A., Duin, R.P.W.: Feedforward neural networks with random weights. In: Proceedings of the 11th IAPR International Conference on Pattern Recognition, Conference B: Pattern Recognition Methodology and Systems, vol. 2, pp. 1–4 (1992)
31. Sezgin, T.M., Davis, R.: HMM-based efficient sketch recognition. In: Intelligent User Interfaces, pp. 281–283 (2005)
32. Sezgin, T.M., Davis, R.: Sketch interpretation using multiscale models of temporal patterns. IEEE Comput. Graph. Appl. **27**(1), 28–37 (2007)
33. Tang, J., Deng, C., Huang, G.B.: Extreme learning machine for multilayer perceptron. IEEE Trans. Neural Netw. Learn. Syst. **27**(4), 809–821 (2016)
34. Valveny, E., Delalandre, M., Raveaux, R., Lamiroy, B.: Report on the symbol recognition and spotting contest. In: Kwon, Y.-B., Ogier, J.-M. (eds.) GREC 2011. LNCS, vol. 7423, pp. 198–207. Springer, Heidelberg (2013). doi:10.1007/978-3-642-36824-0_19
35. Wang, L.P., Wan, C.R.: Comments on the extreme learning machine. IEEE Trans. Neural Netw. **19**(8), 1494–1495 (2008)

Comparative Study of Handwritten Marathi Characters Recognition Based on KNN and SVM Classifier

Parshuram M. Kamble[✉] and Ravindra S. Hegadi

Department of Computer Science, Solapur University,
Solapur 413255, India
parshu1983@gmail.com, rshegadi@gmail.com

Abstract. Robust handwritten Marathi character recognition is essential to the proper function in document analysis field. Many researches in OCR have been dealing with the complex challenges of the high variation in character shape, structure and document noise. In proposed system, noise is removed by using morphological and thresholding operation. Skewed scanned pages and segmented characters are corrected using Hough Transformation. The characters are segmented from scanned pages by using bounding box techniques. Size variation of each handwritten Marathi characters are normalized in 40 × 40 pixel size. Here we propose feature extraction from handwritten Marathi characters using connected pixel based features like area, perimeter, eccentricity, orientation and Euler number. The modified k-nearest neighbor (KNN) and SVM algorithm with five fold validation has been used for result preparation. The comparative accuracy of proposed methods are recorded. In this experiment modified SVM obtained high accuracy as compared with KNN classifier.

Keywords: Geometrical feature · Marathi character · KNN and SVM classification · Feature extraction

1   Introduction

Automatic object detection and recognition from a digital image are the field of pattern recognition. In the pattern recognition feature extraction and classification are two important stages, in pattern recognition area researchers worked on various field like face recognition, Content based image retrieval, biometric and Optical character recognition (OCR). The OCR again divided in two parts machine printed and hand written. Development of off-line and On-line OCR for (MHC) Marathi handwritten characters is challenging work for researchers because handwriting of each person are mimetic. Optical character detection and recognition is used in various applications, such as document indexing, postal address recognition, number plate recognition, information retrieval and office automation. Marathi language is belongs to Devanagari script, it have 63 phonic

© Springer Nature Singapore Pte Ltd. 2017
K.C. Santosh et al. (Eds.): RTIP2R 2016, CCIS 709, pp. 93–101, 2017.
DOI: 10.1007/978-981-10-4859-3_9

letters, further they subdivided into three groups namely (vowels: 12 letters, as shown in Fig. 1, Vyanjan (Consonants: 38 letters), Ankh (numbers: 10 digits) and Modifiers (Diacritic: 12 letters) [6,8].

U. Bhattacharya and S.K. Paru proposed a novel approach Levenshtein Distance metric for on-line handwritten character recognition [1]. In this work shape and position of characters were used as a features. The shape information of character was calculated using quantized values of angular displacement between successive sample point along the trajectory of (HC) handwritten characters. They formulated a distance function based on Levenshtein metric to compute the similarity between unknown sample and training sample. D.V. Rojatkar et al. [10] proposed Handwritten Devanagari consonants recognition using Multilayer Probability neural network (MLPNN) with five fold cross validation. In this work handwritten Marathi consonants characters were used for experiment.

Vikas Dongare et al. [13] proposed based on Geometric Features and Statistical Combination Classifier for (DHNR) Devanagari Handwritten Numeral Recognition. In this paper they used 17 geometric features based on pixel connectivity, line direction, lines, image area, perimeter, orientation etc. and 5 discriminant functions namely, quadratic linear, Mahalanobis and bi-quadratic distance were used for classification. A similar work was proposed by Kamble et al. [8] in which features such as eccentricity, orientation and mass of characters were extracted and minimum distance classifier was used for classification. In another work by Kale et al. [6] Zernike moment based feature extraction for handwritten Devanagari compound character recognition. Here authors proposed Zernike moment based feature descriptor for (HCM) handwritten compound character and Support Vector Machine (SVM), K-NN based classification system.

Dixit A. et al. [3] proposed schemes for handwritten Devanagari character recognition based on wavelet based feature extraction and classification scheme. In this character image was decomposed using wavelet transform and statistical parameters are calculated as feature vector. This feature vector was used as input for back propagation neural networks during training and testing. Hegadi et al. [4] proposed sytem for Marathi handwritten numerals recognition based on multi-layer feed-forward neural network and cubic interpolation feature. N. Sharma et al. [11] proposed recognition of Off-Line handwritten Devanagari characters using Quadratic Classifier. They proposed a quadratic classification based scheme for the recognition of off-line Devanagari HC. The directional chain code information of counter point of the characters were extracted as features. Based on the chain code histogram, they used 64 dimensional features and quadratic classification for recognition. In this experiment they obtained 80.36% recognition accuracy for handwritten Marathi characters. In another work by Kamble et al. Handwritten Marathi Character Recognition Using (R-HOG) Rectangle based Histogram Oriented Gradients Feature and Artificial Neural Network (ANN) and SVM based classification is proposed [7].

In this paper we propose Local Informative k-nearest neighbor (KNN) algorithm for classification of HMC using features such as area, perimeter, eccentricity, orientation and Euler number. The proposed methodology is discussed in Sect. 2, details discussion on feature extraction and classification techniques are discussed in Sect. 3 which are used for this work. The experimental setup and result are discussed in Sect. 4. Finally conclusion of the proposed system is discussed in Sect. 5.

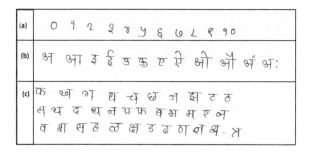

Fig. 1. Sample handwritten Marathi characters (a) Numerals, (b) Vowels and (c) Consonants.

2 Proposed Method

We propose statistical based feature extraction and KNN, SVM based classification for the handwritten Marathi characters. Proposed method consists of pre-processing, segmentation, feature extraction, and classification stages.

The handwritten character recognition system have feature extraction and classification are two important stages. Our work the consists of preparation of the standard database for the Marathi handwritten character images and extraction of geometrical features. In pre-processing stage the images are segmented into individual characters and converted in to binary form. Pre-processing of these character images is essential before feature extraction stage. In this stage we extract a set of geometrical features such as centroid, eccentricity, center mass of gravity for each and every character. These features are used in the classification stage.

The main objectives of pre-processing are binarization of input image, noise reduction, normalization, skew correction and slant removal. The binarization of image is done by applying Otsu technique [9]. In this process image converts into two components, object components and background. In the object components contains actual object and background contains noise and other unwanted information. During the scanning of input handwritten Marathi characters document, noise may be generated due to device error, lighting condition and spread of ink in the pen while writing. There are possibility of small breaks and gaps in the characters.

We applied smoothing median 3×3 pixel size filter and morphological opening with 3×3 square shape structure element to remove such kinds of noises and links breaks in the characters. Scanned input document pages have some skew which is removed by using Hough transformation [5]. After this process each character is segmented from scanned document by using bounding box. During the writing of handwritten Marathi characters some text will be in different size. The size normalization task will reduce each character image in to a vertical letter of uniform height and made up one pixel wide stroke. After this stage each character is normalized in to uniform size of 40 × 40 pixels. This process makes recognition operation process independent of the writing size and scanning resolution. Figure 2(a) shows a character from the original document image. The images after scanning will be in the form of gray-scaling, which will be converted to binary form as shown in Fig. 2(b). Due to scanning errors small gaps may be produced in the formation of characters. These gaps are removed by morphological techniques the character as shown in Fig. 2(c).

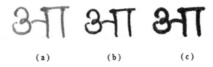

(a)   (b)   (c)

Fig. 2. Shows character pre-processing stages (a) Original character sample (b) Binary (c) Dilated character

3   Feature Extraction

After performing different pre-processing steps over MHC, various geometric features are extracted. In this proposed method we calculate area, perimeter, eccentricity, orientation and Euler number on the basis of pixel connected components.

3.1   Eccentricity

Shape, size and orientation of Marathi characters are heterogeneous. Generally, shape of handwritten Marathi vowels are like an oval shape. We used eccentricity of character as one of the feature for our work. Eccentricity is the ratio of major axis and minor axis of ellipse which covers the entire character. Eccentricity is given by

$$Eccentricity = \frac{Max_{axes}}{Min_{axes}} \tag{1}$$

Eccentricity is calculated for all characters with connected regions and discarded all regions whose eccentricity is greater than 0.89, since this value corresponds to the noise region. In Fig. 3 the doted red line is the ellipse region of handwritten Marathi letter अ and the blue lines are the major and minor axes.

Fig. 3. Red line is the ellipse around the letter अ and blue lines are major and minor axes (Color figure online)

3.2 Orientation

Angle of orientation (in degrees ranging from −90 to 90°) is the angle between major axis of the oval which covers the character and x-axis, as shown in Fig. 4. Solid blue lines are axes of the ellipse and red dots are the foci of covered character region. The orientation is the angle between the horizontal dotted line H_{axes} and the major axis Max_{axes}, which is calculated by using Eq. 2.

$$\tan(\Theta) = \frac{H_{axes} - Max_{axes}}{1 + H_{axes}Max_{axes}} \tag{2}$$

Fig. 4. (a) The sample letter अ (b) Image showing major axes and doted horizontal blue line as x-axis. (Color figure online)

3.3 Perimeter

It is the distance around the boundary of the region around the handwritten Marathi character. Following Fig. 5 shows the sample Marathi character and red line shows the perimeter.

Fig. 5. The sample letter the red line is perimeter. (Color figure online)

3.4   Area

Area of handwritten Marathi character is the actual number of pixel in the region. In binary handwritten Marathi character there are two values for pixels: 0 and 1. 0 represent background region and 1 represent actual character region. The sum of 1's is the area of handwritten Marathi character image.

3.5   Euler Number

It is one of the topological features defined by the number of holes and connected components in the image region. This property will not get affected by character rotation, stretching or transformation. The number of holes H and connected components C can be used to define the Euler number E by Eq. (3).

$$E = C - H \tag{3}$$

3.6   K-Nearest Neighborer Classification

We computed the four features, namely, total mass of character, center of mass, eccentricity and orientation features were computed for different sets of characters samples and features values of each character is computed and stored in database. In pattern recognition the k-NN algorithm is one of the methods for classifying objects based on closest training examples in the feature space. k-NN is a type of instance-based learning where the function is only appreciated locally and all computation is deferred until classification [12].

Classification of object is the heart of any pattern recognition system. The K-NN classification model widely used in various pattern recognition system like OCR and Biometric. The KNN classify the object based on the feature space. In this proposed model we trained the datasets for this algorithms with respect to feature vector and class label. In classification process the query sample assigned to the label of its k nearest neighbors.

The query sample classifies based on the labels of its k nearest neighbors by majority vote. The different distance functions like Euclidean, Manhattan, Mankowski and Chebyshev are used to result preparation.

3.7   Support Vector Machine Classification

In supervised learning model support vector machine algorithms is linear machine learning approach, it also know as support vector network that are used for classification and regression. The SVM are modified in non-linear classification based on kernel function. The kernel is the adjustable parameter of SVM. Given training set of instance label pairs $(C_i, L_i), i = 1 \ldots n$ where C_i and L_i are histograms from training images. The function θ maps training vectors x_i into a higher dimensional feature space while $C > 0$ is the penalty parameter for the error term. We used basic linear and radial basis function (RBF). The radial basis and linear function are given as:

$$K(x_i, x_i) = x_i^T x_i \quad And \quad \exp(\gamma||x_i - x_i||^2), \gamma > 0 \qquad (4)$$

The Radial Basis Function (RBF) provides good performance on handwritten character images. After configuring the kernel function and its parameter, the SVM is applied to classify the trained datasets.

4   Experimental Result

The Experimentation is carried out using Matlab 8.0 tool with Intel core $i5$, 16 GB RAM machine. Bhattacharya and B.B. Chaudhuri [2] prepared 17271 handwritten numeral datasets and 31320 (our datasets) different HC of Marathi Language were used for this experimentation, with five-fold validation. The dataset is manually classified in to three sets Vowels, Consonants, Numerals and finally mixed all sets, Figure shows the sample of datasets (Fig. 6).

Fig. 6. Marathi handwritten dataset sample.

From the each set the characters of three features, namely, eccentricity, orientation and area of character were obtained and average value is computed for each character. Based on the KNN and SVM classifier with diffrent kernel function, classification is done. Table 1 shows the classification accuracy for each of these character set. It can be noticed that the vowel character set such as औ, इ and ओ were classified with very high rate of accuracy, whereas our technique has performed very poor for the characters like ए, ऐ and ई. The rate of correct classification of ऐ is poor due to the fact that the part of character in upper portion of shirorekha will be disjoint from the remaining part of the character, due to which it will be treated as a separate character. Hence in many cases this character may be falsely classified as ए instead of ऐ. In the consonants set few character have small variation in shapes like भ, म due to that fact confusion average rate is 8.20%. When the three sets are combined for this experiment then overall accuracy with respect to KNN 88.53% and SVM 80.25%.

Average Accuracy of Vowels, Consonants and Numerals with respect to SVM is 95.35 and KNN 91.52%.

Table 1. Classification performance of each character set with respect to KNN and SVM classifier

Character set	Samples	SVM	KNN %
Vowels	4800	94.26	88.77
Consonants	6400	93.24	90.12
Numerals	20120	98.56	95.67
Mixed	31320	88.53	80.25
Numerals (U. Bhattacharya and B.B. Chaudhuri)	17271	98.52	97.00

5 Conclusion

In this paper we have proposed geometrical based feature extraction on Marathi Handwritten character recognition. We can apply two stage recognition approaches to improve the performance of the scheme. The main characteristics of the handwritten Marathi characters is their shapes which are mostly formed with more curves. Most of the failures in recognition are due to either characters with sharp edges and corners, or breaking of a characters making it as separate characters. The post processing can definitely improve the performance which we will undertake in our feature work.

References

1. Bhattacharya, U., Parui, S.K.: Online handwriting recognition using levenshtein distance metric. In: Document Analysis and Recognition, pp. 79–83 (2013)
2. Bhattacharya, U., Chaudhuri, B.B.: Handwritten numeral databases of Indian scripts and multistage recognition of mixed numerals. IEEE Trans. Pattern Anal. Mach. Intell. **31**(3), 444–457 (2009)
3. Dixit, A., Navghane, A., Dandawate, Y.: Handwritten Devanagari character recognition using wavelet based feature extraction and classification scheme. In: India Conference (INDICON), pp. 1–4 (2014)
4. Hegadi, R.S., Kamble, P.M.: Recognition of Marathi handwritten numerals using multi-layer feed-forward neural network. In: World Congress on Computing and Communication Technologies (WCCCT), pp. 21–24. IEEE (2014)
5. Jundale, T.A., Hegadi, R.S.: Skew detection and correction of Devanagari script using hough transform. Elsevier Procedia Comput. Sci. **45**, 305–311 (2015)
6. Kale, K.V., Deshmukh, P.D., Chavan, S.V., Kazi, M.M.: Zernike moment feature extraction for handwritten Devanagari compound character recognition. In: Science and Information Conference (SAI), pp. 459–466 (2013)
7. Kamble, P.M., Hegadi, R.S.: Handwritten Marathi character recognition using r-hog feature. Elsevier Procedia Comput. Sci. **45**, 266–274 (2015)
8. Kamble, P.M., Hegadi, R.S.: Handwritten Marathi basic character recognition using statistical method. In: Emerging Research in Computing, Information, Communication and Applications, vol. 3, pp. 28–33. Elsevier (2014)
9. Otsu, N.: A threshold selection method from gray-level histograms. Automatica **11**(285–296), 23–27 (1975)

10. Rojatkar, D.V., Chinchkhede, K.D., Sarate, G.G.: Handwritten Devnagari con-
    sonants recognition using mlpnn with five fold cross validation. In: International
    Conference on Circuits, Power and Computing Technologies, pp. 1222–1226 (2013)
11. Sharma, N., Pal, U., Kimura, F., Pal, S.: Recognition of off-line handwritten Devna-
    gari characters using quadratic classifier. In: Kalra, P.K., Peleg, S. (eds.) ICVGIP
    2006. LNCS, vol. 4338, pp. 805–816. Springer, Heidelberg (2006). doi:10.1007/
    11949619_72
12. Song, Y., Huang, J., Zhou, D., Zha, H., Giles, C.L.: IKNN: informative k-nearest
    neighbor pattern classification. In: Kok, J.N., Koronacki, J., Lopez de Mantaras,
    R., Matwin, S., Mladenič, D., Skowron, A. (eds.) PKDD 2007. LNCS (LNAI), vol.
    4702, pp. 248–264. Springer, Heidelberg (2007). doi:10.1007/978-3-540-74976-9_25
13. Vikas, D., Mankar, V.: Devnagari handwritten numeral recognition using geometric
    features and statistical combination classifier. Int. J. Comput. Sci. Eng. 5(10), 856–
    863 (2013)

Recognition of Handwritten Devanagari Numerals by Graph Representation and Lipschitz Embedding

Mohammad Idrees Bhat and B. Sharada$^{(\boxtimes)}$

Department of Studies in Computer Science, University of Mysore,
Mysore 570006, India
idrees11@yahoo.com, sharadab21@gmail.com

Abstract. In this paper, the task of recognizing handwritten devanagari numerals by giving graph representation is introduced. Lipschitz embedding is explored to extract style, size invariant features from numeral graphs. Graph based features adequately model the cursivenes and are invariant to shape transformations. Recognition is carried out by SVM with radial basis function. Extensive experiments have been carried on standard dataset of CVPR ISI Kolkata. Comparative study of our results is presented with previous reported results on the dataset. From this study, graph representation seems to be robust and resilient.

Keywords: Graph representation · Lipschitz embedding · Shape transformations · Cursivenes

1 Introduction

Understanding the inherent characteristics of a Devanagari script is crucial for its automatic machine recognition such as its constituent parts and complex relationships between them. With different writing styles, ambiguous character shapes, noise, and cursivenes of handwritten script more difficulties get accumulated. Perhaps it may be, due to these bottlenecks that state-of-the-art for handwritten devanagari numeral recognition is not up to the desired level as in other scripts [1]. Applications of it include in reading documents of payment, bank cheques, income tax, postal zip codes etc.

Considerable amount of work has been carried out to develop efficient and robust recognition systems by extracting different types of features such as similarity and stylistic invariant features with neural networks [1], shape invariant features such as normalized distances [2], moment invariant features such as perturbed moments, partitioning of image and coefficient for correlation [3], global and local features obtained from projection profiles used with neuromemetic model [4], directional view based features used with Multi Layer Perceptron classifier model [5], rotation, scale and translation invariant features [6], directional chain codes [7], multi resolution [8], zone based [9], etc. For survey we refer readers to [10–12].

© Springer Nature Singapore Pte Ltd. 2017
K.C. Santosh et al. (Eds.): RTIP2R 2016, CCIS 709, pp. 102–110, 2017.
DOI: 10.1007/978-981-10-4859-3_10

From the literature survey, we observe that recognition of cursive, style and size invariant handwritten devanagari script is way behind from practical use and adding such capability will be extremely useful for its automatic machine recognition. Furthermore, even if the numeral is rotated, translated, scaled and reflected the recognition system should recognize it correctly. Feature vectors are inadequate in modeling complex relationships, cursivenes and shape transformations [13]. Moreover, for all patterns in a recognition system feature vectors need to maintain predefined dimension length which is major obstacle in obtaining size invariant features [13]. These two major limitations of feature vectors are sever in representing devanagari script.

With this backdrop, we feel that graph representation of handwritten devanagari numerals will eliminate representational limitations of features vectors. Due to nodes and edges, they not only represent characteristics of patterns, complex structural relationships between different constituent parts but also can adapt to different sizes of patterns in a system. Moreover, graph representation is invariant to shape transformations and robust to occlusions and deformations [14,15]. We explored a method of extracting features from numeral graphs based on Lipschitz embedding [16]. The rationale behind Lipschitz embedding is that a pattern is transformed into an n-dimensional feature vector F such that i^{th} coordinate in F is the distance of the pattern to already set aside reference set. Extensive experiments have been caried on standard dataset to validate the efficacy of the methodology.

The organization of the paper is as under:- Sect. 2 elaborates method for feature extraction. Section 3 shows experimental results. In Sect. 4, conclusion is drawn and Future work is discussed.

2   Feature Extraction

Effective image preprocessing techniques make OCR systems robust and resilient through noise removal, skew detection and correction, normalization, thinning etc. After image preprocessing, interest point graph representation is given by taking key points in numeral images such as start and end points, connection points as shown in Fig. 1. Lipschitz embedding originally proposed for embedding metric spaces and later adopted for embedding the graph G into feature space $\mathbb{R}^n$ [17]. Let $\mathcal{G} = \{g_1, g_2, g_3, \cdots, g_n\}$ be the set of graphs and $\mathcal{S} = \{\mathcal{P}_1, \mathcal{P}_2, \cdots, \mathcal{P}_n\}$ contains n subsets of $\mathcal{G}$. Each $\mathcal{P}_i$ in $\mathcal{S}$ contains m graphs

Fig. 1. Graph representation of handwritten numeral

from $\mathcal{G}$ and n subsets $P_i \subseteq \mathcal{G}$ known as reference sets of the Lipschitz embedding. Extended Graph Edit Distance is adopted as a dissimilarity measure between input graph g and reference sets $\mathcal{S}$ as $d(g, P_i) = \underset{p \in P_i}{min}\, d(g, \mathcal{P})$ [17] i.e., distance from input graph g to the closest element in P_i, form the ith coordinate value in the feature vector F of g as shown in Fig. 3.

2.1 Graphs and Graph Edit Distance

A Graph is finite set of vertices V, edges E and their labelings. Let L_V and L_E be labels for vertices and edges, respectively.

Definition 1 (Graph). A graph is a four tuple $G = (V, E, \mu, \nu)$ where

- V set of vertices in G
- E set of edges in G
- $\mu : V \rightarrow L_V$ associates label l_v to each vertex in V
- $\nu : E \rightarrow L_E$ associates label l_E to each edge in E

To extract features based on Lipschitz embedding, an error tolerant graph matching method based on computation of edit distance between graphs is employed [13]. Graph Edit Distance computes dissimilarity between graphs by least distortion that is required to transform graph g_1 into graph g_2. Distortion operations are deletion, substitution and insertion of vertices and edges [18]. Edit Distance between graph (g_1, g_2) will result in numerous sequences of edit operations $e_1, e_2, e_3, \cdots, e_k$ known as Graph Edit Paths. Minimum Graph Edit Path between each pair of graphs is chosen from all possible edit paths by introducing cost penalty for each edit operation. An inexpensive edit path should exist between similar graphs while dissimilar graphs, will require high costs [13] as shown in (Fig. 2).

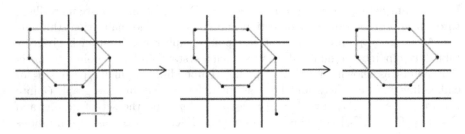

Fig. 2. One edit path between devanagari digit one and zero

Definition 2 (Graph Edit Distance). Let $g_1 = (V, E, \mu_1, \nu_1)$ and $g_2 = (V, E, \mu_2, \nu_2)$ be the two graphs. The graph edit distance (GED) between g_1 and g_2 is given as:-

$$d(g_1, g_2) = \underset{(e_1, e_2, \cdots, e_k) \in \Upsilon(g_1, g_2)}{min} \sum_{i=1}^{k} c(e_i) \qquad (1)$$

where $\Upsilon(g_1, g_2)$ depicts numerous graph edit paths that exist between graph g_1 and g_2 and $c(e_i)$ describes edit cost penalty, to measure the strength of each edit operation between g_1 and g_2, respectively.

Definition 3 (Lipschitz Embedding of Graphs). Lipschitz Embedding between input graph g with respect to reference set $\mathcal{S} = \{\mathcal{P}_1, \mathcal{P}_2, \mathcal{P}_3, \cdots, \mathcal{P}_n\}$ is defined as:-

$$\varphi_s f(g) = (f(g, \mathcal{P}_1), \cdots, f(g, \mathcal{P}_n)) \qquad (2)$$

where, $f(g, P_i) = \underset{P \in P_i}{min}\ d(g, P)$, Each attribute in the range of function φs corresponds $P_i \subseteq \mathcal{G}$ and the values for each attribute are the distances from g to the closest element in P_i as in (2).

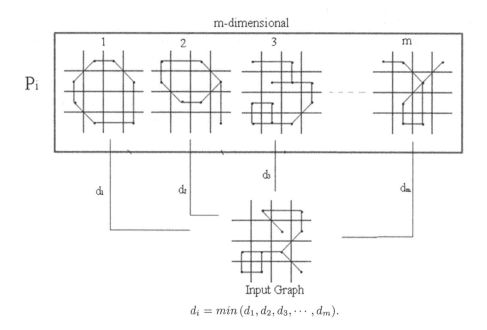

$$d_i = min(d_1, d_2, d_3, \cdots, d_m).$$

Fig. 3. Extraction of features based on Lipschitz embedding.

There are different methods for generation of reference sets [16]. However, we choose random method as it is unbiased towards any graph g in G. In this method n subsets of dimension m are randomly selected from G with replacement of graphs. For calculation of Graph Edit Distance, approximate polynomial time complexity algorithm proposed in [19] is used. Thus for n reference sets of cardinality m the Lipschitz embedding of input graph g is obtained by $n.m$ edit distance computations in polynomial time.

3   Experimental Results

In order to validate the efficacy of the methodology, extensive experiments have been conducted on CVPR (Computer Vision & Pattern Recognition Unit, Indian Statistical Institute, Kolkata) Isolated Handwritten Devanagari Numeral Dataset [20]. The dataset is obtained from individuals of diverse nature and background. Images of numerals are with different writing styles, sizes, with cursivenes, orientation and ambiguous shapes etc., 22,556 are the number of image samples in it (snapshot shown in Fig. 4.).

A set of experiments are conducted for 50 random trials of training, validation and testing in the ratios of 60:20:20 and 50:25:25 respectively. Average recognition rate and F-measure is used for assessment of the method. As a classifier support vector machine (SVM) with radial basis function (RBF) is used due its mathematical robustness and its performance. We have to optimize meta-parameters of SVM i.e., (C, Υ), where C represents weighting factor which controls the misclassification on training data and Υ represents non-linear function in RBF Kernel [21]. For selection of reference sets $\mathcal{S} = \{\mathcal{P}_1, \mathcal{P}_2, \mathcal{P}_3, \cdots, \mathcal{P}_n\}$ random method is used in which n subsets each of cardinality m are randomly chosen with the replacement of graphs. i.e., a graph g may belong to multiple reference sets of S. Total number of reference sets n, parameter pair (C, Υ) for RBFSVM, cardinality of each reference sets m, node deletion and insertion cost in (1) are empirically validated on validation set. Independent test set is then used with the highest performing parameters on validation set.

We observe the graph representation of some numerals show less inter-class variation such as devanagari digits zero, one and four. It is evident from confusion matrices Fig. 5, F-measures for a random run for all classes (Fig. 6 and Table 1) respectively. We also observe for some classes, there is more intra-class variation

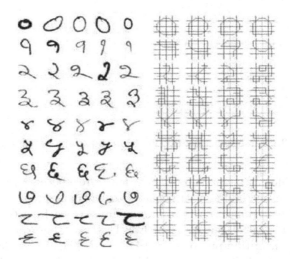

Fig. 4. Handwritten numerals of dataset (0–9) and respective numeral graphs

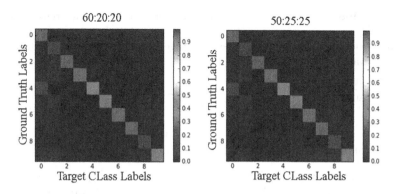

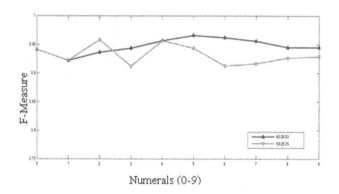

Fig. 5. Confusion matrices

Fig. 6. F-measure of digits (0–9) for a random run

Table 1. Average F-measure (class-wise) for a random run

| Class index | Training:Validation:Testing | | Class index | Training:Validation:Testing | |
	60:20:20	50:25:25		60:20:20	50:25:25
1	0.9512	0.9511	6	0.9358	0.9436
2	0.9523	0.9592	7	0.9619	0.9527
3	0.9364	0.9183	8	0.9160	0.9168
4	0.9435	0.9024	9	0.9251	0.9469
5	0.9567	0.9525	10	0.9452	0.9290

between numeral graphs and hence we could not achieve higher results for such classes. Experiments with 50 random trials are shown in Table 2 after taking average accuracy and F-measure. We notice maximum average accuracy and F-measure is achieved from 60:20:20. However, low average accuracy and F-measures from 50:25:25 is astonishing.

Table 2. Average F-measure and accuracy for 50 random trials

Dataset	Different ratio's for training, validation and testing	Average F-measure	Average recognition rates
CVPR	60:20:20	0.94837 ± 0.00369	94.83%
	50:25:25	0.95857 ± 0.03153	95.85%

3.1 Performance Comparison

The Overall average recognition results are compared with previous two results on the dataset shown in Table 3. The results reported in [22] are better in terms of accuracy, but they have used small portion of dataset, whereas whole dataset is used in this paper. The results reported in [23] are with 0.24% rejection of input samples. Our results are better since we make use of single classifier with no rejection of input samples. Furthermore, from the survey we observe all the methods are based on feature representation of numerals so they are inadequate in handling cursivenes, style, and size variance, different writing styles etc. Our results are based on powerful graph representation, features extracted show invariances to all stated bottlenecks and shape transformations. Moreover expected, results will serve benchmark on the dataset for graph representation of handwritten devanagari numerals.

Table 3. Comparison with previous reported results

Dataset	Approach	Features	Classifier	Recognition accuracy
CVPR	Combination of features	PCA/MPCA + QTLR	SVM	98.5% limited data set
	Multistage classifier	Wavelet	Multistage MLP's	99.04% with 0.24% rejection of input samples
	Graph representation	Dissimilarity features based on Lipschitz embedding	SVM	95.34% Full dataset and with no rejection of input samples

Note: Expansion of Abbreviations used in this table are as follows: PCA: Principal Component Analysis, MPCA: Multi Linear Principal Component Analysis, QTLR: Quad-Tree based Longest-Run, SVM: Support Vector Machine, MLP: Multi-Layer Perceptron.

4   Conclusion and Future Work

In this work, we have explored concept of Graph Embedding based on Lipschitz embedding for handwritten devanagari numeral recognition. In this research, we have shown that the graph representation effectively represent the cursive, size and style variant handwritten devanagari numerals. Applicability of Extended

Graph Edit Distance is studied for embedding of Graphs into feature vectors. Performance of the approach is evaluated in terms of average F-measure by conduction of extensive experiments on CVPR handwritten devanagari isolated numeral dataset. The method obtains the average recognition rate 95.34% and is compared with previous two results on same dataset. We can infer that creation of reference sets is directly proportional to the reliable recognition rate of the method. However, the robustness of the method needs to be studied with additional reference set creation methods and other graph distances measures.

References

1. Bajaj, R., Dey, L., Chaudhary, S.: Devanagiri numerals recognition by combining decision of multiple connectionist classifiers. Sadhana **27**(1), 59–72 (2002)
2. Hanmandlu, M., Grover, J., Madasu, V.K., Vasikarla, S.: Input fuzzy modelling for the recognition of handwritten Hindi numerals. In: Proceedings of the International Conference Information Technology, pp. 208–213 (2007)
3. Ramteke, R.J., Mehrotta, S.C.: Feature extraction based on moment invariants for handwriting recognition. In: Proceedings of IEEE Conference, Cybernetics, Intelligent, System, pp. 1–6 (2006)
4. Banashree, N.P., Vasanta, R.: OCR for script identification of Hindi (devanagiri) numerals using feature sub selection by means of end-point with neuro-memetic model. Int. J. Intell. Technol. **2**, 206–210
5. Bhattacharya, U., Parui, S.K., Shaw, B., Bhattacharya, K.: Neural combination of ANN and HMM for handwritten devanagiri numeral recognition. In: Lorette, G. (ed.) Tenth International Workshop on Frontiers in Handwriting Recognition, La Baule, October 2006
6. Patil, P.M., Sontakke, T.R.: Rotation, scale and translation invariant handwritten devanagiri numeral character recognition using general fuzzy neural network. Pattern Recogn. **40**, 2110–2117 (2007)
7. Sharma, N., Pal, U., Kimura, F., Pal, S.: Recognition of off-line handwritten devnagari characters using quadratic classifier. In: Kalra, P.K., Peleg, S. (eds.) ICVGIP 2006. LNCS, vol. 4338, pp. 805–816. Springer, Heidelberg (2006). doi:10.1007/11949619_72
8. Chaudhary, B.B., Ghosh, R., Ghosh, M., Bhattacharya, U.: On recognition of handwritten devanagiri numerals. In: Proceedings of the Workshop on Learning Algorithms for Pattern Recognition (in Conjunction with the 18th Australian Joint Conference on Artificial Intelligence)
9. Rajashekhararadhya, S.V., Ranjan, P.V.: Efficient zone based feature extraction method for handwritten numeral recognition of four popular south Indian scripts. In: JATIT 2005–2008
10. Jayadevan, R., Satish, R., Patil, M., Pal, U.: Offline recognition of devanagiri script: a survey. IEEE Trans. Syst. Man Cybern. C Appl. Rev. **41**(6), 782–796 (2014)
11. Pal, U., Chaudhuri, B.B.: Indian script character recognition: a survey. Pattern Recogn. **37**, 1887–1899 (2004)
12. Bag, S., Harit, G.: A survey on optical character recognition for Bengali and Hindi documents. In: Sadhana-Academy Proceedings in Engineering Science, vol. 38, no. I, pp. 1333–168. AS & Springer (2013)

13. Riesen, K., Bunke, H.: Graph Classification and Clustering Based on Vector Space Embedding: Series in Machine Perception Artificial Intelligence World Scientific, vol. 77. World Scientific Publishing Co., Inc. River Edge (2010)
14. Raveax, R., Abu-Aisheh, Z.: Graph for pattern recognition. University prancots-rabelais, October 2013
15. Bourgain, J.: On Lipchitz embedding of finite metric spaces in Hilbert spaces. Israel J. Math. **52**, 46–52 (1985)
16. Riesen, K., Bunke, H.: Graph classification by means of Lipchitz embedding. IEEE Trans. Man Cybern. B Cybern. **39**(6), 1472–1483 (2009)
17. Riesen, K., Bunke, H.: On Lipschitz embeddings of graphs. In: Lovrek, I., Howlett, R.J., Jain, L.C. (eds.) KES 2008. LNCS (LNAI), vol. 5177, pp. 131–140. Springer, Heidelberg (2008). doi:10.1007/978-3-540-85563-7_22
18. Gao, X., Xian, B., Tao, D.: A survey of graph edit distance. Pattern Anal. Appl. **13**, 113–129 (2010)
19. Riesen, K., Bunke, H.: Approximate graph edit distance computation by means of bipartite graph matching. Image Vis. Comput. **27**, 950–959 (2009)
20. Bhattacharya, U., Chaudhuri, B.B.: Databases for research on recognition of hand-written characters of Indian scripts. In: Proceedings of the 8th International Conference on Document Analysis and Recognition (ICDAR-2005), Seoul, Korea, vol. II, pp. 789–793 (2005)
21. Hsu, C.-W., Chang, C.-C., Lin, C.-J.: A practical guide to support vector classification. Technical report, Department of Computer Science, National Taiwan University (2003)
22. Das, N., Reddy, J.M., Sarkar, R., et al.: A statistical topological feature combination for recognition of handwritten numerals. Appl. Soft Comput. J. **12**(8), 2486–2495 (2012)
23. Bhattacharya, U., Chaudhuri, B.B.: Handwritten numeral databases of Indian scripts and multistage recognition of mixed numerals. IEEE Trans. Pattern Anal. Mach. Intell. **31**(3), 444–457 (2009)

Unlocking Textual Content from Historical Maps - Potentials and Applications, Trends, and Outlooks

Yao-Yi Chiang[✉]

Spatial Sciences Institute, University of Southern California,
Los Angeles, CA 90089, USA
yaoyic@usc.edu

Abstract. Digital map processing has been an interest in the image processing and pattern recognition community since the early 80s. With the exponential growth of available map scans in the archives and on the internet, a variety of disciplines in the natural and social sciences grow interests in using historical maps as a primary source of geographical and political information in their studies. Today, many organizations such as the United States Geological Survey, David Rumsey Map Collection, OldMapsOnline.org, and National Library of Scotland, store numerous historical maps in either paper or scanned format. Only a small portion of these historical maps is georeferenced, and even fewer of them have machine-readable content or comprehensive metadata. The lack of a searchable textual content including the spatial and temporal information prevents researchers from efficiently finding relevant maps for their research and using the map content in their studies. These challenges present a tremendous collaboration opportunity for the image processing and pattern recognition community to build advance map processing technologies for transforming the natural and social science studies that use historical maps. This paper presents the potentials of using historical maps in scientific research, describes the current trends and challenges in extracting and recognizing text content from historical maps, and discusses the future outlook.

Keywords: Digital map processing · Text recognition · Optical character recognition · Historical maps · Geographic information system · Natural science · Social science · Biology · Spatial humanity

1 Introduction

Historical maps are an irreplaceable primary source of geographical and political information in the past (e.g., historical place names, landmarks, natural features, transportation networks, and war, trade, and diplomacy networks). The image processing and pattern recognition community started to develop computational methods for the extraction and recognition of the content from archived images of maps since the early 80s (Chiang et al. 2014). With the exponential growth of available map scans in the archives and on the internet, a variety of disciplines in the natural and social sciences grow interests in using historical maps in their studies. For example, the Mappa Mundi by Fra Mauro (ca. 1450) (Fig. 1) contains not only place names but also provides *"natural philosophy, description*

© Springer Nature Singapore Pte Ltd. 2017
K.C. Santosh et al. (Eds.): RTIP2R 2016, CCIS 709, pp. 111–124, 2017.
DOI: 10.1007/978-981-10-4859-3_11

of places and people, commercial geography, history, navigation and direction of expansion, and, finally, on what we can nowadays call methodological issues. In addition, Fra Mauro's world map also includes hundreds of images, representing cities, temples, funerary monuments, streets, and ships, as well as a scene in the lower left corner representing Earthly Paradise" (Nanetti et al. 2015).

Fig. 1. East Asia Mainland of the Mappa Mundi (ca. 1450), Fra Mauro

In many cases, historical maps are the only source that provides professionally surveyed historical geographic data. Map archives such as the U.S. Geological Survey (USGS)

National Geologic Map Database,[1] USGS Topographic Maps,[2] David Rumsey Map Collection,[3] OldMapsOnline.org,[4] and the National Library of Scotland,[5] together store millions of this type of historical map in either paper or scanned format. For example, between 1884 and 2006, the USGS has created over 200,000 topographic maps. According to the USGS, in the United States these topographic maps *portray both natural and manmade features. These maps show and name works of nature including mountains, valleys, plains, lakes, rivers, and vegetation. They also identify the principal works of man, such as roads, boundaries, transmission lines, and major buildings.*" The USGS National Geospatial Program has scanned these historical paper maps. Collectively, these publicly available scanned maps portray the evolution of the American landscape over a 125-year period.[6] Similar map series exist in many countries, e.g.; the Ordnance Survey maps in the U.K archived by the National Library of Scotland.

In the case of more recent historical maps produced using modern geospatial survey technologies (e.g., the USGS Topographic Map series, Ordnance Survey six-inch series, and other national agency series dated from the early 1800), the detailed map data on the states of landscapes in the past are essential for understanding the causes and consequences of environmental change and support a variety of natural and social studies on topics such as cancer and environmental epidemiology, urbanization, biodiversity, landscape changes, and history. (See Gregory et al. 2015 for more examples and methodologies in historical geographic information systems.) Many of these historical maps are not georeferenced, and almost all of the maps have content that is not machine-readable. Existing map processing technologies are still limited in making a large number of historical maps fully searchable by their content because the archived documents often suffer from bleaching, blurring, and false coloring (e.g., Khotanzad and Zink 2003; Leyk and Boesch 2009; Leyk et al. 2006). The reader is referred to Chiang et al. (2014) and Chiang et al. (2016) for detailed reviews and case studies on map processing techniques and systems.

Today, a researcher can spend a great deal of time and effort searching and cross-referencing data sources to find relevant maps. Then they need to digitize the map for converting the map content to a machine-readable format (e.g., Godfrey and Eveleth 2015; Nanetti et al. 2015). The researcher may need to search in various publication repositories, map repositories, search engines, and then they will often not find the historical map that they are looking for and work without it. In many cases, these historical maps exist, and it just requires too much effort to locate and digitize them. The result is that researchers waste time and resources and do not get as far as they could have in their work because the relevant information is not discoverable or takes too long to prepare for scientific analysis.

---

[1] USGS NGMDB (2016) [Website]. Retrieved from http://ngmdb.usgs.gov/ngmdb/ngmdb_home.html.

[2] USGS topoView (2016) [Website]. Retrieved from http://ngmdb.usgs.gov/maps/TopoView/.

[3] David Rumsey. (2016). [Website]. Retrieved from http://www.davidrumsey.com/.

[4] OldMapsOnline (2016) [Website]. Retrieved from http://www.oldmapsonline.org/.

[5] NLS (2016) [Website]. Retrieved from http://maps.nls.uk/.

[6] USGS topoView (2016) [Website]. Retrieved from http://ngmdb.usgs.gov/maps/TopoView/.

The challenges in working with historical maps present an enormous collaboration opportunity for the image processing and pattern recognition community to build advance map processing technologies for transforming the scientific studies that currently use textual content in historical maps. Therefore, it is important to understand the current landscape in the broad applications of historical maps. This paper first describes the potentials and current applications of historical maps in a variety of studies, including topics in natural science (Sect. 2) and social science (Sect. 3). Next, the paper describes the current trend in extracting and recognizing textual content from historical maps (Sect. 4). Finally, the paper discusses the future outlook in text recognition technologies in map processing (Sect. 5).

2   Potentials and Applications of Historical Maps in Natural Science

Historical data archives (e.g., museum and herbaria collections, digital photography and newspaper archives) support a variety of scientific studies in natural science on topics such as biodiversity (e.g., Hill et al. 2009), evolutionary biology (e.g., Lavoie 2013), human disease (e.g., Yoshida et al. 2014), plant biology (Davis et al. 2015; Vellend et al. 2013), and ecology (e.g., Newbold 2010; Pyke and Ehrlich 2010), but geolocating the historical localities mentioned in archives (e.g., Calflora Observation Database[7] and the Global Biodiversity Information Facility; Samy et al. 2013) is challenging and very often a tedious manual process using historical maps. Murphey et al. (2004) reviewed the problems in georeferencing museum collections. They compared a number of geoparsing tools including the GEOLocate (Rios and Bart 2010) and BioGeomancer (Guralnick et al. 2006). Since then, a variety of advanced algorithms for geoparsing has been proposed (e.g., Leidner and Lieberman 2011) and open-source software packages (e.g., CLAVIN,[8] CLIFF (D'Ignazio et al. 2014)), and the Edinburgh Geoparser (Alex et al. 2015) are available. These algorithms and tools are widely used in geolocating places in the unstructured text and also used in spatial humanities research (e.g., Gregory et al. 2015). However, these tools need a "gold data" gazetteer to provide the location information of recognized place names, and the lack of historical reference gazetteers remains a challenge. The result is that even if the geoparsing software can correctly identify a historical name as a geolocation reference in the unstructured text, the geocoordinates of the historical name is still unknown if the place name no longer exists. To locate the place names that no longer exist in contemporary data sources, a researcher needs to search and cross-reference a variety of data sources such as archives of historical maps, newspapers, and photography.

For example, a data record in an online database of California herbarium specimens describes an August 16th, 1902 observation of *Artemisia douglasiana* (California mugwort) at the location "near Mesmer" in Los Angeles. The place name Mesmer near or within both the City and County of Los Angeles no longer exists in the contemporary

---

[7] CalFlora (2016) [Data set]. Retrieved from http://www.calflora.org/.

[8] CLAVIN (2016) [Computer software]. Retrieved from https://clavin.bericotechnologies.com/.

geographic data sources, including authoritative sources like the U.S. Census[9] and USGS GNIS (the United States Geological Survey Geographic Names Information System)[10] and open sources, such as GeoNames,[11] OpenStreetMap,[12] and Wikipedia. Searching "Mesmer" in the GeoNames gazetteer results in an airport "Mesmer Airport" in New York and a street "Rue Mesmer" in Haiti. Neither of the results helps to geolocate the observation of California mugwort in 1902. A Google search with the keywords "Mesmer" and "Los Angeles" reveals a few interesting facts that could be helpful for geolocating Mesmer. First, the search results include a person, Louis Mesmer (1829–1900), who was a prominent businessman and the owner of the famous United States Hotel in Los Angeles. Because it was common to name locations after well-known families (e.g., Wilshire, Hancock, and Doheny in Southern California), Mesmer could be a place name in the Los Angeles area in the past. Second, the search results contain a link to a map in the Los Angeles Public Library collections showing a proposed development plan in 1924 for the "Mesmer City" in Los Angeles (Fig. 2). At the time, Mesmer City was advertised as *"In the direct path of the Los Angeles' growth toward the ocean"*.[13] This map further narrows down the search space for Mesmer to somewhere nearby Culver City and Baldwin Hills. Together, the time and location information from the search results points to the USGS topographic map that contains the Mesmer in 1901 (Fig. 3). In this case, Mesmer is geolocated, but the entire process cannot be scaled to handle thousands of records in an efficient manner.

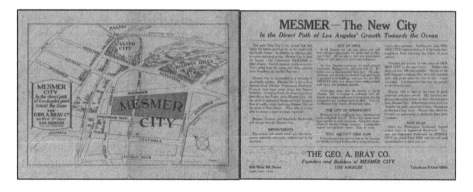

Fig. 2. Map of the Mesmer City development

Historical GIS (Geographic Information System) (Gregory and Ell 2007) could alleviate the problem of geolocating historical locality references by providing a platform for collecting datasets of historical place names, but the datasets are rarely available.

---

[9] U.S. Census Gazetteer (2016) [Data set]. Retrieved from https://www.census.gov/geo/maps-data/data/gazetteer.html.

[10] USGS GNIS (2016) [Data set]. Retrieved from http://geonames.usgs.gov/.

[11] GeoNames (2016) [Data set]. Retrieved from http://www.geonames.org/.

[12] OpenStreetMap (2016) [Website]. Retrieved from https://www.openstreetmap.org/.

[13] Los Angeles Public Library Map Collection (2016) [Website]. Retrieved from https://www.lapl.org/collections-resources/visual-collections/map-collection.

Even when historical gazetteers are available, their spatiotemporal coverage is often sparse. For example, the U.S. Census only provides post-2010 and also 2000 and 1990 census gazetteer files. NHGIS (the National Historical Geographic Information System at the Minnesota Population Center)[14] provides historical demography data down to the census tract level but only a few place names. The Ramsay Place Names File from the State Historical Society of Missouri provides a historical gazetteer covering locations in the State of Missouri from 1928 to 1945 (Adams 1928). The website "A Vision of Britain through Time" from the GB Historical GIS at the University of Portsmouth[15] provides historical place names in the Great Britain dated back in the early 19th century.

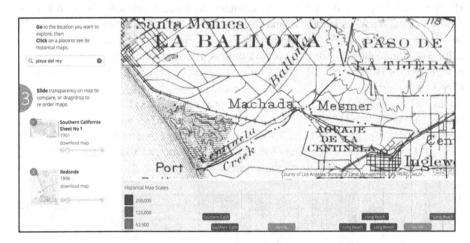

Fig. 3. The USGS historical topographic map shows the location of Mesmer. (Southern California Sheet No. 1, circa 1901)

As shown in the examples of natural science studies in this section, the ability to automatically use the textual content in historical maps as the locality reference source will be able to transform historical data records in documents and collections into georeferenced datasets. This ability will enable natural science researchers to efficiently find, query, and analyze a variety of historical records by location.

3   Potentials and Applications of Historical Maps in Social Science

Historical maps also play an important role in social science studies. Kurashige (2013)[16] used historical census data, voting records, and precinct numbers and

---

[14] NHGIS (2016) [Website]. Retrieved from https://www.nhgis.org/.

[15] A Vision of Britain through Time (2016) [Website]. Retrieved from http://www.visionofbritain.org.uk/.

[16] Dr. Kurashige's article published in the Southern California Quarterly won the 2015 Carl I. Wheat Award for the best demonstration of scholarship in that journal from 2012–2014 by a senior historian.

boundaries extracted from a 1920 map to study "who" (e.g., occupations and political parties) in Los Angeles voted for the 1920 California Alien Land Law that discriminates against Japanese (Fig. 4).

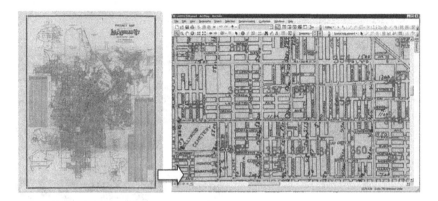

Fig. 4. Automatically unlocking precinct boundaries in a historical map for analyzing historical voting records with demographic datasets.

Ngo et al. (2015) used historical maps and land records to build an interactive visualization of land reclamation in Hong Kong (Fig. 5). This web tool[17] is among the top hits when searching Hong Kong land reclamation on Google.

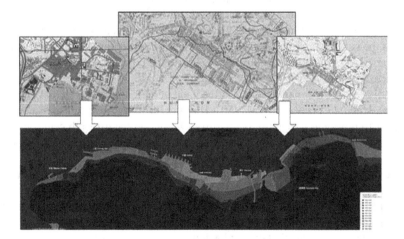

Fig. 5. Building an interactive visualization of land reclamation in Hong Kong from historical maps.

The Spatial Sciences Institute at the University of Southern California (USC) is collaborating with an insurance company to automatically read historical Ordnance

---

[17] http://www.oldhkphoto.com/coast/.

Survey maps (ca. 1900–1970) covering the entire U.K. to identify likely locations of subterranean contamination, such as factories, mines, quarries, and gas works which no longer exist and otherwise would not be known today (Fig. 6).[18]

Fig. 6. Quarries and infill lands in a historical map and the contemporary satellite imagery.

In a joint effort, the USC Shoah Foundation Visual History Archive (VHA) works with the USC Spatial Sciences Institute to link historical maps to places mentioned in genocide survivor testimonies in the VHA archive. The linkages enrich the personal stories of the survivors by using the spatial and temporal context in historical maps to enable the viewers to "go back in time" to recreate the physical world of the historical experience of the survivors (Fig. 7).[19]

Nanetti et al. (2015) manually transcribed and georeferenced the textual content in the *Mappa Mundi by* Fra Mauro (ca. 1450). They use the transcribed data as a knowledge aggregator to represent the world as seen from Venice in the fifteenth centuries. They also plan to use the map data for automatic provenance and validation assessment of large and heterogeneous collections of other historical sources.

The example studies in this section demonstrate the power of historical maps in social science research. They also show that not only extracting and recognizing map content is important, but providing semantic annotations to the map content and linking the map content to other data sources will enable researchers to investigate complex social science problems at a scale that cannot be done today.

---

[18] Spatial technology opens a window into history (2016) [News article]. Retrieved from https://news.usc.edu/91625/spatial-technology-opens-a-window-into-history/.

[19] Peter Feigl's Journey Through Historical Maps (2016) [Website]. Retrieved from http://www.arcgis.com/apps/MapJournal/index.html?appid=6c3b4136b9304df09c9adcf86dd30dd5.

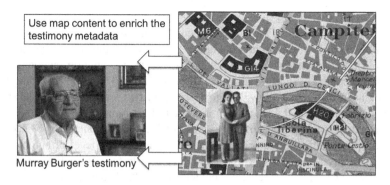

Fig. 7. Using historical maps to identify the wedding location (historical synagogue) described by Holocaust survivor Murray Burger.

4   Current Trends in Text Recognition from Historical Maps

Text recognition from maps is a difficult task, especially for historical maps. This is because map labels often overlap with other map features, such as road lines, do not follow a fixed orientation within a map, and can be stenciled and handwritten text (Chiang et al. 2014, 2016; Nagy et al. 1997). Also, many historical scanned maps suffer from poor graphical quality due to bleaching of the original paper maps and archiving practices. This section presents a number of trends in text recognition from historical maps.

Classic Approaches. Traditional, the approaches on text recognition from historical maps follow the classic document recognition strategy that first analyze the map to identify the potential text areas. Then the approaches use optical character recognition (OCR) algorithms or tools (e.g., TesseractOCR)[20] to convert the detected areas into machine-readable text (Honarvar Nazari et al. 2016; Chiang and Knoblock 2014; Li et al. 2000; Pezeshk and Tutwiler 2010, 2011; Raveaux et al. 2007, 2008). This line of work has demonstrated promising results on single map sheet or map series but still does not handle large numbers and various types of historical maps because of the significant heterogeneity of historical maps.

Crowdsourcing Approaches. To handle the vast variety of historical map types and sources, recent work has adopted the crowdsourcing strategy. Crowdsourcing is not a new idea (but can be very difficult to implement and popularize) in document recognition and map processing. The David Rumsey Map Collection held crowdsourcing events to georeference their map collections by crowdsourcing. The New York Public Library provides semi-automatic tools for the public to extract parcel polygons from their historical insurance maps.[21] They also noted that even with the crowdsourcing approach, semi-automatic tools are required to process their map collections in a reasonable time

---

[20] Tesseract-OCR (2016) [Computer software]. Retrieved from https://github.com/tesseract-ocr.
[21] NYPL map-vectorizer (2016) [Computer software]. https://github.com/NYPL/map-vector-izer.

(Arteaga 2013). Specifically for converting textual content in historical maps using crowdsourcing, the Pelagios Commons[22] is a notable community that provides tools and online infrastructures to facilitate annotating historical locality references in digital materials. Their tools allow semi-automatic extraction, recognition, annotation, and linking of place names in historical maps (Simon et al. 2010, 2014, 2015). These tools and the online infrastructure allow them to provide full-text searchable place data ranges from ancient times to 1500 AD and from Europe to East Asia.

To make the crowdsourcing strategy more effective and efficient, it will be necessary to build adaptive semi-automatic techniques that improve the level of automation as more maps are processed. Also, as the crowdsourcing strategy is used, approaches for cross-validating between user generated content and the "gold data" as well as recording the provenance information are required (e.g., Garijo et al. 2015).

Multi-model Approaches. Another line of work in the recent development of text recognition from historical maps uses additional data sources as the dictionary to help correct the recognition errors. While this dictionary strategy is common in OCR, compiling and effectively using a dictionary for recognizing historical map text is difficult. This is because a dictionary built using contemporary data sources does not contain place names that no longer exist. Also, without knowing the map coverage beforehand, multiple dictionary entries can match to a partially recognized label. For example, a partially recognized label "Glas wo" near London could be matched to "Glasgow" when the label is "Glassworks". Even the map coordinates are known, the map text might not be at the exact location of the geographic features depending on the cartographic labeling practice of the map. Weinman (2013) presents an approach that overcomes this challenge. His approach recognizes text labels in maps to then match the recognized text to a gazetteer by their position patterns using a RANSAC variant called MLESAC (Torr and Zisserman, 2000). He showed that this approach could automatically georeference historical maps and improve the recognition accuracy even when the gazetteer only contains 70% of the text in the test maps.

In previous work, we developed a semi-automatic approach that extracts and recognizes text labels in map images in a system called Strabo (Apache Version 2 License) (Chiang and Knoblock 2014). While Strabo could achieve over 90% precision and recall in recognizing text labels in scanned contemporary maps, it could only produce 47.6% precision and 83.5% recall on well-conditioned text from historical Ordnance Survey six-inch maps (Chiang et al. 2016). The result is that very often only partial labels could be recognized from a historical map (Figs. 8(a) and (b)) and manual post-processing is required to correct the recognition results.

---

[22] Plageois Commons (2016) [Website]. Retrieved from http://commons.pelagios.org/.

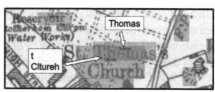

(a) Strabo incorrectly recognizes "St. Thomas Church" as "homa urch" in a 1900 map.

(b) Strabo incorrectly recognizes "St. Thomas Church" as "Thomas t Cltureh" in a 1935 map.

Fig. 8. Matching imperfect OCR results from two map editions to improve recognition accuracy

In an effort to test higher levels of automation in text recognition from historical maps (Yu et al. 2016), we exploit the fact that geographic names for the same area found in different data sources is not independent and use geographic names in OpenStreetMap and other maps covering the same area as the "dependent" knowledge source. Given a historical map, the task at hand is to recognize all map labels in the map accurately without user intervention. First, the system queries a map repository to find all map editions covering the same area and then extracts and recognizes labels in the identified maps. Second, the system compares and uses a fuzzy matching algorithm to match the recognized (imperfect) labels using their locations and string similarity. Finally, the system uses two million geographical names extracted from OpenStreetMap to generate an improved recognition result. For example, by matching "Cltureh" from the 1935 map to "urch" in the 1900 map, the system finds the word "Church" in the geographic names extracted from OpenStreetMap to replace "Cltureh" and "urch" in the 1935 and 1900 recognition results, respectively.

For the multi-model approaches, the current challenges include how to exploit string similarity measures between the extracted map text (which contain recognition errors) and other sources (e.g., gazetteer entries) to (1) prune the search space for finding the matching pattern efficiently and (2) using matches between the OCR text and dictionary entries to learn potential OCR errors specifically for each map type. For example, the character sequences "ni" and "in" is commonly recognized as one character "m" during OCR. With enough training data (matches between OCR text and dictionary entries), the algorithm should be able to learn that the OCR results "Baldwm Hills" is highly likely to be "Baldwin Hills" for a specific map type or condition.

5   Outlooks

This paper presents studies in natural and social sciences demonstrating the opportunities for the image processing & pattern recognition community to transform conventional research practices in using historical maps. For example, a new technology that automatically generates machine-readable or -understandable (e.g., LinkedData (Bizer et al. 2009)) place name databases from historical maps and to do so at scale will enable biology scientists to minimize the time and effort for geo-locating their data records and to efficiently query and analyze historical records by location and time. These opportunities also present unique possibilities for researchers in image processing & pattern recognition to identify collaborators in other scientific domains. This type of interdisciplinary collaboration allows the researchers in image processing & pattern recognition to create algorithms and applications to solving "wicked" research problems and addressing real-world challenges facing our society. Further, the paper discusses a number of trends and their challenges in text recognition from historical maps. These trends have already shown promising results in the automatic unlocking of textual content in heterogeneous historical maps. Solving the challenges in these trends will make it possible to use a large number of heterogeneous historical maps efficiently and study historical spatiotemporal datasets on a large scale.

Acknowledgements. This research is based upon work supported in part by the National Science Foundation under award number IIS-1564164 and in part by the University of Southern California under the Undergraduate Research Associates Program (URAP). The author thanks Travis Longcore for his input on the biology studies and the U.S. National Committee (USNC) to the International Cartographic Association (ICA) for providing travel funding to attend the 27th International Cartographic Conference (ICC).

References

Adams, O.G.: Place Names in the North Central Counties of Missouri (Ph. D.). University of Missouri-Columbia (1928)

Alex, B., Byrne, K., Grover, C., Tobin, R.: Adapting the Edinburgh geoparser for historical georeferencing. Int. J. Humanit. Comput. **9**(1), 15–35 (2015)

Arteaga, M.G.: Historical map polygon and feature extractor. In: Proceedings of the 1st ACM SIGSPATIAL International Workshop on MapInteraction, pp. 66–71. ACM (2013)

Bizer, C., Heath, T., Berners-Lee, T.: Linked data - the story so far. Int. J. Seman. Web Inf. Syst. **5**(3), 1–22 (2009)

Chiang, Y.-Y., Knoblock, C.A.: Recognizing text in raster maps. GeoInformatica **19**(1), 1–27 (2014)

Chiang, Y.-Y., Leyk, S., Knoblock, C.A.: A survey of digital map processing techniques. ACM Comput. Surv. (CSUR) **47**(1), 1 (2014)

Chiang, Y.-Y., Leyk, S., Nazari, N.H., Moghaddam, S., Tan, T.X.: Assessing the impact of graphical quality on automatic text recognition in digital maps. Comput. Geosci. **93**, 21–35 (2016)

Davis, C.C., Willis, C.G., Connolly, B., Kelly, C., Ellison, A.M.: Herbarium records are reliable sources of phenological change driven by climate and provide novel insights into species' phenological cueing mechanisms. Am. J. Bot. **102**(10), 1599–1609 (2015)

D'Ignazio, C., Bhargava, R., Zuckerman, E.: Cliff-clavin: determining geographic focus for news. In: NewsKDD: Data Science for News Publishing (2014)

Garijo, D., Gil, Y., Harth, A.: Challenges for provenance analytics over geospatial data. In: Ludäscher, B., Plale, B. (eds.) IPAW 2014. LNCS, vol. 8628, pp. 261–263. Springer, Cham (2015). doi:10.1007/978-3-319-16462-5_28

Godfrey, B., Eveleth, H.: An adaptable approach for generating vector features from scanned historical thematic maps using image enhancement and remote sensing techniques in a in a geographic information system. J. Map Geogr. Librar. **11**(1), 18–36 (2015)

Gregory, I., Donaldson, C., Murrieta-Flores, P., Rayson, P.: Geoparsing, GIS, and textual analysis: current developments in spatial humanities research. Int. J. Humanit. Comput. **9**(1), 1–14 (2015)

Gregory, I.N., Ell, P.S.: Historical GIS: Technologies, Methodologies, and Scholarship, vol. 39. Cambridge University Press, Cambridge (2007)

Guralnick, R.P., Wieczorek, J., Beaman, R., Hijmans, R.J., Group, B.W., et al.: BioGeomancer: automated georeferencing to map the world's biodiversity data. PLoS Biol. **4**(11), e381 (2006)

Hill, A.W., Guralnick, R., Flemons, P., Beaman, R., Wieczorek, J., Ranipeta, A., Chavan, V., Remsen, D.: Location, location, location: utilizing pipelines and services to more effectively georeference the world's biodiversity data. BMC Bioinf. **10**(Suppl 14), S3 (2009)

Honarvar Nazari, N., Tan, T.X., Chiang, Y.-Y.: Integrating text recognition for overlapping text detection in maps. Electron. Imaging Doc. Recogn. Retrieval XXIII **17**, 1–8 (2016)

Khotanzad, A., Zink, E.: Contour line and geographic feature extraction from USGS color topographical paper maps. IEEE Trans. Pattern Anal. Mach. Intell. **25**(1), 18–31 (2003)

Kurashige, L.: Rethinking anti-immigrant racism: lessons from the Los Angeles vote on the 1920 Alien Land Law. Southern Calif. Q. **95**(3), 265–283 (2013)

Lavoie, C.: Biological collections in an ever changing world: herbaria as tools for biogeographical and environmental studies. Perspect. Plant Ecol. Evol. Syst. **15**(1), 68–76 (2013)

Leidner, J.L., Lieberman, M.D.: Detecting geographical references in the form of place names and associated spatial natural language. Sigspatial Spec. **3**(2), 5–11 (2011)

Leyk, S., Boesch, R.: Colors of the past: color image segmentation in historical topographic maps based on homogeneity. GeoInformatica **14**(1), 1–21 (2009)

Leyk, S., Boesch, R., Weibel, R.: Saliency and semantic processing: extracting forest cover from historical topographic maps. Pattern Recogn. **39**(5), 953–968 (2006)

Li, L., Nagy, G., Samal, A., Seth, S., Xu, Y.: Integrated text and line-art extraction from a topographic map. Int. J. Doc. Anal. Recogn. **2**(4), 177–185 (2000)

Murphey, P.C., Guralnick, R.P., Glaubitz, R., Neufeld, D., Ryan, J.A.: Georeferencing of museum collections: a review of problems and automated tools, and the methodology developed by the mountain and plains spatio-temporal database-informatics initiative (Mapstedi). Phyloinformatics **1**(3), 1–29 (2004)

Nagy, G., Samal, A., Seth, S., Fisher, T.: Reading street names from maps-technical challenges. In: Proceedings of GIS/LIS (1997)

Nanetti, A., Cattaneo, A., Cheong, S.A., Lin, C.-Y.: Maps as knowledge aggregators: from Renaissance Italy Fra mauro to web search engines. Cartographic J. **52**(2), 159–167 (2015)

Newbold, T.: Applications and limitations of museum data for conservation and ecology, with particular attention to species distribution models. Prog. Phys. Geogr. **34**(1), 3–22 (2010)

Ngo, V., Swift, J., Chiang, Y.-Y.: Visualizing land reclamation in Hong Kong: a web application. In: International Cartographic Conference (2015)

Pezeshk, A., Tutwiler, R.L.: Improved multi angled parallelism for separation of text from intersecting linear features in scanned topographic maps. In: IEEE International Conference on Acoustics, Speech and Signal Processing, pp. 1078–1081. IEEE (2010)

Pezeshk, A., Tutwiler, R.L.: Automatic feature extraction and text recognition from scanned topographic maps. IEEE Trans. Geosci. Remote Sens. **49**(12), 5047–5063 (2011). A Publication of the IEEE Geoscience and Remote Sensing Society

Pyke, G.H., Ehrlich, P.R.: Biological collections and ecological/environmental research: a review, some observations and a look to the future. Biol. Rev. Camb. Philos. Soc. **85**(2), 247–266 (2010)

Raveaux, R., Burie, J.C., Ogier, J.M.: A colour document interpretation: application to ancient cadastral maps. In: Ninth International Conference on Document Analysis and Recognition (ICDAR 2007), vol. 2, pp. 1128–1132. IEEE (2007)

Raveaux, R., Burie, J.C., Ogier, J.M.: Object extraction from colour cadastral maps. In: The Eighth IAPR International Workshop on Document Analysis Systems, DAS 2008, pp. 506–514. IEEE (2008)

Rios, N.E., Bart, H.L.: GEOLocate (Version 3.22) [Computer software] (2010)

Samy, G., Chavan, V., Ariño, A.H., Otegui, J., Hobern, D., Sood, R., Robles, E.: Content assessment of the primary biodiversity data published through GBIF network: status, challenges and potentials. Biodivers. Inform. **8**(2) (2013). http://doi.org/10.17161/bi.v8i2.4124

Simon, R., Barker, E., Isaksen, L.: Linking early geospatial documents, one place at a time: annotation of geographic documents with Recogito. E-Perimetron **10**(2), 49–59 (2015)

Simon, R., Pilgerstorfer, P., Isaksen, L., Barker, E.: Towards semi-automatic annotation of toponyms on old maps. E - Perimetron **9**(3), 105–128 (2014)

Simon, R., Sadilek, C., Korb, J., Baldauf, M., Haslhofer, B.: Tag clouds and old maps: annotations as linked spatiotemporal data in the cultural heritage domain. In: Workshop on Linked Spatiotemporal Data, Zurich, Switzerland (2010)

Torr, P.H.S., Zisserman, A.: MLESAC: a new robust estimator with application to estimating image geometry. Comput. Vis. Image Underst. CVIU **78**(1), 138–156 (2000)

Vellend, M., Brown, C.D., Kharouba, H.M., McCune, J.L., Myers-Smith, I.H.: Historical ecology: using unconventional data sources to test for effects of global environmental change. Am. J. Bot. **100**(7), 1294–1305 (2013)

Weinman, J.: Toponym recognition in historical maps by Gazetteer alignment. In: Proceedings of the 12th International Conference on Document Analysis and Recognition, pp. 1044–1048 (2013)

Yoshida, K., Burbano, H.A., Krause, J., Thines, M., Weigel, D., Kamoun, S.: Mining herbaria for plant pathogen genomes: back to the future. PLoS Pathog. **10**(4), e1004028 (2014)

Yu, R., Luo, Z., Chiang, Y.-Y.: Recognizing text on historical maps using maps from multiple time periods. In: Proceedings of the 23rd International Conference on Pattern Recognition (2016)

Document Image Analysis for a Major Indic Script Bangla - Advancement and Scope

Kaushik Roy[(✉)]

Department of Computer Science, West Bengal State University,
Kolkata 700126, WB, India
kaushik.mrg@gmail.com

Abstract. Bangla is one of the most popular script from eastern part of India with a demographic distribution of 212 million of population, used in languages like Bengali, Assamese, Manipuri etc. There are several works reported in literature considering Bangla script in the areas of Bangla OCR, postal automation, writer verification, online document analysis, script identification etc. They need more attention from the researchers as almost all of the mentioned topics are yet far from getting maturity. In this paper, a study on the advancement of those techniques with emphasis on Bangla script is presented. Also, some future directions in this field will be discussed.

Keywords: Bangla script · OCR · Postal automation · Writer identification · Online document analysis · Script identification

1 Introduction

Document image analysis (DIA) refers to reading and analysing text from scanned image documents. So, DIA research involves development of several algorithm and techniques which are applied to document images to obtain some text data from the pixel level data. In our day to day life we can visualize the outcome of research work in document analysis by using different OCRs for different languages, scripts, symbols. But due to the presence of multi-lingual script documents in India, the OCR research faces a real challenge. To overcome such difficulties nowadays researchers are working to propose a pre-processing module which performs the script identification first, before sending the document to language specific OCR.

The rest of the paper is outlined as follows: Sect. 2 describes about the properties of Bangla script. In Sect. 3 different applications of DIA are described. At last the paper will be concluded in Sect. 4 with future directions.

2 Properties of Bangla Script

There are three main languages in India which follows Bangla script. These are Bengali, Assamese and Manipuri. Bengali, originated from the Indo-European

© Springer Nature Singapore Pte Ltd. 2017
K.C. Santosh et al. (Eds.): RTIP2R 2016, CCIS 709, pp. 125–134, 2017.
DOI: 10.1007/978-981-10-4859-3_12

language family, is the state language of West Bengal and Tripura. People living in Bihar, Dhanbad, Manbhum, Singhbhum, Santal Parganas of Jharkhand, Garo Hills of Meghalaya, Goalpara District of Assam, Nagaland and Mizoram also use this language. It is spoken by 181 million population of India. Not only in India, Bengali language is used in Bangladesh also [35].

Assamese can be classified under the Indo-European group of languages. It is the state language of Assam. About 16.8 million of the Indian population living in Arunachal Pradesh, Meghalaya and West Bengal use this language.

Manipuri language is originated from the Sino-Tibetan language group. People of Manipur mostly use the language. It is also used in Karimganji and Cachar of Assam, West and North Tripura districts, Nagaland, West Bengal and Uttar Pradesh. About 13.7 million people use this language.

In India, Bangla is the second most popular script next to Devanagari and used to represent three languages viz., Bengali, Assamese and Manipuri. It is also the national language of Bangladesh. So, working with Bangla has lots of significance in this respect. But despite its importance very limited works are found on Bangla character recognition as the variation of writing and complex nature of Bangla characters make it more challenging. The Bangla script consists of 50 alphabets (39 consonants + 11 vowels) and 10 numerals. The numbers of alphabets are quite higher compared to Roman script. Also the characters (alphabets + numerals) are structurally complex than the Roman script. The sample view of the complex nature of these characters can be found in Fig. 1. Here from the figure differences in printed and handwritten characters are visible [1].

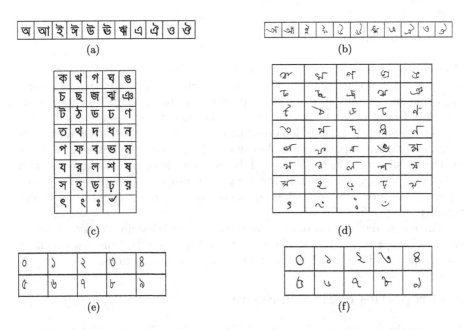

Fig. 1. Bangla printed characters (a, c, e), handwritten characters (b, d, f)

3   Application of DIA on Bangla Script

3.1   OCR

The basic idea of Optical Character Recognition (OCR) is to recognize and extract text to digitally editable text from document images. In current situation there are existing OCRs available for scripts like Roman/Latin, Cyrillic, Chinese, Japanese, Korean, Arabic etc. Some of the commercially available OCR systems are Fine Reader by ABBYY [2], Capture Development System by Scan-Soft [3], Automatic Reader by Sakhr [4], NovoD DX by Novodynamics [5] etc. Considering Indic script like Bangla, very few bits and pieces of researches are conducted [1]. It is also worth mentioning that developing a complete OCR is quite tedious and challenging task. Additionally the complex nature of Bangla script makes it more challenging to work on OCR for Bangla script. It may be one of the prime reasons for lack of interest of researchers in this area. The OCR systems for printed documents can reach more than 99% accuracy mainly for the above mentioned commercially available systems. But the main challenge to develop an OCR system lies for handwritten documents, as these documents are written by writers of different types. The randomness of writing leads to greater variation in feature space which in turn increases the misclassification rate for characters recognition. Also in case of Bangla script the situation is more challenging due to the complex nature of the script itself which is already mentioned earlier in Sect. 2. Till date the reported works on OCR development for Bangla script can be found as: single-stage approach [6–10] and multi-stage approach [11–16]. A two-pass approach for Bangla character recognition is proposed in [17]. In this work the author has reported for recognition of both basic and compound characters. But as we have already mentioned, due to diversified nature of handwriting samples of Bangla script, a significant amount of work is still needed to achieve optimum accuracy.

3.2   Postal Automation

Postal automation system is a system that can be used to automate postal documents by sorting out the letters according to their destination address. We have addressed some fundamental problems of Indian Postal Automation (IPA) considering one of the popular Indic script Bangla. The detailed statistical analysis of the postal documents can be found in [18] on 7,500 Indian postal documents collected for it. Different information obtained from this statistical analysis is very helpful for developing some of the techniques towards IPA. For example, the information that the destination addresses are written in the bottom rightmost portions in 70.6% of the mail pieces has been utilized under the present work for identifying Destination Address Blocks (DAB). Again from the statistical analysis, we noted that 22.04% of the postal documents collected by us were written in more than one script. This information has guided us to develop a method for script identification.

During preprocessing of mail images two-stage binarization technique is applied then text graphics separation, skew correction, DAB identification, pin code box detection and pin code digit extraction, are done. For example, the DAB identification technique, being tested on the images of mail pieces collected by us, has produced correct results in 98.55% of the cases. To get higher accuracy from bi-lingual pin code recognition, we follow a two-stage approach. In the first stage, using a 16-class global recognition scheme, we first identify the script by which the pin code is written. In the second stage, based on the identified script, a local 10-class recognition scheme is applied. The feature sets considered here consists of Structural and Statistical features, Normalized binary pixel images, Direction code based features, Gradient based features etc. For recognition, two categories of classifiers, viz., Multi-Layer Perceptron (MLP) and Modified Quadratic Discriminant Function (MQDF) based classifiers have been selectively tested here. From the result, we noted that MQDF outperforms MLP and hence we finally used MQDF for detailed result computation on digit recognition. Using MQDF classifiers we obtained 99.15% (98.06%) accuracy from Bangla (English), when tested on 14,650 (13,500) samples. In an attempt to make the present postal automation system smart and robust to errors, resulting from omission of complete or a part of a pin code, a lexicon-driven segmentation-recognition scheme is used for Bangla city name recognition. In order to merge segmented primitive components into characters and to find optimum character segmentation, DP (Dynamic Programming) is applied using the total likelihood of characters as the objective function. For testing the performance of the proposed city name recognition technique, a database of 8,625 handwritten samples of 84 Indian city names is considered here. The percentage of recognition rate of the technique as observed through experimental observation is found to be 94.08%.

Some of the related field includes digit recognition system for other Indian scripts, Touching digit recognition, Indian bank cheque recognition system, City name recognition for other Indian scripts and languages, Improvement of the proposed city name recognition, Script identification system for other Indian scripts, Table form document processing, Bangla online handwriting recognition to name a few. Figure 2 shows a sample Bangla postal document.

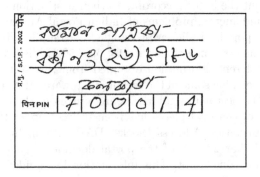

Fig. 2. A sample Bangla postal document

3.3 Writer Identification

In document image processing writer identification is one of the intriguing areas of research. It is the area of document image processing which deals with biometric identification techniques. This research has direct prospect in the area of forensic, judicial system, security etc. So developing a system for writer identification needs proper attention and care regarding confidence of the identification accuracy. Writer identification can be broadly categorized into two parts on-line and off-line writer identification depending on the input method. In on-line the writer needs to write using special equipments like tablet, stylus etc. Along with the text information stroke directions, handwriting speed, hand pressure, pen positions, pen up and pen down moments etc. are also stored. These features of a writer help to classify and identify a writer more easily than in off-line mode. The off-line methods involve handwritten characters and text using conventional pen and paper. In case of off-line mode the collected sample documents need to be digitized using scanners or cameras with different resolution according to the need of the work. Both methods can be text-dependent or text-independent regarding the input database. Here the discussion will be on off-line mode of writer identification problem. Various research works on writer identification can be found in literature but most of them are on Roman/Latin, Chinese, Arabic and other non-Indic scripts [19]. Although few works on Bangla scripts can be found in current scenario, no complete system in this regard is present. More details can be found in [19].

The main area of concern for development of a writer identification system on Bangla is the lack of available standard database. Along with this the complex nature of Bangla script and variability of handwriting of different writers adds to the challenges of this research.

Writer identification can be achieved by matching unknown handwritings with a database of sample handwritings with known authorship. Some methods on Bangla script reported in literature, where for most of the works isolated Bangla characters are used. In [20] a fuzzy logic based writer identification rate of 82.93% is reported for 90 writers. Individuality of Bangla characters are computed along with writer identification on all characters in [21]. An individuality of 55.85% for character GA and writer identification accuracy of 99.75% is reported for 90 writers. In [22] three different modified features like MFFT (Modified Fast Fourier Transform), MGLCM (Modified Gray Level Co-occurrence Matrix), MDCT (Modified Discrete Cosine Transform) are extracted for 150 writers. An individuality of 69.44% is reported for numeral 4 and writer identification accuracy of 98.62% is achieved.

Although writer identification on Bangla recently gained interest from researchers, still various aspects of writer identification needs to be developed. There is a pressing need for a standard database with writer information for Bangla script. Here in our discussion it can be observed that use of isolated characters for writer identification produce high identification accuracy. So quality line, word, character segmentation techniques are required to achieve good identification accuracy from document text that will be parallel to those systems that use isolated characters for identification. Also different type of feature extraction procedures can be applied on text documents to gain better identification accuracies. Other future scope includes introduction of combining classifier and features. From this discussion it is quite evident that there are lots of scope for improvement and development for writer identification on Bangla script.

3.4 Script Identification

In India we have 23 official languages which are written using 11 official scripts [23]. So, an official document can be written using multiple languages and/or multiple scripts. Postal documents, filled up pre-printed forms etc. are good examples of multi-script documents. Optical Character Recognizer (OCR) is a tool used to extract text from document images. For a multi-script country like India, designing of a general OCR system for all official languages is very challenging task. To overcome this, an automatic script identification system can be developed and the output can be feed to script dependent OCR. Document images containing more than one script are generally classified as Intra-document script identification problem to the OCR research community. Whereas in Inter-document script identification, each document is written using one script only.

For Inter-document script, page level identification is possible but in Intra-document script identification, it may be in block, line, word, even in character level also. In many countries automated multi-script identification system is already available [24–27]. But in our country the researchers have recently started showing interest to this area. So a system to identify the script of the document images is of pressing need.

To have an idea of some of the official scripts and languages of India see Fig. 3, where a Rs. 500.00 currency note is shown with some of the official Indian

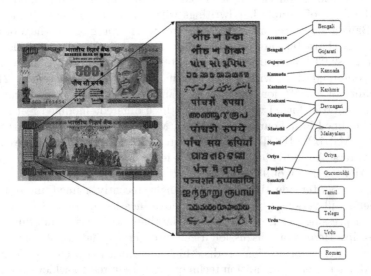

Fig. 3. Different official scripts/languages in an Indian currency note is shown

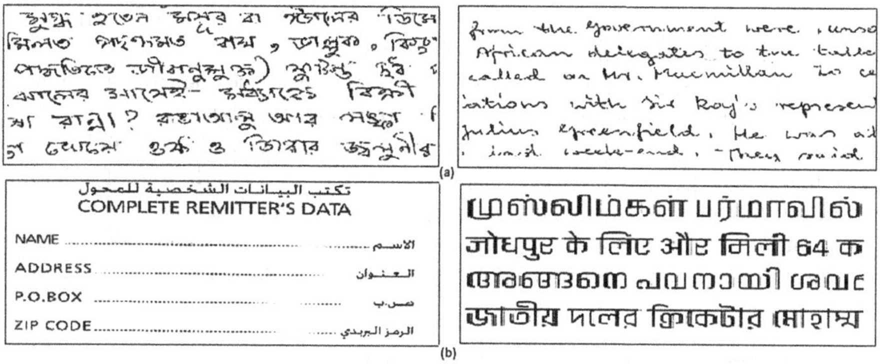

Fig. 4. Different multi-script documents (a) Different document written by different scripts (b) Single document written by different scripts

languages printed on it (highlighted & zoomed) along with the scripts used to write them. Figure 4 provides the glimpse of the multi-script printed/ handwritten documents. A block diagram of a multi-script document processing system is shown in Fig. 3.

Script identification system is broadly classified into two categories mainly on-line [32] and off-line depending upon the nature of the documents are used. In off-line, inputs are provided in the form of images whereas in on-line, inputs are considered to be ordered sequence of points. That is why off-line script identification is more challenging compared to on-line. The present work is based on off-line script identification problem. In the literature few works are reported on script identification techniques [24, 26–31], where most of them are based on non-Indic scripts. Among those, printed documents of non-Indic scripts got more attention from the researchers compared to handwritten ones.

3.5 Database Availability, Development and Future Scope

Developing a standard database for research purpose is one of the most important tasks for any system. It is also a tedious and time consuming job as this needs proper attention to details of the type of data needed for proper evaluation of the system. So during collection of data it should be taken into consideration that replicating the same scenario again is loss of precious time and efforts, so before starting the collection of data every bit of details should be planned accordingly to create a standard database. Considering all of these scenarios, still erroneous samples bound to exist in a preliminary collected database due to natural variations. So to finalize the database before publishing, sometimes manual checking of the whole database is essential.

Here considering the Bangla script there are some databases available for the re-search community to work with, like CMATERdb [33] database by CMATER, dept. of Comp. Sc. And Engg. of Jadavpur University, ISIcalcvpr unit handwritten database of Bangla characters [34]. All of these databases can be used mainly for OCR purpose but for writer identification and verification there is no such database currently available on Bangla for the researchers.

It is quite evident that there are lots of scope for database creation on Bangla. Being the second most popular language (in terms of population) [35] in Indian subcontinent it is quite obvious that research on Bangla script has very high significance in our society. In this current situation there is a very high need of different kind of databases that target Bangla script as prime, like Bangla writer identification and verification database containing original and forged handwriting of different writers, Bangla signature database, Character database etc.

4   Conclusion and Future Direction

In this paper the author present an overview of Bangla script and development of document image analysis applications on this script. The explored areas are mainly: OCR development, writer identification, postal automation, script identification. The work relating to printed Bangla script has reached much attention and success, compared to handwritten one. This makes an open area to work on handwritten Bangla script for various applications. All the works mentioned so far are mainly in off-line environment. So, scopes are there to work in on-line environment also, as nowadays on-line document processing is very popular through different portable devices.

References

1. Halder, C., Obaidullah, S.M., Roy, K.: Effect of writer information on Bangla handwritten character recognition. In: 5th National Conference on Computer Vision, Pattern Recognition, Image Processing and Graphics (NCVPRIPG 2015), pp. 1–4. IIT Patna, India (2015)
2. https://www.abbyy.com/. Accessed 09 Jan 2016
3. http://www.nuance.com/index.htm. Accessed 09 Jan 2016
4. http://www.sakhr.com/index.php/en/. Accessed 09 Jan 2016
5. http://www.novodynamics.com/. Accessed 09 Jan 2016
6. Bhowmik, T.K., Bhattacharya, U., Parui, S.K.: Recognition of Bangla handwritten characters using an MLP classifier based on stroke features. In: Pal, N.R., Kasabov, N., Mudi, R.K., Pal, S., Parui, S.K. (eds.) ICONIP 2004. LNCS, vol. 3316, pp. 814–819. Springer, Heidelberg (2004). doi:10.1007/978-3-540-30499-9_125
7. Basu, S., Das, N., Sarkar, R., Kundu, M., Nasipuri, M., Basu, D.K.: Handwritten Bangla alphabet recognition using an MLP based classifier. In: 2nd National Conference on Computer Processing of Bangla, Dhaka, Bangladesh, pp. 285–291 (2005)
8. Roy, K., Pal, U., Kimura, F.: Bangla handwritten character recognition. In: 2nd Indian International Conference on Artificial Intelligence, Pune, India, pp. 431–443 (2005)
9. Chaudhuri, B.B., Majumdar, A.: Curvelet-based multi SVM recognizer for offline handwritten Bangla: a major Indian script. In: 9th International Conference on Document Analysis and Recognition, pp. 491–495 (2007)

10. Basu, S., Das, N., Sarkar, R., Kundu, M., Nasipuri, M., Basu, D.K.: A hierarchical approach to recognition of handwritten Bangla characters. Pattern Recogn. **42**, 1467–1484 (2009)
11. Rahman, A.F.R., Rahman, R., Fairhurst, M.C.: Recognition of handwritten Bengali characters: a novel multistage approach. Pattern Recogn. **35**, 997–1006 (2002)
12. Bhattacharya, U., Parui, S.K., Shridhar, M., Kimura, F.: Two-stage recognition of handwritten Bangla alphanumeric characters using neural classifiers. In: 2nd Indian International Conference on Artificial Intelligence, Pune, India, pp. 1357–1376 (2005)
13. Bhattacharya, U., Shridhar, M., Parui, S.K.: On Recognition of Handwritten Bangla Characters. In: Kalra, P.K., Peleg, S. (eds.) ICVGIP 2006. LNCS, vol. 4338, pp. 817–828. Springer, Heidelberg (2006). doi:10.1007/11949619_73
14. Das, N., Basu, S., Sarkar, R., Kundu, M., Nasipuri, M., Basu, D.K.: An improved feature descriptor for recognition of handwritten Bangla alphabet. In: International Conference on Signal and Image Processing, pp. 451–454. Excel India Publishers, Mysore (2009)
15. Bhowmik, T., Ghanty, P., Roy, A., Parui, S.: SVM-based hierarchical architectures for handwritten Bangla character recognition. Int. J. Document Anal. Rcogn. **12**, 97–108 (2009)
16. Das, N., Acharya, K., Sarkar, R., Basu, S., Kundu, M., Nasipuri, M.: A Novel GA-SVM based multistage approach for recognition of handwritten Bangla compound characters. In: Satapathy, S., Avadhani, P., Abraham, A. (eds.) International Conference on Information Systems Design and Intelligent Applications-2012 (INDIA-2012), Visakhapatnam, vol. 132, pp. 145–152 (2012)
17. Das, N., Sarkar, R., Basu, S., Saha, P.K., Kundu, M., Nasipuri, M.: Handwritten Bangla character recognition using a soft computing paradigm embedded in two pass approach. Pattern Recogn. **46**, 2054–2071 (2015)
18. Roy, K.: On the Development of OCR System for Indian Postal Automation. LAPLAMBERT Academic Publishing, Saarbrucken (2011)
19. Halder, C., Obaidullah, S.M., Roy, K.: Offline writer identification and verification- a state-of-the-art. In: 3rd International Conference on Information System Design and Intelligent Application (INDIA 2016), Visakhapatnam, India, pp. 153–163 (2016)
20. Halder, C., Das, S., Roy, K.: Application of fuzzy logic in writer identification based on individuality of Bangla numerals. J. Int. Syst. **3**, 37–40 (2013)
21. Halder, C., Roy, K.: Individuality of isolated Bangla characters. In: International Conference on Devices, Circuits and Communication (ICDCCom), Ranchi, India, pp. 1–6 (2014)
22. Halder, C., Obaidullah, S.M., Roy, K.: Offline writer identification from isolated characters using textural features. In: 4th International Conference on Frontiers in Intelligent Computing: Theory and Applications (FICTA 2015), pp. 221–231 (2016)
23. Obaidullah, S.M., Das, S.K., Roy, K.: A system for handwritten script identification from Indian document. J. Pattern Recogn. Res. **8**, 1–12 (2013)
24. Ghosh, D., Dube, T., Shivaprasad, A.: Script recognition- a review. IEEE Trans. PAMI **32**, 2142–2161 (2010)
25. Roy, K., Pal, U., Chaudhuri, B.B.: A system for neural network based word-wise handwritten script identification for Indian postal automation. In: 2nd International Conference on Intelligent Sensing and Information Processing and Control, pp. 581–586 (2005)

26. Hochberg, J., Kerns, L., Kelly, P., Thomas, T.: Automatic script identification from document images using cluster based templates. IEEE Trans. PAMI **19**, 176–181 (1997)
27. Zhou, L., Lu, Y., Tan, C.L.: Bangla/English script identification based on analysis of connected component profiles. In: Bunke, H., Spitz, A.L. (eds.) DAS 2006. LNCS, vol. 3872, pp. 243–254. Springer, Heidelberg (2006). doi:10.1007/11669487_22
28. Patil, B., Subbareddy, N.V.: Neural network based system for script identification in Indian documents. Sadhana **27**, 83–97 (2002)
29. Singhal, V., Navin, N., Ghosh, D.: Script based classification of handwritten text document in a multilingual environment. In: Research Issues in Data Engineering, pp. 47–54 (2003)
30. Spitz, A.L.: Determination of the script and language content of document images. IEEE Trans. PAMI **19**, 235–245 (1997)
31. Lam, L., Ding, J., Suen, C.Y.: Differentiating between oriental and European scripts by statistical features. Int. J. Pattern. Recogn. Artif. Intell. **12**, 63–79 (1998)
32. Namboodri, A.M., Jain, A.K.: Online handwritten script identification. IEEE Trans. PAMI **26**, 124–130 (2004)
33. https://code.google.com/archive/p/cmaterdb/. Accessed 09 Jan 2016
34. http://www.isical.ac.in/cvpr/. Accessed 09 Jan 2016
35. Obaidullah, S.M., Mondal, A., Das, N., Roy, K.: Script identification from printed Indian document images and performance evaluation using different classifiers. Appl. Comput. Intel. Soft Comput. **2014**, 12 (2014)

Pattern Analysis and Machine Learning

Combination of Feature Selection Methods for the Effective Classification of Microarray Gene Expression Data

T. Sheela[(✉)] and Lalitha Rangarajan

Department of Studies in Computer Science, University of Mysore,
Manasagangotri, Mysore, India
sheela.mysore1@gmail.com

Abstract. Gene selection from microarray gene expression data is very difficult due to the large dimensionality of the data. The number of samples in the microarray data set is very small compared to the number of genes as features. To reduce dimensionality, selection of significant genes is necessary. An effective method of gene feature selection helps in dimensionality reduction and improves the performance of the sample classification. In this work, we have examined if combination of feature selection methods can improve the performance of classification algorithms. We propose two methods of combination of feature selection techniques. Experimental results suggest that appropriate combination of filter gene selection methods is more effective than individual techniques for microarray data classification. We have compared our combination methods using different learning algorithms.

Keywords: Gene selection · Microarray data · Dimensionality reduction · Combination of filters · Classification performance

1 Introduction

DNA microarray is used to measure expression levels of genes associated with different types of cancers. The expression data has very high dimensionality, usually around thousands of genes and only hundreds of samples [7]. This causes the problem of over-fitting [1] of the classifier, that is failure of correct classification of new data because of over training the machine. Gene selection techniques can be used to determine a small feature subset while retaining the meaning of the original feature set. Reducing the features can also save storage and computation time as well as improve classification accuracy. Hence, gene selection is an important issue in cancer classification.

Gene selection is an important pre-processing step in microarray data analysis. Common gene selection techniques are filter methods, wrapper methods and embedded methods [21]. Filter methods rank each gene based on univariate metric, and only the top ranked genes are used for classification. The purpose of gene selection is to select a subset of informative genes [21].

© Springer Nature Singapore Pte Ltd. 2017
K.C. Santosh et al. (Eds.): RTIP2R 2016, CCIS 709, pp. 137–145, 2017.
DOI: 10.1007/978-981-10-4859-3_13

Gene ranking methods select genes according to some ranking criteria. Our work is based mainly on filter based gene ranking techniques. The filter models are independent of learning algorithm and other advantages are, these models have a simple structure, easy to design and are fast. Parametric and non-parametric tests [21] are the two main types of ranking criteria. Parametric tests involve estimating parameters such as the mean and assume that the sample means are normally distributed. Non parametric tests are distribution free tests and they work with ranks of the variables but not on their values. A lot of research work has been done on designing more efficient feature selection techniques by combining feature selectors [19, 21–23]. Instead of considering the output of a single feature selector as final subset, different feature selectors can be combined [13, 21] to improve the performance in the classification result. This concept evolved from ensemble classification, which is a method of combining several independent classifiers [12] for improving the final classification accuracy. The underlying principle of combining feature selection methods is that genes that are highly ranked by different selectors will be more biologically relevant than those selected by a single measure [18].

Hence, combination of filter gene selection methods are required to deal with high dimensional gene expression microarray data more effectively and efficiently. In this work, we experimented with the combination of feature selection techniques, where multiple feature selection methods are combined to yield a single sequence of significant genes. We have studied the effect of combined gene selection techniques using different classifiers.

In our study, we are using two parametric tests: t-test, entropy and two non-parametric tests: ROC (Receiver Operator Characteristic) curve and Wilcoxon rank sum method for gene selection [17]. To compare the effectiveness of gene selection, gene sets chosen by each technique are tested with four well-known [4] learning algorithms: An instance based learner k Nearest Neighbor (kNN), Support Vector Machine (SVM), a probabilistic learner Naive Bayes Classifier (NBC) and a decision tree learner Random Forest (RF). These four algorithms represent different approaches to learning and they have been used by many researchers in classification studies. Our experiments are performed on Leukemia DNA microarray gene expression dataset [7] involved in diagnosis of cancer. The classification performance is measured in terms of Accuracy percentage and AUC (Area Under the ROC Curve) value. AUC is a more reliable performance measure for unbalanced datasets, like microarray experiments [9, 17, 23, 27].

2   Related Work

Combination of statistical methods like t-test, penalized t-test, mixture models and linear models are used in [26] to improve the performance of the microarray data classification. Top k items are selected from several feature rankings and one final list is produced by the aggregation of them and sent to the classifier in Markov chain rank aggregation [10] approach. Performance of various classification methods are studied in [2] by combining Wilcoxon test with different feature selection procedures. An investigation is made in [22] to verify whether combining multiple feature selection methods has any effect on the classification performance. Classification accuracy and stability of the gene ranking results are improved [28] by combining multiple filtering algorithms and classifiers. k-nearest neighbor classifier result is enhanced by feature fusion methods proposed in [5] for microarray data classification. The feature selectors, linear SVM and RFE (Recursive Feature Elimination) are combined [23] to design Complete Linear Aggregation and Complete Weighted Linear Aggregation for microarray classification. By incorporating various combinations of multiple filters and classifiers [19], a mapping strategy - multi-filter enhanced genetic ensemble (MF-GE) system is devised to improve sample classification accuracy. An efficient gene selection algorithm NMICFS-PSO [25] is proposed, which integrates correlation based feature selection (CFS), Neighborhood Mutual Information (NMI) and particle swarm optimization (PSO) into an ensemble technique and support vector machine (SVM) with leave-one-out cross-validation is used as a classifier.

3   Ranking Methods

In this subsection, a brief description of the ranking methods used for experimentation is presented. The four popular ranking methods t-test, Entropy, ROC and Wilcoxon ranking methods, have been most commonly applied [15,17] for gene selection of microarray data and are available in bioinformatics toolbox of MATLAB [16]. These are statistical tests in the binary classification problem and in all these criteria, the gene is more important if the statistic score is high.

Two Sample t-test and Entropy Test: These are parametric methods. t-statistic [17] of each gene is computed using Eq. (1). Genes with high absolute t value are considered more informative.

$$t = \frac{\mu_1 - \mu_2}{\sqrt{\frac{\sigma_1^2}{n_1} + \frac{\sigma_2^2}{n_2}}} \tag{1}$$

The entropy score [17] for each gene is computed using Eq. (2). Genes are arranged in decreasing order of entropy score, so the genes with high entropy are se-lected for classification.

$$e = \frac{1}{2} \left[\left(\frac{\sigma_1^2}{\sigma_2^2} + \frac{\sigma_2^2}{\sigma_1^2} - 2 \right) + \left(\frac{1}{\sigma_1^2} + \frac{1}{\sigma_2^2} \right) (\mu_1 - \mu_2)^2 \right] \tag{2}$$

In Eqs. (1) and (2), t is the t-score and e is the entropy score, μ_1 μ_2 are sample mean of class 1 and class 2, σ_1 σ_2 are sample standard deviation of class 1 and class 2 and n_1 n_2 represent number of samples in class 1 and class 2 respectively.

Receiver Operating Characteristic (ROC) Curve: ROC analysis is a non-parametric approach and it can be represented as a measure of separation between two distributions. ROC curve [6] displays the relationship between the proportion of true positive (sensitivity) and false positive (1-specificity) classifications, in a two class classification task. Genes can be ranked using the AUC value [14,15,17,20] a common measure of discrimination which ranges between 0 and 1. Informative genes are those that have greatest AUC.

Wilcoxon Rank Sum Method: In this method, all samples of the two classes are combined and sorted in order of increasing intensity values and ranked accordingly. Wilcoxon statistic [15,17] is calculated as the sum of all ranks of samples of a particular class. If the sums of ranks are similar in both classes, then the gene does not differentiate between samples of different classes and if the rank sums are different then the gene is differently expressed. Genes are ranked based on the absolute values of the Wilcoxon statistics.

4   Proposed Ranking Methods

The combination method proposed in our study is as follows: In the first stage, we rank all the genes using the four selected feature ranking methods. We get four rank lists R1, R2, R3 and R4. So that the best feature is assigned rank-1, the second best feature is assigned rank-2, etc. Table 1 shows an example of four ranking lists generated for Leukemia dataset with 7129 genes. In the second stage, we use two different combination methods to combine these ranked lists.

Table 1. Rank list generated by four feature selectors

Rank	1	2	3	4	5	. . .	7129
R1 (t-test)	g4	g10	g11	g3	g6	. . .	g7
R2 (entropy)	g7	g4	g8	g2	g1	. . .	g100
R3 (ROC)	g3	g6	g15	g10	g30	. . .	g75
R4 (Wilcoxon)	g25	g7	g10	g2	g4	. . .	g3

Combination 1: Select fixed number (m) of genes from each ranking list and count the frequency of each gene in all four methods and determine the sum of ranks in each individual ranking method. Genes are sorted in descending order of frequency and if two or more genes have same number of occurrences, ascending order of rank sum is considered. Table 2 shows steps of gene selection and listing process. If frequency counts are same for two or more genes, then genes are selected in the increasing order of the rank sum (genes g4 and g10 in Table 2). If rank sum is also same for two or more genes, the genes are selected in the order of their number in the expression data (genes g8 and g15 in Table 2).

The top m features from this list is selected for classification. If the cutoff m is at a gene with same frequency count and rank sum as the next few, then all these additional genes are selected (if m = 8, then the first 8 genes g4 to g8 as well as g15 are selected in Table 2).

Table 2. Listing process for gene selection

Gene	g4	g10	g3	g6	g2	g25	g7	g8	g15	g1	g30
Frequency count	3	3	2	2	2	1	1	1	1	1	1
Ranks	(1, 2, 5)	(2, 4, 3)	(4, 1)	(5, 2)	(4, 4)	1	2	3	3	5	5
Rank sum	8	9	5	7	8	1	2	3	3	5	5

Combination 2: Select fixed number (m) of genes from each ranking list. Concatenate the genes having rank-1 from all four ranking lists, then select the non-repetitive genes which have rank 2 etc. These concatenated genes are the final sequence for the classifier. In Table 1, for m = 2, genes (g4, g7, g3, g25) are first selected which have rank-1 and then non-repetitive genes (g10, g6) are selected which have rank-2. So, if m = 5, the genes selected are (g4, g7, g3, g25, g10, g6, g11, g8, g15, g2, g1, g30). This sequence of genes is used by classifier.

4.1   Experimental Design

The experiments were conducted on Leukemia dataset [7]. The data set contains 72 samples. These samples are divided into two variants of leukemia: 25 samples of acute myeloid leukemia (AML) and 47 samples of acute lymphoblastic leukemia (ALL) and there are expression levels for 7129 genes.

In our experiments, a comparison is made between individual ranking methods and the proposed combined ranking methods. For evaluating the performance of the proposed combination methods, we have used four classification models, kNN with k = 1, SVM with linear Kernel, NBC and RF. These algorithms are commonly used in data mining and are readily available in the Weka data mining tool [24] which is used in this study.

The dataset is divided randomly into training and testing samples for classification. The ratio of training and testing samples for all the classifiers in our experiments are 50:50, 60:40, 70:30, 80:20, 90:10. For each classifier, the ratio of training samples to testing samples is 1:1 in each class. Top genes were selected in the range 5, 10, 15, 20, 25, 30, 50 from the ranked data and gene combination has been performed.

The testing process of the classifier is done by applying it on the new test data with known class label and comparing the predicted class with target class. The classification performance of each algorithm for individual ranking methods and the proposed combination methods is evaluated using accuracy measure and also by AUC value. Accuracy is the percentage of correctly classified samples, given as, Accuracy = (TP + TN)/(TP + FP + TN + FN). Where, TP = True Positive, TN = True Negative, FP = False Positive, FN = False Negative. The ROC graph is a two-dimensional plot in which TPR (True Positive Rate) is plotted on the Y axis and FPR (False Positive Rate) is plotted on the X axis. AUC is the area under this ROC curve and is equal to the probability that the classifier will rank a randomly chosen positive instance higher than a randomly chosen negative instance [11]. AUC value ranges from 0 to 1. Larger AUC values indicate better classifier performance.

4.2   Results and Discussion

Results are tabulated for experiments when 90% of the instances are selected randomly for training and remaining 10% for testing. Experiment is repeated 5 times and the average result obtained are tabulated in Tables 3, 4, 5 and 6 for the four classifiers.

Table 3. kNN performance in Accuracy (%) and AUC value

No. of genes	t-test		Entropy		ROC		Wilcoxon		Comb 1		Comb 2	
	Acc	AUC	Acc	AUC	Acc	AUC	Acc	AUC	Acc	AUC	Acc	AUC
5	89.66	0.93	81.82	0.79	72.22	0.73	83.33	0.79	85.71	0.95	86.36	0.93
10	85.71	0.88	82.76	0.78	79.31	0.76	78.57	0.79	83.33	0.92	89.66	0.92
15	75	0.74	81.94	0.81	86.21	0.83	72.41	0.68	91.67	1	89.66	0.96
20	85.71	0.83	100	1	86.21	0.83	85.71	0.83	78.57	1	90.91	0.96
25	100	1	100	1	80.56	0.76	100	1	100	1	100	1
30	100	1	89.66	0.93	100	1	100	1	85.71	0.83	85.71	0.83
50	85.71	0.83	85.71	0.88	85.71	0.88	100	1	85.71	0.83	85.71	0.88

Table 4. SVM performance in Accuracy (%) and AUC value

No. of genes	t-test		Entropy		ROC		Wilcoxon		Comb 1		Comb 2	
	Acc	AUC	Acc	AUC	Acc	AUC	Acc	AUC	Acc	AUC	Acc	AUC
5	76.39	0.8	72.41	0.67	77.78	0.69	89.66	0.86	89.66	0.95	85.71	0.96
10	100	1	85.71	0.83	85.71	0.83	85.71	0.84	85.71	1	86.21	1
15	85.71	0.83	72.73	0.67	93.1	0.9	85.71	0.83	82.76	0.93	89.66	0.97
20	85.71	0.88	100	1	90.91	0.89	82.76	0.91	86.21	0.95	100	1
25	86.36	0.9	72.73	0.6	89.66	0.89	100	1	100	1	89.66	0.86
30	85.71	0.88	75	0.65	90.91	0.86	91.67	0.95	89.66	0.83	86.36	0.79
50	89.66	0.92	86.36	0.83	100	1	85.71	0.83	93.1	0.92	86.36	0.83

With kNN classifier, proposed combination-1 has achieved 100% accuracy for top 25 features and has attained maximum AUC = 1 with only 15 top genes. Combination-2 is showing Accuracy = 100% and AUC = 1 for 25 top genes and it has good AUC (0.93) for top 5 genes. With SVM Classifier, Combination-1 is giving Accuracy = 100% for top 25 genes and AUC = 1 for Top 10 Genes.

Table 5. NBC performance in Accuracy (%) and AUC value

No. of genes	t-test		Entropy		ROC		Wilcoxon		Comb 1		Comb 2	
	Acc	AUC	Acc	AUC	Acc	AUC	Acc	AUC	Acc	AUC	Acc	AUC
5	72.41	0.81	72.41	0.91	71.43	0.89	100	1	90.91	0.91	73.61	0.9
10	76.39	0.86	100	1	89.66	0.91	73.61	0.82	100	1	100	1
15	100	1	79.31	1	86.11	0.93	75	0.85	100	1	100	1
20	75	0.85	86.36	0.96	89.66	0.93	73.61	0.86	80.56	0.94	100	1
25	72.41	0.85	93.1	0.98	90.28	1	79.31	0.87	80.56	0.94	86.21	0.97
30	72.41	0.83	100	1	90.28	1	100	1	75.86	0.91	79.17	0.94
50	72.41	0.88	88.89	1	100	1	75.86	0.85	79.31	0.93	86.11	1

Table 6. RF performance in Accuracy (%) and AUC value

No. of genes	t-test		Entropy		ROC		Wilcoxon		Comb 1		Comb 2	
	Acc	AUC	Acc	AUC	Acc	AUC	Acc	AUC	Acc	AUC	Acc	AUC
5	86.21	0.97	85.71	0.96	79.31	0.88	85.71	0.99	90.91	0.94	100	1
10	100	1	79.31	1	96.55	0.99	90.91	0.95	96.55	0.99	100	1
15	100	1	100	1	100	1	90.91	1	100	1	96.55	0.99
20	100	1	86.36	0.96	91.67	0.98	100	1	100	1	90.91	1
25	95.45	0.95	89.66	1	93.1	1	85.71	0.92	90.91	0.95	95.45	1
30	89.66	1	100	1	93.1	1	86.36	0.93	89.66	0.93	90.91	0.94
50	93.1	0.98	89.66	0.92	100	1	89.66	1	86.36	1	89.66	1

Table 7. Comparison of classification accuracy with other gene selection methods

Reference	Validation method	kNN		SVM	NBC	RF
[22]	10 FCV	k = 5	86		100	NA	85
[5]	10 FCV	k = 1	96.67	NA	NA	NA
[4]	LOOCV with top 4% genes	–		84.72	98.61	100	NA
[19]	3 FCV	k = 3	95.48	NA	96.27	93.13
		k = 7	90.86			
[3]		NA		100 (80)	98.61 (10)	NA
[8]	5 FCV	k = 5	96.53 (30)	98.42 (30)	NA	NA
Combination 1	10 FCV	k = 1	100 (25)	100 (25)	100 (10)	100 (15)
Combination 2	10 FCV	k = 1	100 (25)	100 (20)	100 (10)	100 (5)

Whereas, Combination-2 is giving maximum Accuracy (100%) for top 20 genes and maximum AUC (1.0) for top 10 genes. With NBC, Accuracy is 100% and AUC is 1.0 with top 10 genes for both the proposed combinations, and AUC = 0.91 for top 5 genes. With RF Classifier, Highest accuracy and AUC for combination-1 is for 15 genes and for combination-2 it is 5 genes. All feature selectors are also giving good Accuracy and AUC for very few top genes with RF.

In summary, proposed combination ranking methods are performing well on all the four classifiers. Table 7 gives a comparative analysis of different gene selection methods. It shows the validation method (FCV is Fold Cross Validation), classifier used and accuracy obtained, with number of genes in parenthesis.

Conclusion. In this work, we have compared the classifier performance on the most widely used feature ranking methods and proposed combination of ranking methods. Our results demonstrate that, by combining suitable gene ranking methods, microarray classifier performance can be improved effectively. Performance may be enhanced, if from each ranking method, redundant genes are eliminated before combining. The classification results indicate that there is no single classifier that has the highest accuracy for the microarray expression datasets.

References

1. Ferreira, A.J., Figueiredo, M.A.T.: Efficient feature selection filters for high dimensional data. Pattern Recogn. Lett. **33**, 1794–1804 (2012)
2. Chan, D., Bridges, S.M., Burgess, S.C.: An Ensemble Method for Identifying Robust Features for Biomarker Discovery, pp. 377–392. Chapman & Hall, Boca Raton (2007)
3. Chandra, B., Gupta, M.: An efficient statistical feature selection approach for classification of gene expression data. J. Biomed. Inform. **44**(4), 529–535 (2011)
4. Chopra, P., Lee, J., Kang, J., Lee, S.: Improving cancer classification accuracy using gene pairs. PLoS ONE **5**(12), e14305 (2010)
5. Deegalla, S., Bostrom, H.: Improving fusion of dimensionality reduction methods for nearest neighbor classification. In: Proceedings of the 12th International Conference on Information Fusion, pp. 460–465 (2009)
6. Fawcett, T.: An introduction to ROC analysis. ROC Anal. Pattern Recogn. **27**, 861–874 (2006)
7. Golub, T.R., Slonim, D.K., Tamayo, P., Huard, C., Gaasenbeek, M., Mesirov, J.P., Coller, H., Loh, M.L., Downing, J.R., Caligiuri, M.A.: Molecular classification of cancer: class discovery and class prediction by gene expression monitoring. Science **286**, 531–537 (1999)
8. Han, F., Sun, W., Ling, Q.H.: A novel strategy for gene selection of microarray data based on gene-to-class sensitivity information. PLoS ONE **9**(5), e97530 (2014)
9. Hand, D.J.: Measuring classifier performance: a coherent alternative to the area under the ROC curve. Mach. Learn. **77**, 103–123 (2009)
10. Dutkowski, J., Gambin, A.: On consensus biomarker selection. BMC Bioinform. **8**(Suppl. 5), S5 (2007)
11. Jin, C.L., Ling, C.X., Huang, J., Zhang, H.: AUC: a statistically consistent and more discriminating measure than accuracy. In: Proceedings of 18th International Conference on Artificial Intelligence, pp. 329–341 (2003)
12. Keedwell, E.C., Narayanan, A.: Intelligent Bioinformatics: The Application of Artificial Intelligence Techniques to Bioinformatics Problems. Wiley, London (2005)
13. Kolde, R., Laur, S., Adler, P., Vilo, J.: Robust rank aggregation for gene list integration and meta-analysis. Bioinformatics **28**(4), 573–580 (2012)
14. Mamitsuka, H.: Selecting features in microarray classification using ROC curves. Pattern Recogn. **39**, 2393–2404 (2006)

15. Perez, M.: Machine learning and soft computing approaches to microarray differential expression analysis and feature selection. Ph.D. Thesis 2011, University of the Witwatersrand, Johannesburg (2012)
16. MathWorks: Bioinformatics Toolbox. MATLAB edn. (2007)
17. Nguyen, T., Khosravi, A., Creighton, D.: Heirarchical gene selection and genetic fuzzy system for cancer microarray data classification. PLoS ONE **10**(3), e0120364 (2015)
18. Yang, P., Yang, Y.H., Zhou, B.B., Zomaya, A.Y.: A review of ensemble methods in bioinformatics. Curr. Bioinform. **5**(4), 296–308 (2010)
19. Yang, P., Zhou, B.B., Zhang, Z., Zomaya, A.Y.: A multi-filter enhanced genetic ensemble system for gene selection and sample classification of microarray data. BMC Bioinform. **11**(Suppl. 1), S5 (2010). doi:10.1186/1471-2105-11-S1-S5
20. Pepe, M.S., Longton, G., Anderson, G.L., Schummer, M.: Selecting differentially expressed genes from microarray experiments. Biometrics **59**, 133–142 (2003)
21. Saeys, Y., Lnza, I., Larrañaga, P.: A review of feature selection techniques in bioinformatics. Bioinformatics **23**(19), 2507–2517 (2007)
22. Saeys, Y., Abeel, T., Peer, Y.: Robust feature selection using ensemble feature selection techniques. In: Daelemans, W., Goethals, B., Morik, K. (eds.) ECML PKDD 2008. LNCS (LNAI), vol. 5212, pp. 313–325. Springer, Heidelberg (2008). doi:10.1007/978-3-540-87481-2_21
23. Abeel, T., Helleputte, T., Van de Peer, Y., Dupont, P., Saeys, Y.: Robust biomarker identification for cancer diagnosis with ensemble feature selection methods. Bioinformatics **26**(3), 392–398 (2010)
24. Weka: A multi-task machine learning software. http://www.cs.waikato.ac.nz/ml/weka
25. Xu, J., Sun, L., Gao, Y., Xu, T.: An ensemble feature selection technique for cancer recognition. Biomed. Mater. Eng. **24**(1), 1001–1008 (2014). doi:10.3233/BME-130897
26. Yang, Y.H., Xiao, Y., Segal, M.R.: Identifying differentially expressed genes from microarray experiments via statistic synthesis. Bioinformatics **21**(7), 1084–1093 (2005)
27. Peng, Y., Wu, Z., Jiang, J.: A novel feature selection approach for biomedical data classification. J. Biomed. Inform. **43**, 15–23 (2010)
28. Zhang, Z., Yang, P., Wu, X., Zhang, C.: An agent-based hybrid system for microarray data analysis. IEEE Intell. Syst. **24**(5), 53–63 (2009)

Pattern Recognition Based on Hierarchical Description of Decision Rules Using Choquet Integral

K.C. Santosh[1]([⊠]) and Laurent Wendling[2]

[1] Department of Computer Science, The University of South Dakota,
414 E Clark St, Vermillion, SD 57069, USA
santosh.kc@usd.edu
[2] LIPADE - Université Paris Descartes (Paris V), 45 rue des Saints-Pères,
75270 Paris Cedex 06, France
laurent.wendling@parisdescartes.fr

Abstract. A hierarchical approach to automatically extract subsets of soft output classifiers, assumed to decision rules, is presented in this paper. Output of classifiers are aggregated into a decision scheme using the Choquet integral. To handle this, two selection schemes are defined, aiming to discard weak or redundant decision rules so that most relevant subsets are restored. For validation, we have used two different datasets: shapes (Sharvit) and graphical symbols (handwritten, CVC - Barcelona). Our experimental study attests the interest of the proposed methods.

Keywords: Choquet integral · Selection of decision rules · Hierarchical description

1 Introduction

Often, pattern recognition systems are dedicated to judge the (dis)similarity between two patterns. It can either be a set of measurements performed on the patterns, forming a vector of features, or a symbolic description of how the pattern can be divided into basic shapes. A decision rule is often built from the representation of the pattern. Such rule predicts to which class an observed pattern most likely belongs to. It can either be built by introducing some expert knowledge about the patterns, or learned on a representative subset of labelled patterns. Rather, a collection of techniques has been developed to address domain specific issues. Pattern recognition has rich state-of-the-art. Many classifier combination systems have been proposed and compared [17,18,32,37], and a full presentation of most of these could be found in a reference book by Duda et al. [6]. Handling several classifiers means finding their complements (helping each other) so that recognition/classification can be improved as expected [19,25]. At the same time, we note that methods are generally independently built. Their combination may lead to positive correlations, because both aim at achieving the same goal, and both are based on the same learning data [13,22]. Nonetheless,

© Springer Nature Singapore Pte Ltd. 2017
K.C. Santosh et al. (Eds.): RTIP2R 2016, CCIS 709, pp. 146–158, 2017.
DOI: 10.1007/978-981-10-4859-3_14

even when approaches like Adaboost, arcing [3], and boosting [33] try to limit this dependence by reinforcing diversity, it is difficult to measure and to efficiently incorporate into the classification process [12,25]. Currently deep learning based approaches [27,28] provided interesting results (using large databases), but parameters setting is not so trivial. Such methods often require a consistent as well as large amount of data to optimize their efficiency. In our study, we focus on databases having few samples per classes, which is often the case in industrial applications – real-world cases.

Surveys on pattern representation and classification techniques over the last decade fail to conclude whether a set of generic methods perform best for all applications [2,5,14,21]. This means that methods are application dependent. For a given application, the choice of a pattern representation or a decision scheme relies at best on the extensive testing of several combinations of techniques. It is not surprising that a designer chooses by making an educated guess between the techniques he has at hand, or between those he is the most acquainted with. A tempting approach is to combine several decision rules, based on various representations and classification schemes, instead of electing only one. The expected outcome is a more robust final decision, taking advantage of all the decision rules qualities. This approach appears to be well suited to cope cases, where the available data is too scarce to determine the best method by thorough testing, or to build robust decision rules by learning. Well-known operators applying this scheme include the quasi-arithmetic means, the weighted minimum and maximum, and the ordered weighted averaging [40]. None of these operators families, however, take the possible interactions between the constituents of the aggregation into account. The Choquet integral can be considered, since it allows to take such interactions into account while generalizing many aggregation operators and by choosing specific fuzzy measure such as weighted arithmetic means, ordered weighted averages, order statistics, and median [8,23]. Fuzzy integrals, and the Choquet integral in particular, have been successfully used as fusion operators in various applications. Previous works were dedicated to define an efficient global scheme from the study of learning confusion matrices [31]. This scheme was also combined with a fuzzy inference system and applied to an industrial fabric textile context using non-relevant learning data [34]. The method were adapted to process with speech recognition problem based on overlapping features [9] and also to provide breast cancer diagnosis to be further assessed by an expert [10] Such an approach allows to provide a set of suitable decision rules considering a whole application. The method is extended here to consider independently all possible classes and so to automatically extract a set of decision rules per class. With such an extension, in this paper, a new hierarchical description of decision rules based on two aggregation levels of Choquet integrals is also provided. Proposed methods can be considered as wrapper [20], since they focus on selection of decision rules rather than on filter from the handling of rough data.

The remainder of the paper is outlined as follows. In Sect. 2, we recall background on Choquet integral properties and associated fuzzy measure indexes.

In Sect. 3 two complementary schemes allowing to discard weaker decision rules are defined. Section 4 presents the application of these methods on well-known databases: shapes (from Sharvit) and handwritten graphical symbols (from CVC – Barcelona), and a discussion about the interest of each scheme. Section 5 concludes the paper.

2   Background on Choquet Integral Fusion

2.1   Decision Rule Fusion

Let us consider m classes, $\mathcal{C} = \{C_1, \ldots, C_m\}$, and n Decision Rules (DRs) $X = \{D_1, \ldots, D_n\}$. When a new pattern x^o is observed, we wish to find the class it most likely belongs to. Labelling this unknown pattern is a three-steps process.

- Firstly, for each decision rule j and each class i, we compute ϕ_j^i the degree of confidence in the statement "According to D_j, x^o belongs to the class C_i".
- Secondly, we combine all these partial confidence degrees into a global confidence degree by choosing a suitable aggregation operator $\mathcal{H}$. Thus, the global confidence degree in the statement "x^o belongs to C_i", noted $\Phi(C_i|x^o)$, is given by:

$$\Phi(C_i|x^o) = \mathcal{H}(\phi_1^i, \ldots, \phi_n^i).$$

- Finally, x^o is assigned to the class for which the confidence degree is the highest:

$$label(x^o) = \mathop{\arg\max}_{i=1}^{m} \Phi(C_i|x^o).$$

Many aggregation operators were introduced in the literature. If the classification issue implies more than two classes, two learning approaches can be followed. Either each class C_i is paired with his own aggregation operator $\mathcal{H}^i$, or a single global aggregation operator. In the former case, the final decision is slightly modified as the global confidence degree depends on the operator associated with the class:

$$\Phi(C_i|x^o) = \mathcal{H}^i(\phi_1^i, \ldots, \phi_n^i).$$

2.2   Fuzzy Measures and the Choquet Integral

The Choquet integral was first introduced in the capacity theory [4,30]. Let us denote by $X = \{D_1, \ldots, D_n\}$ the set of n decision rules, and $\mathcal{P}$ the power set of X, i.e. the set of all subsets of X.

Definition 1. *A fuzzy measure or capacity, μ, defined on X is a set function $\mu : \mathcal{P}(X) \longrightarrow [0,1]$, verifying the following axioms:*
$\mu(\emptyset) = 0, \ \mu(X) = 1,$ *and*
$A \subseteq B \Longrightarrow \mu(A) \leqslant \mu(B).$

Fuzzy measures generalize additive measures, by replacing the additivity axiom by a weaker one (monotonicity). Fuzzy measures embed particular cases including probability measure, possibility and necessity measures, or belief and plausibility functions.

In our context of decision rule fusion, $\mu(A)$ represents the importance, or the degree of trust in the decision provided by the subset A of DRs. The next step in building a final decision, is to combine the partial confidence degree according to each DR into a global confidence degree, taking those weights into account.

Definition 2. *Let μ be a fuzzy measure on X. The discrete Choquet integral of $\phi = [\phi_1, \ldots, \phi_n]^t$ with respect to μ, noted $\mathcal{C}_\mu(\phi)$, is defined by:*

$$\mathcal{C}_\mu(\phi) = \sum_{j=1}^{n} \phi_{(j)} [\mu(A_{(j)}) - \mu(A_{(j+1)})],$$

where $(.)$ is a permutation and $A_{(j)} = \{(j), \ldots, (n)\}$ represents the $[j..n]$ associated criteria in increasing order and $A_{(n+1)} = \emptyset$.

2.3   Determining the Fuzzy Measure

There are several methods to determine the most adequate fuzzy measure to be used for a given application and the most straightforward learning approach is based on optimization techniques. The aim is to find the fuzzy measure that minimizes best a criterion on the training set, such has the square error. Considering $(x^k, y^k), k = 1, \ldots, l$, l learning samples where $x^k = [x_1^k, \ldots, x_n^k]^t$ is a n-dimensional vector, and y^k the expected global evaluation of object k, the fuzzy measure can be determined by minimizing [11]:

$$E^2 = \sum_{k=1}^{l} (\mathcal{C}_\mu(x_1^k, \ldots, x_n^k) - y^k)^2.$$

This criterion can be put under a quadratic program form and solved by the Lemke method. Nevertheless the method requires at least $n!/[(n/2)!]^2$ learning samples. When little data is available, matrices may be ill-conditioned, causing a negative impact on the algorithm. To cope with the above problems, "heuristic" algorithms have been developed.

To the best of our knowledge, the algorithm providing the best approximation was proposed by Grabisch in [7]. It assumes that in the absence of any information, the most reasonable way to aggregate the partial matching degrees is to compute the arithmetic mean on all the inputs.

2.4   Behavioral Analysis of the Aggregation

The importance index is based on the definition proposed by Shapley in game theory [35]. It is defined for a fuzzy measure μ and a rule i as:

$$\sigma(\mu, i) = \frac{1}{n} \sum_{t=0}^{n-1} \frac{1}{\binom{n-1}{t}} \sum_{\substack{T \subseteq X \setminus i \\ |T|=t}} [\mu(T \cup i) - \mu(T)].$$

It can be interpreted as a average value of the marginal contribution $\mu(T \cup i) - \mu(T)$ of the decision rule i alone in all combinations. The interaction index [29] represents the degree of interaction between two decision rules. If the fuzzy measure is non-additive then some sources interact. The *marginal interaction* between I and j, conditioned to the presence of elements of the combination $T \subseteq X \backslash ij$ is:

$$(\Delta_{ij}\mu)(T) = \mu(T \cup ij) + \mu(T) - \mu(T \cup i) - \mu(T \cup j).$$

Averaging this criterion over all the subsets of $T \subseteq X \backslash ij$ gives the interaction index of sources i and j:

$$I(\mu, ij) = \sum_{T \subseteq X \backslash ij} \frac{(n - t - 2)! t!}{(n - 1)!} (\Delta_{ij}\mu)(T).$$

A positive interaction index for two DRs i and j means that the importance of one DR is reinforced by the second. A negative interaction index indicates that the sources are antagonist, and their combined use impairs the final decision.

3   Selection of Decision Rules

3.1   Local Scheme

Handling with Learning Error. All the lattices associated to fuzzy measures are initialized at the arithmetic mean, and are approximated using a training set via a gradient descent. From training pattern, m training samples are created $\Phi^1, \ldots, \Phi^m$, with $\Phi^i = (\phi_1^i, \ldots, \phi_m^i)$ where ϕ_j^i represents the confidence in the fact that the sample belongs to class i, according to DR j. Each of these samples is paired with a target value, i.e. the value an ideal operator would output using this sample as input. For techniques that use a single fuzzy measure no real formula exists and often the following one is used:

$$C_\mu(\Phi^i) = \begin{cases} 1, & \text{if sample belongs to class } i, \\ 0, & \text{otherwise.} \end{cases}$$

For techniques that use a different fuzzy measure per class, the optimal target value minimizing the quadratic error is known for two classes [7]. Best criterion is defined as follows:

$$E^2 = \sum_i \sum_j |\Psi(\Delta\Phi_{12}(X_k^j)) - 1|^2$$

with X_k^j is the kth training data of class j, Ψ a sigmoid-type function and $\Delta\Phi_{12}$ is given by:

$$\Delta\Phi_{12} = \Phi_{\mu_1}(C_1 | X_k^j) - \Phi_{\mu_2}(C_2 | X_k^j).$$

Two class errors used in the gradient descent algorithm is given by:

$$e = \Psi(\Delta\Phi_{12}(X_k^j)) - 1.$$

The criterion is modified as follows to process with m classes,

$$\Delta\Phi_{qr_{r\in X-\{q\}}} = \Phi_{\mu_q}(C_q|X_k^j) - \bigotimes_{\{r\in X-\{q\}\}} \Phi_{\mu_r}(C_r|X_k^j)$$

with q and r two classes. Operator $\bigotimes$ can be a median, min... Here the max was kept to move away ambiguous classes and so to favor a discriminate behavior. Median is interesting to preserve acceptable results even some sources can be contradictory. The sign of $\Delta\Phi_{qr_{r\in X-\{q\}}}$ is studied to set the error to be propagated in the lattice as follows:

$$sign(\Delta\Phi_{qr_{r\in X-\{q\}}}) = \begin{cases} +e = 1./f(\Delta\Phi_{qr_{r\in X-\{q\}}}) \\ -0, \ e = 0 \text{ for } q, \ 1 \text{ for others,} \end{cases}$$

with f an increasing function. Obviously the relevant and the irrelevant learning data are alternated while training the fuzzy measures.

Weaker Decision Rules. Once the lattice is learned, the individual performance of each DR is analyzed in the produced fuzzy measure. This analysis is performed using the importance and interaction indexes defined in Sect. 2.4. The aim is to track the DRs having the weak importance in the final decision, and that positively interact the least with the other rules. Such DRs are assuming to blur the final decision. First low significant rules S_L having an importance index lower than 1 are selected:

$$S_L = \{k|n \cdot \sigma(\mu, k) < 1\}.$$

The set of rules to be removed MS_L is composed of the rules having an interaction index lower than the mean of the interaction indexes of S_L:

$$MS_L = argmin_k\{\sum_{j=1,n} I(\mu, kj) < h\}_{k\in S_L}$$

with the global mean interaction index:

$$h = \frac{1}{|S_L|} \sum_{k\in S_L} \sum_{j=1,n} I(\mu, kj).$$

Main Selection Algorithm. We use the classic fuzzy pattern matching setup. All the classes $C_1, \ldots, C_m$ are associated with a fuzzy measure $\mu_1, \ldots, \mu_m$. The evaluation measures are generally classifier dependent [26]. For their computation the classification of training data must be performed to identify the fuzzy measure for each class. Furthermore, we need to fix thresholds for the interaction indexes. This must be done by an expert and for each class. In this case, selection is performed dependently. The application of our learning algorithm followed by the extraction of the most relevant DRs forms a training epoch. As it is not easy to evaluate each combination of classes without an expert, we consider them independently. The overall algorithm is described below.

% Initialization %
For Each C_i **in** $\mathcal{C} = \{C_1, \ldots, C_m\}$
 – Learned associated capacity μ_i
 – Extract weakest descriptor
End For Each
% Main %
While Minimization is on the way
 – Replace old capacity with new capacity
 – Evaluate gain (how the new capacity minimizes a cost function)
 – Keep the new capacity that provides best minimization
 – Extract feature for that new capacity
End while

A Greedy feature selection algorithm is used to ensure a continuous extraction of unexpected features per class. At each epoch, the weakest descriptor calculated from indices is removed and so on, while improving a gain (recognition rates).

3.2 Hierarchical Scheme

Usually decision rules are embedded in an aggregation way to combine them. The problem is rewritten here in a 2-class description scheme by aggregating local decisions between two classes C_i and C_j. We aim here to reconsider the problem by specifying fuzzy measure μ_i^j to distinguish pairs of classes. That remains to specialize a set of fuzzy measures to assess each one the comparison between two classes with respect to Choquet integral. Roughly speaking, each capacity becomes an "expert" able to compare one class to another one.

The learning of μ_i^j is performed from the decisions rules computed from the set of training samples ϕ_j^i, that is the samples belonging to C_i and C_j, using the sigmoid-type function Ψ as two classes are studied (see Sect. 3.1). The symmetry is not warranted due to gradient algorithm (that is μ_i^j can differ from $1 - \mu_j^i$) and the computation of μ_j^i is done separately.

For each class C_i, a vector of fuzzy measures V^i is built by considering all the other classes:

$$V^i = [\mu_i^1, \mu_i^2, \ldots, \mu_i^m].$$

All the vectors can be stored in a matrix M containing all the possible cases:

$$M = \begin{pmatrix} T & \mu_1^2 & \cdots & \mu_1^m \\ \mu_2^1 & T & \cdots & \mu_2^m \\ \vdots & \vdots & \ddots & \vdots \\ \mu_m^1 & \mu_m^2 & \cdots & T \end{pmatrix}.$$

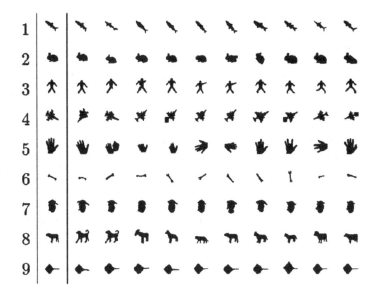

Fig. 1. The first Sharvit' database (B1).

Obviously we assume that recognizing the class i from class i is always true (tautology) and brings no interest for the approach. It is denoted by T in the above matrix.

Considering a pattern x_0, the achieved vectors should be handled to give a decision about its target class by aggregating 2-class models assumed to be new decision rules. For each class a new learning is done at this step from the values taken by each vector. So each vector were assumed to be input of an high level Choquet integral to confront them and to express a decision per class. Then a new learning step is performed for each class.

To summarize, let us consider one pattern to be classified during the recognition step. Basic decision rules defined from shape descriptors are calculated and given as input to the capacities compounding M. Let us consider one class. The values obtained by calculating Choquet integral for all the elements of the vector are then aggregated by a high level capacity and associated Choquet integral. Same process is carried out for all the classes. At last a classical *argmax* is applied to assign this pattern to its nearest class.

The previous algorithm (see Fig. 1) is adapted to remove none relevant capacities that brings no interest to the learning and so to the recognition. The stopping criterion relies on the number of samples correctly classified. Then weakest capacities are taken off until no improvement is achieved. Obviously each removing requires a new learning step.

4   Experimental Results

4.1   Set of Decision Rules

The proposed approaches being aimed at situations where little information is available for training, databases having a fair number of categories and a small number of samples have been used. For the experiments, several decision rules are set from different photometric descriptors associated to a basic similarity measure to belong in the same range. A set of nine pattern recognition methods $R = \{R_i\}_{i=1,9}$ is used here, most of them having a low processing time, easy to implement, and invariant to affine transforms such as translation, rotation, or scaling. The descriptors computed on the samples are: $DC = \{$ART [16], angular signature [1], Generic Fourier Descriptors [42], degree of ellipticity [39], f_0 and f_2-histograms [24], moments of Zernike [15], Yang histograms [41], Radon signature [38]$\}$.

4.2   Experimental Data Sets

Experimental results gathered during shape recognition process are presented to show the efficiency of the proposed algorithm. The method was tested on several databases. First, two databases of Sharvit et al. kindly made available to us on his website [36], URL: http://www.lems.brown.edu/vision/researchAreas/SIID/ have been used: B1(9 classes × 11samples) and B2(18 classes × 12 samples). As shown in Fig. 1 (i.e., from B1), a few of the shapes are occluded (classes airplanes and hands) and some shapes are partially represented (classes rabbits, men, and hands). There are also distorted objects (class 6) and very heterogeneous shapes in the same class (animals).

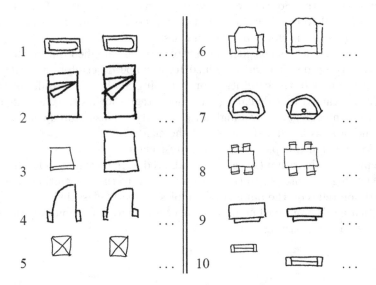

Fig. 2. Samples of the CVC database (B3).

$B3(10 \times 300)$ is a database kindly provided by the CVC Barcelona. Symbols have been drawn by ten people using "anoto" concept. Few samples are provided in Fig. 2.

4.3 Applications

An experimental study is carried out from each decision rules R_i, basic aggregation operators as Min, Max, $Median$ and the proposed methods based on $Choquet$ integral.

Table 1. Recognition rates reached for each method.

	R_1	R_2	R_3	R_4	R_5	R_6	R_7	R_8	R_9	Mi	Ma	Me	Ch_1	Ch_2
B1	93	59	98	48	74	50	96	85	66	43	99	78	100	100
B2	88	56	90	48	62	46	86	66	56	59	87	76	93	–
B3	80	30	38	22	20	46	80	76	56	46	82	78	89	88

For each test, a cross validation was applied (1/3 and 2/3). Table 1 shows the good behavior of the method on these databases. The results reached independently by each decision rule R_i are coherent with the amount of information processed by associated features. Simple aggregation operators: minimum, maximum and median exhibit various behavior depending on the database. In terms of recognition rates, only the maximum achieves better results than the best simple DR on two databases. In comparison to the simple DRs and the simple aggregation operators, our fusion operators based on the Choquet integral consistently achieve better results on each database, in terms of recognition rates. On each dataset, our recognition method at worse improves a little the recognition rates; it never worsens them.

4.4 Discussion

The first scheme allows to define a kind of identity map per class consisting in the most suitable decision rules and their importance weight following the application under consideration. When the number of classes grows this method allows to reach better results than considering a global scheme removing the same decision rules for all the classes.

The hierarchical scheme has the highest computing time considering the training step due to its own representation. Nonetheless it gives rise to good results while allowing to reach a powerful description which is more efficient to process with inconsistent data. Furthermore, oracles may be easily introduced in this structure to improve the recognition. Such scheme is very promising and might be the base of a wrapper-filter hybrid method by combining the selection of decisions rules and the extraction of irrelevant data from a study of the matrix.

Both models are easy to implement and the decision part is very fast as only a sort of decision rule values and the search of associated path in the lattice are useful to calculate the Choquet integral. At last, the best choice so far of cost function (experimentation based) is simple zero-one loss function. Other functions were tested as MSE for all items, or MSE for just badly classified items but not really gave improvements certainly due to the weak amount of learning data.

5   Conclusion

In this paper, we have discussed a hierarchical approach to automatically extract subsets of soft output classifiers, assumed to decision rules. Output of classifiers are aggregated into a decision scheme using the Choquet integral. The algorithm appears to be well suited for different situations: (a) when no *a priori* knowledge is provided about the relevance of a set of decision rules for a given dataset; (b) when the training set available is to small to build reliable decision rules; and (c) in case we are required to determine the best performer. It finds the best consensus between the rules, taking their interaction into account, and discards the undependable or redundant ones. A new way to merge both numerical and expert decision rules in order to improve the recognition process is under consideration.

References

1. Bernier, T., Landry, J.A.: A new method for representing and matching shapes of natural objects. Pattern Recogn. **36**(8), 1711–1723 (2003)
2. Andreopoulos, A., Tsotsos, J.K.: 50 years of object recognition: directions forward. Comput. Vis. Image Underst. **117**(8), 827–891 (2013)
3. Breiman, L.: Bagging predictors. Mach. Learn. **24**(2), 123–140 (1996)
4. Choquet, G.: Theory of capacities. Annales de l'Institut Fourier **5**, 131–295 (1953)
5. Cordella, L.P., Vento, M.: Symbol recognition in documents: a col of technics? Int. J. Doc. Anal. Recogn. **3**(2), 73–88 (2000)
6. Duda, R.O., Hart, P.E., Stork, D.G.: Pattern Classification, 2nd edn. Wiley-Interscience, New York (2001)
7. Grabisch, M.: A new algorithm for identifying fuzzy measures and its application to pattern recognition. In: FUZZ'IEEE International Conference, vol. 95, pp. 145–150 (1995)
8. Grabisch, M.: The application of fuzzy integrals in multicriteria decision making. Eur. J. Oper. Res. **89**(3), 445–456 (1996)
9. Mauclair, J., Wendling, L., Janiszek, D.: Fuzzy integrals for the aggregation of confidence measures in speech recognition. IEEE FUZZ **2011**, 1149–1156 (2011)
10. Trabelsi BenAmeur, S., Cloppet, F., Sellami Masmoudi, D., Wendling, L.: Choquet integral based feature selection for early breast cancer diagnosis from MRIs. ICPRAM **2016**, 351–358 (2016)
11. Grabisch, M., Nicolas, J.M.: Classification by fuzzy integral - performance and tests. Fuzzy Sets Syst. **65**, 255–271 (1994)

12. Hadjitodorov, S.T., Kuncheva, L.I., Todorova, L.P.: Moderate diversity for better cluster ensembles. Inf. Fusion **7**(3), 264–275 (2006)
13. Ho, T.K.: Multiple classifier combination: lessons and next steps. In: Kandel, A., Bunke, H. (eds.) Hybrid Methods in Pattern Recognition. World Scientific, Singapore (2002)
14. Jain, A.K., Duin, R.P.W., Mao, J.: Statistical pattern recognition: a review. IEEE Trans. Pattern Anal. Mach. Intell. **22**(1), 4–37 (2000)
15. Khotanzad, A., Hong, Y.H.: Invariant image recognition by Zernike. IEEE Trans. Pattern Anal. Mach. Intell. **12**(5), 489–497 (1990)
16. Kim, W.Y., Kim, Y.-S.: A new region-based shape descriptor. In: TR 15–01, Pisa, Italy (1999)
17. Kittler, J., Hatef, M., Duin, R., Matas, J.: On combining classifiers. IEEE Trans. Pattern Anal. Mach. Intell. **20**(3), 226–239 (1998)
18. Kuncheva, L.I., Whitaker, C.J.: Measures of diversity in classifier ensembles. Mach. Learn. **51**, 181–207 (2003)
19. Britto, A.S., Sabourin, R., Soares de Oliveira, L.E.: Dynamic selection of classifiers - a comprehensive review. Pattern Recogn. **47**(11), 3665–3680 (2014)
20. Langley, P.: Selection of relevant features in machine learning. In: AAAI Fall Symposium on Relevance, pp. 140–144 (1994)
21. Lladós, J., Valveny, E., Sánchez, G., Martí, E.: Symbol recognition: current advances and perspectives. In: Blostein, D., Kwon, Y.-B. (eds.) GREC 2001. LNCS, vol. 2390, pp. 104–128. Springer, Heidelberg (2002). doi:10.1007/3-540-45868-9_9
22. Littewood, B., Miller, D.: Conceptual modeling of coincident failures in multiversion software. IEEE Trans. Softw. Eng. **15**(12), 1596–1614 (1989)
23. Marichal, J.L.: Aggregation of interacting criteria by means of the discrete Choquet integral. In: Aggregation Operators: New Trends and Applications, pp. 224–244. Physica-Verlag GmbH, Heidelberg (2002)
24. Matsakis, P., Wendling, L.: A new way to represent the relative position between areal objects. IEEE Trans. Pattern Anal. Mach. Intell. **21**(7), 634–643 (1999)
25. Melnik, O., Vardi, Y., Zhang, C.H.: Mixed group ranks: preference and confidence in classifier combination. IEEE Trans. Pattern Anal. Mach. Intell. **26**(8), 973–981 (2004)
26. Mikenina, L., Zimmermann, H.J.: Improved feature selection and classification by the 2-additive fuzzy measure. Fuzzy Sets Syst. **107**, 197–218 (1999)
27. Schmidhuber, J.: Deep learning in neural networks: an overview. Technical report IDSIA-03-14 (2014)
28. Erhan, D., Szegedy, C., Toshev, A., Anguelov, D.: Scalable object detection using deep neural networks. In: CVPR 2014 (2014)
29. Murofushi, T., Soneda, S.: Techniques for reading fuzzy measures (iii): interaction index. In: Proceedings of the 9th Fuzzy Set System, pp. 693–696 (1993)
30. Murofushi, T., Sugeno, M.: A theory of fuzzy measures: representations, the Choquet integral, and null sets. J. Math. Anal. Appl. **159**, 532–549 (1991)
31. Rendek, J., Wendling, L.: On determining suitable subsets of decision rules using Choquet integral. Int. J. Pattern Recogn. Artif. Intell. **22**(2), 207–232 (2008)
32. Ruta, D., Gabrys, B.: An overview of classifier fusion methods. Comput. Inf. Syst. **7**, 1–10 (2000)
33. Schapire, R.E., Fruend, Y., Bartlett, P., Lee, W.: Boosting the margin: a new explanation for the effectiveness of voting methods. Ann. Stat. **26**(5), 1651–1689 (1998)

34. Schmitt, E., Bombardier, V., Wendling, L.: Improving fuzzy rule classifier by extracting suitable features from capacities with respect to Choquet integral. IEEE Trans. Syst. Man Cybern. Part B **38**(5), 1195–1206 (2008)

35. Shapley, L.: A value for n-person games. In: Khun, H., Tucker, A. (eds.) Ann. Math. Stud., pp. 307–317. Princeton University Press, Princeton (1953)

36. Sharvit, D., Chan, J., Tek, H., Kimia, B.: Symmetry-based indexing of image databases. J. Vis. Commun. Image Represent. **12**, 366–380 (1998)

37. Stejic, Z., Takama, Y., Hirota, K.: Mathematical aggregation operators in image retrieval: effect on retrieval performance and role in relevance feedback. Sig. Process. **85**(2), 297–324 (2005)

38. Tabbone, S., Wendling, L.: Binary shape normalization using the radon transform. In: Nyström, I., Sanniti di Baja, G., Svensson, S. (eds.) DGCI 2003. LNCS, vol. 2886, pp. 184–193. Springer, Heidelberg (2003). doi:10.1007/978-3-540-39966-7_17

39. Teague, R.: Image analysis via the general theory of moments. J. Opt. Soc. Am. **70**(8), 920–930 (1979)

40. Yager, R.: On ordered weighted averaging aggregation operators in multicriteria decision making. IEEE Trans. Syst. Man Cybern. **18**(1), 183–190 (1988)

41. Yang, S.: Symbol recognition via statistical integration of pixel-level constraint histograms: a new descriptor. IEEE Trans. Pattern Anal. Mach. Intell. **27**(2), 278–281 (2005)

42. Zhang, D., Lu, G.: Shape-based image retrieval using generic Fourier descriptor. Sig. Process. Image Commun. **17**, 825–848 (2002)

Classification of Summarized Sensor Data Using Sampling and Clustering: A Performance Analysis

Lavanya P.G.$^{(\boxtimes)}$ and Suresha Mallappa

DoS in Computer Science, University of Mysore, Mysore, India
lavanyarsh@compsci.uni-mysore.ac.in

Abstract. As humans and machines generate a tremendous amount of digital data in their daily life, we are in the era of Big Data which poses unique challenges of storing, processing and analyzing this voluminous data. Sensors which continuously generate data are one important source of Big Data and have innumerous applications in real life scenario. As storing the entire data becomes expensive, summarization is the need of the hour. Data Summarization is a compact representation of the entire data which can reduce storage and processing requirements. In this work, we try to effectively summarize Sensor Data using simple but effective techniques such as sampling and clustering and analyze the performance of the summarized data in comparison to the complete dataset. Popular classification techniques like KNN, SVM and Naive Bayes are used to evaluate the efficiency of the summarization techniques by training the classifiers using the summarized data and testing with the test data set. The performance of the summarized dataset and the complete dataset are compared. The experimental results show that summarized data set performs almost equally well as the complete data set.

Keywords: Big Data · Classification · Clustering · KNN · Naive Bayes · Sensor data · Sampling · Summarization · SVM

1 Introduction

With the advent of technology, humans and machines have become data sensors as they generate tremendous amount of data every second. According to a survey, 2.5 Quintillion bytes of data is generated every day, and this rate goes on increasing. Gartner, Inc. forecasts that "6.4 billion connected things will be in use worldwide in 2016, which is 30% more compared to 2015, and will reach 20.8 billion by 2020". This huge data generated has all the "4 V" characteristics of Big Data, i.e., Volume, Velocity, Variety and Veracity. But the same data becomes useless unless we extract a fifth 'V' from it i.e., Value. Effectively processing Big Data poses challenges in every step of the analysis pipeline right from acquisition, extraction, representation, modeling and interpretation [1]. As the data generated is too huge, it becomes expensive to store and analyze the

© Springer Nature Singapore Pte Ltd. 2017
K.C. Santosh et al. (Eds.): RTIP2R 2016, CCIS 709, pp. 159–172, 2017.
DOI: 10.1007/978-981-10-4859-3_15

entire data. Though we may have large data centers, as data is continuously growing, today's Big Data will become "small data" tomorrow and we will have to face the problem of "Big" Big Data.

Sensor data is a major source of Big Data with Internet of Things coming to reality where every object in daily life can be equipped with sensors to collect data [2]. This data is voluminous, has a temporal attribute and is also heterogeneous in nature. Sensor data is usually collected in a distributed setting and have physical resource constraints in communication, power consumption and computation. Data transmission to a centralized server for further analysis proves to be extremely expensive and hence in-network sensor processing and data aggregation at source becomes essential [3]. These characteristics of sensor networks have contributed to research issues like Data collection and cleaning, sensor data management and analysis which are also application specific. The existing algorithms and techniques have to be further explored and modified to handle the challenges in the context of sensor data.

As the data generated from sensor networks is voluminous and continuous in nature, it is desirable that only relevant information be retained for future use. Summarization plays an important role in capturing the essence of the data for further processing and analyzing data thereby reducing both time and storage requirements. Summarization is different from compression and is intended to provide a very significant reduction in the size of the data, but does not promise to reconstruct the original data [4]. Hence, efficient summarization techniques which compress the data but still retain the important information have to be developed.

In this work, we explore two intuitive techniques for Data Summarization - sampling and clustering. These two methods, though are simple and used extensively, prove to be effective in providing good representatives of the entire data. The added advantage of these techniques are, they are not processor heavy and quick in producing results which is a major requirement for summarizing sensor data which is continuous in nature. Sampling is the process of selecting representatives from the entire data population where the key challenge is identifying the right samples. Clustering is an unsupervised technique which groups similar data together and hence can form a base for choosing a representative set. The performance of the summarized data are evaluated using three different classification techniques KNN, SVM and Naive Bayes on a multiclass vehicle classification sensor dataset. The objective is to achieve data summarization for sensor data with large samples and evaluate the performance of the summarized data using classification techniques using a dataset which can be considered as a benchmark dataset for vehicle classification.

The related work is reviewed in Sect. 2. The methods used are described in Sect. 3. Section 4 gives the details of the dataset, experimental results and discussions. Section 5 presents conclusion and future work.

2   Related Work

With the enormous amount of digital data which is ever growing, Summarization in the context of Big Data has become a high priority area. Data Summarization has applications in variety of fields like Medical Informatics, Astronomy and Earth Science, Social Networks, Sensor Networks and Business and Marketing to name a few [5]. As the data produced from sensor networks is growing rapidly, mining and analyzing data is very important. The use of Machine Learning algorithms on Sensor data is analyzed in [6] which also highlights the applications of analyzing data produced by sensor networks. The challenges of Sensor data such as uncertainty, volume, power issues, communication and applications of mining and analyzing sensor data like activity monitoring, event detection, prediction of weather changes are highlighted in [7].

Different sampling methods like simple random sampling, systematic sampling and stratified sampling are studied and the sampled data using these techniques are evaluated for clustering with Fuzzy C-means algorithm in [8]. An adaptive stratified reservoir sampling method for heterogeneous data streams which consist of multiple sub-streams with large statistical variations is proposed in [9] which handles two technical issues, (i) determining the optimal sizes of sub-samples for each sub-stream and (ii) maintaining the uniformity of each sub-sample as its size changes. Polynomially biased reservoir sampling is proposed in [10] to summarize unordered vehicle-to-vehicle data streams and the summarized data is then used to analyze the traffic flow. A comprehensive survey of existing data mining techniques along with their multilevel classification is presented in [11]. As the existing techniques have limitations in the context of wireless sensor networks, an adaptive hybrid data mining architecture is also proposed which combines offline learning with distributive and online data processing. Fuzzy logic based protoforms are used to create linguistic summaries from long duration sensor data for elder care in [12]. The sensor data collected is from a single person for 15 months. Sensor data is mostly used in classification tasks like vehicle classification, activity recognition and Summarization of sensor data in large scale is still in its initial stage which provides lot of scope for research.

3   Proposed Method

In this work, we summarize the sensor data using Sampling and Clustering techniques which are well known techniques used for summarization. The key idea behind choosing these techniques is that the summarization techniques used should not consume more memory or time, but still effectively summarize data for further use. In order to evaluate the performance of summarized data, multi class classification is done on a benchmark dataset with three different types of classifiers, KNN, SVM and Naive Bayes. In order to achieve this, the summarized data is used to train the multi class classifiers and later classification is done on the test dataset. The accuracy of the classification is compared with the classification accuracy obtained when the training is done with the complete data. The results show that the techniques prove to be effective in summarizing the data.

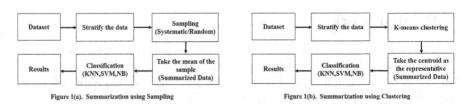

Figure 1(a). Summarization using Sampling   Figure 1(b). Summarization using Clustering

Fig. 1. Overall flow of the proposed method

The overall flow of the method using Sampling for summarization is given in Fig. 1(a) and summarization using Clustering is given in Fig. 1(b).

3.1   Sampling

Sampling is defined as "selection of a subset of individuals from within a statistical population to estimate characteristics of the whole population". This clearly indicates that sampling is done to choose the representatives for the entire population which is exactly the principle behind summarization of data. The challenge here is to choose the proper representatives. Sampling techniques are mainly classified as Probabilistic and Non-probabilistic. Probabilistic sampling techniques are those in which each element of the population has the same chance of being chosen as the sample. Probabilistic sampling techniques include Simple random sampling, Systematic sampling and Stratified Sampling. In our work, we use stratified sampling technique which can be used when the population has distinct categories. As the dataset used is multiclass in nature, stratifying technique is suitable as we perform classification further. Stratified sampling divides the population to different 'strata' which are nothing but non overlapping categories. Later sampling is done considering each strata as a population. This leads to efficient statistical analysis as all the subpopulation are considered in the sample. We use both random sampling and systematic sampling on this stratified data. We even consider 'proportionate stratification' approach which ensures that samples drawn are proportional to their respective strata size and thereby increases the effectiveness of the sample. Strata sample sizes are determined by the Eq. (1):

$$n_h = \frac{N_h}{N} * n \tag{1}$$

The drawback of stratified sampling is identifying different strata which is overcome by the inherent quality of our dataset which is made up of three classes. The data is sampled with different sample sizes and the mean of the sample is drawn and selected as the representative sample. This representative sample forms the training data set for classification and tested for efficiency.

3.2   Clustering

Clustering is the process of grouping a set of data objects that are similar to one another within the same cluster and are dissimilar to the objects in other clusters [13]. Clustering is also a popular technique used for selecting representatives from a large set of data. In this context, Clustering can be chosen as a summarization technique which can compress the data through cluster prototypes and still be informative [14]. There are different types of clustering methods which include Hierarchical, Partitioning, Density based, Grid based and Model based techniques. In our work, we use all the three popular partition based clustering techniques i.e., k-means, k-medoids and Fuzzy C-means for selecting representatives. In partition based methods, the data is grouped into k partitions where minimizing the sum of the squared error over all k partitions is the objective function [13]. Partition based methods are further classified into soft and hard clustering techniques. K-means and k-medoids are hard clustering techniques and Fuzzy C-means is a soft clustering technique which is devoid of distinct boundaries [15]. Given a set of observations $(x_1, x_2, ...x_n)$, where each observation is a d-dimensional vector, k-means clustering aims to partition the n observations into k sets $(k \leq n)$ $S = S_1, S_2, ...S_k$ so as to minimize the objective function given in Eq. (2)

$$\sum_{i=1}^{k} \sum_{x \in S_i} \| x - \mu_i \|^2 \tag{2}$$

K-medoids algorithm is similar to k-means algorithm but it minimizes the sum of dissimilarities between points labeled to be in a cluster and a point designated as the center of that cluster [12]. That is an absolute-error criterion is used, given in Eq. (3)

$$E = \sum_{j=1}^{k} \sum_{p \in C_j} | p - o_j | \tag{3}$$

Fuzzy c means algorithm overcomes the limitations of the hard clustering algorithm by associating a membership function to each sample with each cluster. It is based on minimization of the following objective function given in Eq. (4)

$$J_m = \sum_{i=1}^{N} \sum_{j=1}^{C} U_{ij}^m \| x_i - C_j \|^2, 1 \leq m < \infty \tag{4}$$

where, m is any real number greater than 1, U_{ij} is the degree of membership of x_i in the cluster j, x_i is the ith of d-dimensional measured data, C_j is the d-dimension center of the cluster and $*$ is any norm expressing the similarity between any measured data and the center [16]. Partition based techniques are chosen as they are based on centroids and these centroids themselves can be considered as representatives of the respective clusters which enables us to summarize the data. The limitation of the partition based techniques is that the number of partitions should be given in advance which is not a hindrance in our case as we know the number of classes. This summarized dataset is used for training the classifiers and tested against the test dataset.

3.3   Multi-class Classification

Classification is a supervised learning technique where the problem is to identify the class to which a new sample (observation/data) belongs to, provided we already have a training set of data which contains labelled observations. There are several popular classifiers like Decision trees, K-Nearest Neighbour (KNN), Support Vector Machine (SVM) and Naive Bayes (NB). Classification is further divided as Binary and Multi-class, where Binary has two classes and Multi-class requires assigning the new observation with one class out of many classes available. We have used Multi-class classifiers and evaluated our summarized dataset with three classifiers KNN, SVM and Naive Bayes.

The KNN algorithm classifies a data sample based on the labels of the k nearest data samples measured by a distance function [17]. The most commonly used distance measures are Euclidean, Manhattan and Minkowski which are valid for continuous variables. In the instance of categorical variables the Hamming distance is used. This method uses low computational power and makes it suitable for wireless sensor networks. In this work, we have experimented with k ranging from 1 to 5.

Multi-class SVM is classified into two types: One-Versus-One (1V1) and One-Versus-Rest (1VR) [18]. We have used One-Versus-One approach as it is less sensitive to imbalanced datasets and thus a preferred choice [19]. In this approach each class is compared to every other class which is also known as pairwise decomposition. It evaluates all possible pairwise classifiers and thus induces k(k-1)/2 individual binary classifiers. When an unseen object has to be classified, a voting is made and the class with the maximum number of votes is considered. Naive Bayes is a widely used classification method based on Bayes theory which is useful for large datasets. It is an eager learning classifier, simple and outperforms other sophisticated classification methods. It is fast and hence can be used to predict in real time.

4   Results and Discussion

The experiments are carried out on a well known benchmark dataset for vehicle classification using sensor data. The dataset is chosen as it is a real life sensor dataset which is used for vehicle classification. But in our work, we are using the same dataset for summarization and then perform classification using the summarized data. The classification accuracy is used as a measure to compare the performance of summarized data and the original data. Accuracy is given by the formula:

$$Accuracy = \frac{t}{n}$$

where 't' is the number of sample cases correctly classified, and 'n' is the total number of sample cases. Detailed explanation of the dataset used and the experiments carried out along with the results obtained are discussed in the following subsections.

4.1 Dataset

The dataset used is 'SensIT' dataset which comprises of sensor data for multiclass vehicle classification [20]. The dataset extracted from a real-life vehicle tracking wireless sensor network is generated using two types of sensors, 'seismic' and 'acoustic'. Totally, we have three sets of data - Seismic, Acoustic and Combined which is the combined data of the two sensors. The Seismic and Acoustic data has 78,823 samples with 50 features. The Combined dataset has 78,823 samples with 100 features. Class 1 has 18,261 samples, Class 2 has 21,159 samples and Class 3 has 39,403 samples. All the data are normalized and range between -1 and 1. The test dataset contains 19,705 samples in which 4,580 samples belong to Class 1, 5,264 samples belong to Class 2 and 9,861 samples belong to Class 3.

4.2 Experiments and Results

The classification performance of the summarized data using sampling technique for KNN, SVM and Naive Bayes classifiers for all the three datasets are given in the Tables 1, 2, 3, 4, 5, 6 and 7. The experiments were carried out on an Intel Core i5 - 4210@ 1.70 GHz machine with 8 GB RAM. The code is implemented in MATLAB. It can be observed that the summarized data performs equally well as the complete data. There is a marginal difference in the accuracy which is in the range of $\pm 3\%$. This difference seems to be acceptable as there is a tremendous decrease in the number of samples considered for classification. The summarized data considered is 10%, 2% and 1% of the complete data. We can also observe that both systematic sampling and random sampling work almost similar and proportional stratification gives a better performance among the three.

With respect to classifiers, for KNN, the best K is always data dependent. Here we observe that $K = 3$ and $K = 5$ gives better results for the complete data. The performance improves with sampled data with mean of 10 samples in case

Table 1. Classification accuracy on seismic dataset using systematic sampling

Number of samples	Seismic dataset - classification accuracy					SVM	NB
	KNN						
	K = 1	K = 2	K = 3	K = 4	K = 5		
78823	0.65	0.66	0.7	0.7	0.72	0.73	0.67
7882	0.7	0.7	0.7	0.7	0.7	0.7	0.68
1576	0.69	0.69	0.69	0.69	0.69	0.69	0.68
780	0.69	0.69	0.69	0.69	0.69	0.7	0.68

Table 2. Classification accuracy on acoustic dataset using systematic sampling

Number of samples	Acoustic dataset - classification accuracy					SVM	NB
	KNN						
	K = 1	K = 2	K = 3	K = 4	K = 5		
78823	0.68	0.70	0.73	0.74	0.74	0.70	0.63
7882	0.70	0.70	0.70	0.70	0.70	0.65	0.67
1576	0.62	0.63	0.63	0.64	0.63	0.63	0.66
780	0.63	0.62	0.62	0.62	0.62	0.63	0.66

Table 3. Classification accuracy on combined dataset using systematic sampling

Number of samples	Combined dataset - classification accuracy					SVM	NB
	KNN						
	K = 1	K = 2	K = 3	K = 4	K = 5		
78823	0.76	0.78	0.81	0.81	0.83	0.82	0.76
7882	0.78	0.78	0.78	0.78	0.78	0.79	0.74
1576	0.75	0.75	0.75	0.75	0.75	0.74	0.74
780	0.75	0.75	0.75	0.75	0.75	0.74	0.74

Table 4. Classification accuracy on seismic dataset using random sampling

Number of samples	Seismic dataset - classification accuracy					SVM	NB
	KNN						
	K = 1	K = 2	K = 3	K = 4	K = 5		
78823	0.65	0.66	0.70	0.70	0.72	0.73	0.67
7882	0.70	0.69	0.70	0.70	0.70	0.70	0.68
1576	0.69	0.69	0.69	0.69	0.69	0.69	0.68
780	0.69	0.69	0.69	0.69	0.69	0.70	0.68

Table 5. Classification accuracy on acoustic dataset using random sampling

Number of samples	Acoustic dataset - classification accuracy					SVM	NB
	KNN						
	K = 1	K = 2	K = 3	K = 4	K = 5		
78823	0.68	0.70	0.73	0.74	0.74	0.70	0.63
7882	0.65	0.65	0.65	0.65	0.65	0.66	0.67
1576	0.63	0.63	0.64	0.64	0.64	0.63	0.66
780	0.63	0.62	0.63	0.62	0.62	0.63	0.66

Table 6. Classification accuracy on combined dataset using random sampling

Number	Combined dataset - classification accuracy						
	KNN					SVM	NB
	K = 1	K = 2	K = 3	K = 4	K = 5		
78823	0.76	0.78	0.81	0.81	0.83	0.82	0.76
7882	0.78	0.78	0.78	0.78	0.78	0.78	0.74
1576	0.76	0.75	0.76	0.75	0.75	0.76	0.74
780	0.75	0.75	0.75	0.75	0.75	0.75	0.74

Table 7. Classification accuracy on combined dataset using proportional stratification for 1% of the dataset

Dataset	KNN					SVM	NB
	K = 1	K = 2	K = 3	K = 4	K = 5		
Seismic	0.65	0.65	0.69	0.69	0.70	0.72	0.66
Acoustic	0.66	0.67	0.70	0.70	0.71	0.70	0.65
Combined	0.75	0.77	0.79	0.79	0.80	0.81	0.75

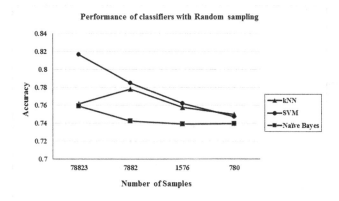

Fig. 2. Performance of classifiers using random sampling technique for combined dataset

of K = 1 for all datasets but slightly decreases in case of K = 5. In the case of seismic data, the performance is same for both complete data and sampled data with mean of 10 samples. The accuracy marginally decreases in case of SVM and Naive Bayes is a better performer when the difference in accuracy is considered across all the three datasets. The performance of all the three classifiers for random sampling is given in Fig. 2.

The performance of different sampling technique for 780 samples which is 1% of the complete dataset is given in Fig. 3. It can be observed that Systematic sampling and Random sampling are giving same accuracy with all classifiers. Proportionate stratification gives better performance in all the cases. Naive Bayes remains a consistent performer across different sampling techniques.

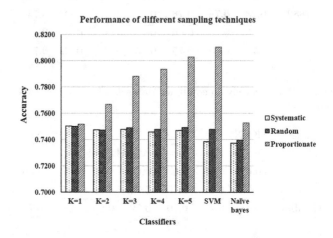

Fig. 3. Performance of different sampling techniques for combined dataset with 780 samples

The execution time reduces drastically as the number of samples decreases which is shown in the Table 8 and Fig. 4.

Table 8. Execution time for KNN classifier for combined dataset before and after summarization

Dataset	No. of samples	Time taken (in seconds)
Complete data	78823	1029
Mean of 10 samples	7882	118
Mean of 50 samples	1576	31
Mean of 100 samples	780	19

The performance of the different clustering techniques (KM - K-means, KMD - K-medoids, FCM - Fuzzy C-means) used for selecting representatives are evaluated using three different classifiers. The classification accuracy measure used to assess the techniques for Seismic dataset is given in Table 9.

It can be observed that all three clustering techniques perform equally well in choosing the right representatives for summarization. However, FCM takes more time when compared to the other two methods and k-medoids which takes

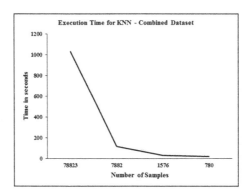

Fig. 4. Execution time for KNN classifier with combined dataset before and after summarization

Table 9. Classification accuracy for seismic dataset using different clustering techniques

NOC	KNN						SVM			NB		
	K = 1			K = 3								
	KM	KMD	FCM	KM	KMD	FCM	KM	KMD	FCM	KM	KMD	FCM
10	0.64	0.62	0.61	0.62	0.62	0.66	0.68	0.68	0.69	0.66	0.67	0.67
20	0.65	0.63	0.62	0.61	0.62	0.64	0.70	0.70	0.69	0.66	0.66	0.66
30	0.63	0.60	0.63	0.60	0.60	0.63	0.70	0.69	0.69	0.66	0.66	0.67
40	0.65	0.61	0.63	0.60	0.63	0.63	0.69	0.69	0.69	0.66	0.66	0.65
50	0.64	0.63	0.62	0.60	0.63	0.64	0.70	0.70	0.69	0.66	0.66	0.66
60	0.64	0.60	0.64	0.60	0.62	0.62	0.69	0.69	0.70	0.66	0.66	0.67
70	0.65	0.62	0.62	0.61	0.62	0.64	0.70	0.69	0.70	0.66	0.69	0.66
80	0.64	0.61	0.65	0.62	0.62	0.63	0.70	0.70	0.70	0.67	0.66	0.66
90	0.65	0.62	0.62	0.62	0.63	0.63	0.70	0.69	0.70	0.66	0.66	0.66
100	0.65	0.62	0.63	0.62	0.64	0.63	0.70	0.70	0.70	0.66	0.67	0.66
110	0.65	0.61	0.62	0.63	0.63	0.62	0.70	0.70	0.70	0.66	0.66	0.65
120	0.64	0.60	0.62	0.62	0.62	0.62	0.69	0.69	0.70	0.66	0.66	0.66

longer duration, when the number of clusters are small, goes on improving with the increase in the number of clusters. This can be observed in Fig. 5.

The classification accuracy of the summarized data using k-means clustering technique for all the three classifiers and all the three datasets (Sei-Seismic, Aco-Acoustic, Com-Combined) is given in Table 10. As the performance of k-means depends on the initial points selected, the experiment was conducted 10 times and the average accuracy is taken.

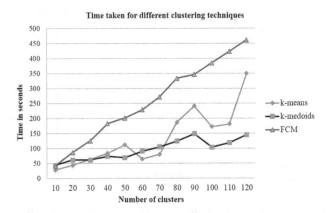

Fig. 5. Time taken by different clustering techniques for different cluster sizes

Table 10. Classification accuracy for all three datasets using different size of clusters

NOC	KNN						SVM			NB		
	K = 1			K = 3								
	Sei	Aco	Com	Sei	Aco	Com	Sei	Aco	Com	Sei	Aco	Com
Full data	0.65	0.68	0.76	0.70	0.73	0.81	0.73	0.70	0.82	0.67	0.63	0.76
10	0.64	0.58	0.74	0.62	0.58	0.69	0.68	0.62	0.78	0.66	0.68	0.75
20	0.65	0.6	0.75	0.61	0.54	0.72	0.70	0.62	0.79	0.66	0.69	0.71
30	0.63	0.63	0.76	0.60	0.58	0.73	0.70	0.62	0.80	0.66	0.69	0.72
40	0.65	0.64	0.76	0.60	0.6	0.75	0.69	0.63	0.79	0.66	0.69	0.73
50	0.64	0.63	0.77	0.60	0.6	0.77	0.70	0.65	0.8	0.66	0.7	0.73
60	0.64	0.64	0.77	0.60	0.61	0.76	0.69	0.65	0.77	0.66	0.69	0.74
70	0.65	0.64	0.77	0.61	0.61	0.77	0.70	0.65	0.80	0.66	0.70	0.74
80	0.64	0.65	0.77	0.62	0.62	0.77	0.70	0.66	0.80	0.67	0.71	0.74
90	0.65	0.65	0.77	0.62	0.63	0.77	0.7	0.65	0.80	0.66	0.7	0.74
100	0.65	0.64	0.76	0.62	0.63	0.77	0.7	0.66	0.80	0.66	0.71	0.74
110	0.65	0.66	0.77	0.63	0.64	0.78	0.7	0.66	0.80	0.66	0.70	0.75
120	0.64	0.65	0.77	0.62	0.65	0.79	0.69	0.66	0.80	0.66	0.70	0.74

Here also there is only a marginal decrease of 3% to 5% which improves with increase in number of clusters. It is to be noted that if the number of clusters is 10, then only 10 representatives of each class are considered i.e., 30 samples are used in place of 78823 samples. It can be observed that the performance improves with the increase in number of clusters but becomes almost consistent after a certain number i.e., 70 clusters which is depicted in Fig. 6.

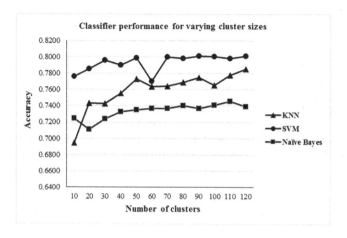

Fig. 6. Time taken by different clustering techniques for different cluster sizes

5   Conclusion

In this work, we make an attempt to summarize sensor data using well known and widely used sampling and clustering techniques. It is observed that sampling and clustering techniques can be effectively used to summarize data. These techniques provide quick results and are not processor heavy which is the need of the hour in the context of streaming sensor data. The effectiveness of the summarized data is evaluated using Classification techniques like KNN, SVM and Naive Bayes. The classification accuracy is used to compare the performance of the summarized data. The results also show that the summarized data perform almost equivalent to their respective original data set. Systematic and Random sampling techniques give similar performance whereas proportionate random sampling performs well compared to the other two. In case of clustering, in terms of accuracy all three clustering techniques behave consistently whereas FCM takes more time which would not be preferable in case of voluminous sensor data. As the number of samples decrease, the time and space also considerably reduces which is crucial to process large data sets. However, as future work, we have to explore whether these techniques perform equally well in case of different datasets which are much larger in size and explore new techniques to effectively summarize sensor data for further processing and analyzing. The summarized dataset can be further compressed using dimensionality reduction techniques for larger datasets. These intuitive and simple techniques seem to be efficient in summarizing large data sets.

References

1. Challenges and opportunities with Big Data - a community white paper developed by leading researchers across the United States, March 2012
2. Aggarwal, C.C., Naveen, A., Amit, P.S.: The internet of things: a survey from the data-centric perspective. In: Aggarwal, C.C. (ed.) Managing and Mining Sensor Data, pp. 383–428. Springer, New York (2013)

3. Aggarwal, C.C., Naveen, A., Amit, P.S.: An introduction to sensor data analytics. In: Aggarwal, C.C. (ed.) Managing and Mining Sensor Data, pp. 1–8. Springer, New York (2013)

4. Cormode, G.: Summary data structures for massive data. In: Bonizzoni, P., Brattka, V., Löwe, B. (eds.) CiE 2013. LNCS, vol. 7921, pp. 78–86. Springer, Heidelberg (2013). doi:10.1007/978-3-642-39053-1_9

5. Hesabi, R.Z., Tari, Z., Goscinski, A., Fahad, A., Khalil, I., Queiroz, C.: Data summarization techniques for big data - a survey. In: Khan, S.U., Zomaya, A.Y. (eds.) Handbook on Data Centers, pp. 1109–1152. Springer, New York (2015)

6. Moraru, A., Pesko, M., Porcius, M., Fortuna, C., Mladenic, D.: Using machine learning on sensor data. In: 32nd International Conference on Information Technology Interfaces (ITI), Cavtat/Dubrovnik, pp. 573–578 (2010)

7. Aggarwal, C.C., Naveen, A., Amit, P.S.: Mining sensor data streams. In: Aggarwal, C.C. (ed.) Managing and Mining Sensor Data, pp. 143–172. Springer, New York (2013)

8. Josien, K., Wang, G., Liao, T.W., Triantaphyllou, E., Liu, M.C.: An evaluation of sampling methods for data mining with fuzzy C-means. In: Braha, D. (ed.) Data Mining for Design and Manufacturing, pp. 355–369. Springer, Dordrecht (2001)

9. Al-Kateb, M., Lee, B.S.: Adaptive stratified reservoir sampling over heterogeneous data streams. Inf. Syst. **39**, 199–216 (2014)

10. Zhang, J., Xu, J., Liao, S.S.: Sampling methods for summarizing unordered vehicle-to-vehicle data streams. Trans. Res. Part C Emerg. Technol. **23**, 56–67 (2012)

11. Mahmood, A., Shi, K., Khatoon, S., Xiao, M.: Data mining techniques for wireless sensor networks: a survey. Int. J. Distrib. Sens. Netw. **9**(7), 1–24 (2013)

12. Wilbik, A., James, M.K., Gregory, L.A.: Linguistic summarization of sensor data for eldercare. In: 2011 IEEE International Conference on Systems, Man, and Cybernetics (SMC). IEEE (2011)

13. Jiawei, H., Micheline, K.: Data Mining-Concepts and Techniques. Elsevier, 2nd edn

14. Jain, A.K.: Data clustering: 50 years beyond K-means. Pattern Recogn. Lett. **31**(8), 651–666 (2010)

15. Panda, S., Sahu, S., Jena, P., Chattopadhyay, S.: Comparing fuzzy-C means and K-means clustering techniques: a comprehensive study. In: Wyld, D., Zizka, J., Nagamalai, D. (eds.) Advances in Computer Science. Engineering & Applications, pp. 451–460. Springer, Heidelberg (2012)

16. Velmurugan, T., Santhanam, T.: A survey of partition based clustering algorithms in data mining: an experimental approach. Inf. Technol. J. **10**(3), 478–484 (2011)

17. Alsheikh, M.A., Lin, S., Niyato, D., Tan, H.P.: Machine learning in wireless sensor networks: algorithms, strategies, and applications. IEEE Commun. Surv. Tutor. **16**(4), 1996–2018 (2014)

18. Wang, Z., Xiangyang, X.: Multi-class support vector machine. In: Ma, Y., Guo, G. (eds.) Support Vector Machines Applications, pp. 23–48. Springer, Switzerland (2014)

19. Anthony, G., Gregg, H., Lidzi, M.: Image classification using SVMs: one-against-one vs one-against-all. arXiv preprint (2007). arXiv:0711.2914

20. Duarte, M.F., Hu, Y.H.: Vehicle classification in distributed sensor networks. J. Parallel Distrib. Comput. **64**(7), 826–838 (2004)

Feature Reduced Weighted Fuzzy Binarization for Histogram Comparison of Promoter Sequences

K. Kouser[(✉)] and Lalitha Rangarajan

Department of Studies in Computer Science, University of Mysore,
Mysore 570 006, India
kouser@compsci.uni-mysore.ac.in

Abstract. Effective biological sequence analysis methods are in great demand. This is due to the increasing amount of sequence data being generated from the improved sequencing techniques. In this study, we select statistically significant features/motifs from the Position Specific Motif Matrices of promoters. Later, we reconstruct these matrices using the chosen motifs. The reconstructed matrices are then binarized using triangular fuzzy membership values. Then the binarized matrix is assigned weights to obtain the texture features. Histogram is plotted to visualize the distribution of texture values of each promoter and later histogram difference is computed across pairs of promoters. This histogram difference is a measure of underlying dissimilarity in the promoters being compared. A dissimilarity matrix is constructed using the histogram difference values of all the promoter pairs. From the experiments, the combination of feature reduction and fuzzy binarization seems to be useful in promoter differentiation.

Keywords: Biological sequence analysis · Entropy · Feature selection · Fuzzy membership · Motifs · Position Specific Motif Matrices (PSMMs) · Promoter sequences · Variance

1 Introduction

Obtaining the hidden details from the large repository of biological sequence data is gaining importance. Also, there is great demand for the techniques which assist biologists in making appropriate biological inferences [1]. Promoters (noncoding DNA) are one such biological sequence data. These promoters are crucial regulatory elements that consist of the necessary sequence features which help cells to initiate transcription [2]. Gene regulation and expression is determined by transcription factors (TFs) to a large extent. TFs are proteins that regulate the process of transcription initiation by binding to promoter regions at specific sites called transcription factor binding sites (TFBSs). The knowledge that governs the RNA synthesis using RNA polymerase is positioned in the promoter region that lies between 200–2000 nucleotides upstream of the Transcription

© Springer Nature Singapore Pte Ltd. 2017
K.C. Santosh et al. (Eds.): RTIP2R 2016, CCIS 709, pp. 173–184, 2017.
DOI: 10.1007/978-981-10-4859-3_16

Start Site (TSS) of a gene [3]. These TFs interact with the sequence specific elements/motifs, which are usually 5–12 nucleotides in length [3].

There have been some recent efforts in identifying the role of promoter sequences which have some important function in gene expression analysis, phylogenetic analysis and tissue development which is the motivation to this research work [4]. Also, studies show that the transcriptional frequencies and the structure of the promoters are positively correlated [5].

"The lack of nucleotide sequence conservation between functionally related promoter regions makes it challenging to come out with an efficient computational model for promoter sequence analysis. Thus, the promoter regions of genes with similar expression pattern may not show sequence similarity even though they may be regulated by similar configuration of TFs" [6].

The motifs that are arranged in a specific pattern are known to be of particular importance in promoter analysis [3], we consider these motifs as the features in this work. As the promoter length increases the number of motifs also increases. Not all motifs are useful for analysis. Therefore, selecting some important motifs before performing analysis might aid experts/biologists make better inferences. Feature selection or feature transformation techniques are useful in selection of important motifs. Feature selection is preferred to feature transformation as it helps cope with huge amounts of irrelevant features [7] and retains the original structure of the features which helps us in easy interpretation of results.

Feature selection techniques can be classified into filter, wrapper and embedded methods. Filter methods are easy to use on big data as they are computationally simple and are independent of the learning algorithms [8]. Wrapper methods consider feature dependencies but they are computationally intensive and have a higher risk of over fitting. Embedded approaches interact with classifier and are far more computationally less expensive than the wrapper methods [9].

Feature selection for sequence analysis is finding prominence in more applications such as promoter region recognition [10]. Entropy of a feature is one such measure which is a good candidate to provide useful information about state and/or disorder in a system [11]. Entropy based feature selection methods have been widely used for various applications. An entropy based iterative algorithm is used to classify cancer using microarray [8] and also successfully explored in finding motifs [12].

Most of the existing biological sequence comparison methods are alignment based. Some of the notable attempts in the recent past to align promoter sequences include, Clustal W and Clustal X [13] based on the Needleman-Wunsch algorithm. Analysis tools are divided into two categories viz., searching and learning tools for discovering multiple, distinct motifs in a set of biological sequence. PSI-BLAST [14] is one such searching tool and MEME [15] is a learning tool. In [16] a detailed comparative assessment survey with analysis of several sequence alignment methods is described. Most of these methods work on the principle of nucleotide comparison which is not suited for promoter regions. In promoters, functionality is known to be based on motif conservation rather than nucleotide conservation. Hence, a comparison that considers motif conservation as its basis is useful in promoter sequence analysis. There have been a few works that consider motif conservation for effectively analyzing promoter sequences [17–19].

In this work, we perform feature selection on FSM (feature sample matrix) of promoter sequences using low entropy and high variance values which results in dimensionality reduction of promoter sequences. Later, we reconstruct the position specific motif matrices (PSMMs) using the low entropy/high variance motifs/features and then use triangular fuzzy membership function to binarize the PSMMs using the fuzzy membership values. Later, we apply binary weights across 2×2 overlapping masks to obtain the texture features existing in PSMM. A histogram is plotted for these texture values. Finally, histogram difference is calculated to find the similarity/dissimilarity existing in the promoters being analysed. Using the histogram difference values a dissimilarity matrix is constructed. The proposed method and dataset is described in detail in the next section.

2   Proposed Methods

The overall architecture of the proposed methods is as shown in Fig. 1.

2.1   Overall Architecture

Creation of the PSMMs of the promoter sequences is carried out using the method described in [19], next we construct the FSM for these sequences which has the arrangements and frequencies of different motifs across various bands. FSM is used to find the entropy and variance values of each feature to select certain percentage of important features. After feature selection the original PSMMs are reconstructed using the selected motifs. The similarity analysis of promoter pairs is carried out by computing the dissimilarity from the histogram features. The two major steps of the method, feature selection and texture feature extraction are described in the next section.

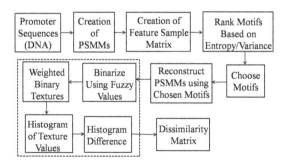

Fig. 1. Overall architecture of the proposed method.

2.2 Feature/Motif Selection

As discussed in the introduction section, feature selection is an important step in biological sequence analysis (BSA). Feature selection helps reduce the size of the data before it is analyzed hence, making the task of analysis less computationally intensive. To perform feature selection, the PSMM of a promoter/sample is vectorized into a single row in the FSM as detailed in Fig. 2. Once the variance and entropy computation for all the features in the FSM is computed, we order the variance values in descending order and entropy values in the ascending order. Then only those top features/motifs that satisfy a certain threshold are chosen. The threshold is empirically chosen by performing experiments.

A hypothetical example is described below, which demonstrates the feature selection on PSMMs of 4 promoters (P1, P2, P3 and P4) considered which contain 2 motifs/features (M1 and M2) each. Chosen motifs are highlighted which are further used for PSMM reconstruction. You may observe that for this particular case in entropy based feature selection both motifs M1 and M2 are selected for threshold = 50. However, it is important to note that not all the bands are selected. However, when variance based approach is used only the motif 'M2' is selected in all the bands. This reduces the number of chosen features to 50% of the original number of features.

The dataset we consider for our experiment is of length 500 nucleotides/basepairs, the number of motifs is 73 for dataset 1, 79 for dataset 2

Promoter1 PSMM

P1	0-50	51-100
M1	0	1
M2	3	0

Promoter2 PSMM

P1	0-50	51-100
M1	1	0
M2	0	0

Promoter3 PSMM

P1	0-50	51-100
M1	0	0
M2	0	1

Promoter4 PSMM

P1	0-50	51-100
M1	2	1
M2	0	3

Feature Sample Matrix of Promoter 1, 2 , 3 and 4

Motif	M1	M1	M2	M2
Bands	0-50	51-100	0-50	51-100
P1	0	1	3	0
P2	1	0	0	0
P3	0	0	0	1
P4	2	1	0	3
Entropy	1.5	1	0.81	1.5
Variance	0.92	0.33	2.25	2.00

Ranked Entropy Features

Motif	M2	M1	M1	M2
Bands	0-50	51-100	0-50	51-100
Entropy	0.81	1	1.5	1.5

Selected features/motifs for threshold= 50

Ranked Variance Features

Motif	M2	M2	M1	M1
Bands	0-50	51-100	0-50	51-100
Variance	2.25	2.00	0.92	0.33

Selected features/motifs for threshold= 50

Fig. 2. Illustration of entropy and variance feature selection in FSM having 4 promoters.

and each motif has entries across 10 different bands (each band consists of 50 nucleotides). The size of the FSM for 10 organisms will be 10×730 (10 organisms, 73 motifs and 10 bands ($73 \times 10 = 730$)). Dataset 2 has size to be 10×790 (10 enzymes, 79 motifs and 10 bands ($79 \times 10 = 790$)). For a threshold of 2% only 14, 15 motifs are chosen for dataset 1 and 2 respectively. As the threshold increases the number of motifs also increases.

2.3   Fuzzy Binarization

Fuzzification is the process of generating membership values for a fuzzy variable using an appropriate membership function. Membership function (MF) is one of the basic elements of fuzzy set theory. The purpose of using a fuzzy system is to convert the crisp data into fuzzy data based on membership function [20]. A MF defines how each point in the input space is mapped to a membership value (or degree of membership) between 0 and 1. In this work, we have considered the reconstructed PSMM as a fuzzy set. Each feature is represented as a member of its respective PSMM. For a promoter's PSMM 'A', a fuzzy PSMM A_{FS} in a finite set X is defined as:

$$A_{FS} = \{x_{ij}, \mu_A(x_{ij}) | x_{ij} \in X\} \tag{1}$$

where x_{ij} is the feature value of the PSMM and the function $\mu_A(x)\epsilon[0,1]$ is the degree of belongingness of the feature. The significant issue of fuzzy system is its direct impact on the obtained results based on the definition of fuzzy sets that model the variables in terms of shape and partitioning their attributes [21]. There are no general rules or guidelines for fuzzification that are appropriate for multiple domains [22]. The robustness of fuzzy logic lies in choosing appropriate membership function. The triangular and trapezoidal shapes are widely used in most of the domains according to literature for their inherent characteristics of producing good results [23].

Therefore, in this work, the PSMM (fuzzy set) is modeled by choosing the triangular membership function as specified:

$$\mu_A(x_{ij}) = \begin{cases} \frac{x_{ij}-a}{b-a} & \text{if } a \leq x_{ij} \leq b \\[2mm] \frac{c-x_{ij}}{c-b} & \text{if } b \leq x_{ij} \leq c \\[2mm] 0 & \text{otherwise} \end{cases} \tag{2}$$

2.4   Binary Weighted Textures and Histograms

After obtaining the fuzzy equivalent of the PSMM, we binarize the fuzzy matrix using the mean of the fuzzified matrix. If the entry in the fuzzy PSMM is greater than or equal to the mean then '1' is entered else a '0' is entered. The binary weighted textures are obtained from the binarized PSMM by using 2×2 overlapping masks which assigns an appropriate binary weight in the clockwise pattern.

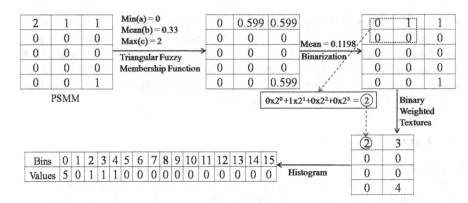

Fig. 3. Illustration of fuzzification and texture extraction.

The maximum weight assigned is '15' when the mask contains a 1 in all four positions of the 2×2 mask $[(1, 1); (1, 2); (2, 1); (2, 2)]$ and the least possible weight assigned is a 0 when the mask contains a 0 in all four positions of the 2×2 mask. This process is repeated for all the PSMMs.

After obtaining the binary weighted textures for all the promoter PSMMs, the textures are represented by using a histogram which keeps account of the texture distribution across '16' bins starting from '0' till '15'. Later, the histograms of the promoters are compared using the Euclidean distance between the histograms. An illustration demonstrating fuzzification and texture extraction is shown in Fig. 3.

3   Experiments and Results

The experiments were performed on the datasets described in the previous section. The original number of motifs in the PSMM of dataset 1 is 73 but in the reconstructed PSMMs the number of motifs reduce to a number less than 73

Table 1. Dissimilarity matrix of histogram difference using entropy weighted fuzzy binarization features (100% motif features) on dataset 1

100%	Human	Gorilla	Monkey	Cattle	Cat	Fruitfly	Bacteria	Chimp	Dog	Rat
Human	0	7.48	17.89	9.7	49.76	18.6	54.26	6.63	8.94	32.74
Gorilla	7.48	0	22.36	13.04	54.22	15.43	58.21	11.31	11.4	36.47
Monkey	17.89	22.36	0	16.61	33.32	32.74	38.5	15.23	14.42	17.09
Cattle	9.7	13.04	16.61	0	48.25	22.41	53.08	10.1	7.07	31.21
Cat	49.76	54.22	33.32	48.25	0	64.16	9.7	45.63	46.9	19.95
Fruitfly	18.6	15.43	32.74	22.41	64.16	0	69.14	22.18	23.15	48.33
Bacteria	54.26	58.21	38.5	53.08	9.7	69.14	0	49.78	51.3	22.85
Chimp	6.63	11.31	15.23	10.1	45.63	22.18	49.78	0	10	28.84
Dog	8.94	11.4	14.42	7.07	46.9	23.15	51.3	10	0	28.95
Rat	32.74	36.47	17.09	31.21	19.95	48.33	22.85	28.84	28.95	0

Table 2. Dissimilarity matrix of histogram difference weighted fuzzy binarization using entropy reduced features (20% motif features) on dataset 1

20%	Human	Gorilla	Monkey	Cattle	Cat	Fruitfly	Bacteria	Chimp	Dog	Rat
Human	0	4.9	8.72	6.16	15.03	15.62	31.11	5.48	6.32	7.87
Gorilla	4.9	0	11.31	4.24	18.71	11.66	34.93	9.9	8.25	10.49
Monkey	8.72	11.31	0	11.92	9.06	20.59	23.96	5.83	6.63	3.46
Cattle	6.16	4.24	11.92	0	18.22	11.4	35.04	10.68	7.21	10.68
Cat	15.03	18.71	9.06	18.22	0	26.57	17.44	10.77	11.83	9.27
Fruitfly	15.62	11.66	20.59	11.4	26.57	0	43.47	20.3	16.67	19.54
Bacteria	31.11	34.93	23.96	35.04	17.44	43.47	0	26	28.46	25.06
Chimp	5.48	9.9	5.83	10.68	10.77	20.3	26	0	6.93	6
Dog	6.32	8.25	6.63	7.21	11.83	16.67	28.46	6.93	0	4.69
Rat	7.87	10.49	3.46	10.68	9.27	19.54	25.06	6	4.69	0

Table 3. Dissimilarity matrix of histogram difference using entropy weighted fuzzy binarization features (100% motif features) on dataset 2

100%	HK1	GP1	PFKM	ALDOA	TPI1	GAPDH	PGK1	PGAM2	ENO1	PKM
HK1	0	32.31	29.26	63.67	93.68	86.75	67.19	55.52	20.74	68.35
GP1	32.31	0	7.35	32.65	63.02	56.71	35.67	23.83	18.38	36.63
PFKM	29.26	7.35	0	36.63	66.45	59.82	39.42	27.68	15.68	40.2
ALDOA	63.67	32.65	36.63	0	30.66	24.9	5.83	13.34	50.1	11.58
TPI1	93.68	63.02	66.45	30.66	0	8.6	28.28	41.21	80.04	29.63
GAPDH	86.75	56.71	59.82	24.9	8.6	0	23.28	35.97	73.85	25.69
PGK1	67.19	35.67	39.42	5.83	28.28	23.28	0	14.63	52.71	8.49
PGAM2	55.52	23.83	27.68	13.34	41.21	35.97	14.63	0	39.47	13.04
ENO1	20.74	18.38	15.68	50.1	80.04	73.85	52.71	39.47	0	52.23
PKM	68.35	36.63	40.2	11.58	29.63	25.69	8.49	13.04	52.23	0

Table 4. Dissimilarity matrix of histogram difference using entropy weighted fuzzy binarization features (20% motif features) on dataset 2

20%	HK1	GP1	PFKM	ALDOA	TPI1	GAPDH	PGK1	PGAM2	ENO1	PKM
HK1	0	19.95	8.49	31.34	48.74	38.65	14.42	22.72	16.79	32.06
GP1	19.95	0	13.56	12.17	29.6	19.75	6.93	6.48	6.32	13.49
PFKM	8.49	13.56	0	25.1	42.8	32.92	7.62	16.25	11.14	25.81
ALDOA	31.34	12.17	25.1	0	18.28	10.58	17.78	9.8	15.3	3.46
TPI1	48.74	29.6	42.8	18.28	0	11.14	35.67	27.75	32.86	17.89
GAPDH	38.65	19.75	32.92	10.58	11.14	0	26.12	19.29	23.54	10.95
PGK1	14.42	6.93	7.62	17.78	35.67	26.12	0	8.83	5.66	18.49
PGAM2	22.72	6.48	16.25	9.8	27.75	19.29	8.83	0	7.48	10.1
ENO1	16.79	6.32	11.14	15.3	32.86	23.54	5.66	7.48	0	15.94
PKM	32.06	13.49	25.81	3.46	17.89	10.95	18.49	10.1	15.94	0

Table 5. Dissimilarity matrix of histogram difference using variance weighted fuzzy binarization features (100% motif features) on dataset 1

100%	Human	Gorilla	Monkey	Cattle	Cat	Fruitfly	Bacteria	Chimp	Dog	Rat
Human	0	7.48	17.89	9.7	49.76	18.6	54.26	6.63	8.94	32.74
Gorilla	7.48	0	22.36	13.04	54.22	15.43	58.21	11.31	11.4	36.47
Monkey	17.89	22.36	0	16.61	33.32	32.74	38.5	15.23	14.42	17.09
Cattle	9.7	13.04	16.61	0	48.25	22.41	53.08	10.1	7.07	31.21
Cat	49.76	54.22	33.32	48.25	0	64.16	9.7	45.63	46.9	19.95
Fruitfly	18.6	15.43	32.74	22.41	64.16	0	69.14	22.18	23.15	48.33
Bacteria	54.26	58.21	38.5	53.08	9.7	69.14	0	49.78	51.3	22.85
Chimp	6.63	11.31	15.23	10.1	45.63	22.18	49.78	0	10	28.84
Dog	8.94	11.4	14.42	7.07	46.9	23.15	51.3	10	0	28.95
Rat	32.74	36.47	17.09	31.21	19.95	48.33	22.85	28.84	28.95	0

Table 6. Dissimilarity matrix of histogram difference using variance weighted fuzzy binarization features (20% motif features) on dataset 1

20%	Human	Gorilla	Monkey	Cattle	Cat	Fruitfly	Bacteria	Chimp	Dog	Rat
Human	0	10.49	20.15	11.49	39.67	19.39	56.14	7.07	8	33.76
Gorilla	10.49	0	28.91	20.15	48.56	14.56	64.53	16.12	11.83	41.86
Monkey	20.15	28.91	0	10.86	20.69	36.25	37.55	16.67	19.44	15.36
Cattle	11.49	20.15	10.86	0	30.33	28.18	47.18	8.72	10.86	24.86
Cat	39.67	48.56	20.69	30.33	0	54.44	18.38	34.93	39.62	10.49
Fruitfly	19.39	14.56	36.25	28.18	54.44	0	71.32	24.17	21.4	49.56
Bacteria	56.14	64.53	37.55	47.18	18.38	71.32	0	51.22	55.96	23.32
Chimp	7.07	16.12	16.67	8.72	34.93	24.17	51.22	0	11.31	29.5
Dog	8	11.83	19.44	10.86	39.62	21.4	55.96	11.31	0	33.05
Rat	33.76	41.86	15.36	24.86	10.49	49.56	23.32	29.5	33.05	0

Table 7. Dissimilarity matrix of histogram difference using variance weighted fuzzy binarization features (100% motif features) on dataset 2

100%	HK1	GP1	PFKM	ALDOA	TPI1	GAPDH	PGK1	PGAM2	ENO1	PKM
HK1	0	32.31	29.26	63.67	93.68	86.75	67.19	55.52	20.74	68.35
GP1	32.31	0	7.35	32.65	63.02	56.71	35.67	23.83	18.38	36.63
PFKM	29.26	7.35	0	36.63	66.45	59.82	39.42	27.68	15.68	40.2
ALDOA	63.67	32.65	36.63	0	30.66	24.9	5.83	13.34	50.1	11.58
TPI1	93.68	63.02	66.45	30.66	0	8.6	28.28	41.21	80.04	29.63
GAPDH	86.75	56.71	59.82	24.9	8.6	0	23.28	35.97	73.85	25.69
PGK1	67.19	35.67	39.42	5.83	28.28	23.28	0	14.63	52.71	8.49
PGAM2	55.52	23.83	27.68	13.34	41.21	35.97	14.63	0	39.47	13.04
ENO1	20.74	18.38	15.68	50.1	80.04	73.85	52.71	39.47	0	52.23
PKM	68.35	36.63	40.2	11.58	29.63	25.69	8.49	13.04	52.23	0

depending on the threshold chosen when entropy values are ordered in ascending order ignoring features with '0' entropy and variance values in descending order. The results are encouraging in terms of differentiating ability of these features when it is used to obtain the fuzzy weighted histogram values. A comparison of results using complete features and reduced features is presented in Tables 1 and 2 for dataset 1 using entropy, Tables 3 and 4 for dataset 2 using entropy, Tables 5 and 6 for dataset 1 using variance and Tables 7 and 8 for dataset 2 using variance. Also, the dissimilarity results of human with rest of the organisms is compared for entropy based 100% features in Fig. 4 and entropy, variance based features with 20% reduced features in Figs. 5 and 6 respectively. The dissimilarity values between organisms belonging to the same class (Human, Gorilla, Monkey and Chimpanzee) is low and that of organisms belonging to different classes is reasonably high. Also there is a huge difference between dissimilarity values of lower level organism (Bacteria) with that of rest of the higher level organisms as seen in Figs. 4, 5 and 6. We can observe that even with the reduced set of features the differences are retained and in some places as seen in Fig. 5 the results

Table 8. Dissimilarity matrix of histogram difference using variance weighted fuzzy binarization features (20% motif features) on dataset 2

20%	HK1	GP1	PFKM	ALDOA	TPI1	GAPDH	PGK1	PGAM2	ENO1	PKM
HK1	0	34.79	29.87	57.48	86.56	70.89	61.89	49.46	15.94	67.17
GP1	34.79	0	7.48	24.25	53.55	38.6	28.14	16.25	24.49	33.59
PFKM	29.87	7.48	0	29.36	58.1	42.71	33.11	20.69	20.05	38.18
ALDOA	57.48	24.25	29.36	0	29.7	15.49	6.63	12.88	47.81	13.78
TPI1	86.56	53.55	58.1	29.7	0	16.19	26.38	39.9	76.94	23.79
GAPDH	70.89	38.6	42.71	15.49	16.19	0	13.86	26.19	61.89	15.23
PGK1	61.89	28.14	33.11	6.63	26.38	13.86	0	14.56	51.28	8.72
PGAM2	49.46	16.25	20.69	12.88	39.9	26.19	14.56	0	37.76	18.11
ENO1	15.94	24.49	20.05	47.81	76.94	61.89	51.28	37.76	0	55.59
PKM	67.17	33.59	38.18	13.78	23.79	15.23	8.72	18.11	55.59	0

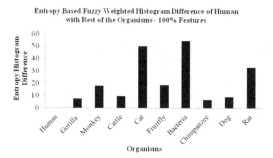

Fig. 4. Entropy based fuzzy weighted histogram difference of human with rest of the organisms - 100% features.

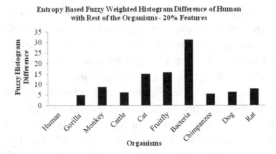

Fig. 5. Entropy based fuzzy weighted histogram difference of human with rest of the organisms - 20% features.

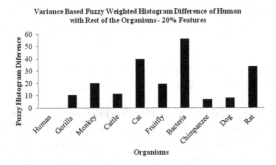

Fig. 6. Variance based fuzzy weighted histogram difference of human with rest of the organisms - 20% features.

get enhanced between other organisms and bacteria. The results on dataset 2 suggest that there is some similarity in the promoters of all the organisms that take part in the glycolysis pathway (Tables 3, 4, 7 and 8).

4   Conclusion

The proposed weighted fuzzy binarization for histogram comparison of promoter sequences seems to be an effective measure to study the underlying similarity/differences in the promoter sequences. The results obtained are better in terms of promoter differentiation when compared to some of the recent similar studies [17–19]. The obtained results could aid biologists to make better biological inferences in applications like analysis of metabolic pathways and understanding biomedical mechanisms in different organisms.

References

1. Qin, Y., Yalamanchili, H.K., Qin, J., Yan, B., Wang, J.: The current status and challenges in computational analysis of genomic big data. Big Data Res. **2**(1), 12–18 (2015)
2. Landolin, J.M., Johnson, D.S., Trinklein, N.D., Aldred, S.F., Medina, C., Shulha, H., Myers, R.M.: Sequence features that drive human promoter function and tissue specificity. Genome Res. **20**(7), 890–898 (2010)
3. Wray, G.A., Hahn, M.W., Abouheif, E., Balhoff, J.P., Pizer, M., Rockman, M.V., Romano, L.A.: The evolution of transcriptional regulation in Eukaryotes. Mol. Biol. Evol. **20**(9), 1377–1419 (2003)
4. Ghiurcuta, C.G.: Models and Algorithms for Noncoding Genes. Edic Research Proposal (2009)
5. Hu, J., Zhao, H., Liang, X., Chen, D.: The analysis of similarity for promoter sequence structures in yeast genes. In: 2012 5th International Conference on IEEE Biomedical Engineering and Informatics (BMEI), pp. 919–922 (2012)
6. Reiter, L.T., Potocki, L., Chien, S., Gribskov, M., Bier, E.: A systematic analysis of human disease-associated gene sequences in Drosophila melanogaster. Genome Res. **11**(6), 1114–1125 (2001)
7. Guyon, I., Elisseeff, A.: An introduction to variable and feature selection. J. Mach. Learn. Res. **3**(Mar), 1157–1182 (2003)
8. Liu, X., Krishnan, A., Mondry, A.: An entropy-based gene selection method for cancer classification using microarray data. BMC Bioinform. **6**(1), 1 (2005)
9. Saeys, Y., Inza, I., Larrañaga, P.: A review of feature selection techniques in bioinformatics. Bioinformatics **23**(19), 2507–2517 (2007)
10. Conilione, P., Wang, D.: A comparative study on feature selection for E.coli promoter recognition. Int. J. Inf. Technol. **11**, 54–66 (2005)
11. López-de-Ipiña, K., Solé-Casals, J., Faundez-Zanuy, M., Calvo, P.M., Sesa, E., de Lizarduy, U.M., Bergareche, A.: Selection of entropy based features for automatic analysis of essential tremor. Entropy **18**(5), 184 (2016)
12. Chitralegha, M., Thangavel, K.: A novel entropy based segment selection technique for extraction of protein sequence motifs. IJCSI Int. J. Comput. Sci. Issues **9**(4), 314 (2012)
13. Larkin, M.A., Blackshields, G., Brown, N.P., Chenna, R., McGettigan, P.A., McWilliam, H., Thompson, J.D.: Clustal W and Clustal X version 2.0. Bioinformatics **23**(21), 2947–2948 (2007)
14. http://blast.ncbi.nlm.nih.gov
15. http://meme-suite.org
16. Yan, R., Xu, D., Yang, J., Walker, S., Zhang, Y.: A comparative assessment and analysis of 20 representative sequence alignment methods for protein structure prediction. Sci. Rep. **3**, 2619 (2013)
17. Kouser, K., Rangarajan, L., Chandrashekar, D.S., Kshitish, K.A., Abraham, E.M.: Alignment free frequency based distance measures for promoter sequence comparison. In: Ortuño, F., Rojas, I. (eds.) IWBBIO 2015: Bioinformatics and Biomedical Engineering. LNCS, vol. 9044, pp. 183–193. Springer, Cham (2015). doi:10.1007/978-3-319-16480-9_19
18. Kouser, K., Rangarajan, L.: Promoter sequence analysis through no gap multiple sequence alignment of motif pairs. Procedia Comput. Sci. **58**, 356–362 (2015)

19. Kouser, K., and Rangarajan, L.: Similarity analysis of position specific motif matrices using lacunarity for promoter sequences. In: Proceedings of the 2014 International Conference on Interdisciplinary Advances in Applied Computing, p. 37. ACM (2014)
20. Zadeh, L.A.: Fuzzy sets. Inf. Control **8**(3), 338–353 (1965)
21. Cintra, M.E., Camargo, H.A., Monard, M.C.: A study on techniques for the automatic generation of membership functions for pattern recognition. Congresso da Academia Trinacional de Ciências **C3N**(1), 1–10 (2008)
22. Medasani, S., Kim, J., Krishnapuram, R.: An overview of membership function generation techniques for pattern recognition. Int. J. Approxiamate Reasoning **19**(3), 391–417 (1998)
23. Kaya, M., Alhajj, R.: A clustering algorithm with genetically optimized membership functions for fuzzy association rules mining. In: 12th IEEE International Conference on Fuzzy Systems 2, pp. 881–886 (2003)

A Fast k-Nearest Neighbor Classifier Using Unsupervised Clustering

Szilárd Vajda[1]([⊠]) and K.C. Santosh[2]

[1] Computer Science Department, Central Washington University,
Ellensburg, WA 98926, USA
Szilard.Vajda@cwu.edu
[2] Computer Science Department, University of South Dakota,
Vermillion, SD 57069, USA
Santosh.KC@usd.edu

Abstract. In this paper we propose a fast method to classify patterns when using a k-nearest neighbor (kNN) classifier. The kNN classifier is one of the most popular supervised classification strategies. It is easy to implement, and easy to use. However, for large training data sets, the process can be time consuming due to the distance calculation of each test sample to the training samples. Our goal is to provide a generic method to use the same classification strategy, but considerably speed up the distance calculation process. First, the training data is clustered in an unsupervised manner to find the ideal cluster setup to minimize the intra-class dispersion, using the so-called "jump" method. Once the clusters are defined, an iterative method is applied to select some percentage of the data closest to the cluster centers and furthest from the cluster centers, respectively. Beside some interesting property discovered by altering the different selection criteria, we proved the efficiency of the method by reducing by up to 71% the classification speed, while keeping the classification performance in the same range.

Keywords: k-nearest neighbor · Unsupervised clustering · Fast handwritten character classification · Lampung handwriting · Digit recognition

1 Introduction

The k-nearest neighbor classifier (kNN) can be considered as one of pioneers among the supervised methods – proposed originally by Fix and Hodges [7]. The idea behind the method is rather simple. Considering an annotated data collection, for an unknown data sample the class label is assigned based on the majority of its k-nearest neighbors. The so-called nearest neighbor classifier is a special case of the previously mentioned one for $k = 1$. Even though it is a rather simple method, it has some indisputable advantages such as: simplicity, effectiveness, intuitivity, non-parametric nature, and high performance for different classification tasks [20]. The proper selection of parameter k responsible

© Springer Nature Singapore Pte Ltd. 2017
K.C. Santosh et al. (Eds.): RTIP2R 2016, CCIS 709, pp. 185–193, 2017.
DOI: 10.1007/978-981-10-4859-3_17

for the neighborhood size, and the distance function responsible for the quality of the topological representation can have a significant impact on the underlying results [11].

Formally, the problem can be stated as follows. Let $T = \{t_1, t_2, \cdots, t_m\}$ be a template or reference set, containing m number of points taking values in R^d, d denotes the dimension of the data. Let $Q = \{q_1, q_2, \cdots, q_n\}$ a query set containing n different points with the same dimension. The k-nearest neighbor problem consist in searching for each point $q_i \in Q$ in the template set T given a specific distance metric. The Euclidean distance, Manhattan distance, cosine similarity measures are commonly used, but other distances measures such as Hamming, cityblock (sum of absolute differences) can also be considered. The computational complexity of the method in case of linear search is $\mathcal{O}(md)$, which for large data collections (m), and high dimensional data (d) can be an expensive operation. Its parameters (neighborhood size, distance function) – though they are simple, are also the major challenges.

In this paper, we propose a fast k-nearest neighbor classifier by reducing the number of reference points that need to be considered in the distance computation. The reduction is achieved by clustering the data points first, - using unsupervised clustering to find a stable cluster setup, followed by selecting the closest points and the furthest points, respectively. The rest of the paper is organized as follows. Section 2 briefly reviews different attempts to reduce the linear search in the k-nearest neighbor method, Sect. 3 describes the proposed reference points reduction strategy, while Sect. 4 describes the different data collections involved in the experiments, as well the results, and some comparisons. Finally, Sect. 5 draws the conclusions.

2   Related Work

In order to lower the linear search complexity, different solutions have been proposed. Some methods use graph based methods to approximate the nearest neighbor [12], while some others sub-sample the reference set to diminish the number of distance calculation between the reference points and the query point [2,8,13], and others invoke parallel calculation supported by GPU [9].

Peredes et al. [18] proposed a method to minimize the number of distance calculations considering a graph, built from the data set. Knowing that the distance between two elements is the shortest path, they filter out points which are far away from the query point, hence reducing the search space, and apply linear search for the remaining points. In the work [17], the authors build a *visibility graph* followed by a greedy type search. An extension of their work is proposed by Hajebi et al. [12], where instead of the a visibility graph, the search is made on a k-NN graph, which is a directed graph structure. The complexity of building such a graph is $\mathcal{O}(md)$, but more efficient methods were proposed by several other authors [4,6].

Another type of solution proposed by Indyk and Motwani [13] involves hash functions, in order to create a hash value for each point. Each hash function reduces the dimensionality by projecting the original point into a lower dimensional random space. The projected points are partitioned into bins considering a uniform grid. To reduce even further the search space, a second hashing is applied. The query point is matched only with those ones falling in the same bin, where a classical linear search is applied to distinguish the closest match.

The KD-tree proposed by Friedman et al. [8] and Bentley [2] is based on partitioning the search space by hyperplanes that are perpendicular to the coordinate axes. The root of the tree is a hyperplane orthogonal to one of the dimensions, splits the data into two separate half planes. Each half is recursively partitioned into another two half planes, and so forth. The partitioning stops at $log(m)$, so at each leaf there will be only one data point. The query point is compared to the root element, and all the subsequent ones, while traversing the tree to find the best match. As the leaf points are not always the nearest points, a simple backtracking is applied to analyze the closest ones. Instead of using backtracking Hajebi applied *best bin first*, proposed first by Beis and Lowe [1].

Zhang and Srihari [22] propose for handwritten digits classification a hierarchical search using a non-metric measure applied to a binary feature space. In the training phase, the set is organized in a multi-level tree, while for the test phase, a hierarchical search is applied based on a subset of templates selected on the upper levels.

A rather modern and new GPU based solution is proposed by Garcia and Debreuve [10], where instead of reducing the size of the reference points, or organizing the points in a tree structure, the authors concentrate more on the distance calculation part, which can be formulated as a highly parallel process. Each distance calculation can be done separately as each point is independent.

The proposed method is aligning with the methods proposed in [2, 8, 13]. Instead of using hash functions, or tree representations, a data sampling has been proposed, by discarding those samples which based on some distance metric do not contribute to build reliable cluster representations. For the best cluster representation a so-called "jump method" has been invoked. For the selected data points we also apply linear search to find the nearest neighbors.

3   Method

In this section we introduce the proposed method. First, we will briefly describe the "jump method" [19], followed by the data selection criterion to reduce the number of reference points.

The original method proposed by Sugar and James [19] provides a systematic analysis to automatically discover the number of clusters for an unknown data collection. They propose an efficient, non-parametric solution involving distortion, a quantity that measures the average distance, per dimension, between each sample of a cluster and its cluster center. The algorithm can be summarized as follows:

(1) Apply k-means algorithm [14] to the unknown data, and after each iteration calculate

$d_k = \frac{1}{d} \min_{c_1,c_2,\cdots,c_K} \{\frac{1}{n} \sum_{i=1}^{K} \sum_{i \in k} (x_i - c_k)^T (x_i - c_k)\}$, where x_i is the ith sample belonging to the kth cluster, c_k is the kth cluster center, n is the number of samples, while d is the dimension of the data.

(2) Pick a suitable transformation power $Y > 0$. If the clusters are assumed to be generated by a Gaussian process, the theory suggests $Y = \frac{d}{2}$.

(3) Apply the first order forward difference operator to the transformed curve d_k^{-Y} in order to get the "jump" statistic $J_K = d_K^{-Y} - d_{K-1}^{-Y}$. For practical reasons $d_0^{-Y} = 0$ should be defined.

(4) For the K for which the J_K is the largest will provide the optimal number for the clusters. The number of clusters $C = argmax_K \{J_k\}$.

Once the optimal number of clusters is estimated for the data points, the data is clustered in exactly C clusters, as per suggested by the algorithm. Due to the nature of the method, the C number of clusters assures a low intra-class variability reported to each dimension. In other words, those clusters represent the most the underlying data. This information is used to select from each cluster a certain number of points. Two selection criteria were considered. For each cluster, the distance between each sample x_i and $c_k, k \in \{1, \cdots, C\}$ were calculated considering Euclidean distance. The different distances were sorted first, and different percentages considering the closest (*min* rule) and furthest samples (*max* rule) from the centroids were retained as reference points for the upcoming k-nearest neighbor clustering. Instead of calculating the distances in a brute force manner, we propose a selection, a subsampling. The *min* rule selects those samples closer to the cluster center, therefore the cluster is represented by strong representatives, while the *max* rule selects those candidates which are lying on the shell of the d dimensional hyper sphere defining the cluster. Those samples are far from the center, and one might think they can not attract many samples from the test set, as they themselves could be considered as possible outliers, but according to Bishop [3], "for points which are uniformly distributed inside a sphere of d dimension, where d is large, almost all of the points are concentrated in a thin shell close to the surface".

The amount of data added by the *min/max* rule is increased incrementally, and accuracy performances are calculated. One could argue, that the selection method should not consider similar percentage of points from each cluster. Large clusters should get more importance over smaller clusters, but this one is assured by the percentile based selection. This type of selection is also supported by the fact that k-means clustering -by its nature-, tries to build uniform and equally distributed (balanced) clusters, and therefore a heuristic based selection could underestimate or overestimate the importance of one cluster or another. The optimal reference set is selected based on the accuracy performance. Speed factor which is linear in relation to the points selected in the reference set will decrease.

4   Experiments

This section is meant to first present the datasets used, followed by the achieved results, and a comparison at accuracy level as well as speed with the classical k-nearest neighbor utilizing brute force - by comparing each query example with all the reference samples [9].

4.1   Data Description

MNIST Digits. MNIST [16] is a well-known benchmark dataset[1] containing separated Latin digits assigned to 10 different classes. The images coming mainly from census forms, are size normalized and centered to 28×28 gray level images. The data set contains $60,000$ and $10,000$ images for training and test, respectively.

Lampung Characters. The Lampung characters[2] used in our experiments were extracted from a multi-writer handwritten collection produced by 82 high school students from Bandar Lampung, Indonesia. The Lampung texts are created as transcriptions of some fairy tales. One exemplary document snippet can be seen in Fig. 1.

Some $23,447$ characters were used as training set, while $7,853$ characters were considered for test. Altogether 18 different character classes were identified. Each character is represented by a centered and normalized 32×32 gray scale image. More details about this publicly available data is to be found in [15,21].

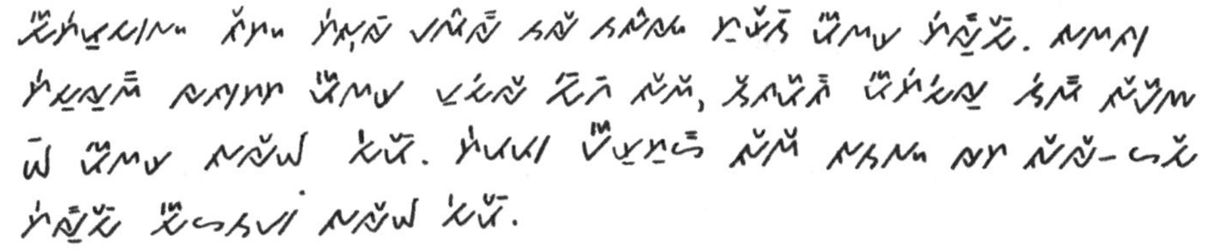

Fig. 1. A Lampung document snippet.

4.2   Results

First, the results achieved by the previously described "jump" method are shown in Fig. 2. For features we considered the intensity values of the gray scale images. This choice is motivated by the fact, that the best scores achieved on both data sets were using intensity values [5,15,16,21]. Our goal is not to find the best feature describing these digits and characters, but to show that using a common feature such as the intensity value we can considerably speed-up the recognition process by avoiding unnecessary distance calculations.

---

[1] http://yann.lecun.com/exdb/mnist/.
[2] http://patrec.cs.tu-dortmund.de/files/Lampung-Dataset.zip.

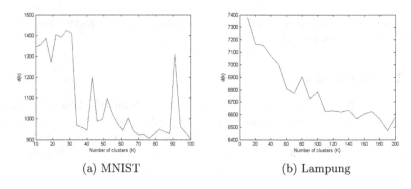

(a) MNIST   (b) Lampung

Fig. 2. The results of the "jump" method.

One might observe that the curve proposed by Sugar and James is not as smooth as discussed in their previous paper [19]. This can be explained by the fact that the authors analyzed their method only for low dimensional data, while here the dimensionality is rather high, comprising 784 and 1024 dimensions, respectively. However, in both cases a diminishing tendency is observed, hence the possibility to select the optimal number of clusters for both collections. In case of MNIST 76 clusters were found to be optimal, while for the Lampung collection 186 is the cluster number which indicates an optimal setup. The optimal cluster number assures that those centers are representative enough, and the surrounding data points should not be split further in smaller clusters.

Once the optimal cluster number is detected using the "jump" method, the selected cluster arrangement is considered, and for each cluster 5%, 10%, ..., 100% of the data is considered using the *min* and *max* rule for the k-nearest neighbor scenario ($k = 1$). While the *min* rule is responsible to select those samples close to the centroids, the *max* rule selects the samples lying furthest from the cluster centers. The data points collected using these two methods are than used to build two different reference data collections, used in a kNN classification - performing linear search as in case of the classical k-nearest neighbor. The results can be observed in Fig. 3.

A similar trend can be observed for both collections. The more data is considered, the more precise the results reported. However, it is really important to note that, for a small amount of data (up to 40%), the results provided by the *min* selection are much better, while for larger data selections comprising more than 40% for each cluster, the trend changes completely, and those samples selected by the *max* rule take over by producing far better scores than the other collection selected by the min rule. The *min* selection rule provides those samples closer to the cluster centers, while the *max* rule goes for those sample close to the cluster boundaries. One explanation for this rather interesting finding could be the fact supported also by Bishop [3], stating that for large collections with high dimensionality the samples are arranged on a thin shell close to the surface bounding the cluster in question.

To compare the performance versus the time necessary to perform the linear search applicable for k-nearest neighbor, we analyzed the performance charts depicted in Fig. 3. Selecting for both collections those settings when only 65% of the data is used in the search - using the max rule, we can state that our selection can reduce the time performance by 71% for MNIST, and 56% for Lampung, while still performing in the same range. The exact results are reported in Table 1. The results go up as high as 96.91% when 100% of the data is considered (classical case), while for the selection proposed by us, the scores are in the same range, obtaining 96.12% accuracy, but reducing the search time by 71%. Similarly, for the Lampung collection, considering the classical k-nearest neighbor classifier, the results for the complete set can go up to 83.94%, while selecting only 65% of the data (using the max rule), there is only a 0.86% drop in performance, but there is a gain in speed of 56%.

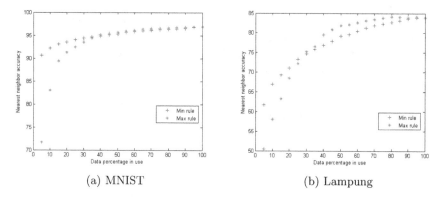

(a) MNIST   (b) Lampung

Fig. 3. The performance improvements using different data selection criteria and different amount of data.

In order to compare the efficiency of our selection method, we conducted a Monte Carlo simulation by randomly selecting 65% of the data, and observed for those randomly selected data how the performance measures look like. The average scores achieved by repeating the experiments 100 times can be seen also in Table 1. The lower scores indicates that our selection method is better, and therefore our method is empirically validated.

Table 1. Comparing performance and speed using the complete data collections and using the selection strategy.

Data	Accuracy (100%)	Accuracy (65%) random	Accuracy (65%) max rule
MNIST	96.91	94.03	96.12
Lampung	83.94	80.24	83.08

5   Conclusion

In this paper, we proposed a straightforward way to reduce the linear search applied to k-nearest neighbor by reducing the number of reference points considering using different benchmark handwritten character collections as test bed. The method can be considered a data reduction strategy based on optimization. The data points are first clustered in an optimal number of clusters using the so-called "jump" method, which is based on the optimization of inter-class variability. Once the samples are clustered using the optimal number of clusters, we select the closest and the furthest samples alike, and using a certain percentage of the data, we build several subsets of the original data, and run the k-nearest neighbor classifier. Analyzing the performances for the different amounts of data, we can clearly detect an optimum point in the size of the data for which the scores are similar as the whole data would be considered, but due to the reduction the search time is also reduced up to 71%.

Along the speed gain achieved by the data reduction, an interesting fact was observed when altering the *min* and *max* rules. For a smaller amount of data the *min* rule selects better candidates. However, when the selected data becomes larger the samples residing on the boundaries outperform those close to the center. This supports the idea that for larger data sets with high dimensional representatives, it is very likely that the data is organized in the outer shell of the sphere incorporating the data.

References

1. Beis, J.S., Lowe, D.G.: Shape indexing using approximate nearest-neighbour search in high-dimensional spaces. In: Proceedings of the 1997 Conference on Computer Vision and Pattern Recognition, CVPR 1997, p. 1000. IEEE Computer Society, Washington, DC (1997)
2. Bentley, J.L.: Multidimensional divide-and-conquer. Commun. ACM **23**(4), 214–229 (1980)
3. Bishop, C.M.: Neural Networks for Pattern Recognition. Oxford University Press Inc., New York (1995)
4. Chen, J., Fang, H.R., Saad, Y.: Fast approximate kNN graph construction for high dimensional data via recursive Lanczos bisection. J. Mach. Learn. Res. **10**, 1989–2012 (2009)
5. Ciresan, D.C., Meier, U., Gambardella, L.M., Schmidhuber, J.: Convolutional neural network committees for handwritten character classification. In: ICDAR, pp. 1135–1139 (2011)
6. Connor, M., Kumar, P.: Fast construction of k-nearest neighbor graphs for point clouds. IEEE Trans. Vis. Comput. Graph. **16**(4), 599–608 (2010)
7. Fix, E., Hodges, J.L.: Discriminatory Analysis - Nonparametric Discrimination: Consistency Properties. USAF School of Aviation Medicine (1951)
8. Friedman, J.H., Bentley, J.L., Finkel, R.A.: An algorithm for finding best matches in logarithmic expected time. ACM Trans. Math. Softw. **3**(3), 209–226 (1977)
9. Garcia, V., Debreuve, E., Barlaud, M.: Fast k nearest neighbor search using GPU. In: CVPR Workshop on Computer Vision on GPU (CVGPU). Anchorage, Alaska, USA (2008)

10. Garcia, V., Debreuve, E., Barlaud, M.: Fast k nearest neighbor search using GPU. In: 2008 IEEE Computer Society Conference on Computer Vision and Pattern Recognition Workshops, pp. 1–6 (2008)
11. Gou, J., Du, L., Zhang, Y., Xiaong, T.: A new distance-weighted k-nearest neighbor classifier. J. Inf. Comput. Sci. **9**(6), 1429–1436 (2012)
12. Hajebi, K., Abbasi-Yadkori, Y., Shahbazi, H., Zhang, H.: Fast approximate nearest-neighbor search with k-nearest neighbor graph. In: Proceedings of the Twenty-Second International Joint Conference on Artificial Intelligence, IJCAI 2011, vol. 2, pp. 1312–1317. AAAI Press (2011)
13. Indyk, P., Motwani, R.: Approximate nearest neighbors: towards removing the curse of dimensionality. In: Proceedings of the Thirtieth Annual ACM Symposium on Theory of Computing, STOC 1998, pp. 604–613. ACM, New York (1998)
14. Jain, A.K.: Data clustering: 50 years beyond k-means. Pattern Recogn. Lett. **31**(8), 651–666 (2010)
15. Junaidi, A., Vajda, S., Fink, G.A.: Lampung - a new handwritten character benchmark: database, labeling and recognition. In: International Workshop on Multilingual OCR (MOCR), pp. 105–112. ACM, Beijing (2011)
16. LeCun, Y., Bottou, L., Bengio, Y., Haffner, P.: Gradient-based learning applied to document recognition. In: Intelligent Signal Processing, pp. 306–351. IEEE Press (2001)
17. Lifshits, Y., Zhang, S.: Combinatorial algorithms for nearest neighbors, near-duplicates and small-world design. In: SODA, pp. 318–326 (2009)
18. Paredes, R., Chávez, E.: Using the k-nearest neighbor graph for proximity searching in metric spaces. In: Consens, M., Navarro, G. (eds.) SPIRE 2005. LNCS, vol. 3772, pp. 127–138. Springer, Heidelberg (2005). doi:10.1007/11575832_14
19. Sugar, C.A., James, G.M.: Finding the number of clusters in a dataset: an information-theoretic approach. J. Am. Stat. Assoc. **98**(463), 750–763 (2003)
20. Torralba, A., Fergus, R., Freeman, W.T.: 80 million tiny images: a large data set for nonparametric object and scene recognition. PAMI **30**(11), 1958–1970 (2008)
21. Vajda, S., Junaidi, A., Fink, G.A.: A semi-supervised ensemble learning approach for character labeling with minimal human effort. In: ICDAR, pp. 259–263 (2011)
22. Zhang, B., Srihari, S.N.: A fast algorithm for finding k-nearest neighbors with non-metric dissimilarity. In: IWFHR, pp. 13–18 (2002)

DSS for Prognostication of Academic Intervention by Applying DM Technique

Pawan Wasnik, S.D. Khamitkar[✉], P.U. Bhalchandra[✉], S.N. Lokhande[✉],
Preetam Tamsekar[✉], Govind Kulkarni[✉], Kailas Hambarde[✉],
and Shaikh Husen

School of Computational Sciences, S.R.T.M. University, Nanded 431606, MS, India
pawan_wasnik@yahoo.com, s_khamitkar@yahoo.com, srtmun.parag@gmail.com,
sana_lokhande@rediff.com, pritam.tamsekar@gmail.com,
govindcoolkarni@gmail.com, kailas.srt@gmail.com, husen09@gmail.com

Abstract. The decision making process in any field related to human behavior is an integral part of complex environment. Education has become a major concern of the development process in every field. The competent decision making to plan, execute and evaluate policies in this field became a necessity of this field which may be achieved by applying data mining techniques to educational environment. EDM uses many techniques such as decision trees, neural networks, k-nearest neighbor, naive bays, support vector machines and many others. The principal purpose of the study is identifying how each of these traditional processes can be improved through data mining techniques. And also to analyze the student behavior for future benefit by applying Data mining technique and using this valuable information for Decision Support to Prognostication of Academic Intervention for Higher Education using Data Mining Techniques. The study has suggested models and algorithms for every educational sphere we found while analyzing Education database. Data modeling processes is our main outcome, and enhanced processes achieved through data mining have been presented as research outcome. The techniques appropriate in achieving this enhanced processes has also been presented as modeling processes for finding the behavioral aspects and to effectively implement the organizational policies.

Keywords: DMT · Educational data mining · KDM · DPAI model

1 Introduction

We know that the quality of service is the main concern of any service provider. This quality depends on fast decision-making and efficiency, which depends on easy access to knowledge domain. However an educational organization like us has tremendous volume of electronic data available with us. Extracting meaning full information form it is quite difficult manually. We demand for automatic discovery of information or knowledge from it so that decision-making can be

© Springer Nature Singapore Pte Ltd. 2017
K.C. Santosh et al. (Eds.): RTIP2R 2016, CCIS 709, pp. 194–201, 2017.
DOI: 10.1007/978-981-10-4859-3_18

efficient and faster. Data mining techniques can be used to extract unknown pattern from the set of data and discover useful knowledge, which would assist decision makers to improve the decision-making and policy-making procedures. It results in extracting greater value from the raw data set, and making use of strategic resources efficiently and effectively. It finally improves the quality of higher educational processes.

2   Data Mining

Data mining is a process of discovering various hidden patterns, summaries, and derived values from given collection of data. This is sufficiently broad definition of data mining [1]. Data mining is iterative process within which progress is defined by discovery, through either automatic or manual methods. Best results are achieved by balancing the knowledge of human experts in describing problems and goals with the search capabilities of computers. Data mining synonyms is Knowledge Discovery from Data, or KDD. While other consider data mining as just a necessary steps in the process of knowledge discovery. The KDD process is shown below.

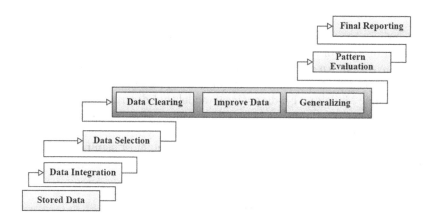

Fig. 1. KDD process

There are two primary practices generally used in data mining one is prediction and other is description. Therefore contemporary work is in either one of them (Fig. 2).

The goals of prediction and description are achieved by using following tasks:

1. Classification: Finding of a predictive learning function that classifies a data item into one of several predefined classes.
2. Regression: Discovery of a predictive learning function that maps a data item to a real-value prediction variable.

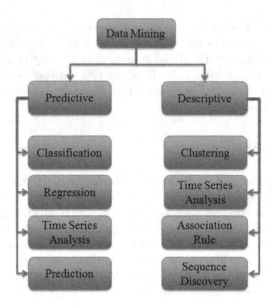

Fig. 2. Data mining task

3. Clustering: A common descriptive task in which one seeks to identify a finite set of categories of clusters to describe the data.
4. Summarization: An additional descriptive task that involves methods for finding a compact description for a set (or subset) of data.
5. Dependency Modeling: Finding a local model that describes significant dependencies between variables or between the values of a feature in a data set of in a part of a data set.
6. Change and Deviation Detection: Discovering the most significant changes in the given data set.

3 Educational Data Mining

The emerging fields of academic analytic and educational data mining are rapidly producing new possibilities for gathering, analyzing, and presenting educational data. Data is a key source of intelligence and has competitive advantage for every higher educational organization. With the explosion of electronic data available to educational organizations and the demand for better and faster decisions, the role of data driven intelligence is becoming central in educational organizations. Virtually every educational organization these days is in the process of exploring and implementing data mining solutions to core problems including student support, course registration processes, alumina associations, designing new courses, etc. Today almost all educational organizations, institutions or universities have been computerized and they have database systems capturing all essential data. Even though, one of the biggest challenges that higher education faces today is predicting knowledge from databases. The objective of this study is to introduce models for data mining. Using these models, one can realize what data has to be captured, what surrounding information has also to be captured, how mining can be carried out, etc.

4 System Outline

The methodology proposed for prognostication of academic intervention for higher education will be validated through the analysis of actual data of students gathered from questionnaires. The results from overall stage lead to minor refinements of the original theoretical framework and also provide a new research question for future work. This research is a case study of analysis of student data in Swami Ramanand Teerth Marathwada University, Nanded In this work, we attempt to address the capabilities of data mining and its applications to higher education data, a view that data mining is a potent instrument for academic intervention. We will be indicating a model and an algorithm for every educational sphere we found while analyzing Education database. Data modeling processes will be our main outcome. This must not be wrongly interpreted like proposed work will be creating database structures, feeding data or mining millions of information stored in the databases, as this will be a very big and complex activity. In routine sense, our work relies on four basic methods of data mining: classification, categorization, estimation, and visualization. While dealing with modeling processes we will use Classification to identify associations and clusters to separate subjects under study. We can come with some modeling processes that use classification for a comprehensive analysis of student characteristics or use estimation to predict the likelihood of a variety of outcomes, such as transfer-ability, persistence, retention, and course success, etc. Since nobody knows how to derive these results, we will suggest a model for every process found.

5 System Planning and Architectural Components

In order to develop the decision support system for identification of academic intervention in higher education for prognostication, we will use SPSS for the implementation of our idea [2]. Our student's dataset in MS-Excel can be exported in SPSS. There are other Open sources platforms like R Miner, WEKA, etc. for implementation of our experiments. The following process has been adopted (Fig. 3).

The primary data based on the present study for the analysis. The method is adopting the questionnaire has collected primary data. This questionnaire prepared in school of computational sciences Swami Ramanand Teerth Maratwada University Nanded. This questionnaire will be filled up by the student of computational sciences Swami Ramanand Teerth Maratwada University Nanded, related to their Academic, Personal, Hobbies, Interest, Residential, Family background records (Fig. 4).

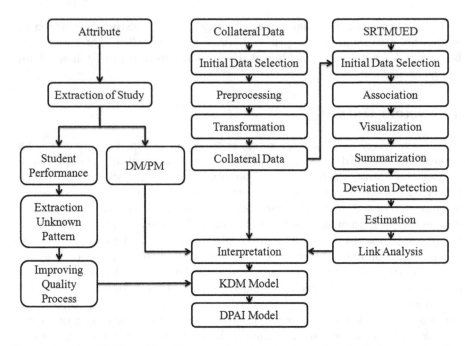

Fig. 3. Proposed DSS for identification of prognostication of academic intervention for higher education

1	Course name		
2	Your name		
3	Gender (sex)	Male	Female
4	Marital status	Married	unmarried
5	Age		
6	Home address	Urban/	rural
7	Mobile no.		
8	Personal email id		
9	Degree passer and percentage	General B.Sc. / B.Sc.(computer CS) / BCA/ BCS/ Other / Percentage:	
10	Degree collage name		
11	Father's Education	Below or SSC/ HSC/ Graduate/ Post Graduate/ other	
12	Fathers job and annual income	Service / Business/ Agriculture/ In house/ Other/ Income	
13	Mothers education	Below or SSC/ HSC/ Graduate/ Post Graduate/ other	
14	Mothers job and annual income	Service / Business/ Agriculture/ In house/ Other/ Income	
15	Family size		
16	Family relationship	Excellent / Good/ Satisfactory/ Bad/ Very Bad	
17	Family support to your education	Excellent / Good/ Satisfactory/ Bad/ Very Bad	
18	Reason to choose this course	Career in IT/ Near to Home/ Reputation of course / Blind Decision/ Parents wish:	
19	Travel mode and time needed	Bus/ Railway/ City Bus/ Rickshaw/ Self Vehicle / Walking Time needed:	
20	Study time	Excellent / Good/ Satisfactory/ Bad/ Very Bad	
21	Details of past failure exam		
22	Do you attended extra tutorial class	Yes /	no
23	Do you get scholarship	Yes /	no
24	Do you have part time job	Yes /	no

Fig. 4. Sample questionnaire

In India, the educational system consists of $10 + 2 + 3$ pattern of undergraduate education for no-professional streams and $10 + 2 + 4$ pattern for undergraduate professional streams. The students admitted to Computational Sciences allied subjects are mainly from the first pattern. Most of the students are under graduate from the public, grant-in-aids sanctioned and nominal expensive education system. There are several courses like BCS, BCA, B.Sc (CS or IT or CM) under science and technology faculty from where the students mainly come. Their data will be collected for the past few years. The database was built from two sources: previous examination's progress reports and our questionnaires.

5.1 KDM (Knowledge Discovery Management)

We will show that the performance degrading pattern we have discovered will be helpful to predict some students which will also have failure. Our questionnaire will have questions with predefined options [3] related to student's attributes as defined in Pritchard and Wilson [3,4]. The attributes in questionnaire have relations with the performance of students. The questionnaire will be reviewed by experts from educational sciences. There will be some trial testing of questionnaire on some small groups of students. These trials will help us to understand over all feedback as such. Some revisions with trial testing will be made to devise out the final version of questionnaire. The final questionnaire consisted of finite number of closed type questions [3]. The questionnaire will be distributed to students and demonstrated for feedback. After this, a dataset will be integrated with thousands of student records and each record consists of many fields. Originally, there will be fields equal to the total number of questions in questionnaire. Some additional fields will be added for seeking information of students. Microsoft Excel 2007 software can be used to record the dataset. Data set values like Yes/No were converted in to numeric values like 1 or 0. Other numerical codes in the range $0, 1, 2, 3, 4..., 6$ will also be given depending upon the number of possible answers a question can have. Likewise other answers are also converted into numeric values. A sample questionnaire is given in Fig. 1. During the pre-processing of data, we may find some ambiguities and false information in student's data. We forecast around 10% confusing data or falsely filled data or partly filled questionnaire in first step. In order to correct them, the students will be called on one to one basis and convinced to fill the missing data. There can be some confidential issues discovered after going through the filled questionnaire. Appropriate actions will be taken time to time and significant number of students will get convinced.

Since we aim for discovery of attributes which affects performance of students, we primarily investigated literature across the globe to see what other people have done. To understand performance of a student, we underwent discussions with educationalist. The performance in broader sense is how well a student does in over all courses. For proper understanding the performance terminology, we primarily relied on the work of Shoukat Ali et al. [5]. This work is a lucid discussion on performance analysis of students. This work is base for our analysis and some terminology is also borrowed from the same. As per above refereed studies, there are numerous factors which affect student's academic growth and learning outcome. This consideration matches with few attributes of our dataset. In the literature review Shoukat Ali et al. [5] cites other references for proper understanding of factors important for performance analysis. A similar works of Graetz et al. [6] suggested that the social status of parents and performance of students are reliant with each other. This also matches with our understanding of proportionate relationship of performance with social and economical conditions of students. The Shoukat Ali et al. [5] also cites that Considine and Zappala [10] have noticed that parent's economical conditions have positive effects on the performance. The work of Staffolani and Bratti [7] highlights that the future achievements of students have correlation with previous year's scores.

The combined finding that affects performance as per [5] highlights many social, economical and self related factors that have effect on student's academic performance. We felt that, once we discover these hidden truths, we can undertake appropriate, corrective actions to improve overall performance. This is the motto behind our prognostication work. Further, it was matter of curiosity that whether such investigations were made in past or not. So we started investigating profiling studies for student's performances. In effect, several studies have been found which have addressed related issues. Some of them includes, Ma et al. [7] which used association rules [3], the Minaei-Bidgoli et al. [9] used classification technique, the Kotsiantis et al. [3,8] used prediction approach, and more recently, Pardos et al. [3,9] used regression technique for prognostication purpose. Keeping the knowledge earned after careful review of above primary source.

5.2   DPAI (Development for Identification of Prognostication of Academic Intervention)

We aim to predict attributes which are directly related to student's performance. We are of the opinion that not only productive teaching or learning but also other social and economical aspects will hamper the performance. Our analysis will carried out with some thoughts in mind including social aspects of students, economical desirableness of students to peruse education, personal desires & ambitions and finally resources available with students which can help them to get success.

6   Conclusion

It was openly understood that many social, habitual and economical aspects are associated with performance of students and mere studying cannot be the sole criteria for good performance. However these are hidden and no attempt was made at to scientifically visualize them. The study took it as a challenge and using interdisciplinary approach, we will collect data and data mining algorithms will be implemented to get such insight. The specific objective of the undertaken research work is to find out any hidden patterns in the available data which could be useful for predicting student's performance. We will scientifically make visible the hidden aspects which affects the performance. The ultimate goal of our study is in terms of prognostication actions to improve academic performance of our students in their weaker aspects.

References

1. Al-Radaideh, Q.A., Al Ananbeh, A., Al-Shawakfa, E.M.: A classification model for predicting the suitable study track for school student's. IJRRAS **8**(2) (2011)
2. IBM SPSS Statistics 22 Documentation on internet. Accessed www.ibm.com/support/docview.wss?uid=swg27038407
3. Cortez, P., Silva, A.: Using data mining to predict secondary school student performance. Accessed http://www.researchgate.net/publication/Using_data_mining_to_predict_secondary_school_student_performance
4. Pritchard, M.E., Wilson, G.S.: Using emotional and social factors to predict student success. J. Coll. Student Dev. **44**(1), 18–28 (2003)
5. Ali, S., et al.: Factors contributing to the students academic performance: a case study of Islamia University Sub-campus. Am. J. Edu. Res. **1**(8), 283–289 (2013)
6. Graetz, B.: Socio-economic status in education research and policy in John Ainley et al., socio-economic status and school education DEET/ACER Canberra. J. Pediatr. Psychol. **20**(2), 205–216 (1995)
7. Bratti, M., Staffolani, S.: Student Time Allocation and Educational Production Functions. University of Ancona Department of Economics Working Paper No. 170. Ma, Y., Liu, B., Wong, C.K., Yu, P.S., Lee, S.M., Targeting the right (2000)
8. Minaei-Bidgoli, B., Kashy, D.A., Kortemeyer, G., Punch, W.F.: Predicting student performance: an application of data mining methods with the educational web-based system LON-CAPA. In: Proceedings of ASEE/IEEE Frontiers in Education Conference, Boulder, CO. IEEE (2003)
9. Kotsiantis, S.: A case study for predicting dropout prone students. Int. J. Knowl. Eng. Soft Data Paradigms **1**(2), 101–111 (2009)
10. Considine, G., Zappala, G.: Influence of social and economic disadvantage in the academic performance of school students in Australia. J. Sociol. **38**, 129–148 (2002)

Cluster Based Symbolic Representation for Skewed Text Categorization

Lavanya Narayana Raju, Mahamad Suhil[✉], D.S. Guru, and Harsha S. Gowda

Department of Studies in Computer Science, University of Mysore, Mysore, India
swaralavz@gmail.com, mahamad45@yahoo.co.in, dsg@compsci.uni-mysore.ac.in,
harshasgmysore@gmail.com

Abstract. In this work, a problem associated with imbalanced text corpora is addressed. A method of converting an imbalanced text corpus into a balanced one is presented. The presented method employs a clustering algorithm for conversion. Initially to avoid curse of dimensionality, an effective representation scheme based on term class relevancy measure is adapted, which drastically reduces the dimension to the number of classes in the corpus. Subsequently, the samples of larger sized classes are grouped into a number of subclasses of smaller sizes to make the entire corpus balanced. Each subclass is then given a single symbolic vector representation by the use of interval valued features. This symbolic representation in addition to being compact helps in reducing the space requirement and also the classification time. The proposed model has been empirically demonstrated for its superiority on bench marking datasets viz., Reuters 21578 and TDT2. Further, it has been compared against several other existing contemporary models including model based on support vector machine. The comparative analysis indicates that the proposed model outperforms the other existing models.

Keywords: Feature selection · Skewed text data · Clustering · Symbolic data representation · Text classification

1 Introduction

With the advancement of digital technology, the amount of text content available on the web has become unimaginably big. Automatic text categorization systems are being developed since last three decades in order to effectively manage such a huge quantity of text documents. Text categorization (TC) is the process of classifying a huge collection of text documents into predefined categories. It carries higher importance due to its huge impact on subsequent activities of text mining and also due to many applications involving text categorization such as spam filtering in emails, classification of medical documents, sentiment analysis etc., [1,16].

Curse of dimensionality, preserving semantics and effective representation are the issues which make the problem of text classification a suitable one. The complexity of the problem gets doubled if the text corpora are skewed or imbalanced

© Springer Nature Singapore Pte Ltd. 2017
K.C. Santosh et al. (Eds.): RTIP2R 2016, CCIS 709, pp. 202–216, 2017.
DOI: 10.1007/978-981-10-4859-3_19

as a class with a large number of samples normally dominates the classes with a small number of samples. In this paper, we address this problem of skewness by transforming imbalanced corpora into balanced corpora through application of a clustering algorithm class wise. Subsequent to partitioning of a large class into a number of smaller sized subclasses, we also recommend, to have a compact representation of text documents by the use of interval valued features. The compact representation not only supports achieving reduction in storage, but also in efficient way of classification through a simple symbolic classifier [12]. Nevertheless, to overcome the curse of dimensionality, we adapt a novel representation scheme proposed in [14,18] which reduces the dimension of the vector space into the number of classes present in the collection.

Overall organization of the paper is as follows. In Sect. 2 we present brief summary of existing works. The proposed model is presented in Sect. 3. The experimental results are discussed in Sect. 4 followed by conclusions in Sect. 5.

2   Related Works

From the literature we can understand that, the effort to design systems for automatic text categorization has the history of more than two decades [1,17]. Machine learning based TC systems carry the following general structure. All the training documents are preprocessed using stemming, pruning, stopwords removal to retain only content terms. Then a matrix representation to the entire training data is given using vector space model which uses the bag of words (terms) [20,29]. The dimension of such a matrix will be very high even for a dataset of reasonable size which makes the learning algorithms less effective. Hence, dimensionality reduction has been widely explored on text data as a mandatory step in the design of TC to increase the classification performance in addition to reduction in the dimension [15].

Most of the works in literature of TC have used either feature selection through ranking or feature extraction through transformation as the means of dimensionality reduction. A number of works can be traced in recent years addressing the problem of text classification through feature selection. Feature selection algorithms such as chi-square, information gain, and mutual information [38] though seem to be powerful techniques for text data, a number of novel feature selection algorithms based on genetic algorithm [5,10], ant colony optimization [7,21,22,34], Bayesian principle [8,9,19,30,39], clustering of features [4], global information gain [32], adaptive keyword [33], global ranking [24,25] are proposed.

On the other hand, a classifier is trained and evaluated with a small set of features obtained after dimensionality reduction [31]. Thus, it is a very long and time consuming process. However, many applications do not provide such a huge processing capability but still expect the process of classification to be very quick and effective. For such type of applications, it is essential to design a simple yet effective TC system which can predict the probable class of a test document quickly.

It shall be observed from the literature survey, that the existing works are being generic in nature, perform well on balanced text corpora, and are not that effective for skewed/imbalanced text corpora. Hence here in this work, our objective is to convert an imbalanced text corpus into a balanced one through clustering of text documents classwise and then giving it a compact representation.

3 Proposed Method

The proposed model has two major stages learning and classification.

3.1 Learning

The learning stage has 3 different stages; (i) representation of the text documents in lower dimensional space [14,18] (ii) clustering, where the documents of large sized classes are clustered into sub groups to overcome the problem of skewness, and (iii) compact representation of documents, where a cluster of documents is given a single vector of interval valued feature representation.

Representation of the Text Documents in Lower Dimensional Space. In this section, we present the representation scheme adapted for the text documents. We have intentionally kept this description as a separate section so that the reader should clearly understand that we do not represent the documents using conventional vector space model (VSM) using the bag of words (BoW) constructed for the entire collection. This is due to the fact that, VSM leads to a very high dimensional sparse matrix which is not effective if directly used in computations and hence dimensionality reduction has to be applied through either feature selection or transformation [31]. To alleviate this problem, [18] have proposed an effective text representation scheme which can reduce the dimension of the documents equal to the number of classes at the time of representation itself. In addition to this, [14] have proposed a novel term-weighting scheme called Term_class Relevance Measure (TCR) to be used with the representation scheme of [18] for achieving better performance. Hence, we adapt the representation from [18] with term weighting scheme of [14]. A brief overview of the representation and weighting scheme is presented in Fig. 1.

Consider a huge collection of text documents say 'N' in number due to 'K' different semantically meaningful categories $C_1, C_2, ..., C_K$. Each document is first preprocessed using stemming and stop word removal to end up with a collection of content terms. In the representation provided by [18], initially, a matrix F of size MXK is created for every document in the collection; where, M is the number of terms assumed to be available in the document as shown in Fig. 1. Then, every entry $F(j, i)$ of the matrix denotes weight of t_j with respect to C_i which is computed using TCR measure as follows [14].

Terms in d	C_1	C_2	...	C_K
t_1	$W(t_1,C_1)$	$W(t_1,C_1)$	...	$W(t_1,C_K)$
t_2	$W(t_2,C_1)$	$W(t_2,C_2)$	...	$W(t_2,C_K)$
$\vdots$	$\vdots$	$\vdots$	$\vdots$	$\vdots$
t_M	$W(t_M,C_1)$	$W(t_M,C_2)$	...	$W(t_M,C_K)$
Feature Vector	$\dfrac{\sum W(t_1,C_1)}{M}$	$\dfrac{\sum W(t_1,C_2)}{M}$	...	$\dfrac{\sum W(t_1,C_K)}{M}$

Fig. 1. Representation scheme for a document d

TCR is defined as the ability of a term t_i in classifying a document D as a member of a class C_j as follows.

$$TCR(t_i, C_j) = c \times Class\_TermWeight(t_i, C_j) \times Class\_TermDensity(t_i, C_j)$$

where c is the proportionality constant defined as the weight of the class C_j, Class_TermWeight and Class_TermDensity are respectively the weight and density of t_i with respect to the class C_j which are computed using the below equations respectively.

$$ClassWeight(C_j) = \frac{\#Documents\ in\ C_j}{\#Documents\ in\ Training\ Set}$$

$$Class_TermWeight(t_i, C_j) = \frac{\#Document\ in\ C_j\ containing\ t_i}{\#Documents\ in\ the\ training\ set\ containing\ t_i}$$

$$Class_TermDensity(t_i, C_j) = \frac{\#occurrences\ of\ t_i\ in\ C_j}{\#occurrences\ of\ t_i\ in\ the\ training\ collection}$$

Then, a feature vector f of dimension K is created as a representative for the document where $f(i)$ is the average of the relevancies of all its terms to C_i from F. The main advantage of this representation is that, a document with any number of terms is represented with a feature vector of dimension equal to the number of classes in the population and which is negligibly small in contrast to the feature vector that is created in any other VSM. Therefore, a great amount of dimensionality reduction is achieved at the time of representation itself without the application of any dimensionality reduction technique.

Clustering. Availability of balanced text corpora plays a crucial role in the success of any text classification system. This is due to the fact that during the process of training a classifier, the classes with a more number of samples will dominate generally the other classes with a less number of training samples. One solution to handle the class imbalance problem is to convert the corpus into a balanced one. It is true in most of the cases of text classification problems that the variation within a class will increase with the increase in the size of the class.

Hence, we perform clustering of documents within each class to convert the class into a collection of dense groups, subclasses. In the process, we also ensure that the sizes of clusters are more or less same.

Given a collection of N labeled documents belonging to K classes say, $C_1, C_2, ..., C_K$ where i^{th} class C_i contains N_i number of documents each is represented by K features as described in Sect. 3.1. Let $D_i = D_{i1}, D_{i2}, ..., D_{Ni}$ be the set of documents of the class C_i. A class C_i with N_i number of documents is grouped into Q_i number of dense clusters using hierarchical clustering which is denoted by

$$Cl^i = \{cl_1^i, cl_2^i, ..., cl_{q_i}^i\}.$$

The number of clusters is automatically decided using the inconsistency coefficient. The inconsistency coefficient i_c characterizes each link in a cluster tree by comparing its height with the average height of other links at the same level of the hierarchy. The higher the value of this coefficient, the less similar the objects connected by the link. The value inconsistency coefficient i_c is empirically decided for each class.

Let $Q_1, Q_2, ..., Q_K$ respectively be the number of clusters obtained for the K different classes and let $Q = \sum Q_i \, \forall i \in [1, ..., K]$ be the total number of clusters. For imbalanced datasets the number of clusters obtained will vary from one class to the other class based on the size and variations within a class. Then, a cluster itself can be treated as an independent class and hence the original K-class classification problem on an imbalanced corpus has thus become a Q-class classification problem on a balanced corpus.

Compact Representation. Recently, the concept of symbolic data analysis has gained much attention by the community of researchers since it has proven its effectiveness and simplicity in designing solutions for many pattern recognition problems [13,23,26]. We can also trace a couple of attempts for text classification using the concepts of symbolic representation and classification [11,16,28]. In this section, we propose to use interval valued type symbolic data to effectively capture the variations within a cluster of text documents. Another advantage of having such a representation is its simplicity in classifying an unknown document. Given a cluster cl_j^i of a class C_i with N_j^i number of documents $D^{ij} = \{D_1^{ij}, D_2^{ij}, ..., D_{n_j^i}^{ij}\}$ it is represented by an interval valued symbolic representative vector R_{ij} as follows. Let every document is represented by a feature vector of dimension K given by $\{f_1, f_2, ..., f_K\}$. Then, with respect to every feature f_s, the documents of the cluster are aggregated in the form of an interval $[\mu^s - \sigma^s, \mu^s + \sigma^s]$ where, μ^s and σ^s are respectively the mean and standard deviation of the values of t_s in the cluster. Hence, R_{ij} contains K intervals corresponding to the K features as,

$$R^{ij} = \{R_1^{ij}, R_2^{ij}, ...R_K^{ij}\}$$

where, $R_s^{ij} = [\mu^s - \sigma^s, \mu^s + \sigma^s]$ is the interval formed for the sth feature of the jth cluster cl_j^i of the ith class C_i. This process of creation of interval valued symbolic representative is applied on all the Q clusters individually to obtain Q interval representative vector $\{R^{11}, R^{12}, R^{1Q_1}, R^{21}, R^{22}, R^{2Q_2}, ..., R^{K1}, R^{K2}, R^{KQ_K}\}$ which are then stored in the knowledgebase for the purpose of classification.

3.2 Classification

Given an unlabeled text document D_q its class label is predicted by comparing it with all the representative vectors present in the knowledgebase. Initially, D_q is converted and represented as a feature vector $\{f_1^q, f_2^q, ..., f_K^q\}$, of dimension K as explained in Sect. 3.1. Then the similarity between the crisp vector D_q and an interval based representative vector R is computed using the similarity measure proposed by [12] as follows.

$$SIM(D_q, R) = \frac{1}{K} \sum_{s=1}^{K} D_q^s, R_s$$

where,

$$SIM(D_q^z, R_z) = \begin{cases} 1 & \text{if } (\mu^z - \sigma^z) \le f_z^q \le (\mu^z + \sigma^z) \\ \max\left[\dfrac{1}{1+abs((\mu^z - \sigma^z) - f_z^q)}, \dfrac{1}{1+abs((\mu^z + \sigma^z) - f_z^q)}\right] & \text{otherwise} \end{cases}$$

Similarly, the similarity of D_q with all the Q representative vectors present in the knowledgebase is computed. The class of the cluster clm which gets highest similarity with D_q is decided as the class of D_q as shown in equation below.

$$ClassLabel(D_q) = Class(Argmax_{i,j}(max(SIM(D_q, R^{ij}))))$$

where, R^{ij} is the representative of the jth cluster of the ith class.

4   Experimentation and Results

We have conducted a series of experiments to validate the applicability and efficiency of the proposed model. We have also implemented the Support Vector Machines (SVM) based classification to demonstrate the superiority of the proposed model. The performance of the proposed model has been evaluated using Precision, Recall and F-measure in terms of both micro and macro averaging. The following sections describe details about the skewed datasets considered for experimentation and the results obtained.

4.1   Text Corpora

To assess the performance of the proposed model, we have conducted experiments on two commonly used benchmarking skewed text corpora viz., Reuters-21578 and TDT2. The Reuters corpus is a collection of 21578 news articles taken from Reuters newswire (available at http://www.daviddlewis.com/resources/testcollections/reuters21578/). The total number of topics was 135 where a document may belong to multiple classes. In our experiments we use documents from top 10 categories. There are totally 7285 documents distributed into different classes with a large degree of skew as shown in the Fig. 1. The TDT2 corpus (Nist Topic Detection and Tracking corpus) consists of data collected during the first half of 1998 and taken from 6 sources including 2 newswires (APW, NYT), 2 radio programs (VOA, PRI) and 2 television programs (CNN, ABC). It consists of 11201 on-topic documents which are classified into 96 semantic categories. In our experiments we have chosen top 20 categories based on the number of documents to arrive at a subset of 8741 documents distributed with high degree of skew for different classes as shown in Fig. 2. In our experiments, we vary the training set from 10 to 80 percent to verify the performance of the classifier.

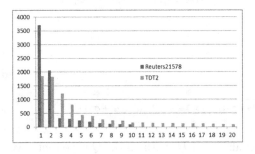

Fig. 2. Distribution of samples in Reuters-21578 and TDT2 corpora

4.2   Results and Discussion

In this section, we present the details of the results obtained by the proposed method and compare it with that of the conventional SVM based classification on Retuers-21578 and TDT2 text corpora. The experiments have been conducted by varying the percentage of training from 10 to 80 percent with 5 random trials each. For every set of training samples, performance is studied in terms of precision, recall and F-measures using both micro and macro averaging.

Figures 3 and 4 show the performance of the proposed method in comparison with SVM classifier on Reuters-21578 corpus using macro and micro averaged F measures respectively. It can be observed from the Figs. 3 and 4 that the proposed method performed well on each training collection than the SVM based classification. Similar study is made on the TDT2 corpus and the results have been shown in Figs. 5 and 6 for macro averaged and micro averaged F-measures respectively. The similar observation can be made for the TDT2 corpus also as the performance of the proposed method is better when compared to that of the SVM based method.

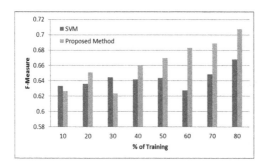

Fig. 3. Comparison of performances of the proposed model and SVM based model for Reuters-21578 dataset using macro averaged F-measure

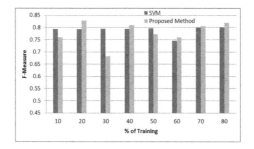

Fig. 4. Comparison of performances of the proposed model and SVM based model for Reuters-21578 dataset using micro averaged F-measure

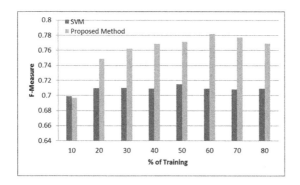

Fig. 5. Comparison of performances of the proposed model and SVM based model for TDT2 dataset using macro averaged F-measure

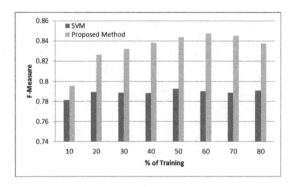

Fig. 6. Comparison of performances of the proposed model and SVM based model for TDT2 dataset using micro averaged F-measure

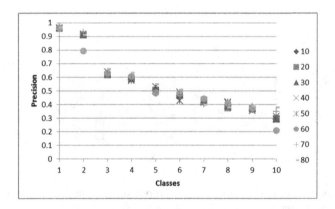

Fig. 7. Classwise Precision obtained by SVM classifier on Reuters-21578 corpus under varying percentage of training samples

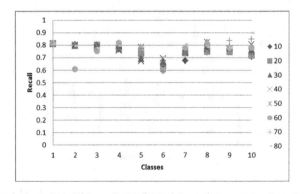

Fig. 8. Classwise Recall obtained by SVM classifier on Reuters-21578 corpus under varying percentage of training samples

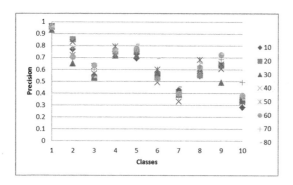

Fig. 9. Classwise Precision obtained by the proposed model on Reuters-21578 corpus under varying percentage of training samples

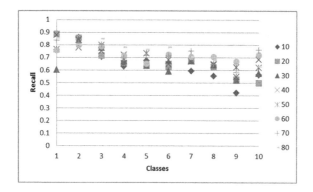

Fig. 10. Classwise Recall obtained by the proposed model on Reuters-21578 corpus under varying percentage of training samples

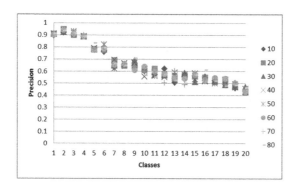

Fig. 11. Classwise Precision obtained by SVM classifier on TDT2 corpus under varying percentage of training samples

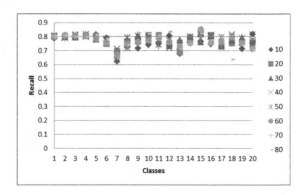

Fig. 12. Classwise Recall obtained by SVM classifier on TDT2 corpus under varying percentage of training samples

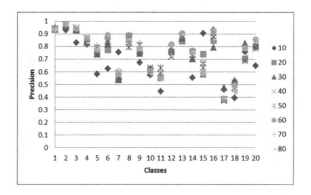

Fig. 13. Classwise Precision obtained by the proposed model on TDT2 corpus under varying percentage of training samples

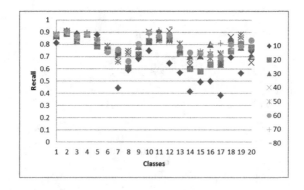

Fig. 14. Classwise Recall obtained by the proposed model on TDT2 corpus under varying percentage of training samples

Further, we have also studied the classwise performance of the proposed method along with SVM classifier based method in terms of precision and recall. This helps in demonstrating the performance of the proposed method with respect to larger and smaller classes and to compare it with that of the SVM classifier. Figures 7 and 9 show the performance in terms of precision respectively for SVM classifier and the proposed method, whereas, Figs. 8 and 10 show the respective performances in terms of recall values on Reuters-21578 corpus. Similarly, Figs. 11 and 13 show the performance in terms of precision respectively for SVM classifier and the proposed method whereas Figs. 12 and 14 show the respective performances in terms of recall values on TDT2 corpus. Overall observations made from all the figures showing classwise performances with the increase in the number of features are as follows. For SVM based classification, the value of precision has dropped suddenly for small classes and has reached maximum for large classes whereas, the value of recall has seen an increase for small classes and sudden drop for large classes. On contrary to this, the proposed method has initially seen increase in the performance till 500 features followed by a steady performance thereafter both in terms of precision as well as Recall and hence the overall performance in terms of F-measure is improved significantly.

Table 1. The best performance of the proposed method on Reuters-21578 and TDT2 corpora in terms of Macro-F and Macro-F

Text corpus	No. of training samples	Maximum no. of clusters formed	Macro-F	Micro-F
Reuters-21578	5828	636	70.75	82.03
TDT2	7867	582	76.92	83.74

Table 2. Comparison of the results of the proposed method with the state of the art techniques on Reuters 21578

Author and year	Method	Macro-F (no. of features)	Micro-F (no. of features)
Uysal (2016)	IG + IGFSS + SVM	67.53 (500)	86.473 (300)
Uysal and Gunal (2012)	DFS + SVM	66.55 (200)	86.33 (500)
Pinheiro et al. (2015)	MFD + BNS	64 (254)	81.51 (254)
Pinheiro et al. (2012)	ALOFT + MOR	62.13 (135)	80.47 (135)
Rehman et al. (2015)	DFS, RDC + SVM	63.47 (500)	81.98 (500)
Aghdam et al. (2009)	ACO	78.42 (>=3600)	89.08 (>=3600)
Proposed method	**Reduced representation + clustering + symbolic representation**	**70.75 (10)**	**82.03 (10)**

Table 1 shows the best performance obtained by the proposed method for both Reuters-21578 and TDT2 corpora in terms of macro and micro F-measures. Also, we have shown the maximum number of clusters formed with respect to each corpus. It can be observed that the number of clusters formed is very less when compared to the total number of training samples considered for training. In Table 2, we also compare the results of the proposed method with that of the state of the art methods. It can be seen from Table 2 that the proposed method outperforms most of the contemporary methods in addition to being very effective since it works with only K features (where K is the number of classes present in the corpus) whereas the other methods need at least few hundreds of features to achieve better performance.

5   Conclusions

In this work, a method of converting an imbalanced text corpus into a balanced one is presented by exploiting the notion of data clustering. The problem due to skewness of a corpus is addressed. For the purpose of overcoming the curse of dimensionality, we just have adopted our previous model which accomplishes the reduction while representation of documents itself. A method of compact representation of text data by the use of interval-valued data representation is presented in a feature space of dimension equal to the number of classes. It has been experimentally argued that the proposed model is effective in addition to being simple. A comparative analysis indicates that the proposed model outperforms several other existing contemporary models. The finding of this work is that splitting of a larger class of text documents into several smaller subclasses during training would enhance the performance of a classifier.

Acknowledgements. The second author of this paper acknowledges the financial support rendered by the University of Mysore under UPE grants for the High Performance Computing laboratory. The first and fourth authors of this paper acknowledge the financial support rendered by Pillar4 Company, Bangalore.

References

1. Aggarwal, C.C., Zhai, C.X.: Mining Text Data. Springer, New York (2012). ISBN 978-1-4614-3222-7
2. Aghdam, M.H., Aghaee, N.G., Basiri, M.E.: Text feature selection using ant colony optimization. Expert Syst. Appl. **36**(2–3), 6843–6853 (2009)
3. Azam, N., Yao, J.: Comparison of term frequency and document frequency based feature selection metrics in text categorization. Expert Syst. Appl. **39**, 4760–4768 (2012)
4. Bharti, K.K., Singh, P.K.: Hybrid dimension reduction by integrating feature selection with feature extraction method for text clustering. Expert Syst. Appl. **42**, 3105–3114 (2015)
5. Bharti, K.K., Singh, P.K.: Opposition chaotic fitness mutation based adaptive inertia weight BPSO for feature selection in text clustering. Appl. Soft Comput. **43**, 20–34 (2016)

6. Corrêa, G.N., Marcacini, R.M., Hruschka, E.R., Rezende, S.O.: Interactive textual feature selection for consensus clustering. Pattern Recogn. Lett. **52**, 25–31 (2015)
7. Dadaneh, B.Z., Markid, H.Y., Zakerolhosseini, A.: Unsupervised probabilistic feature selection using ant colony optimization. Expert Syst. Appl. **53**, 27–42 (2016)
8. Feng, G., Guo, J., Jing, B.Y., Hao, L.: A Bayesian feature selection paradigm for text classification. Inf. Process. Manage. **48**, 283–302 (2012)
9. Fenga, G., Guoa, J., Jing, B.Y., Sunb, T.: Feature subset selection using naive Bayes for text classification. Pattern Recogn. Lett. **65**, 109–115 (2015)
10. Ghareb, A.S., Bakar, A.A., Hamdan, A.R.: Hybrid feature selection based on enhanced genetic algorithm for text categorization. Expert Syst. Appl. **49**, 31–47 (2016)
11. Guru, D.S., Harish, B.S., Manjunath, S.: Symbolic representation of text documents. In: Proceedings of the Third Annual ACM Bangalore Conference (COMPUTE 2010). ACM, New York (2010). Article 18, 4 pages
12. Guru, D.S., Nagendraswamy, H.S.: Symbolic representation of two-dimensional shapes. Pattern Recogn. Lett. **28**, 144–155 (2006)
13. Guru, D.S., Prakash, H.N.: Online signature verification and recognition: an approach based on symbolic representation. IEEE TPAMI **31**(6), 1059–1073 (2009)
14. Guru, D.S., Suhil, M.: A Novel Term-Class relevance measure for text categorization. Procedia Comput. Sci. **45**, 13–22 (2015)
15. Guyon, I., Elisseeff, A.: An introduction to variable and feature selection. JMLR **3**, 1157–1182 (2003)
16. Harish, B.S., Guru, D.S., Manjunath, S.: A brief review. IJCA, Special Issue on RTIPPR **2**, 110–119 (2010)
17. Hotho, A., Nurnberger, A., Paab, G.: A brief survey of text mining. J. Comput. Linguist. Lang. Technol. **20**, 19–62 (2005)
18. Isa, D., Lee, L.H., Kallimani, V.P., Rajkumar, R.: Text document preprocessing with the Bayes formula for classification using the support vector machine. IEEE TKDE **20**, 1264–1272 (2008)
19. Jiang, L., Li, C., Wang, S., Zhang, L.: Deep feature weighting for naive Bayes and its application to text classification. Eng. Appl. Artif. Intell. **52**, 26–39 (2016)
20. Li, Y.H., Jain, A.K.: Classification of text documents. Comput. J. **41**(8), 537–546 (1998)
21. Meena, M.J., Chandran, K.R., Karthik, A., Samuel, A.V.: An enhanced ACO algorithm to select features for text categorization and its parallelization. Expert Syst. Appl. **39**, 5861–5871 (2012)
22. Moradi, P., Gholampour, M.: A hybrid particle swarm optimization for feature subset selection by integrating a novel local search strategy. Appl. Soft Comput. **43**, 117–130 (2016)
23. Nagendraswamy, H.S., Guru, D.S.: A new method of representing and matching two dimensional shapes. Int. J. Image Graph. **7**(2), 377–405 (2007)
24. Pinheiro, R.H.W., Cavalcanti, G.D.C., Ren, T.I.: Data-driven global-ranking local feature selection methods for text categorization. Expert Syst. Appl. **42**, 1941–1949 (2015)
25. Pinheiro, R.H.W., Cavalcanti, G.D.C., Correa, R.F., Ren, T.I.: A global-ranking local feature selection method for text categorization. Expert Syst. Appl. **39**, 12851–12857 (2012)
26. Punitha, P., Guru, D.S.: Symbolic image indexing and retrieval by spatial similarity: an approach based on B-tree. Pattern Recogn. **41**(6), 2068–2085 (2008)
27. Rehman, A., et al.: Relative discrimination criterion - a novel feature ranking method for text data. Expert Syst. Appl. **42**, 3670–3681 (2015)

28. Revanasidappa, M.B., Harish, B.S., Manjunath, S.: Document classification using symbolic classifiers. In: International Conference on Contemporary Computing and Informatics (IC3I), pp. 299–303 (2014)
29. Rigutini, L.: Machine learning techniques. Ph.D. thesis, University of Siena
30. Sarkar, S.D., Goswami, S., Agarwal, A., Aktar, J.: A Novel Feature Selection Technique for Text Classification Using Naive Bayes, pp. 1–10. Hindawi Publishing Corporation (2014)
31. Sebastiani, F.: Machine learning in automated text categorization. ACM Comput. Surv. **34**(1), 1–47 (2002)
32. Shang, C., Li, M., Feng, S., Jiang, Q., Fan, J.: Feature selection via maximizing global information gain for text classification. Knowl. Based Syst. **54**, 298–309 (2013)
33. Tasci, S., Gungor, T.: Comparison of text feature selection policies and using an adaptive framework. Expert Syst. Appl. **40**, 4871–4886 (2013)
34. Uysal, A.K.: An improved global feature selection scheme for text classification. Expert Syst. Appl. **43**, 82–92 (2016)
35. Uysal, A.K., Gunal, S.: A novel probabilistic feature selection method for text classification. Knowl. Based Syst. **36**, 226–235 (2012)
36. Wang, D., Zhang, H., Li, R., Lv, W., Wang, D.: t-Test feature selection approach based on term frequency for text categorization. Pattern Recogn. Lett. **45**, 1–10 (2014)
37. Yang, J., Liu, Y., Zhu, X., Liu, Z., Zhang, X.: A new feature selection based on comprehensive measurement both in inter-category and intra-category for text categorization. Inf. Process. Manage. **48**, 741–754 (2012)
38. Yang, Y., Pedersen, J.O.: A comparative study on feature selection in text categorization. In: Proceedings of the 14th International Conference on Machine Learning, vol. 97, pp. 412–420 (1997)
39. Zhang, L., Jiang, L., Li, C., Kong, G.: Two feature weighting approaches for naive Bayes text classifiers. Knowl. Based Syst. **100**, 137–144 (2016)
40. Zong, W., Wu, F., Chu, L.K., Sculli, D.: A discriminative and semantic feature selection method for text categorization. Int. J. Prod. Econ. **165**, 215–222 (2015)

Semi-supervised Text Categorization
Using Recursive K-means Clustering

Harsha S. Gowda, Mahamad Suhil$^{(\boxtimes)}$, D.S. Guru, and Lavanya Narayana Raju

Department of Studies in Computer Science, University of Mysore, Mysore, India
harshasgmysore@gmail.com, mahamad45@yahoo.co.in,
dsg@compsci.uni-mysore.ac.in, swaralavz@gmail.com

Abstract. In this paper, we present a semi-supervised learning algorithm for classification of text documents. A method of labeling unlabeled
text documents is presented. The presented method is based on the principle of divide and conquer strategy. It uses recursive K-means algorithm
for partitioning both labeled and unlabeled data collection. The K-means
algorithm is applied recursively on each partition till a desired level partition is achieved such that each partition contains labeled documents
of a single class. Once the desired clusters are obtained, the respective
cluster centroids are considered as representatives of the clusters and the
nearest neighbor rule is used for classifying an unknown text document.
Series of experiments have been conducted to bring out the superiority of the proposed model over other recent state of the art models on
20Newsgroups dataset.

Keywords: Unlabeled text documents · Recursive K-means algorithm ·
Semi-supervised learning · Text categorization

1 Introduction

The amount of text content available over the web is so abundant that anybody
can get information related to any topic. But, the performance of retrieval systems is still far below the level of expectation. One of the major reasons for this
is the amount of labeled text available is negligibly small when compared to that
of the unlabeled text. Thus, automatic text categorization has received a very
high demand by many applications to well organize a huge collection of text
content in hand. To this end, many machine learning based algorithms are being
developed to best make use of the unlabeled text in addition to the available
labeled text to draw clear boundaries between different classes of documents
present in the corpus [8,10,14]. Hence, further categorization of unlabeled samples can be done effectively. The process of using unlabeled samples along with
a small set of labeled samples to better understand the class structure is known
as semi-supervised clustering [15].

Generally there are two approaches to semi-supervised learning; one is a similarity based approach and the other one is a search based approach. In similarity

© Springer Nature Singapore Pte Ltd. 2017
K.C. Santosh et al. (Eds.): RTIP2R 2016, CCIS 709, pp. 217–227, 2017.
DOI: 10.1007/978-981-10-4859-3_20

based approach an existing clustering algorithm that uses a similarity matric is employed, while in search based approach, the clustering algorithm itself is modified so that the user provided labels are used to bias the search for an appropriate partition. A detailed comparative analysis on these two approaches can be found in [2]. Further, readers can find a review on semi supervised clustering methods for more details [1].

A method based on hierarchical clustering approach is proposed by [13] where labeled and unlabeled texts are respectively used for capturing silhouettes and adapting centroids of text clusters. A simple semi-supervised extension of multinomial Naive Bayes has been proposed [10]. This model improves the results when unlabeled data are added. The notion of weakly related unlabeled data is introduced in [12]. The strength of this model is that it works even on a small training pool. A model based on combination of expectation maximization and a Naive Bayes classifier is introduced by [8]. This algorithm trains a classifier using available label documents first and subsequently labels the unlabeled documents probabilistically. A variant of expectation maximization by integrating Bayesian regression is also proposed [14]. Based on co-clustering concept a fuzzy semi supervised model can also be traced in literature [11].

Based on the above literature survey we learnt that the notion of semi-supervised learning is receiving greater attention by the researchers in recent years. It is also noted that consideration of unlabeled data at the time of learning along with labeled data has a tendency of improving the results. In this direction, here in this work, we made a successful attempt for text categorization through semi-supervised learning and as a result of it, we propose a search based approach. The proposed approach is based on a partitional clustering where in, the K-means algorithm is tuned up to be a recursive algorithm. The proposed model works based on divide and conquer strategy. Initially K-means clustering algorithm is used to partition the sample space into as many as the number of classes and subsequently, on each obtained cluster we employ K-means algorithm recursively till the partitions meet a pre-defined criterion.

Rest of the paper is organized as follows: Sect. 2 presents the detailed description of the proposed model for labeling of unlabeled samples through recursive semi-supervised K-means clustering. In Sect. 3, the representation of documents, experimental setup including datasets and evaluation measures have been presented. Section 4 provides the results and analysis of the proposed model on different datasets. Finally Sect. 5 presents the conclusion of the paper followed by references.

2   Proposed Method

The proposed model has two major stages; learning, through recursive K-means clustering and classification, to label a given unknown text document.

2.1 Recursive K-means Clustering

Let be a collection of N text documents where, be the set of N_1 labeled documents and be the set of N_2 unlabeled documents (where, $N_1 \ll N_2$ and $N_1 + N_2 = N$). Let be the set of K classes present in. In semi-supervised clustering, the task is to label the documents in with one of the K different class labels using documents of. For this purpose, we initially consider the labeled documents along with a subset of with number of randomly chosen documents say to form a training collection with N_{tr} $(N_1 + N_3)$ documents. In the next subsection, a recursive K-means clustering algorithm is proposed to cluster the documents in into many partitions consisting of both unlabeled and labeled documents such that each partition should contain labeled samples from a single class.

Initially K-means clustering is applied on with $K = K$ (the number of classes) since has labeled samples of all K classes. If a partition P_i has labeled samples from more than one class then K-means is applied again with K being the number of distinct classes present in P_i. This process is applied recursively on each sub partition till the entire training collection is partitioned into many small clusters say M in number and represented by such that each cluster contains labeled samples from strictly a single class. So, this recursive K-means is a based on the divide and conquer strategy. The major difference is that, divide and conquer normally partitions the problem into predefined number sub-problems at each stage, whereas, the proposed recursive K-means decides the number of sub-problems dynamically based on the number of unique classes present in each cluster. Hence, we may end up with multiple clusters for each class depending on the variations present within the class. Let, where, be the class labels of each cluster in the $FinalClusters$ set. Figure 1 shows a simple illustration of the recursive K-means clustering on a 4 class problem.

Further, every unlabeled sample of D^T is labeled by the class label of its respective cluster as their final labels. The centroids of respective clusters say are computed as mean of each cluster. A knowledge base of $FinalClusters$, $ClusterCentroids$ and $ClusterLabels$ is then created for the purpose of labeling of unlabeled samples in D^U during classification. The proposed recursive K-means clustering for semi-supervised learning is detailed in Algorithm 1.

Input to the recursive K-means algorithm is a collection of labeled and unlabeled samples, D^T. In Initialization part, the number of unique labels present in D^T is set to K, and K-means clustering is performed by randomly choosing K samples, each from a different class, as initial seeds to arrive at K disjoint clusters of the data say Partition. The process of recursive K-means clustering is applied to each cluster in Partition as explained below.

For every cluster P_i in Partition, the unique class labels are computed. The label of a class with maximum labeled samples out of all the labeled samples in Pi is assigned as the $ClassLabel$ of P_i. If P_i has labeled samples from two or more classes and if the ratio of the number of samples from a class other

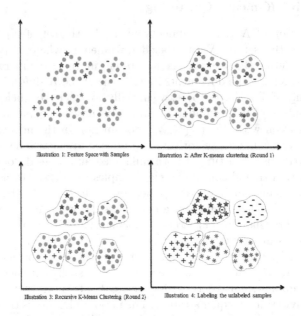

Fig. 1. Illustration of the proposed recursive K-means clustering for semi-supervised learning

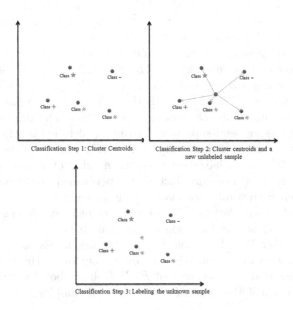

Fig. 2. Labeling of an unlabeled sample

than class of P_i to the number of samples from the class of P_i is greater than a predefined threshold 'Th'; then P_i is treated as a new collection of labeled and unlabeled samples and hence the Algorithm 1 is re-invoked with K being the number of unique class labels in P_i. The threshold Th is included to eliminate the outliers, which is set empirically. The clusters which do not undergo this recursive clustering are added to the *FinalClusters*.

Once, all the clusters in Partition are processed by the proposed recursive K-means clustering, all the unlabeled sample of each cluster in *FinalClusters* are assigned by the *ClassLabel* of the respective cluster.

Algorithm 1. Recursive K-Means for Semi-Supervised Learning: RKMSSL
Input:

    $D^T = \{D^L, \overline{D}^U\}$: A collection of labeled and unlabeled samples.

Output:

    FinalClusters : a collection of labeled clusters
    Labels for the unlabeled samples in D^T

Method

(i).   Initialization

Step 1.   K ← Number of unique labels in D^T (number of classes)

Step 2.   InitialSeeds ← randomly chosen K samples (one from each unique class present in D^T)

Step 3.   SeedLabels ← cluster indices of IntialSeeds

(ii).   Initial K-means clustering

Step 4.   Apply K-means on D^T with IntialSeeds as initial cluster centroids to get K clusters say, Partition

(iii).   Recursive K-means clustering

Step 5.   For every cluster P_i in Partition

Step 6. NCP_i ← Number of unique class labels in P_i and
      LSP_i ← Number of labeled samples of each unique class in P_i

Step 7.   If $NCP_i > 1$ then,

Step 8.   ClassLabel(P_i) ← Label (max (LSP_i))

Step 9.   For each class j other than in ClassLabel(P_i)

Step 10. $RelativePercentage_j$ ← (LSP_i [j] / LSP_i [ClassLabel(P_i)])*100

Step 11.   If $RelativePercentage_j$ > greater than Th then,

Step 12.   RKMSSL (P_i)

Step 13.   Goto step 15;
       end

    End for

    Add P_i to the FinalClusters set

Step 14.   End if

(iv)   Labeling

Step 15.   For every unlabeled document d_u in cluster P_i

Step 16.   Label(d_u) ← ClassLabel(P_i)

Step 17.   End for

Step 18. End for

Algorithm Ends

2.2 Classification

Given a collection of unlabeled samples D^U, they are classified into one of the K classes by comparing with the centroids of the clusters formed in the learning stage using Algorithm 2. Initially, the distance of an unlabeled sample d_u in D^U to the centroids of all the clusters in $FinalClusters$ is computed. Then d_u is labeled by the label of a cluster which has the least distance to it or simply the nearest neighbor classifier is employed on the cluster centroids to label an unknown document. An illustration of labeling a given unlabeled sample is shown in Fig. 2.

Algorithm 2. Classification

Input:

        FinalClusters : a collection of labeled clusters

        ClusterLabels: class labels of each cluster in FinalCluster

        D^U: Collection of unlabeled samples

Output:

        ComputedLabels: Labels for the unlabeled samples in D^U

Method:

Step 1.   for every document d_u in D^U

Step 2.   for every cluster F_c in FinalClusters

Step 3. $Dist(d_u, F_c) = distance(d_u, Centroid(F_c))$

Step 4.   End for

Step 5. $ComputedLabel(d_u) = ClusterLabels(argmin(Dist))$

Step 6.   End for

3 Experimental Setup

3.1 Representation of Documents in Lower Dimensional Space

In this section, we present the representation scheme followed for the text documents. The importance of this section is that, it has to be brought into the notice of the reader that we do not represent the documents using conventional vector space model (VSM) using the bag of words (BoW) constructed for the entire collection. This is due to the fact that, VSM leads to a very high dimensional sparse matrix which is not effective if directly used in computations and hence dimensionality reduction has to be applied [9]. To alleviate this problem, [6] have proposed an effective text representation scheme which can reduce the dimension of the documents equal to the number of classes at the time of representation itself. Recently, we can track a couple of attempts in the literature which have proven the effectiveness of this representation in addition to its time efficiency [4,5]. Besides, [3] have proposed a novel term-weighting scheme called Term_class Relevance Measure (TCR) to be used with the representation scheme of [6] for achieving better performance. Hence, we adapt the representation from [6] with term weighting scheme of [3].

3.2   Dataset and Evaluation Measures

To validate the applicability and efficiency of the proposed method, we conducted a series of experiments on 20Newsgroups dataset. Since we are using supervised datasets to evaluate the performance of the proposed method, we use the well-known information retrieval measures to quantize the results obtained viz., Precision (P), Recall (R) and F-measures (F) in both micro and macro averaging [7]. The original 20Newsgroups collection is nearly balanced corpus consists of 18846 documents from 20 different news topics. In our experiments we have considered the documents from top 10 categories of the 20Newsgroups to form a dataset of 9645 text documents. We divided the entire dataset into two halves where the first half was used for model building and the second half is used for classification which we call respectively as 'training set' and 'test set'. The first half is again divided into two subsets; one is a very small subset of labeled samples and the other one is a large subset of unlabeled. We varied the ratio of labeled and unlabeled from 1:49 to 20:30 in steps of 1 and hence 20 different cases were experimented. For each case, 20 different random trials were considered to study the consistency of the results obtained by the proposed method on the test set.

4   Results and Analysis

In this section, we present the results and analysis of the various experiments conducted on 20Newgroups dataset to evaluate the proposed method. Figure 3 shows the performance of the proposed method for varying percentage of labeled samples in terms of classification accuracy. It can be observed from the Fig. 3 that the average accuracy of the proposed method is very high and consistent under varying percentage of labeled samples though it has attained a minimum value for some trails. Figures 4 and 5 show respectively the precision and recall curves of the proposed method for varying percentage of labeled samples in terms of maximum, minimum, average and standard deviations of the 20 random trails conducted. The high average values and the less standard deviation among the values of different trials indicate that the proposed method is consistent in addition to being very efficient except a few cases where the performance has declined to a minimum value. Furthermore, performance in terms of macro and micro averaged F-measure values has also been studied and are respectively shown in Figs. 6 and 7. The similar observation as in precision and recall can also be drawn for macro and micro averaged F-measures. Moreover the similarity in the values of macro and micro averaged F-measures validate the fact that the 20Newsgroups dataset is a balanced corpus.

Besides, a quantitative comparative analysis of the proposed method is also made with one of the recently proposed semi-supervised method [13] which has shown very good performance for text categorization applications. The other reason for the consideration of TESC for comparison is that TESC follows the similar basic principle of arriving at clusters by using unlabeled samples along with a small set of labeled samples. Further the unlabeled samples are labeled in

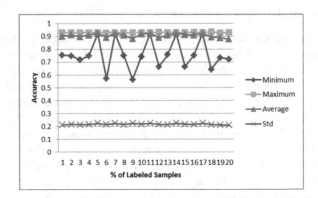

Fig. 3. Accuracy of the proposed method for varying percentage of labeled samples

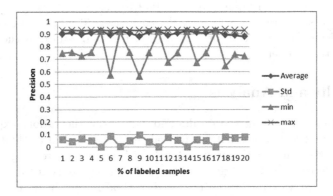

Fig. 4. Macro averaged precision of the proposed method for varying percentage of labeled samples

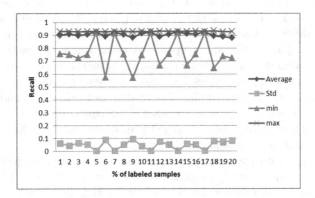

Fig. 5. Macro averaged recall of the proposed method for varying percentage of labeled samples

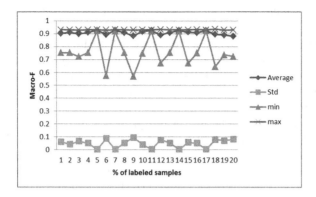

Fig. 6. Macro averaged F-measure of the proposed method for varying percentage of labeled samples

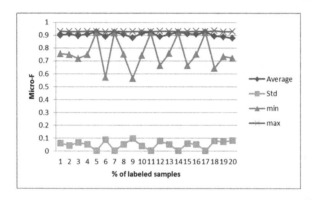

Fig. 7. Micro averaged F-measure of the proposed method for varying percentage of labeled samples

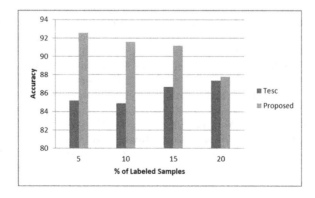

Fig. 8. Comparison of the proposed method with the TESC [13] for varying percentage of labeled samples in terms of accuracy

a similar fashion followed by the proposed method, i.e., a test sample is labeled as a member of a class by comparing it with the centroids of each cluster formed during training process. The major difference lies in the proposed method when compared to TESC is that, they follow an approach very similar to hierarchical clustering to arrive at the clusters whereas, the proposed method proposes a recursive K-means clustering. We conducted the experiments on TESC with four different percentages of labeled samples viz., 5%, 10%, 15% and 20% respectively and are compared with that of the proposed method using accuracy as shown in Fig. 8. It can be clearly observed from the Fig. 8 that, the proposed method outperforms TESC in all the four cases. Another observation is that the proposed method can learn effectively with a small quantity of labeled samples itself whereas TESC requires sufficiently large number of labeled samples to learn the silhouettes of the clusters effectively.

5   Conclusions

A semi-supervised model for classification of text documents is presented. The model works on divide and conquer strategy and uses K-means algorithm recursively. The finding of the work is on adaptation of partitional clustering algorithm for semi-supervised learning of text documents.

Acknowledgements. The second author of this paper acknowledges the financial support rendered by the University of Mysore under UPE grants for the High Performance Computing laboratory. The first and fourth authors of this paper acknowledge the financial support rendered by Pillar4 Company, Bangalore.

References

1. Bair, E.: Semi-supervised clustering methods. Wiley Interdiscip. Rev. Comput. Stat. **5**(5), 349–361 (2013)
2. Basu, S., Bilenko, M., Mooney, R.J.: Comparing and unifying search-based and similarity-based approaches to semi-supervised clustering. In: Proceedings of the ICML-2003 Workshop on the Continuum from Labeled to Unlabeled Data in Machine Learning and Data Mining Systems, pp. 42–49 (2003)
3. Guru, D.S., Suhil, M.: A novel Term_Class relevance measure for text categorization. Procedia Comput. Sci. **45**, 13–22 (2015). Elsevier
4. Guru, D.S., Harish, B.S., Manjunath, S.: Symbolic representation of text documents. In: Proceedings of the Third Annual ACM Bangalore Conference, COMPUTE 2010. ACM, New York (2010). Article 18, 4 pages
5. Harish, B.S., Guru, D.S., Manjunath, S.: Representation and classification of text documents: a brief review. IJCA **2**, 110–119 (2010). Special Issue on RTIPPR
6. Isa, D., Lee, L.H., Kallimani, V.P., RajKumar, R.: Text document preprocessing with the Bayes formula for classification using the support vector machine. IEEE TKDE **20**, 23–31 (2008)
7. Manning, C.D., Raghavan, P., Schutze, H.: Introduction to Information Retrieval. Cambridge University Press, Cambridge (2008)

8. Nigam, K., McCallum, A.K., Thrun, S., Mitchell, T.: Text classification from labeled and unlabeled documents using EM. Mach. Learn. **39**, 103–134 (2013)
9. Sebastiani, F.: Machine learning in automated text categorization. ACM Comput. Surv. **34**(1), 1–47 (2002)
10. Su, J., Shirabad, J.S., Matwin, S.: Large scale text classification using semi-supervised multinomial Navie Bayes. In: Proceedings of the International Conference on Machine Learning (2011)
11. Yan, Y., Chen, L., Tjhi, W.C.: Fuzzy semi-supervised co-clustering for text documents. Fuzzy Sets Syst. **215**, 74–89 (2013)
12. Yang, L., Jin, R., Sukthankar, R.: Semi-supervised learning with weakly-related unlabeled data: towards better text categorization. In: Advances in Neural Information Processing Systems (NIPS). MIT Press, Cambridge (2009)
13. Zhang, W., Tang, X., Yoshida, T.: TESC: An approach to TExt classification using Semi-supervised Clustering. Knowl. Based Syst. **75**, 152–160 (2015)
14. Zhang, W., Yang, Y., Wang, Q.: Using Bayesian regression and EM algorithm with missing handling for software effort prediction. Inf. Softw. Technol. **58**, 58–70 (2015)
15. Zhu, X.: Semi-supervised learning literature survey, Technical Report 1530, University of Wisconsin-Madison (2006)

Class Specific Feature Selection for Interval Valued Data Through Interval K-Means Clustering

D.S. Guru and N. Vinay Kumar[(✉)]

Department of Studies in Computer Science, University of Mysore,
Manasagangotri, Mysore 570 006, India
dsg@compsci.uni-mysore.ac.in, vinaykumar.natraj@gmail.com

Abstract. In this paper, a novel feature selection approach for supervised interval valued features is proposed. The proposed approach takes care of selecting the class specific features through interval K-Means clustering. The kernel of K-Means clustering algorithm is modified to adapt interval valued data. During training, a set of samples corresponding to a class is fed into the interval K-Means clustering algorithm, which clusters features into K distinct clusters. Hence, there are K number of features corresponding to each class. Subsequently, corresponding to each class, the cluster representatives are chosen. This procedure is repeated for all the samples of remaining classes. During testing the feature indices correspond to each class are used for validating the given dataset through classification using suitable symbolic classifiers. For experimentation, four standard supervised interval datasets are used. The results show the superiority of the proposed model when compared with the other existing state-of-the-art feature selection methods.

Keywords: Feature selection · Interval data · Symbolic similarity measure · Symbolic classification

1 Introduction

In the current era of digital technology- pattern recognition plays a vital role in the development of cognition based systems. These systems quite naturally handle a huge amount of data. While handling such vast amount of data, the task of data processing has become curse to process. To overcome curse in data processing, the concept of feature selection is being adopted by researchers. Nowadays, feature selection has become a very trending topic in the field of machine learning and pattern recognition. Feature selection helps us to select the most relevant features from a given set of features. The different feature selection techniques can be listed as: filter, wrapper, and embedded methods [1].

Generally, the existing conventional methods fail to perform feature selection on unconventional data like interval, multi-valued, modal, and categorical data. These data are also called in general symbolic data. The notion of symbolic

© Springer Nature Singapore Pte Ltd. 2017
K.C. Santosh et al. (Eds.): RTIP2R 2016, CCIS 709, pp. 228–239, 2017.
DOI: 10.1007/978-981-10-4859-3_21

data was emerged in the early 2000, which mainly concentrates in handling very realistic type of data for effective classification, clustering, and even regression for that matter [2]. As it is a powerful tool in solving realistic problems, we thought of developing a feature selection model for any one of the modalities. In this regard, we have chosen with an interval valued data, due its strong nature in preserving the continuous streaming data in discrete form [2]. In this regard, we built a feature selection model for interval valued data in this work.

In literature, works done on feature selection of interval valued data is very few compared to conventional feature selection methods. Ichino [3] had given only the theoretical interpretation of feature selection on interval valued based on the pretended simplicity algorithm which works in a Cartesian space. Bapu et al. [4] proposed a two stage feature selection algorithm which can handle both interval as well multi-valued data based on the Mutual Similarity Value proximity measure. But the method is restricted to unsupervised dataset. Lyamine et al. [5] speak about the feature selection of interval valued data based on the concept of similarity margin computed between an interval sample and a class prototype. The similarity margin is computed using certain symbolic similarity measure. The authors have constructed basis for the similarity margin and then they worked out at the multi-variate weighting scheme. The weights guarantee with the number of subset features to be selected. The experimentation is done on three standard benchmarking interval dataset and validated using LAMDA classifier. Recently, Chih-Ching et al. [6] have come up with a feature selection model, where it adopts the framework of [5] for selecting the features. But, the authors have used different kernel viz., Gaussian kernel for measuring the similarity between an interval sample and a class prototype. The authors also have given the experimentation and comparative analysis on only single interval valued dataset.

Apart from the above mentioned works, no work can be seen on feature selection of interval valued data based on clustering in general, class specific features selection in particular. The class specific feature selection helps in improving the prediction accuracy as it selects features which are most relevant to the specific classes instead of selecting features relevant to all classes. With this motivational background, here in this paper, a feature selection model is proposed and validated on supervised interval datasets.

The proposed feature selection model initially transforms the given supervised feature matrix and later divides the transformed matrix into several (equal to number of classes) interval feature sub-matrices. The transformed feature sub-matrices are then fed into interval K-means clustering algorithm. Thus, results with K clusters for each sub-matrix. Next, for every cluster, a cluster representative is computed that results with K number of representatives corresponding to each class. During testing, a single interval feature vector is considered for classification based on the class specific features selected from the knowledgebase and they are validated using suitable symbolic classifiers.

The major contributions of this paper are as follows:

1. Proposal of a novel interval feature selection model based on class specific feature selection.
2. Design of an interval K-Means clustering algorithm by incorporating interval similarity kernel into conventional K-Means clustering.
3. Conduction of an experimentation, to show that the proposed model outperforms the state-of-the art models.

The organization of the paper is as follows: In Sect. 2, the proposed model is well explained. The details of experimental setup, datasets and results are given in Sect. 3. Section 4 presents a comparative analysis. Finally, Sect. 5 concludes the paper.

2   Proposed Model

The proposed interval feature selection model comprises of various steps in both training and testing respectively. Pre-processing, Interval K-Means clustering, selection of cluster representatives (Feature Selection) are done at a former stage and selection of feature indices (pre-processing), and classification tasks are performed at a latter stage. The architecture of the proposed model is given in Fig. 1.

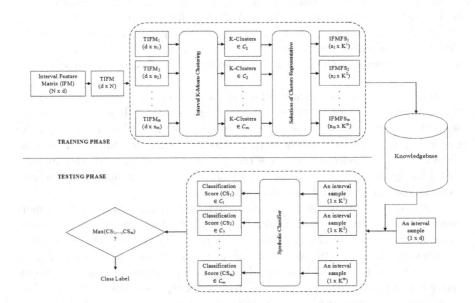

Fig. 1. Architecture of the proposed model

2.1   Pre-processing During Training Phase

Let us consider a supervised interval feature matrix IFM, with N number of rows and $d + 1$ number of columns. Each row corresponds to a sample and each column corresponds to a feature of type interval. Such a matrix is given by: IFM:(ξ_i, y_i), ξ_i represents a sample and y_i represents a class label ($i = 1, 2, ..., N$).

Each sample ξ_i is described by d interval features and is given by:

$$\xi_i = (\xi_i^1, \xi_i^2, ..., \xi_i^d) = ([f_1^-, f_1^+], [f_2^-, f_2^+], ..., [f_d^-, f_d^+])$$

where, f_k^- and f_k^+ are the lower and upper limits of an interval respectively.

The basic idea of the proposed model is to cluster the similar features. To accomplish this, a feature matrix should be transformed in such a way that the positions of samples become features and features become samples. That is, the rows of a feature matrix should correspond to features and the columns should correspond to samples.

Now, we have a transposed feature matrix of dimension dxN. But, our main objective is to select class specific features. In this regard, we separated samples based on their class correspondence and obtain with a sub-matrix $TIFM_j$ of dimension dxn_j (n_j is the number of samples per class) corresponding to a particular class C_j ($j = 1, 2, ..., m; m = no.\ of\ classes$).

Further, the $TIFM_j$ is fed into interval K-Means clustering algorithm to obtain K clusters from each matrix, where d features are spread across K different clusters. The details of clustering procedure are given in next section.

2.2   Interval K-Means Clustering

In this section, details about the construction of an interval K-Means clustering algorithm are given.

As we know, conventional K-Means clustering is an instance of partitional clustering techniques. Initially, it fixes up with the number of clusters (K) and the centroid points. Then the algorithm uses one of the different kernels such as squared Euclidean/city block/cosine/correlation/Hamming distance to compute the proximity among the samples [7]. Later those samples which have greater affinity go to same cluster and samples with a little affinity go to different clusters. Then the new centroids will be computed for each K clusters. The same procedure is repeated until certain convergence criteria are satisfied. The convergence criteria may be the maximum iterations or ϵ difference. Usually, the above said procedures are followed in conventional K-Means clustering algorithm. But, in our work, as we are handling with interval valued data, a slight modification has been brought out at kernel level. The kernel used to compute the affinity among the samples is symbolic similarity measure [8] instead of the above said kernels. The symbolic similarity kernel (SSK) used in our work is given by:

$$SSK(A, B) = \frac{(ISV_{AB}^- + ISV_{AB}^+) + (ISV_{BA}^- + ISV_{BA}^+)}{4} \tag{1}$$

where $A = ([a_1^-, a_1^+], [a_2^-, a_2^+], ..., [a_k^-, a_k^+], ...)$ and $B = ([b_1^-, b_1^+], [b_2^-, b_2^+], ..., [b_k^-, b_k^+], ...)$ be any two interval objects with $(a_k^- \leq a_k^+)$ and $(b_k^- \leq b_k^+)$. $ISV_{AB}^-, ISV_{AB}^+ (ISV_{BA}^-, ISV_{BA}^+)$ be the lower and upper limits of interval similarity value computed from object A to object B (B to A) and are given by:

$$ISV_{AB}^- = min(Sim(A_k, B_k)); k = 1, 2, ..., d$$

$$ISV_{AB}^+ = max(Sim(A_k, B_k)); k = 1, 2, ..., d$$

$$ISV(A, B) = [ISV^-, ISV^+]$$

$$Sim(A_k, B_k) = \begin{cases} 1, & \text{If } A \text{ contains } B \\ \frac{\text{Length of overlapping portion of } A \text{ and } B}{\text{Length of } B}, & \text{If there exists overlapping} \\ 0, & \text{If there is no overlapping} \end{cases}$$

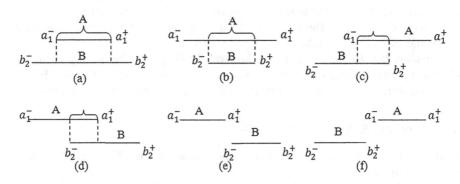

Fig. 2. Different instances of similarity computation between two intervals [4], (a)–(d): Overlapping cases, (e)–(f): Non-overlapping cases

The symbolic similarity kernel used in this work is very realistic in nature, as it preserves the topological relationship between the two intervals. The illustration of different cases of topological relationships exist between two intervals are shown in Fig. 2.

The rest of the interval K-Means clustering follows the same procedure as conventional K-Means clustering as explained above.

2.3   Selection of Cluster Representative (Feature Selection)

The K-clusters obtained from the class are considered here for selecting respective clusters' representative. The procedure for selecting the cluster representatives is discussed below:

Consider a cluster $Cl_q \in C_j$ $(q = 1, 2, ..., K; j = 1, 2, ..., m)$, containing z number of features. A feature is said to be a cluster representative (ClR_q), then it must exhibit a maximum similarity to all the remaining features. In this regard, the similarity computation among the features in a cluster Cl_q results with a similarity matrix SM^q, which is given by:

$$SM_{ab}^q = SSK(F_a, F_b) \in \mathbb{R}; \forall a = 1, 2, ..., z; b = 1, 2, ..., z$$

Where, $SSK(F_a, F_b)$ is given by Eq. 1.

Further, the computation of average similarity value is given by:

$$ASV_a = \frac{1}{z} \sum_{b=1}^{z} SM_{ab}^q \tag{2}$$

Now, we have obtained with z average similarity values corresponding to cluster Cl_q. Thus ClR_q is given by:

$$ClR_q = argmax_{F_a}\{(ASV_1, ASV_2, ..., ASV_z)'\} \tag{3}$$

$$\text{i.e., } ClR_q = argmax_{F_a}\left\{ \left(\frac{1}{z} \sum_{b=1}^{z} SM_{1b}^q, \frac{1}{z} \sum_{b=1}^{z} SM_{2b}^q, ..., \frac{1}{z} \sum_{b=1}^{z} SM_{zb}^q \right)' \right\}$$

From Eq. 3, it is very clear that the feature (F_a) which gives maximum ASV_a value is considered as a cluster representative (ClR_q) corresponding to cluster Cl_q. Thus the above procedure is repeated for all the clusters corresponding to remaining classes. Now we have $m \times K$ such clusters representative

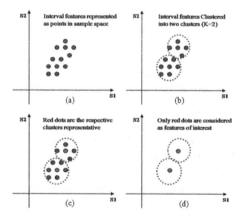

Fig. 3. Illustration of interval features selection using clustering: (a) Interval features (visualized as points) are spread in two dimensional sample space, (b) Clusters obtained after applying interval K-Means clustering, (c) Red dots are the clusters representative selected based on the procedure explained in Sect. 2.3, (d) Two red dots are further retained as the features of interest. (Color figure online)

$(ClR_1, ClR_2, ..., ClR_{mK})'$. The feature indices of these cluster representatives are further used to select features from original interval feature matrices and archived the same in the knowledgebase for classification. The illustration of selection of cluster representatives (features selection) is shown in Fig. 3.

2.4 Pre-processing During Testing Phase

Basically, our classification strategy is influenced from biometric verification, where, initially it identifies a class of the sample and then authenticates the claimed sample during verification. Similarly, in our work, initially a query sample is claimed as not only the member of a single class instead it is claimed to be as the member of all m different classes. While claiming the membership of all m classes, the (K) features of a query sample are selected based on the feature indices preserved during training. Thus for classification, there are totally m different query instances (of a sample) entering into the symbolic classifiers.

2.5 Symbolic Classifiers

In this paper, as we are handling with interval type data, it is difficult to compatible with conventional classifiers such as $K - NN$ (K-Nearest Neighbour), SVM (Support Vector Machines), Random Forest etc [9]. In this regard, we have recommended symbolic classifiers which handle interval type data successfully for classification. Here, we use two symbolic classifiers proposed in [10,11]. Henceforth, these two are called as $C - 1$ and $C - 2$ classifiers respectively.

The classifier proposed in [10], operates directly on interval data and the similarity measure proposed by them is of interval type in nature, hence the computed similarity matrix is again a symbolic. Further, authors aggregate the obtained matrix using the concept of mutual similarity value (MSV) and obtain with the conventional symmetric similarity matrix. Later on, the authors follow the nearest neighbour approach for classification.

In [11], authors propose a symbolic classifier which mainly concentrates on nearest neighbour approach in classifying an unknown sample to a known class. In our work, a slight modification has been done on the similarity measure proposed by [11]. The slight modification of the above said similarity measure is done at feature level. As the similarity measure in [11], is capable of measuring the similarity of multi-interval valued data, but in our case, only single interval valued data is enough to measure the similarity between two objects. Hence, we have restricted the measure to only single interval valued data.

Finally, we end up with m different classification scores obtained for m different classes. The classification of an unknown sample is labelled based on these scores. A class which possesses a maximum classification score is given as the class membership for an unknown sample.

3 Experimentation and Results

3.1 Datasets

We have used totally four different supervised interval datasets for experimentation. The four different benchmarking datasets used are: Iris [2], Car [12], Water [13], and Fish [12] datasets. The Iris interval dataset consists of 30 samples with 4 interval features. The 30 samples are spread across the three different classes, with 10 samples per class. The Car dataset consists of 33 samples with 8 interval features. The samples are spread across the 4 different classes with 10, 8, 8, and 7 samples per class respectively. The Fish dataset consists of 12 samples with 13 interval features. The samples are spread across 4 different classes, each with 4, 2, 4, and 2 samples respectively. Finally, the Water dataset consists of 316 samples with 48 interval features. The samples are spread across 2 different classes, each with 223 and 93 samples respectively. Among four datasets, the fish dataset seems to provide very less instances for classification. Thus for this dataset, the classification results vary a lot compare to other datasets.

3.2 Experimental Setup

In this sub-section, details of experimentation conducted on the four benchmarking supervised interval datasets are given. The experimentation is conducted in two phases viz., training, and testing. During training phase, we consider a supervised interval feature matrix and obtained the class specific features as explained in Sect. 2. These features are then preserved in a knowledgebase for classification. During testing phase, an unknown interval sample is considered and selected its class specific features and performed classification as explained in Sects. 2.4 and 2.5.

During training and testing, the samples of the dataset are varied from 30% to 70% (in steps 10%) and 70% to 30% (in steps 10%) respectively. For, interval K-Means clustering the maximum number of iterations is fixed to be 100. The value of K in interval K-Means clustering is varied from 2 to one less than number of features for all datasets except water dataset (In case water dataset, the K is varied till 21, as the clustering algorithm does not converge above that value). The parameter β in the symbolic classifier $(C - 2)$ is fixed to be 1.

3.3 Results

The validation of the proposed feature selection model is performed using classification accuracy, defined as the ratio of correctly classified samples to the number of samples. The experimental results are tabulated for the best feature subset (results with feature selection (WFS)) obtained from the proposed model and also we have compared the classification results of the same datasets without using any feature selection models (results without feature selection $(WoFS)$). The tabulated results are shown from Tables 1, 2, 3 and 4.

Table 1. Comparison of classification accuracies obtained from the classifiers $C - 1$ and $C - 2$ with different training-testing percentage for Iris dataset

Train-Test	C − 1 [10]				C − 2 [11]			
	WFS		WoFS		WFS		WoFS	
	# of features	Accuracy	# of features	Accuracy	# of features	Accuracy	# of features	Accuracy
30–70	3	100	4	100	3	100	4	100
40–60	2	100	4	100	2	100	4	100
50–50	2	100	4	100	3	100	4	100
60–40	2	100	4	91.67	2	100	4	100
70–30	2	100	4	88.89	3	100	4	100

Table 2. Comparison of classification accuracies obtained from the classifiers $C - 1$ and $C - 2$ with different training-testing percentage for Car dataset

Train-Test	C − 1 [10]				C − 2 [11]			
	WFS		WoFS		WFS		WoFS	
	# of features	Accuracy	# of features	Accuracy	# of features	Accuracy	# of features	Accuracy
30–70	2	76.19	8	42.86	2	61.9	8	71.43
40–60	4	72.22	8	38.89	4	61.11	8	77.78
50–50	3	81.25	8	50	4	56.25	8	81.25
60–40	2	66.67	8	50	4	83.33	8	83.33
70–30	2	66.67	8	55.56	2	55.56	8	88.89

Table 3. Comparison of classification accuracies obtained from the classifiers $C - 1$ and $C - 2$ with different training-testing percentage for Fish dataset

Train-Test	C − 1 [10]				C − 2 [11]			
	WFS		WoFS		WFS		WoFS	
	# of features	Accuracy	# of features	Accuracy	# of features	Accuracy	# of features	Accuracy
30–70	3	66.67	13	66.67	6	50	13	66.67
40–60	5	100	13	66.67	7	66.67	13	66.67
50–50	10	66.67	13	66.67	10	66.67	13	66.67
60–40	3	100	13	100	2	50	13	100
70–30	8	100	13	100	2	50	13	100

Table 4. Comparison of classification accuracies obtained from the classifiers $C - 1$ and $C - 2$ with different training-testing percentage for Water dataset

Train-Test	C − 1 [10]				C − 2 [11]			
	WFS		WoFS		WFS		WoFS	
	# of features	Accuracy	# of features	Accuracy	# of features	Accuracy	# of features	Accuracy
30–70	11	68.78	48	66.52	2	71.5	48	63.8
40–60	14	68.09	48	65.96	14	71.81	48	60.11
50–50	5	70.7	48	65.61	6	73.89	48	56.05
60–40	4	69.84	48	54.76	20	77.78	48	62.7
70–30	2	76.34	48	63.44	10	79.57	48	59.14

From the above tables (Tables 1, 2, 3 and 4), it is very clear that the classification performance has been increased due to the incorporation of feature selection method com-pared to that of not using any feature selection method. It is also so clear that the best results are quoted for lesser number of features.

To test effectiveness of the proposed model, we have used the datasets containing different feature dimensions (from 4 to 48). From the results, one can notice that the model performs well even for such kind of datasets in-spite of selecting very few features. This shows the robustness of the proposed model under varied feature sizes of the dataset.

4   Comparative Analysis

To corroborate the effectiveness of the proposed model, the comparative analyses are given. Initially, the proposed model is compared against the state-of-the-art methods in terms of classification accuracy and the same is tabulated in Table 5. Further, we have compared our model with the other models which do not use any feature selection during classification. In literature, we found

Table 5. Comparison of proposed feature selection method v/s other existing methods

	Lyamine et al. [5]		Chih-Ching et al. [6]		**Proposed model**			
Classifier	LAMDA		LAMDA		**C − 1** [10]		**C − 2** [11]	
Dataset	Feature subset	Accuracy	Feature subset	Accuracy	Feature subset	Accuracy	Feature subset	Accuracy
Car	5	78	–	–	3	81.25	4	**83.33**
Fish	4	74	–	–	3	**100**	7	66.67
Water	14	77	11	78.66	2	76.34	10	**79.57**

Table 6. Comparison of classification with the proposed feature selection method v/s the existing classification methods without using any feature selection methods for Car interval dataset

Methods		Accuracy
Proposed method	**C − 1 (WFS)**	**81.25**
	C − 2 (WFS)	**83.33**
Barros et al. [14]	Binary model	48.49
	Multinomial	54.55
Renata et al. [15]	IDPC-CSP	63.64
	IDPC-VSP	63.6
	IDPC-PP	72.8
Silva and Brito [16]	Distributional approach	73
	Mid points and ranges	55

Table 7. Selected feature subsets and their corresponding feature indices

Dataset (# of class)	C − 1	C − 2
Car (4)	{(1,3,4), (2,4,1), (3,1,2), (1,8,4)}	{(4,3,6,1), (1,2,3,4), (2,1,5,4), (1,8,6,5)}
Fish (4)	{(12,4,7), (8,1,9), (4,12,1), (9,3,6)}	{(1,9,3,12,2,4,7), (1,3,5,9,11,6,7), (9,11,1,5,8,6,12), (3,12,2,9,8,13,7)}
Water (2)	{(5,18), (23,34)}	{(38,42,18,8,34,35,40,24,4,14), (13,32,27,31,22,34,36,18,3,16)}

such classification models re-ported only on Car dataset. Hence, we have given comparison with only Car dataset and is given in Table 6.

The Table 6 justifies that the classification model with feature selection outperforms well compared to that of other models which do not use any feature selection methods during classification. This is because; the proposed feature selection model selects only the features of interest through clustering instead of considering all features.

From Tables 5 and 6, it is very clear that the proposed model not only outperforms the existing models in terms of accuracy but also in terms of selecting number of features. This shows that the proposed model is much better than the similarity margin based models [5,6]. The selected feature subset and their class specific features indices corresponding to $C − 1$ and $C − 2$ classifiers are given in Tables 6 and 7.

5   Conclusion

In this paper, a novel idea for selection of supervised interval data through clustering is introduced. The proposed model incorporates the concept of symbolic similarity measure to build the interval K-Means clustering. The cluster representatives are computed based on the symbolic similarity measure. Later on, the indices of cluster representatives are preserved in the knowledgebase. During testing, for a sample, the class specific feature indices are selected from knowledgebase and classified using symbolic classifier. The proposed model has been well exploited for different interval supervised datasets and also it outperformed against other existing models in terms of classification accuracy and also in terms of dimension.

Acknowledgement. The second author would like to acknowledge the Department of Science Technology, INDIA, for their financial support through DST-INSPIRE fellowship.

References

1. Artur, J.F., Figueiredo, A.T.M.: Efficient feature selection filters for high-dimensional data. Pattern Recogn. Lett. **33**, 1794–1804 (2012)
2. Billard, L., Diday, E.: Symbolic Data Analysis: Conceptual Statistics and Data Mining. Wiley, Hoboken (2007)
3. Ichino, M.: Feature selection for symbolic data classification. In: Diday, E., Lechevallier, Y., Schader, M., Bertrand, P., Burtschy, B. (eds.) New Approaches in Classification and Data Analysis, Sect. 2, pp. 423–429. Springer, Heidelberg (1994)
4. Bapu, B., Kiranagi Guru, D.S., Ichino, M.: Exploitation of multivalued type proximity for symbolic feature selection. In: Proceedings of the International Conference on Computing: Theory and Applications, pp. 320–324. IEEE (2007)
5. Hedjazi, L., Aguilar-Martin, J., Le Lann, M.V.: Similarity-margin based feature. Pattern Recogn. Lett. **32**, 578–585 (2011)
6. Hsiao, C.-C., Chuang, C.-C., Shun-Feng, S.: Robust Gaussian Kernel based approach for feature selection. Adv. Intell. Syst. Comput. **268**, 25–33 (2014)
7. Jain, A.K., Dubes, R.C.: Algorithms for Clustering Data. Prentice-Hall Inc., Upper Saddle River (1988)
8. Guru, D.S., Kiranagi, B.B., Nagabhushan, P.: Multivalued type proximity measure and concept of mutual similarity value useful for clustering symbolic patterns. Pattern Recogn. Lett. **25**, 1203–1213 (2004)
9. Duda, O.R., Hart, E.P., Stork, G.D.: Pattern Classification, 2nd edn. Wiley, New York (2000)
10. Kiranagi, B.B.: Classification of symbolic data through symbolic similarity and dissimilarity measures. Ph.D. thesis, University of Mysore, Mysore (2006)
11. Guru, D.S., Nagendraswamy, H.S.: Symbolic representation and classification of two- dimensional shapes. In: Proceedings of the 3rd Workshop on Computer Vision, Graphics, and Image Processing (WCVGIP), pp. 19–24 (2006)
12. Carvalho, F.A.T., De Souza, R.M.C.R., Chavent, M., Lechevallier, Y.: Adaptive Hausdorff distances and dynamic clustering of symbolic interval data. Pattern Recogn. **27**, 167–179 (2006)
13. Quevedo, J., Puig, V., Cembrano, G., Blanch, J., Aguilar, J., Saporta, D., Benito, G., Hedo, M., Molina, A.: Validation and reconstruction of flow meter data in the Barcelona water distribution network. J. Control Eng. Pract. **18**, 640–651 (2010)
14. Barros, A.P., Carvalho, F.A.T., Neto, E.A.L.: A pattern classifier for interval-valued data based on multinomial logistic regression model. In: IEEE International Conference on Systems, Man, and Cybernetics, pp. 541–546 (2012)
15. de Souza, R.M.C.R., Queiroz, D.C.F., Cysneiros, F.J.A.: Logistic regression-based pattern classifiers for symbolic interval data. Pattern Anal. Appl. **14**, 273–282 (2011)
16. Duarte, S.A.P., Paula, B.: Linear discriminant analysis for interval data. Comput. Stat. **21**, 289–308 (2006)

Image Analysis

Performance Analysis of Impulse Noise Attenuation Techniques

M.S. Sonawane[1,2(✉)] and C.A. Dhawale[1]

[1] P.R. Pote College of Engineering and Management, SGBAU, Amravati, India
manojkumar.sonawane@rediffmail.com, cadhawale@rediffmail.com
[2] Computer Department, Institute of Management Research
and Development Shirpur, Shirpur, India

Abstract. At present, digital image processing is elevated vicinity. Image possession, a broadcast may corrupt an image with impulse noise. Several realistic appliances necessitate a superior, squat complex denoising practice as a pre-processing maneuver. While impulse noise filtering, the need is to conserve edges and image features. The merely damaged pixel should be filtered, to evade image smoothing. Analyses of few impulse noise cutback procedures are discussed in the study, their outcomes are inspected as well as competences are estimated in MATLAB R2014a. An appraisal affords inclusive acquaintance of noise diminution methods and also assists pollsters in paramount impulse noise reduction technique selection.

Keywords: Noise reduction · Impulse noise · Linear filter · Non-linear filter

1 Introduction

Digital image processing is the discipline of amending digital images with a digital machine. Digital imaging system and appliances fabricates amended, encoded image as a result by typically gaining an image as input. Images are exploited in countless areas like medical, remote sensing, entertainment, etc. [1] Image processing embraces practices that aim to revise the image nature, facade in order to augment its illustrative information substance for human elucidation or make it right adequate for building up appliances [3].

To attempt diverse image allied crisis domains, image processing techniques has been deliberated. Each procedures competence depends on image superiority. Assorted images renovation, enrichment practices is exercised to boost an image class and as par image noise form, image augmentation practice varies. Every surplus signal occurs in inventive signal is deemed as noise. Noise is discarded signal or information occurs in inventive image that harms image prominence. Visual data are broadcasted in channel for data transmission system which might be despoiled in the communication channel by noise. Noisy sensor, scanner, camera, lighting, channel error, storage media etc. is diverse ways

© Springer Nature Singapore Pte Ltd. 2017
K.C. Santosh et al. (Eds.): RTIP2R 2016, CCIS 709, pp. 243–250, 2017.
DOI: 10.1007/978-981-10-4859-3_22

to construct image noises. Random valued, fixed valued impulse noise or salt-pepper noises are impulse noise types [4]. Gaussian noise, impulse noise, speckle noise, etc. are noises caused by varying supplies. On an image, impulse noise fabricates dark smudges, petite dots. Speckle noise creates big patches while Gaussian noise diminishes or amplifies the image brightness. Speckle noise is un-even noise while impulse, Gaussian noises are dispersed evenly.

Blunder in broadcast cables, camera sensors is the core impulse noise source. Linear, non-linear techniques are subcategories of impulse noise reduction methods. Noise decline rule is functional for all image pixels in the former category. Linear methods hitch is, it harms the quiet pixels since the routine is practical for quiet plus noisy pixels. Average, mean, median filters, etc. are paradigms of such category. Noise detection and replacement are two phases, those fit in non-linear noise diminution [7–19]. Noise spot exposure happens at first, while in succeeding phase sensed noisy pixels are substituted by approximated value. Several schemes are explicated in writing. Although with the low noise stipulation they efforts sound, in towering noise provisions recital are pitiable. As noise ratio swells, noise process time too raises. It is snag of such routines that necessitates extreme time, so incongruous for factual appliances. To perk up the scale of nonlinear systems, Min-max filter [7], Center weighted filter [8], Adaptive filter [9], Progressive switching filter [10], Tri-state median filters, etc. [6] and Decision based algorithm [11] algorithms are projected.

The rest paper part is organized as; assessment rubrics utilized in the study are conveyed in Sect. 2. The linear filters conversation is in Sect. 3; in Sect. 4 non-linear filters are depicted whereas concluding remarks are addressed in Sect. 5.

2   Performance Measurement

To evaluate impulse noise removal technique outcomes, several appraisal factors exist. Signal to noise ratio improvement and peak signal to noise ratio are estimated in this study.

2.1   Signal to Noise Ratio Improvement

It termed as the divergence between restored images signal to noise ratio (SNR) and noisy images SNR. Here,

$$\text{Restored Image SNR} = 10log10 \times \frac{\sum_i \sum_j X_{ij}^2}{\sum_i \sum_j (X_{ij} - R_{ij})^2} \tag{1}$$

$$\text{Noisy Image SNR} = 10log10 \times \frac{\sum_i \sum_j X_{ij}^2}{\sum_i \sum_j (X_{ij} - N_{ij})^2} \tag{2}$$

Nij, X, R are noisy image pixel, original image and restored image correspondingly. The higher SNRI value reveals the improved restoration, visual consequences.

2.2   Peak Signal to Noise Ratio

Decibel unit is employed to decide the peak signal to noise ratio, In case of gray level illustration it is delineated like,

$$MSE = \frac{\sum_i \sum_j (X_{ij} - R_{ij})^2}{M \times N} \tag{3}$$

$$PSNR = 10 log10 \times \frac{255 \times 255}{MSE} \tag{4}$$

Here,

MSE - Mean Square Error. PSNR - Peak Signal to Noise Ratio. M × N Image size. X - Imaginative Image. R - Restored Image. The superior PNSR value in the renovated image offers enhanced class.

3   Linear Filters

3.1   Median Filter

Median filters implementation is effortless moreover effectual for impulse noise elimination at low density levels. Principally with a bigger window size, it obliterates the image details comprising corners, thin lines, etc. It performs similar to a low pass filter that blocks all high frequency image components such as edges and noise, consequently blurs the image. The filtering window size is raised to have adequate encrypted pixels in the neighborhood, as the noise density augments [5]. Median filter also works similar to an average filter, but middle pixel assessment is changed by its nearby pixel median value those belong to the window.

3.2   Mean Filter

Frequently a 3 * 3 square kernel is exploited in mean filter. When the mask coefficients sum to zero, then the average brightness vanished, and it returns a dark image implementation. Else image average brightness ratio is not revised in the inventive image. On the shift-multiply-sum rule, mean filter efforts. Mean filter labors like an average filter except middle pixel consideration is modified by its adjacent pixels mean value those fit in the window.

3.3   Average Filter

A square window with $2k + 1$ size is exercised in an average filter where k value varies from 1 to n. $2k + 1$ window size has been applied since window height, width should be odd with aim to catch precise middle pixel $(k + 1, k + 1)$. Imaginative image is scanned row, column wise by such window and at every scan time, windows middle pixel value is substituted by an average value of adjoining pixels in the window.

Table 1. SNRI evaluation [2]

Noise ratio	Median filter	Mean filter	Average filter
10	16.09	7.00	7.01
20	15.00	6.94	7.00
30	12.22	6.66	6.67
40	9.19	6.25	6.25
50	6.56	5.89	5.82
60	4.54	5.47	5.47
70	3.11	5.08	5.06
80	1.97	4.71	4.65
90	1.23	4.34	4.32
Average	7.76	5.81	5.80

Table 2. PSNR evaluation [2]

Noise ratio	Median filter	Mean filter	Average filter
10	31.20	22.51	22.54
20	27.12	19.58	19.71
30	22.58	17.70	17.72
40	18.30	16.14	16.16
50	14.70	14.91	14.86
60	11.82	13.83	13.81
70	9.62	12.84	12.85
80	7.75	12.01	11.95
90	6.30	11.22	11.21
Average	16.59	15.63	15.64

4   Non Linear Filters

4.1   Min-max Median Filter

To do image scanning from top to bottom and left to right, 3×3 window works out in Min-max filter (MMF). 2×2 windows middle pixel is deemed to be a trial pixel. Whenever trial version is smaller versus the least value occurs in windows remaining pixels and larger in comparison with the ceiling value occurs in windows else pixels, then the middle pixel is assumed like despoiled pixel and corresponding value will be restored by the windows pixel median value otherwise pixel will be assumed as pure and will be unaffected. MMF is conditional non-linear filter [7].

4.2 Center Weighted Median Filter

The weighted median filters expansion is the center weighted median (CWM) filter [8] that confers added mass to middle assessments inside the window. CWM filter tolerates smoothing behavior control by the weights which could be put, consequently promises superior enrichment practice. Such methodologies entail degraded pixels credentials with an aim to avoid factual pixel value amendment and $2k + 1$ square windows middle pixel judged as experimental pixel. When middle pixel $(k + 1, k + 1)$ diminutive versus the lowest value occur in remaining pixels in the window and bigger as compare to highest value, then such a pixel is assumed as ruined pixel, consequently shall be restored with projected median value. The median computed by arranging all window elements in uphill sequence, gaining elements median.

4.3 Adaptive Median Filter

For noise reduction, this filter uses changeable window size. Window size swells until approved median value is estimated and noise pixel is restored by gauged median value. An adaptive median filter is nonlinear uncertain filter [9]. Two stipulations are exercised one to perceive ruined pixels and another to prove median value suitability. Whenever experimental pixel is smaller than least value and larger than the ceiling value occurs in else pixels in the window, afterward the middle pixel is deemed like degraded pixel and its applicable for analyzing median value as well. Amplify the window dimension, re-compute the median value till the exact median value attains or window dimension accomplish utmost perimeter.

4.4 Progressive Switching Median Filter

It works in two stages, noise pixels are acknowledged initially by 3×3 size window. Middle pixel is assumed as tarnished pixel, if trial pixel is smaller than lowest value and larger than the highest value in windows remaining pixels. Noisy pixels prior facts are exercised and such pixels are changed by approximated median value, in subsequent steps. The median value is determined alike adaptive median filter with no degraded pixel considered. When an estimated median value is small as compare to least value, bigger versus the ceiling value, at that time median value is supposed like ruined value, if so augment the window dimension, re-estimate the median unless acceptable median value gained or window size achieve ceiling boundary [10].

4.5 Tri-state Median Filter

To verify whether the pixel is ruined, prior to concerning filtering unconditionally, it integrates center weighted median, the standard median filter into the noise recognition skeleton. Impulse detector realizes noise detection, that gets center weighted median filter and standard median results, evaluates all by the

Table 3. PSNR evaluation [2]

Noise ratio	DBMF	AMF	TMF	MMF	PSMF	CWMF
10	31.66	31.97	22.50	32.17	28.31	31.95
20	31.43	30.27	22.44	28.69	27.66	28.62
30	30.00	28.49	22.32	23.81	25.38	23.96
40	28.76	27.28	22.18	19.56	22.07	19.46
50	27.19	26.01	22.08	15.95	18.59	15.96
60	26.17	24.71	21.80	12.94	15.38	12.85
70	24.99	23.32	21.09	10.42	12.71	10.37
80	23.79	21.02	20.07	8.30	10.20	8.32
90	21.89	17.22	16.96	6.51	8.11	6.56
Average	27.32	25.58	21.27	17.59	18.71	17.56

middle pixel value to construct a tri-state resolution. Tri-state median filter outcome, threshold T controls the switching logic [6]. With typical median filter, noise pixels are recognized primarily. Subsequently noisy pixels prior comprehension is exploited and are restored by center weighted median filter [6].

4.6   Decision Based Algorithm

Its a two phase mechanism, where primarily with 3×3 size window noise pixels are accredited. Afterwards noisy pixels prior data are exercised and such pixels are swapped by the core value of ordering window pixels [11].

Table 4. SNRI evaluation [2]

Noise ratio	DBMF	AMF	TMF	MMF	PSMF	CWMF
10	54.29	54.60	45.12	54.79	50.93	54.57
20	54.05	52.89	45.06	51.31	50.28	51.25
30	52.62	51.12	44.95	46.44	48.01	46.58
40	51.39	49.90	44.81	42.18	44.70	42.08
50	49.81	48.63	44.70	38.58	41.21	38.59
60	48.79	47.34	44.42	35.56	38.01	35.48
70	47.61	45.95	43.72	33.05	35.34	32.99
80	46.41	43.65	42.70	30.93	32.83	30.94
90	44.52	39.84	39.59	29.13	30.73	29.18
Average	49.94	48.21	43.89	40.21	41.33	40.18

5   Conclusion

Impulse noise diminution is more crucial in conventional digital image processing vicinity. Few existing linear, non-linear filters for impulse noise exposure with their individual worth and weaknesses are examined and evaluate in the study. Tables 1, 2, 3 and 4 shows result analysis in a tabular form. Median filter competence is higher in contrast to the mean, average filters, in linear methodology; consequently median filter is ideal in nearly all linear techniques. In nonlinear filters, as evaluated by else filters decision based median filter offers higher signal to noise ratio improvement, peak signal to noise ratio and thus decision based median filters performance is superior than else. For future trade one could do invention of an innovative impulse noise reduction technique, amendment in presenting systems with improved truth or appropriate merge of offered practices.

References

1. Soni, T., Joshi, V.: A comparative performance analysis of high density impulse noise removal using different type median filters. Int. J. Comput. Sci. Trends Technol. (IJCST) **2**(6) (2014)
2. Koli, M.A.: Review of impulse noise reduction techniques. Int. J. Comput. Sci. Eng. (IJCSE) **4**(2) (2012). ISSN 0975-3397
3. Gonzalez, R.C., Woods, R.E.: Digital Image Processing. Pearson Education, Upper Saddle River (2007)
4. Kesharwani, A., Agrawal, S., Dhariwal, M.K.: An improved decision based asymmetric trimmed median filter for removal of high density salt and pepper noise. Int. J. Comput. Appl. **84**(8) (2013). ISSN 0975-8887
5. Jain, A.K.: Fundamentals of Digital Image Processing. Prentice-Hall, Upper Saddle River (1989)
6. Chen, T., Ma, K.-K., Chen, L.-H.: Tri-state median filter for image de-noising. IEEE Trans. Image Process. **8**(12) (1999)
7. Satpathy, S.K., Panda, S., Nagwanshi, K.K., Ardil, C.: Image restoration in nonlinear filtering domain using MDB approach. Int. J. Sig. Process. **6**(1) (2010)
8. Ko, S.-J., Hoon, Y.: Center Weighted Median Filters and Their applications to image enhancement. IEEE Trans. Circ. Syst. **38**(9) (1991)
9. Hwang, H., Haddad, R.A.: Adaptive median filter new algorithms and results. IEEE Trans. Image Process. **4**(4) (1995)
10. Wang, Z., Zhang, D.: Progressive switching median filter for the removal of impulse noise from highly corrupted images. IEEE Trans. Circ. Syst. II Analog Digit. Sig. Process. **46**(1) (1999)
11. Srinivasan, K.S., Ebenezer, D.: A new fast and efficient decision-based algorithm for removal of high-density impulse noises. IEEE Sig. Process. Lett. **14**(3) (2007)
12. Lee, J.S.: Digital image enhancement and noise filtering by use of local statistics. IEEE Trans. Pattern Anal. **PMAI-4**, 141–149 (1982)
13. Nahi, N.E., Habbi, A.: Decision directed recursive image enhancement. IEEE Trans. Circ. Syst. **CAS-2**, 286–293 (1975)
14. Eng, H.L., Ma, K.K.: Noise adaptive soft-switching median filter. IEEE Trans. Image Process. **10**(2), 242–251 (2001)

15. Chan, R.H., Ho, C.-W., Nikolova, M.: Salt and pepper noise removal by median type noise detectors and detail preserving regularization. IEEE Trans. Image Process. **14**(10) (2005)
16. Huang, T.S., Yang, G.J., Tang, G.Y.: A fast two dimensional median filtering algorithm. IEEE Trans. Accustics Speech Sig. Process. **ASSP-27**(1) (1997)
17. Xu, X., Mller, E.L.: Adaptive two pass median filter to remove impulse noise. In: IEEE ICIP (2002)
18. Ping, W., Li, L.J., Dongming, L., Gang, C.: A Fast and reliable switching median filter for highly corrupted images by impulse noise. IEEE (2007)
19. Pandey, R.: An Improved switching median filter for uniformly distributed impulse noise removal. World Acad. Sci. Technol. **38** (2008)

Neuro-Fuzzy Approach for Speckle Noise Reduction in SAR Images

Vijayakumar Singanamalla and Santhi Vaithyanathan$^{(\boxtimes)}$

VIT University, Vellore, Tamil Nadu, India
singanamalla.5a8@gmail.com, vsanthinathan@gmail.com

Abstract. In recent years, SAR image processing plays a major role in coastal region monitoring through object identification for the betterment of the livelihood of sea shore people. In order to carry out the above said task, SAR images need to be analysed for extracting features which could be accomplished only after the removal of speckle noise. In this work, a new approach using Neuro-Fuzzy method is proposed for the removal of speckle noise. It is developed on fuzzy logic rule-based system. It is designed based on 3-input 1-output first order Sugeno type fuzzy inference system (FIS). The experimental analysis shows an effective performance of the proposed approach. The obtained results of the proposed approach are compared with results of the traditional approaches and it is proved that the NeuroFuzzy approach is giving better results compared with traditional methods.

Keywords: Speckle noise · Neuro-fuzzy system · Fuzzy logic · Fuzzy inference system · Ocean monitoring · SAR images

1 Introduction

In general, the speckle noise suppresses underlying features in imagery systems, while operating with coherent radiation, such as Synthetic Aperture Radar (SAR), and Light Detection And Ranging (LiDAR). The speckle noise a is form of multiplicative model, which is inherently correlated with pixel intensity values. The main objective of the proposed work is to remove the speckle noise from images to enhance its quality without destroying its important features in a specified region or the entire region of images [1]. However, in some of the digital image applications, removal of speckle noise introduces counterproductive effects. In SAR image processing, one of the key tasks is to effectively remove the speckle noise as it affects the subsequent processing also. For example, in one of the model called speckle preservation in which speckle noise presents is so important to extract features or to perform tracking, since image features are represented as a speckle patterns. In order to remove the speckle noise there are many traditional filtering approaches existing that include Lee filtering [2], Frost filtering [3], Kuan filtering [4], Gamma MAP filtering [5] and other models presented in [6,7].

© Springer Nature Singapore Pte Ltd. 2017
K.C. Santosh et al. (Eds.): RTIP2R 2016, CCIS 709, pp. 251–260, 2017.
DOI: 10.1007/978-981-10-4859-3_23

However, in some of the applications of SAR images, traditional linear techniques are proved imperfect as they cannot survive with the non-linear image creation models. The nature of the problem cannot be fully visualized with the human system interaction, while formation of the image model into traditional image processing models.

Thus, it is observed that the speckle noise could also be removed using computational intelligence approaches. In particular fuzzy logic based approaches are predominantly used in speckle noise reduction. In general, because of the coherent radiation of radar images, the fuzzy logic based approaches are best suitable for speckle noise reduction. In this proposal, speckle noise removal is carried out for performing boundary detection, segmentation and classification using NeuroFuzzy approach.

In general, the speckle noise removal process is conflict task while enhancing the image quality. In order to filter the various regions of coherent radar images, single filter is not appropriate [8,9]. This filtering operation could vary from the pixel to pixel depending upon the local context. The fuzzy logic approach is used to reduce the speckle noise based on the frequency domain processing. Usually, the conventional filtering operations have been carried on the uncorrupted regions of SAR images. The basic idea of noise filtering and noise detector is shown in Fig. 1.

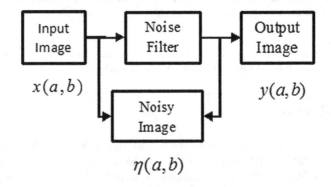

Fig. 1. Block diagram representation of noise removal approach

In recent years, one of the main problems of SAR speckle filtering is to enhance image quality and also to handle the local non-stationary regions. In order to address this type of problem, an existing system uses multi-scale local co-efficient of variation (MLCV) approach. But, it is not developed for speckle noise removal on the high heterogeneous areas. In order to overcome this drawback, a new computational concept called Neuro-Fuzzy logic technique is used. It is developed by combining the feature of fuzzy logic with neural network algorithms. In this paper, a new de-speckling approach using the fuzzy logic with neural network has been presented for SAR images.

In Sect. 2, review of related works is presented. Section 3 presents basics of Neuro-Fuzzy systems. Section 4 discusses about proposed methodology. Performance analysis has been presented in Sect. 5. Section 6 concludes the proposed works.

2   Review of Related Works

A brief literature review has been made in speckle noise filtering and it is discussed below. Most of the existing image enhancement techniques are embedded with non-linear models. In [10], statistical model is presented to suppress the speckle noise in SAR images. In theoretical, this model shows an intensity of speckle noise can be observed from the false positive exponential circulation. There are two kinds of SAR images namely, SIR-B and SEASAT SAR images. These images could be analysed in two ways, either through statistical correlation approach or through noise models. The statistical correlation model can analyse image noise that can be based on noise intensities of statistically significant pixels. Next, the analysis of noise models can be perceived based on intensity of an observed image.

In [11], the de-speckling by wavelet rescaling method is presented which is based on the un-decimated wavelet scaling. It is carried out through the maximum decomposition of noise images. The computational filters are applied on wavelet based co-efficient sub-bands. At the final stage, the de-speckling exploits the translation invariance of un-decimated frequency wavelet decomposition. It could reject the multiplicative noise, which is free from typical artifacts from denoising schema with wavelet transforms. But, this approach is entirely different from the speckle suppression approach using statistical models proposed in [10]. In speckle noise filtering, most of the existing approaches uses mean and variances of the noise image as models.

The adaptive method could also be used for the removal of speckle noise to enhance the SAR image features. It is presented in [12], which uses both curvelet transform and particle swarm optimization (PSO) techniques. It is originated from the non-linear shrink and stretches the curvelet co-efficient. The main objective of the approach is presented in [12], to improve the quality of image feature. In order to bring the adaptiveness, the optimal parameters are represented with operation of SAR satellite imagery function. In addition, the proposed approach uses PSO method for global search strategy for best despeckled and enhanced image. Thus based on the literature review carried out it is observed that, the SAR image de-noising is very much required for enhancing image features. In the proposed work, the raw SAR image is taken as an input data, in which the pixels components are highly correlated. In subsequent section, the basics of Neuro-Fuzzy system is presented elaborately.

3   Basics of Neuro-Fuzzy System

In 1989, Buckley and Hayashi [13] showed that the fuzzy neural networks are universal approximations for any continuous fuzzy functions on a compact domain.

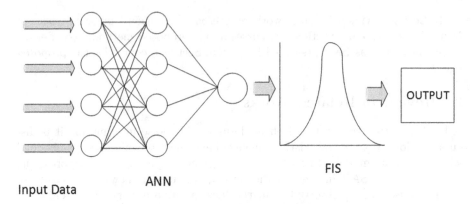

Input Data   **ANN**   **FIS**

Fig. 2. The sample neuro-fuzzy architecture

The sample Neuro-Fuzzy architecture is shown in Fig. 2. In Fig. 2 $X_i = x_1, x_2, x_3, \ldots\ldots, x_n$ represents signals and $W_i = w_1, w_2, w_3, \ldots\ldots, w_n$ represents weights of fuzzy members. The information neurons don't change the data flags so their yield is the same as their information. The signals $x_1, x_2, x_3, \ldots\ldots x_n$ interacts with the appropriate weights $w_1, w_2, w_3, \ldots\ldots, w_n$ to generate the product

$$P_i = P_1, P_2, P_3, \ldots\ldots, P_n = W_i * X_i, \quad i = 1, 2, 3, \ldots\ldots, n \tag{1}$$

The extension principle is used to compute P from Eq. (1). The aggregation of input information or net input of the neuron is given by

$$net = \sum_{i=1}^{n} P_i = \sum_{i=1}^{n} W_i * X_i \tag{2}$$

The net input is given as an input to its transfer function f as shown in Eq. (2) using the sigmoidal function and then the output is calculated by using the Eq. (3).

$$Y = f(net) = f \sum_{i=1}^{n} W_i * X_i \tag{3}$$

Basically, the fuzzy neural network is a neural network with fuzzy signals and/or fuzzy weights, which can be processed by the following three steps:

1. Combine signals X_i and weights W_i using t-norms, t-conorm or some other continuous operation;
2. Aggregate the P_is with a t-norm, t-conorm, or any other continuous function;
3. Apply transfer function to obtain output.

4   Proposed Methodology

The proposed architecture for speckle noise removal is shown in Fig. 3, where $x(a, b)$ represents the luminance values of the pixels and $y(a, b)$ represents the de-speckled intensity values. Here, the index variable a vary from $1 \leq a \leq A$ and index variable b vary from $1 \leq b \leq B$ for an input image having a size of AXB pixels. The noise detector is constructed by combining two NF wedge with a decision maker. The internal structures of the NF wedge are identical to each other.

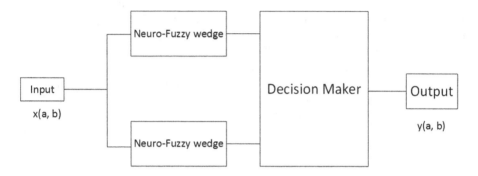

Fig. 3. The architecture of noise filtering using neuro-fuzzy technique

In the above architecture, each NF wedge working principle is first order Sugeno type fuzzy system [14]. And also, each input has been used three generalized Gaussian (i.e., bell) type membership functions, whereas the output has a linear membership function. The input and output relationship of any of the two NF wedges is as follows.

Let $x(a, b)$ represents the input of the NF wedge and $y(a, b)$ as shown in Eq. (7) denote its output. Each possible combination of inputs and their associated membership functions is represented by a rule in the rule base of the NF wedge. Since, the wedge has N number of inputs and each input has N number of membership functions, the rule base contains a total of (N^N) rules, which are given as follows: For example, three input FIS is shown below

1. IF $(S_1 \in A_{11}) \cap (S_2 \in A_{21}) \cap (S_3 \in A_{31})$ THEN $\eta_1 = L_1(S_1, S_2, S_3)$
2. IF $(S_1 \in A_{11}) \cap (S_2 \in A_{21}) \cap (S_3 \in A_{32})$ THEN $\eta_2 = L_2(S_1, S_2, S_3)$
3. IF $(S_1 \in A_{11}) \cap (S_2 \in A_{21}) \cap (S_3 \in A_{33})$ THEN $\eta_3 = L_3(S_1, S_2, S_3)$
4. IF $(S_1 \in A_{11}) \cap (S_2 \in A_{22}) \cap (S_3 \in A_{31})$ THEN $\eta_4 = L_4(S_1, S_2, S_3)$

....

27. IF $(S_1 \in A_{13}) \cap (S_2 \in A_{23}) \cap (S_3 \in A_{33})$ THEN $\eta_{27} = L_{27}(S_1, S_2, S_3)$

Here A_{ij} as shown in Eq. (4) represents the jth membership function of the ith input, η^k represents the output of the kth rule, and L_k represents the kth output of membership value. The input membership values are generalized by the Gaussian bell type and the output membership functions are linear

$$A_{ij}(\alpha) = \frac{1}{1 + [\frac{\alpha - P_{ij}}{q_{ij}}]^{2r_{ij}}} \tag{4}$$

$$L(\alpha_1, \alpha_2, \alpha_3) = d_{k1} * \alpha_1 + d_{k2} * \alpha_2 + d_{k3} * \alpha_3 + d_{k4}, k = 1, 2, 3, ..., 27 \tag{5}$$

Here p, q, r and d represents the constant values basically depends on the member function. The optimality of the parameters is defined by the training data. S1, S2 and S3 represent the actual parameters and $\alpha1$, $\alpha2$ and $\alpha3$ represents the formal parameters in Eq. (5). The wedge function is calculated based on the average of weighted individual ruled outputs. For each rule, the weighted function is evaluated using the member function of antecedent rule. The discussed process is accomplished by converting the input values in to the member function of the fuzzy with the help of input member function. The obtained member values are processed with ∩ operator. The ∩ operator relates to the input member value multiplication. Therefore, the rules weighting factors is evaluated as

$$w_1 = A_{11}(S_1) * A_{21}(S_2) * A_{31}(S_3)$$
$$w_1 = A_{11}(S_1) * A_{21}(S_2) * A_{31}(S_3)$$
$$w_1 = A_{11}(S_1) * A_{21}(S_2) * A_{31}(S_3)$$
$$w_1 = A_{11}(S_1) * A_{21}(S_2) * A_{31}(S_3)$$
$$.................. \ ...$$
$$w_1 = A_{11}(S_1) * A_{21}(S_2) * A_{31}(S_3)$$

Once the weighting factors are obtained, the output of the system can be found by calculating the weighted average of the individual rule outputs

$$Y = \frac{\sum_{k=1}^{27} w_k * \eta_k}{\sum_{k=1}^{27} w_k} \tag{6}$$

The two Neuro-Fuzzy widgets output are assigned to the decision maker for providing the final detector output. The functionality of the decision maker is to calculate the minimum and maximum values of the given widget outputs and to adjust their range according to the luminous values of the pixels. The comparison is made against the threshold value. Equation (7) shows the decision maker computation, is following formula to process the output.

Let Y_H and Y_V represent the outputs of horizontal and vertical wedges, respectively. The output of the decision maker, which is also the output of the proposed NF speckle noise removal, is calculated as follows:

$$y(a, b) = \begin{cases} MIN & if \frac{Y_H + Y_V}{2} < \frac{MIN + MAX}{2} \\ MAX & if \frac{Y_H + Y_V}{2} \geq \frac{MIN + MAX}{2} \end{cases} \tag{7}$$

From Eq. (7), the MIN and MAX represent as the minimum and maximum values of image pixels that the allowable dynamic luminance range, respectively. For 8-bit images, MIN is 0 and MAX is 255.

The entire filtering operation is performed through the noise input image and it is processed by three stages. At very first stage level, the noise input image is processed by using the noise removal operator. The second stage, the noise input image and de-speckled image are given as input to noise detector to detect the noise patterns. As discussed before, the locations of the white pixels in the noise detection image indicate the locations of the corrupted pixels in the noise input image. At final stage, the enhancement process is carried out by interfacing the pixels of noise input image and the output image of the noise removal operator. The output image pixels that are corresponds to the white pixels in the noise detection image are copied from the output image of the noise filtering operator, and other image pixels are shown directly from the original input image.

5 Performance Analysis

The performance analysis of proposed Neuro-Fuzzy based approach is presented in this section. The proposed approach is implemented using Matlab. In order to test the proposed approach SAR image of size 512×512 is considered.

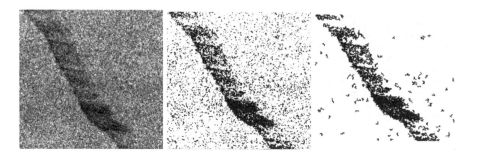

Fig. 4. (a) Original SAR image, (b) De-speckled image and (c) Difference image or noise image

The input parameter and output membership functions of two wedges are optimized by the heuristic testing schema. Figure 3 shows the training setup for using the original SAR image. In Fig. 4(a) the original SAR image with noise is presented. The filtered image is shown in Fig. 4(b). The difference between original and filtered image is shown in Fig. 4(c).

The quality of the de-speckled image is evaluated through Mean Absolute Error (MAE) which is a measure of difference between two images and is defined as shown in Eq. (8) and it is shown in Table 1.

$$MAE = \frac{1}{AB} \sum_{a=1}^{A} \sum_{b=1}^{B} ||x(a,b) - y(a,b)|| \qquad (8)$$

Table 1. The calculated Mean Absolute Error (MAE) is compared with the results obtained using above said algorithms

Filter	MAE (%)
SAR-BM3-D	85.7
SA-WBMMAE	74.50
MAP-S	82.00
PPB	78.80
Sigma filter	81.14
2D-GARCH-M	82.49
ATWD	80.32
2D-HS	79.56
UKF	78.80
GM	84.15
Proposed	91.20

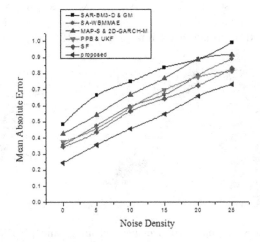

Fig. 5. Comparison of calculated MAE with existing approaches

The obtained results are compared with the results of SAR-BM3-D filter [15], spatially adaptive wavelet homomorphic shrinkage algorithm (SA-WBMMAE) [16], the wavelet-based MAP filtering algorithm (MAP-S) [17], the PPB nonlocal filter [18], Sigma filter [19], 2D-GARCH-M filter [20], Adaptive thresholding of wavelet-domain (ATWD) filter [21], 2-D Heteroscedasticity Sparse (2D-HS) filter [22], Unscented Kalman Filter (UKF) [23,24], and GaussMarkov (GM) filter [25].

In Fig. 5 the graphical representation of obtained MAE is shown. It is evident from the obtained results that the proposed approach is performing well in removing speckle noise from SAR images.

6   Conclusion and Future Work

In this work a novel Neuro-Fuzzy based approach is proposed. It could effectively remove noise in SAR images. The objective evaluation is carried out for performance analysis of images. The calculated MAE shows the proposed approach is giving better results compared to existing algorithms. In future, the proposed approach could be extended with numerous fuzzy rules to enhance the quality of images.

References

1. Yu, Y., Acton, S.T.: Speckle reducing anisotropic diffusion. IEEE Trans. Image Process. **11**(11), 1260–1270 (2002)
2. Mastin, G.A.: Adaptive filters for digital image noise smoothing: an evaluation. Comput. Vis. Graph. Image Process. **31**(1), 103–121 (1985)
3. Frost, V.S., Stiles, J.A., Shanmugan, K.S., Holtzman, J.C.: A model for radar images and its application to adaptive digital filtering of multiplicative noise. IEEE Trans. Pattern Anal. Mach. Intell. **2**, 157–166 (1982)
4. Lee, J.-S.: Digital image enhancement and noise filtering by use of local statistics. IEEE Trans. Pattern Anal. Mach. Intell. **2**, 165–168 (1980)
5. Lopes, A., Nezry, E., Touzi, R., Laur, H.: Maximum a posteriori speckle filtering and first order texture models in SAR images. In: 10th Annual International Geoscience and Remote Sensing Symposium on Remote Sensing Science for the Nineties, IGARSS 1990, pp. 2409–2412. IEEE (1990)
6. Oliver, C., Quegan, S.: Understanding Synthetic Aperture Radar Images. Artech House, Norwood (1998)
7. Lopes, A., Touzi, R., Nezry, E.: Adaptive speckle filters and scene heterogeneity. IEEE Trans. Geosci. Remote Sens. **28**(6), 992–1000 (1990)
8. Pandey, R., Ghanekar, U.: Fuzzy Filtering Algorithms for Image Processing: Performance Evaluation of Various Approaches
9. Tyan, C.-Y., Wang, P.P.: Image processing-enhancement, filtering and edge detection using the fuzzy logic approach. In: Second IEEE International Conference on Fuzzy Systems, pp. 600–605. IEEE (1993)
10. Lee, J.S.: Speckle suppression and analysis for synthetic aperture radar images. Opt. Eng. **25**(5), 255636–255636 (1986)
11. Argenti, F., Alparone, L.: Speckle removal from SAR images in the undecimated wavelet domain. IEEE Trans. Geosci. Remote Sens. **40**(11), 2363–2374 (2002)
12. Li, Y., Gong, H., Feng, D., Zhang, Y.: An adaptive method of speckle reduction and feature enhancement for SAR images based on curvelet transform and particle swarm optimization. IEEE Trans. Geosci. Remote Sens. **49**(8), 3105–3116 (2011)
13. Buckley, J.J., Hayashi, Y.: Fuzzy neural networks: a survey. Fuzzy Sets Syst. **66**(1), 1–13 (1994)
14. Basturk, A., Yksel, M.E.: A generalized neuro-fuzzy filter for removing different types of noise in digital images by a single operator. In: 2006 IEEE 14th Conference on Signal Processing and Communications Applications, pp. 1–4. IEEE, April 2006
15. Jang, J.-S.R., Sun, C.-T., Mizutani, E.: Neuro-Fuzzy and Soft Computing. Prentice-Hall, Upper Saddle River (1997)

16. Bhuiyan, M., Ahmad, M., Swamy, M.: Spatially adaptive wavelet based method using the cauchy prior for denoising the SAR images. IEEE Trans. Circuits Syst. Video Technol. **17**(4), 500–507 (2007)

17. Argenti, F., Bianchi, T., Alparone, A.: Segmentation-based MAP despeckling of SAR images in the undecimated wavelet domain. IEEE Trans. Geosci. Remote Sens. **46**(9), 2728–2742 (2008)

18. Deledalle, C., Denis, L., Tupin, F.: Iterative weighted maximum likelihood denoising with probabilistic patch-based weights. IEEE Trans. Image Process. **18**(12), 2661–2672 (2009)

19. Lee, J.-S.: Speckle suppression and analysis for synthetic aperture radar images. Optical Eng. **25**(5), 255636–255636 (1986)

20. Amirmazlaghani, M., Amindavar, H.: Two novel Bayesian multiscale approaches for speckle suppression in SAR images. IEEE Trans. Geosci Remote Sens. **47**(7), 2980–2993 (2010)

21. Gnanadurai, D., Sadasivam, V.: An efficient adaptive thresholding technique for wavelet based image denoising. Int. J. Sig. Process. **2**(2), 114–119 (2005)

22. Amirmazlaghani, M., Amindavar, H.: A novel sparse method for despeckling SAR images. IEEE Trans. Geosci. Remote Sens. **50**(12), 5024–5032 (2012)

23. Julier, S.J., Uhlmann, J.K.: A general method for approximating nonlinear transformations of probability distributions. Technical report, RRG, Department of Engineering Science, University of Oxford, Oxford, UK (1996)

24. Julier, S.J., Uhlmann, J.K.: A new extension of the Kalman filter to nonlinear systems. In: Presented at the AeroSense: 11th International Symposium on Aerospace/Defense Sensing, Simulation and Controls, Orlando, FL (1997)

25. Gleich, D., Datcu, M.: Gauss Markov model for wavelet-based SAR image despeckling. IEEE Sig. Process. Lett. **13**(6), 365–368 (2006)

A Hybrid Approach for Hyper Spectral Image Segmentation Using SMLR and PSO Optimization

Rashmi P. Karchi[1][(✉)] and B.K. Nagesh[2]

[1] Deaprtment of Computer Science, Bharathiar University,
Coimbatore 641046, Tamilnadu, India
rashmikarchi@gmail.com
[2] Department of Computer Science and Engineering, S.I.T.,
Mangalore 574143, Karnataka, India
nagesh.bk@gmail.com

Abstract. A hybrid approach for hyperspectral image segmentation is presented in this paper. The contribution of the proposed work is in two folds. First, learning of the class posterior probability distributions with Quadratic Programming or joint probability distribution by employing sparse multinomial logistic regression (SMLR) model. Secondly, estimation of the dependencies using spatial information and edge information by minimum spanning forest rooted on markers by acquiring the information from the first step to segment the hyper spectral image using a Markov Random field segments. The particle swarm optimization (PSO) is performed based on the SMLR posterior probabilities to reduce the large number of training data set. The performance of the proposed approach is illustrated in a number of experimental comparisons with recently introduced hyperspectral image analysis methods using both simulated and real hyper spectral data sets of Mars.

Keywords: Feature selection · Hyperspectral image classification · Particle swarm optimization · Spatio-spectral analysis

1 Introduction

Spectroscopy has a long history of providing the fundamental compositional discoveries in the solar system, from atmospheric constituents to surface mineralogy, from ground based to spacecraft-based observations [1]. Some spectroscopic compositional discoveries have come only after many years of research. It is critical that each mission provides answers to relevant questions to optimize the success of the next mission to get more accurate interpretations needed for such ambitious and time critical exploration objectives. Some of the major problems dealing with satellite images are:

– **End-to-End testing:** Determination of uncertainties as related to studies of Mars requires demonstration through coordinated of End-to-End testing.

© Springer Nature Singapore Pte Ltd. 2017
K.C. Santosh et al. (Eds.): RTIP2R 2016, CCIS 709, pp. 261–269, 2017.
DOI: 10.1007/978-981-10-4859-3_24

- **High fidelity data:** There are gaps in terrestrial hyper spectral airborne or satellite data sets for CRISM and OMEGA (mainly 2.5–5 μm) and essentially no thermal-IR hyper spectral satellite data sets comparable to TES exist in the NASA community.
- **Lander development data:** The NASA community has essentially no field, data sets available measured with high fidelity to the Lander Mini-TES or Pancam.
- **Mismatch of flight data release and R&A research:** Many factors make the spatial resolution one of the most expensive and hardest to improve in imaging systems [3]. This circumstance can occur independently of the spatial resolution of the sensor. According to scientists, the minerals were indentified because they either reflect or absorb part of the electromagnetic spectrum. Beneath the layer of dust, the Martian crust consists mostly of volcanic basalt rock. The soil of Mars also holds nutrients such as sodium, potassium, chloride and magnesium. As we go deeper and deeper based on the interaction of electromagnetic radiation with matter different minerals like Iron Oxide, Hydrated Minerals, Serpentines, Olivines and other minerals are found and their spectrum range are given below;
- **Iron Oxide:** The go ethic and hematite spectra have broad band cantered at about 0.9 μm to 1.3 μm.
- **Hydrated Minerals:** The minerals have spectral features at 1.4, 1.9 and 2.5 μm and a more variable band at 2.2 μm.
- **Surpentines:** All the serpentine spectra have a strong M shape duet absorptions at 1.91 μm (H-O-H), 2.32 (FE) bonds.
- **Olivines:** The olivine fayalite & forsterite spectra have in common broad spectral feature at 1 μm.
- **Other Minerals:** The hypersthene and the diopside spectra are directly related to the detection of LCP-OPx and HCP-CPx, respectively kieserite, jarosite, kaolinite, calcite, kaolinite having spectral range from 0.02 to 2.02 μm.

Among all possible signal processing applications that exploit hyper spectral data, we are more interested in the thematic area of spectral unmixing. This leads to get corresponding endmembers. Endmembers normally correspond to familiar macroscopic objects in the scene, such as water, soil, metal etc. In the case of hyper spectral sensing in the reflective regime, and ignoring atmospheric effects, the incident signal is electromagnetic radiation that originates from the sun and is measured by a sensor after it has been reflected upwards by natural and man-made materials on the surface of the mars. Nevertheless, the complete end to-end unmixing problem is decomposed in three stages namely dimension reduction, end member determination, and inversion. Most of the researchers working separately to explore the techniques involved in exploiting these stages [4].

In this paper the algorithm is illustrated with data of synthetic and simulated type. A set of experiments are carried out in reference to the size of the training set in distinct conditions of data with synthetic and simulated type. The performance is evaluated individually for the both estimation of SMLR and the segmentation steps and further compared with hyper-spectral classification/segmentation methods. The proposed algorithm also provides highlight on other major advantages like: (1) MLL spatial prior helps to model accurately the piecewise continuous nature of the image elements, and (2) Usage of a-expansion algorithm for hard integer optimization problem gives high-quality approximate solutions with optimal computations [7]. The objective of this article is to systematically introduce the reader to the wide variety of techniques being employed for spectral unmixing. The rest of the paper is organized as follows, Sect. 2 explains the background knowledge regarding the related work. Section 3 explains and formulates the proposed System. The experimental results are discussed in Sect. 4; we conclude the work with future work of the paper at Sect. 5.

2   Related Work

Recent advances in hyperspectral image classification and segmentation has stimulated an interest by the research community. It is due to the spectral resolution of the hyperspectral data. The spectral resolution is higher and that competence in discrimination between similar classes. In past decades, many classification techniques have been proposed using unsupervised and semi supervised approaches of data mining. The posterior class densities algorithms follow less complexity than their generative counterparts [8,9]. The encodement of the boundary between classes are conceptually considered as simpler approach to classification [10]. As approaches are discriminant methods, which offers a high classification accuracy but lags in the inter cluster analysis and intra cluster similarity of the image features in the hyperspectral images.

In Unsupervised classification, training sample has to undergo with accurate and highly robust discriminative model, as it depends on the spectral bands. However the number of the labeled data is increased as training data, it gradually increase the pixel labeling or feature labeling of the image which results in over fitting issues. The Above problem is alleviated by hybrid approach which exploits the function of SMLR model to acquire and know the information about the class posterior probability distributions with Quadratic Programming or joint probability distribution which obtained without significant cost. Next, the proposed work uses the information acquired in the prior step to segment the hyper spectral image using a Markov Random field segments the data to estimate the dependencies using spatial information. To minimize the cost of acquiring large training sets, PSO optimization is performed based on the SMLR posterior probabilities [11].

3   Proposed Model

In the proposed work, a hybrid approach to hyperspectral image viz. combination of simulated and real hyperspectral Mars data, segmentation with active learning is presented. Firstly, learning the class posterior probability distributions using the models sparse multinomial logistic regression (SMLR) model with Quadratic Programming or joint probability distribution is performed.

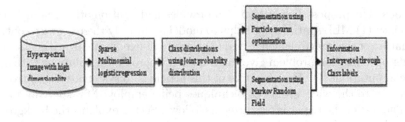

Fig. 1. Steps involved in proposed model.

In further stage, the information acquired in the prior step to segment the hyper spectral image using a Markov Random field segments to estimate the dependencies using spatial information and edge Information by minimum spanning forest rooted on markers is used. The cost required for acquiring large training data set of Mars, particle swarm optimization (PSO) is performed based on the SMLR posterior probabilities, which is shown in Fig. 1. The detailed description of both the steps are explained in the following subsections.

3.1   Sparse Multinomial Logistic Regression (SMLR) Model

To learn the class posterior probability distributions a sparse multinomial logistic regression (SMLR) model with Quadratic Programming or joint probability distribution is used in the proposed work. Normally the class probability distribution is learned using Multinomial logistic regression to generate the feature detection and selection to classify/identify the subsets of the small subset of the similar features.

Lets represents the $x = [x_1, x_2.x_d]$ is the set of the features. Each feature xi is classified by MLR to the probability of K Classes. It provides accurate solution for two-class (i.e. binary) case but better approximation for more number of classes. The Gaussian radial basis function is mainly used kernel function for image classification [12]. In order to achieve sparsity in the estimation of vector, a sparsity-promoting prior is incorporated in the inference of vector. The prior will control the classifier complexity. In addition, to avoid the unbounded development of the log-likelihood function, the prior on vector is employed on the training data when they are separable in nature.

3.2   Markov Random Field Segments

Markov Random field is more suitable to hyperspectral image classification through integer optimization tools based on graph cut technique. The proposed paper employs the information/characteristics extracted in the prior step to segment the hyper spectral image using a Markov Random field segments for blending the spatial and edge information into the classification [13]. The data is to estimate the dependencies of the features using spatial information. Moreover the spatial characteristics of hyperspectral data is processed by employing an additional regularization phrase on the arrangement of labeled and unlabelled data of the SMLR classification [6].

1. **Clustering criteria for Hyperspectral Images.** The association of spatial neighbors can be classified into two categories:

   (a) The related pixels of the class is grouped based on spatial and spectral similarity;

   (b) The pixels belong to different intensity is grouped under discriminate classes. The classification of the hyperspectral pixels is performed based on the spatial smoothness. The belongingness of the spatial adjacent to its own class is having higher level of spatial smoothness compared to other classes. Hence, the Euclidean distance metric is computed among the spectra of pixels and represented as spatial similarity matrix [6].

2. **Constraints in the characterizing the Images labels**

   (a) A proximity spatial constraint is employed on the estimation of sample labels, to avoid the spot-like dissimilarity of the hyper-spectral images.

   (b) The categorization is performed on spectral vectors to devise a manifold regularization to use both the labeled samples and unlabeled samples, to achieve higher level of classification with few number of labeled samples; and

   (c) The algorithm PSO is carried in next section to solve dual-regularized problem with its a non-iterative optimization algorithm, which makes a rapid Hybrid classification possible [6].

3. **PSO optimization.** Cost of acquiring large training sets, PSO optimization is performed based on the SMLR posterior where probabilities are reduced. PSO optimization is carried out in the low density separation techniques as it often non convex and it is difficult to solve in large no of unlabelled samples. It is iterative optimization operation to predict the class to the low density image features [14].

   (a) **Feature selection and Feature labeling through PSO.** Feature selection is an important steps to detect and extract the discriminative characteristics of the hyper-spectral images. Estimate of the class statistical characteristics during the optimization process will be performed by employing the particle swarm optimization (PSO). The fitness function is employed for the estimation of class number and selection of the most discriminative features as a training data. Whereas, the estimation of the class number is computed by using a the minimum description length (MDL) approach. The interesting point is that, statistical distance among the classes is computed with fitness function for the subspace of detected features [17].

As described in algorithm the hyperspectral image is processed to transform into vector V1 with labeled features and V2 with unlabelled features. Further compute Spatial and Spectral similarity matrix for vectors V1 and V2. In order to classify select the kernel function and then apply Markov Random field for pixel weighting. The optimization process will be performed by employing the PSO. Finally the classification/segmentation is carried out by predicting the labels of unlabelled samples in the classes with low density.

Algorithm 1. SMLR+PSO optimization for Hyperspectral classification

Input: Hyperspectral Images

Output: Classes of the Images features in vector form

Begin

1: Step 1: Process Hyperspectral Image(I);
2: Step 2: Transform I into Vector V_1 with Labeled features;
3: Step 3: Transform I into Vector V_2 with unlabelled features;
4: Step 4: Compute Spatial and Spectral similarity matrix for vectors V_1 and V_2;
5: Step 5: Choose the kernel function for classifying;
6: Step 6: Apply Markov Random field for pixel weighting;
7: Step 7: Optimize the class through PSO;
8: Step 8: Predict the labels of unlabelled samples in the classes with low density;

End

4   Experimental Analysis

The experiments is been carried out on the MARS hyperspectral data [2,5] The hyperspectral images are taken with fixed spatial dimensions, and it preprocessed for the noise removal and it is further taken to the feature extraction process. To generate a feature, hyperspectral value of the image is derived through multivariate Gaussian distribution and it modeled using fitness function by this features were selected and extracted, classes determined by the MDL criteria and its performance compared against mean and variance. The error in classification is given by Err_c in 1,

$$Err_c = \frac{\mu_{i,j} - \mu_{ijtrue}}{\mu_{max} - \mu_{min}} \tag{1}$$

Where μ_{ij} is a mean value estimation for the jth class along the ith feature, μ_{ijtrue} is the corresponding true mean value associated with over all features and all classes μ_{max} is the maximum true mean value and μ_{min} is the minimum true mean value. The MRF segmentation of the hyperspectral image is given in the Fig. 2.

Fig. 2. Hyperspectral images classification based on the MRF.

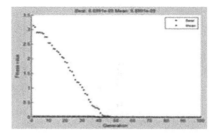

Fig. 3. Performance of the PSO approach in generation of the class label by reducing time in the distribution of the feature labels.

From Fig. 3, it is clear that PSO based classification optimization yields a higher level of accuracy of classification map compared with the ground truth.

It is noteworthy that the numbers of iterations required by the SMLR and optimization using PSO algorithms leads to common results are relatively similar with MRF segmentation. In addition, it exhibits the relation that, the number of complete runs of the SMLR posterior capabilities is independent of the number of iterations required.

Fig. 4. PSO with MRF segmentation of the MARS image.

MRF-based spatial characterization with PSO optimization can increase the performance through linear mapping with less number of training samples whereas the feature extraction with discriminant analysis applied to increase spectral separation which is been shown in Fig. 4.

The classification accuracy is given in the Fig. 5. The accuracy results are depicted in Table 1, which point out the performance of the proposed segmentation in terms of precision, recall and Specificity.

It is noticed that the higher level of accuracy values are achieved with the optimized classification of hyperspectral image categorized to unsupervised classification. It can be applicable any type of Mars dataset. The process is tested with different spectral images from MARS surface to classify the minerals.

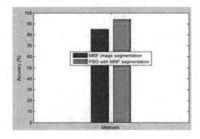

Fig. 5. Performance evaluation of the PSO with MRF segmentation and MRF segmentation.

Table 1. Performance values of the proposed classification- PSO with MRF for mineral classes

Metrics	Class 1	Class 2	Class 3	Class 4	Class 5
True positive	63084	5000	50597	57975	29373
False positive	4461	11652	10681	8007	4422
False negative	10351	3700	9326	10613	5233
True negative	182768	224900	190060	184069	221636
Precision	0.93	0.64	0.83	0.88	0.87
Recall or Sensitivity	0.86	0.85	0.84	0.85	0.85
Specificity	0.98	0.95	0.95	0.96	0.98

5   Conclusion

Hyperspectral image segmentation with active learning is performed by an hybrid approach consists of two main steps. Firstly, the proposed work emphasize the class posterior probability distributions by employing sparse multinomial logistic regression (SMLR) model with Quadratic Programming or joint probability distribution. Secondly, the usage of information acquired in the first step to segment the hyper spectral image using a Markov Random field segments to estimate the dependencies using spatial information and edge information by minimum spanning forest rooted on markers. To reduce the higher number of training sets and the cost requirement towards the collection of training samples the PSO optimization is performed based on the first step viz. SMLR posterior probabilities. Hence, the performance of the proposed method is explained by using the hybrid approach viz. combination of simulated and real hyper-spectral Mars data achieves better results. In future, the experimentation can be performed with data sets acquired by other instruments of Mars.

References

1. Kirkland, L., Mustard, J., McAfee, J., Hapke, B., Ramsey, M.: Mars infrared spectroscopy: from theory and the laboratory to field observations (2002)
2. Murchie, S., et al.: Compact Reconnaissance Imaging Spectrometer for Mars (CRISM) on Mars Reconnaissance Orbiter (MRO). J. Geophys. Res. **112**(03), 1–57 (2007)
3. Villa, A.: Spectral unmixing for the classification of hyperspectral images at a finer spatial resolution. IEEE **5**(3), 521–533 (2010)
4. Karchi, R.P., Nagesh B.K.: A review of spectral unmixing algorithms in the context of Mars dataset. Int. J. Latest Trends Eng. Technol. 55–60 (2013). Special Issue - IDEAS-2013
5. http://pds-geosciences.wustl.edu/missions/mro/crism.htm
6. Yang, L., Yang, S., Jin, P., Zhang, R.: Semi-supervised hyperspectral image classification using spatio-spectral Laplacian support vector machine. IEEE Geosci. Remote Sens. Lett. **11**(3), 651–655 (2014)
7. Borges, J.S., Bioucas-Dias, J.M., Marcal, A.R.S.: Bayesian hyperspectral image segmentation with discriminative class learning. IEEE Trans. Geosci. Remote Sens. **49**(6), 2151–2164 (2011)
8. Villa, A., Benediktsson, J.A., Chanussot, J., Jutten, C.: Hyperspectral image classification with independent component discriminant analysis. IEEE Trans. Geosci. Remote Sens. **49**(12), 4865–4876 (2011)
9. Mianji, F.A., Zhang, Y.: Robust hyperspectral classification using relevance vector machine. IEEE Trans. Geosci. Remote Sens. **49**(6), 2100–2112 (2011)
10. Bishop, C.M.: Pattern Recognition and Machine Learning (Information Science and Statistics), 1st edn. Springer, New York (2007)
11. Li, J., Dias, J.M.B., Plaza, A.: Semi-supervised hyperspectral image classification using soft sparse multinomial logistic regression. IEEE Geosci. Remote Sens. Lett. **10**(2), 318–322 (2013)
12. Gu, Y.F., Feng, K.: L1-graph semisupervised learning for hyperspectral image classification. In: IEEE International Geoscience and Remote Sensing Symposium, Munich, Germany, pp. 1401–1404 (2012)
13. Kim, W., Crawford, M.M.: Adaptive classification for hyperspectral image data using manifold regularization kernel machines. IEEE Trans. Geosci. Remote Sens. **48**(11), 4110–4121 (2010)
14. Rajadell, O., Garca-Sevilla, P., Pla, F.: Spectral-spatial pixel characterization using Gabor filters for hyperspectral image classification. IEEE Geosci. Remote Sens. Lett. **10**(4), 860–864 (2013)
15. Fauvel, M., Tarabalka, Y., Benediktsson, J.A., Chanussot, J., Tilton, J.C.: Advances in spectral-spatial classification of hyperspectral images. Proc. IEEE **101**(3), 652–675 (2013)
16. Melacci, S., Belkin, M.: Laplacian support vector machines trained in the primal. J. Mach. Learn. Res. **12**(3), 1149–1184 (2011)
17. Paoli, A., Melgani, F., Pasolli, E.: Clustering of hyperspectral images based on multiobjective particle swarm optimization. IEEE Trans. Geosci. Remote Sens. **47**(12), 4175–4188 (2009)

An Integrated Framework to Image Retrieval Using L*a*b Color Space and Local Binary Pattern

N. Neelima$^{(\boxtimes)}$, P. Koteswara rao, N. Sai Praneeth, and G.N. Mamatha

Jain University, Bangalore 562112, Karnataka, India
neelima.niz@gmail.com
http://www.jainuniversity.ac.in

Abstract. Information retrieval in the form of documents, images is playing a key role in day-to-day life of humans. Real world applications scenario is changing daily, so as the improvement is also becomes a necessary. Various approaches were proposed for retrieval, but all the input images were considered under proper illumination conditions. If the images suffered with illumination angle color and viewing angle changes then it's very difficult to retrieve similar images. We propose a system which can deal with illumination angle and color variations. Experiments were conducted on ALOI (Amsterdam Library of Object Images) dataset, which is a collection of one thousand objects each with hundred similar images. These images were recorded under changing the illumination angle, color and viewing angle. Experimental results prove that the proposed approach outperforms well in terms of retrieval efficiency ...

Keywords: Segmentation · L*a*b color space · Similarity matching · Cityblock distance

1 Introduction

Visual content based information retrieval is a process which is used to search, index and retrieve semantically relevant images from large databases [1]. Intensive research is being carried out in this field, as it has tremendous applications in digital media, medical investigation and object tracking. Any retrieval system has two significant challenges: feature selection/extraction and similarity matching. These challenges were addressed by a handful of approaches, but still finding a proper solution is still a bottleneck. Huneiti proposed a method which uses hsv space and wavelets. First all the images are converted into hsv space and then decompose by using wavelets [1]. The LL sub-band is quantized and texture features are extracted. These features are compared to measure the similarity between the images and with respect to the ascending order of the distance the most relevant images are retrieved. The main disadvantage of this approach is if the images are rotated or any illumination change occurs, then the corresponding precision dropped down.

© Springer Nature Singapore Pte Ltd. 2017
K.C. Santosh et al. (Eds.): RTIP2R 2016, CCIS 709, pp. 270–276, 2017.
DOI: 10.1007/978-981-10-4859-3_25

Sudipta [3] proposed a texture based image retrieval system using fuzzy logic. This approach works well only with texture databases. As the real-time applications use mostly color images this approach cannot be used for several applications. A new approach using Gabor Wavelets and its correlogram for image retrieval is proposed in [8]. Gabor wavelets are used to decompose the images into different scales and orientations. Then these coefficients are quantized using threshold values and the corresponding autocorrelogram is computed. By matching the autocorrelogram between the images the relevance between the images is indexed and displayed. Another retrieval system based on shape and texture features is proposed by Xiang wang in [5]. These features are extracted from the query and database images and compared by means of euclidean distance. To extract the shape features morphological operations are used. Block Truncation coding (BTC) is applied over the feature extracted images to construct the feature vectors. The main drawback of the above two methods is they are evaluated only for wang data set. Huang [6] discussed the system with HSV color model, a method of object-based spatial-color feature (OSCF) for color image retrieval. Firstly, objects are extracted from color, and then image features are represented by objects in it. This method concentrates mainly on central objects. The main drawback of the above two methods is the efficiency decreases as the number of retrieved images increases. The author proposed a novel fuzzy approach to classify the color images based on their content and neural network is used for fast and efficient retrieval in [7]. As this approach concentrates only on color, it is not applicable for some of the data sets such as MPEG CE. We propose an integrated approach which use L*a*b space for color image segmentation and local binary pattern for texture feature extraction. The experimental evaluation proves that the proposed system outperformed than the state-of-art systems in terms of precision.

2   Proposed Retrieval Approach

The proposed system architecture is described in Fig. 1. It consists of two phases: offline and on-line. The offline process is also known as feature database preparation. At first, all the input RGB color images are segmented using L*a*b color space to identify the visual differences between the colors.

Then for each segmented color region the texture features are calculated using local binary pattern (LBP). As LBP is invariant to illumination changes the texture features are calculated easily. These features are stored as feature vectors in feature database. In the on-line phase, when the user enters the query image, the above process is repeated to compute the feature vector. This feature vector is compared with the feature vectors in feature database. The similarity between the features is calculated using city block distance and it decides the most relevant images which are to be displayed.

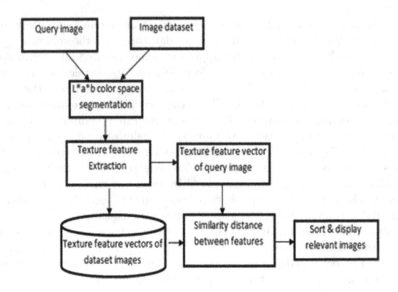

Fig. 1. Block diagram of the proposed approach

2.1   L*a*b Color Space Segmentation

The L*a*b color space has three dimensions, where L stands for brightness, and "ab" stands for chromacity (or) color content. 'a' indicates the range of colors which falls along the red-green axis and 'b' indicates the range of colors which falls along the blue-yellow axis. The first step is to identify the sample colors in lab space. Classify each pixel value based on its nearest neighborhood pixel so that it can fall on to either 'a' or 'b'. The general possible values for L are from 0 to 100 and for 'a' and 'b' are from -128 to $+127$. The positive values of 'a' indicates that the corresponding pixel color is close to magenta and negative values indicates that the color is in range of green. Similarly positive and negative values of 'b' indicate the color ranges from yellow to blue. This space allows us to quantify the visual differences between the colors properly. The difference between 'a' and 'b' gives the similar visual effect as human visual system. As it is the three dimensional space the conversion from RGB to L, a, b is given by the following Eqs. (1), (2) and (3).

$$L = 116[f(Y/Y_n) - 16] \tag{1}$$

$$a = 500[f(X/X_n) - f(Y/Y_n)] \tag{2}$$

$$b = 200[f(Y/Y_n) - f(Z/Z_n)] \tag{3}$$

where Xn, Yn, Zn are the co-ordinates of the CIE-XYZ color space which are derived from X, Y, Z. These are calculated as follows given in Eq. (4).

$$X = 0.608R + 0.174G + 0.201B \quad Y = 0.299R + 0.587G + 0.114B \quad Z = 0.000R + 0.066G + 1.117B \tag{4}$$

Then by using genetic algorithm the color spaces are segmented. For each color segmented region texture features are calculated. This is discussed in the following section.

2.2 Local Binary Pattern

Local binary pattern is used to extract the texture content of the image. Now, for each color region the texture features are extracted and stored in a feature vector. For each pixel a radius of neighborhood is defined and in that neighborhood the pixel values are compared. If the center pixel value is greater than the neighborhood value it is replaced with '1' else it is '0'. So, a series of 0's and 1's are generated. The corners and edges are represented by a group of similar patterns which are known as uniform patterns. The LBP histogram enables us to classify the texture content. This texture features are stored in feature vectors. Then the similarity is measured between the texture features.

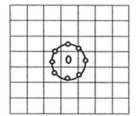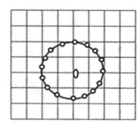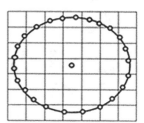

Fig. 2. Examples of LBP operator with different radius and sampling points $(8, 1)$, $(16, 2)$, $(24, 3)$

$$LBP_{(P,R)}(x_c, y_c) = \sum_{p=0}^{p-1} s(g_p - g_c) \tag{5}$$

Equation 5 is used to calculate LBP, where gp is the gray level intensity of the particular pixel and gc is the gray level value with in the $3 * 3$ neighborhood of the center pixel. Figure 2 provides the different neighborhoods with the specified radius.

3   Results

The proposed approach is evaluated on ALOI (Amsterdam Library of Object Images) database. It consist 1000 different classes of objects each with 100 different images. These images were recorded under changing the illumination angle, illumination color and viewing angle. These images were recorded from left to right of an object by changing the number of cameras focused and changing

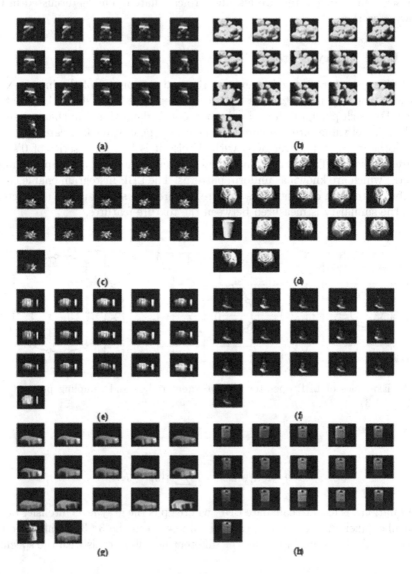

Fig. 3. The retrieval results at precision P(2/3) for sample query images in ALOI dataset

Table 1. Retrieval efficiency comparison of proposed approach with state-of-art system [2]

Probability	State-of-art system	Proposed approach
P(1/3)	100	100
P(2/3)	94.66	98
P(1)	83.14	89

the sensor temperature. City block distance is used to calculate the similarity between the feature vectors. The images are displayed as per the ascending order of the distance. The retrieval efficiency is defined as Precision = number of similar images retrieved/total number of images retrieved (Fig. 3).

The city block distance between the feature vectors of query image (Qi) and database images (Dbi) is given by (6)

$$Cityblock(Qi, Dbi) = \sum_{i=1}^{n} |Q_i - Db_i| \qquad (6)$$

Where Dbi= [Db1, Db2 ... Dbi] are the feature vectors of the database images. The proposed approach is compared with the system in [2] which use wavelet transforms. In this data set each category consists of 24 similar images. The precision of the system is evaluated in terms of three levels P(1/3), P(2/3) and P(1). The precision after retrieving 1/3rd of the relevant images is denoted by P(1/3). The precision after retrieving 2/3rd of relevant documents is denoted by P(2/3) and P(1) is the precision after retrieving all the relevant images. Figure 4 displays the retrieved images at precision level P(2/3) for some of the sample query images. In ALOI database each image has 24 similar images, so the precision P(2/3) means 16 similar images are to be retrieved. In Fig. 4(a–c), (e, f, h) the number of relevant images retrieved are 16/16, so the precision rate is 100. Figure 4(d, g) precision is 16/17 which is 94.11 The detail comparison of the proposed approach with the state-of-art method is given in Table 1.

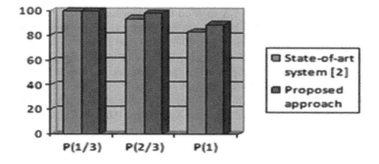

Fig. 4. Precision comparison analysis of proposed and existing approach

The maximum efficiency at precision level P(1) for the existing and proposed systems are 83 and 89. It clearly indicates better performance for the proposed system than the state-of-art system. Figure 4 provides the graphical view of precision comparison between existing and proposed approach.

4   Conclusion

We propose an integrated framework for content based image retrieval using L*a*b space and Local binary pattern. The segmentation plays key role in this approach. L*a*b space allows us to identify the visual differences between the colors properly and local binary pattern enables us to extract texture features. LBP is invariant to illumination changes and L*a*b segmentation provides better segmentation of color space. The precision is evaluated with ALOI database and the overall efficiency is improved from 83 to 89. From Table 1, we conclude that the proposed approach outperforms in terms of efficiency compared to state-of-art system [2].

References

1. Huneiti, A., Daoud, M.: Content based image retrieval using SOM and DWT. J. Soft. Eng. Appl. **8**, 51–61 (2015)
2. Farsi, H., Mohamadzadeh, S.: Color and texture feature-based image retrieval by using Hadamard matrix in discrete wavelet transform. IET Image Process. **7**, 212–218 (2013). doi:10.1049/iet-ipr.2012.0203
3. Mukhopadhyay, S.: Content-based texture image retrieval using fuzzy class membership. J. Pattern Recogn. Lett. **34**(6), 646–654 (2013). doi:10.1016/j.patrec.2013.01.001
4. An, Y., Riaz, M., Park, J.: CBIR based on adaptive segmentation of HSV color space. In: Proceedings of IEEE International Conference on Computer Modelling and Simulation, pp. 248-251. IEEE computer society, ACM pub (2010). doi:10.1016/j.csi.2010.03.004
5. Wang, X.Y., Yu, Y.J., Yang, H.Y.: An effective image retrieval scheme using color, texture and shape features. J. Comput. Stand. Interfaces **33**(1), 59–68 (2011). doi:10.1109/UKSIM.2010.53. Elsevier
6. Huang, C., Han, Y., Zhang, Y.: A method for object-based color image re-trieval, Fuzzy Systems and Knowledge Discovery (FSKD). In: IEEE 9th International Conference on, IEEE computer society, pp. 1659–1663 (2012)
7. Fernando, R., Kulkarni, S.: Hybrid technique for color image classification and efficient retrieval based on fuzzy logic and neural networks. In: The 2012 International Joint Conference on Neural Networks, pp. 1–6 (2012)
8. Moghaddam, H., Nikzad Dehaji, M.: Enhanced Gabor wavelet correlogram feature for image indexing and retrieval. Pattern Anal. Appl. **16**(2), 163–177 (2013)

Texture Classification Using Deep Neural Network Based on Rotation Invariant Weber Local Descriptor

Arnab Banerjee$^{(\boxtimes)}$, Nibaran Das, and Mita Nasipuri

Department of Computer Science and Engineering, Jadavpur University,
Jadavpur, Kolkata 700032, WB, India
arnab.jdvu@yahoo.in, nibaran@gmail.com, mitanasipuri@gmail.com

Abstract. In recent times deep neural network is widely used in different challenging problem domain like object detection, character recognition, and texture classification. There are several texture descriptors present in the pattern recognition domain to classify challenging texture datasets. Recently an efficient texture descriptor called Rotation Invariant Weber local descriptor (WLDRI), an improvement over original Weber local descriptor (WLD) has been developed to classify skin diseases. In this work, we explore the combination of WLDRI kernel in a simple deep neural network. Though the normal WLD and WLDRI efficiently classify the textures but applying WLDRI kernel into deep neural network significantly improves the performance than normal WLD and WLDRI. The present method provides an average improvement of 8.06% over WLDRI with OUTEX-10 dataset and provides 5.03% better accuracy over normal WLD with KTH-TIPS2-a dataset. In addition CMATER skin diseases dataset is used for experiment and it shows 5.74% better performance over the normal WLDRI.

Keywords: Texture classification · WLD · WLDRI · Deep neural network

1 Introduction

In computer vision many texture features have been popularly used in different applications such as object detection, robot vision, industrial automation, satellite image classification, and medical image analysis etc. Generally, local feature descriptor plays an important role in texture classification due to its robustness and short execution time. There are two type descriptors which are popularly used for texture classification; one is sparse descriptor and another is dense descriptor. The sparse descriptor first detects the interest points in a given image, and then samples a local patch and describes its features and dense descriptor extracts local features pixel by pixel over the input image. The scale invariant feature transform (SIFT) introduced by Lowe [1] is the typical sparse descriptor which performs well for object recognition task for its invariance to

© Springer Nature Singapore Pte Ltd. 2017
K.C. Santosh et al. (Eds.): RTIP2R 2016, CCIS 709, pp. 277–292, 2017.
DOI: 10.1007/978-981-10-4859-3_26

scale and rotation. Dalal and Triggs [2] proposed a "histogram of oriented gradients" (HOG) for human detection. Lazebnik et al. [3] proposed a rotation invariant descriptor called the Rotation Invariant Feature Transform (RIFT) for texture recognition. Among different dense descriptors the two most popular descriptors are Gabor Wavelet [4] and local binary pattern [5]. The Gabor filters can be considered as orientation and scale tunable edge and line detectors, and the statistics of these micro features in a given region are often used to model the texture information. The Gabor wavelet has been broadly used in texture classification and segmentation, image registration and face recognition [6]. The dense local descriptor LBP, has also gained increasing attention due to its simplicity and excellent performance in various texture and face image analysis tasks [5]. The local directional pattern (LDP), one of recent dense local descriptor has been used in facial expression analysis task [8] and face recognition task [8]. One of recent robust dense descriptor based on Weber's law introduced by Chen et al. is weber local descriptor (WLD) [9]. The WLD is very robust against noise and illumination change but it is not rotation invariant. A rotation invariant WLD feature descriptor is proposed by Anabik et al. [10] and used for recognizing popular skin diseases such as Leprosy, Tineaversicolor, and Vitiligo along with normal skin image.

In this paper, we proposed a novel approach to apply the WLDRI kernel into a simple deep neural network architecture to improve the classification accuracy with texture datasets. Deep neural network has the inherent capability to learn the optimum features from the training dataset. The above proposed approach is applied on two popular texture dataset OUTEX-10 and KTH-TIPS2-a. We have also applied the proposed method on the CMATER Skin Dataset to check the reliability of the approach. The results of the proposed method outperform the existing WLDRI approach on the same dataset.

2   Weber Local Descriptor

2.1   Weber's Law

Ernst Weber, an experimental psychologist in the 19th century, observed that the ratio of the increment threshold to the background intensity is a constant. So in a noisy environment one must communicate loudly to be heard while a mutter works in quiet room. And when an incremental threshold is observed on various intensity backgrounds, the threshold increased in proportion with to the background. This relationship known as Weber's law can be expressed as:

$$\frac{\Delta.I}{I} = k \tag{1}$$

2.2   WLD

WLD has two components called differential excitation (ξ) and orientation (θ). These two components are described here. The computation of WLD Descriptor is illustrated in Fig. 1.

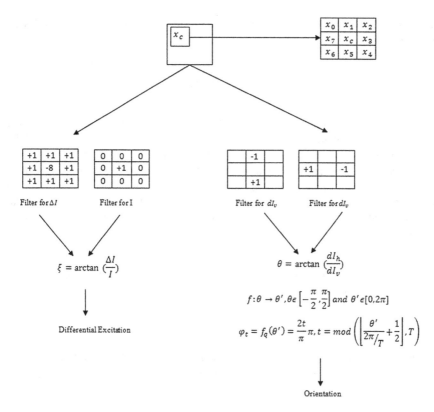

Fig. 1. Computation of WLD Descriptor. Here ΔI represent difference in intensity and I represent the intensity of the current pixel and dI_v and dI_h represents difference of intensity of two pixels at vertical and horizontal direction

Differential Excitation. By the use of the intensity differences between its neighbors and a current pixel as the changes of the current pixel, the salient variations within an image is found to simulate the pattern perception of human beings. Specifically saying, the differential excitation $\xi(X_c)$ of a pixel X_c in an image is computed as follows-At first the intensity differences between the central pixel and its neighbors is computed using the following equation-

$$\Delta I = \sum_{i=0}^{p-1}(\Delta I(X_i)) = \sum_{i=0}^{p-1}(I(X_i) - I(X_c)) \tag{2}$$

Where X_i ($i = 0, 1 \ldots p-1$) denotes the ith neighbors of x_c and p is the number of neighbors. $I(x_i)$ represent the intensity of the current pixel and $I(x_c)$ represent the intensity of the neighboring pixels of x_i. Now the ratio of the differences and the intensity of current pixel are computed using the following equation-

$$\xi(x_c) = arctan\left(\frac{\Delta I}{I}\right) = arctan\left(\sum_{i=0}^{p-1} \frac{I(x_i) - I(x_c)}{I(x_c)}\right) \tag{3}$$

Where I is the intensity of the current pixel $I(x_c)$. The arctan() function is used to limit the output to prevent it from increasing or decreasing too quickly when the input becomes larger or smaller. The Differential excitation may take a negative value if the current pixel intensity is higher than the neighbor intensities. So to find the absolute value of $\xi(x_c)$ more discriminating information have been preserved. If $\xi(x_c)$ is positive, it simulates the case that the current pixel is darker than the neighbors. In contrast, if $\xi(x_c)$ is negative, it simulates the case that current pixel is lighter than the neighbors.

Orientation. Orientation component of WLD is the gradient orientation as in [1]. The orientation is computed as

$$\theta(x_c) = arctan\left(\frac{dI_h}{dI_v}\right) \tag{4}$$

Where $dI_h = I(x_7) - I(x_3)$ and $dI_v = I(x_5) - I(x_1)$ is calculated from the two filter for orientation in the Fig. 1. Now we perform the mapping $f : \theta \rightarrow \theta'$ as-

$$\theta' = arctan2(dI_h, dI_v) + \pi, and \tag{5}$$

$$arctan2(dI_h, dI_v) = \begin{cases} \theta, & dI_h > 0 \quad and \quad dI_v > 0 \\ \pi - \theta, & dI_h > 0 \quad and \quad dI_v < 0 \\ \theta - \pi, & dI_h < 0 \quad and \quad dI_v < 0 \\ -\theta, & dI_h < 0 \quad and \quad dI_v > 0 \end{cases} \tag{6}$$

Where $\theta \in \left[\frac{-\pi}{2}, \frac{\pi}{2}\right]$ and $\theta \in [0, 2\pi]$. The quantization function is as follows:

$$\phi_t = f_q(\theta') = \frac{2t}{T}\pi, and \ t = mod\left(\left\lfloor \frac{\theta'}{\frac{2\pi}{T}} + \frac{1}{2}\right\rfloor, T\right) \tag{7}$$

WLD Histogram. The differential excitation (ξ_j) and orientation (ϕ_t) of each pixel in an image is computed as shown in Fig. 1. Now the 2D histogram is created WLD(ξ_j, ϕ_t), where ($j = 0, 1 \ldots N - 1$) and ($t = 0, 1 \ldots T - 1$). The Fig. 2 illustrates how the WLD 1D histogram is generated. N is dimensionality of an image (for example if an image is of m no. of row and n no. of columns, then dimension is $m \times n$) and T is number of dominant orientations.

Each column of the 2D histogram represents a dominant orientation and each row represents a differential excitation histogram with C bins. So each cell represents the number of pixels present in a certain differential excitation interval

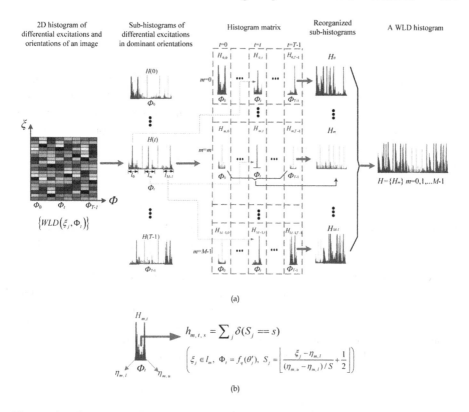

Fig. 2. An illustration of a WLD Histogram of an image (Image Courtesy: WLD: a robust local image descriptor [9])

on a dominant orientation. The 2D histogram is decomposed into T number of 1D histogram. That is for each dominant orientation there is one 1D histogram $H(t)$ where $t = 0, 1 \ldots T - 1$. Now each 1D histogram divided into m number of segments. So each 1D histogram is consists of m number of segments $H_{m,t}$ where $m = 0, 1 \ldots M - 1$. The histogram matrix is then reorganized as 1D histogram H_m where $m = 0, 1 \ldots M - 1$. Specifically each row of the 1D histogram is concatenated as a sub-histogram H_m (i.e. $H_m = \{H_{m,t}\}, t = 0, 1 \ldots T - 1$). Concatenating the M sub-histograms, we have the final 1D histogram $H = \{H_m\}, m = 0, 1 \ldots M - 1$. Each sub-histogram segment $\{H_{m,t}\}$ is composed of S bins, i.e. $H_{m,t} = \{H_{m,t,s}\}, s = 0, 1 \ldots S - 1$. So $H_{m,t,s}$ is computed as:

$$H_{m,t,s} = \sum_j \delta(S_j = S), \left(S_j = \left\lfloor \frac{\xi_j - \eta_{m,l}}{(\eta_{m,u} - \eta_{m,l})/S} + \frac{1}{2} \right\rfloor\right) \qquad (8)$$

Where m is determined according to the interval to which $\xi_j \in l_m$ and t is index of quantized orientation and $\delta(.)$ computed as

$$\delta\left(X\right) = \begin{cases} 1 & X \text{ is true} \\ 0 & \text{otherwise} \end{cases} \tag{9}$$

Here, $H_{m,t,s}$ represents the number of pixels whose differential excitation ξ_j belong to the same interval l_m and $(\eta_{m,u} - \eta_{m,l})/S$ is the width of the each bin and $\frac{\xi_j - \eta_{m,l}}{(\eta_{m,u} - \eta_{m,l})/S}$ is the linear mapping, used to map the differential excitation to its corresponding bin since the value of S_j is real. The size of the WLD 1D histogram is $T \times M \times S$. An illustration of a WLD Histogram of an image is shown in [9].

2.3   Rotation Invariant Weber Local Descriptor (WLDRI)

As mentioned above the original WLD [9] is very robust against noise and illumination change, but not rotation invariant. The rotation invariant WLD is proposed by Anabik et al. [10] and used for recognizing popular skin diseases like Leprosy, Tineaversicolor, Vitiligo and normal image. As the differential excitation computed as the sum of intensity difference between the center pixel and its neighboring pixels, so the value of differential excitation is same for any orientation. But orientation component value is changed if the image is rotated. So all possible mutually perpendicular diagonal pairs are considered for computing orientation and the minimum value among them are taken [10].

$$\theta_i = \arctan\left(\frac{I\left(x_{((\frac{p}{2})+i) \bmod p}\right) - I(x_i)}{I\left(x_{((\frac{3p}{4})+i) \bmod p}\right) - I\left(x_{((\frac{p}{4})+i) \bmod p}\right)}\right) \tag{10}$$

$$\theta\left(x_c\right) = min_{i=0}^{p-1}(\theta_i) \tag{11}$$

3   Deep Neural Network

Deep neural network is different from shallow neural network in the context of depth, i.e. number of layers. A simple deep neural network consists of more than three layers (including input and output layer) and specifically it should have more than one hidden layer. Any hierarchical model with cascaded nonlinear transformation is called deep architecture. Here the network can be extended by adding layers consisting of multiple units and the parameters of each and every layer are trainable. The deep network used the intermediate layers to build up multiple layer of abstraction. It extracts the features from the data automatically without any human intervention. Deep Neural Networks has been used in texture classification using convolutional neural network by [13]. Recently [14] uses multimodal deep autoencoder for human pose recovery.

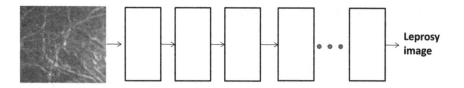

Fig. 3. Layers of deep neural network

4 Proposed Methodology

- The color images are converted into gray scale images with .bmp file extension (we have used irfanview software).
- The raw features are extracted from the images using rotation invariant Weber local descriptor (WLDRI) kernel [10].
- Features are then fitted into a simple deep neural network (3 layers deep) with 3000 neurons present in each hidden layer. Theoretically the WLDRI mask is fitted into the deep neural architecture.
- The deep network is trained with total training set for maximum 1000 epochs. If the error rate will be not decreasing for consecutive 30 epochs the training process is stopped otherwise it is trained for 1000 epochs.
- The trained network is used to classify the unknown texture samples.

The work flow diagram of the proposed system is shown in Fig. 4.

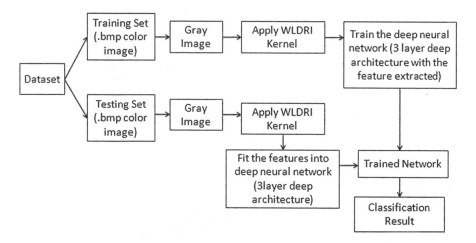

Fig. 4. The work flow diagram of the proposed methodology using deep neural network

4.1   Dataset and Experiment Protocol

As previously described we have used two popular texture dataset Outex-10 Dataset [11] and KTH-TIPS2-a Dataset [12] for texture classification using the proposed methodology. The Outex-10 dataset consists of 4320 images belonging to 24 different textures classes. The images are rotated at nine different angles (0°, 5°, 10°, 15°, 30°, 45°, 60°, 75°, 90°) and the illumination is kept constant. In this experiment, 20 images from each class are used for training and the rest 3840 images are used for testing. The KTH-TIPS2-a texture dataset [12] contains 11 texture classes (e.g. cork, wool, linen, etc.) with 4,395 images. The images are 256×256 pixels in size, and they are transformed into 256 gray levels. Each texture class consists of images from four different samples. The images for each sample are taken at nine scales, under four different illumination directions, and three different poses. The variations in scales, illumination and pose make it a challenging dataset. We use the same experimental protocol for KTH-TIPS2-a dataset as [9]. The outex-10 and KTH-TIPS2-a is more challenging dataset because of rotation, scale, and illumination difference between the samples. The sample images from these two datasets are shown in Fig. 5. We have also applied the developed technique on CMATER Skin Dataset. Example of some sample images used in the experiment is shown in Fig. 6. This dataset contains images of three popular skin diseases - Leprosy, Tineaversicolor, and Vitiligo along with

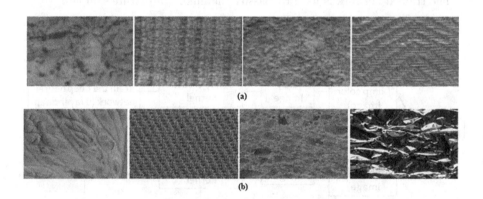

Fig. 5. Sample images of (a) Outex-10 dataset and (b) KTH-TIPS dataset

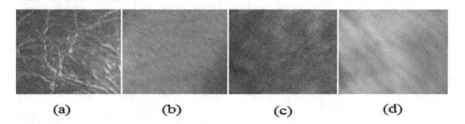

Fig. 6. Sample skin diseases images (a) Leprosy (b) Normal (c) Tineaversicolor (d) Vitiligo

Table 1. Distribution of CMATER skin dataset

Image class	Training data	Testing data
Leprosy	270	52
Normal	130	32
Tineaversicolor	160	40
Vitiligo	202	50

normal skin images. The images are resized into 144×144 pixels in size and converted to grayscale. The images of the affected regions are collected from the outdoor patients of department of Dermatology, School of Tropical Medicine (STM) during the period April 2011–March 2012. There are total 876 images used in the experiment. The images are divided into training and testing set maintaining 4:1 ratio. The distribution of the dataset [10] is shown in Table 1.

5 Results

5.1 Results on OUTEX-10 Dataset

It has already been mentioned that the outex-10 dataset consist of 24 texture classes with 4320 images. In the present work, we have used 20 images per class for training and rest of the images of that class for testing. The recognition accuracy found after applying normal WLDRI using multiscale analysis is 81.27% and using the proposed method is 89.33%. The comparison of normal WLDRI and the proposed method is shown in Table 2.

Table 2. Comparison of result of OUTEX-10 dataset using normal WLDRI (IB1 classifier) and proposed method

Features used	Recognition accuracy (in %)		Hike in percentage
	Normal WLDRI	Proposed method	
WLDRI T = 8, M = 6, P = 8, R = 1	72.13	79.87	7.74
WLDRI T = 8, M = 6, P = 16, R = 2	74.21	81.57	7.36
WLDRI T = 8, M = 6, P = 24, R = 3	77.13	83.03	5.9
Concatenation of above features	81.27	89.33	8.06

5.2 Results on KTH-TIPS2-a Dataset

The KTH-TIPS2-a dataset contains 11 texture classes with 4395 images. Each texture class consists of images from four different samples. The images for each sample are taken at nine scales, under four different illumination directions, and three different poses. We have used 3 samples from each of four samples for training and the remaining images for testing. The recognition accuracy is compared with that of normal WLD [9] with KTH-TIPS2-a dataset using Multiscale analysis(concatenate the histograms from multiple operators with

Table 3. Comparison of result of CMATER skin dataset

Features used	Recognition accuracy (in %)			
	Normal WLDRI		Proposed method	
	Without CG based partition	With CG based partition	Without CG based partition	With CG based partition
WLDRI T = 8, M = 6, P = 8, R = 1	74.71	79.88	80.46	80.46
WLDRI T = 8, M = 6, P = 16, R = 2	79.31	82.76	78.17	83.91
WLDRI T = 8, M = 6, P = 24, R = 3	79.88	87.36	86.79	86.79
Concatenation of above features	85.06	89.08	87.94	94.82

different (P, R). Three histograms with $P = 8$, $R = 1$, $P = 16$, $R = 2$, $P = 24$, $R = 3$ is concatenated) is 64.7%. The recognition accuracy of the above proposed method with KTH-TIPS2-a method is 69.73%. We have achieved 5.03% performance hike using the proposed method.

5.3   Results on CMATER Skin Dataset

The dataset contains total 874 images of three popular skin diseases Leprosy, Tineaversicolor, Vitiligo and normal skin images. We have used 702 images for training and 174 images for testing (4:1 ratio). In this experiment center of gravity (CG) is used to divide the images into four regions with similar gray level distribution and extract features for every region using WLDRI and combine them. Multiscale analysis has been applied to extract features with different granularities. The recognition accuracy of using WLDRI without CG based partition is 85.06% and with CG based partition is 89.08%. The recognition accuracy of the above proposed method using WLDRI without CG based partition is 87.94% and with CG based partition is 94.82%. The comparison of the result of [10] and the proposed method is shown in Table 3.

5.4   Statistical Measures

KTH-TIPS2-a, OUTEX10 and CMATER Skin dataset are purely imbalanced because the numbers of samples in the classes are differing significantly. That is why only classification accuracy is not sufficient to measure the efficiency of a method. There are several statistical measures present in the literature for measuring the efficiency of a method or better say a classifier. Here precision, recall and F1-measure are shown below for every class of the different datasets.

We have compared the performance of WLD on KTH-TIPS2-a dataset with the method proposed by us. Using WLD the accuracy is 64.7% by [9] and that by using our proposed method it is 69.73%. The statistical measure of the proposed method is shown in Table 6.

6   Discussion

The above results conclude that the use of WLDRI kernel in deep learning architecture gives a promising result in texture recognition. The proposed method
outperforms normal WLD with KTH-TIPS2-a dataset and WLDRI with the two
popular challenging texture dataset OUTEX-10 and CMATER skin dataset. The
proposed method with Concatenation of multiscale features using CG based partition gives 94.82% performance which is 5.60% better than normal WLDRI with
concatenation of multi-scale features using CG based partition. The comparative
results using the proposed method and normal WLDRI with the OUTEX-10,
KTH-TIPS2-a, and CMATER Skin dataset are shown in the Figs. 7, 8 and 9
respectively. The mean false positive rate (FPR) and mean true positive rate
(TPR) of the Normal WLDRI and Proposed method is presented in the Tables 4,
5 and 6 respectively for OUTEX-10 dataset, CMATER Skin dataset and KTH-
TIPS2-a dataset. These two rates are used to compare two classification algorithms efficiently. If one classification algorithm 1 has lower FPR and higher TPR
than the classification algorithm 2 then it is obvious to state that classification
algorithm 1 is better than classification algorithm 2, i.e. classification algorithm
1 has better recognition accuracy than classification algorithm 2. From Table 4
it can be observed that the proposed technique has FPR .004 and TPR .893
whereas Normal WLDRI has FPR .008 and TPR .813for OUTEX-10 data set.
Therefore it is clear that our proposed technique is better than Normal WLDRI
for dataset OUTEX-10. The proposed technique has FPR .017 and TPR .946 for

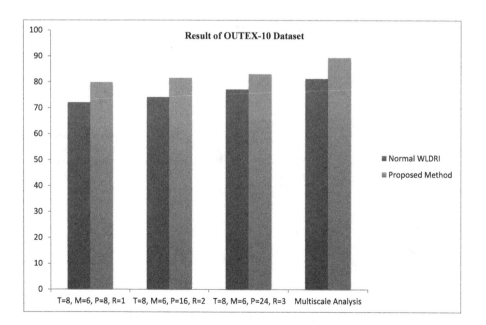

Fig. 7. Comparative result of OUTEX-10 dataset

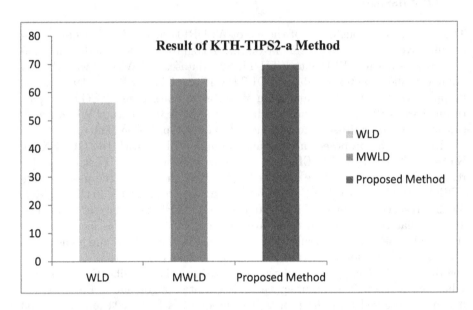

Fig. 8. Comparative result of KTH-TIPS2-a dataset

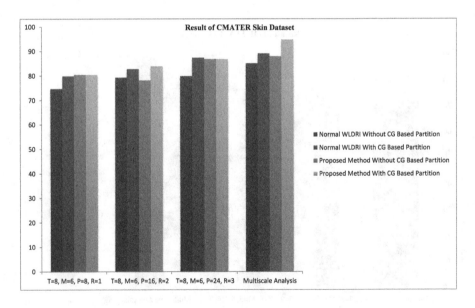

Fig. 9. Comparative result of CMATER skin dataset

Table 4. Statistical measures of OUTEX-10 dataset

Class	Precision measure		Recall measure		F1-Score measure		TPR		FPR	
	Normal WLDRI	Proposed method	Normal WLDRI	Proposed method	Normal WLDRI	Proposed method	Normal WLDRI	Proposed method	Normal WLDRI	Proposed method
1	0.975	1	0.988	0.994	0.981	0.997	0.988	0.994	0.001	0
2	0.778	0.780	0.919	0.844	0.842	0.811	0.919	0.844	0.011	0.010
3	0.773	0.994	1	1	0.872	0.997	1	1	0.013	0
4	0.853	0.884	0.688	0.95	0.761	0.916	0.688	0.95	0.005	0.005
5	1	0.975	1	0.994	1	0.985	1	0.994	0	0.001
6	1	0.989	1	1	1	0.994	1	1	0	0
7	1	1	1	1	1	1	1	1	0	0
8	0.994	0.976	1	1	0.997	0.988	1	1	0	0.001
9	0.94	0.994	0.975	1	0.957	0.997	0.975	1	0.003	0
10	0.832	0.972	0.525	0.875	0.644	0.921	0.525	0.875	0.005	0.001
11	0.843	0.726	0.738	0.744	0.787	0.735	0.738	0.744	0.006	0.012
12	1	0.976	1	1	1	0.988	1	1	0	0.001
13	0.464	0.851	0.969	1	0.628	0.910	0.969	1	0.049	0.008
14	0.414	0.645	0.663	0.556	0.51	0.597	0.663	0.556	0.041	0.013
15	0	0.732	0	0.188	0	0.299	0	0.188	0	0.002
16	0.744	0.684	0.744	0.838	0.744	0.753	0.744	0.838	0.011	0.017
17	0.555	0.753	0.475	0.894	0.512	0.817	0.475	0.894	0.017	0.013
18	0.921	0.801	0.581	0.881	0.713	0.839	0.581	0.881	0.002	0.009
19	0.967	0.953	0.725	0.888	0.829	0.919	0.725	0.888	0.001	0.002
20	0.785	0.874	0.981	0.95	0.872	0.910	0.981	0.95	0.012	0.006
21	0.826	0.993	0.888	0.944	0.855	0.968	0.888	0.944	0.008	0
22	0.846	0.941	0.688	0.9	0.759	0.920	0.688	0.9	0.005	0.002
23	0.935	0.909	0.981	1	0.957	0.952	0.981	1	0.003	0.004
24	0.94	1	0.981	1	0.96	1	0.981	1	0.003	0
Mean	0.808	**0.891**	0.813	**0.893**	0.799	**0.884**	0.813	**0.893**	0.008	**0.004**

Table 5. Statistical measure of CMATER skin dataset

Class	Precision measure		Recall measure		F1-Score measure		TPR		FPR	
	Normal WLDRI	Proposed method	Normal WLDRI	Proposed method	Normal WLDRI	Proposed method	Normal WLDRI	Proposed method	Normal WLDRI	Proposed method
1	0.774	0.96	0.923	0.923	0.842	0.941	0.923	0.923	0.115	0.016
2	0.945	0.935	0.656	0.906	0.778	0.920	0.656	0.906	0.007	0.007
3	0.925	0.906	0.925	0.975	0.925	0.939	0.925	0.975	0.022	0.022
4	0.980	0.942	0.980	0.98	0.980	0.960	0.980	0.98	0.008	0.024
Mean	0.906	**0.936**	0.871	**0.946**	0.881	**0.94**	0.891	**0.946**	0.043	**0.017**

CMATER skin data set, whereas Normal WLDRI has FPR .043 and TPR .891 on the same set. The result concludes that the proposed technique is performs better than Normal WLDRI. The performance of WLD [9] and the proposed technique is compared for KTH-TIPS2 dataset also. For this case only the TPR and FPR of the proposed technique is shown in Table 6. From the classification accuracy it can be inferred that the proposed technique is better than normal WLD approach.

Table 6. Statistical measure of KTH-TIPS2-a method (Precision, Recall and F1-Score)

Class	Precision measure	Recall measure	F1-Score measure	TPR	FPR
1	0.981	0.823	0.895	0.823	0.002
2	0.645	0.784	0.708	0.784	0.046
3	0.652	0.642	0.647	0.642	0.035
4	0.835	0.819	0.827	0.819	0.018
5	0.758	0.421	0.541	0.421	0.013
6	0.5	0.686	0.578	0.686	0.041
7	0.732	0.618	0.670	0.618	0.024
8	0.668	0.678	0.673	0.678	0.033
9	0.566	0.824	0.671	0.824	0.066
10	0.742	0.740	0.741	0.740	0.028
11	0.717	0.617	0.663	0.617	0.027
Mean	0.709	0.696	0.692	0.696	0.03

7   Conclusions

The main objective of this work is to explore the performance of deep neural network when rotation invariant weber local descriptor kernel is applied. The proposed system have been tested on two most popular and challenging texture dataset Outex-10 and KTH-TIPS2-a. The images of the Outex-10 dataset are rotated in nine different angles and KTH-TIPS2-a dataset contains image which differs in scale, illumination direction and poses. The proposed technique performs better than rotation invariant Weber local descriptor and provides 8.06% improved recognition accuracy on Outex-10 dataset and 5.03% improved recognition accuracy on KTH-TIPS2-a dataset. Both the above performances achieved using multiscale analysis. The proposed technique has been also applied in one of challenging application of texture identification Skin diseases classification. The proposed technique achieved 2.88% improved accuracy than the normal rotation invariant weber local descriptor using multiscale analysis and 5.74% improved accuracy using multiscale analysis and CG based partition. The essence of deep learning resides in the property of intermediate representation of the input in several layers in order to represent a given problem. The idea of the present work is to fit the features using the rotation invariant weber local descriptor to a deep neural network architecture. It can be theoretically considered that the kernel of rotation invariant weber local descriptor is being fitted into the deep neural network. From the comparative result on the above three challenging texture dataset it can be concluded that the present system is better optimized for the features and performs better than the existing methodologies. But optimization of hyper-parameters (the number of hidden layer, number of hidden neurons etc.) is not considered in the present work. Though the present system has achieved better recognition accuracy but it may be case that better optimization of the hyper-parameters leads to better recognition accuracy and a stable system. So future work can be the optimization of the hyper-parameter (number of hidden layers, number of hidden neurons etc.) since these parameters were fixed during the present work. There are several deep learning techniques, like stacked auto encoder, greedy layer wise training, and Convolution neural network which can be implemented in future and comparison of that with this present work may lead to a brighter prospect. The rotation invariant Weber local descriptor mask only has been applied here; different existing texture descriptor mask (such as LBP, LDP etc.) could be used to compare them with the present work.

References

1. Lowe, D.G.: Distinctive image features from scale-invariant keypoints. Int. J. Comput. Vis. **60**(2), 91–110 (2004)
2. Dalal, N., Triggs, B.: Histograms of oriented gradients for human detection. In: 2005 IEEE Computer Society Conference on Computer Vision and Pattern Recognition (CVPR 2005), vol. 1, pp. 886–893. IEEE, June 2005
3. Lazebnik, S., Schmid, C., Ponce, J.: A sparse texture representation using local affine regions. IEEE Trans. Pattern Anal. Mach. Intell. **27**(8), 1265–1278 (2005)
4. Manjunath, B.S., Ma, W.Y.: Texture features for browsing and retrieval of image data. IEEE Trans. Pattern Anal. Mach. Intell. **18**(8), 837–842 (1996)
5. Ojala, T., Pietikainen, M., Maenpaa, T.: Multiresolution gray-scale and rotation invariant texture classification with local binary patterns. IEEE Trans. Pattern Anal. Mach. Intell. **24**(7), 971–987 (2002)
6. Zhang, W., Shan, S., Gao, W., Chen, X., Zhang, H.: Local Gabor binary pattern histogram sequence (LGBPHS): a novel non-statistical model for face representation and recognition. In Tenth IEEE International Conference on Computer Vision (ICCV 2005), vol. 1, pp. 786–791. IEEE, October 2005
7. Jabid, T., Kabir, M.H., Chae, O.: Facial expression recognition using local directional pattern (LDP). In: 2010 IEEE International Conference on Image Processing, pp. 1605–1608. IEEE, September 2010
8. Jabid, T., Kabir, M.H., Chae, O.: Local directional pattern (LDP) for face recognition. In: Proceedings of the IEEE International Conference on Consumer Electronics, pp. 329–330, January 2010
9. Chen, J., Shan, S., He, C., Zhao, G., Pietikainen, M., Chen, X., Gao, W.: WLD: a robust local image descriptor. IEEE Trans. Pattern Anal. Mach. Intell. **32**(9), 1705–1720 (2010)
10. Pal, A., Das, N., Sarkar, S., Gangopadhyay, D., Nasipuri, M.: A new rotation invariant weber local descriptor for recognition of skin diseases. In: Maji, P., Ghosh, A., Murty, M.N., Ghosh, K., Pal, S.K. (eds.) PReMI 2013. LNCS, vol. 8251, pp. 355–360. Springer, Heidelberg (2013). doi:10.1007/978-3-642-45062-4_48
11. Ojala, T., Maenpaa, T., Pietikainen, M., Viertola, J., Kyllonen, J., Huovinen, S.: Outex-new framework for empirical evaluation of texture analysis algorithms. In: Proceedings of the 16th International Conference on Pattern Recognition, vol. 1, pp. 701–706. IEEE (2002)

12. Caputo, B., Hayman, E., Mallikarjuna, P.: Class-specific material categorisation. In: Tenth IEEE International Conference on Computer Vision (ICCV 2005), Vol. 2, pp. 1597–1604. IEEE, October 2005
13. Tivive, F.H.C., Bouzerdoum, A.: Texture classification using convolutional neural networks. In: 2006 IEEE Region 10 Conference, TENCON 2006, pp. 1–4. IEEE, November 2006
14. Hong, C., Yu, J., Wan, J., Tao, D., Wang, M.: Multimodal deep autoencoder for human pose recovery. IEEE Trans. Image Process. **24**(12), 5659–5670 (2015)

Industrial Applications of Colour Texture Classification Based on Anisotropic Diffusion

P.S. Hiremath[1] and Rohini A. Bhusnurmath[2(✉)]

[1] Department of Computer Science (MCA), KLE Technological University,
BVBCET Campus, Hubli 580031, Karnataka, India
hiremathps53@yahoo.com
[2] Department of P.G. Studies and Research in Computer Science,
Gulbarga University, Kalaburagi 585106, Karnataka, India
rohiniabmath@gmail.com

Abstract. A novel method of colour texture classification based on anisotropic diffusion is proposed and is investigated with different colour spaces. The objective is to explore the colour spaces for their suitability in automatic classification of certain textures in industrial applications, namely, granite tiles and wood textures, using computer vision. The directional subbands of digital image of material samples are obtained using wavelet transform. The anisotropic diffusion is employed to obtain the texture components of directional subbands. Further, statistical features are extracted from the texture components. The linear discriminant analysis (LDA) is employed on feature space to achieve class separability. The proposed method has been experimented on RGB, HSV, YCbCr and Lab colour spaces. The k-NN classifier is used for texture classification. For experimentation, image samples from MondialMarmi database of granite tiles and Parquet database of hard wood are considered. The experimental results are encouraging due to reduced time complexity, reduced feature set size and improved classification accuracy as compared to the state-of-the-art-methods.

Keywords: Industrial applications · Colour texture classification · Granite tiles · Wood textures · Anisotropic diffusion · Wavelet transform · Linear discriminant analysis

1 Introduction

Texture analysis is an active area of research in machine vision for over four decades. Texture plays a central role in many applications that include object tracking, face detection, food inspection and industrial applications in surface grading [1,2]. In many industries such as parquet [3], marble [4], fabric [5], etc., there is a need to perform the task of surface grading automatically. In these industries, visual appearance of the product decides the price of the material. Granite and wood industries are also concerned in the development of automatic machine vision system for grading, since the manual quality control procedures are time-consuming, subjective and non repetitive.

© Springer Nature Singapore Pte Ltd. 2017
K.C. Santosh et al. (Eds.): RTIP2R 2016, CCIS 709, pp. 293–304, 2017.
DOI: 10.1007/978-981-10-4859-3_27

A number of effective texture analysis methods have been reported in the literature. The wavelet co-occurrence histogram is used for texture feature extraction in [6]. Linear discriminant analysis (LDA) is found to be efficiently used in pattern recognition [7]. Perona and Malik [8] introduced anisotropic diffusion for image smoothing while keeping the edges sharp in texture analysis. The anisotropic diffusion and local directional binary patterns are effectively used for colour texture classification in [9]. The partial differential equation (PDE) for diffusion and wavelet transform are employed to obtain texture features in [10]. Fernandez et al. [11] have explored various texture descriptors such as local binary patterns, improved local binary patterns and coordinated clusters representation for granite texture classification. They have analyzed the robustness of the texture descriptors to image rotation. Bianconi et al. [12] have proposed the method for classification of granite tiles, wherein colour and textural features are considered. Gonzalez et al. [13] have presented applications of material characterization using colour and texture analysis on granite tiles. Fernandez et al. [14] have described a texture analysis using improved local ternary patterns and completed local binary patterns based on histograms of equivalent patterns. Bianconi et al. [15] have investigated the discriminative features from local binary patterns on several databases that include granite tiles database. Kylberg and Sintorn [16] have used local binary pattern approach to texture analysis of granite tiles and demonstrated that the method performs better when the level of noise is low. Paci et al. [17] have attempted many feature extraction approaches and their combinations for granite texture classification. Bianconi et al. [3] have proposed sorting of hard wood parquet slabs based on various texture descriptors and colour spaces. It is demonstrated that the use of simple statistical descriptors and RGB colour space yields better classification results.

In the present paper, an effective method for colour texture classification of industrial materials is proposed. The proposed method is useful in designing an intelligent vision system for automatic classification of granite tiles and wood textures using digital image processing techniques. Such systems can be employed for automatic grading of the granite tiles and wood textures at reduced computational cost. The digital image of industrial material sample is subjected to the wavelet transform to obtain directional subbands of the transformed image. The anisotropic diffusion of wavelet transformed image yields texture components of these directional subbands. Further, statistical features are obtained from the texture components. The proposed algorithm has been tested on the different colour spaces, namely, RGB, HSV, YCbCr and Lab. The LDA is used on feature space to enhance the class separability. The k-NN classifier is used for texture classification. For experimentation, image samples from MondialMarmi database of granite tiles and Parquet database of hard wood are considered. The experimental results indicate the efficiency of the proposed method in terms of reduced computational cost, reduced features set size and improved classification accuracy.

2   Proposed Method

The proposed method extracts features using relationships between colour components of neighboring pixels, i.e. luminance based texture features, that are combined with pure chrominance based statistical moment features. The extraction of luminance based texture features is achieved through following steps:

- The Haar wavelet transform is applied to input image of material sample to yield directional information (H, V and D subbands).
- The anisotropic diffusion is applied on directional information (H, V and D) up to t diffusion steps, which yields texture components.
- The statistical features are obtained from the resultant texture components.

The k-NN classifier is employed to classify textures in the feature space. These steps are described briefly as given below.

2.1   Wavelet Transform

The one level decomposition of Haar wavelet transform is applied to the input sample image, that yields horizontal (H), vertical (V) and diagonal (D) subbands. The one level decomposition extracts better directional information, while multilevel decomposition results in compression of the information. The theory of the wavelet transform is discussed in [18]. The wavelet transform is described briefly in the Appendix A.

2.2   Anisotropic Diffusion

The anisotropic diffusion is applied to the directional subbands H, V and D of wavelet transformed image, which yields texture components. The basic idea of the anisotropic diffusion filter [8] is described in the Appendix B.

2.3   Feature Sets

The texture components obtained after anisotropic diffusion of H, V and D subbands of wavelet transformed image are considered for feature extraction. The two types of texture feature measures used are first order and second order statistics. The first order statistics captures texture properties considering individual pixel values. The second order statistics considers the relationship between neighboring pixel values. The various feature sets based on first order statistics (F1) and second order statistics (F2–F9) considered in the present study are tabulated in the Table 1 [10]. Further, the various combinations of these feature sets (F10–F30) listed in the Table 2 are also considered for the study.

Table 1. The different feature sets based on first order statistics (F1) and second order statistics (F2–F9) [10].

Feature set	Description	Features extracted
F1	First order statistics	Skewness, mean, standard deviation, kurtosis and median.
F2	Haralick features	Entropy, homogeneity, contrast, energy, maximum probability, cluster shade and cluster prominence
F3	Gray level difference statistics	Contrast, homogeneity, energy, entropy and mean
F4	Neighborhood gray tone difference matrix	Busyness, complexity, coarseness, contrast and texture strength
F5	Statistical feature matrix	Coarseness, contrast, period and roughness
F6	Law's texture energy measures	Six texture energy measures
F7	Fractal dimension texture analysis	Roughness of a surface
F8	Fourier power spectrum	Radial sum and angular sum
F9	Shape	size(x,y), area, perimeter and $perimeter^2/area$

3   Texture Classification Procedure

Texture classification procedure comprises the training and testing phases. The colour and texture features are obtained from colour image samples of industrial materials. The different colour spaces, namely, RGB, HSV, YCbCr and Lab are considered for investigation. In HSV, YCbCr and Lab colour spaces, V, Y, L represent luminance, respectively, while the remaining two channels in each colour space represent chrominance. Texture features are computed from the luminance channel, while the first order statistical features, namely, mean and standard deviation, are computed from the chrominance channels. The training and testing procedures are described below.

3.1   Training Procedure

The input colour image I of an industrial material sample (in RGB) is converted to HSV (or YCbCr or Lab) space. The luminance (I_{lmn}) and chrominance components of I are obtained. The luminance (I_{lmn}) component is decomposed using one level Haar wavelet transform, into horizontal (H), vertical (V) and diagonal (D) components. The anisotropic diffusion is performed on H, V and D components up to t steps. The texture approximations I_{Htxr}, I_{Vtxr}, I_{Dtxr} for H, V and D components are obtained. The statistical features defined in the Tables 1 and 2 are extracted from I_{Htxr}, I_{Vtxr}, I_{Dtxr}. From the chrominance components,

Table 2. The combinations (F10–F30) of feature sets given in the Table 1.

Feature set name	Feature set combination	Feature set name	Feature set combination
F10	F1 + F3	F21	F1 + F3 + F5
F11	F1 + F3 + F4	F22	F1 + F3 + F6
F12	F1 + F3 + F4 + F5	F23	F1 + F4 + F5
F13	F1 + F3 + F4 + F5 + F6	F24	F3 + F4 + F5
F14	F1 + F3 + F4 + F5 + F6 + F7	F25	F6 + F7
F15	F1 + F3 + F4 + F5 + F6 + F7 + F8	F26	F4 + F5
F16	F1 + F3 + F4 + F5 + F6 + F7 + F8 + F9	F27	F3 + F4
F17	F1 + F3 + F5 + F6	F28	F5 + F6
F18	F3 + F4 + F5 + F6	F29	F8 + F9
F19	F1 + F4 + F5 + F6	F30	F2 + F4
F20	F6 + F7 + F8 + F9		

statistical moment features (mean and SD) are computed. The feature vector F is formed using features obtained from luminance and chrominance components and stored with class label. This procedure is repeated for all the training sample images and training feature vector set (TF) is formed. The LDA is applied on TF to obtain the discriminant feature set TFLDA, which is then used for texture classification.

3.2   Testing Procedure

The test colour image I_{test} of an industrial material sample (in RGB) is converted to HSV (or YCbCr or Lab) space. The luminance ($I_{testlmn}$) and chrominance components of I_{test} are obtained. The $I_{testlmn}$ is decomposed using one level Haar wavelet transform, into horizontal (H), vertical (V) and diagonal (D) components. The anisotropic diffusion is performed on H, V and D components of $I_{testlmn}$, which yields texture approximations $I_{testHtxr}$, $I_{testVtxr}$, $I_{testDtxr}$. The statistical features defined in the Tables 1 and 2 are extracted from $I_{testHtxr}$, $I_{testVtxr}$, $I_{testDtxr}$. From the chrominance components, statistical moment features (mean and SD) are computed. The feature vector F_{test} is formed containing features computed from luminance and chrominance components. The F_{test} is projected on TFLDA components and test image feature vector $F_{testLDA}$ is obtained. The k-NN classifier [19] with k = 3 is used to classify $F_{testLDA}$ vectors of the test images I_{test} of industrial material samples.

4   Experimental Results and Discussion

The proposed methodology is experimented on two benchmark databases of colour texture images of industrial material samples, namely, MondialMarmi database [20] for granite tiles and Parquet database [21] for hardwood. The experimentation of the proposed method is carried out on Intel(R) Core(TM) i3-2330M @ 2.20 GHz with 4 GB RAM using MATLAB 7.9 software. The values of parameters of anisotropic diffusion are: λ (lambda) $= 0.25$ and c (conduction coefficient) $= 60$. The k-NN classifier is in popular usage, because of the absence of tuning parameter and ease of implementation (Bianconi et al. [3], Kylberg and Sintorn [16], Gonzalez et al. [13], Fernandez et al. [14], Bianconi et al. [15]). The training and testing strategy comprises two-fold experimentation repeated five times.

4.1   Industrial Materials

The Fig. 1 shows sample colour images of materials, namely, granite tiles and hard wood, taken from each of the two databases.

(a)   (b)

Fig. 1. Sample colour texture images from two databases: (a) MondialMarmi images from left to right: Acquamarina, Azul Platino, Bianco Sardo, Giallo Ornamentale. (b) Parquet images from left to right: IRK 01, OAK 02, OAK 04, OAK 10.

MondialMarmi is a database of commercial granite tiles images [20]. The current version (1.1) contains 12 granite classes, namely, Acquamarina, Azul Capixaba, Azul Platino, Bianco Cristal, Bianco Sardo, Giallo Napoletano, Giallo Ornamentale, Giallo Santa Cecilia, Giallo Veneziano, Rosa Beta, Rosa Porrino A, Rosa Porrino B. The database contains four granite images for each class. The images are available in 24 bit colour bmp with hardware and software rotations. The nine rotation angles used are 0°, 5°, 10°, 15°, 30°, 45°, 60°, 75° and 90°. The acquisition procedure is available in [11]. The whole MondialMarmi database (2011) of 48 images with rotation angle zero degree with bicubic interpolation is taken for the experimentation.

The Parquet database [21] for wood is the collection of commercial engineered parquet images. These hard woods are of various treatment, type and finish. The database contains fourteen classes, namely, IRK 01, OAK 01, OAK 02, OAK 03, OAK 04, OAK 05, OAK 06, OAK 07, OAK 08, OAK 09, OAK 10, OAK 11, TEK 01, TEK 02. Each class contains two to four different subclasses (tones) with least colour and texture difference from each other. The image samples per tone vary from six to eight. The database contains a total of 295 images. The images are available as 24 bit colour bmp with image size varying from class to class. Rotation, scale, viewing direction and illumination conditions are invariable.

Table 3. Properties of the databases used for experimentation.

Database name	No. of classes	No. of sub images per class	Total no. of sub images	Image size (pixels)	Sub image size (pixels)
MondialMarmi [20]	12	64	768	544 × 544	136 × 136
Parquet [21]	14	192	2688	1200 × 300	150 × 150

The acquisition procedure is described in detail in [3]. For the experimentation, twelve samples per class are considered. This includes images from each tone.

The basic properties of the experimental databases are listed in the Table 3. The unbiased texture classification is achieved by randomly dividing images into independent training and testing sets. The half of the sample images are considered as training set and the remaining half are used for testing.

4.2   Results for MondialMarmi Database

The Table 4 shows the comparison of optimal classification accuracy obtained among the thirty feature sets that are experimented for different colour spaces using MondialMarmi database. The corresponding training time, testing time, optimal number of diffusion steps and feature set are presented in the Table 4. It is observed from the Table 4 that the YCbCr colour space yields better classification accuracy of 99.58% as compared to the other colour spaces, which is obtained for the feature set F21 with training time of 36.03 s. and testing time of 0.0040 s. Further, the feature sets F1, F3, F4 and F5 are found to be dominant feature sets (Table 2) responsible for attaining higher classification accuracy.

The Table 5 presents the comparison of classification accuracy (%) and feature set size obtained by the proposed method and other state-of-the-art-methods [11–17], along with classifier used, in case of MondialMarmi database.

It is observed from the Table 5 that the classification accuracy of the proposed method is improved as compared to the other state-of-the-art-methods [11–17], which can be attributed to the diffusion approach and the wavelet transform.

Table 4. Comparison of classification accuracy of the proposed method on different colour spaces and the corresponding training time, testing time, optimal feature set and diffusion steps for MondialMarmi database.

Parameters	Colour spaces			
	RGB	HSV	YCbCr	Lab
Classification accuracy (%)	98.69	99.54	99.58	99.19
Training time (s)	120.45	67.64	36.03	55.52
Testing time (s)	0.0039	0.0037	0.0040	0.0045
Optimal feature set	F5	F26	F21	F24
Optimal no. of diffusion step	8	8	6	2

Table 5. Comparison of classification accuracy (%) and feature set size for the proposed method and other state-of-the-art-methods [11–17], along with classifier used, in case of MondialMarmi database.

Reference	Classification accuracy (%)	Feature set size	Classifier
Fernández et al. [11]	97.40	325	k-NN, k = 1
Bianconi et al. [12]	98.50	30	SVM
González et al. [13]	97.50	216	k-NN, k = 1
Fernández et al. [14]	93.35	725	k-NN, k = 1
Bianconi et al. [15]	93.90	4116	k-NN, k = 1
Kylberg and Sintorn [16]	95.80	60	k-NN, k = 1
Paci et al. [17]	96.56	512	SVM+GPC
Proposed method	**99.58**	**11**	**k-NN, k = 3**

In addition, the computational cost in terms of testing and training times is considerably reduced due to the diffusion approach [10] and the reduced feature set obtained by using LDA.

4.3   Results for Parquet Database

The Table 6 shows the comparison of optimal classification accuracy obtained among the thirty feature sets that are experimented for different colour spaces using Parquet database. The corresponding training time, testing time, optimal number of diffusion steps and feature set are presented in the Table 6.

It is observed from the Table 6 that the HSV colour space yields better classification accuracy (96.57%) than other colour spaces experimented. The optimal classification accuracy of 96.57% is obtained for the feature set F12 with training time of 237.56 s. and testing time of 0.02 s. Further, the same feature sets, namely, F1, F3, F4, F5 and F6, as observed in MondialMarmi database, are found to be dominant for attaining higher classification accuracy.

The Table 7 presents the comparison of classification accuracy (%) and feature set size obtained by the proposed method and the other state-of-the-art-method [3], along with classifier used, in case of Parquet database.

Table 6. Comparison of classification accuracy of the proposed method on different colour spaces and the corresponding training time, testing time, optimal feature set and diffusion steps using Parquet database.

Parameters	Colour spaces			
	RGB	HSV	YCbCr	Lab
Classification accuracy (%)	95.15	96.57	96.55	96.48
Training time (s)	433.75	237.56	262.84	234.28
Testing time (s)	0.04	0.02	0.03	0.02
Optimal feature set	F21	F12	F18	F17
Optimal no. of diffusion step	6	8	8	9

Table 7. Comparison of classification accuracy (%) and feature set size and classifier used for the proposed method and other state-of-the-art-method [3] using Parquet database.

Reference	Classification accuracy (%)	Feature set size	Classifier
Bianconi et al. [3]	89.80	12	k-NN, k = 1
Proposed method	**96.57**	**13**	**k-NN, k = 3**

It is observed from the Table 7 that the classification accuracy of the proposed method is improved as compared to the other state-of-the-art-method [3], which can be attributed to diffusion approach and wavelet transform.

5   Conclusions

In this paper, an effective method for colour texture classification for industrial applications, namely, grading of granite tiles and wood textures, is proposed. The proposed method is experimented on different colour spaces, namely, RGB, HSV, YCbCr and Lab. The classes of the benchmark image databases of these materials are of similar visual appearance making it complex for experimentation. The proposed method is robust due to feature extraction based on wavelet transform and anisotropic diffusion. The YCbCr and HSV colour spaces yield better classification accuracy for MondialMarmi and Parquet databases, respectively. The proposed method is simple and computationally inexpensive, making it suitable for real time processing. Hence, it is suitable for designing an intelligent vision system for automatic classification of colour texture characteristics of the material products where visual appearance plays an important role, for example, granite, parquet, marble, leather and fabric. Also, it becomes evident that the choice of colour space for texture analysis is crucial and application-dependent. The experimental results exhibit the effectiveness of the proposed method in terms of improved classification accuracy, reduced computational cost and reduced feature set size as compared to the state-of-the-art-methods.

Acknowledgments. The authors are grateful to the reviewers for their valuable comments and suggestions, which improved the quality of the paper considerably.

Appendix

A   Wavelet transform

Wavelet analysis is a particular time-scale representation of signals. It has wide range of applications in physics, signal processing and applied mathematics. The theoretical aspect and implementation of wavelet transform are available in [18]. The wavelet transform uses the Haar function in edge extraction, image coding and binary logic design, The one level of Haar wavelet decomposition decomposes the input image into four subbands, namely, A, H, V and D respectively. The Fig. 2 shows test input image and its one level wavelet decomposition. The subband A (Approximation) contains the global properties of the input image. The H (horizontal) subband contains the horizontal details of input image. The V (vertical) subband includes information of vertical details whereas D (diagonal) subband embraces the diagonal details of image. Due to the low computing requirements, the Haar transform has been used for image processing and pattern recognition.

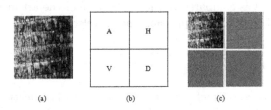

(a)   (b)   (c)

Fig. 2. Wavelet transform: (a) Test image, (b) One-level decomposition, (c) One level decomposition of image in (a).

B   Anisotropic diffusion

Perona and Malik [8] proposed anisotropic diffusion process, where diffusion takes place to smooth image while preserving edge sharpness. It was demonstrated [8] that this process clearly outperforms the canny edge detector, making image boundaries sharp. The nonlinear PDE for smoothing image on a continuous domain as suggested in [8] is shown in the Eq. (1):

$$\begin{cases} \frac{\partial I}{\partial t} = div\left[c\left(|\nabla I|\right)\nabla I\right] \\ I_{(t=0)} = I_0 \end{cases} \tag{1}$$

where ∇ denotes the gradient operator, div is divergence operator, c(x) represents diffusion coefficient, $||$ is the magnitude and I_0 denotes initial image. The two diffusion coefficients are given by the Eqs. (2) and (3):

$$c(x) = \frac{1}{1 + (\frac{x}{k})^2} \tag{2}$$

and

$$c(x) = exp\left\lfloor -(x/k)^2\right\rfloor \tag{3}$$

where k is an edge magnitude parameter. In the anisotropic diffusion method, the gradient magnitude is used to detect an image edge or boundary as a step discontinuity in intensity. If $|\nabla I| >> k$ then $c\left(\nabla I\right) \to 0$, and we have an all-pass filter. If $|\nabla I| << k$ then $c\left(\nabla I\right) \to 1$ and we achieve isotropic diffusion (Gaussian filtering). A discrete form of the Eq. (1) is given by the Eq. (4):

$$I_s^{t+\Delta t} = I_s^t + \frac{\lambda}{|\overline{\eta_s}|} \sum_{p \in \overline{\eta_s}} c(\nabla I_{s,p}^t)\nabla I_{s,p}^t \tag{4}$$

where I_s^t is the discretely sampled image, s denotes the pixel position in a discrete two-dimensional (2-D) grid, and $0 \le \lambda \le 1/4$ is a scalar that controls the numerical stability, $\overline{\eta_s}$ is the number of pixels in the window (usually four, except at the image boundaries), and $\nabla I_{s,p}^t = I_p^t - I_s^t, \forall p \in \overline{\eta_s}$.

References

1. CIE: A framework for the measurement of visual appearance. Technical report, CIE 175 (2006)
2. Eugene, C.: Measurement of "total visual appearance": a CIE challenge of soft metrology. In: Proceedings of the 12th IMEKO TC1-TC7 Joint Symposium on Man, Science and Measurement, Annecy, France, pp. 61–65 (2008)
3. Bianconi, F., Fernandez, A., Gonzalez, E., Saetta, S.A.: Performance analysis of colour descriptors for parquet sorting. Expert Syst. Appl. **40**(5), 1636–1644 (2013)
4. Martinez-Alajarin, J., Luis-Delgado, J.D., Tomas-Balibrea, L.M.: Automatic system for quality based classification of marble textures. IEEE Trans. Syst. Man Cybern. C **35**, 488–497 (2005)
5. Bennamoun, M., Bodnarova, A.: Digital image processing techniques for automatic textile quality control. Syst. Anal. Model. Simul. **43**, 1581–1614 (2003)
6. Hiremath, P.S., Shivashankar, S.: Wavelet based co-occurrence histogram features for texture classification with an application to script identification in a document image. Pattern Recogn. Lett. **29**, 1182–1189 (2008)
7. Shivashankar, S., Hiremath, P.S.: PCA plus LDA on wavelet co-occurrence histogram features for texture classification. Int. J. Mach. Intell. **3**(4), 302–306 (2011)
8. Perona, P., Malik, J.: Scale-space and edge detection using anisotropic diffusion. IEEE Trans. Pattern Anal. Mach. Intell. **12**(7), 629–639 (1990)
9. Hiremath, P.S., Bhusnurmath, R.A.: RGB - based color texture image classification using anisotropic diffusion and LDBP. In: Murty, M.N., He, X., Chillarige, R.R., Weng, P. (eds.) MIWAI 2014. LNCS (LNAI), vol. 8875, pp. 101–111. Springer, Cham (2014). doi:10.1007/978-3-319-13365-2_10
10. Hiremath, P.S., Bhusnurmath, R.A.: PDE based features for texture analysis using wavelet transform. Int. J. Cybern. Inform. **5**(1), 143–155 (2016). doi:10.5121/ijci.2016.5114
11. Fernández, A., Ghita, O., Gonzalez, E., Bianconi, F., Whelan, P.F.: Evaluation of robustness against rotation of LBP, CCR and ILBP features in granite texture classification. Mach. Vis. Appl. **22**, 913–926 (2011). doi:10.1007/s00138-010-0253-4
12. Bianconi, F., Gonzalez, E., Fernández, A., Saetta, S.A.: Automatic classification of granite tiles through colour and texture features. Expert Syst. Appl. **39**, 11212–11218 (2012)
13. Gonzalez, E., Bianconi, F., Ivarez, M.X., Saetta, S. A.: Automatic characterization of the visual appearance of industrial materials through colour and texture analysis: an overview of methods and applications. Adv. Opt. Technol. **2013** (2013). Hindawi Publishing Corporation. Article ID 503541, 11 pages. doi:10.1155/2013/503541

14. Fernandez, A., Alvarez, M.X., Bianconi, F.: Texture description through histograms of equivalent patterns. J. Math. Imaging Vis. **45**, 76–102 (2013). doi:10. 1007/s10851-012-0349-8
15. Bianconi, F., Gonzalez, E., Fernandez, A.: Dominant local binary patterns for texture classification: labelled or unlabelled. Pattern Recogn. Lett. **65**, 8–14 (2015)
16. Kylberg, G., Sintorn, I.M.: Evaluation of noise robustness for local binary pattern descriptors in texture classification. EURASIP J. Image Video Process. **2013**, 17 (2013). http://jivp.eurasipjournals.com/content/2013/1/17
17. Paci, M., Nanni, L., Severi, S.: An ensemble of classifiers based on different texture descriptors for texture classification. J. King Saud Univ. Sci. **25**, 235–244 (2013)
18. Mallat, S.G.: A theory of multiresolution signal decomposition: the wavelet representation. IEEE trans. pattern anal. Mach. intell. **11**, 674–693 (1989)
19. Duda, R.O., Hart, P.E.: Stork: Pattern Classification. Wiley publication, New York (2001)
20. MondialMarmi: Mondial Marmi, a granite image database for colour and texture analysis, v1.1. (2011). http://dismac.dii.unipg.it/mm
21. Parquet: Parquet image database (2012). http://dismac.dii.unipg.it/parquet/data. html

Shot-Based Keyframe Extraction Using Bitwise-XOR Dissimilarity Approach

Rashmi B.S.[1,2(✉)] and Nagendraswamy H.S.[1]

[1] DoS in Computer Science, University of Mysore,
Mysore 570 006, India
rashmibsrsh@compsci.uni-mysore.ac.in
[2] Karnataka State Open University, Mysore, India

Abstract. Keyframe extraction is an essential task in many video analysis applications such as video summarization, video classification, video indexing and retrieval. In this paper, a method of extracting keyframes from the shots using bitwise XOR dissimilarity has been proposed. The task of segmenting continuous video into shots and selection of key frames from segmented shots has been addressed. The above task has been accomplished through a feature extraction technique, based on bitwise XOR operation between consecutive gray scale frames of the video. Thresholding mechanism is employed to segment the videos into shots. Dissimilarity matrix is constructed to select a representative keyframe from every shot of a video sequence. The proposed shot boundary detection and keyframe extraction approach is implemented and evaluated on a subset of TRECVID 2001 data set. The proposed approach outperform other contemporary approaches in terms of efficiency and accuracy. Also, the experimental results on the data set have demonstrated the efficacy of the proposed keyframe extraction technique in terms of fidelity measure.

Keywords: Bitwise-XOR · Cumulative sum · Dissimilarity matrix · Fidelity measure · Keyframes · Shot boundary detection · Variance · Video summarization

1 Introduction

Recent advances in computing and internet technologies have rapidly increased the demand for multimedia applications. Large repositories of video require efficient and effective mechanisms, which can effectively represent, index and retrieve the information. Generally video sequence may contain redundant information. Video summarization is a mechanism to eliminate redundancy in video data through a compact representation of video sequence and is used for video indexing and retrieval purposes [1,2]. Video summaries can be generated by extracting keyframes. Keyframes can be defined as a subset of a video sequence that represents visual content [3]. In order to reduce redundancy in video data, the extraction of keyframes must be content based and automatic [4]. The entire

© Springer Nature Singapore Pte Ltd. 2017
K.C. Santosh et al. (Eds.): RTIP2R 2016, CCIS 709, pp. 305–316, 2017.
DOI: 10.1007/978-981-10-4859-3_28

video sequence is mapped to a small number of representative images in keyframe video representation. Extraction of key frames from video can be performed in two different approaches. In the first approach, video sequence has already been segmented into shots using shot boundary detection technique. The key frame extraction process uses the video shots independently and the key frames are extracted depending upon the nature of the shots. In the second approach, video sequences are first segmented into shots and key frames are then extracted from the segmented shots. The proposed method of key frame extraction follows the second approach. Several works have been addressed in literature for shot boundary detection and keyframe extraction and most of them are computationally expensive [5]. The proposed approach is found to be simple and effective for shot boundary detection and keyframe extraction from a video sequence. Rest of the paper is organized as follows: Sect. 2 gives a detailed description of the related work. Section 3 presents the proposed methodology covering the details about feature extraction, shot boundary detection and keyframe extraction process. Experimental analysis and results of shot boundary detection and keyframe extraction are discussed in Sect. 4, followed by conclusion in Sect. 5.

2 Related Works

In shot based approaches, initially the video is segmented into shots and keyframe extraction from the shots is performed using various methodologies. In this section, a brief overview of literature on shot boundary detection and keyframe extraction approaches by various researchers is presented.

2.1 Shot Boundary Detection

Shot boundary detection is a fundamental step in video analysis. Shots may be abrupt or gradual. Several attempts have been made by researchers to propose efficient shot boundary detection methods (e.g. pixel based [7], histogram based [8], edge based [9], motion based [10] etc.). Lot of work has been reported on abrupt [11,12] and gradual [13–15] transition detection. Detection of gradual transition is tedious compared to that of abrupt transition. Also, accuracy of detection methods varies from one video data set to another and has been affected by several parameters. The most affecting factors for shot detection is lighting changes and camera/object motion. Hence, there is a need for efficient shot boundary detection algorithms that yield maximum detection rates. A detailed survey on recent developments of shot boundary detection is reported in [6].

2.2 Keyframe Extraction

The review of existing techniques on keyframe extraction from video shots has been reported in [1,16,17]. The keyframe extraction methods are classified into shot based and segment based. In shot based approach, some of the existing keyframe algorithms consider either the first, middle or the last frame as keyframe for each video shot. In some other approaches, low level features such as color, motion, texture etc., are used to extract keyframes [18]. The difference in color histograms of consecutive frames were compared to obtain keyframes [19]. In [4], cumulative frame differences based on color histograms and histogram of edges and wavelets were computed to extract keyframes. In [20], an aggregation mechanism to combine visual features extracted from correlation of RGB color channels, color histogram and moments of inertia were used. However, in shot based approach, the keyframes are extracted based on the content change between consecutive frames. Some of the researchers have explored the concept of clustering for keyframe extraction. In [21], time constrained clustering method was used to extract keyframes. An unsupervised clustering approach [22] used color histogram for key frame extraction. Delaunay triangulation based clustering of color histogram features were proposed in [23]. In [24], the video is summarized with a clustering algorithm based on singular value decomposition (SVD). The refined feature space obtained by SVD is clustered and a keyframe is extracted from each cluster. In [25], keyframes are extracted using inter cluster similarity analysis from clusters having larger dispersion rate. In [26], the subset of keyframes is extracted using combinatorial algorithm. In [27], video summaries are generated by exploiting connectivity matrix and keyframe extraction from cluster is accomplished by dominant set clustering algorithm.

3   The Proposed Methodology

The proposed methodology for shot boundary detection and keyframe extraction involves several steps as illustrated in Fig. 1. The given color video frames are first converted into gray scale images as preprocessing. In the first step, feature extraction using bitwise XOR variance method between adjacent frames of video sequence is performed and further used for partitioning the shots. In the second step, the same feature extraction approach is applied for each video shots and dissimilarity matrix is constructed based on the obtained feature values. Using the information in dissimilarity matrix, the representative keyframe is selected for every shot. The details of the proposed methodology are described in the following sub sections.

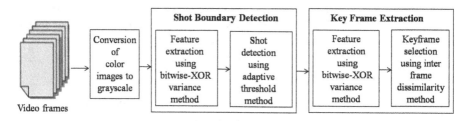

Fig. 1. Illustration of the proposed methodology.

3.1 Feature Extraction and Representation

Effective description of frame information plays a vital role for accurate detection of shots and selection of relevant keyframes. The proposed method exploits the XOR operation on the corresponding gray scale values at each pixel position of current and succeeding frame of the video sequence to derive features for frame description as depicted numerically in Fig. 2. The corresponding gray pixel values of the frames will be converted into their equivalent binary representations. The bitwise XOR operation is then applied on two binary bits, which produces value 1, if the corresponding binary bits have different value (e.g. either 1's or 0's), otherwise produces value 0. The resultant binary bits will be converted back to gray scale values. Likewise, all the corresponding pixels of adjacent image frames will undergo the same process. Later the cumulative sum value is evaluated on the obtained resultant matrix and finally variance value is computed and stored as the representative feature value of corresponding adjacent frames respectively.

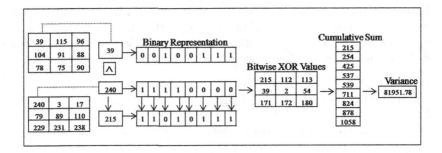

Fig. 2. Numerical illustration of Bitwise XOR variance operation.

Illustration of the above process is depicted in Fig. 3. The figure illustrates few sample frames (865, 866 and 867) of anni006 of TRECVID 2001 data set. In the first case, the bitwise XOR operation between adjacent dissimilar frames (865, 866) will exhibit large difference in variance value. In the second case, the bitwise XOR operation between adjacent similar frames (866, 867) will result in small difference in variance value. The approach exhibits the visual content changes between the adjacent frames of a video shot. The variance feature value is further exploited for shot boundary detection in a video sequence and keyframe extraction from every shot of a video sequence as well.

3.2 Shot Detection Process

Shot boundary in a continuous video is a frame, which possesses significant difference in terms of its content when compared to previous frames. A shot boundary is detected, if the difference between consecutive frames is greater than a predefined threshold. Computing a good threshold, which can detect precise shot boundary, is a challenging task. In this work, we propose a global threshold

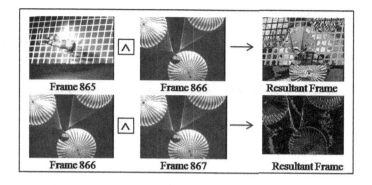

Fig. 3. Illustration of Bitwise XOR operation on image frames.

approach for detection of shot cuts. The variance feature values obtained as discussed in the previous section are considered for shot cut detection. The Z-score for each feature value is computed as follows:

$$ZS_i = |F_i - \mu|/\sigma \tag{1}$$

Where,

$$\mu = \frac{\sum\limits_{i=1}^{n} F_i}{n} \tag{2}$$

$$\sigma = \sqrt{\frac{\sum\limits_{i=1}^{n}(F_i - \mu)^2}{n}} \tag{3}$$

Further, the difference between the consecutive Z-score values is computed as follows:

$$D_i = (Z_i - Z_{i+1}) \tag{4}$$

Where D_i is the difference Z-score value computed and is represented as positive, negative or zero values. When these difference values were plotted, we observed that only the positive D_i values may be the indicators for the shot cuts and hence, the D_i values, which are equal to zero or less than zero, are ignored. In order to choose the threshold value, further the mean (μ) and standard deviation (σ) of the D_i values of entire feature values of video sequence are computed. The value $\mu + h * \sigma$ is set as threshold, where h is a constant value. The experimental analysis showcases that the global threshold approach has yielded good accuracy in detecting abrupt shot cuts in several categories of videos. Our main aim is to segment the video into shots and hence gradual transition is not addressed.

3.3   Keyframe Selection

After shot detection process, the appropriate keyframe is extracted from each shot of a video sequence. In this section, we present a method for keyframe extraction. The keyframe extraction process is accomplished by constructing a dissimilarity matrix. The variance feature values obtained from feature extraction section are used to construct dissimilarity matrix. Each feature value of a video shot is compared against the remaining feature values by establishing Euclidean distances between them. Thus, the dissimilarity matrix is constructed for every video shot. A sample dissimilarity matrix is shown in Fig. 4, which depicts the frame-to-frame Euclidean distance between the feature values obtained for a video shot. It can be observed that the distance value between the same frames is zero.

Dissimilarity Matrix											Row Sum
	f1	f2	f3	f4	f5	f6	f7	f8	f9	f10	
f1	0.00	2.39	3.68	1.01	1.33	0.63	0.20	0.92	1.63	0.38	12.17
f2	2.39	0.00	1.29	1.39	1.06	1.76	2.19	3.31	0.76	2.77	16.93
f3	3.68	1.29	0.00	2.67	2.35	3.05	3.48	4.60	2.05	4.06	27.21
f4	1.01	1.39	2.67	0.00	0.32	0.38	0.80	1.92	0.63	1.39	10.51
f5	1.33	1.06	2.35	0.32	0.00	0.70	1.13	2.24	0.30	1.71	11.15
f6	0.63	1.76	3.05	0.38	0.70	0.00	0.43	1.54	1.00	1.01	10.50
f7	0.20	2.19	3.48	0.80	1.13	0.43	0.00	1.12	1.43	0.58	11.35
f8	0.92	3.31	4.60	1.92	2.24	1.54	1.12	0.00	2.55	0.54	18.74
f9	1.63	0.76	2.05	0.63	0.30	1.00	1.43	2.55	0.00	2.01	12.36
f10	0.38	2.77	4.06	1.38	1.71	1.01	0.58	0.54	2.01	0.00	14.42

Min value → 10.50

f6=Key Frame

Fig. 4. Illustration of keyframe selection from a video shot.

In the proposed approach, a single keyframe is selected from every shot without the involvement of a threshold or parameter. For the keyframe extraction process, we compute the row sum for each row in the dissimilarity matrix. The minimum value out of all the row sum values per each shot is evaluated. The frame number corresponding to this minimum value is considered as the keyframe of that particular shot of a video sequence. Likewise the keyframes will be identified for every shot. Thus, the selected keyframes from each individual shot can be archived as video abstract and can be further used for video indexing and retrieval applications.

4   Experimental Analysis and Results

The performance evaluation process for the above approach is presented in two stages: shot boundary detection and keyframe extraction. The proposed method has been implemented in MATLAB 2012a version using Intel Core i5 processor with 2.20 GHz and 2 GB RAM. To evaluate the performance of the proposed method, we carried out a series of experiments on TRECVID video dataset sponsored by the National Institute of Standards and Technology (NIST). The dataset contains object motion, camera motion and illumination variation of various degree, which makes detection process very cumbersome. The frame size of the data set is (320 × 262). The description of the dataset sponsored by NIST is presented in Table 1.

Table 1. Description of subset of TRECVID 2001 video dataset

File name	Video title	MB	MM:SS
anni005	"NASA_25th_Anniversary_Show_Segment_5" [28]	66.9	6:01
anni006	"NASA_25th_Anniversary_Show_Segment_6" [28]	97.6	9:13
anni009	"NASA_25th_Anniversary_Show_Segment_9" [28]	72.4	6:50
NAD53	"A&S_Reports_Tape_#4_Report_#260" [28]	128	14:20

4.1 Evaluation Criterion of Shot Boundary Detection

Efficiency of the shot detection process depends upon the feature extraction scheme. The performance of our shot boundary detection process is promising due to its efficiency as compared to other state of the art algorithms. The comparative results are tabulated in Table 2. Comparison of Recall, Precision, F-measure and Average graphs are depicted in Figs. 5, 6, 7 and 8. We have compared the results with the available ground truth to classify the detection as correct, false or missed cuts. The following measures are used to demonstrate the performance of the proposed methodology:

$$Recall = \frac{N_C}{N_C + N_M} \tag{5}$$

$$Precision = \frac{N_C}{N_C + N_F} \tag{6}$$

$$F\text{-}Measure = \frac{2 * Recall * Precision}{Recall * Precision} \tag{7}$$

where N_C, N_M and N_F are the number of correctly detected shot cuts, missed shot cuts and falsely detected shot cuts respectively.

As a summary, the results illustrated in Table 2 shows that the proposed approach is comparatively high in accuracy and yields better detection rate compared to that of existing state of the art approaches.

4.2 Evaluation Criterion of Keyframe Extraction

Evaluation of the keyframe extraction is one of the important issues in video analysis and summarization. It is difficult to check the correctness of keyframe extraction due to lack of ground truth and evaluation is tedious [26]. In this work,

Table 2. Comparative results of proposed method along with other shot detection algorithms

Video sequence	Number of shots	Color histograms [29]			MotionVector likelihoods [30]			Proposed method		
		R	P	Fm	R	P	Fm	R	P	Fm
anni005	38	0.83	0.64	0.72	0.53	0.46	0.49	0.92	1	0.96
anni006	41	0.7	0.78	0.74	0.56	0.57	0.56	0.71	0.81	0.75
anni009	38	0.71	0.84	0.77	0.64	0.59	0.61	0.79	0.91	0.85
NAD53	83	0.62	0.69	0.65	0.73	0.46	0.56	0.86	0.89	0.87
Average		0.72	0.74	0.72	0.61	0.52	0.56	0.89	0.94	0.92

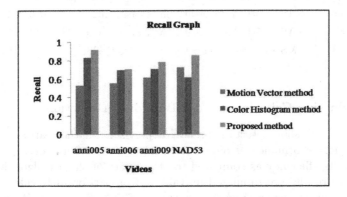

Fig. 5. Comparison of recall measure.

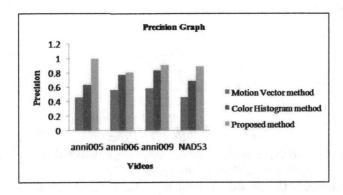

Fig. 6. Comparison of precision measure.

the summary of video is accomplished by the extraction of one keyframe per shot. A video summary is efficient, if the set of keyframes represent the visual contents of video sequence effectively. We have used fidelity measure, which is based on Semi-Hausdorff distance for evaluation of keyframe extraction process on the bench mark data set. Fidelity measure [27] is computed as maximum of minimal

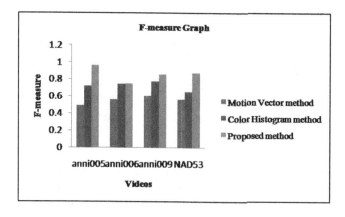

Fig. 7. Comparison of F-measure measure.

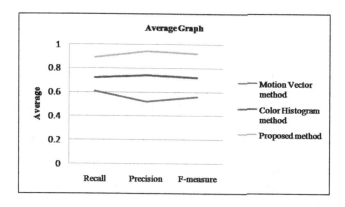

Fig. 8. Comparison of average measure.

distance between keyframe set and shot frame set. Let $R = \{F_1, F_2, F_3, ... F_n\}$ be the n frames of input video and $S = \{F_1, F_2, F_3, ... F_m\}$ be the set of m keyframes extracted from shots of video sequence. The distance between the sets are defined as follows:

$$d_j = min(d(R_i, S_{km}))$$
(8)

Each frame of a video is characterized using the features as discussed earlier in feature extraction section. The Semi-Hausdorff distance between S and R is defined as:

$$d_{sh} = max(d_j)$$
(9)

And, the fidelity measure is defined as:

$$Fidelity = \frac{(1 - d_{sh})}{max(max(d_i))}$$
(10)

Table 3. Performance evaluation of keyframe extraction

Video sequence	No. of shots	Dimension of frames	No. of frames	Fidelity measure
anni005	38	340×262	11362	0.85
anni006	41	340×262	16586	0.81
anni009	38	340×262	12305	0.90
NAD53	83	340×262	26114	0.91

The bigger fidelity value indicates the accurate description of visual content of video sequence. In our experiment, the fidelity measure is computed for the corresponding keyframes of each shot. If an algorithm does not extract keyframes from a shot, the corresponding fidelity measurement is set to the worst case value (zero). The fidelity measure values of the proposed method, implemented on TRECVID 2001 data set are presented in Table 3.

5   Conclusion

In this paper, we have proposed an approach for generating video summary from each video sequence, which can be used for video indexing and retrieval applications. The proposed methodology comprises of shot boundary detection and keyframe extraction phases. The properties of bitwise XOR operation is employed to derive features, which are used for shot detection and also for selecting keyframes from every shot. For experimental analysis and evaluation of shot boundary detection and keyframe extraction methods, TRECVID 2001 bench mark data set has been used. The shot boundary detection algorithm yields F-measure score of 92% compared to other existing approaches. Keyframe extraction method yields average fidelity score of 0.87%.

References

1. Money, A.G., Agius, H.: Video summarisation: a conceptual framework and survey of the state of the art. J. Vis. Commun. Image Represent. **19**(2), 121–143 (2008)
2. Amiri, A., Fathy, M.: Hierarchical keyframe-based video summarization using QR-decomposition and modified k-means clustering. EURASIP J. Adv. Sig. Process. **2010** (2010). Article No. 102
3. Girgensohn, A., Boreczky, J.: Time-constrained keyframe selection technique. Multimedia Comput. Syst. IEEE Int. Conf. IEEE **1**, 756–761 (1999)
4. Gianluigi, C., Raimondo, S.: An innovative algorithm for key frame extraction in video summarization. J. Real-Time Image Process. **1**(1), 69–88 (2006)
5. Furini, M., Geraci, F., Montangero, M., Pellegrini, M.: STIMO: STIll and MOving video storyboard for the web scenario. Multimedia Tools Appl. **46**(1), 47–69 (2010)
6. Hu, W., Xie, N., Li, L., Zeng, X., Maybank, S.: A survey on visual content-based video indexing and retrieval. IEEE Trans. Syst. Man Cybern. C (Applications and Reviews), **41**(6), 797–819 (2011)

7. Lian, S.: Automatic video temporal segmentation based on multiple features. Soft Comput. **15**(3), 469–482 (2011)
8. Küçüktunç, O., Güdükbay, U., Ulusoy, Ö.: Fuzzy color histogram based video segmentation. Comput. Vis. Image Underst. **114**(1), 125–134 (2010)
9. Yoo, H.W., Ryoo, H.J., Jang, D.S.: Gradual shot boundary detection using localized edge blocks. Multimedia Tools Appl. **28**(3), 283–300 (2006)
10. Amel, A.M., Abdessalem, B.A., Abdellatif, M.: Video shot boundary detection using motion activity descriptor. arXiv preprint arXiv:1004.4605 (2010)
11. Barbu, T.: Novel automatic video cut detection technique using Gabor filtering. Comput. Electr. Eng. **35**(5), 712–721 (2009)
12. Shekar, B.H., Uma, K.P.: Kirsch directional derivatives based shot boundary detection: an efficient and accurate method. Procedia Comput. Sci. **58**, 565–571 (2015)
13. Cernekova, Z., Pitas, I., Nikou, C.: Information theory based shot cut/fade detection and video summarization. IEEE Trans. Circ. Syst. Video Technol. **16**(1), 82–91 (2006)
14. Jiang, X., Sun, T., Liu, J., Chao, J., Zhang, W.: An adaptive video shot segmentation scheme based on dual detection model. Neurocomputing **116**, 102–111 (2013)
15. Birinci, M., Birinyaz, S.: A perceptual scheme for fully automatic video shot boundary detection. Sig. Process. Image Commun. **29**(3), 410–423 (2014)
16. Truong, B.T., Venkatesh, S.: Video abstraction: a systematic review and classification. ACM Trans. Multimedia Comput. Commun. Appl. (TOMM) **3**(1), 3 (2007)
17. Li, Y., Lee, S.H., Yeh, C.H., Kuo, C.C.: Techniques for movie content analysis and skimming: tutorial and overview on video abstraction techniques. IEEE Sig. Process. Mag. **23**(2), 79–89 (2006)
18. Jiang, R.M., Sadka, A.H., Crookes, D.: Advances in video summarization and skimming. In: Grgic, M., Delac, K., Ghanbari, M. (eds.) Recent Advances in Multimedia Signal Processing and Communications, vol. 231, pp. 27–50. Springer, Heidelberg (2009)
19. Hanjalic, A., Lagendijk, R.L., Biemond, J.: A new keyframe allocation method for representing stored video streams. In: Proceedings of 1st International Workshop on Image Databases and Multimedia Search (1996)
20. Ejaz, N., Tariq, T.B., Baik, S.W.: Adaptive key frame extraction for video summarization using an aggregation mechanism. J. Vis. Commun. Image Represent. **23**(7), 1031–1040 (2012)
21. Yeung, M.M., Yeo, B.L.: Video visualization for compact presentation and fast browsing of pictorial content. IEEE Trans. Circ. Syst. Video Technol. **7**(5), 771–785 (1997)
22. Zhuang, Y., Rui, Y., Huang, T.S., Mehrotra, S.: Adaptive key frame extraction using unsupervised clustering. In: Proceedings of the International Conference on Image Processing, ICIP 1998, vol. 1, pp. 866–870. IEEE (1998)
23. Mundur, P., Rao, Y., Yesha, Y.: Keyframe-based video summarization using Delaunay clustering. Int. J. Digit. Libr. **6**(2), 219–232 (2006)
24. Gong, Y., Liu, X.: Generating optimal video summaries. In: 2000 IEEE International Conference on Multimedia and Expo, ICME, vol. 3, pp. 1559–1562. IEEE (2000)
25. Priya, G.L., Domnic, S.: Shot based keyframe extraction for ecological video indexing and retrieval. Ecol. Inf. **23**, 107–117 (2014)
26. Besiris, D., Makedonas, A., Economou, G., Fotopoulos, S.: Combining graph connectivity and dominant set clustering for video summarization. Multimedia Tools Appl. **44**(2), 161–186 (2009)

27. Chang, H.S., Sull, S., Lee, S.U.: Efficient video indexing scheme for content-based retrieval. IEEE Trans. Circ. Syst. Video Technol. **9**(8), 1269–1279 (1999)
28. http://www-nlpir.nist.gov/projects/trecvid/collection.html
29. Adjeroh, D., Lee, M.C., Banda, N., Kandaswamy, U.: Adaptive edge-oriented shot boundary detection. EURASIP J. Image Video Process. **2009**(1), 1 (2009). Article No. 5
30. Li, W.K., Lai, S.H.: Integrated video shot segmentation algorithm. In: Electronic Imaging 2003 International Society for Optics and Photonics, pp. 264–271 (2003)

Biomedical Image Analysis

Automatic Compound Figure Separation in Scientific Articles: A Study of Edge Map and Its Role for Stitched Panel Boundary Detection

A. Aafaque and K.C. Santosh[(⊠)]

Department of Computer Science, The University of South Dakota,
414 E Clark St, Vermillion, SD 57069, USA
aafaque.aafaque@coyotes.usd.edu, santosh.kc@usd.edu

Abstract. We present a technique that uses edge map to separate panels from stitched compound figures appearing in biomedical scientific research articles. Since such figures may comprise images from different imaging modalities, separating them is a critical first step for effective biomedical content-based image retrieval (CBIR). We study state-of-the-art edge detection algorithms to detect gray-level pixel changes. It then applies a line vectorization process that connects prominent broken lines along the panel boundaries while eliminating insignificant line segments within the panels. We have validated our fully automatic technique on a subset of stitched multipanel biomedical figures extracted from articles within the Open Access subset of PubMed Central repository, and have achieved precision and recall of 74.20% and 71.86%, respectively, in less than 0.272 s per image, on average.

Keywords: Automation · Edge detection · Stitched multipanel figures · Biomedical publications · Content-based image retrieval

1 Introduction

1.1 Context

In biomedical publications alone, authors report an increasing use of medical images [4,12]. The average number of figures in reputable biomedical journals ranges from 6 to 31 [7,21]. More importantly, according to [10,11,15], multipanel figures represent about 50% of the figures in the biomedical open access articles used for the imageCLEF (URL: http://www.imageclef.org) benchmark. Figures are often composed of multiple panels, each describing different methodologies, modalities or results, including the possibility of providing direct comparisons among them. Figure 1 shows one of the examples. However, such figures pose a challenge for image retrieval [1,2,6,14,16] and modality classification systems [8,18,20]. In this context, figure panel separation is considered as a crucial step to biomedical content-based image retrieval (CBIR) [3,5,6,13].

In the literature, uniform-space-separated multipanel figures comprise regular (images) and graphical (illustrations, charts, plots) type figures. Pixel intensity

© Springer Nature Singapore Pte Ltd. 2017
K.C. Santosh et al. (Eds.): RTIP2R 2016, CCIS 709, pp. 319–332, 2017.
DOI: 10.1007/978-981-10-4859-3_29

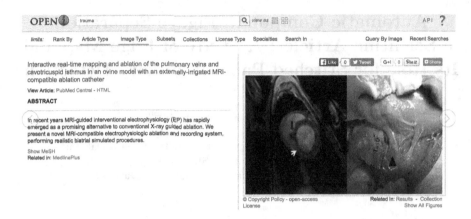

Fig. 1. Using National Library of Medicine's (NLM) Open-i^{SM} image retrieval search engine, the illustration highlights the possibility of figures with multipanels.

profile-based and homogeneity-based (for crossing bands) methods are commonly used (and often sufficient) to separate the panels [3,5,5,17]. Other methods uses optical character recognition (OCR) for stitched or fully connected multipanel figures [3,13]. But, their solution is sensitive to common errors generated by the OCR and are rigid about the alignment of subfigure panel labels relative to each other. To the best of our knowledge, no real works have been reported that separate stitched multipanel figures purely from an image analysis standpoint. A primary challenge for image analysis-based techniques is that no clear boundaries and homogeneous gaps exist between fully connected panels. Therefore, the scope of the current work is focused on stitched multipanel figures (see Fig. 1 from Open-i^{SM} (url: https://openi.nlm.nih.gov) and Fig. 2) that largely affect the performance of the state-of-the-art techniques.

1.2   Structure of the Paper

The remainder of the paper is organized as follows. In Sect. 2, our proposed method is described. It includes basics on state-of-the-art edge detection algorithms (see Sect. 2.1); how panel boundaries are separated from edge map (see Sect. 2.2); and how multipanel figure separation is accomplished (see Sect. 2.3). It also include qualitative sample outputs. In Sect. 3, we report our results and analyze them. Section 4 concludes the paper.

2   The Proposed Method

Following the concept reported in [19], our method separates multipanel figures by computing panel boundaries using edge map (see Fig. 3 for the workflow). In general, we detect line segments (i.e., edges), representing panel boundary using several different state-of-the-art edge detection algorithms i.e., profile-based line

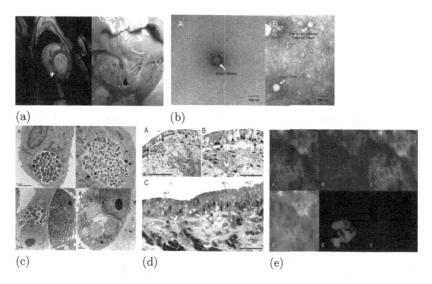

Fig. 2. Examples showing stitched multipanel figures. These are appeared with and without panel labels, including irregular panel boxes.

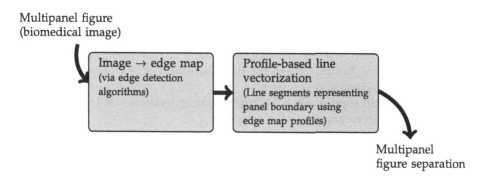

Fig. 3. Workflow: images are first transformed into binary image via edge detection algorithms. These are then processed to get profiles and apply profile-based line vectorization (based on the peak locations of the profiles) that ultimately separates panels.

vectorization technique is used to confirm the panel boundaries (based on the location of peaks). Panels are then separated iteratively until we catch prominent peaks in both horizontal and vertical profiles. Compared to [19], our method advanced in detecting peaks, and at the same time, it does not require corner detection for separating multipanel figure.

2.1 Basics: State-of-the-Art Edge Detection Algorithms

For this paper, we use six different types of state-of-the-art edge detection algorithms: (1) Canny, (2) Roberts, (3) Sobel, (4) Prewitt, (5) Zero-cross and

(6) Laplacian of Gaussian. In what follows, we describe them, with sample outputs. Those sample outputs allows visual comparison among them.

Canny edge operator. The process of Canny edge detection algorithm can be broken down to 5 different steps.

(1) *Apply smoothing*
We start with smoothing, which refers to blurring of the image. Blurring is aimed to remove noise. For this, a Gaussian filter is applied to convolve with the image. In general, Gaussian filter can be expressed as,

$$G(x) = \frac{1}{\sqrt{2\pi}\sigma}e^{-\frac{x^2}{2\sigma^2}}.$$

This step will slightly smooth the image to reduce the effects of obvious noise on the edge detector.
(2) *Compute the intensity gradients*
An edge in an image may point in a variety of directions. In case of Canny algorithm, four filters are used to detect horizontal, vertical and diagonal edges in the blurred image. The edge gradient and directions (by using G_x and G_y) can be determined:

$$G = \sqrt{G_x^2 + G_y^2} \text{ and } \theta = atan2(G_y, G_x).$$

Note that the edge direction angle is rounded to one of four angles representing vertical, horizontal and the two diagonals: $0, \pi/4, \pi/2$ and $3\pi/2$.
(3) *Apply non-maximum suppression*
Non-maximum suppression is an edge thinning technique. It is used to get rid of spurious response to edge detection.
(4) *Apply double threshold*
To determine potential edges, there are two thresholds: high and low that are empirically set. High threshold yields strong edges, and in the same way, low threshold yields weak edges. Edges are suppressed if the pixel value is smaller than the low threshold value.
(5) *Track edge by hysteresis*
It finalizes the detection of edges by suppressing all the other edges that are weak and not connected to strong edges.

Roberts edge operator. As a differential operator, reported in [], the idea behind the Roberts cross operator is to approximate the gradient of an image through discrete differentiation which is achieved by computing the sum of the squares of the differences between diagonally adjacent pixels.

To perform edge detection with the Roberts operator we first convolve the original image, I with the following two kernels as follows:

$$G_x = \begin{bmatrix} -1 & 0 \\ 0 & -1 \end{bmatrix} \star I \text{ and } G_y = \begin{bmatrix} 0 & -1 \\ 1 & 0 \end{bmatrix} \star I.$$

This means that for an image, I, G_x and G_y be a point after convolving with the kernels. Like before, we can compute the edge gradient and directions.

Prewitt edge operator. The operator uses two 3×3 kernels, and are convolved with the original image, I to calculate approximations of the derivatives: horizontal and vertical. In general, we have

$$G_x = \begin{bmatrix} -1 & 0 & 1 \\ -1 & 0 & 1 \\ -1 & 0 & 1 \end{bmatrix} \star I \text{ and } G_y = \begin{bmatrix} 1 & 1 & 1 \\ 0 & 0 & 0 \\ -1 & -1 & -1 \end{bmatrix} \star I$$

Once we have G_x and G_y, as before, we can compute the edge gradient and directions.

Sobel edge operator. Like in Prewitt case, Sobel does the task. The major difference is that in Sobel operator, the coefficients of kernels are not fixed and they can be adjusted according to our requirement unless they do not violate any property of derivative kernels. In other words, the only difference is it has '2' and '−2' values in center of first and third column of the kernel matrix, that can be expressed as,

$$G_x = \begin{bmatrix} -1 & 0 & 1 \\ -2 & 0 & 2 \\ -1 & 0 & 1 \end{bmatrix} \star I \text{ and } G_y = \begin{bmatrix} 1 & 2 & 1 \\ 0 & 0 & 0 \\ -1 & -2 & -1 \end{bmatrix} \star I$$

Such kernels emphasize the pixels that are closer to the center of the kernel. As a result, Sobel operator is expected to produce more edges (or more visible edges) as compared to Prewitt operator (see Fig. 5).

Zero cross edge operator. The second derivative of a smoothed step edge is a function that crosses zero at the location of the edge. The Laplacian is the two-dimensional equivalent of the second derivative. The formula for the Laplacian of a function $f(x, y)$ is

$$\nabla^2 f = \frac{\delta^2 f}{\delta x^2} + \frac{\delta^2 f}{\delta y^2}.$$

For this, the following kernel can be used to approximate the zero cross:

$$\nabla^2 \approx \begin{bmatrix} 0 & 1 & 0 \\ 1 & -4 & 1 \\ 0 & 1 & 0 \end{bmatrix}.$$

While creating a kernel, we can also provide more weight to the center pixels in the neighborhood.

Laplacian of Gaussian edge operator. Like in Canny edge detection, the process is composed of five steps:

(1) Smooth the image using the Gaussian filter with some fixed width;
(2) compute local gradient;

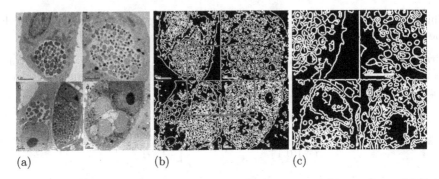

(a)   (b)   (c)

Fig. 4. Figures shows (a) original multipanel stitched image (b) edge map via Canny edge detection and (c) cropped area from (b) (in red) for clear visual understanding. (Color figure online)

(3) compute second directional derivative in the direction of local gradient;
(4) identify zero crossings; and
(5) accept or reject the resulting edges based on some signal-to-noise evaluation technique.

Note that zero crossings of the second derivative of the image intensity are very sensitive to noise. It is, therefore, desired to filter out the noise before edge enhancement. For this, the Laplacian of Gaussian (LoG) combines Gaussian filtering with the Laplacian for edge detection. The output of the LoG operator, $h(x,y)$, is obtained by the convolution operation:

$$h(x,y) = \nabla^2 \left[(g(x,y) * I(x,y)) \right].$$

Using the derivative rule for convolution, we have $h(x,y) = \left[\nabla^2 g(x,y) \right] * I(x,y)$, where $\nabla^2 g(x,y) = \left(\frac{x^2+y^2-2\sigma^2}{\sigma^4} \right) e^{\frac{x^2+y^2}{2\sigma^2}}$.

Comparison. This section aims to provide a clear-cut visual illustration-based comparison among the edge detection algorithms. In Fig. 4, we first provide a complete idea of edge map from the use of Canny edge detection, where it is important to take a look into cropped edge map region (for clear visual understanding). For a comparison, in Fig. 5, we take that cropped region (as shown in Fig. 4) for all remaining edge detection algorithms. We observe that Canny edge detection algorithm yields clear edges as compared to others. Beside, zero cross and laplacian of Gaussian operators provide good edges, but in contrast to Canny, some edges: horizontal and vertical lines seem broken.

Note that such a visual comparison does not guarantee the performance of the multipanel figure separation. For this, we refer readers to Sect. 3.

2.2 Boundary Panel Detection

From the edge map (as shown in Fig. 5, it is required to select the edges that are representing boundary panels. In this section, we discuss about edges along the boundary panels are filtered. Our process is composed of two steps:

(1) Compute edge map profiles (horizontal and vertical); and
(2) Locate peak points.

The peak locations along the profiles help us to confirm the boundary panel, since we assume that boundary panel must have strong edges as compared to other regions.

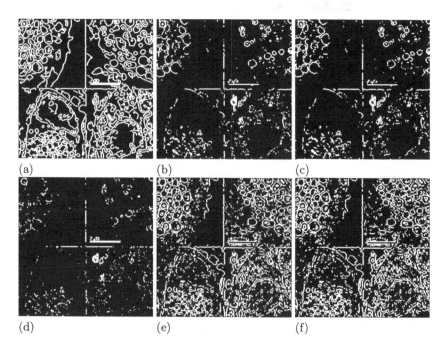

(a)   (b)   (c)

(d)   (e)   (f)

Fig. 5. Edge map comparison: (a) Canny, (b) Prewitt, (c) Sobel, (d) Roberts, (e) Zero cross, and (f) Laplacian of Gaussian. It follows the cropped region as shown in Fig. 4.

Edge map profiles: horizontal and vertical. We compute orthogonal projection profiles in both directions: 0 and $\pi/2$. Projection profiles from a 2D image $I(x, y)$ of size $m \times n$ can be computed as,

$$p_{\theta=\pi/2} = \sum_{1 \le x \le m} I(x, y) \text{ and } p_{\theta=0} = \sum_{1 \le y \le n} I(x, y).$$

To eliminate dominant edges that typically result from objects within the panels, we compute their corresponding profile transforms(i.e., p_θ^2), which is then normalized (Fig. 6).

Peak detection. Peaks (or local maxima) from horizontal and vertical profiles (as mentioned before) can be computed in a five step process.

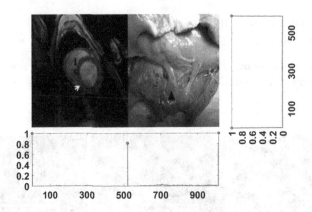

Fig. 6. Example showing the profile-based line vectorization process: both vertical and horizontal profiles are taken, where peak locations are shown (in red dots). (Color figure online)

(1) Calculate peaks based on the threshold, t (manually set), and therefore any peak location l^t can be expressed as

$$l^t = \underset{i=1\ldots n}{\arg} \begin{cases} p_i & \text{if } p_i \geq t \\ \emptyset & \text{otherwise.} \end{cases}$$

(2) Compute distances between the successive peak locations:

$$\mathbf{D}^t = \left\{ \delta\left(l_i^t\right) - \left(l_{i+1}^t\right) \right\}_{i=1\ldots n'} \text{ and } n' \leq n,$$

where $\delta(*, \triangleleft) = || * - \triangleleft ||$.
(3) Calculate mean from $\mathbf{D}^t$, $m_d = \mathbf{mean}\left(\mathbf{D}^t\right)$.
(4) Using m_d (in place of t), repeat the procedure explained in step 1, and it results l^d. At this point, we consider both l_t and l_d. The peaks that are too close to each other are ignored (meaning one of two will be taken):

$$l^d = \begin{cases} \arg\{p_i\} & \text{if } (\arg\{p_{i+1}\} - \arg\{p_i\}) \geq m_d \\ \emptyset & \text{otherwise.} \end{cases}$$

(5) Common peak locations l^p that are resulted from steps 1 and 4 can be computed as $l = l^d \cap l^t$. These final peak locations would be use to crop the panels from stitched panel images.

2.3   Multipanel Figure Separation

Consider we have two different sets, $\mathcal{H}$ and $\mathcal{V}$ of peak locations, l (which is an argument of the peak value, $\arg(\wp)$) from both profiles horizontal and vertical profiles defined by $p_{\theta=0}$ and $p_{\theta=\pi/2}$:

$$\mathcal{H} = \left\{l_i^0\right\}_{i=1,\ldots,n} \text{ and } \mathcal{V} = \left\{l_j^{\pi/2}\right\}_{j=1,\ldots,m}.$$

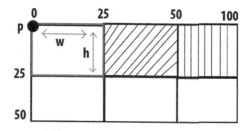

Fig. 7. An example (toy) showing image to rectangle transformation (i.e., six rectangles). These rectangles help image regions crop. In this example, $\mathcal{H} = [0, 25, 50]$ and $\mathcal{V} = [0, 25, 50, 100]$. The rectangle in red, $r = [0, 0, 25, 25]$. (Color figure online)

It also includes image border locations: top and bottom (for $\mathcal{H}$), and left and right (for $\mathcal{V}$). From these locations (along x and y axes), we can compute all possible rectangles from the studied image. Now, the set $\mathcal{R}$ of rectangles can be expressed as

$$\mathcal{R} = \left\{ \left[l_i^0, l_j^{\pi/2}, \left(l_{i+1}^0 - l_i^0 \right), \left(l_{j+1}^{\pi/2} - l_j^{\pi/2} \right) \right] \right\}_{j=1...(m-1)} \quad \text{for } i = 1...(n-1),$$

where end locations are not required since any rectangle, r, in general, is defined in the form: $r = [start\_point, width, height]$. Therefore, the number of rectangles represents the panels of any studied compound figure. In Fig. 7 illustrates an example of it.

In Fig. 8, qualitative outputs are shown. This allows us to prove the effectiveness/robustness of the proposed method.

3 Experiments

3.1 Dataset

Even though the goal remains the same, evaluations of the state-of-the-art methods vary with the dataset collection. But, most of the reported methods used imageCLEF. However, none of them evaluated stitched multipanel figures.

Besides the imageCLEF, we used NLM's *Open-i* (URL: http://openi.nlm.nih.gov) search engine to collect more samples, where panels are completely connected. Altogether, our collection is composed of 150 images, and are available upon request. A few samples are shown in Fig. 2. For validation purpose, we developed an annotator that can automatically annotate the panels in the presence of the user.

3.2 Evaluation Protocol

For any image I, we have a set $\mathcal{R}$ of the detected rectangles: $I \mapsto \mathcal{R}$ and $\mathcal{R} = \{r_i\}_{i=1,...,\mathbf{R}}$, representing an output. Similarly, in our ground-truth, we have a set $\mathcal{R}^\circ$ of rectangles, $\mathcal{R}^\circ = \{r_{i^\circ}^\circ\}_{i^\circ=1,...,\mathbf{R}^\circ}$. Each rectangle refers to a panel.

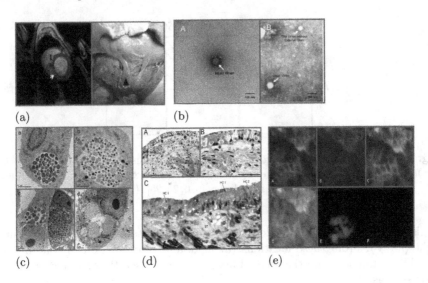

(a) (b)

(c) (d) (e)

Fig. 8. Qualitative outputs: stitched multipanel figure separation. The bold lines (in red) shows panel separation. These multipanel figures correspond to Fig. 2. (Color figure online)

We then use overlapping ratio (OR) to identify correct matches. Consider two rectangles: r° and r, their OR can be computed as [9]

$$\mathrm{OR}(r^\circ, r) = \frac{2 \times |r^\circ \cap r|}{|r^\circ| + |r|} \text{ and } \mathrm{OR}(,) \in [0,1],$$

where $|r^\circ \cap r|$ is the intersected or common area, and $|r^\circ|$ and $|r|$ are the individual areas. When separating panels, we may not achieve 100% OR since a few border pixels can possibly be chopped. Therefore, we follow the following condition:

$$\mathbf{c} = \begin{cases} 1 & \text{if } \mathrm{OR}(,) \geq 0.8 \text{ and} \\ 0 & \text{otherwise.} \end{cases}$$

This means that we assume panel separation is correct in case at least 80% OR exists. Such an OR score does not let images semantic different, and it does not affect CBIR performance. Having OR scores, for validation, for any given image in the dataset, our performance evaluation criteria are precision, recall and F_1-score:

$$\text{precision} = \frac{\mathbf{c}}{\mathbf{R}}, \quad \text{recall} = \frac{\mathbf{c}}{\mathbf{R}^\circ} \text{ and}$$

$$F_1\text{-score} = 2\left(\frac{(\mathbf{c}/\mathbf{R}) \times (\mathbf{c}/\mathbf{R}^\circ)}{(\mathbf{c}/\mathbf{R}) + \mathbf{c}/\mathbf{R}^\circ)}\right),$$

where c is the number of correct matches from the detected set $\mathbf{R}$ and $\mathbf{R}^\circ$ is the total number of rectangles (in the ground-truth) that are expected to be detected. The score computed from every metric is normalized by total number of images in the database.

3.3   Results and Analysis

Using the dataset (*cf.* Sect. 3.1) and the evaluation protocol defined in (Sect. 3.2), experimental results are reported in Table 1.

Table 1. Performance comparison: state-of-the-art edge detection algorithms.

Algorithms	Precision (in %)	Recall (in %)	F_1-score (in %)	Time (in s)
Canny	74.20	71.86	73.00	0.272
LoG	67.20	62.62	64.83	0.268
Zero cross	67.20	62.63	64.83	0.266
Prewitt	59.77	55.92	57.78	0.208
Sobel	57.94	54.03	55.92	0.212
Roberts	54.25	50.75	52.44	0.208

In Table 1, we have achieved maximum precision and recall, respectively 74.20% and 71.86% in approximately 0.27 s per image, on average using Canny edge detection. All tests were made using MATLAB R2016b on UNIX environment Ubuntu 16.04 on Intel Core i7-4510U CPU with (2.00 GHz × 4) and 8 GB RAM. We have taken state-of-the-art edge detection algorithms (see Sect. 2.1 and have performed the test.

Having such a set in our study allows us to make a comprehensive comparison, where Canny edge detector performs the best. The results for all methods in Table 1 are obtained using a threshold of 0.15 as shown in Fig. 9.

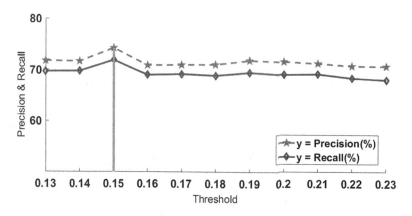

Fig. 9. Precision vs. Recall for Canny edge detection method using different threshold including best 0.15 threshold.

In the reported results (see Table 1), the lowest error rate is approximately 26% (considering precision). Such error rates can be expressed by taking some of the issues in the following. For sample outputs, we refer to Fig. 8, and we note that the last panel that is labelled with F has not been separated. This is due to the fact that there exists no panel boundary (edge). Further, under segmentation and over segmentation are other sources of errors. Under segmentation occurs with no clear pixel differences exist along the panel boundaries (since identical backgrounds are used for all panels). While, over segmentation exists when clear (end to end) separation is appeared within the panels. A more comprehensive results (including comparative study with previous work [19]) has been published in a peer-reviewed journal article [22]

4   Conclusion

Based on the line segment-based concept separating multipanel biomedical figures appearing in biomedical research articles, in this paper, we have studied state-of-the-art edge detection algorithms that detect gray-level pixel changes. We have then applied a new line vectorization process that connects prominent broken lines along the panel boundaries. We have validated our fully automatic technique on a subset of stitched multipanel biomedical figures extracted from articles within the Open Access subset of PubMed Central repository, and have achieved precision and recall of 74.20% and 71.86%, respectively, in less than 0.272 s per image, on average.

References

1. Aigrain, P., Zhang, H., Petkovic, D.: Content-based representation and retrieval of visual media: a state-of-the-art review. Multimedia Tools Appl. **3**(3), 179–202 (1996)
2. Akgül, C.B., Rubin, D.L., Napel, S., Beaulieu, C.F., Greenspan, H., Acar, B.: Content-based image retrieval in radiology: current status and future directions. J. Digit. Imaging **24**(2), 208–222 (2011)
3. Apostolova, E., You, D., Xue, Z., Antani, S., Demner-Fushman, D., Thoma, G.R.: Image retrieval from scientific publications: text and image content processing to separate multipanel figures. JASIST **64**(5), 893–908 (2013)
4. Aucar, J.A., Fernandez, L., Wagner-Mann, C.: If a picture is worth a thousand words, what is a trauma computerized tomography panel worth? Am. J. Surg. **6**(194), 734–740 (2007)
5. Cheng, B., Antani, S., Stanley, R.J., Thoma, G.R.: Automatic segmentation of subfigure image panels for multimodal biomedical document retrieval. In: Agam, G., Viard-Gaudin, C. (eds.) Proceedings of the 18th Document Recognition and Retrieval Conference, Part of the IS&T-SPIE Electronic Imaging Symposium on Document Recognition and Retrieval XVIII - DRR 2011, San Jose, CA, USA. SPIE Proceedings, vol. 7874, pp. 1–10, 24–29 January 2011
6. Chhatkuli, A., Markonis, D., Foncubierta-Rodríguez, A., Meriaudeau, F., Müller, H.: Separating compound figures in journal articles to allow for subfigure classification. In: SPIE, Medical Imaging (2013)

7. Cooper, M.S., Sommers-Herivel, G., Poage, C.T., McCarthy, M.B., Crawford, B.D., Phillips, C.: The zebrafish DVD exchange project: a bioinformatics initiative. Methods Cell Biol. **77**, 439–457 (2004)

8. Demner-Fushman, D., Antani, S., Simpson, M.S., Thoma, G.R.: Design and development of a multimodal biomedical information retrieval system. J. Comput. Sci. Eng. **6**(2), 168–177 (2012)

9. Dice, L.R.: Measures of the amount of ecologic association between species. Ecology **26**(3), 297–302 (1945)

10. de Herrera, A.G.S., Kalpathy-Cramer, J., Demner-Fushman, D., Antani, S., Müller, H.: Overview of the imageCLEF 2013 medical tasks. In: Forner, P., Navigli, R., Tufis, D., Ferro, N. (eds.) Proceedings of the Working Notes for CLEF 2013 Conference, Valencia, Spain. CEUR Workshop, vol. 1179. CEUR-WS.org, 23–26 September 2013

11. Kalpathy-Cramer, J., Müller, H., Bedrick, S., Eggel, I., de Herrera, A.G.S., Tsikrika, T.: Overview of the CLEF 2011 medical image classification and retrieval tasks. In: Petras, V., Forner, P., Clough, P.D. (eds.) CLEF 2011 Labs and Workshop, Notebook Papers, Amsterdam, The Netherlands. CEUR Workshop Proceedings, vol. 1177, 19–22 September 2011

12. Licklider, J.C.R.: A picture is worth a thousand words: and it costs. In: Proceedings of the Joint Computer Conference, AFIPS 1969 (Spring), pp. 617–621. ACM, New York (1969)

13. Lopez, L.D., Yu, J., Arighi, C.N., Tudor, C.O., Torii, M., Huang, H., Vijay-Shanker, K., Wu, C.H.: A framework for biomedical figure segmentation towards image-based document retrieval. BMC Syst. Biol. **7**(s–4), s8 (2013)

14. Müller, H.: Medical (visual) information retrieval. In: Agosti, M., Ferro, N., Forner, P., Müller, H., Santucci, G. (eds.) PROMISE 2012. LNCS, vol. 7757, pp. 155–166. Springer, Heidelberg (2013). doi:10.1007/978-3-642-36415-0_10

15. Müller, H., de Herrera, A.G.S., Kalpathy-Cramer, J., Demner-Fushman, D., Antani, S., Eggel, I.: Overview of the imageCLEF 2012 medical image retrieval and classification tasks. In: Forner, P., Karlgren, J., Womser-Hacker, C. (eds.) CLEF 2012 Evaluation Labs and Workshop, Online Working Notes, Rome, Italy. CEUR Workshop Proceedings, vol. 1178, 17–20 September 2012

16. Müller, H., Michoux, N., Bandon, D., Geissbühler, A.: A review of content-based image retrieval systems in medical applications - clinical benefits and future directions. Int. J. Med. Inform. **73**(1), 1–23 (2004)

17. Murphy, R.F., Velliste, M., Yao, J., Porreca, G.: Searching online journals for fluorescence microscope images depicting protein subcellular location patterns. In: Proceedings of the 2nd IEEE International Symposium on Bioinformatics and Bioengineering, BIBE 2001, pp. 119–128 (2001)

18. Rahman, M.M., You, D., Simpson, M.S., Antani, S., Demner-Fushman, D., Thoma, G.R.: Interactive cross and multimodal biomedical image retrieval based on automatic region-of-interest (ROI) identification and classification. Int. J. Multimedia Inf. Retr. **3**(3), 131–146 (2014)

19. Santosh, K.C., Antani, S.K., Thoma, G.R.: Stitched multipanel biomedical figure separation. In: 28th IEEE International Symposium on Computer-Based Medical Systems, CBMS, pp. 54–59 (2015)

20. Simpson, M.S., Demner-Fushman, D., Antani, S., Thoma, G.R.: Multimodal biomedical image indexing and retrieval using descriptive text and global feature mapping. Inf. Retr. **17**(3), 229–264 (2014)

21. Yu, H.: Towards answering biological questions with experimental evidence: auto-matically identifying text that summarize image content in full-text articles, pp. 834–838 (2006)
22. Santosh, K.C., Aafaque, A., Antani, S., Thoma, G.R.: Line segment-based stitched multipanel figure separation for effective biomedical CBIR. Int. J. Pattern Recogn. Artif. Intell. **31**(5), 1757003 (2017). 17 pages. http://dx.doi.org/10.1142/S0218001417570038

Automated Chest X-ray Image View Classification using Force Histogram

K.C. Santosh[1(✉)] and Laurent Wendling[2]

[1] Department of Computer Science, The University of South Dakota,
414 E Clark St, Vermillion, SD 57069, USA
santosh.kc@usd.edu
[2] LIPADE – Université Paris Descartes (Paris V),
45, rue des Saints-Pères, 75270 Paris Cedex 06, France
laurent.wendling@parisdescartes.fr

Abstract. To advance and/or ease computer aided diagnosis (CAD) system, chest X-ray (CXR) image view information is required. In other words, separating CXR image view: frontal and lateral can be considered as a crucial step to effective subsequent processes, since the techniques that work for frontal CXRs may not equally work for lateral ones. With this motivation, in this paper, we present a novel machine learning technique to classify frontal and lateral CXR images, where we introduce a force histogram to extract features and apply three different state-of-the-art classifiers: support vector machine (SVM), random forest (RF) and multi-layer perceptron (MLP). We validated our fully automatic technique on a set of 8100 images hosted by National Library of Medicine (NLM), National Institutes of Health (NIH), and achieved an accuracy close to 100%.

Keywords: Automation · Chest X-ray · Force histograms · Image view · Classification

1 Introduction

1.1 Context

Chest radiography (or chest X-ray (CXR)) has always been a widely used test to perform screening: pulmonary abnormalities detection, for instance. The WHO revisited the usefulness of CXR mainly because of chest radiography has made x-ray much cheaper and easier to use [16]. In addition, very specifically, for automated CXR screening (for the evidence of Tuberculosis (TB)), we can avoid the rise of smear negative TB [1]. Using digital CXRs, an abnormality suspect can be screened within one second. Two image views are commonly used for diagnosing: frontal and lateral view. Figure 1 shows one patient's frontal and lateral chest radiographs, respectively. Moreover, we found that CXR image view information is not always available in the text. To have such an automated screening system efficient and effective, one needs to separate CXR image view: frontal and lateral

© Springer Nature Singapore Pte Ltd. 2017
K.C. Santosh et al. (Eds.): RTIP2R 2016, CCIS 709, pp. 333–342, 2017.
DOI: 10.1007/978-981-10-4859-3_30

CXR, since further processing for frontal and lateral views could potentially be different. As a consequence, such a image view separation will then guarantee further image analysis and machine learning tasks that are related to several purposes: TB screening [8,15], for instance. In the previously reported CXR screening system [8,15], we note that the system is trained with frontal CXRs, and may not work with lateral ones, even though their goal is common. The primary reason behind this is (as shown in Fig. 1), features vary from frontal to lateral CXR due to the change in lung shape and size, including texture. The aforementioned arguments motivate us to separate CXRs: frontal and lateral. Not to be confused with CXR orientation, which is another important concern to automate the screening [14], and is not the theme of the paper.

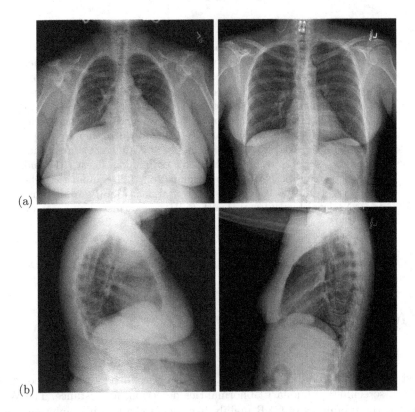

(a)

(b)

Fig. 1. Examples showing two samples per class: (a) frontal and (b) lateral CXRs.

1.2   Related Works and Our Contribution

Separating/identifying CXR image view does not have rich state-of-the-art literature [2,7,9,12,17]. More often, state-of-the-art techniques used features, such as topological and/or geometrical property (e.g. min./max. profile length ratio) [12], template matching concept [2] or matching with reference images [9], projection profile [4] and body symmetry index [7]. On the whole, their features can be described in terms of low-level shape features, and spatial relation of medial axes of anatomic structures and pixel intensity of the region of interest. Further, they have used different similarity metrics, such as cross-correlation coefficient [2] and classifiers, such as k-nearest neighbor, neural networks and Bayesian networks. Regardless the classifiers, their features are not robust enough to separate CXR image view. Very recently, the problem has been reported with a comprehensive and/or extended features, such as image profile, body-size ratio, pyramid of histograms of orientation gradients (PHOG) and contour-based shape features (CBSF). The features used in the recent work [17] are not different from the existing works reported earlier except the use of PHOG and CBSF. At the same time, one has to note that PHOG and CBSF are not rotation invariant (and not robust to scale invariant). In Fig. 1(b), lateral CXR orientations are different from one another. Moreover, even though the reported classification scores are close to perfect (i.e., 99.2% from test set) after integrating all features (altogether feature dimensionality of 1276 per image), the real burden on to the classifier has not been clearly mentioned. Instead, in the paper, we propose a single feature called 'force histogram' to reduce computational burden of the classifiers.

In this paper, the proposed force histogram can capture both: spatial relationships between the pixels and shape of the region-of-interest (see Sect. 2, for more detail). This results a complete feature of dimensionality of 64, in a one shot. Moreover, unlike the state-of-the-art techniques, the proposed technique does not require any costlier pre-processing (except CXR image border cleaning). To determine how accurate (or distinguishable between the class) the feature is, three different well-known classifiers are used: multi-layer perceptron (MLP), random forest (RF) and support vector machine (SVM). In our study, like the previously reported work [17], we validated our fully automatic technique on a set of 8100 images hosted by National Library of Medicine (NLM), National Institutes of Health (NIH), and achieved F-score of 99.79%.

1.3   Outline

In Fig. 2, we propose a fully automated system in an efficient way, where only one feature (force histogram) is used to separate/identify CXR image via three different classifiers.

Following Fig. 2, we organize the remainder of the paper as follows. In Sect. 2, we first explain in detail about force histogram and its properties (see Sect. 2.1). It also includes how we interpret CXR using the force histogram (see Sect. 2.2. We briefly discuss about three different classifiers: MLP, RF and SVM in Sect. 3. In Sect. 4, we provide information about dataset, evaluation protocol and/or metrics (see Sect. 4.1), and test results (see Sect. 4.2). Section 5 concludes the paper.

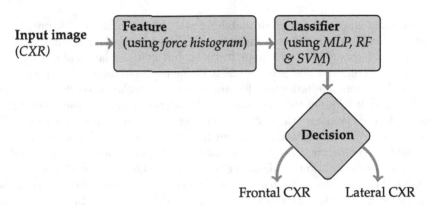

Fig. 2. Work flow: it starts with feature extraction using force histogram and classify them via three different classifiers: multi-layer perceptron (MLP), random forest (RF) and support vector machine (SVM) to make a decision either the input CXR is frontal or lateral.

2 Force Histogram

2.1 Materials

The histogram of forces, originally, allows to assess with accuracy the spatial location of an object from another one [10,11]. The studied objects are broad and can be composed of several connected components. In general, the attraction between two points at a distance d between is given by:

$$\forall d \in R_+^*,\ \varphi_r(d) = 1/d^r,$$

with r, the kind of force processed, e.g. $r = 0$ for constant forces and $r = 2$ for gravitational ones. The handling of segments is considered to decrease the computation time instead of directly studying any pair of points between the two patterns. Let I and J be two segments with a line of angle θ from the frame, D_{IJ}^θ the distance between them and $|.|$ the length of a segment. The calculation of the attraction force f_r of a segment with regard to another is given by:

$$f_r(|I|, D_{IJ}^\theta, |J|) = \int_{D_{IJ}^\theta+|J|}^{|I|+D_{IJ}^\theta+|J|} \int_0^{|J|} \varphi_r(u - v)dvdu$$

Considering two objects A and B, following a direction θ they can be entirely described by the set of segments using a pencil of parallel lines of angle θ. Let us take one line, denoted $\mathcal{D}_\eta^\theta$. The two sets of segments correspond to: $A_\theta(\eta) = \cup\{I_i\}_{i=1,n}$ and $B_\theta(\eta) = \cup\{J_j\}_{j=1,m}$ and the mutual attraction of these segments is given by:

$$F(\theta, A_\theta(\eta), B_\theta(\eta)) = \sum_{i \in 1..n} \sum_{j \in 1..m} f_r(|I_i|, D_{I_i J_j}^\theta, |J_j|)$$

All the pencils of lines $\mathcal{D}_\theta^\eta$ which entirely describe A and B are then processed. The histogram corresponds to a set of angles and the calculation of $F^{AB}(\theta)$ remains to an assessment of the forces exerted by an object with regard to another one in the direction θ. Finally the calculation of F^{AB} onto a set of angles θ_i ($\theta_i \in [-\pi, +\pi]$) defines a spatial relational descriptor, denoted $\mathcal{F}^{AB}$.

By axiomatic definitions of the function F, the following properties, useful to characterize the images, can be easily checked (Fig. 3):

- **translation** as objects are processed independently of their location in the image. This property allows avoid the consideration of symmetry axis in the proposed study.
- **symmetry** considering opposite directions. Disparities can be interesting here.
- **scale factor** if the histograms are normalized. This process is carried out to take into account images of different sizes.
- **rotation** (after circular shifts), because the approach is isotropic. Here this property has a weak importance. Only few degrees might be considered bringing no real accuracy due to the discretization. So we avoid taking into account it.

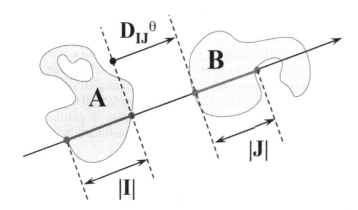

Fig. 3. Force histogram: illustrating its working principle, in general.

2.2 Chest X-ray Image Interpretation

A simple sum scheme [6], widely used to calculate fuzzy value from level set description, is used here to process with grey level images. The variation of gray level from background is considered following local binarization assumed to level sets. The process is run using all the grey to reach a whole level set description. The attraction (force constant) is calculated on each straight line and combined as shown previously to define a Force histogram descriptor.

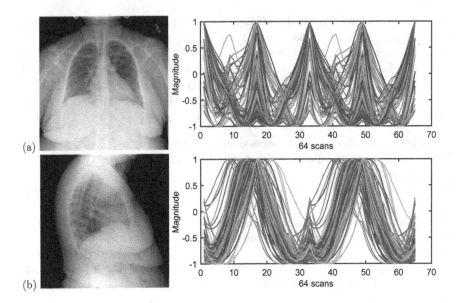

Fig. 4. Force histogram (on the right side): interpreting CXRS from two different classes: (a) frontal and (b) lateral. To plot histogram, we have used 100 CXR samples per class. At a glance, the histograms are fairly distinct from one class to another.

In Fig. 4, we provide histograms for both classes: frontal and lateral CXRs. The histograms on the right are produced from 100 CXR images (but at the moment, we provide one sample per class). The primary aim of illustrating these histograms is to show how different they (frontal and lateral CXRs) are. The force histogram clearly shows that we have high intra-class similarity and inter-class dissimilarity. On the whole, this allows accurate classification (see Sect. 4.2).

3   Classifiers

Note the feature is represented by a single vector of dimensionality of 64, where each attribute refers to value extracted from a particular pencil of line (see Sect. 2.1). Considering such a compact feature vector, one could directly compute the differences between two features: f_1 and f_2 of dimensionality $N = 64$ (i.e., $f_i, i = 1, \ldots, N$), by computing their overlapping score: $f_1 \cap f_2$. This underscores the simplicity of the feature matching procedure. Instead, in our study, we used three different classifiers: (a) Neural network (based on multilayer perceptron (MLP)) [3], (b) Random forest (RF) [5] and (c) Support vector machine (SVM) [13].

MLP. It uses layer wise connected nodes to build the architecture of the model [3]. Each node (except for the input nodes) can be viewed as a neuron with a nonlinear activation function (i.e., the sigmoid function): $\sigma(x) = \frac{1}{1+\exp(-(\omega * x + v))}$, where the weight vector w and bias vector b in each layer pair are trained by the back propagation algorithm. We considered error-backpropagation strategy, where learning rate of 0.3 and momentum 0.2 were used.

RF. It operates by constructing a group of decision trees at training time and outputting the class that is the mode of the classes output by individual trees [3]. The forest error rate depends on the correlation between any two trees, and strength of each individual tree. This means that increasing the correlation increases the forest error rate, and a tree with a low error rate is a strong classifier.

SVM. It is a discriminative classifier formally defined by a separating hyperplane. In general, any hyperplane can be written as the set of points $\vec{x}$ satisfying $\vec{w} \cdot \vec{x} + b = 0$, where $\vec{w}$ is the (not necessarily normalized) normal vector to the hyperplane.

4 Experiments

4.1 Dataset, Evaluation Protocol and Metrics

The National Library of Medicine (NLM) has been maintaining a large dataset of chest X-ray DICOM images containing both frontal view and lateral view and related textual radiology reports. The data was collected by the medical school at the University of Indiana. In our study, as mentioned in [17], we used 8100 images for validation, where frontal and lateral CXRs are equally distributed.

For validation, k-fold cross-validation was considered, where $k = 10$. The original sample is randomly partitioned into k equal sized subsamples, where a single subsample is retained as the validation data for testing the model, and the remaining $k - 1$ subsamples are used as training data. The process is repeated for k times (i.e., folds) and results are averaged at the end.

To measure the performance, the following five different metrics are used: (a) sensitivity, (b) specificity and (c) accuracy, that can be computed as follows:

$$sensitivity = \frac{t_p}{t_p + f_n},$$

$$specificity = \frac{t_n}{f_p + t_n}, \text{ and}$$

$$accuracy = \frac{t_p + t_n}{t_p + f_n + f_p + t_n},$$

where t_p (true positive) is the total number of CXRs correctly classified, f_p (false positive) is the total number of CXRs of other classes falsely recognized as its own, t_n (true negative) is the total number CXRs of the other classes truly rejected as intruders and f_n (false negative) is the total number of CXRs falsely rejected.

Sensitivity quantifies the avoiding of false negatives, as specificity does for false positives. Note that recall refers to the sensitivity measure (i.e., true positive rate), which is refer to the measures the proportion of positives that are correctly identified as such. Specificity (i.e., true negative rate) measures the proportion of negatives that are correctly identified as such.

Table 1. Performance (in $x \times 100\%$) of force histogram using three different state-of-the-art classifiers, where evaluation protocol: 10-fold cross-validation has been used.

Classifier	Sensitivity	Specificity	Accuracy
MLP	0.9985	0.9973	0.9979
RF	0.9815	0.9830	0.9822
SVM	0.9516	0.9711	0.9610

4.2 Results and Analysis

Following the evaluation protocol mentioned in Sect. 4.1, in Table 1, we provide a complete test results. Out of three different classifiers, we found out MLP performs the best with the maximum accuracy of 99.79%. Note that other two classifiers are closer to the MLP, with a marginal difference of less than 4%. To make a clear note, we also provide confusion matrices that are resulted for three different classifiers. Since we cannot categorize negative and positive samples, we simply computed the average scores by changing its category: negative to positive and vice-versa (Fig. 5).

For a comparison, we refer to the recently reported work [17], where the maximum accuracy is 99.90% by using a feature vector with dimension 1277. At this point, one should note that the feature vector dimension and its subsequent computational burden for classification task. In the previous work, there are four different features extracted together with the pre-processing block. In contrast, the proposed force histogram produces a feature vector with dimension 64, with no pre-processing. This makes our system compact and efficient.

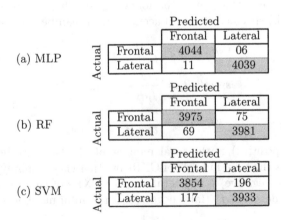

Fig. 5. Confusion matrices from using three different state-of-the-art classifiers, where evaluation protocol: 10-fold cross-validation has been used.

5 Conclusion

To advance and/or ease computer aided diagnosis (CAD) system, chest X-ray (CXR) image view information is required. In other words, separating CXR image view: frontal and lateral can be considered as a crucial step to effective subsequent processes, since the techniques that work for frontal CXRs may not equally work for lateral ones. With this motivation, in this paper, we present a novel machine learning technique to classify frontal and lateral CXR images, where we introduce a force- histogram to extract features and apply three different state-of-the-art classifiers: support vector machine (SVM), random forest (RF) and multi-layer perceptron (MLP). We validated our fully automatic technique on a set of 8200 images hosted by National Library of Medicine (NLM), National Institutes of Health (NIH), and achieved an accuracy close to 100%.

References

1. Improving the diagnosis and treatment of smear-negative pulmonary and extra-pulmonary tuberculosis among adults and adolescents: recommendations for HIV-prevalent and resource-constrained settings. World Health Organization, Geneva (2006)
2. Arimura, H., Katsuragawa, S., Li, Q., Ishida, T., Doi, K.: Development of a computerized method for identifying the posteroanterior and lateral views of chest radiographs by use of a template matching technique. Med. Phys. 29(7), 1556–1561 (2002). http://dx.doi.org/10.1118/1.1487426
3. Bishop, C.M.: Neural Networks for Pattern Recognition. Oxford University Press Inc., New York (1995)
4. Boone, J.M., Seshagiri, S., Steiner, R.M.: Recognition of chest radiograph orientation for picture archiving and communications systems display using neural networks. J. Digit. Imaging 5(3), 190–193 (1992). http://dx.doi.org/10.1007/BF03167769
5. Breiman, L.: Random forests. Mach. Learn. 45(1), 5–32 (2001)
6. Dubois, D., Jaulent, M.: A general approach to parameter evaluation in fuzzy digital pictures. Pattern Recogn. Lett. 6, 251–259 (1987)
7. Kao, E.F., Lee, C., Jaw, T.S., Hsu, J.S., Liu, G.C.: Projection profile analysis for identifying different views of chest radiographs. Acad. Radiol. 13(4), 518–525 (2006). http://dx.doi.org/10.1016/j.acra.2006.01.009
8. Karargyris, A., Siegelman, J., Tzortzis, D., Jaeger, S., Candemir, S., Xue, Z., Santosh, K.C., Vajda, S., Antani, S.K., Folio, L., Thoma, G.R.: Combination of texture and shape features to detect pulmonary abnormalities in digital chest x-rays. Int. J. Comput. Assist. Radiol. Surg. 11(1), 99–106 (2016). http://dx.doi.org/10.1007/s11548-015-1242-x
9. Lehmann, T.M., Güld, M.O., Keysers, D., Schubert, H., Kohnen, M., Wein, B.B.: Determining the view of chest radiographs. J. Digit. Imaging 16(3), 280–291 (2003). http://dx.doi.org/10.1007/s10278-003-1655-x
10. Matsakis, P., Wendling, L.: A new way to represent the relative position between areal objects. IEEE Trans. Pattern Anal. Mach. Intell. 21(7), 634–643 (1999)

11. Matsakis, P., Wendling, L., Ni, J.: A general approach to the fuzzy modeling of spatial relationships. In: Jeansoulin, R., Papini, O., Prade, H., Schockaert, S. (eds.) Methods for Handling Imperfect Spatial Information, pp. 49–74. Springer, Heidelberg (2010)

12. Pietka, E., Huang, H.K.: Orientation correction for chest images. J. Digit. Imaging 5(3), 185–189 (1992). http://dx.doi.org/0.1007/BF03167768

13. Platt, J.: Fast training of support vector machines using sequential minimal optimization. In: Schoelkopf, B., Burges, C., Smola, A. (eds.) Advances in Kernel Methods - Support Vector Learning. MIT Press (1998). http://research.microsoft.com/~jplatt/smo.html

14. Santosh, K.C., Candemir, S., Jäger, S., Karargyris, A., Antani, S.K., Thoma, G.R., Folio, L.: Automatically detecting rotation in chest radiographs using principal rib-orientation measure for quality control. Int. J. Pattern Recogn. Artif. Intell. 29(2) (2015). http://dx.doi.org/10.1142/S0218001415570013

15. Santosh, K.C., Vajda, S., Antani, S., Thoma, G.R.: Edge map analysis in chest x-rays for automatic pulmonary abnormality screening. Int. J. Comput. Assist. Radiol. Surg., 1–10 (2016). http://dx.doi.org/10.1007/s11548-016-1359-6

16. Schaefer-Prokop, C., Neitzel, U., Venema, H., Uffmann, M., Prokop, M.: Digital chest radiography: an update on modern technology, dose containment and control of image quality. Eur. Radiol. 18(9), 1818–1830 (2008)

17. Xue, Z., You, D., Candemir, S., Jaeger, S., Antani, S.K., Long, L.R., Thoma, G.R.: Chest x-ray image view classification. In: 28th IEEE International Symposium on Computer-Based Medical Systems, pp. 66–71 (2015). http://dx.doi.org/10.1109/CBMS.2015.49

An Automatic Computerized Model for Cancerous Lung Nodule Detection from Computed Tomography Images with Reduced False Positives

Senthilkumar Krishnamurthy[1(✉)], Ganesh Narasimhan[2],
and Umamaheswari Rengasamy[3]

[1] Anna University, Chennai, India
tkseneee@gmail.com
[2] Saveetha Engineering College, Chennai, India
enganesh50@gmail.com
[3] Velammal Engineering College, Chennai, India
umavijai.iitm@gmail.com

Abstract. The objective of this work is to identify the malignant lung nodules accurately and early with less false positives. In our work block histogram based auto center seed k-means clustering technique is used to segment all the possible nodule candidates. Efficient shape and texture features (2D and 3D) were computed to eliminate the false nodule candidates. The two-stage classifier is used in this work to classify the malignant and benign nodules. First stage rule-based classifier producing 100% sensitivity, but with high false positive of 13.1 per patient scan. The BPN based ANN classifier is used as the second-stage classifier which reduces a false positive to 2.26 per patient scan with a good sensitivity of 88.8%. The nodule growth predictive measure was modeled through the features such as tissue deficit, tissue excess, isotropic factor and edge gradient. The overlap of these measures for larger, average and minimum nodule growth cases are less. Therefore this developed growth prediction model can be used to assist the physicians while taking the decision on the cancerous nature of lung nodules from an earlier CT scan.

Keywords: Computed tomography · 3D shape feature · 3D texture feature · Lung nodule classifier · Lung nodule growth

1 Introduction

Lung cancer is most diagnosed cancer worldwide (13% of all diagnosed cancers). Lung cancer also leads to maximum deaths compare to all other cancer (19% of overall cancer deaths) [1]. These statistics makes many researchers all over the world to do work on lung cancer diagnosis. Computerized Tomography (CT) is the scanning technology widely used to diagnose the lung cancer symptoms. If the physicians suspect any sign of lung cancer from the CT scan, the follow-up scan is recommended for the patient after a time span of 3 to 18 months based on patient living habits. Then

© Springer Nature Singapore Pte Ltd. 2017
K.C. Santosh et al. (Eds.): RTIP2R 2016, CCIS 709, pp. 343–355, 2017.
DOI: 10.1007/978-981-10-4859-3_31

by comparing the follow-up scan images with the earlier scan, the physicians will take the decision to recommend for biopsy or suggest one more follow-up scan. The radiologists are comparing the growth of the abnormal tissue cluster in both the scans. The abnormal spherical tissue clusters of size 3 mm to 30 mm present inside the lung parenchyma region is known as 'lung nodule.' If the size is more than 30 mm, then it is called as 'lung mass.' Many research works were reported in the literature to segment these nodules effectively [2]. The 3D visualization of nodule will help to analyze its growth. 3-D algorithms for size and growth characterization was well reported in [3, 4]. Reeves et al. [5] proposed a methodology for nodule location and sizing, pleural segmentation, adaptive thresholding, image registration, and knowledge-based shape matching in their work. All the nodules segmented from the lung CT is not malignant. The nature of the nodule malignancy can be modeled through shape and texture features. Many works were presented to extract the different features from nodules and to classify it [6]. Recent works on automatic computer aided tool to detect the malignant nodules from series of CT cross-sectional images are presented in [7–9]. In this work, we are concentrating on measuring the lung nodule growth quantitatively and characterize the nature of the lung nodule which may grow in future. Early and accurate detection (less false positive) of cancerous nature of the lung nodule through its features from earlier CT scan is presented in this paper.

2 Lung Nodule Detection System

2.1 Lung Nodule Segmentation

'Nodule' is the tissue clusters accumulated inside the lung parenchyma region. Usually, the size of the nodules is 3 mm to 30 mm. If the size is more than 30 mm, then it is known as 'lung mass' [10]. These nodules are the primary indicator for detecting lung cancer. Therefore the first step of any computerized lung cancer diagnostic system is to segment these nodules from parenchyma region of the lung. The segmentation of nodule from CT scan is a complex process as the nodules structure and position are non linear. Also the pixel intensity of nodules overlap with the other regions of lung CT image. The position of the nodules inside the lung makes the segmentation process tedious. Developing a common algorithm to segment well-circumscribed, pleural tail, vascularized and juxta pleural nodules make the segmentation work challenging.

In this work, we are using the concept of data clustering to segment those nodules from each slice of CT scan. Block histogram processing is carried out in this work to choose the initial cluster center seed automatically. In this research 3-D segmentation of nodule is carried out by consecutive 2-D segmentation of nodule structure from each CT scan image.

Block histogram processing is carried out in this work to choose the initial cluster center seed automatically. In this research 3-D segmentation of nodule is carried out by consecutive 2-D segmentation of nodule structure from each CT scan image. The proposed auto center seed k-means clustering based segmentation algorithm steps are:

Step 1:   Compute the histogram (H) of lung CT image.
Step 2:   Split the histogram into five blocks as shown in Fig. 1.

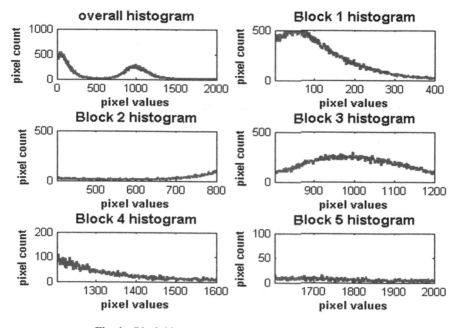

Fig. 1. Block histogram processing to select initial seed

$$H = \{H1,\ H2,\ H3,\ H4,\ H5\} \tag{1}$$

Step 3: Compute the pixel value corresponding to the maximum peak of each histogram block.

$$Mi = maximum(Hi) \tag{2}$$

$$Pi = find\_position(Hi == lung\ CT\ image\ Mi) \tag{3}$$

where i = 1 to 5

Step 4: Choose the mean of first two histogram blocks maximum peak pixel position as cluster 1 (C1) seed and the mean of the last two blocks maximum peak pixel position as cluster 2 (C2) seed.

$$C1 = \frac{P1 + P2}{2} \tag{4}$$

$$C2 = \frac{P1 + P2}{2} \tag{5}$$

Step 5: Group the image pixels which have minimum distance with C1 and C2 separately, without changing its spatial positions.

$$d1 = \sqrt{(I - C1)^2} \tag{6}$$

$$d2 = \sqrt{(I - C2)^2} \tag{7}$$

$$K1(i,j) = I(i,j), \text{ if } d1 < d2 \tag{8}$$

$$K2(i,j) = I(i,j), \text{ if } d2 < d1 \tag{9}$$

Step 6: Find the new cluster seed C1new and C2new using the Eqs. 10 and 11. Repeat from step 1 until the two consecutive cluster seeds (C1 and C2) are equal.

$$C1_{upd} = \frac{1}{L}\sum_{i=1}^{m}\sum_{j=1}^{n}(K1(i,j) \neq\neq 0) \tag{10}$$

$$C2_{upd} = \frac{1}{L}\sum_{i=1}^{m}\sum_{j=1}^{n}(K2(i,j) \neq\neq 0) \tag{11}$$

Step 7: Perform morphological closing/opening operation and border clearing morphology on a cluster 2 reference image to segment nodule candidates.
Step 8: Repeat the steps 1 to 7 for all the CT images slices.
Step 9: Stack the each nodule candidates segmented from each CT slice to form a 3-D visualization.

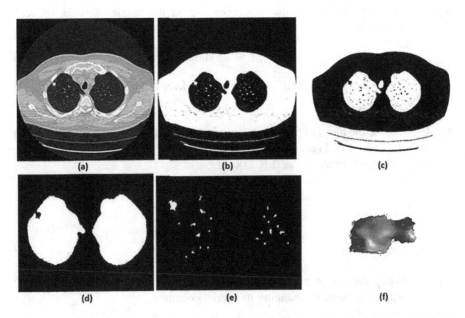

Fig. 2. (a) CT 2-D slice, (b) cluster-2 seed mask, (c) cluster-1 seed mask, (d) Lung mask with juxta nodule hole, (e) Segmented nodule candidates, (f) 3-D visualization of one segmented nodule.

For a CT lung image with juxta-pleural nodule (nodule connected to the lung wall), the morphological closing process was performed. Since juxta-pleural nodules are located in the parenchyma and connected with lung wall, the hole (black region) was created in place of juxta nodule as shown in Fig. 2(d). This juxta-hole region is usually connected with the background black region; hence it should be closed before filling the parenchyma region. Morphological closing process with disk structural element was performed on an image segmented from step 6. The left and right lungs were separated using connected component analysis to avoid connection between two lung lobes during the closing process. Finally, after closing the juxta nodule holes both the left and right lung masks were added as shown in Fig. 2(e).

The performance of the auto-cluster seed k-means algorithm is compared with other traditional segmentation algorithms and the results are tabulated in Table 1.

Table 1. Nodules shape and texture feature

Algorithms implemented in this work	Time in seconds per CT slice	Number of segmented cluster per CT slice	Nature of segmentation
Multi threshold	5	75	Not automatic
AMRG	8	41	Fully automatic
Level set	4	34	Automatic, but iteration dependent
ACKMS	4.5	38	Fully automatic

2.2 Quantitative Shape and Texture Based Lung Nodule Candidates Feature Extraction

In this section, the different shape and texture based features are extracted on the nodule candidates segmented in the last section. The nodule's 2D shape and texture features are computed from the median CT slice, whereas the 3D features are computed from consecutive CT slice images. All the shape features are extracted from the binary version of nodules and the texture features are obtained from the original DICOM version of the nodule portion.

The probability of lung nodule being benign increases with the regularity in its shape across consecutive CT slices. The more regular the shape of the nodule, the more likely it is benign. In this work, the variation in shape features in the consecutive slices are quantitatively modeled through the features such as a change in centroid, change in area and change in equivalent diameter of the nodule. Edge sharpness is also one another measure which helps to discriminate malignant nodules from benign as the benign nodules have smooth edges. Frequency domain feature of DC constant also computed in this chapter, which is used to identify the calcifications. As the calcifications are uniform throughout its region, the DC constant value of it is on the higher side, and also the calcifications have a higher value of homogeneity and autocorrelation due to its uniform surface nature. The shape and texture features used in this work are tabulated in Table 2.

Table 2. Nodules shape and texture feature

Feature	Expression
Area	$\sum_{x=1}^{M} \sum_{y=1}^{N} fb(x,y)$ Where fb = binary image of nodule candidate M = Number of rows in fb N = Number of columns in fb
Diameter	$\sqrt{\frac{4*Area}{\pi}}$
Centroid	$\left[\frac{\sum_{i=1}^{M} \sum_{j=1}^{N} i*f(i,j)}{\sum_{i=1}^{M} \sum_{j=1}^{N} f(i,j)}, \frac{\sum_{i=1}^{M} \sum_{j=1}^{N} j*fb(i,j)}{\sum_{i=1}^{M} \sum_{j=1}^{N} fb(i,j)} \right]$
Elongation	$\frac{\max(x_{length}, y_{length}, z_{length})}{\min(x_{length}, y_{length}, z_{length})}$
Volume	$\sum_{x=1}^{m} \sum_{y=1}^{n} \sum_{z=1}^{p} fb(x,y,z)$
Edge sharpness	$\frac{\text{Magnitude(gradient}(f(i,j)))}{length(x_{gradient})}$
Compactness	$\frac{\text{radius of sphere with equivalent radius}}{\text{root mean square distance from center}}$
Bounding box dimension rate	$\frac{\min([xLength,yLength,zLength])}{\max([xLength,yLength,zLength])}$
Compactness 2	$\frac{Surface\,Area^3}{Volume^2 * 36 * \pi}$
x-y plane projection compactness	$\frac{4*\pi*A}{P^2}$
Homogeneity	$\sum_{i=1}^{m} \sum_{j=1}^{n} \frac{P[i,j]}{1+|i-j|}$
Correlation	$\sum_{i=1}^{m} \sum_{j=1}^{n} \frac{(i*j)*P[i,j]-(\mu x * \mu y)}{(\sigma x * \sigma y)}$
Mean contrast	$\frac{Mean\,Inside - Mean\,outside}{Mean\,Inside + Mean\,outside}$
Moment 6	$\frac{\sum_{x=1}^{m} \sum_{y=1}^{n} y^6 * f(x,y)}{\sum_{x=1}^{m} \sum_{y=1}^{n} f(x,y)}$
Moment 7	$\frac{\sum_{x=1}^{m} \sum_{y=1}^{n} y^7 * f(x,y)}{\sum_{x=1}^{m} \sum_{y=1}^{n} f(x,y)}$
3D variance	$[\frac{1}{n}(\sum_{i=1}^{n}(xi - x\_mean)^2 \sum_{y=1}^{n}(yi - y\_mean)^2 \sum_{z=1}^{n}(zi - z\_mean)^2)]^{\frac{1}{2}}$
3D skewness	$\frac{E[(x-x_{mean}),(y-y_{mean})(z-z_{mean})]^3}{3D\_variance^3}$
Fourier DC constant	$fc(x,y) = (-1)(x+y) * f(x,y)$ $F(u,v) = \sum_{x=0}^{M-1} \sum_{y=0}^{N-1} fc(x,y) * \exp[-j2\Pi(\frac{mu}{M} + \frac{nv}{N})]$ DC constant $= F(M/2, N/2)$

2.3 Two Stage Lung Nodule Classification

In this chapter, a two-stage hybrid classifier is developed to classify the malignant and benign nodules using the selective features extracted in the previous section. The rule-based scheme followed by ANN based classifier is utilized in this chapter to classify the lung nodules.

The first stage rule-based classifier is framed with the following rules:

Table 3. Rules of the first stage classifier

Feature	Rule
Nodule diameter	dia_min to dia_max (3 mm to 30 mm)
Nodule area	$\pi * (\frac{dia\_min}{2})2$ to $\pi * (\frac{dia\_max}{2})2$
Nodule volume	$3 * \frac{\pi}{4} * (\frac{dia\_min}{2})3$ to $3 * \frac{\pi}{4} * (\frac{dia\_max}{2})3$
Nodule elongation	$\frac{max(x_{length}, y_{length}, z_{length})}{min(x_{length}, y_{length}, z_{length})} < 4$ mm
Nodule round degree	$\frac{4*\pi*area}{perimeter^2} > (1/6)$ mm
Nodule centroid change	Centroid change in consecutive three slices < 10 pixels

After performing the first stage rule-based classifier, most of the vessel structures, a line like irrelevant structures are removed from nodule candidate list. The nodule elongation criteria as 4 mm and round degree criteria as (1/6) mm are fixed after applying and analyzing these rules on a training image database considered for this work. All the vessels like structures and highly non-linear irrelevant tissue clusters are removed successfully from nodule candidates group, but still more non-nodule and benign tissue clusters exist in the output of the first stage of classifier.

All the shape and texture features are calculated on the nodule candidates remained after the first stage of classifier. As the radiologist report on training dataset is available, the correlation analysis is performed for each feature variable against the target (malignant or benign). The correlation coefficient between each feature and the target is computed. From the correlation matrix, the features which have high correlation coefficient are picked as input features to the ANN classifier. Finally, a hybrid input feature vector is formed with twelve features (change in diameter, change in area, circularity, compactness, bounding box dimension rate, compactness2, x-y plane projection compactness, mean contrast, moment 6, moment 7, 3D variance and 3D skewness). A two-layer feedforward network, with sigmoid hidden and output neurons, is used for classification (second stage). The scaled conjugate gradient back-propagation algorithm is used to train the neural network.

3 Early Malignant Nodule Detection Model

In this work even a small size nodules from size 3 mm (diameter) is consider for further investigation which enables the possibility of finding the cancerous nature of nodule at an early stage. Also during the second stage of the classifier, explicit size measurements are not considered to take a decision on malignancy, i.e., volume, area or diameter of the nodule is not considered as one feature (only change in area and diameter from consecutive CT slices is considered as features). The chance for the malignancy is more for a nodule whose area and volume is high, but an area and volume value is high only after nodule grown well. As this work is concentrating on early detection of malignant nodules, the area, and volume features are not considered during the ANN training phase of the classifier. The diameter, area and volume features used during the first

Table 4. Nodule volume growth and prediction

Case ID	V1	V2	NVG	TD	TE	IF	EG
1	630	9840	14.619	0.308	0.668	0.400	0.820
2	2108	2576	0.222	0.271	0.395	0.600	0.534
6	95	234	1.4632	0.532	0.732	0.324	0.610
7	149	181	0.2148	0.201	0.278	0.740	0.634
8	90	91	0.0111	0.152	0.143	0.895	0.342
10	1490	1508	0.0121	0.093	0.072	0.920	0.123
11	5640	5970	0.0585	0.093	0.173	0.912	0.321
13	8197	8746	0.067	0.189	0.188	0.820	0.432
15	447	646	0.4452	0.198	0.306	0.718	0.540
16	284	318	0.1197	0.215	0.301	0.720	0.632
18	3709	3839	0.035	0.097	0.132	0.944	0.240
20	1340	1353	0.0097	0.117	0.211	0.775	0.234
21	2239	2233	0.0027	0.176	0.128	0.759	0.211
23	2807	3031	0.0798	0.183	0.192	0.812	0.500
24	930	901	0.0322	0.102	0.152	0.783	0.267
25	1485	1961	0.3205	0.283	0.452	0.740	0.654
28	956	1340	0.4017	0.195	0.214	0.800	0.701
29	64	66	0.0313	0.125	0.141	0.856	0.345
32	112	124	0.1071	0.203	0.200	0.670	0.458
33	643	649	0.0093	0.042	0.135	0.750	0.345
34	106	160	0.5094	0.345	0.655	0.654	0.610
36	1028	1098	0.0681	0.172	0.182	0.764	0.590
37	1818	2430	0.3366	0.214	0.534	0.670	0.467
38	1742	1835	0.0534	0.048	0.115	0.785	0.340
39	1920	2533	0.3193	0.276	0.521	0.723	0.587
40	773	954	0.2342	0.243	0.319	0.562	0.454
41	1236	1566	0.267	0.341	0.627	0.540	0.620
42	611	850	0.3912	0.321	0.678	0.730	0.560
44	690	1356	0.9652	0.478	0.878	0.263	0.712
45	866	1223	0.4122	0.234	0.403	0.884	0.532
46	136	149	0.0956	0.194	0.196	0.830	0.432
47	1688	2111	0.2506	0.301	0.347	0.630	0.534
48	653	381	0.7139	0.107	0.509	0.556	0.640
49	4280	4950	0.1565	0.341	0.432	0.693	0.576

stage of the rule-based classifier is only to make sure that even the small nodule structures were considered for the further investigation on its malignancy.

Volume growth is one measure on which radiologists are taking a decision about the malignancy and forward the patient to biopsy [11, 12]. Nodule growth can be computed only by comparing the two scans of the same patient taken at a different time interval of 3 to 18 months. 34 cases from VOLCANO database are used in this work. The Nodule Volume Growth (NVG) is computed from earlier and follow-up CT scans and tabulated in Table 4.

$$NVG = \frac{V2 - V1}{V1} \tag{12}$$

where V1 and V2 are the volumes of nodules segmented from earlier and follow-up scan respectively.

In Fig. 3, the nodules segmented from earlier and later scan are depicted for three patient cases. In the first row of Fig. 3(a) and (b), the nodule segmented from an earlier scan is shown. These nodules surface is not uniform, and few tissue parts are coming out of the nodule surface in a radial direction, whereas in figure(c), the tissue components which coming out of nodule surface is minimum and the surface looks uniform. From the follow-up scans of all these patient cases, it has been proven that first two cases depicted in Fig. 3(a) and (b) are grown in future, on the other hand, the nodule showed in Fig. 3(c) not grown. These characteristics of nodules segmented from earlier scans are used as a quantitative measure to predict the nodule growth. In this work, the nodule growth is predicted using four measures: tissue excess (TE), tissue deficit (TE), isotropic factor(IF) and edge gradient (EG). The template and expression of these measures are tabulated in Table 5 and these values are computed and tabulated in Table 4.

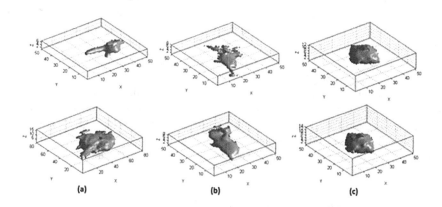

(a) (b) (c)

Fig. 3. Nodules from earlier and later scan (a) with large growth (b) with medium growth (c) No growth

Table 5. Nodule growth prediction measures

Tissue Deficit (TD)	Tissue Excess(TE)	Isotropic Factor(IF)	Edge Gradient (EG)
$TD = \dfrac{Sc - A}{Sc}$	$TE = \dfrac{A - Si}{A}$	$IF = \dfrac{Rm}{RM}$	$\dfrac{Magnitude(gradient(f(i,j)))}{length(x_{gradient})}$

4 Results and Discussion

In this work 24 patient lung CT scan series from VOLCANO database [13] and five patient cases from LIDC database [14, 15] are used as a training image set. VOLCANO cases contain 25 to CT image slices per scan as an average, and LIDC scans have 120 to 280 CT slices per scan. In this work, a total of 1450 CT cross-sectional images (slices) are used for training. The auto center seed k-means clustering based segmentation was effectively applied on all these 1450 CT slice images to segment all the possible nodule candidates.

The nodule candidates segmented from these 1450 CT slices are applied to the rule-based classifier (first stage classifier). The nodule candidates, which are not satisfying the rules mentioned in Table 2 are eliminated. The training database set used in this work contains 32 malignant nodules. The first stage of classifier output preserving all the 32 nodules, which marked in radiologist report. Along with these 32 nodules, 362 other nodules also remained in the output of the rule-based classifier. Hence, the True Positive (TP) (the nodules detected which matched with radiologist report) at the output of classifier first stage is 32, and the False Positive (FP) (the nodules detected, which not matched with radiologist report) is 362. As all the nodules marked by the radiologists report are detected, the False Negative (FN) is zero. The performance of the first stage rule-based classifier is shown in Table 6.

The first stage rule based classifier producing a poor (high) false positive of 12.5 per patient case. Artificial Neural Network based second stage of classifier is used to reduce the false positive. The input feature matrix size for an ANN is 12 × 394, where 12 is the total number of finalized features and 394(362 + 32) is the number of nodule candidates remained at the output of the rule-based classifier. The target matrix of size

Table 6. Performance measure of the first stage of classifier

Statistic	Formula	Value
Sensitivity	$\dfrac{TP}{TP+FN}$	100%
False positive	FP/scan	12.48

Table 7. Statistical results

Statistic	Formula	Value
Sensitivity	$\dfrac{TP}{TP+FN}$	88.8%
Specificity	$\dfrac{TN}{TN+FP}$	83.3%
FP/patient scan	Total FP/Number of patient scan	2.26
Disease prevalence	$\dfrac{TP+FN}{TP+FN+TN+FP}$	8.1%

2×394 is framed with the help of radiologist findings. The target output of [0 1] and [1 0] is fixed for benign and malignant nodules respectively. The BPN based ANN classifier is trained towards the minimum error. The trained net input and output weights are saved for testing the new cases.

10 cases of VOLCANO and 5 cases of LIDC are tested using the parameters of trained classifier. This testing set contains 18 malignant nodules. Total of 975 cross-sectional CT images are present in the testing database. After the segmentation process, all the suspected nodule candidates are applied under the rule based classifier. Total of 204 nodule candidates remained at the output of the rule-based classifier. The 12 features discussed previously are computed for each nodule and the feature vector of size 12×204 is applied to a trained ANN system. The benign nodules feature vector are converged very near to [0 1], and the malignant nodules are to [1 0]. The output of our designed lung nodule detection system is compared with the radiologist report. Algorithm developed in this work correctly detected 16 malignant nodules out of 18 and missed to detect 2, with a TP of 16 and FN of 2. This algorithm successfully eliminated 170 nodule candidates and wrongly identified 34 nodule candidates as a malignant nodule. Therefore, the TN is 170; FP is 34; and the FP per patient scan is 2.26. The overall performance measure of the developed algorithm is given in Table 7.

From Table 3 NVG value for case no 1, 3 and 44 was 14.6, 1.46, and 0.96 which was found to grow approximately by 15, 1.5 and 1 times, respectively, compared with the initial scan. This noticeable growth confirms that these nodules are malignant in nature. There were 14 cases for which the NVG ranged between 0.2 and 0.8, suggesting a reasonable growth that requires repetition of a scan after few days to confirm malignancy. Of the remaining 17 cases, 7 had NVG of less than 0.2, i.e., almost no change and 10 cases showed minimum nodule growth which may require follow-up scans.

The nodules from VOLCANO database are analyzed further for it's growth measurement and prediction, as this database have two CT scan series for each patient which taken at different time intervals. The nodule growth measures are tabulated in Table 5. The nodules which had larger growth (in follow-up scan) having TD > 0.3, TE > 0.6, IF < 0.4 and EG > 0.6 in its earlier scan. The nodules which had average growth having TD in between 0.2 to 0.4, TE in between 0.2 to 0.7, IF in between 0.5 to 0.75, and EG in between 0.45 to 0.7. Finally, the nodules which had very minimum or no growth have the TD < 0.2, TE < 0.2, IF > 0.65, and EG < 0.6. The overlap of these measures for larger, medium and minimum nodule growth cases are less.

5 Conclusion

An early and accurate lung nodule detection system was successfully implemented in this work. Histogram based 'auto center seed k-means clustering' was successfully implemented to segment the nodule candidates. Two stage classifier used in this work reduced the false positive to 2.26 per patient scan with a good sensitivity of 88.8%. The nodules growing nature was modeled in this work using four shape measures computed from earlier CT scan, which can be used to assist the physicians while taking the decision on cancerous nature of lung nodules at an early stage. In future, this work can be extended by modeling the nodule growth prediction algorithm, more accurately by training and testing with more patient cases.

References

1. Torre, L.A., Bray, F., Siegel, R.L., Ferlay, J., Tieulent, J.L., Jemal, A.: Global cancer statistics 2012. CA-Cancer J Clin. **65**(2), 87–108 (2015)
2. Van Rikxoort, E.M., Van Ginneken, B.: Automated segmentation of pulmonary structures in thoracic computed tomography scans: a review. Phys. Med. Biol. **58**(17), R187 (2013)
3. Yankelevitz, D.F., Reeves, A.P., Kostis, W.J., Zhao, B., Henschke, C.I.: Small pulmonary nodules: volumetrically determined growth rates based on CT evaluation. Radiology **217**(1), 251–256 (2000)
4. Kostis, W.J., Reeves, A.P., Yankelevitz, D.F., Henschke, C.I.: Three-dimensional segmentation and growth-rate estimation of small pulmonary nodules in helical ct images. IEEE Trans. Med. Imaging **22**(10), 1259–1274 (2003)
5. Reeves, A.P., Chan, A.B., Yankelevitz, D.F., Henschke, C.I., Kressler, B., Kostis, W.J.: On measuring the change in size of pulmonary nodules. IEEE Trans. Med. Imaging **25**(4), 435–450 (2006)
6. El-Baz, A., Beache, G.M., Gimel'farb, G., Suzuki, K., Okada, K., Elnakib, A., Soliman, A., Abdollahi, B.: Computer-aided diagnosis systems for lung cancer: challenges and methodologies. Int. J. Biomed. Imaging (2013)
7. Krishnamurthy, S., Narasimhan, G., Rengasamy, U.: Three-dimensional lung nodule segmentation and shape variance analysis to detect lung cancer with reduced false positives. P I Mech. Eng. H **230**(1), 58–70 (2016)
8. Demir, Ö., Çamurcu, A.Y.: Computer-aided detection of lung nodules using outer surface features. Bio-Med. Mater. Eng. **26**(s1), S1213–S1222 (2015)
9. Lu, L., Tan, Y., Schwartz, L.H., Zhao, B.: Hybrid detection of lung nodules on CT scan images. Med. Phys. **42**(9), 5042–5054 (2015)
10. Furman, A.M., Yafawi, J.Z.D., Soubani, A.O.: An update on the evaluation and management of small pulmonary nodules. Future Oncol. **9**(6), 855–865 (2013)
11. Gould, M.K., Donington, J., Lynch, W.R., Mazzone, P.J., Midthun, D.E., Naidich, D.P., Wiener, R.D.: Evaluation of individuals with pulmonary nodules: when is it lung cancer?: Diagnosis and management of lung cancer: American College of chest physicians evidence-based clinical practice guidelines. Chest J. **143**(5_suppl), e93S–e120S (2013)
12. MacMahon, H., Austin, J.H., Gamsu, G., Herold, C.J., Jett, J.R., Naidich, D.P., Patz Jr., E.F., Swensen, S.J.: Guidelines for management of small pulmonary nodules detected on CT scans: a statement from the Fleischner Society 1. Radiology **237**(2), 395–400 (2005)

13. Reeves, A.P., Jirapatnakul, A.C., Biancardi, A.M., Apanasovich, T.V., Schaefer, C., Bowden, J.J., Kietzmann, M. et al.: The VOLCANO 2009 challenge: preliminary results. In: Second International Workshop of Pulmonary Image Analysis, pp. 353–364 (2009)

14. Armato, I.I.I., Samuel, G., McLennan, G., Bidaut, L., McNitt-Gray, M.F., Meyer, C.R., Reeves, A.P., Zhao, B., et al.: The lung image database consortium (LIDC) and image database resource initiative (IDRI): a completed reference database of lung nodules on CT scans. Med. Phys. **38**(2), 915–931 (2011)

15. Clark, K., Vendt, B., Smith, K., Freymann, J., Kirby, J., Koppel, P., Moore, S., Phillips, S., Maffitt, D., Pringle, M., Tarbox, L., Prior, F.: The Cancer Imaging Archive (TCIA): maintaining and operating a public information repository. J. Digit. Imaging **26**(6), 1045–1057 (2013)

Synthesis of a Neural Network Classifier for Hepatocellular Carcinoma Grading Based on Triphasic CT Images

Vitoantonio Bevilacqua[1(✉)], Leonarda Carnimeo[1], Antonio Brunetti[1],
Andrea De Pace[1], Pietro Galeandro[1], Gianpaolo Francesco Trotta[2],
Nicholas Caporusso[1], Francescomaria Marino[1], Vito Alberotanza[3],
and Arnaldo Scardapane[3]

[1] Department of Electrical and Information Engineering, Polytechnic of Bari,
Via Orabona 4, 70125 Bari, Italy
vitoantonio.bevilacqua@poliba.it
[2] Department of Mechanical and Management Engineering, Polytechnic of Bari,
Via Orabona 4, 70125 Bari, Italy
[3] Interdisciplinary Department of Medicine - Section of Diagnostic Imaging,
University of Bari Aldo Moro, Piazza Giulio Cesare 11, 70120 Bari, Italy
arnaldo.scardapane@uniba.it

Abstract. Computer Aided Decision (CAD) systems based on Medical Imaging could support radiologists in grading Hepatocellular carcinoma (HCC) by means of Computed Tomography (CT) images, avoiding that patient undergo any medical invasive procedures such as biopsies. The individuation and characterization of Regions of Interest (ROIs) containing lesions is an important phase that enables an easier classification between two classes of HCCs. Two phases are needed for the individuation of lesioned ROIs: a liver isolation in each CT slice, and a lesion segmentation. Ultimately, all individuated ROIs are described by morphological features and, finally, a feed-forward supervised Artificial Neural Network (ANN) is used to classify them. Testing determined that the ANN topologies found through an evolutionary strategy showed a high generalization on the mean performance indices regardless of applied training, validation and test sets, showing good performances in terms of both accuracy and sensitivity, permitting a correct grading of HCC lesions.

Keywords: Hepatocellular carcinoma · Computed Tomography · Image processing · Artificial Neural Network · Genetic Algorithm

1 Introduction

Hepatocellular carcinoma (HCC) is the fifth most common malignant disease in men and the eighth most common in women. It is the third most common cause of death from cancer, after lung tumor and stomach cancer [1]. HCCs mostly

© Springer Nature Singapore Pte Ltd. 2017
K.C. Santosh et al. (Eds.): RTIP2R 2016, CCIS 709, pp. 356–368, 2017.
DOI: 10.1007/978-981-10-4859-3_32

develop in patients with chronic liver disease caused by viral hepatitis, alcohol abuse and inborn metabolic errors. Eighty percent of all HCCs worldwide occur when the underlying chronic liver disease has reached the cirrhotic stage [2,3]. Moreover, less common causes are Wilson's disease, hereditary hemochromatosis, alpha1-antitrypsin deficiency, primary biliary cirrhosis and autoimmune hepatitis [4]. The nodules associated with liver cirrhosis are histologically divided into six categories according to the classification proposed by the Liver Cancer Study Group of Japan: large regenerative nodules, adenomatous hyperplasia (AH), atypical AH, early HCC, well differentiated HCC, and moderately or poorly differentiated HCC (so-called classical HCC) [5,6]. Namely, HCC differentiation directly impact on patients' prognosis.

Thanks to recent progress, Computed Tomography (CT) and Magnetic resonance Imaging (MRI) are the gold standard for non-invasive evaluation of diffuse and focal diseases of the liver and biliary tract [7,8]. Unlike most cancers, imaging can be used to non-invasively diagnose HCC; treatment, including major surgical options such as hepatic resection and liver transplantation, can be realized without confirmatory biopsy [9,10].

The hallmark diagnostic features of HCC at multiphasic CT or MR imaging are arterial phase hyper-enhancement, followed by portal venous or delayed phase washout appearance; in patients with cirrhosis or other risk factors for HCC, such temporal enhancement pattern provides near 100% specificity for diagnosis of HCC [9]. However, the presence of specific imaging features which may predict the differentiation of HCC is still widely debated.

As HCC tends to be untreatable when it is diagnosed at a late stage, it is necessary to diagnose it in an early stage by means of blood exams using liver cancer biomarkers, or other exams.

According to World Health Organization (WHO), an HCC can be analyzed from both macroscopic and microscopic point of view; at first, the degree of tumor depends on size and presence (or absence) of liver cirrhosis. From a microscopic point of view, a histological classification of tumors includes trabecular (plate-like), pseudoglandular and acinar, compact and scirrhous types [11]. For several years, grading of HCC relied on Edmondson and Steiner system, which divided HCC into four grades - from I to IV - based on histological differentiation [12]. Grade I is the best differentiated form, consisting of small tumor cells arranged in thin trabeculae. Cells in grade II are larger, and they have abnormal nuclei and glandular structures. In grade III, nuclei are larger and more hyperchromatic than grade II cells; also, the cytoplasm is granular and acidophilic, though less than grade II. In grade IV, tumor cells are much less differentiated with hyperchromatic nuclei and loss of trabecular pattern. In particular, most of HCCs appears as grade II or III.

As stated before, thanks to imaging, it is possible to study and determine the stage of liver tumor; one of the most utilized imaging technique in this field is Computed Tomography (CT). Indeed, new technology enables multi-phases acquisition protocols consisting of different acquisitions repeated at specified time intervals.

2 Materials

2.1 Patients

In the time interval between January and August 2016, four patients (men aged 55–78 years, mean ± standard deviation (SD), 66.3 ± 6.4 years) were subject to liver transplant, partial hepatectomy, or US-guided needle biopsy with pre-operative abdominal CT showing hepatic lesion and the typical HCC pattern. In all the cases histopathological specimen analysis confirmed the diagnosis of overt HCC. On the basis of histopathology, the patients were divided into 2 groups:

– well/moderately differentiated nodule;
– poorly differentiated nodules.

2.2 Computed Tomography Acquisition Protocol

All CT scans were acquired with a 320 slices Scanner (Toshiba Aquilion One) after an automated injection of 1.5 ml/kg of iodinated contrast medium (Iomeprole 400 mgI/ml) through a 16G Needle in antecubital vein at a flow rate of 4 ml/s with the following protocol:

1. **arterial** dominant phase (Fig. 1(a)) acquired 20 s after the aortic peak calculated by a bolus tracking system with a ROI positioned in the abdominal aorta at a trigger density of 150 Hounsfield Units (HU);
2. **portal** phase (Fig. 1(b)) acquired 70 s after contrast injection;
3. **equilibrium** phase (Fig. 1(c)) acquired 180 s after contrast injection.

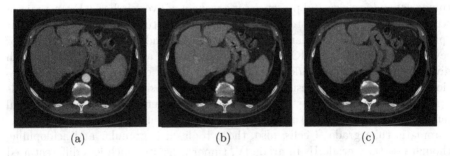

(a)   (b)   (c)

Fig. 1. CT images acquired in the different phases: (a) arterial phase; (b) portal phase; (c) equilibrium phase

For each CT series, we realized a volumetric acquisition using a collimation of 0.6 mm, a pitch value of 1.2, 120 kV, 160–440 mAs. Images were reconstructed with 1 mm as thickness and a reconstruction index of 0.8. Then, they were sent to a post-processing workstation.

3   Methods

Figure 1 shows that the lesion is easily distinguishable in both the arterial and the equilibrium phases; as the middle phase is insignificant for our purposes, the most significant images to be processed for feature extraction and the subsequent lesion classification are acquired from the first and last phases.

3.1   Image Segmentation

Preliminarily, we contrasted the acquired images (Fig. 2(a)) to enhance them. By doing this, we rendered all the areas of the CT image clearly distinguishable; the result is shown in Fig. 2(b).

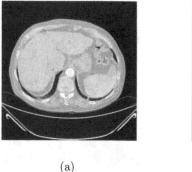 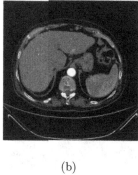

(a)   (b)

Fig. 2. Image Contrasting: (a) acquired image; (b) result after contrast enhancement

In the second step, images of the arterial phase were processed to isolate the liver from other organs in the same section. The algorithm for isolating the liver is described below.

Step 1. The process of liver segmentation starts with selecting the image which contains the maximum extension of the liver (Fig. 3).

Step 2. On the starting image (Fig. 4(a)), a morphological opening was applied using a disk (r = 20) as structuring element (Fig. 4).

Step 3. Starting from image at Step 1 Fig. 5(a), a morphological erosion was applied with the same structuring element. Subsequently, the image is reconstructed using both the starting image and the one coming from the erosion operation. The result is shown in Fig. 5(b).

Step 4. On the image from Step 2 Fig. 6(a), a morphological closure was applied using the same structuring element. The result is shown in Fig. 6(b).

Step 5. On the image from Step 3, a morphological dilatation was applied using the same structuring element of previous steps; the resulting image was then complemented with the one coming from Step 3. Both images were then used

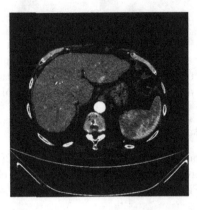

Fig. 3. CT slice with the larger extension of liver

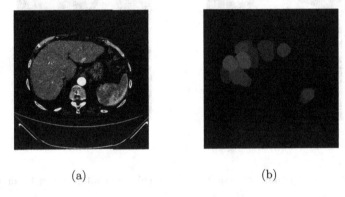

(a)   (b)

Fig. 4. Application of morphological opening: (a) starting image; (b) result of morphological opening

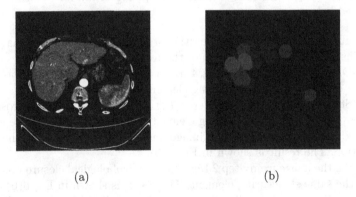

(a)   (b)

Fig. 5. Application of morphological erosion and reconstruction: (a) starting image; (b) result of reconstruction

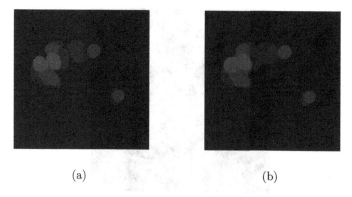

(a)   (b)

Fig. 6. Application of morphological closure: (a) starting image; (b) result of morphological closure.

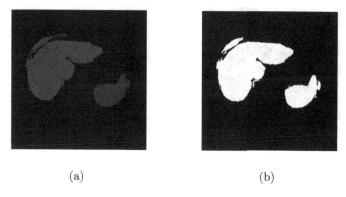

(a)   (b)

Fig. 7. Individuation of regions with high extension: (a) result of image reconstruction after the morphological operations; (b) obtained binary mask

together in the reconstruction. Finally, the resulting image was complemented (Fig. 7(a)) and the connected regions with the larger extension of areas were found on the resulting image (Fig. 7(b)).

Step 6. We applied a morphological closure on the image obtained in the previous step using a 5-by-5 unitary matrix as structuring element; then, a morphological opening was applied using the same structuring element. Subsequently, all the areas with less than 20 pixels were removed. The resulting image is then superimposed on the starting image (Fig. 8).

Step 7. On the image from Step 5, the watershed transformation was applied; this allowed to obtain 2 separated areas containing the liver and the other organ respectively (Fig. 9(a)). The ridge line obtained from the watershed transformation was used to cut off the other organs from the CT image (Fig. 9(b))

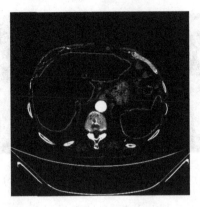

Fig. 8. A representation of the starting image with the superimposed areas

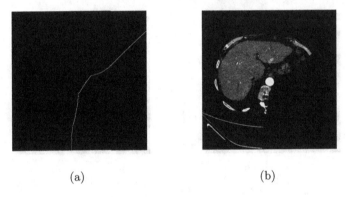

(a)   (b)

Fig. 9. Image showing the result of: (a) watershed transformation; (b) the application of the obtained ridge line

Step 8. Steps 4 and 5 were repeated on the resulting image; the area with maximum extension was found and the final image which contains the liver was obtained (Fig. 10).

Finally, a mono-seed region growing algorithm [13] was applied for a complete segmentation and isolation of liver; a restrained threshold value enabled us to completely isolate the liver; this, is turn, is clearly separated from the other parts which were not excluded in the previous steps of the algorithm. An example of the final result obtained from the segmentation algorithm could be seen in Fig. 11.

From the segmented liver, a binary mask was obtained which was then applied to all the others slices from the arterial phase of acquisition protocol for obtaining only images that contain parts of liver.

The described processing algorithm, together with the correct execution of the acquisition protocol, results in a correct extraction of the regions of interest (ROIs), including liver lesions (Fig. 12), from the portion of the liver in the CT images acquired during the arterial phase.

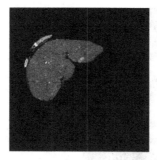

Fig. 10. Image containing the result of segmentation algorithm

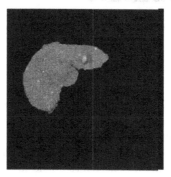

Fig. 11. Completely isolated liver

The segmentation of ROIs containing lesions was realized using a multi-seed region growing algorithm. Actually, the seeds are positioned by a physician using a graphical user interface (GUI) specifically developed for this purpose. After the ROI has been selected, it is automatically reported on the respective slice acquired during the equilibrium phase. By doing this, using some textural descriptors, we could describe the same region but under different conditions during the CT exam.

3.2 Feature Extraction

We used textural features extracted using gray level co-occurence matrices, as proposed by Haralick [14] and derived from his work [15,16], in order to describe the ROIs. They were extracted from the ROIs detected in the previous step (in both the arterial and the delayed phases). Specifically, 22 features were extracted from each ROI. Consequently, each entry in the dataset corresponding to a lesion found in 2 slices (acquired in both the arterial and the equilibrium phases) was described by a total of 44 features.

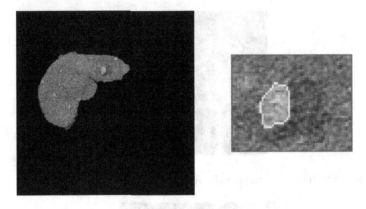

Fig. 12. Lesioned ROI selected on the liver

4   Classification

As stated in Sect. 2.2, we divided patients in two groups, in order to perform a binary classification. The first group contains subjects with well/moderately differentiated nodule; conversely, patients with poorly differentiated nodules are grouped in the second set. In this section, we describe the Artificial Neural Network (ANN) used to classify the degree of lesions between the two groups mentioned above.

4.1   Data Analysis and Preprocessing

Prior to the analysis, we excluded CT images from one patient, because their acquisition was not performed correctly. The resulting dataset was composed of **31** entries with a lesion in the first group (negatives) and **17** samples with a lesion in the second one (positives). Indeed, the performance of machine learning algorithms in medicine is evaluated using predictive accuracy, that is, a measure of diagnostic ability to correctly predict the output. As reported in [17], a small dataset affected by unbalance between classes could undermine the validity of a classification process. Therefore, we balanced the dataset using the Adaptive Synthetic Sampling (ADASYN) algorithm [18], an improved version of the Synthetic Minority Oversampling Technique (SMOTE) [19], in order to increase the number of positive patterns (second group examples) until the amount of negatives ones (first group examples) to improve the learning ability of the classifier. As a result, the final dataset was perfectly balanced, and it shows the same number of samples for each class (**31** positives and **31** negatives), so a total number of **62** samples. Moreover, starting from the initial dataset, the number of features was reduced to:

- 22 features coming from an algorithm of ranking based on the relative entropy, also known as Kullback-Leibler distance or divergence [20];

- 5 features of Haralick, that is, Contrast, Correlation, Energy, Homogeneity and Entropy, which have been used in a previous work for blood vessels and tubules classification [21].

In all the cases mentioned above, the dataset was standardized before classification using the z-score technique [22], in which the aim is to rescale the absolute values in data in an interval centered in 0 and with a variance equal to 1.

4.2 Classifiers

Several approaches for finding the best topology for an ANN classifier with Genetic Algorithms are described in literature; in [23], the authors search the optimal topology of ANN using a multi-objective genetic algorithm (MOGA). In this work, we found the topology of the ANN using a mono-objective Genetic Algorithm (GA) which finds the best topology maximizing the average test accuracy on a certain number of training, validation and test iteration for each topology of the ANN using different permutations of the dataset [24].

For each input dataset, the GA was executed to find the optimal topology in each case. Specifically, the GA finds topology of the ANN in terms of number of hidden layers (ranging from 1 to 3), number of neurons per layer (ranging from 1 to 256 for the first hidden layer, and from 0 to 255 for the other hidden layers), and activation functions in *log-sigmoid* (logsig), the *hyperpolic tangent sigmoid* (tansig), the *pure linear* (purelin) and the *symmetric saturating linear* (satlins), for all the neurons per-single layer.

The performances of the classifiers were evaluated in terms of accuracy (Eq. 1), specificity (Eq. 2) and sensitivity (Eq. 3), using the confusion matrix as follow (Table 1):

Table 1. The configuration of confusion matrix.

Predicted	True	
	Positive	Negative
Positive	TP	FP
Negative	FN	TN

$$Accuracy = \frac{TP + TN}{TP + TN + FP + FN} \tag{1}$$

$$Specificity = \frac{TN}{FP + TN} \tag{2}$$

$$Sensitivity = \frac{TP}{TP + FN} \tag{3}$$

5 Results

The optimal topologies for ANNs specified by the Genetic Algorithm in the three cases are:

Case 1. Balanced dataset with all the 44 features (22 for arterial phase and 22 for equilibrium phase)
ANN with: 4 layers, 117 neurons for the first hidden layer, 199 for the second, 6 for the third and 1 neuron for the output layer. The activation functions found by the GA were *logsig* for all the hidden layers, while the *tansig* function was set for the neuron in the output layer.

Case 2. Balanced dataset with the ranked 22 features
ANN with 3 layers: 16 neurons for the first hidden layer, 14 for the second and 1 neuron for the output layer. The activation functions found by the GA were *logsig* for all the hidden layers, while the *tansig* function was set for the neuron in the output layer.

Case 3. Balanced dataset with the 10 Haralick features (5 for arterial phase and 5 for equilibrium phase)
ANN with: 4 layers, 20 neurons for the first hidden layer, 17 for the second, 13 for the third and 1 neuron for the output layer. The activation functions found by the GA were *tansig* for the first hidden layer, *logsig* for the second, *satlins* for the third, while the *tansig* function was set for the neuron in the output layer.

The ANN training, validation, and test sets were obtained from the input dataset with 60% of samples for training, 20% for validation, and 20% for test set. Specifically, at each iteration, the above sets are obtained through a random permutation of the dataset, maintaining the number of samples of each class balanced. Moreover, the classification thresholds were determined using Receiver Operating Characteristic (ROC) curves [25], by evaluating the True Positive Rate (TPR) against the False Positive Rate (FPR) at various thresholds setting, in order to find the value which could achieve the best discrimination between the two classes.

Results are expressed in terms of mean values, considering 100 iterations, for accuracy, specificity, and sensitivity. In the first case, accuracy was 91.43% (std = 3.04), specificity was 0.974 (std = 0.059), and sensitivity was 0.8543 (std = 0.0201). In the second case accuracy was 92.14% (std = 2.15), specificity was 0.986 (std = 0.043), and sensitivity was 0.857 (std = 0.0001). In the third

Table 2. Confusion matrix for the best case.

Predicted	True	
	Positive	Negative
Positive	TP = 6	FP = 0
Negative	FN = 1	TN = 7

case accuracy was 88.93% (std = 4.80), specificity was 0.95 (std = 0.079), and sensitivity was 0.8286 (std = 0.073).

Due to the small number of samples, the performances in all the cases are quite similar; in particular, the maximum value for the accuracy was the same in the three cases and equal to 92.8571%. The confusion matrix is shown in Table 2.

6 Conclusions

The results of our study show that HCC grading can be discriminated using the extracted features which were discussed in the previous section: the HCC wash-in and wash-out dynamic suggests that this type of lesion could be characterized by analyzing the differences in textural features in both the arterial and the equilibrium phases, ignoring the portal phase. Specifically, the group of feature which enable the best discrimination between the classes consists in the 22 features extracted by the ranking algorithm. Although the number of cases we could analyze is relatively small, the preliminary results obtained in this work and shown in Sect. 5 are indeed very promising. In conclusion, recruiting new patients will result in confirming the results discussed in this paper, and in improving both the method and the outcome of our study.

References

1. Ferenci, P., Fried, M., Labrecque, D., Bruix, J., Sherman, M., Omata, M., Heathcote, J., Piratsivuth, T., Kew, M., Otegbayo, J.A., et al.: Hepatocellular carcinoma (HCC): a global perspective. J. Clin. Gastroenterol. **44**(4), 239–245 (2010)
2. Llovet, J.M., Burroughs, A., Bruix, J.: Hepatocellular carcinoma. The Lancet **362**(9399), 1907 (2003)
3. Bartolozzi, C., Crocetti, L., Lencioni, R., Cioni, D., Della Pina, C., Campani, D.: Biliary and reticuloendothelial impairment in hepatocarcinogenesis: the diagnostic role of tissue-specific MR contrast media. Eur. Radiol. **17**(10), 2519–2530 (2007)
4. Sanyal, A.J., Yoon, S.K., Lencioni, R.: The etiology of hepatocellular carcinoma and consequences for treatment. Oncologist **15**(Suppl. 4), 14–22 (2010)
5. Kudo, M.: Multistep human hepatocarcinogenesis: correlation of imaging with pathology. J. Gastroenterol. **44**(19), 112–118 (2009)
6. Kudo, M., Chung, H., Haji, S., Osaki, Y., Oka, H., Seki, T., Kasugai, H., Sasaki, Y., Matsunaga, T.: Validation of a new prognostic staging system for hepatocellular carcinoma: the JIS score compared with the CLIP score. Hepatology **40**(6), 1396–1405 (2004)
7. Memeo, M., Stabile Ianora, A.A., Scardapane, A., Suppressa, P., Cirulli, A., Sabba, C., Rotondo, A., Angelelli, G.: Hereditary haemorrhagic telangiectasia study of hepatic vascular alterations with multi-detector row helical CT and reconstruction programs. La Radiologia Medica **109**(1–2), 125–138 (2004)
8. Stabile Ianora, A.A., Memeo, M., Scardapane, A., Rotondo, A., Angelelli, G.: Oral contrast-enhanced three-dimensional helical-CT cholangiography: clinical applications. Eur. Radiol. **13**(4), 867–873 (2003)
9. Choi, J.-Y., Lee, J.-M., Sirlin, C.B.: CT and MR imaging diagnosis and staging of hepatocellular carcinoma: part II. Extracellular agents, hepatobiliary agents, and ancillary imaging features. Radiology **273**(1), 30–50 (2014)

10. Bruix, J., Sherman, M.: Management of hepatocellular carcinoma. Hepatology **42**(5), 1208–1236 (2005)
11. Kleihues, P., Sobin, L.H.: World health organization classification of tumors. Cancer **88**(12), 2887 (2000)
12. Edmondson, H.A., Steiner, P.E.: Primary carcinoma of the liver. A study of 100 cases among 48,900 necropsies. Cancer **7**(3), 462–503 (1954)
13. Adams, R., Bischof, L.: Seeded region growing. IEEE Trans. Pattern Anal. Mach. Intell. **16**(6), 641–647 (1994)
14. Haralick, R.M., Shanmugam, K., et al.: Textural features for image classification. IEEE Trans. Syst. Man Cybern. **6**, 610–621 (1973)
15. Soh, L.-K., Tsatsoulis, C.: Texture analysis of SAR sea ice imagery using gray level co-occurrence matrices. IEEE Trans. Geosci. Remote Sens. **37**(2), 780–795 (1999)
16. Clausi, D.A.: An analysis of co-occurrence texture statistics as a function of grey level quantization. Can. J. Remote Sens. **28**(1), 45–62 (2002)
17. Mazurowski, M.A., Habas, P.A., Zurada, J.M., Lo, J.Y., Baker, J.A., Tourassi, G.D.: Training neural network classifiers for medical decision making: the effects of imbalanced datasets on classification performance. Neural Netw. **21**(2), 427–436 (2008)
18. He, H., Bai, Y., Garcia, E.A., Li, S.: Adasyn: adaptive synthetic sampling approach for imbalanced learning. In: 2008 IEEE International Joint Conference on Neural Networks (IEEE World Congress on Computational Intelligence), pp. 1322–1328. IEEE (2008)
19. Chawla, N.V., Bowyer, K.W., Hall, L.O., Philip Kegelmeyer, W.: SMOTE: synthetic minority over-sampling technique. J. Artif. Intell. Res. **16**, 321–357 (2002)
20. Kullback, S., Leibler, R.A.: On information and sufficiency. Ann. Math. Stat. **22**(1), 79–86 (1951)
21. Bevilacqua, V., Pietroleonardo, N., Triggiani, V., Gesualdo, L., Palma, A.M., Rossini, M., Dalfino, G., Mastrofilippo, N.: Neural network classification of blood vessels and tubules based on Haralick features evaluated in histological images of kidney biopsy. In: Huang, D.-S., Han, K. (eds.) ICIC 2015. LNCS (LNAI), vol. 9227, pp. 759–765. Springer, Cham (2015). doi:10.1007/978-3-319-22053-6_81
22. Zill, D., Wright, W.S., Cullen, M.R.: Advanced Engineering Mathematics. Jones & Bartlett Learning, Burlington (2011)
23. Bevilacqua, V., Mastronardi, G., Menolascina, F., Pannarale, P., Pedone, A.: A novel multi-objective genetic algorithm approach to artificial neural network topology optimisation: the breast cancer classification problem. In: The 2006 IEEE International Joint Conference on Neural Network Proceedings, pp. 1958–1965. IEEE (2006)
24. Bevilacqua, V., Brunetti, A., Triggiani, M., Magaletti, D., Telegrafo, M., Moschetta, M.: An optimized feed-forward artificial neural network topology to support radiologists in breast lesions classification. In: Proceedings of the 2016 on Genetic and Evolutionary Computation Conference Companion, pp. 1385–1392. ACM (2016)
25. Bradley, A.P.: The use of the area under the ROC curve in the evaluation of machine learning algorithms. Pattern Recogn. **30**(7), 1145–1159 (1997)

A Comprehensive Method for Assessing the Blepharospasm Cases Severity

Vitoantonio Bevilacqua[1]([✉]), Antonio Emmanuele Uva[2], Michele Fiorentino[2],
Gianpaolo Francesco Trotta[2], Maurizio Dimatteo[1], Enrico Nasca[1],
Attilio Nicola Nocera[1], Giacomo Donato Cascarano[1], Antonio Brunetti[1],
Nicholas Caporusso[1], Roberta Pellicciari[3,4], and Giovanni Defazio[3]

[1] Department of Electrical and Information Engineering, Polytechnic of Bari,
Via Orabona 4, 70125 Bari, Italy
vitoantonio.bevilacqua@poliba.it
[2] Department of Mechanical and Management Engineering, Polytechnic of Bari,
Via Orabona 4, 70125 Bari, Italy
antonio.uva@poliba.it
[3] Department of Basic Medical Sciences, Neuroscience and Sensory Organs,
University of Bari Aldo Moro, Piazza Giulio Cesare, 11, 70120 Bari, Italy
giovanni.defazio@uniba.it
[4] Department of Neurology and Psychiatry, Sapienza University of Rome,
Rome, Italy
ro.pellicciari@gmail.com

Abstract. Blepharospasm is characterized by bilateral, synchronous, and symmetric involuntary orbicularis oculi muscle spasms leading to partial/total eyelid closure. We proposed a comprehensive method for assessing the severity of blepharospasm cases, based on expert observation of fixed-length video recordings and natural feature detection algorithms. The developed software detects involuntary spasms and blinks in order to evaluate BSP severity. In this work we have considered a new BSP severity scale to realize an objective evaluation of BSP severity.

1 Introduction

Blepharospasm (BSP) is characterized by bilateral, synchronous, and symmetric involuntary orbicularis oculi (OO) muscle spasms leading to partial/total eyelid closure [1–3]. Spasms may be brief or prolonged. Usually, they are aggravated by bright light, stress, or voluntary muscle contractions; conversely, they are reduced by attention-demanding tasks, such as writing. Additional symptoms include: increased blinking rate, sensory tricks, apraxia of eyelid opening (AEO) and dystonia in other body parts [4,5]. As clinical management is symptomatic and often incomplete, research focuses on new treatment strategies. Periodic botulinum neurotoxin (BoNT) injections, into the affected muscles, provides symptomatic treatment with reasonable efficacy and safety. Yet, the development of new more effective therapies [6] requires sensitive and objective methods to rate symptoms severity [7].

© Springer Nature Singapore Pte Ltd. 2017
K.C. Santosh et al. (Eds.): RTIP2R 2016, CCIS 709, pp. 369–381, 2017.
DOI: 10.1007/978-981-10-4859-3_33

Determining the efficacy of treatments requires a system for measuring the severity of symptoms. Existing clinical rating scales are inherently subjective. Objective methods, such as kinematic measures, are expensive and not easily adoptable for widespread clinical use. This critical need for development of an objective, sensitive BSP rating scale has not moved forward. Current rating scales, such as the Burke-Fahn-Marsden Dystonia Rating Scale (BFM) [8], Global Dystonia Rating Scale (GDRS) [9], Jankovic Rating Scale (JRS) [10] and the recently developed rating scale for BSP remain based on the subjective evaluation of a clinician. To this end, video analysis might offer a better alternative. Videos, recorded during clinical examinations, enable more authorized expert to review a consistent set of data, without requiring them to attend recordings or examinations. Moreover, video recordings do not require additional resources and patient set-up time, as would be the case with equipment for kinematic measurements, so that the clinical setting time is not affected. The wide availability of inexpensive digital video cameras also enables video analysis to be performed with a rapidly growing suite of more recent and advanced artificial intelligence algorithms.

2   Related Works

Potential solutions include the Computer Expression Recognition Toolbox (CERT), previously available from the University of California, San Diego (UCSD) for academic use, now available as the Facet commercial software from iMotions.com. CERT combines artificial intelligence algorithms taken from the domains of computer vision, pattern recognition and machine learning. CERT is able to evaluate blepharospasm severity according to the following scales:

- Burke-Fahn-Marsden (BFM):
  - no dystonia present
  - slight: occasional blinking
  - mild: frequent blinking without prolonged spasms of eye closure
  - moderate: prolonged spasms of eye closure, but eyes open most of the time
  - severe: prolonged spasms of eye closure, with eyes closed at least 30% of the time
- Global Dystonia Rating Scale (GDS):
  - no dystonia present
  - minimal dystonia
  - moderate dystonia
  - severe dystonia
- Jankovic Rating Scale (JRS):
  - none
  - minimal, increased blinking present only with external stimuli
  - mild, but spontaneous eyelid fluttering (without actual spasm), definitely noticeable, possibly embarrassing, but not functionality disabling
  - moderate, very noticeable spasm of eyelids only, mildly incapacitating
  - severe, incapacitating spasm of eyelids and possibly other facial muscles

Previous BSP severity scales do not include factors, such as duration, because of the relatively short observation periods. Indeed video-recordings have been performed according to the following standardized video protocol:

- at rest, eyes open for 10 s
- at rest, eyes gently close for 10 s
- at rest, after opening eyes, for an additional 10 s
- forced eyelid closure for 3 times, then observation effect for 5 s after each closure

However, with the new BSP severity scale, video-recordings were performed according to a standardized video protocol lasting approximately 5 min:

- Patient at rest, eyes open (10 s)
- Patient voluntarily performs a forceful eye closure followed by eye re-opening (repeated 5 times, one cycle per second)
- Patient at rest, eyes open (10 s)
- Voluntary gentle eye closure followed by eye reopening (repeated 5 times, one cycle per second)
- Patient at rest, eyes open (10 s)
- The doctor asks the patient the following questions: are you able to suppress eye closure? How? Are you able to voluntary suppress it? Or do you need to touch your eyes, face or neck?
- The patient answers the questions (at least 50 s)
- The doctor asks the patient to write a standard sentence 3 times (today it is a nice sunny day)
- Patient at rest, eyes open (at least 150 s). In the last 120 s, we counted the number of tonic OO spasms (and measured their duration), the number of blinks and clonic OO spasms. Patients were instructed to avoid antagonistic gestures

In this work we used the aforementioned video-recordings standard protocol to analyse the last 120 s of video and to evaluate BSP severity, according to the BSP severity scale described in Fig. 1 [11].

3 Methods

The process of analysing BSP symptoms consists in two steps:

- Signal extraction: frame-by-frame video analysis to measure the geometry of specific facial features [12]. Data are collected as digital signals which will exhibit local minima at frames where phenomena occur
- Signal processing: signal trend analysis and threshold evaluation to distinguish BSP-related phenomena from natural movements of the face [13]

3.1 Signal Extraction

In the signal extraction step, the dlib frontal face detector outputs a region of interest, which is scanned by the dlib shape predictor [14] to estimate the

Intensity rating

ITEM A1) Type of eyelid spasm
▯ Brief (< 3 sec duration) eyelid spasms with complete rim closure = score 1
▯ Prolonged (≥ 3 sec duration) eyelid spasms with partial rim closure = score 2
▯ Prolonged (≥3 sec duration) eyelid spasms with complete rim closure = score 3

ITEM A2) Apraxia of eyelid opening
▯ Yes = score 2
▯ No = score 0

ITEM A3) OO spasms occur during writing:
▯ Yes = score 1
▯ No = score 0

ITEM A4) Average duration of prolonged eyelid spasm with complete rim closure recorded while patient at rest, eyes open, for two minutes. Calculate the correspondent tertile as follows:
▯ I tertile = 3 to 4 sec = score 1
▯ II tertile = 4.1 to 5 sec = score 2
▯ III tertile = > 5 sec = score 3

Frequency rating

ITEM B1) Count "number of blinks + brief eyelid spasm / min" (patient at rest, eyes open, for two minutes) and calculate the corresponding tertile as follows:
▯ I tertile = 1 – 18 blinks + brief spasm / min = score 1
▯ II tertile = 19 – 32 blinks + brief spasm /min = score 2
▯ III tertile = > 32 blinks + brief spasm / min = score 3
ITEM B2) Count number of prolonged eyelid spasm with complete rim closure / min" (patient at rest, eyes open, for two minutes) and calculate the corresponding quartile as follows:
▯ I tertile = 1 – 3/ min = score 1
▯ II tertile = 3.1 – 7/min = score 2
▯ III tertile = > 7/ min = score 3

Total score = Intensity + Frequency = (A1 + A2 + A3 + A4) + (B1 + B2)

Fig. 1. BSP severity scale

coordinates of 68 facial landmark points. A subset of such points is then used to perform simple geometric calculations.

For each frame i, the function $Y(i)$ is computed as shown in Eq. 1.

$$Y(i) = \frac{T(i)}{L(i)} \tag{1}$$

where:

– $T(i)$: height of the triangle shown in Fig. 2(b)
– $L(i)$: distance between the nose tip and the bridge as shown in Fig. 2(c)

The tip-bridge distance is a normalising divisor that prevents sudden signal variation due to head rotation. The output of this step is a signal that will exhibit local minima in correspondence of spasm events.

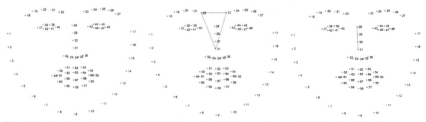

(a) 68 landmark points from dlib shape predictor tool

(b) Triangle with vertices defined by the two inner landmarks of eyebrows and the tip of the nose

(c) Tip - bridge distance

Fig. 2. Using of dlib shape predictor tool

Figure 3 shows a simulation of spasm event.

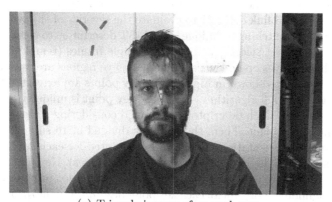

(a) Triangle in case of opened eyes

(b) Triangle during spasm event

Fig. 3. Spasm simulation

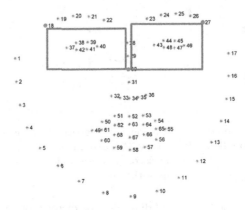

Fig. 4. Estimated regions of interest.

An involuntary OO muscle spasm occurs when both eyes are closed. Additionally, we developed a blink detector to evaluate the severity of the symptoms. We employ a template matching technique using SIFT descriptors to mark closed eyes. First, a domain expert selects one or many sample frames (templates) in which the patient has his eyes open. For each template, eye regions are estimated using selected landmarks, as shown in Fig. 4; then, key points are extracted from these regions using the FAST algorithm [15]. Every key point is uniquely described by the SIFT algorithm. Each descriptor is obtained considering a region of 16×16 pixels around a key point. Then, the region is divided in 16 subregions of 4×4 pixels and an 8-bin orientation histogram is computed for each subregion. Each 8 bin sequence forms the key point descriptor (128 values). Key points and their relative descriptors are extracted in each frame during video processing. Using a K-nearest neighbour algorithm for each key point descriptor of the i_{th} frame, we use a classification technique to find similar key points, based on Euclidean distance, between template and the i_{th} frame. In order to remove outliers, we consider the distance between the i_{th} and the closest-to-template key point descriptor and the distance between the i_{th} and the second closest-to-template key point descriptor [16]. If the ratio of the distances exceeds a 0.7 threshold the match shall not be valid. As a result, the output of the algorithm is the product between similar key points in right and left eye.

Figure 5 shows a simulation of blink event and regions from which extract key points.

The face region, which the dlib shape predictor requires as an input parameter, is computed by the dlib frontal face detector, which is based on the Histogram of Oriented Gradients (HOG). For the purposes of this work, the dlib face detector provides an advantage in terms of accuracy and speed over the OpenCV face detector, which is based on Haar Cascade [17]. Still, video processing is affected by some delay caused by the face detector, which is executed on every frame. However, the video recording protocol adopted in our set-up requires the patient to sit in front of a fixed camera: hence we can assume that the position of the face does not

(a) Triangle in case of opened eyes   (b) Triangle in case of closed eyes

(c) Eyes regions of interest

Fig. 5. Blink simulation and eyes regions of interest

significantly change between consecutive frames. A naive solution to decrease processing time consists in running the face detector every k frames. A more elegant approach for detecting changes in the shape of the face is based on the Frobenius distance, shown in Eq. 2.

$$F = \sqrt{\sum_{i=0}^{67}((x_i - \bar{x})^2 + (y_i - \bar{y})^2)} \tag{2}$$

where:

- (x_i, y_i): the i_{th} point coordinates
- $(\bar{x}, \bar{y})$: the centroid coordinates

If the dlib shape predictor tool is executed on a region that does not contain a full face, the Frobenius distance higher. If it exceeds a certain threshold, it is necessary to execute the face detector. In this work, we used the following algorithm to reduce processing time:

- read the i_{th} frame and run both the face detector and the dlib shape predictor tool on it
- read the $(i_{th} + 1)$ frame and use the previously detected landmark points to evaluate face region position on the frame
- run dlib shape predictor tool on the $(i_{th} + 1)$ frame
- evaluate Frobenius distance for the $(i_{th} + 1)$ and i_{th} frame: if the difference between the $(i_{th} + 1)$ and i_{th} exceeds a certain threshold read the $(i_{th} + 2)$ frame and run face detector alternatively use the previously detected landmark points to evaluate face region position

Table 1. Difference between detector runs number using Frobenius distance or sub samples on 4 videos

Total number of frame	Detector runs (with Frobenius distance)	Detector runs (every 3 frames)
3881	56	1293
3861	77	1287
3915	266	1305
3829	26	1276

Table 1 compares the number of detector runs using Frobenius distance and a constant sub samples (every 3 frames) on 4 different videos. The improvement is considerable and the use of Frobenius distance does not result in any deterioration in the quality of the extracted signals.

3.2   Signal Processing

The beginning of a spasm is detected by signal analysis on $Y(i)$. The main goal is to find $Y(i)$'s local minima and to determine a threshold value to distinguish BSP phenomena from natural movements. During a spasm the patient's eyes are closed. The ending of a spasm is detected by the analysis of the signal generated by the number of similar key points found during video processing. The main goal is to find local minima in which the frame is characterized by open eyes. This information, in turn, enables to evaluate the BSP severity using the BSP severity scale in Fig. 1.

The $Y(i)$ signal, an example is shown in Fig. 6, shows a noise component due to two main factors:

- Head movements causing shifts in the signal. To cancel this noise source, we apply a detrending filter to the signal.
- Small variations of landmark points position happen also when the patient is steady. To delete this noise source, we apply a smoothing filter to the signal.

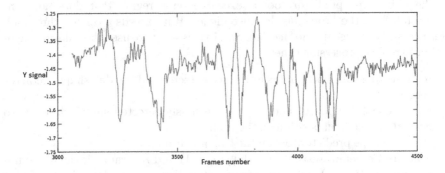

Fig. 6. The raw signal example relative to spasms detection

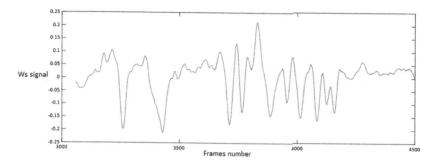

Fig. 7. The output signal example relative to spasms detection after pre-processing operations

To mitigate the noise component caused by head movements, the $Y(i)$ signal is estimated by a low order polynomial function $p(i)$. The output of this process is a new signal $W(i) = Y(i) - p(i)$. To mitigate the noise component caused by small variations of landmark points position, we apply a Savitzky-Golay filter to $W(i)$ signal. An example of $W_s(i)$ signal is shown in Fig. 7.

In order to determine a threshold value to distinguish BSP phenomena from natural face movements, we apply the find-peaks MATLAB function to find all $-W_s(i)$'s peaks that are $W_s(i)$'s local minima. Using the find-peaks MATLAB function, we obtain an array of peak prominences, which is then used to create an histogram where the binning is realized to set the ranges of values in different bins to an equal amplitude. By doing this, less prominent peaks due to signal noise are isolated in the bottom half of the histogram. To determine a threshold value we consider P_k for $k = 1, 2, ..., n$ the values set of most important prominences and B_k for $k = 1, 2, ..., n$ the number of elements in bin k. The threshold value T, shown in Eq. 3, is a halved weighted average where $B_1, B_2, ..., B_n$ are the weights.

$$T = \frac{\sum_k P_k B_k}{2 * \sum_k B_k} \qquad (3)$$

This approach is useful to isolate prominences that are repeated frequently in the signal, indicating possible spasms. The threshold value evaluation to distinguish BSP phenomena from natural face movements is done using the first part of the video in which the patient performs voluntary spasms and blinks. The same pre-processing tasks are applied to the signal extracted from open eye detection. In this case, finding a constant threshold value is useful to detect when eyes are open or closed. Figure 8 shows an output signal related to the detection of eyes open.

This signal does not enable to choose a constant threshold value. As a result, we manually solved the issue. During video processing the application runs a software frame grabber that enables the user to choose an indefinite number of frames with eyes open. The higher the number of selected templates the better the performance.

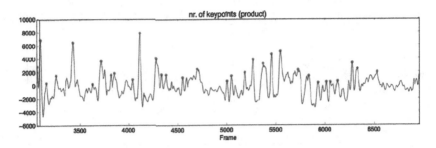

Fig. 8. The output signal example relative to eyes open detection step after pre-processing operations

4   Results

Two videos were considered. The first one shows a subject exhibiting both short and long spasms along with apraxia. Conversely the patient in the second video shows both enduring and multiple very short spasms. Figure 9 shows the results obtained with data from the first patient.

The BSP phenomena are detected accurately. However to evaluate intensity and frequency rating according to the BSP severity scale in Fig. 1 it is useful to detect one additional phenomenon, in order. Apraxia of lid opening (ALO) is a nonparalytic motor abnormality characterized by difficulty initiating the act of lid elevation after lid closure [18]. The algorithm that detects apraxia consists of the following steps:

– Run the algorithm to detect spasm
– Run the algorithm to detect opened eyes

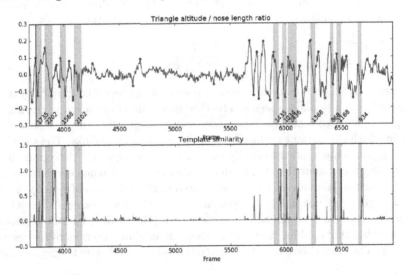

Fig. 9. The results relative to the first patient

- Consider the highest peaks of signal related to spasm detection after pre-processing that are not in any spasm time interval
- For each highest peak, find a maximum in the open eye detection signal after pre-processing in the next 2 s
- If there is a maximum then apraxia is detected.

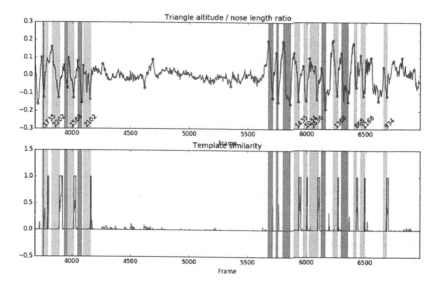

Fig. 10. The results relative to the first patient with apraxia detection (Color figure online)

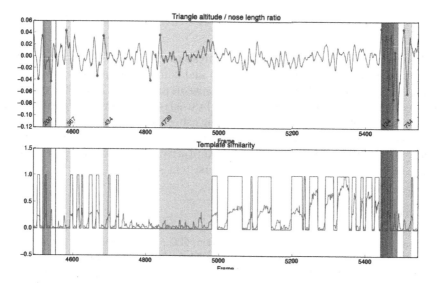

Fig. 11. The results relative to the second patient

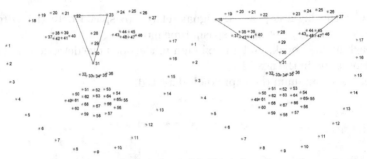

(a) Triangle with vertices defined by the two outer landmarks of eyebrows and the tip of the nose.

(b) Triangle where the endpoints defined by the left and right outer eyebrows form the base, whereas the tip of the nose is the remaining vertex

Fig. 12. Two different triangles to resolve the issue of persistent spasm

Data resulting from the apraxia detection algorithm are shown in Fig. 10. Green bars are relative to apraxia phenomena.

Figure 11 shows the results from the second patient. Similarly, all phenomena are detected accurately. However, data show a problem caused by a phenomenon knowns as *persistent spasm*. Indeed a spasm occurs when the triangle in Fig. 12(b) is subject to height reduction. A persistent spasm is characterized by a fixed height of the triangle in Fig. 12(a). So, in this case, all eyes open detected by software should be brief spasms.

5   Conclusion

In this work we conducted a qualitative analysis to evaluate blepharospasm (BSP) severity. Based on both video observation and comparison of results from algorithms, we were able to detect involuntary spasms and blinks. The software developed has been used to extract data that will be used to implement an algorithm that evaluates BSP intensity and frequency rating using a new BSP severity scale. In the future, our results will help define a gold standard on a relevant number of patients, which, in turn, will enable to conduct a quantitative analysis and to improve algorithms in order to resolve issues such as, persistent spasm.

References

1. Grandas, F., Elston, J., Quinn, N., Marsden, C.D.: Blepharospasm: a review of 264 patients. J. Neurol. Neurosurg. Psychiatry **51**(6), 767–772 (1988)
2. Hallett, M., Evinger, C., Jankovic, J., Stacy, M.: Update on blepharospasm: report from the BEBRF international workshop. Neurology **71**(16), 1275–1282 (2008)

3. Jinnah, H.A., Berardelli, A., Comella, C., De Fazio, G., DeLong, M.R., Factor, S., Galpern, W.R., Hallett, M., Ludlow, C.L., Perlmutter, J.S.: The focal dystonias: current views and challenges for future research. Mov. Disord. **28**(7), 926–943 (2013)
4. Defazio, G., Berardelli, A., Hallett, M.: Do primary adult-onset focal dystonias share aetiological factors? Brain **130**(5), 1183–1193 (2007)
5. Abbruzzese, G., Berardelli, A., Girlanda, P., Marchese, R., Martino, D., Morgante, F., Avanzino, L., Colosimo, C., Defazio, G.: Long-term assessment of the risk of spread in primary late-onset focal dystonia. J. Neurol. Neurosurg. Psychiatry **79**(4), 392–396 (2008)
6. Price, K.M., Ramey, N.A., Richard, M.J., Woodward, D.J., Woodward, J.A.: Can methylphenidate objectively provide relief in patients with uncontrolled blepharospasm? A pilot study using surface electromyography. Ophthalmic Plast. Reconstr. Surg. **26**(5), 353–356 (2010)
7. Wabbels, B., Jost, W.H., Roggenkämper, P.: Difficulties with differentiating botulinum toxin treatment effects in essential blepharospasm. J. Neural Transm. **118**(6), 925–943 (2011)
8. Burke, R.E., Fahn, S., Marsden, C.D., Bressman, S.B., Moskowitz, C., Friedman, J.: Validity and reliability of a rating scale for the primary torsion dystonias. Neurology **35**(1), 73–73 (1985)
9. Comella, C.L., Leurgans, S., Wuu, J., Stebbins, G.T., Chmura, T.: Rating scales for dystonia: a multicenter assessment. Mov. Disord. **18**(3), 303–312 (2003)
10. Jankovic, J., Orman, J.: Botulinum a toxin for cranial-cervical dystonia a double-blind, placebo-controlled study. Neurology **37**(4), 616–616 (1987)
11. Defazio, G., Hallett, M., Jinnah, H.A., Stebbins, G.T., Gigante, A.F., Ferrazzano, G., Conte, A., Fabbrini, G., Berardelli, A.: Development and validation of a clinical scale for rating the severity of blepharospasm. Mov. Disord. **30**(4), 525–530 (2015)
12. Loconsole, C., Chiaradia, D., Bevilacqua, V., Frisoli, A.: Real-time emotion recognition: an improved hybrid approach for classification performance. In: Huang, D.-S., Bevilacqua, V., Premaratne, P. (eds.) ICIC 2014. LNCS, vol. 8588, pp. 320–331. Springer, Cham (2014). doi:10.1007/978-3-319-09333-8_35
13. Bevilacqua, V., D'Ambruoso, D., Mandolino, G., Suma, M.: A new tool to support diagnosis of neurological disorders by means of facial expressions. In: 2011 IEEE International Workshop on Medical Measurements and Applications Proceedings (MeMeA), pp. 544–549, May 2011
14. Kazemi, V., Sullivan, J.: One millisecond face alignment with an ensemble of regression trees. In: Proceedings of the IEEE Conference on Computer Vision and Pattern Recognition, pp. 1867–1874 (2014)
15. Rosten, E., Drummond, T.: Machine learning for high-speed corner detection. In: Leonardis, A., Bischof, H., Pinz, A. (eds.) ECCV 2006. LNCS, vol. 3951, pp. 430–443. Springer, Heidelberg (2006). doi:10.1007/11744023_34
16. Lowe, D.G.: Distinctive image features from scale-invariant keypoints. Int. J. Comput. Vis. **60**(2), 91–110 (2004)
17. Viola, P., Jones, M.: Rapid object detection using a boosted cascade of simple features. In: Proceedings of the 2001 IEEE Computer Society Conference on Computer Vision and Pattern Recognition, CVPR 2001, vol. 1, p. I-511. IEEE (2001)
18. Defazio, G., Livrea, P., Lamberti, P., De Salvia, R., Laddomada, G., Giorelli, M., Ferrari, E.: Isolated so-called apraxia of eyelid opening: report of 10 cases and a review of the literature. Eur. Neurol. **39**(4), 204–210 (1998)

Identification and Classification of Fruit Diseases

Y.H. Sharath Kumar[✉] and G. Suhas

Department of Information Science and Engineering,
Maharaja Institute of Technology, Belawadi,
Sri-rangapatna Tq, Mandya, Karnataka, India
sharathyhk@gmail.com, suhasnidhi789@gmail.com

Abstract. In this paper, we propose a method for identification and classification of fruit diseases. Initially, the fruit image is segmented using K-means and C-Means clustering algorithms, later performance evaluation of segmentation algorithm is conducted using the parameters such as Measure of under-segmentation (MUS), Measure of overlapping (MOL), Dice similarity measure (DSM), Measure of over segmentation (MOS), Error-rate (ER). The performance evaluation of segmentation parameters are calculated based on the comparison between the manually segmented ground truth and segmentation result generated by the image segmentation approaches. After segmentation, features are extracted using Gray Level Co-occurrence Matrix. The K-Nearest Neighbors Algorithm classifier is used to classification. The collected database consists of 10 classes with 243 images. The result of classification has relatively higher accuracy in all cases when segmented using K-Means compared to C-Means clustering algorithms . . .

Keywords: K-means · C-means · GLCM · KNN

1 Introduction

India is agricultural dependent country, it stands as a second largest producers of fruits by producing over 44.04 million tons of fruits with an area of 3.72 million hectares and 10.

Farmers find difficulty in finding the fruits affected with disease which result in loss of revenue to the farmers and the nation. The types of diseases on fruits determine the quantity and quality of yield. The diseases in fruits reduce the market of fruit and also minimizes the number of fruit production. Early disease detection can facilitate the control of fruit disease through proper management approaches, such as fungicide applications, pesticide application and disease specific chemical applications there by improve production. Visual perception by expert people was the classical approach for detection of diseases in fruits which are very expensive. Fruit diseases cause major problem in economy and production in agriculture industry worldwide, manually identifying diseases in the fruits is used by the experts till date, but it is expensive for farmer to consult an expert, so automatically detect the symptoms of the fruit disease is required. Diseases in fruit can cause major losses in marketing.

© Springer Nature Singapore Pte Ltd. 2017
K.C. Santosh et al. (Eds.): RTIP2R 2016, CCIS 709, pp. 382–390, 2017.
DOI: 10.1007/978-981-10-4859-3_34

2 Literature Survey

Bhange and Hingoliwala [1] suggested a solution for the detection of pomegranate fruit disease. Intent Search module helps to capture the intension of the user while searching the information related to his fruit diseases. Feature extraction includes Color, Morphology and Texture feature vectors. K-means clustering algorithm is used for image segmentation and K-nearest neighbor algorithm is proposed for classification. Deshpande et al. [2] proposed a method for automatic grading. The grading is based on the disease of the Pomegranate plant leaves and fruit. In fruits the black spots are identified. If there is a crack passing through the black spot then the fruit is infected by Bacterial Blight and Cracks are found using canny edge detector. K-means clusteringmethod is used for segmentation. Kanakaraddi et al. [3] proposed method for analysis and grading of pathogenic disease of chili crop, specifically Fruit Rot. The method proposed automates the manual way of analyzing the severity of fungal disease of chili crop. Preprocessing includes filtering, intensifying the image and binarization. Gray Level Co-occurrence Matrix is used for extracting texture features. Classification of the disease is done based on the percentage of area affected. Pujari et al. [4] proposed a Statistical Methods for Quantitatively Detecting Fungal Disease from Fruits Images. This method considers fungal disease symptoms affected on fruits like mango, pomegranate and grape. Statistical features using block wise, Gray Level Co-occurrence Matrix (GLCM), Gray Level Run-length Matrix (GLRM) are extracted. Nearest Neighbor classifier using Euclidean distance is used to classify images. Pujari et al. [5] proposed a method for Grading and Classification is based on Statistical Texture Features. In this method, infected areas affected by anthracnose are segmented using segmentation techniques, graded based on percentage of affected area and neural network classifier is used to classify normal fruits and anthracnose affected on fruits. Pujari et al. [6] presented a reduced feature set based approach for classification and recognition of fruits. The RGB (Red Green Blue) color features and GLCM (Gray-level Co-occurrence Matrix) texture features are reduced from 18 to 2 and from 30 to 2. Dubey and Jalal [7] proposed a solution for the detecting and classification of apple fruit diseases. The proposed approach have following main steps; initially image segmentation is performed by k means clustering, from segmented image features are extracted, and finally images are classified in to different classes. Liu et al. [8] proposed automated blemish orange detection system. The system focused on ripe and unripe oranges. Unay and Gosselin [9] introduced a grading system for 'Jonagold' apples. The system involves following steps pre-processing, classification, post-processing and decision taking steps are involved. Dubey and Jalal [10] proposed approach for the identification of fruit diseases. In the proposed approach the K-Means clustering technique is used to identify the defect, from the segmented image features are extracted, and images are classified into classes using Multi-class Support Vector Machine. Seng and Mirisaee [11] proposed a new Fruit recognition system which combines three features analysis methods: color-based, shape based and size-based in order to increase accuracy of recognition.

3   Proposed Work

The process of identification and classification of fruit diseases involves various stages. Initially, segmentation of input image is performed by removing background and later obtaining of infected part. In the next stage, features are extracted using gray level co-occurrence matrix. Later, identified fruits are classified using K-Nearest Neighbor. The complete process is depicted in Fig. 1.

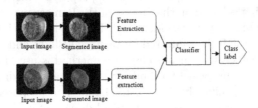

Fig. 1. Flow diagram of identification and classification of fruit disease

3.1   Segmentation

In this work, the purpose of segmentation is to find the regions in the image which are infected. Here the Fuzzy c-means clustering and K-means clustering methods are used to perform segmentation.

Fuzzy C-Means Clustering Method. Fuzzy c-means clustering segmentation method is based on a region growing method. The method uses membership grades of pixels. It is used to classify pixels into appropriate segments. Image segmentation process consists of several steps. The first is input image conversion to chosen feature space, which depends on used clustering method. In this method input image converted from RGB color space to L*u*v* color space and L*, u* and v* values are features respectively, attributes for fuzzy c-means clustering method. After input image conversion, feature space is applied for clustering. After two steps (input image conversion to feature space of clustering method and accomplishing clustering method) is accomplished next segmentation method (Fig. 2).

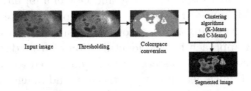

Fig. 2. Flow diagram of segmentation

K-Means Clustering Algorithm. Clustering technique classifies the objects into different groups, partitioning of a data set into subgroup, so that the data in each cluster shares some common trait. K-means is used to determine the groupings of pixels naturally present in the image. K-means clustering algorithm partitions the input dataset into k clusters and each cluster is represented by a cluster center, starting from initial values named seed points. The algorithm computes the distances between the input data points and centers. After distance calculation it group inputs to the nearest center. K-means clustering algorithm method is an unsupervised clustering method and it groups the input data objects into multiple classes based on the distance from each other. Figure 5 shows some of the disease infected fruit images and Fig. 6 shows K means clustering method applied to disease infected images.

Performance Evaluation of Segmentation. Measuring the performance of a segmentation algorithm is necessary for mainly two reasons first is based on a performance metric, good parameter settings can be found for a segmentation algorithm and second is performance of different segmentation approaches can be compared. The region based measures are used when the size and location measurement of the area of the object is essential to detect the disease and is the objective of the segmentation. Therefore, region based measures are used to evaluate the segmentation algorithm.

Measure of Overlap. Area overlap measure (AOM) or the Jaccard similarity measure and is defined as ratio of intersection of segmented infected area S and

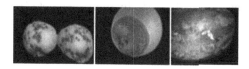

Fig. 3. Few samples of images before applying Fuzzy *c*-means clustering method

Fig. 4. Few samples of images after applying Fuzzy c-means clustering method

Fig. 5. Few samples of images before applying Fuzzy k-means clustering method

Fig. 6. Few samples of images after applying Fuzzy k-means clustering method

ground truth infected area G and the union of segmented infected area S and ground truth area G.

$MOL = \frac{(S \cap G)}{(S \cap G)}$ Where MOL = Measure of overlap, S = Segmented area, G = Ground truth area

Measure of under Segmentation. Measure of under segmentation (MUS) is defined as the ratio of the unsegmented infected area U and the ground truth infected area G.

$M \cup S = \frac{|U|}{|G|}$ Where U = Unsegmented infected area, G = Ground truth area $U = |G/(S \cap G)|$ Where S = Segmented area

Measure of over Segmentation. Measure of over Segmentation is the ratio of segmented non-infected area V and the ground truth area G. Measure of over segmentation (MOS) is given in equation. $MOS = \frac{|V|}{|G|}$ Where, V = Segmented non infected area, S = Segmented infected area $V = |\frac{S}{(S \cap G)}|$ Where, G = Ground truth infected area

Dice Similarity Measure (DSM). This measure is derived from a reliability measure known as the kappa statistic and computes the ratio of the intersection area divided by the mean sum of each individual area. Let C denote the contour of the segmented area, Cr the reference contour, A(C) the set of pixels enclosed by contour C, $A(C_r)$ the set of pixels enclosed by contour C and $|C|$ the cardinality of the set C. Then Dice similarity measure (DSM) is defined as

$$DSM = \frac{2 \times |A(C) \cap A(C_r)|}{A(C) + A(C_r)}$$

Error Rate (ER). The error rate is the normalized agreement of segmentation results and the ground truth. Let C denote the contour of the segmented area, C_r the reference contour, A(C) the set of pixels enclosed by contour, $|C|$ the cardinality of set C, and $\oplus$ exclusive or logical operation. The error rate is given in equation.

$$ER = \frac{|A(C) \oplus A(C_r)|}{A(C) + A(C_r)}$$

4   Experimentation for Segmentation

Performance evaluation parameters are applied to C-means and K-means algorithms by measuring -Measure of Overlap, Measure of under Segmentation, Measure of over Segmentation, Dice Similarity Measure, Error Rate is conducted.

Table 1. Performance evaluation of segmentation results of c-means clustering method

MeasOverSeg	MeasUnderSeg	Error rate	Dice similarity measure	MeasOverlap
0.1692	0.3485	0.5198	0.6732	0.8175
0.1842	0.3367	0.5356	0.6873	0.8212
0.1350	0.3396	0.5100	0.6556	0.8106
0.1509	0.3143	0.5027	0.6927	0.8741
0.1494	0.4139	0.5589	0.6919	0.8279
0.1699	0.3828	0.5166	0.6448	0.8331
0.1655	0.3383	0.5320	0.6712	0.8283
0.1519	0.3215	0.5108	0.7049	0.8450
0.1248	0.2803	0.4707	0.6322	0.8373
0.1595	0.2796	0.4839	0.6691	0.8704

Table 2. Performance evaluation of segmentation results of k-means clustering method

MeasOverSeg	MeasUnderSeg	Error rate	Dice similarity measure	MeasOverlap
0.1898	0.3494	0.5380	0.7192	0.8538
0.2072	0.3613	0.5134	0.7020	0.8441
0.0869	0.2351	0.4445	0.5865	0.7412
0.1975	0.3755	0.5677	0.6882	0.8197
0.1879	0.3787	0.5481	0.7217	0.8549
0.1817	0.3387	0.5224	0.7057	0.8655
0.1310	0.2837	0.5063	0.6336	0.8328
0.1673	0.3158	0.4911	0.6405	0.8157

Table 1 shows the performance evaluation for C-means and Table 2 shows the performance evaluation for k-means.

5   Feature Extraction

Texture feature calculations use the contents of the GLCM to give a measure of the variation in intensity at a pixel of interest. First proposed by Unay and Gosselin [9] in 1973, they characterize texture using a variety of quantities derived from second order image statistics. Co-occurrence texture features are extracted from an image in two steps. First, the pairwise spatial co-occurrences of pixels separated by a particular angle and distance are tabulated using a gray level co-occurrence matrix (GLCM). Second, the GLCM is used to compute a set of scalar quantities that characterize different aspects of the underlying texture. The GLCM is a tabulation of how often different combinations of gray levels co-occur in an image or image section [9]. The GLCM is a $N \times N$ square matrix, where

N is the number of different gray levels in an image. An element $p(i, j, d, \theta)$ of a GLCM of an image represents the relative frequency, where i is the gray level of the pixel p at location (x, y), and j is the gray level of a pixel located at a distance d from p in the orientation. While GLCMs provide θ a quantitative description of a spatial pattern, they are too unwieldy for practical image analysis. The following five GLCM derived features such as contrast, homogeneity, energy, entropy and correlation are extracted.

6   Dataset

In this work we have created our own database despite of existence of other databases as these are less intra class variations or no change in view point. We collected fruit images from World Wide Web in addition to taking up some photographs of fruit that can be found in and around our place. The images are taken to study the effect of the proposed method with large intra class variations. The data set consists of 243 images of 10 different fruit types. Fruit images of Apple, banana, citrus, grape, guava, mango, papaya, peach, pomegranate, watermelon are collected. The images are rescaled to the size 250250. Figure 3(a) shows a sample image of each 10 classes. It is clearly understandable that there is a large intra class variations. The large intra-class variability and the small inter-class variability make this data set very challenging.

7   K-Nearest Neighbour Algorithm

In pattern recognition, the k-Nearest Neighbors algorithm is a non-parametric method used for classification. The K-nearest-neighbor (KNN) algorithm measures the distance between a query scenario and a set of scenarios in the data set. The algorithm can be summarized as: 1. A positive integer k is specified, along with a new sample. 2. Select the k entries in our database which are closest to the new sample. 3. Find the most common classification of these entries. 4. This is the classification given to the new sample.

8   Experimentation

During experimentation, we conducted three different sets of experiments. For the first set of experiments, we used 30% of the images for training and remaining 70% of images for testing. In the second set of experiments, the number of training and testing ratio is 50:50. In the third set of experiments, we used 70% for training and 30% for testing. Table 3.1 shows the results of classification when segmented using C-Means clustering. Table 3.2 shows the results of classification when segmented using K means clustering. Table 3.3 shows the comparison results of two segmentation techniques. By analyzing above table, segmentation using K-Means clustering shows better result when compare to C-means clustering.

Table 3. Results of classification when segmented using c-means, k-means and comparisons of both clustering algorithms

Training samples	C-Means
70	84.66
50	82.45
30	79.86

Training samples	K-Means
70	87.46
50	84.69
30	82.74

Training samples	C-Means	K-means
70	84.66	87.4651
50	82.45	84.6987
30	79.864	82.741

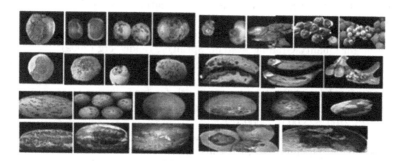

Fig. 7. Sample flower images of fruit classes.

9 Conclusion

In this work, we proposed a system for identification and classification of fruit diseases. The proposed approach is composed of following main steps, initially, segmentation using K-means and C-Means clustering algorithms is performed, later performance evaluation of segmentation algorithm is conducted. After segmentation, features are extracted using Gray Level Co-occurrence Matrix. The k-Nearest Neighbors Algorithm classifier is used to classify the diseases in fruits. Extracted features are fed to classifier for classification. The collected database consists of 10 classes with 243 images. The result of classification has relatively higher accuracy in all cases when segmented using K-Means compared to C-Means clustering algorithms.

References

1. Bhange, M.A., Hingoliwala, H.A.: A review of image processing for pomegranate disease detection. Int. J. Comput. Sci. Inf. Technol. **6**(1), 92–94 (2015)
2. Deshpande, T., Sengupta, S., Raghuvanshi, K.S.: Grading & identification of disease in pomegranate leaf and fruit. Int. J. Comput. Sci. Inf. Technol. **5**(3), 4638–4645 (2014)

3. Kanakaraddi, S., Iliger, P., Gaonkar, A., Alagoudar, M., Prakash, A.: Analysis and grading of pathogenic disease of chilli fruit using image processing. In: Proceedings of International Conference on Advances in Engineering & Technology (2014)
4. Pujari, J.D., Yakkundimath, R., Byadgi, A.S.: Statistical methods for quantitatively detecting fungal disease from fruits images. Int. J. Intel. Syst. Appl. Eng. Adv. Technol. Sci. (IJISAE) 1(4), 60–67 (2013)
5. Pujari, J.D., Yakkundimath, R., Byadgi, A.S.: Grading and classification of anthracnose fungal disease of fruits based on statistical texture features. Int. J. Adv. Sci. Technol. **52** March 2013
6. Pujari, J.D., Yakkundimath, R., Byadgi, A.S.: Reduced color, texture features based identification, classification of affected, normal fruits images. Int. J. Agric. Food Sci. 3(3), 119–127 (2013)
7. Dubey, S.R., Jalal, A.S.: Detection and Classification of Apple Fruit Diseases using Complete Local Binary Patterns. IEEE (2012)
8. Liu, M.H., Ben-Tal, G., Reyes, N.H., Barczak, A.L.C.: Navel Orange Blemish Identification for Quality Grading System. Springer, Heidelberg (2009)
9. Unay, D., Gosselin, B.: A quality grading approach for 'Jonagold' apples. In: Proceedings of SPS (2004)
10. Dubey, S.R., Jalal, A.S.: Adapted approach for fruit disease identification using images. Int. J. Comput. Vis. Image Process. (IJCVIP) 2(3), 44–58 (2012). 978-1-4244-4913-2/09/$25.00 © 2009 IEEE
11. Seng, W.C., Mirisaee, S.H.: A new method for fruits recognition system
12. Haralick, R.M., Shanmungam, K., Dinstein, I.: Textural features of image classification. IEEE Trans. Syst. Man Cybern. **3**, 610–621 (1973). IEEE

Circular Foreign Object Detection in Chest X-ray Images

Fatema Tuz Zohora and K.C. Santosh[✉]

Department of Computer Science, The University of South Dakota,
414 E Clark St, Vermillion, SD 57069, USA
fatema.zohora@coyotes.usd.edu, santosh.kc@usd.edu

Abstract. In automated chest X-ray screening (to detect i.e., Tuberculosis for instance), the presence of foreign objects (buttons, medical devices) hinders it's performance. In this paper, we present a new technique for detecting circular foreign objects, in particular buttons, within chest X-ray (CXR) images. In our technique, we use a pre-processing step that enhances the CXRs. Using these enhanced images, we find the edge images performing four different edge detection algorithms (Sobel, Canny, Prewitt, and Roberts) and after that, we apply some morphological operations to select candidates (image segmentation) in the chest region. Finally, we apply circular Hough transform (CHT) to detect the circular foreign objects on those images. In all tests, our algorithm performed well under a variety of CXRs. We also compared our proposed technique's performance with existing techniques in literature (Viola-Jones and CHT). Our technique was able to excel performance in terms of both detection accuracy and computational time.

Keywords: Chest X-ray (CXR) images · Foreign object detection · Edge detection · Button detection · Circular Hough Transform (CHT) · Viola-Jones

1 Introduction

1.1 Context

Lung diseases are major threats because significant numbers of people suffer from these diseases such as tuberculosis [11], pneumonia, lung cancer and pulmonary edema across the world. The advent of new powerful hardware and software techniques has triggered attempts to develop computer-aided diagnostic (CAD) systems for automatic chest x-ray screening [10,12,13]. However, foreign objects such as buttons on the gown that the patients were wearing or coins/buttons mistakenly swallowed by patients, within the chest x-ray images hinders the performance of the automatic screening process. Figure 1 shows one such CXR which contain several buttons and Fig. 2 shows a closer view of all the buttons in these CXRs. The presence of such objects (especially the ones located within the lung region) hinder the CAD system performance, as they are not due to

© Springer Nature Singapore Pte Ltd. 2017
K.C. Santosh et al. (Eds.): RTIP2R 2016, CCIS 709, pp. 391–401, 2017.
DOI: 10.1007/978-981-10-4859-3_35

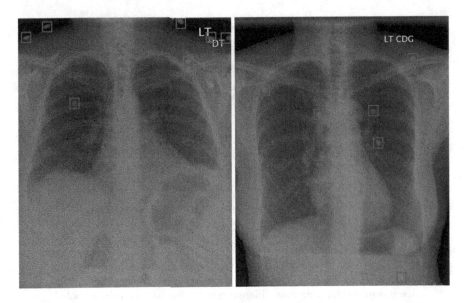

Fig. 1. CXRs containing buttons, boxes marked by red indicate the location of buttons in the images. (Color figure online)

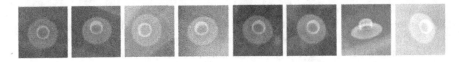

Fig. 2. Closer view of all the buttons in above chest x-ray images.

any lung abnormalities and therefore should not be considered. Therefore, in the screening process precise detection of foreign objects is an important issue for screening of chest diseases in CAD systems.

1.2   Related Works and Our Contributions

Detecting foreign objects in CXRs is a challenging and open research problem. It does not have rich state-of-the-art. In [1], Xue et al. used techniques Viola-Jones and circular Hough transform (CHT) for circular object detection in CXRs. Among them, CHT algorithm has average recall and precision rate and its performance depends on the image intensity. If there is not enough contrast between the objects (buttons in CXRs) and the background image, then the performance of CHT degrades drastically. On the other hand, Viola-Jones algorithm has high false detection rate, which is confusing for the CAD system.

To improve the CAD systems, precise and faster methods require. Unlike [1], we enhance the circular candidate objects from the CXRs applying edge detection, followed by some morphological operations, and then perform CHT on these enhanced circular candidates (see Sect. 2). We compared the performance for four different edge detection algorithms. Finally, we compared our proposed method with the two benchmarking techniques that are used in [1]. In all our tests, the proposed algorithms showed better performance the other existing techniques and achieved 100% precision and 100% recall[1].

1.3 Organization of the Paper

The rest of this paper is structured as follows: In Sect. 2, we give detailed overview of our proposed technique. At first, we briefly discuss the image enhancement (see Sect. 2.1) and then we provide a detailed description of the circular object detection process (see Sect. 2.2). Next, Sect. 3 provides information about the data set and the evaluation protocol (see Sect. 3.1) and results (see Sect. 3.2). Finally, Sect. 4 concludes the paper.

2 The Proposed Technique

In our algorithm, we first enhance the CXRs to increase the contrast between the button objects with their background, using intensity normalization and image adjustment. Next, we apply candidate selection (CS)/circular shape enhancement step to make the circular candidates more distinct and then we perform Circular Hough Transform (CHT) for extracting circular shape objects (e.g., buttons) in these images. For improving the performance, we segment the chest area to identify the region of interest. Figure 3 briefly presents the proposed method workflow.

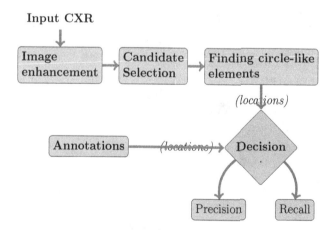

Fig. 3. Workflow: It begins with image enhancement, using intensity normalization and image adjustment. After that candidate (circular object) selection is performed and finally decision is made whether the candidates are circular shape objects.

---

[1] Note that, we have tested using 50 CXR images.

2.1   Image Enhancement

We applied some pre-processing steps on the CXRs to improve the image quality, so that the objects of interest (e.g., buttons) become more evident. The quality of the pre-processing steps strongly affects the performance of the subsequent circular object detection steps.

In our tests, we applied two pre-processing steps: intensity normalization and image adjustment. For intensity normalization, we used the same approach as in [1]. For image adjustment; however, we adopted slightly different approach than [1]. For images without any windowing (intensity window manually optimized by radiologists to visually enhance the lung tissue region) information, [1] performs adjustment only for low contrast images. We, however, observed that applying such adjustments always improve performance. Hence, we applied it as a common pre-processing step to all images.

Figure 4 shows one such low contrast input and the resultant image after enhancement. It also shows the histogram of pixel intensities before and after the adjustment. It can be seen from the figure that the adjusted image has more uniformly distributed intensity values and a higher contrast.

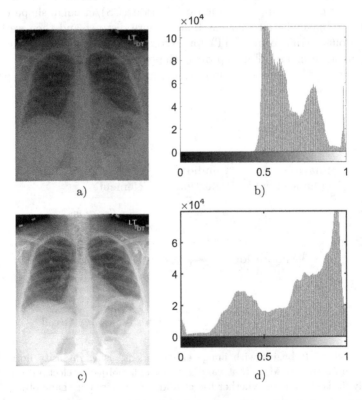

Fig. 4. Image Enhancement: (a) original image, (b) original image histogram, (c) enhanced image, and (d) enhanced image histogram.

2.2 Candidate (Circular Object) Selection

By analyzing the input CXRs, we observe that the buttons in the lung region are mostly of circular/elliptical shape and their boundaries are sharper than other areas. Based on these facts, we extracted circular shape object from CXRs. In our proposed technique, we applied edge detection and then performed some

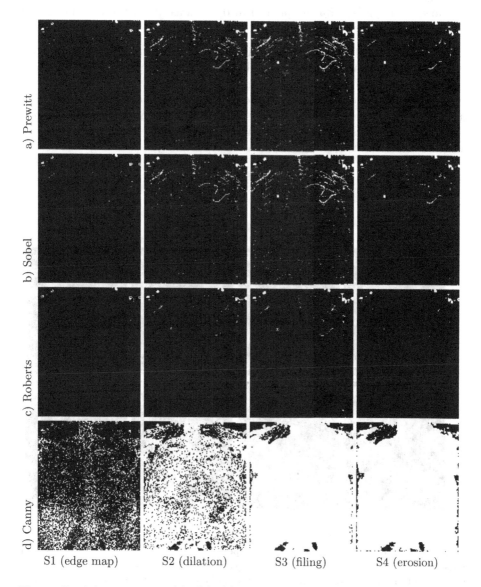

Fig. 5. Candidate selection: (a), (b), (c), and (d) show results for Prewitt, Sobel, Roberts, and Canny edge detection correspondingly. Steps S1, S2, S3, and S4 correspond to the edge detection, dilation, filling, and erosion.

morphological operations on these edge-images to enhance the circular candidates for candidate selection.

Edge detection. We applied edge detection to extract high gradient regions in the image. For this, we tested with four edge detection operators: Canny [5], Prewitt [6], Sobel [7], and Roberts [8]. Figure 5 S1 represents the four resultant edge-images.

Now, we apply several morphological operations [9] on the edge-images to segment and enhance all distinct objects in the image.

Dilation. We first threshold the edge images to create binary edge masks. Such binary edge masks usually mark the object boundaries in the image. However, due to noise or low background to foreground contrast, the edge mask in general is not continuous and hence the corresponding object boundaries have small gaps in between. To overcome this issue, we dilated the edge mask using line shaped structuring elements. We used two linear structuring element **Sl1** and **Sl2** of length 3, oriented at angles 90° and 0° correspondingly.

$$\mathbf{Sl1} = \begin{bmatrix} 1 \\ 1 \\ 1 \end{bmatrix} \quad , \quad \mathbf{Sl2} = \begin{bmatrix} 1 & 1 & 1 \end{bmatrix} \quad \text{and} \quad \mathbf{Sd} = \begin{bmatrix} 0 & 1 & 0 \\ 1 & 1 & 1 \\ 0 & 1 & 0 \end{bmatrix}$$

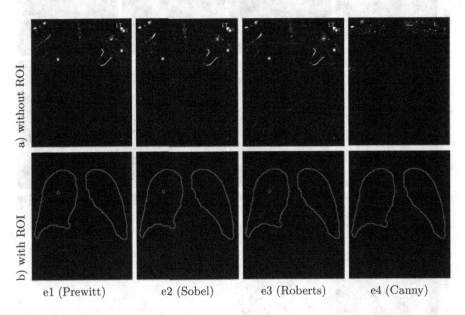

Fig. 6. Decision: e1, e2, e3, and e4 correspond to the Prewitt, Sobel, Roberts and Canny edge images followed by circular object selection steps with CHT. (a) and (b) show resultant circular object detection intermediate step without and with region of interest (ROI) respectively. Circles marked by green indicate the location of circular shape object on the candidate selection images. (Color figure online)

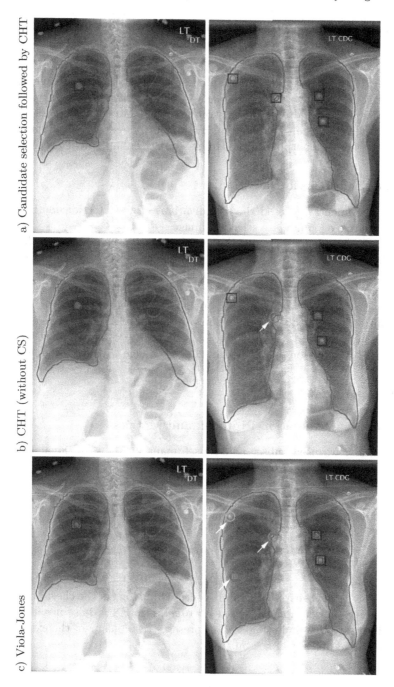

Fig. 7. Circular object detection: (a), (b) and (c) show candidate (circular object) selection (CS) followed by CHT, CHT and Viola-Jones respectively. Here, circles marked by yellow pointed by white arrow indicate false negative, circles marked by red pointed by white arrow indicate false positive and rectangles marked by blue indicate true positive. (Color figure online)

Filling. In this step, we first label all the connected objects in the dilated image. Next, for each such object we perform a flood-fill operation that fills the holes in the objects and generates objects with solid interior.

Erosion. In order to remove noisy small object from the edge images, next we eroded the image. For erosion, we used a diamond-shaped structuring element **Sd**. In this step, we also suppress structures that are connected to the image border. After these steps, we apply CHT for button extraction. Figure 5 S1–S4 shows the step-wise outputs of the circular object enhancement process.

2.3 Decision (Circle Detection)

In our experiments, we used the size invariant circle detection method [2] for detecting circle on candidate selection image.

Our goal is to detect circular shape objects in the lung region of the CXRs, since that is the main area of interest for detecting chest diseases in the CAD systems. The accuracy of the lung segmentation has a big impact on the overall performance of the system. For lung segmentation, we applied anatomical atlases with nonrigid registration algorithm [4]. In Fig. 6, shows the intermediate resultant circular objects detection on candidate selection image with and with out lung segmentation. In Fig. 7(a), shows the complete view of circular foreign object detection on candidate selection image with lung segmentation.

3 Experiments

3.1 Dataset, Evaluation Protocol, and Metrics

In our study, we used subset of data-set maintained by National Library of Medicine which is composed of 50 DICOM images. This subset of data set has total 32 buttons in chest area. We annotated corresponding ground-truths, since they are not available in this data set.

We used precision and recall to measure the performance:

$$Precision = \frac{TP}{TP + FP} \quad and \quad Recall = \frac{TP}{TP + FN},$$

where TP = true positive (accurately detected buttons in the chest area), FP = false positive (inaccurately detected buttons), and FN = false negative (undetected buttons). The following section presents a summary of the experimental setup, test and quick comparison.

3.2 Results and Analysis

In our proposed technique, we applied four different edge operations and additional circular object enhancement step is performed on these edge images. Figure 5 S1–S4 shows all four steps of this approach. It can be seen from the

Table 1. Circular foreign object detection result: candidate selection (CS) followed by CHT

Ground-truth	Detection	TP	FP	FN	Precision	Recall
32	32	32	0	0	1.0	1.0

Table 2. Circular foreign object detection result: CHT (without CS)

Ground-truth	Detection	TP	FP	FN	Precision	Recall
32	22	22	0	10	1	0.69

S4 step of the figure that Prewitt edge detection performs the best with distinct circular objects and less amount of outlier high gradient regions. It also is the fastest method, due to the less amount of high gradient regions. Sobel operator also had similar strong circular objects but it had more outlier high gradient regions too, which leads to false detection and more computation time. On the other hand, Roberts does not have distinct circular objects. However, Canny performs the worst with this approach, because Canny edge-image has many strong connected object all over the image. Hence, after the dilation and filling steps a big portion of the image gets filled and CHT does not work well on such images. Hence, we only include results of this approach with Prewitt edge-images. The computation time is presented in Table 4 and the detection performance in Table 1. Figure 7(a) shows circular foreign object detection results for this approach. Applying this method, we got 100% precision and 100% recall using Prewitt edge image.

Now, we compare our result with two benchmarking techniques Viola-Jones and CHT that are used in [1] for circular object detection.

For CHT algorithm, we followed similar approach as in [1] and used the implementation in MATLAB image processing toolbox. However, instead of using a single radii range, we used a set of three radii ranges ([12, 19], [25, 45] and [46, 60]) and accumulated the results. It not only increases the speed but also accuracy of the detection process. Figure 7(b) shows two output images of this algorithm and Table 2 presents a summary of the results.

For Viola-Jones [3] algorithm, we also applied similar approach in [1]. Due to data set of 50 DICOM CXRs, we trained it using 50 positive images and 50 negative images, and set the number of cascade stages to 6. We observed that Viola-Jones detector perform best using Haar-like feature. Table 3 provides a comparison of the results for this method while varying the number of training and testing images. Figure 7(c) shows two of the resultant outputs of this method.

We also measured the computational time for all circular object detection techniques. Our system has following configuration: intel core i7 processor, windows 7 operating system and MATLAB R2016a. We calculated computational time in seconds per image, on average. Average CXR size is around 3K × 3K.

Table 3. Circular foreign object detection result:: Viola-Jones

Test	Train	Ground-truth	Detection	TP	FP	FN	Precision	Recall
10	40	7	9	6	3	1	0.67	0.86
20	30	18	17	12	5	6	0.71	0.67
30	20	22	22	17	5	5	0.77	0.77
40	10	27	13	11	2	16	0.85	0.41

Table 4. Computational time of button detection techniques

Method	Time (in sec)
CS followed by CHT	8.52
Viola-Jones	18.83
CHT	29.02

Table 4 shows the computational time of all circular object detection techniques. Note that in [1], authors did not report computational time.

4 Conclusion

In this work, we have focused on identifying circular foreign objects such as buttons appearing in lung regions of the chest X-ray images. We presented a novel technique for circular foreign object detection. Our proposed technique is encouraging, both in terms of detection accuracy and computation time. Using Prewitt edge detection followed by circular candidate selection and CHT, we achieved perfect detection of 100% precision and recall. As future work, we plan to test the robustness of our algorithms on larger data sets and extend this work to detect other types of circular and non-circular foreign objects (e.g., medical tubes) that usually appears in CXRs.

References

1. Xue, Z., Candemir, S., Antani, S., Long, L. R., Jaeger., S., Demner-Fushman, D., Thoma, G. R.: Foreign object detection in chest X-rays. In: 2015 IEEE International Conference on Bioinformatics and Biomedicine (BIBM), pp. 956–961. IEEE (2015)
2. Atherton, T.J., Kerbyson, D.J.: Size invariant circle detection, image and vision computing. Image Vis. Comput. **17**(11), 795–803 (1999). Elsevier
3. Viola, P., Jones, M.: Rapid object detection using a boosted cascade of simple features. In: Proceedings of the 2001 IEEE Computer Society Conference on Computer Vision and Pattern Recognition, CVPR 2001, vol. 1, pp. I-511. IEEE (2001)

4. Candemir, S., Jaeger, S., Palaniappan, K., Musco, J.P., Singh, R.K., Xue, Z., Karargyris, A., Antani, S., Thoma, G., McDonald, C.J.: Lung segmentation in chest radiographs using anatomical atlases with nonrigid registration. IEEE Trans. Med. Imaging **33**(2), 577–590 (2014). IEEE

5. Canny, J.: A computational approach to edge detection. IEEE Trans. Pattern Anal. Mach. Intell. **8**(6), 679–698 (1986). IEEE

6. Prewitt, J.M.S.: Object enhancement and extraction. In: Picture Processing and Psychopictorics, 1st edn., vol. 10, pp. 15–19. Academic Press, New York (1970)

7. Sobel, I.: History and definition of the sobel operator. Retrieved from the World Wide Web (2014)

8. Lawrence, G.R.: Machine perception of three-dimensional solids, Ph.D. Thesis, Massachusetts Institute of Technology Cambridge, MA, USA (1963)

9. Soille, P.: Morphological Image Analysis: Principles and Application. Springer, Heidelberg (2013)

10. Schaefer-Prokop, C., Neitzel, U., Venema, H.W., Uffmann, M., Mathias, P.: Digital chest radiography: an update on modern technology, dose containment and control of image quality. Eur. Radiol. **18**(9), 1818–1830 (2008). Springer

11. World Health Organization (WHO): global tuberculosis report (2014)

12. Santosh, K.C., Vajda, S., Antani, S., Thoma, G.R.: Edge map analysis in chest X-rays for automatic pulmonary abnormality screening. Int. J. Comput. Assist. Radiol. Surg., 1–10 (2016). ISSN 1861–6429

13. Karargyris, A., Siegelman, J., Tzortzis, D., Jaeger, S., Candemir, S., Xue, Z., Santosh, K.C., Vajda, S., Antani, S., Folio, L., et al.: Combination of texture and shape features to detect pulmonary abnormalities in digital chest X-rays. Int. J. Comput. Assist. Radiol. Surg. **11**(1), 99–106 (2016). Springer

Biometrics

FaceMatch: Real-World Face Image Retrieval

Eugene Borovikov$^{(\boxtimes)}$ and Szilárd Vajda

U.S. National Library of Medicine, 8600 Rockville Pike, Bethesda, MD 20894, USA
FaceMatch@NIH.gov

Abstract. We researched and developed a practical methodology for face and image retrieval (FIR) based on optimally weighted image descriptor ensemble. We describe a single-image-per-person (SIPP) face image retrieval system for real-world applications that include large photo collection search, person location in disaster scenarios, semi-automatic image data annotation, etc. Our system provides efficient means for face detection, matching and annotation, working with unconstrained digital photos of variable quality, requiring no time-consuming training, yet showing a commercial performance level at its sub-tasks. Our system benefits public by providing practical FIR technology, annotated image data and web-services to a real-world family reunification system.

Keywords: Face recognition · Image retrieval · Family reunification

1 Introduction

Recent advances in content based image retrieval (CBIR) technology have produced many meaningful image-based web-scale search techniques [10], and several web search engines (e.g. google.com/insidesearch, bing.com/images, yandex.com/images) now provide such capabilities. The recent decade has also seen a considerable progress in the face recognition (FR) technology, in some cases approaching human-level accuracy in face detection and verification tasks, especially in the controlled environments [24,30,33].

The modern web-based FR solutions (e.g. facebook.com, plus.google.com) work well in limited users circles that tend to contain tagged pictures of the same few individuals (e.g. family and friends) with multiple shots per person, which allows for recognition model training. There are still very few publicly available *single image per person* (SIPP) training-less face image retrieval systems that can work effectively with millions of faces pictured in unconstrained settings, presenting many challenges for such systems in practice, e.g. disaster recovery:

- data-set size: millions of photos, many near-duplicates[1]
- no constraints on uploaded or query pictures, as in Fig. 1

The rights of this work are transferred to the extent transferable according to title 17 U.S.C. 105.

[1] Vsisually almost identical.

© Springer Nature Singapore Pte Ltd. 2017
K.C. Santosh et al. (Eds.): RTIP2R 2016, CCIS 709, pp. 405–419, 2017.
DOI: 10.1007/978-981-10-4859-3_36

Fig. 1. Unconstrained images present challenges to face recognition systems.

- often suboptimal quality query and database images
- inconsistency in query/gallery face appearance.

Many of those challenges are being addressed by the modern FR systems thanks to the emergence of labeled datasets with unconstrained images [7,8,14] utilized for various competitions.

Typical FR systems would approach the face recognition problem in one of the two formulations [34]: *verification* (photos depict the same person), and *identification* (pick the closest in appearance pictures to the query image). Such systems usually require some form of model training, using multiple photos per individual. They would typically work with a set of visual features extracted from images, imposing (or learning) a measure of visual proximity, modeling human visual perception of faces. While modern automatic face classification/verification methods can work fairly well on good quality face images (fairly well lit, sharp, 80×80 pixels or better), their performance degrades quite rapidly as the image quality drops (e.g. due to burring, scaling, re-compression, etc.) causing a significant degeneration of the visual attributes [27] they rely on.

We formulate our face matching problem as a *face image retrieval* (FIR) problem: given a query photo, return visually similar faces (preferably of the same individual) from a dynamically changing photo collection, thus efficiently reducing the user's search space from many thousands to just tens of likely candidates. This dynamic, open set approach essentially demands the method to be *training-less* and uses the accuracy evaluation methods that are more typical of CBIR (e.g. top-N hit-rate, defined in Sect. 3.2), rather than those used in FR (e.g. receiver operating characteristic [12], ROC).

We implement our SIPP face image retrieval methodology in a real-world *face retrieval* system (FaceMatch), putting no restrictions on input images, detecting and matching faces in arbitrary poses or lighting conditions. Handling large scale photo collections, our system requires no training while dealing with any open sets of images. Our FaceMatch R&D effort addresses many of the mentioned challenges and provides the following functionality:

- semi-automatic annotation for faces and landmarks,
- accurate face detection robust to scale and rotation,
- image descriptors ensemble for improved face image match.

We present FaceMatch evaluation results for the face detection, matching and retrieval tasks, using several publicly available data sets, some of which were annotated at our laboratory. The resulting image retrieval system is geared towards face detection and matching, but it can be used for generic object/scene detection and matching, providing a rich set of tools for practical large-scale image collection management.

In what follows, we discuss our data repository and present the major components of our FaceMatch (FM) system. In each section, we review the relevant publications, describe our approach, and present our experimental results.

2   Image Data Collections

Our approach to face image processing and retrieval is data driven, automatically extracting and weighting features from the data, based on statistics. Annotated image repositories provide ground truth (GT) for the accuracy evaluation and optimization of individual components, e.g. skin mapping for face localization.

Image annotations for *face detection* typically consists of localized face regions (and optionally face landmarks: eyes, nose, mouth, and ears), optional gender and age groups, and some skin patches. Such annotations are done semi-automatically, providing the human annotator with initial face/landmark localization, which can be manually corrected or completed.

Ground truth for *face matching and retrieval* involves labeling face images with face/person ID[2] that are used to assess the quality of retrieval accuracy. Our system targets unconstrained image data-sets, e.g. photos from natural disaster events collected by People Locator (PL). PL data-set consists of 40 thousand weakly text-labeled mostly color, low quality images, some of which are shown in Fig. 1. PL image repository is changing over time, as disasters happen [31].

To help organize PL repository, we have developed several cross-platform image processing and annotation tools to

- reduce data by removing near-duplicates,
- outline faces, profiles as rectangular regions,
- localize facial features: eyes, nose, mouth, and ears,
- extract skin patches from the skin-exposed regions.

These tools were used to partially annotate various image collections with the correct face/profile locations and facial landmarks (eyes, nose, mouth, and ear), as shown in Fig. 2. Using our web-based and desktop annotation tools, our team annotated several thousand PL images, producing:

PL-Faces consists of 2882 low resolution, color PL images, with 3/4 of face regions being frontal and about 1/4 are profile views. The average face and profile diameters are 40 and 50 pixels respectively.

HEPL-500 is a subset of PL containing 500 images from 2011 Haiti earthquake, containing a large variety of faces. Some of them are over-exposed, blurry or occluded as shown in Fig. 1.

---

[2] Unique alpha-numerical sequence, *not* revealing the true person identity.

Fig. 2. Face and landmarks annotation examples

The images were selected to include a large range of skin tones, environments, cameras, resolutions, lighting conditions. Some of the images contain multiple human subjects. The quality of the images varies significantly in illumination, resolution and sharpness.

The annotated PL data-sets are freely available for research purposes. Additional meta-data annotation (e.g. ethnicity, age/group, gender) is also available for some sets. The annotated repository is regularly updated and used for improving face detection and matching performance. We also utilize some publicly available datasets depicting humans in unconstrained environments for algorithm evaluation and tuning:

CalTech Faces set [1] consists of 450 frontal views of 29 subjects, which are taken under varying lighting and background conditions.

Indian Faces set [19] contains 676 face images of 61 individuals (male and female), shot in a studio, exhibiting large variations in head pose, face expression, and lighting.

ColorFERET set [2] contains 2413 facial images of 856 individuals showing frontal and left/right profile head pose variation, optional glasses, and various facial expressions.

Face Detection Data Set and Benchmark (FDDB) set [18] contains 2845 images with 5171 unconstrained faces.

Lehigh Faces set C1 contains 512 images obtained trough our collaboration with Lehigh University [20] containing unconstrained images of celebrities, exhibiting wide variations in background and pose, with mostly light skin tones. Set C2 is similar to C1, containing 550 images, but with a greater variety in faces and their sizes.

For some of the mentioned sets (e.g. CalTech and Indian Faces) we have provided landmark annotations in addition to the supplied head/face regions. Our experiments use those sets to test FaceMatch performance, and the evaluation results are presented in the respective sections.

3   Face Matching

A typical face recognition (FR) system addresses the problem of face matching in one of two formulations: *verification* 1 : 1 (is the same person depicted in two photos) or *identification* 1 : N (find the depicted person in a fixed set of enrolled faces). Our FaceMatch (FM) system understands *face matching* as *single image per person* (SIPP) face retrieval approach utilized for interactive-time searches in large dynamic collections of face images shot in unconstrained environments, i.e. arbitrary resolution, scale, illumination, etc. Thus it is different from *verification* (as our decision is not binary) or *identification* (our image sets are dynamic).

3.1   Background

In the last couple of decades, the face recognition (FR) community has considerably advanced the filed and produced a large number of great papers. Here, we review the research that is most relevant to our approach, describing the methods we drew upon and utilized in the implementation of our FaceMatch.

Face recognition (FR) in general conditions remains to be an open problem that's being researched actively [4,16,28]. Beham [6] gives a good overview of FR techniques and divides them in the following major groups (holistic, feature-based, and soft-computing), providing normalized accuracy (NA) figures, pointing out their advantages and drawbacks.

Unconstrained, *single image per person* (SIPP) face retrieval from a large, dynamically changing (open-set) reference gallery basically requires its face matching to be training-less, robust to pose, occlusion, expression, lighting, and fast, i.e. essentially modeling human perception of unfamiliar faces from a single photo and utilizing some fast approximate indexing for efficiency.

Several very promising methods [13,17,30,32] have been proposed over the past decade, and more recent papers describe systems that are as accurate as a human [29] at the face verification task or sometimes even better [22]. This kind of accuracy typically implies (deep) learning systems with a substantial training stage using hundreds or thousands shots per person, and their matching time may still be not very practical for large scale interactive searches.

Wolf et al. [32] presented an interesting approach to face matching called the one-shot similarity kernel, using a special similarity measure to produce some impressive face matching results on Labeled Faces in the Wild (LFW) collection [14]. We cannot utilize this approach directly, as it requires some training with the background examples.

3.2   Face Image Retrieval

Given a dynamically changing repository of images, we propose a methodology for scalable visual search, effectively solving the face image retrieval problem. Face matching queries can be performed after the face/profile regions in the image collection are localized and their descriptors are indexed. The proposed method accommodates wide variations in face appearance mentioned in Sect. 1.

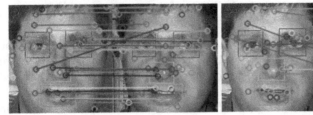

(a) same person, different photos   (b) different faces

Fig. 3. SIFT based matching performance of the system on two example faces: observing more correct correspondences for the same person

Given a query face image, the goal is to match it against the repository of the existing face descriptors, and output a list of likely face candidates ordered by similarity. The matching technique cannot assume that many faces of the same subject are present in the database, and it needs to be robust to illumination, scale and affine transformations.

Among the training-less single-descriptor face matching methods, we decided to focus on rotation and scale invariant key-spot descriptor based matching (e.g. SIFT [21], SURF [5], and ORB [26]), compare them with the holistic descriptors (color HAAR [15] and LBPH [3]), and consider an weighted ensemble of them.

Figure 3 presents two unrestricted key-spot matching examples with SIFT descriptors. The left pair shows matches between two different photos of the same person: the number of correctly matched locations is relatively high. The right pair shows the faces that belong to different people: there are evidently fewer sensible matching locations, e.g. note the non-matched key-spots at the chin location of the faces. Experiments with several datasets revealed that

- single descriptor is insufficient for accurate retrieval,
- some key-spot matches need to be filtered as outliers,
- face landmarks help filter and weigh the matches.

Having several image descriptors per face (HAAR, SURF, SIFT, ORB, LBPH), we experimented with similarity distance-based and similarity rank-based feature combination strategies. The combinations used individual distances $d_i \in [0,1]$ (or ranks) and descriptor matching confidence weights $w_i \in [0,1]$:

DIST: *weighted distance product* $d = \prod d_i{}^{w_i}$
RANK: *rank-based* combination based on Borda count [11].

Evidently, the *decreasing confidence radical* is a particular case of the *weighted distance product*, but it skips the need to specify the weights explicitly, and uses the inverse confidence ordering of the descriptors to compute its distance combination efficiently. The weighted descriptor ensemble hence allows:

- combination of holistic with the key-spot based image descriptors,
- utilization of color along with the texture information,
- optimal descriptor weighting procedure according to the matching confidence,

The optimization procedures are performed using the non-linear simplex [25] method maximizing the retrieval accuracy expressed as F-score or *hit rate*, i.e. the frequency of retrieving the correct subject given a probe photo in a top-N query, i.e. for a set of query images $\mathcal{Q}$, define the hit rate for top-N matches as

$$HitRate(N) = HitCount(N, \mathcal{Q})/|\mathcal{Q}|, \tag{1}$$

where $HitCount(,)$ is a function that counts the successful top-N matches using the query set of size $|\mathcal{Q}|$.

Boosting Key-Spot Matching Accuracy. As Fig. 3 suggests, there may be some key-spot mis-matches, that may in turn cause some false hits in face image queries. To improve matching confidence, our key-spot descriptor matching scheme includes the descriptor symmetric match *cross-check* to ensure that best match relationship works both ways. Our matching scheme also removes the descriptor matches whose distance is greater than two minimum distances across the matching pool, but still can produce some false hits.

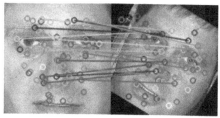 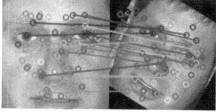

(a) RANSAC scale and rotation   (b) MEADOW scale and rotation

Fig. 4. Spurious SURF key-spot match filtering to ensure geometric consistency

To further improve the key-spot descriptor matching accuracy, we filter out the outliers among the two-way descriptor matches via the inter-view homography [9] based RANdom SAmple Consensus (RANSAC) algorithm [35]. This iterative statistical method computes and uses an affine transform between two images (homography) of the same (or similar) object to assert the key-spot consensus. It works quite well for the near-frontal views of in-plane rotated and scaled faces, as shown in Fig. 4(a), but it may slow down the face matching process because of is iterative nature and having to estimate the homography matrix at each iteration.

Increasing Key-Spot Matching Speed. As quicker alternative to RANSAC, we researched and developed MEdian-based Anomalous Distance Outliers Weeding (MEADOW) method. As the name suggests, the method weeds out the key-spot outliers, i.e. matches with too unlikely geometric distances between the corresponding key-spots. Compared to RANSAC, MEADOW is intended to be

- more efficient: no iterative estimation of homography
- less constrained: no key-spot co-planarity assumption

MEADOW is expected to be less accurate than RANSAC in general, but for practical face image matching applications, their accuracies are comparable.

In MEADOW, for each two-way descriptor match, we compute the Euclidean distance between their key-points (not descriptors) p and q, and we discard that match as a false positive, if that distance $D = |p - q|$ is an outlier among all the distances in the match sample: $|D - M| > T$, as shown in Fig. 5, where M is the sample's distance median (dashed green lines), and T is computed as a median deviation from M. MEADOW is a simpler (than RANSAC) method for filtering out the largest outliers from a sample, which is what we intend for the key-spot distances to ensure the key-spot geometric consistency. As we can see in Fig. 4(b), MEADOW efficiently handles the outliers, filtering out most of the false matches, typically five times faster than RANSAC, resulting in a similar matching accuracy.

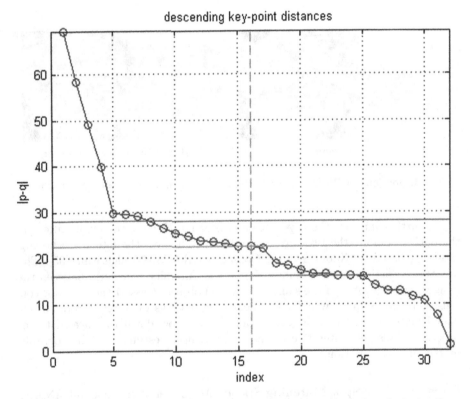

Fig. 5. MEADOW filters distance outliers above and below the median deviation lines (red) with respect to the sample's median (green). (Color figure online)

Distance Normalization. The *cumulative difference* between two face images is computed as a median (also to be robust to the outliers) among their closest descriptor matches:

$$\hat{d}(f, g) = \mu_{i=1,...,I}\{\min_{j=1,...,J} \tilde{d}(s_i(F), s_j(G))\} \tag{2}$$

where μ stands for the *median*, $\tilde{d}$ is the matching distance between descriptors $s_i(F)$ and $s_j(G)$ computed for their images F and G, with the (filtered) descriptor match counts I and J respectively.

Since a difference measure (e.g. $\hat{d}$) may range in $[0, \infty)$, it can be *normalized* to $[0, 1)$ via the monotone increasing and smooth arctangent mapping

$$d(x) = \arctan(ax)/a \tag{3}$$

where $a = \frac{\pi}{2}$, which maps an infinite range to a unit, and behaves quite linearly near 0, having $d(0) = 0$ and $d'(0) = 1$.

For easier distance thresholding, one can scale the normalized distance to satisfy some perceptual similarity constraints, depending on the descriptor and the image set $\delta(x) = d(\alpha x)$ by picking $\alpha > 0$ such that $\delta(x) \leq 0.5$ for the similar faces, and $\delta(x) > 0.5$ for the dissimilar ones, but that would involve some human judgment and semi-manual grouping of similar faces. Clearly, this monotone distance normalization approach applies to any distance measure.

Descriptor Search Space Partitioning. While dealing with large unconstrained face image datasets (over $40\,\mathrm{K}$ images), our system, to be practical, needs to retrieve face images within interactive (about $1\,\mathrm{s}$) turn-around time intervals. To accomplish that we researched and developed the *attribute bucketing* strategy and utilized the *approximate nearest neighbor* (FLANN) searches [23].

We have noticed that our image typically carry gender and age-group meta-information, which allowed us to partition the search space into a number of age and gender groups (called buckets), which we could query in parallel using multi-threading. This allowed us to optimize our query turn-around times by a factor of 9 or more, especially when we introduced sub-bucketing within groups.

Utilization of FLANN resulted in the additional (five-fold on average) queries speed-up with a small penalty (a couple of percentage points) to the retrieval accuracy and a small one-time clustering overhead during the index loading and incremental update. Overall, the face image query turn-around times are kept under a second for our image data-sets. Provided enough of the multi-core power it should be scalable to the web-scale sets of millions of images.

3.3 Experiments

Due to the sources of our target image collections, we very rarely have more than one picture of the same person. Hence, in our face retrieval evaluations, we had to rely on a mixture of datasets, e.g. the CalTech Faces data mixed with some typical PL photos, described in Sect. 2.

Color-Aware Face Matching. For the color-aware face matching experiments, we considered IndianFacesDB and ColorFERET datasets (described in Sect. 2), containing color images of male and female faces with good variations in lighting, pose, and expression (Table 1).

Table 1. Color-aware face matching top-1 hit rates

descriptor	IndianFaces		ColorFERET	
	alone	+CW	alone	+CW
CW	0.52	-	0.78	-
SIFT	0.61	**0.66**	0.91	**0.95**
SURF	0.75	**0.78**	0.96	**0.98**
SURF+SIFT	0.76	**0.79**	0.97	**0.98**

We observe that our CW descriptor alone is a weaker matcher than any of the key-point based descriptors, but it considerably improves the query hit rates, when included in the ensemble with the stronger (but color-blind) descriptors. This behavior suggests that bringing color-awareness to the descriptor ensemble helps improve the face matching performance on color images.

Descriptor Ensemble Matching. For the FaceMatch overall visual feature ensemble (with optimally weighted descriptors), the top-N hit rate accuracy results on the available benchmark datasets are summarized in Table 2 in comparison with the commercial face matching engine FaceSDK.

Table 2. FaceSDK (FSDK) vs. FaceMatch (FM) hit rate accuracy in top-N queries

top-N	CalTech		ColorFERET		IndianFacesDB	
	FSDK	FM	FSDK	FM	FSDK	FM
1	.98	.98	.74	.98	.69	.79
3	.99	.98	.75	.98	.73	.85
5	.99	.99	.75	.99	.76	.87
10	.99	.99	.76	.99	.79	.90
20	.99	1.0	.76	1.0	.83	**.92**

On the relatively easy CalTech dataset (with large, mostly frontal faces), accuracy figures of both FaceMatch and FaceSDK are predictably high and close to each other. On the more challenging (than CalTech) ColorFERET benchmark dataset with considerable variations in head pose and lighting, FaceSDK clearly yields to FaceMatch, which performs just as well as it does on CalTech, reaching the statistically guaranteed retrieval of the correct person within top 20 retrieved records. The accuracy on even more challenging (than CalTech or ColorFERET) IndianFacesDB dataset is noticeably lower for both competitors probably due to some extreme head pose variations, but FaceMatch clearly outperforms FaceSDK, providing the 92% likelihood of retrieving the right person in top 20 visual query results.

4 System

Our system is cross-platform and production-level. The core FaceMatch (FM) imaging code is written in C++. It relies on open source libraries (e.g. STL, OpenCV, OpenMP) and is packaged as a shared library. This makes it deployable for desktop applications or over as web services. The key focus during the web integration was to ensure the top performance across all FaceMatch operations, e.g. list, ingest, query and remove. Our design takes advantage of multi-core architectures by exploiting task level and functional parallelism inside all critical modules. For instance, the web service can answer multiple queries while ingesting or removing descriptors.

The FaceMatch (FM) services are currently utilized in a real-world family re-unification system, which adds a visual modality to the otherwise text based searches. The user is free to browse the database by inspecting the details of the retrieved records and optionally re-submitting queries using the retrieved faces as examples. The output of the FaceMatch module can be optionally fused with the text query results for an increased query accuracy.

A sample visual query results are shown in Fig. 6, and we can see how the system retrieves the faces similar to the query in the ascending distance-to-query order, observing the same person photos being at the top of the result set.

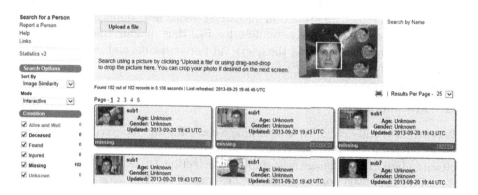

Fig. 6. FaceMatch sample visual query results on the CalTech+PL data

5 Summary

Targeting a practical system handling web-scale photo collections with real-world images, we researched and developed a *single-image-per-person* (SIPP) query-by-photo methodology (FaceMatch) working with unconstrained images of variable quality, implemented it as a cross-platform software library, exposing its face image retrieval functionality via web-services, which can be consumed by real-world applications, such as efficient photo collection search for the disasters management, missing children location, and law enforcement organizations.

5.1 Applications

FaceMatch services currently benefit public by providing its SIPP face image query capability to a real-world family re-unification system, which includes a set of mobile applications and a website accepting missing/found people records and answering (visual) queries about them. Since text-based records may be inexact or incomplete, queries by photo greatly improve the user experience and provide the visual modality reducing the search space.

With tens of thousands records in a real-world collection, FaceMatch can reduce the user browsing set of most likely candidates to about 20 with the user-friendly query turn-around time of about a second. FaceMatch is quite robust to *cross-cultural face matching*, retrieving visually matching records much faster (and in some cases more accurately) than a human emergency coordinator under stress in case of an emergency. This helps save time and effort for the disaster event managers, health emergency coordinators and people who search for their missing relatives.

FaceMatch also provides its robust face detection and general image matching services, which have been successfully utilized at detecting pictures with faces in a multi-million document collection of medical documents. Our rapid image search services are utilized in identifying visual near-duplicates, efficiently reducing image collections, e.g. by 40% for PL, thus making the system more user-friendly by nearly halving the query turn-around time and presenting non-duplicate results.

5.2 Methodology

We researched and developed several image matching and face recognition methods, evaluated a few state-of-the-art systems on available datasets, developed a software library for: (i) image near-duplicate detection, (ii) general image queries, (iii) robust face detection, (iv) efficient face matching. The major features that make FaceMatch practical for the real-world face image retrieval:

- *unconstrained* images handling,
- *training-less* single-image-per-person (SIPP) approach,
- *cross-platform* approach to the implementation.

Our technology matches the performance of the leading open-source and commercial solutions. We have made several important improvements to the existing methods and developed some new ones:

Face detection was improved by using human skin tone information and facial landmarks along with default (color-blind) face detection algorithm. The skin regions are mapped using an artificial neural network (ANN). On public data sets, our face detector was more accurate than the available state-of-the-art engines, both commercial and open-source.

Face matching utilized a SIPP approach using weighted image descriptor ensemble to optimize the matching accuracy without training. Our MEADOW key-point filtering, attribute bucketing and FLANN indexing helped speed-up queries up to 20-times (compared to the linear search), keeping turn-around time within one second for a typical real-world collection.

We have annotated thousands of face images in the PL dataset with face, profile and landmark regions. The annotated datasets are public domain and can be made available upon request.

5.3 Prospects

We plan to expand the number of applications for our public FaceMatch services. Those may include visual search by photo for missing children, pets, criminal suspects, as well as detecting disaster and crime scenes. From the technical prospective, our R&D team is actively engaged in research and development that lead to (i) robust gender, age and ethnicity estimation, and (ii) general object and animal detection/matching.

We are currently researching the *human-in-the-loop* (HiL) approach for naturally merging face image retrieval with annotation, making both more efficient via semi-supervised and incremental machine learning techniques as well as via more natural human-computer interactions, which may include the development of more convenient game-like visual annotation tools, and use of crowd-sourcing for developing more comprehensive testing and evaluations data sets, including video, because mobile technology tends to generate an increasing amount of moving pictures often with characteristic audio tracks, quite useful for practical face and object image retrieval.

Acknowledgments. This research is supported by the Intramural Research Program of the National Library of Medicine at National Institutes of Health. We thank our colleagues from Lister Hill National Center for Biomedical Communications (LHNCBC) Michael C. Bonifant, Girish Lingappa, Sema Candemir, Le Lan and Tehseen Sabeer for their technical assistance during the experiments. Our special thanks to Michael Gill, Sameer Antani and George Thoma for their valuable advice and general guidance.

References

1. Caltech frontal face dataset. http://www.vision.caltech.edu/archive.html
2. The color FERET database. http://www.nist.gov/itl/iad/ig/colorferet.cfm
3. Ahonen, T., Hadid, A., Pietikäinen, M.: Face recognition with local binary patterns. In: Pajdla, T., Matas, J. (eds.) ECCV 2004. LNCS, vol. 3021, pp. 469–481. Springer, Heidelberg (2004). doi:10.1007/978-3-540-24670-1_36
4. Azeem, A., Sharif, M., Raza, M., Murtaza, M.: A survey: face recognition techniques under partial occlusion. Int. Arab J. Inf. Technol. 11(1), 1–10 (2014)
5. Bay, H., Tuytelaars, T., Gool, L.V.: SURF: speeded up robust features. In: European Conference on Computer Vision, pp. 404–417 (2006)
6. Beham, M.P., Roomi, S.M.M.: A review of face recognition methods. Int. J. Pattern Recogn. Artif. Intell. 27(04), 1356005 (2013). http://www.worldscientific.com/doi/abs/10.1142/S0218001413560053
7. Beveridge, J., Phillips, P., Bolme, D., Draper, B., Givens, G., Lui, Y.M., Teli, M., Zhang, H., Scruggs, W., Bowyer, K., Flynn, P., Cheng, S.: The challenge of face recognition from digital point-and-shoot cameras. In: 2013 IEEE Sixth International Conference on Biometrics: Theory, Applications and Systems (BTAS), pp. 1–8, September 2013
8. Borovikov, E., Vajda, S., Lingappa, G., Antani, S., Thoma, G.: Face matching for post-disaster family reunification. In: IEEE International Conference on Healthcare Informatics, pp. 131–140, September 2013
9. Chum, O., Pajdla, T., Sturm, P.: The geometric error for homographies. Comput. Vis. Image Underst. 97(1), 86–102 (2005). http://www.sciencedirect.com/science/article/pii/S1077314204000244
10. Dharani, T., Aroquiaraj, I.: A survey on content based image retrieval. In: 2013 International Conference on Pattern Recognition, Informatics and Mobile Engineering (PRIME), pp. 485–490, February 2013
11. van Erp, M., Schomaker, L.: Variants of the borda count method for combining ranked classifier hypotheses. In: 7th International Workshop on Frontiers in Handwriting Recognition, pp. 443–452 (2000)
12. Fawcett, T.: An introduction to ROC analysis. Pattern Recogn. Lett. 27(8), 861–874 (2006). ROC Analysis in Pattern Recognition. http://www.sciencedirect.com/science/article/pii/S016786550500303X
13. Gao, Y., Qi, Y.: Robust visual similarity retrieval in single model face databases. Pattern Recogn. 38(7), 1009–1020 (2005)
14. Huang, G.B., Ramesh, M., Berg, T., Learned-Miller, E.: Labeled faces in the wild: a database for studying face recognition in unconstrained environments. University of Massachusetts, Amherst, Technical report (2007)
15. Jacobs, C.E., Finkelstein, A., Salesin, D.H.: Fast multiresolution image querying. In: Proceedings of the 22nd Annual Conference on Computer Graphics and Interactive Techniques, pp. 277–286. ACM, New York (1995)
16. Jafri, R., Arabnia, H.R.: A survey of face recognition techniques. JiPS 5(2), 41–68 (2009)
17. Jain, A., Klare, B., Park, U.: Face matching and retrieval in forensics applications. MultiMedia 19(1), 20–20 (2012). IEEE
18. Jain, V., Learned-Miller, E.: FDDB: a benchmark for face detection in unconstrained settings. Technical report UM-CS-2010-009, University of Massachusetts, Amherst (2010)

19. Jain, V., Mukherjee, A.: The indian face database (2002). http://vis-www.cs.umass.edu/~vidit/IndianFaceDatabase/
20. Kim, E., Huang, X., Heflin, J.: Finding VIPs - a visual image persons search using a content property reasoner and web ontology. In: 2011 IEEE International Conference on Multimedia and Expo (ICME), pp. 1–7, July 2011
21. Lowe, D.G.: Distinctive image features from scale-invariant keypoints. Int. J. Comput. Vis. **60**(2), 91–110 (2004)
22. Lu, C., Tang, X.: Surpassing human-level face verification performance on LFW with GaussianFace. CoRR abs/1404.3840 (2014)
23. Muja, M., Lowe, D.G.: Fast approximate nearest neighbors with automatic algorithm configuration. In: International Conference on Computer Vision Theory and Applications, pp. 331–340 (2009)
24. Naruniec, J.: A survey on facial features detection. Int. J. Electron. Telecommun. **56**(3), 267–272 (2010)
25. Nelder, J.A., Mead, R.: A simplex method for function minimization. Comput. J. **7**(4), 308–313 (1965)
26. Rublee, E., Rabaud, V., Konolige, K., Bradski, G.: ORB: an efficient alternative to SIFT or SURF. In: IEEE International Conference on Computer Vision, pp. 2564–2571, November 2011
27. Scheirer, W.J., Kumar, N., Iyer, V.N., Belhumeur, P.N., Boult, T.E.: How reliable are your visual attributes? In: Proceedings of SPIE, vol. 8712, pp. 87120Q-1–87120Q-12 (2013)
28. Sharif, M., Mohsin, S., Javed, M.Y.: A survey: face recognition techniques. Res. J. Appl. Sci. Eng. Technol. **4**(23), 4979–4990 (2012)
29. Taigman, Y., Yang, M., Ranzato, M.A., Wolf, L.: Deepface: closing the gap to human-level performance in face verification. In: Proceedings of the IEEE Computer Society Conference on Computer Vision and Pattern Recognition (2014)
30. Tan, X., Chen, S., Zhou, Z.H., Zhang, F.: Face recognition from a single image per person: a survey. Pattern Recogn. **39**(9), 1725–1745 (2006)
31. Thoma, G., Antani, S., Gill, M., Pearson, G., Neve, L.: People Locator: a system for family reunification. IT Prof. **14**, 13–21 (2012)
32. Wolf, L., Hassner, T., Taigman, Y.: The one-shot similarity kernel. In: International Conference on Computer Vision, pp. 897–902. http://www.openu.ac.il/home/hassner/projects/Ossk
33. Zhang, C., Zhang, Z.: A survey of recent advances in face detection. Technical report, Microsoft (2010)
34. Zhou, H., Mian, A., Wei, L., Creighton, D., Hossny, M., Nahavandi, S.: Recent advances on singlemodal and multimodal face recognition: a survey. IEEE Trans. Hum. Mach. Syst. **44**(6), 701–716 (2014)
35. Zuliani, M., Kenney, C.S., Manjunath, B.S.: The multiRANSAC algorithm and its application to detect planar homographies. In: IEEE International Conference on Image Processing. http://vision.ece.ucsb.edu/publications/05ICIPMarco.pdf

Evaluation of Texture Features for Biometric Verification System Using Handvein and Finger Knuckleprint

H.D. Supreetha Gowda$^{(\boxtimes)}$ and G. Hemantha Kumar

Department of Computer Science, University of Mysore, Mysore 560 007, India
supreethad3832@gmail.com

Abstract. In this paper, we have evaluated a biometric verification system of universal acceptable hand based modalities. We have employed the Dorsal Handvein and finger Knuckle print modalities that are recently emerging modalities in the biometrics field. The Handvein and finger knuckle print databases are subjected to extract the texture features from the texture classification techniques like LBP, LPQ and Gabor filter. We compare both the modalities separately and conclude from the results obtained which modality performs better on texture descriptors. The results are presented graphically using the ROC curve which is plotted for GAR (Genuine Acceptance Rate) v/s FAR (False Acceptance Rate) with the threshold benchmark values of FAR $(0.01\%, 0.1\%, 1\%)$ in illustrating the performance of verification rate. From our experimental results, it is clearly evident that the LPQ texture features are more suitable for both modalities.

Keywords: Handvein · Texture features · LPQ · Finger knuckleprint · GAR · FAR

1 Introduction

In a technological generation at various levels of government and private sector biometric recognition is being promoted as a reliable authentication system that can help to identify unauthorized users, biometric technology is a real-time tool mainly used for national security, law enforcement, network security, access control etc. Confidential transaction needs highly secure biometric systems to avoid fraudulent actions. Traditionally, individual's identity is determined by Tokens (What You Have), Passwords (What You Know) and Biometric trait (What You Are). These conventional methods are not reliable and fail to meet the desirable requirements. Biometric identifiers are more reliable than token based and knowledge based identification systems, because they rely on surrogate representations. Capturing the biometric data and saving it securely tied with the individual is called Enrollment. The biometric authentication is done either by identification or verification. Biometric Identification systems are described as a 1-to-n matching system, that reads a sample and compares the sample against

© Springer Nature Singapore Pte Ltd. 2017
K.C. Santosh et al. (Eds.): RTIP2R 2016, CCIS 709, pp. 420–428, 2017.
DOI: 10.1007/978-981-10-4859-3_37

every template already in the database and the authentication is done to access the system [16]. Biometric verification refers to verify an individual by matching the new biometric sample with the specific biometric already stored in the database, it is also called as 1-to-1 matching system, the cost of verification is less compared to identification.

In this work, we have used two recently developing modalities namely handvein and Finger Knuckle Print (FKP). Handvein is one of the safest biometric and the patterns are underlying in the skin, so the falsification is difficult [1]. This modality is network of blood vessels, stable, contactless image acquisition, difficult to forge, hard to damage and even the twins have different handveins. Hand veins are not used widely, due to less availability of the databases and the cost of acquisition device is high. On the other hand the finger knuckle print is a newly emerged biometric trait, the pattern present on back surface of fingers, the texture is very rich and has better discriminative power compared to fingerprint, because the fingerprint is prone to damage for the laborers and the cultivators who practice agricultural work [6]. Knuckle print is a new modality used in recent days and less research work is explored on this trait. The Characteristics of these physiological biometric traits is shown in Table 1.

Table 1. Characteristics of handvein and knuckleprint biometrics

Biometric	Characteristics						
	Universality	Unicity	Persistent	Collectability	Permanence	Acceptability	Circumvention
Finger knuckleprint	Medium	Medium	Medium	Medium	Low	Medium	Low
Handvein	Medium	Medium	Medium	High	Medium	High	Medium

In general every biometric system works in this flow, Sensor module: a quality checking module which acquires the biometric data of an individual. Preprocessing of raw data is necessary. Feature extraction module: captures biometric data and processes to extract salient features. Matching module: also called as decision making module that measures the similarity of features during recognition with a reference template by applying various methods like probabilistic measures, neural networks, etc. Decision module maintains the expressive templates for enrolled users as a reference for future comparison in a central database. Identified features are compared by the system with the stored reference to establish whether claimed identity is accepted or rejected [17].

Performance parameters used for verification of biometric are Equal Error Rate (EER): Predetermination of threshold values for its false acceptance rate and its false rejection rate, FAR = FRR, also called as crossover error rate (CER). False Acceptance Rate (FAR): A statistic used to measure biometric performance where invalid inputs are incorrectly matched to another biometric subject when operating in the verification task. Genuine Acceptance Rate (GAR): is an overall accuracy measurement of a biometric system. It is calculated by the formula: $GAR = 1 - FRR$. Receiver Operating Characteristics (ROC): ROC curve is plotted to analyze the performance of the system graphically, the threshold is computed and performance metrics used in plotting ROC graph are GAR and FAR [11].

Handvein and Finger Knuckle Print (FKP) biometrics have many advantages that makes it preferable in many biometric applications such as acceptability, availability of strong feature extraction algorithms, easy for image acquisition etc. On the other hand, even though there exists several studies in the literature that have showed on applying particular texture based algorithms on these two modalities, there are no evidences of solitary work that reports fusion method for handvein and FKP. In order to evaluate the texture feature extraction algorithms of these two modalities in real time scenarios, performance analysis needs to be carried out. In this work, we have evaluated the performance of texture feature extraction algorithms for handvein and FKP.

The outline of the paper is as follows: Sect. 2 gives review of literature related to handvein and FKP biometric systems. Section 3 presents the methods employed. Section 4 discusses experimental results. Conclusion and future work are drawn in Sect. 5.

2 Review of Literature

Di Huang et al. [1] proposed a handvein recognition model employing LBP (Local Binary Pattern) and BC (Binary Coding) to extract either the texture or shape features of hand vein modality and the features are represented using the Graphical notation. The vein shape features are extracted by minutiae features and by a BC (binary coding) to analyze skeletal image, the image is intensified using the Gaussian filter. LBP, BC are fused to arrive at a final decision. The number of images are increased in the gallery and accuracy at higher level is achieved. Jun Wang et al. [2] proposed hand vein recognition system, they have used a relatively cheap charge coupled device (CCD) camera lens of infrared light to record the underlying hand vein images at lower resolution, Segmentation is the challenging task and vital aspect in biometric authentication, where the background image has to be separated and the ROI (Region of Interest) should be extracted. The Gaussian low pass filter is applied on original images to remove the high spatial frequency and the binary images obtained from Niblack algorithm are subjected to sobel operator to emphasize regions, The boundary is determined to extract the ROI of the image, PCA, LDA and Gabor algorithms are used for classification.

The structure of Hand vein is a time invariant property and detected only live. Due to uneven illumination and difficulty in extracting ROI (region of interest), preprocessing is a challenging task and obtaining feature points in Handvein Biometric modality. Inshirah Rossan and Maleika Heenaye-Mamode Khan [3] proposed preprocessing techniques for hand vein images. The contrast of the original image is enhanced by histogram equalization, The Contrast limited adaptive histogram equalization (CLAHE) is employed for preprocessing followed by mean-c, median-c and wellner's adaptive threshold. Threshold is done to separate the background from foreground image, FAR (False Acceptance Rate) and FRR (False Reject Rate) are used as performance measures. Yun peng Hu et al. [4] proposed a hand vein recognition model. The Geometric operation, rotation when subjected on hand vein images leads to degradation of system performance. These drawbacks have been addressed in their work, the interconnection points in the hand vein images like intersection point and terminating end points are used as features. False acceptance rate is one of the performance measure which cannot be ignored while considering the biometric authentication system's accuracy.

Ahmed M. Badawi [5] proposed a hand vein verification system, the shape and size of the hand vein modality are the features to be extracted. The vein tree is different from each individual and the vein pattern of both the hands of an individual is also different, Gaussian filter is used in smoothening and the edges are also retained to analyze statistical performance measures. ROC curve is plotted to analyze the performance of the system graphically. Aditya Nigam et al. [6] proposed a finger knuckleprint based system. The ROI regions, central knuckle line and central knuckle point is extracted by Gabor filter, the image samples are enhanced using CLAHE (Central Limited Adaptive Histogram Equalization) for better discrimination, the images are binarized and edges are detected using the canny edge detection method, ROC curve is plotted and EER(Equal Error Rate) is reported. Zahra S. Shariatmadar and Karim Faez [7] proposed a finger knuckle-print recognition system. Left and right index fingers and middle fingers are used for experimentation based on multi-instance fusion. Gabor features are extracted and the dimensionality is reduced using the combination of subspace algorithms PCA and LDA. Scores of the feature vectors are normalized and the client is decided whether he is a genuine or imposter.

Lin Zhang et al. [8] fused the local features of finger knuckle print that are independent of each other like local phase, local orientation, phase congruency that are extracted from gabor filter, by combining those local features with fourier transformed global features, the system recognition performance is increased instead of using the local features individually. S. KhellatKihel et al. [9] proposed a multimodal biometric system employing the finger knuckleprint, fingerprint and finger vein structure modalities by selecting the discriminating features among those modalities, which in turn reduces the memory usage. 2D gabor filter is used for extracting the texture features. Feature level and decision level fusion is used for fusing the features of three modalities. Classification is done by SVM a discriminating classifier defined by separating hyperplane, cosine distance and KNN. Vandana Yadava et al. [10] proposed a finger knuckle print identification system using Kekre's Hybrid Wavelet transform type I and type II for feature vector coefficients. Hybrid wavelet features are generated and subjected to Intra-class testing and Inter-class testing to verify the claimed identity as genuine or imposter.

3   Methodologies

We have chosen the hand based modalities for our experimentation, from the review of literature these modalities are subjected to discriminate by the texture. Nevertheless, we have applied texture descriptors such as LBPV, LPQ and Gabor filter. The working approach of each feature extraction algorithms in detailed is as follows.

3.1   Local Binary Pattern and Its Variant (LBPV)

The original LBP operator, introduced by Ojala et al. [13] in 1996. Lbp is a texture based classification model for gray scale image, which is translation invariant and computationally simple. A central pixel is selected in the input image and the binary code is calculated by thresholding the neighborhood over the center pixel. If the center pixel's value is greater than the neighboring value, then the binary value is set to '1' else the binary value is set to '0'. If the value of the neighboring pixels does not change, then it is featureless. If there is at most two transitions in the cell then it is called uniform pattern, else if it contains more than two transitions it is said to be non-uniform pattern. The basic 8-bit version of the LBP operator considers only eight neighbors which is of 256 dimensional vector, which is used as a texture descriptor. Histogram of all the independent cells is computed and the feature vectors are normalized. LBPV is a rotation invariant descriptor that descriptors the local contrast information, higher variance has more discriminative texture features. Guo et al. [15] proposed the calculation adaptive weight in histogram of LBP code, the LBPV histogram is computed as,

$$LBPV_{P,R}(K) = \sum_{I=1}^{N} \sum_{J=1}^{M} W[(LBP_{P,R}(I, J), K \in (0, K)]$$ (1)

where K indicates the maximal value of LBP codes.

3.2   The Local Phase Quantization (LPQ)

Ojansivu originally proposed LPQ operator and Heikkila [14] as a texture based classification method, which is blur insensitive and rotation invariant. Lpq is a fourier transform quantizer. Fourier domain using the convolution theorem is given by, $G(u) = F(u) H(u)$, where G, F, and H are discrete Fourier transforms. $H(u)$ is the point spread function of the blur image and $F(u)$ is the original image.

The magnitude and phase of the image can be separated by,

$$|G(u)| = |F(u)| * |H(u)|$$ (2)

The Fourier transform is a two valued function and and H must equal 0 or Π. The phase is computed by imaginary and real points of the feature vector f_x.

$$f_x = [Ref_x^c, Imf_x^c] \text{ where } [F(u_1, x), F(u_2, x), F(u_3, x), F(u_4, x)]$$

and the frequency vectors are given by, $u_1 = [a, 0]^T, u_2 = [0, a]^T, u_3 = [a, a]^T, u_4 = [a, a]^T$.

3.3   Gabor

Gabor filter is a local texture descriptor named after Dennis Gabor. Gabor wavelet represents spatial orientation and frequency characteristics and similar to human visual system, similar to windowed Fourier transform [13]. It is a multi-resolution filter used in many applications. 2D wavelet decomposition with Gabor filter is applied to extract local features. The 2D gabor filter is modulated by gaussian kernel and complex sinusoidal function, on applying gabor filter to obtain real and imaginary features with orientation θ and frequency f is given by

$$f(x, y, f, \theta, \sigma_x, \sigma_y) = \frac{1}{2\pi\sigma_x, \sigma_y} exp\{-\frac{x^2 + y^2}{2\sigma^2} + f(x\cos\theta + y\sin\theta)\} \quad (3)$$

σ_x and σ_y are standard deviations along x and y directions.

4   Experimental Results

In this section, we have presented the extensive performance analysis of hand based biometric system. In our experiments, we have selected two recent emerging texture modalities, Handvein and finger knuckle print. We have employed the databases such as Cluj university-Handvein database and PolyU- Finger Knuckle Print (FKP). In Handvein modality we have considered 100 users such that each user has 5 samples of handvein image, in that 3 samples for training and 2 for testing. In PolyU- Finger Knuckle print, out of 165 users we have considered first 100 users for our experiments. Such that each user has 5 samples, out of which we have considered 3 samples for training and 2 samples for testing purpose.

Texture is mainly classified into statistical and structural way. To analyze the nature of texture in the selected biometric modality, we have used state-of-art best texture based algorithms namely LBPV, LPQ, and Gabor. We have adopted ROC method for evaluating model performance, the curve is traced by plotting GAR(Genuine acceptance rate) and FAR(False acceptance rate) at 0.01%, 0.1% and 1% threshold ratings. Area under the curve indicates the classifying power. The ROC curve to the upper left corner indicates the highest performance of the verification rate. The length of feature vector for LBPV and LPQ is 256, and 5076 for Gabor filter (Fig. 2).

The performance of texture-based algorithms on the handvein modality is summarized in Table 2. It can be seen that LPQ feature extraction method performs better than other methods with highest GAR% for different threshold values of FAR%, setting the FAR thresholding value at 1% gives better classification, the LBPV under performs among all texture based algorithms for

Table 2. Performance of different texture feature extraction algorithms for handvein

FAR%	GAR%		
	LBPV	Gabor	LPQ
0.01	5	33.5	26.5
0.1	17	54	38
1	37	74.5	55

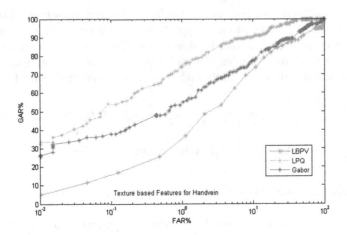

Fig. 1. ROC curve for different modalities on fusion of multiple feature extraction algorithms modality

Table 3. Performance of different texture feature extraction algorithms for finger knuckle print

FAR%	GAR%		
	LBPV	Gabor	LPQ
0.01	10	83	84
0.1	19.5	86	88.5
1	40	90.5	92

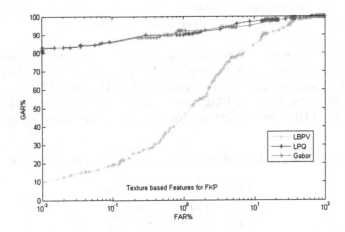

Fig. 2. ROC curve for different texture based feature extraction algorithms to finger knuckle print modality

handvein. Clear graphical representation is given in ROC curve is depicted in Fig. 1 for the results tabulated in Table 2. Table 3 shows the performance of various texture based methods on the FKP. One can observe from the results listed in Table 2, the Gabor feature extraction algorithm performs slightly better than LPQ with highest GAR% at 1% FAR. LBPV feature extraction algorithm under performs with lowest GAR% for different values of FAR%, the ROC curve is plotted in Fig. 1.

5   Conclusion

Handvein and finger Knuckle print modalities are used in recent days and there is much more to explore, the modalities are recognized separately using the performance measures GAR and FAR, the ROC curve is plotted to analyze the system performance graphically. From the empirical study of obtained experiments, we can conclude that LPQ performs better for Handvein modality and Gabor performs better for Finger knuckle print modality at FAR threshold value 1% when compared to other texture descriptors. However, the LBPV features are not much discriminative for both handvein and FKP modality, which has obtained 5% and 10% GAR at 0.1% FAR respectively. From our experimental results it is evident that, for these kind of modalities the LPQ feature extraction algorithms seem to be very much reliable which performs better for handvein as well as FKP. From this one can conclude that understanding of texture based feature methods that are suitable for the particular modality is very much important to have more reliable and accurate biometric authentication system. Our future work would be intended in investigating these modalities subjecting them on subspace and kernel based methods and combining other modalities so as to make it most efficient.

References

1. Huang, D., Zhu, X., Wang, Y., Zhang, D.: Dorsal hand vein recognition via hierarchical combination of texture and shape clues. Neurocomputing **214**(C), 815–828 (2016). ISSN 0925-2312
2. Wang, J., Wang, G., Li, M., Wenkai, D.: Hand vein recognition based on PCET. Optik **127**, 7663–7669 (2016)
3. Rossan, I., Khan, M.H.M.: Impact of changing parameters when preprocessing dorsal hand vein pattern. Procedia Comput. Sci. **32**, 513–520 (2014)
4. Hu, Y.-P., Wang, Z.-Y., Yang, X.-P., Xue, Y.-M.: Hand vein recognition based on the connection lines of reference point and feature point. Infrared Phys. Technol. **62**, 110–114 (2014)
5. Badawi, A.M.: Hand vein biometric verification prototype: a testing performance and patterns similarity. IPCV **14**, 3–9 (2006)
6. Nigam, A., Tiwari, K., Gupta, P.: Multiple texture information fusion for finger knuckleprint authentication system. Neurocomputing **188**, 190–205 (2016)
7. Shariatmadar, Z.S., Faez, K.: Finger-Knuckle-Print recognition performance improvement via multi-instance fusion at the score level. Optik **125**, 908–910 (2014)

8. Zhang, L., Zhang, L., Zhang, D., Guo, Z.: Phase congruency induced local features for finger-knuckle-print recognition. Pattern Recogn. **45**, 2522–2531 (2012)
9. KhellatKihel, S., Abrishambafc, R., Monteiro, J.L., Benyettoua, M.: Multimodal fusion of the finger vein, fingerprint and the finger-knuckle-print using Kernel Fisher analysis. Appl. Soft Comput. **42**, 439–447 (2016)
10. Yadav, V., Bharadi, V., Yadav, S.K.: Feature vector extraction based texture feature using hybrid wavelet type I and II for finger knuckle prints for multi-instance feature fusion. Procedia Comput. Sci. **79**, 351–358 (2016)
11. Raghavendra, R., Imran, M., Rao, A., Hemantha Kumar, G.: Multimodal biometrics: analysis of handvein and palmprint combination used for person verification. In: 2010 3rd International Conference on Emerging Trends in Engineering and Technology (ICETET). IEEE (2010)
12. Ojala, T., Pietikäinen, M., Maaenpaa, T.: Multiresolution gray-scale and rotation invariant texture classification with local binary patterns. IEEE Trans. Pattern Anal. Mach. Intel. Arch. **24**(7), 971–987 (2002)
13. Ojala, T., Pietikäinen, M., Harwood, D.: A comparative study of texture measures with classification based on feature distributions. Pattern Recogn. **29**(1), 51–59 (1996)
14. Ojansivu, V., Heikkila, J.: Proceedings of the 3rd International Conference on Image and Signal Processing, ICISP 2008, pp. 236–243 (2008)
15. Guo, Z., Zhang, L., Zhang, D.: A completed modeling of local binary pattern operator for texture classification. IEEE Trans. Image Process. **19**, 1657–1663 (2010)
16. Lumini, A., Nann, L.: Overview of the combination of biometric matchers. Inf. Fusion **33**, 71–85 (2017). Original Research Article
17. Khandelwal, C.S., Maheshewari, R., Shinde, U.B.: Review paper on applications of principal component analysis in multimodal biometrics system original research article. Procedia Comput. Sci. **92**, 481–486 (2016)
18. Saevanee, H., Clarke, N., Furnell, S., Biscione, V.: Continuous user authentication using multi-modal biometrics. Comput. Secur. **53**, 234–246 (2015). Original Research Article

Face Sketch Matching Using Speed up Robust Feature Descriptor

N.K. Bansode$^{(\boxtimes)}$ and P.K. Sinha

Department of Computer Engineering, College of Engineering, Pune, India
nk_bansode@rediffmail.com, pksinha58@gmail.com

Abstract. In this paper, face sketch and face image matching problem is presented. Matching of the sketch with face is crucial for the law enforcement applications and received attention of the researchers in the recent years. Face sketch and face images are the two different modality representations of the same face. Face sketch is drawn based on description given by the witness when no other source of information is available about the suspect. Matching of the sketch with the face image is challenging problem due to the visual difference between a face sketch and face image. To find the potential suspect, the sketch is compared with the different face images. Speed Up Robust Feature (SURF) descriptor used for matching similarity between sketch and the face image. The result shows that, SURF descriptor gives better result as compared to Scale Invariant Feature Transform descriptor for the viewed and forensic sketches.

Keywords: Face sketch · Scale · Rotation · Invariant · Robust features · Matching

1 Introduction

The human face is a source of the demographic information such as gender, age and emotions. The biometric techniques such as fingerprint, iris scan, speech recognition, signature, hand geometry, DNA analysis, etc. are used for the identification of an individual. Person identification using face biometric requires less assistance as compared to the other biometrics. The human face plays important role in the identification of a person for the law enforcement agencies.

In investigation, matching of face image with the sketch is very important for finding the potential suspect. The forensic sketch and viewed sketch are two types of sketch images used for the identifications. Viewed sketch is drawn by looking at face image, but in forensic sketch, it is generated from the description of the face. In many cases, face image of the suspect is not available and forensic sketch is prepared by the sketch artist [1].

The different methods of sketch generation were developed in the past several years. Methods such as manual, mechanical, feature set generation and automatic sketch generation are used for the sketch drawing. In a manual method, face

© Springer Nature Singapore Pte Ltd. 2017
K.C. Santosh et al. (Eds.): RTIP2R 2016, CCIS 709, pp. 429–439, 2017.
DOI: 10.1007/978-981-10-4859-3_38

sketch is drawn by the sketch artists with the description provided by the witness or victim of the crime. The problem with a manual system is that, there are shortages of the people who can draw a face sketch. The method of the drawing face sketch varies from artist to artist. The sketch produced is limited by the skill set of an artist. Mechanical systems are designed for uniform generation of the face composite. The quality of face composite produced by the mechanical system was poor. The problem with mechanical face composite system was a limited set of the feature for face composite generation. To overcome the problem of the mechanical face composite system, new features set based face composite system are designed. The facial features are extracted from the feature database and face composite is generated.

1.1   Matching Face Sketch and Face Image

Sketches are drawn by the artist that limns facial representation of the suspects face. The sketches are depicted by using two or three types of pencils. When the sketch is ready, it is displayed in the media for somebody familiar with the person in image will identify. The sketch is simply represented with very low-level texture. The sketches are drawn with information provided by the witness which difficult to represent visually. This degrades the sketch recognition rate. Identifying the sketch is a very difficult task due to the several issues with the sketches [11–13, 18].

There is a modality gap in between face sketch and image. The face sketch is depicted by skilled sketch artist based on the appearance description given by witness or victim about the suspect, while the photo (image) is captured by the camera. The visual cue is perceived from the fine and coarse texture features of the face. The fine texture feature of the face includes low contrast details such as wrinkles, flaws and reflection of the face image. The coarse texture include the boundaries of the internal facial features.

The coarse texture features are important for the boundary representation of face features and artist works on these coarse textures. Thus, the coarse texture features may be considered modality invariant features. We have developed a new algorithm for automatic face sketch generation from the face image. The algorithm simulates the artist's process of the face sketch generation. The contributions of this paper are:

- The modality difference present between face sketch and image. Modality invariant features descriptor SURF is used for the similarity matching of face sketch with face image.
- New automatic face sketch generation algorithm is developed for face images.
- The comparisons of face sketch and face image is done using SIFT and SURF feature descriptors for similarity matching.

2   Related Work

The criminal face appearance is described by the witness or victim of the crime and sketch is drawn by the trained artists. Forensic sketch recognition is a challenging problem due to the face information collected from the different resources such as surveillance camera, mobile, or social media sites, etc.

The research on sketch matching mostly based on the viewed sketches. In sketch matching, the photograph is transformed into sketches or vice versa and comparison is done between these images. The different transformation method includes Eigen face transforms, local linear embedding, random fields matching, etc. Brendan F. Klare and Anil Jain [2] used SIFT descriptor with local binary pattern for matching heterogeneous face images. The discriminate projections on the face feature patch are used for matching. SIFT feature descriptor is suitable for sketch matching. The cumulative matching curve is used for accuracy measurement. Brendan F. Klare and Anil K. Jain [3] performed identification of the heterogeneous face using kernel prototype similarities. A framework for heterogeneous face recognition is proposed using nonlinear kernel similarities of the gallery and probe images. The accuracy of the heterogeneous face recognition is improved based on linear transform from probe prototype to the gallery prototype representation.

H.S. Bhatt et al. [6] presented a new technique for comparing sketch and face image. The features from different level of granularity are extracted using extended local binary pattern in the form of circular pattern. Genetic optimization method is then used for weights assignment in the local face region. Hu Han et al. [8] addressed problems of matching sketch composite with the photographs using component based approach. The facial landmarks are detected in face composite and photograph using active shape model. The features of each face component are extracted using multi-scale local binary pattern and similarity score is computed. Finally, all components score fused for sketch and photo image. The performance of the matching improved using a component based approach as compared to commercial systems. J. Choi et al. [9] performed recognition of the sketch and photo image. Modality gap modelling is performed by maximizing co-variance between sketch and face image. They suggested shortage of the face sketch data set for the comparative study. Tiago de Freitas and Sebastien Marcle [14] performed recognition of the face images of heterogeneous types such as face sketch, near infrared images using intern-session variability modelling. The problem with the heterogeneous face recognition is due to the different nature of representation. The Gaussian mixture models are used to model the image inter-session variability. Xiaogang Wang and Xiaoou Tang [16] presented photo retrieval system using face sketches. The photo image and sketch image represent different forms of the image. The image is made of pixel intensity and texture pattern. The sketch image is represented only by the gray scale values. The photo image is converted into a sketch image that is a database of photo image is converted into a database of sketch images. Zhen Lei et al. [19] performed heterogeneous face recognition using coupled discriminant analysis. The coupled discriminant analysis is an effective framework provides improved accuracy for the heterogeneous face recognition.

3 Methodology

Invariant features to the scale and rotation is becoming more important for image recognition. Recently, two types of the image invariant feature are represented using SIFT and SURF descriptors. The feature descriptor should be invariant to the scale, rotation, noise or error in detection and distinctive. These image feature descriptor are described in the following paragraphs.

3.1 Scale Invariant Feature Transform (SIFT) Descriptor

Image feature descriptor Scale Invariant feature Transform (SIFT) was proposed by Lowe [4]. SIFT descriptor generates invariant features to the scale and rotation and affine transform. It has been used for feature extraction from images to compare images of different scale, pose, etc. It consists of the following steps:

(a) Scale space representation by difference of Gaussian
(b) Key point localization and filtering
(c) Orientation assignments and 128 element descriptor.

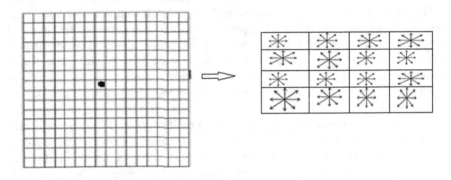

Fig. 1. Representation of scale invariant feature descriptor

The incremented Gaussian blur is used with the original image to create scale space difference of Gaussian. Consider input image I(x, y). Function L(x, y, σ) calculates the scale space of the image and produced using the convolution of Gaussian G(x, y, σ) and I(x,y) in Eq. (2). The scale space difference of the two images is calculated using Gaussian D (x, y, σ) difference of the factor k as given in Eq. (3) [17].

$$G(x,y,\sigma) = \frac{1}{2\pi\sigma^2}e^{\frac{-(x^2+y^2)}{2\sigma^2}} \tag{1}$$

$$L(x,y,\sigma) = G(x,y,\sigma) * I(x,y) \tag{2}$$

$$D(x,y,\sigma) = (G(x,y,k\sigma) - G(x,y,\sigma) * I(x,y) = L(x,y,k\sigma) - L(x,y,\sigma) \tag{3}$$

The image local maxima or minima of D(x, y, σ) for scale space is calculated using above and blow neighbours. The image gradient magnitude m(x, y) and orientation θ(x, y) is given by Eqs. (4) and (5)

$$m(x, y) = \sqrt{((L(x+1, y) - L(x-1, y))^2 + ((L(x, y+1) - L(x, y-1))^2} \quad (4)$$

$$\theta = \tan^{-1} \frac{(L(x, y+1) - L(x, y-1))}{(L(x+1, y) - L(x-1, y))} \quad (5)$$

The key point descriptor and orientation histograms are created on 4×4 regions as shown in Fig. 1. The histogram is represented using 8 directions. The key point descriptor generated vector of 128 elements [15].

3.2 Speed Up Robust Feature (SURF) Descriptor

We have proposed approach for matching face sketch with the facial image based on the Speed Up Robust Feature (SURF) key point matching technique. The SURF detects the features which are scale and rotation invariant, so that the images of the different scales and orientations are compared [5]. It is a robust feature detector and descriptor recently used for different application in the computer vision [7]. The following paragraph describes the steps in the SURF feature descriptor.

3.3 Interest Point Detection

The interest points are the key feature points in the image. The SURF detector finds the bob like structure in the image. To find the bob like structure in the image, the image is convolved with the various Gaussian filters. Hessain-matrix approximation and integral images are used to detect the interest points [10].

3.4 Scale Space Representation

The scale invariant features are detected using the features at the different image scales. The scale spaces of the image are represented by using the pyramid of the images at the different scales. The difference of Gaussian is calculated by subtracting images of the pyramid layers as shown in Fig. 2.

3.5 Orientation Assignment

The process of the orientation assignment involves Harr wavelet response both in x and y axis with the radius 6 s in the neighbourhood of the interest point where, s represents the scale of orientation calculations. The strength of orientation at the interest point is obtained by summing all the responses around the orientation as shown in Fig. 3. The response in the horizontal direction and the vertical direction are summed together and represented in the vector as a local orientation vector.

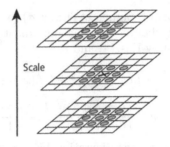

Fig. 2. Scale space representation

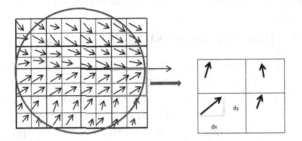

Fig. 3. Orientation assignment

3.6   Feature Descriptor

The feature descriptor of the interest points determines the features using the neighbouring pixels. The descriptor vector contains the pixels in the windows of the size of 20 σ. The square window is divided into the 4×4 regular sub regions. Harr wavelet response in x and y directions are resented by dx and dy respectively. Thus, each sub region contributes to the 4 values in the descriptor vector. The overall descriptor vector length is $4 \times 4 \times 4 = 64$. The resulting feature descriptor is invariant to scale and rotations.

4   Face Sketch Generation Algorithm

We have implemented artists approach for the sketch generation from the face image as shown in Fig. 4. The size of input image used as (256×256) pixels. Face image is pre-processed for eliminating the noise and converted into a grayscale image and then converted into monochrome image. The square grid of 32×32 is placed on input image and it divides the image into several blocks. The size

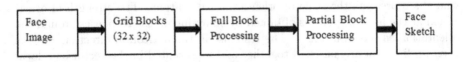

Fig. 4. Face sketch generation system

of each block is 8×8 pixels. The image blocks are divided as a (i) Background blocks (ii) Foreground blocks (iii) Partial blocks. This is simple, an efficient and fast method similar to the artistic style of sketch generation.

Algorithm   *SketchGeneration (Image, Size, BlockSize)*

// This Algorithm generates face sketch from the image
// Image   : input image
// Size   : size of image
// BlockSize   : size of each block in a image
// Output   : sketch of the image
1.   Calculate number of blocks in the image.
                number of blocks =Image Size/BlockSize
2.   Divide image into number of blocks
3.   Call FullBlockProcessing (ImageBlocks)
4.   Call Sketch (PartialBlocks)
5.   End

Function   *FullBlockProcessing (ImageBlocks)*

// This Function process only full background or foreground image blocks
// Input   : ImageBlocks
// Output   : Image with partial blocks
1.   For all the blocks in the image do
2.   If the current full block represents background or foreground
3.   discard this block from the image
4.   End
5.   If the block is partial block
6.   store it in the partial block array
7.   End
8.   End
9.   End

Function   *Sketch (PartialBlocks)*

// This function generates face sketch.
// Input   : PartialBlocks
// Output   : Face sketch
1.   For all partial blocks do
2.   Read each block
3.   For all pixels in the block do
4.   Find the start pixel in the block
5.   Find the nearest neighbour pixel to the previous pixel
6.   If found connect these pixels by line
7.   otherwise select next pixel.
8.   End
9.   End
10.   End
11. End

5   Results and Discussions

In this paper, we have proposed the problem of the face sketch matching with face image. The experiment is performed for matching face sketch with the face image using SURF feature descriptors. We have developed new sketch generation algorithm based on artist skills of drawing the face sketch. The result of the face sketch generation algorithm from face image is shown in Fig. 5.

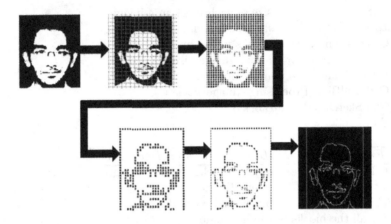

Fig. 5. Face sketch generation

The SIFT and SURF feature descriptor used to obtain a description of the sketch and face image. The Fig. 6 shows matching of the key points of the sketch with the face image. The accuracy of the key points matching is shown in Table 1.

Fig. 6. Key point matching sketch and face image using SURF descriptor

Table 1. Sketch matching result

Sr. no	DataSet	Feature descriptor	Rank accuracy (%)
1	CUHK	SIFT	65.00
2	CUHK	SURF	84.00
3	Caltech	SIFT	68.00
4	Caltech	SURF	92.00

The Cumulative Matching Curve (CMC) is plotted as shown in Fig. 7 for sketch matching for the CUHK sketch database [20] and Caltech dataset [21]. The sketch generation algorithm is used to generate face sketches from the image. The result of the sketch matching with the image is shown in Fig. 8.

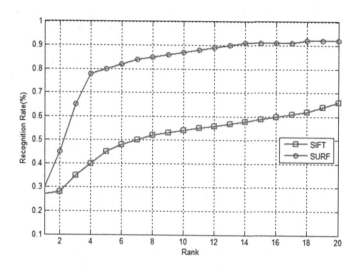

Fig. 7. CMC graph for sketch generation algorithm

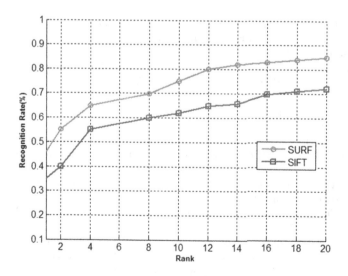

Fig. 8. CMC graph for viewed sketch matching

6 Conclusions

In case of investigation, identification of person in sketch is crucial for the law enforcement to find the potential suspect. The image and sketch comparison is done using the SURF and SIFT feature descriptor algorithm which reduces modality gap between the sketch and face image. In the matching sketch with the image, there would be the maximum number of matching points in the corresponding face sketch and the face image. The result of the face image and viewed sketch matching is shown in Fig. 8. The SURF feature descriptor is more efficient than SIFT feature descriptor of matching sketch with the image.

References

1. Jain, A.K., Klare, B., Park, U.: Face matching and retrieval in forensic applications, multimedia in forensics, security, and intelligence. IEEE Multimedia 19(1), 20 (2012)
2. Klare, B., Jain, A.K.: Sketch to photo matching: a feature-based approach. In: Proceedings of SPIE, Biometric Technology for Human Identification VII, 766702 (2010)
3. Klare, B.F., Jain, A.K.: Heterogeneous face recognition using kernel prototype similarities. IEEE Trans. Pattern Anal. Mach. Intell. 35(66), 1410–1422 (2013)
4. Lowe, D.: Distinctive image features from scale-invariant key points. Int. J. Comput. Vision 60(2), 91–110 (2004)
5. Schmitt, D., McCoy, N.: Object classification and localization using SURF descriptor, pp. 1–5, December 2011
6. Bhatt, H.S., Bhardwaj, S., Singh, R., Vasta, M.: On matching sketches with digital face images. In: Fourth IEEE International Conference on Biometrics: Theory and Applications, September 2010
7. Bay, H., Tuytelaars, T., Van Gool, L.: SURF: Speeded Up Robust Features. Comput. Vis. Image Underst. 110(2), 346–359 (2008)
8. Han, H., Klare, B.F., Bonnen, K., Jain, A.K.: Matching composite sketches to face photos: a component based approach. IEEE Trans. Inf. Forensic Secur. 8(1), 191–204 (2013)
9. Choi, J., Sharma, A., Jacobs, D.W., Davis, L.S.: Data insufficiency in sketch versus photo face recognition. In: Computer Vision and Pattern Recognition Workshop (2012)
10. Li, J., Zang,Y.: Learning SURF cascade for fast and accurate object detection. In: IEEE Conference on Computer Vision and Pattern Recognition, June 2013
11. Suresh ThangaKrishnan, M., Ramar, K.: A survey of forensic sketch matching. IIOAB J. 6, 50–54 (2015)
12. Purkait, P., Chanda, B., Kulkarni, S.: A novel techniques for sketch to photo synthesis. In: International Conference on Computer Vision Graphics and Image Processing (ICVGIP), Chennai, India, December 2010
13. Lahlali, S.E., Sadiq, A., Mbarki, S.: Review of face sketch recognition systems. J. Theoretic Appl. Inf. Technol. 81(2), 255–264 (2015)
14. de Freitas, T., Marcle, S.: Heterogeneous face recognition using intern-session variability modelling. In: IEEE Computer Society Workshop on Biometrics (2016)

15. Liu, T., Kim, S.-H., Lim, S.-K., Lee, H.-S.: Selection of distinctive SIFT based on its distribution on feature space and local classifier for face recognition. Int. Arab J. Inf. Technol. **10**, 1 (2013)
16. Wang, X., Tang, X.: Face photo-sketch synthesis and recognition. IEEE Trans. Pattern Anal. Mach. Intell. **31**(11), 1955–1967 (2009)
17. Ke, Y., Sukthankar, R.: PCA-SIFT: a more distinctive representation for local image descriptor. In: IEEE Computer Society Conference on Computer Vision and Pattern Recognition (CVPR), vol. 2, pp. 506–513 (2004)
18. Li, Z.: Matching forensic sketches to mug shot photos. IEEE Trans. Pattern Anal. Mach. Intell. **33**(3), 639–646 (2011)
19. Lei, Z., Liao, S., Jain, A.K., Li, S.Z.: Coupled discriminant analysis for heterogeneous face recognition. IEEE Trans. Inf. Forensic Secur. **7**(6), 1707–1716 (2012)
20. http://mmlab.ie.cuhk.edu.hk/archive/facesketch.html
21. http://www.vision.caltech.edu/html-files/archive.html

Enhanced Gray Scale Skeletonization of Fingerprint Ridges Using Parallel Algorithm

Shoba Dyre$^{(\boxtimes)}$ and C.P. Sumathi

Department of Computer Science, SDNB Vaishnav College for Women,
Chennai, India
shobales14@gmail.com, drcpsumathi@gmail.com

Abstract. Thinning of fingerprint ridges plays a vital role in fingerprint identification systems as it simplifies the subsequent processing steps like fingerprint classification and feature extraction. In this paper, we analyze some of the parallel thinning algorithms and have proposed a methodology for skeletonization of fingerprint ridges directly on gray scale images as significant amount of information and features are lost during the binarization process. This algorithm is based on conditionally eroding the gray level ridges iteratively until a one pixel thick ridge is obtained. Refinement procedures have also been proposed to improve the quality of ridge skeleton. Experiments conducted on sample fingerprint images collected using an optical fingerprint Reader exhibit desirable features of the proposed approach.

Keywords: Gray scale image · Fingerprint · Skeletonization · Parallel algorithm · Iterative

1 Introduction

Automatic fingerprint recognition has received considerable attention over the past decades as fingerprint is one of the most popular and reliable methods used for personal identification. A fingerprint is composed of a pattern of interleaved ridges and valleys [1] as shown in Fig. 1. As fingerprint based applications are mostly real time, they require faster algorithms for processing. Hence it is useful to convert the original image data to a more compact representation to remove redundant information as much as possible and therefore fingerprint ridge skeletonization becomes an essential step in the recognition process for subsequent steps. Most fingerprint recognition systems are based on minutiae matching [1] (i.e.) ridge endings and ridge bifurcations and hence extraction of reliable minutiae relies heavily on the quality of the ridge skeleton.

Ridge skeletons are obtained by the application of thinning reduction operator. The result of skeletonization using thinning algorithms should satisfy the following conditions [1]:

1. Preserve topological characteristics (i.e.) doesn't cause disconnections or create holes.

© Springer Nature Singapore Pte Ltd. 2017
K.C. Santosh et al. (Eds.): RTIP2R 2016, CCIS 709, pp. 440–449, 2017.
DOI: 10.1007/978-981-10-4859-3_39

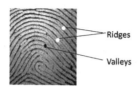

Fig. 1. Ridges and valleys in a fingerprint image

2. Preserve geometry (i.e.) aligned to medial axis and retain original shape.
3. Single pixel wide lines and curves.
4. Preserve end points to sufficiently represent the ridge shape.

Most of the proposed methods work on the binarized version of fingerprint images [3,4]. The methodology proposed in this paper for gray-scale skeletonization of fingerprint ridges is motivated by the consideration that a significant amount of information is lost during the binarization process. Though there are many thinning algorithms proposed in the literature [5,10], not all are suitable for fingerprint images. A fingerprint image of low quality due to factors such as different properties of sensors, temporary or permanent cuts and bruises in the skin creates a large number of false minutiae. The performance of distance transform algorithm proposed in [5] based on Pseudo distance map for gray scale images is not satisfactory for fingerprint images. The results of the thinning algorithms proposed in [7,12,13] are not single pixel wide. The parallel algorithm criteria for thinning specified in [8] exhibit discontinuity along the ridges. The gray scale fingerprint thinning algorithm proposed in [9] assumes that the gray intensity is minimum towards the center of the ridges, but in reality it is not so.

In this work, a novel approach to obtain gray-scale fingerprint ridge skeleton has been proposed by applying the parallel criteria specified in [6] with refinement procedures to improve the quality of ridge skeleton. The outputs of various existing parallel thinning algorithms in [6–8,13] and the proposed method applied on real gray scale fingerprint images have been analyzed and compared.

Section 2 presents some definitions and notations used throughout the paper. Section 3 is devoted to presenting the proposed gray scale ridge skeletonization methodology. Experimental results of the proposed sketonization method in comparison with other methods is shown in Sect. 4 and conclusions are presented in Sect. 5.

2   Definitions and Preliminary Concepts

Definitions and concepts used in this work are presented here [12]. An input image is represented by a matrix, where entries are gray intensities of the image ranging from 0 to 255. Let S be a set of non-zero pixels.

Definition 1. *A pixel P has four neighbors denoted as P2, P4, P6, and P8 in Fig. 2. These points are called 4-neighbors of P. The pixel P has four diagonal neighbors denoted as P1, P3, P5, and P7 in Fig. 2. These, together with the four neighbors, are called 8-neighbors of P.*

P1 (i-1,j-1)	P2 (i-1,j)	P3 (i-1,j+1)
P8 (i,j-1)	P (i,j)	P4 (i,j+1)
P7 (i+1,j-1)	P6 (i+1,j)	P5 (i+1,j+1)

Fig. 2. 8-neighbors of a pixel P in 3 × 3 template

Definition 2. *Two non-zero pixels P and Q are said to be 8-connected (4-connected) if a sequence of pixels p_0 (=P), p_1,.......p_n (=Q) exists such that each p_i is an 8-neighbor (4-neighbor) of $p_{i-1}(1 \leq i \leq n)$ and all p_i have non-zero values.*

Definition 3. *Each set of pixels defined by 8-connectedness (4-connectedness) is called an 8-connected component (4-connected component).*

Definition 4. *A non-zero pixel P is deletable from S, if its removal preserves connectivity of S.*

3 Proposed Thinning Method

In many existing Fingerprint authentication systems, the fingerprint image is binarized before skeletonization. The proposed method works directly on gray scale fingerprint images.

This section provides detailed description of the proposed methodology for fingerprint ridge skeletonization using parallel iterative thinning algorithm [6] that has been modified to work directly on grayscale fingerprint images. Refinement procedures have also been proposed to enhance the quality of the ridge skeleton to remove undesirable artifacts to be more suitable for further processing like classification and feature extraction. Figure 3 shows the steps involved in the proposed thinning process.

3.1 Segmentation and Enhancement

The segmentation and enhancement of the gray-scale fingerprint image are carried out using the method discussed in [2]. The fingerprint image consists of an area of interest that has ridges and valleys of the fingerprint impression. Segmentation is the process of extracting the foreground region from the background. A method that is based on gray intensity variance level is used to segment the foreground from the background.

The fingerprint image is then enhanced using Gaussian band pass filter in the frequency domain [2]. This is done to reduce noise and improve the legibility of the fingerprint.

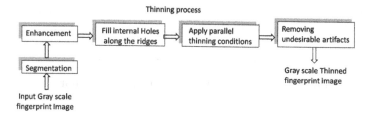

Fig. 3. Overview of the proposed ridge skeletonization process

3.2   Filling Holes Along the Ridges

Due to different properties of fingerprint sensors and the variations in the quality of fingerprints, the gray-scale intensity along the ridges may be characterized by regional minima or an area of dark pixels that are not connected to the boundary of the ridge called isolated holes. Such unwanted holes cause spurious lakes in the thinned image as shown in Fig. 4(a) and hence should not be present. This step is to fill any internal holes before applying the thinning criteria to eliminate the spurious lakes in the output ridge skeleton. Intensity values of dark area that are surrounded by lighter areas are replaced by the mean intensity levels of the surrounding pixels. Most of the algorithms proposed in the literature are based on flood filling algorithm or morphological operations. Using flood filling algorithm more than one connected components of dark pixels as in Fig. 4(c) cannot be tracked.

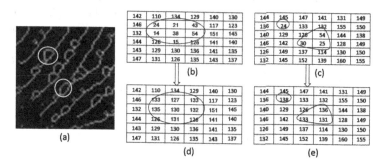

Fig. 4. (a) Thinned fingerprint image with lakes (b) one connected component or hole (c) two connected components or holes (d) and (e) dark pixels replaced

In the proposed algorithm, possible isolated holes or points are tracked using an overlapping pixel window of size w × w that moves from top left to bottom right of the segmented fingerprint image. The size of the window is chosen based on the image features. A threshold t (110 is used in this work) is used to identify dark pixels. One or more areas of dark pixels found within a window of fully bounded light intensity pixels, are replaced by the mean value of the light pixels in the neighborhood as shown in Fig. 4(d) and (e). Using this method more than one regional minima or connected components can be identified.

$$I(i, j) = \text{mean}\{n_k \mid k = 1, 2, \ldots, 8\}$$

where I(i,j) is a dark pixel, n_k are the pixels in the 8-neighborhood of the dark pixel and $n_k \geq t$.

3.3   Gray Scale Parallel Thinning Algorithm for Ridge Skeletonization

The proposed thinning algorithm is defined over gray intensity valued fingerprint image. The image exhibits very low gray-scale intensities in the background and valleys. Hence a threshold value is chosen to classify the pixels as ridge (valley) pixel if its gray value is larger (smaller) than the value. Valley pixels are encoded as zero while the ridges maintain same gray-scale intensities. The gray level ridges are eroded iteratively using parallel reduction operators until a one pixel thick ridge is obtained.

As speed and simplicity of operations is utmost important in fingerprint recognition systems, parallel thinning criteria that allows simultaneous deletion of many pixels at a time is used. It is based on two sub-iterations algorithm proposed in [6] to obtain single pixel ridge pattern. It has been modified to work directly on gray-scale fingerprint image. For pixel deletion, a 3×3 template representing the 8-neighborhood of the center non-zero pixel P is used as shown in Fig. 2.

Symbols $\neg$, $\wedge$ and $\vee$ are used to refer different logical operators which are complement, AND and OR, respectively. Let C(P) be the number of distinct 8-connected components of non-zeros in its neighborhood. C(P) counts the number of occurrences of a side zero with a non-zero in at least one of the two adjacent pixels in the clockwise direction around P's eight-neighborhood. It takes on values over the range 0 to 4.

N(P) is an operator that is used to remove redundant pixels and at the same time to preserve end points.

$$N(P) = min(N1(P), N2(P)) \tag{1}$$

where

$$N1(P) = (P1 > 0 \vee P2 > 0) + (P3 > 0 \vee P4 > 0) + (P5 > 0 \vee P6 > 0)$$
$$+ (P7 > 0 \vee P8 > 0) \tag{2}$$

and

$$N2(P) = (P2 > 0 \vee P3 > 0) + (P4 > 0 \vee P5 > 0) + (P6 > 0 \vee P7 > 0)$$
$$+ (P8 > 0 \vee P1 > 0) \tag{3}$$

The pixel P is deleted iff all of the following conditions are satisfied [6]:

1. $C(P) = 1$ (preserves skeleton connectivity)
2. $2 \leq N(P) \leq 3$
3. Apply one of the following
   (i) $(P2 > 0 \vee P3 > 0 \vee \neg(P5 > 0)) \wedge P4 > 0$ (for odd numbered iteration checking and deleting north and east boundary pixels i.e. P2 to P5)
   (or)
   (ii) $(P6 > 0 \vee P7 > 0 \vee \neg(P1 > 0)) \wedge P8 > 0$ (for even numbered iteration checking and deleting south and west boundary pixels i.e. P6 to P8 and P1)

$N1(P)$ and $N2(P)$ each break the ordered set of P's neighboring pixels into four pairs of adjoining pixels and count the number of pairs which contain one or two non-zeros [6]. The neighbourhood criteria for deletion of pixels n the odd iteration is given by Fig. 5(a) and (b) as proposed in [6].

Thinning of an object proceeds by successively removing in distinct iterations north and east, and then south and west boundary pixels. The algorithm stops when there are no more pixels to be deleted. The output of a fingerprint segment as a result of thinning is shown in Fig. 5(d).

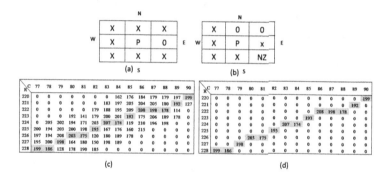

Fig. 5. (a) and (b) Neighborhood conditions required for deletion of P in odd iterations (symbol X represents 0 or non-zero) (c) segment of a ridge in the input fingerprint image (d) output of the segment as a result of thinning

3.4   Refinement Procedure

On completion of the thinning process, many unwanted isolated spurs and ridge-sprawled spurs were visible as seen in Fig. 6(a) and this may lead to the detection of many spurious features in the subsequent steps. Some techniques have been proposed to remove false minutiae after thinning as in [11,15]. These existing works have proposed separate algorithms to remove different artifacts. Hence, to reduce computational complexity, a one pass algorithm is proposed to eliminate those artifacts to improve the quality of the ridge skeleton before classification or feature extraction.

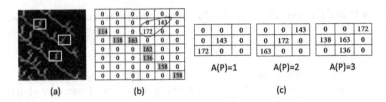

Fig. 6. (a) Spurs in the thinned ridge skeleton (b) pixel representation of a ridge line and a spur (c) values of A(P)

An operator $A(P)$ is defined using the 3×3 neighborhood template for the non-zero center pixel P. Move all around the neighborhood of a non-zero pixel in the clockwise direction and count the number of background to non-zero pixel transitions to obtain $A(P)$. Figure 6(c) shows the values of $A(P)$.

(i) $A(P) = 1$ indicates that it is an endpoint.
(ii) $A(P) = 2$ indicates it is an intermediate point on the ridge line.
(iii) $A(P) = 3$ indicates it has encountered another ridge line.

A threshold value n is chosen as the maximum length (10 in this work) of the island or spur. It is appropriately chosen to be less than the average distance between the thinned ridges.

Steps of the proposed one-pass refinement procedure are as follows:

1. For each ridge ending point in the thinned image take a window of size w × w (3×3 in this work).
2. n = 1.
3. Store the position of the ridge ending point and place it at the center of window.
4. Move in the direction of connected branches of the end point and calculate A(P) by placing the connected point at the center of the window.
5. Preserve its pixel coordinates.
   (a) if A(P) = 1, another end point has been encountered. Delete all pixels along the connected path, go to step 1
   (b) if A(P) = 2 and $n < 10$, go to step 4
   (c) if A(P) = 3, another ridge line has been encountered. Delete all pixels along the connected path, go to step 1

Using the proposed algorithm spurs, isolated points and islands can be eliminated to obtain a good quality ridge skeleton for subsequent processing steps.

4   Performance Evaluation and Experimental Results

The performance of our proposed technique is tested on Fingerprint images collected from heterogeneous population that includes manual workers and people from different age groups using an optical Fingerprint Reader. The size of each image is 480×320 and are stored as 8-bit gray scale images. Four parallel thinning algorithms [6–8,13] and the proposed methodology were applied on the fingerprint images and its performance is evaluated in terms of thinning rate, data reduction efficiency/computational cost and the quality of skeleton obtained.

1. Thinning Rate (TR): The degree to which an image can be thinned is measured in terms of thinning rate based on finding triangles to remove excessive pixels. This principle is used by this equation [6]:

$$TTC = \sum_{i=1}^{n} \sum_{j=1}^{m} TC(P[i][j]) \tag{4}$$

where:
TTC stands for total triangle count [14], n and m are dimensions of fingerprint image, P[i][j] is non-zero pixel with coordinates (i, j), TC is function which counts number of non-zero triangles which can be created from P[i][j] and its neighboring pixels.

TR is defined as follows:

$$TR = 1 - \frac{TTC_T}{TTC_O} \tag{5}$$

where TTC_T stands for total triangle count of thinned image and TTC_O stands for total triangle count of original image.

2. Measure of Computational cost m_d: A measure to evaluate both the data reduction efficiency and the computational cost is defined as [12]

$$m_d = min[1, \frac{Area[S] - Area[S_m]}{n \times Area[S]}] \tag{6}$$

where n is the number of parallel operations required for convergence, S is the original input fingerprint image and S_m the thinned image. This measure has a value between 0 and 1. A large value indicates high efficiency.

Table 1. Performance comparison of various parallel thinning methods

Method	Total Triangle Count (TTC)	Thinning Rate (TR)	Computational Cost (m_d)
Original image	346383		
Zhang-Suen [13]	5588	0.9839	0.0486
Guo-Hall [6]	336	0.9990	0.0741
Kwon J. [8]	487	0.9983	0.0452
Zhang-Wang [7]	5975	0.9828	0.0486
Proposed method	182	0.9995	0.0759

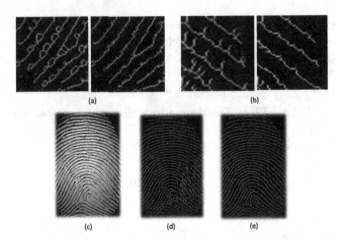

Fig. 7. (a) Before and after applying the module to fill holes (b) before and after applying the module to remove spurs after thinning (c) original image (d) thinned fingerprint image with spurs (e) ridge skeleton after applying refinement procedure

3. Quality of the thinned skeleton: The thinned gray scale ridges are evaluated based on connectivity and spurious branches. For fingerprint systems, preservation of fingerprint patterns is very crucial as disconnected ridges and spurious branches produce false features.

A window size of 6×6 is used to track region of dark pixels along the ridges to eliminate lakes in the output skeleton. Table 1 shows the results of the two performance measures TR and m_d obtained experimentally using Eqs. (5) and (6) by applying various existing parallel thinning algorithms available in the literature [6–8,13] along with the proposed method on the sample Fingerprint images implemented in MATLAB. The proposed method exhibit ideal characteristics in terms of connectivity, unitary thickness and superior parallel computational speed. The experimental results of the proposed gray scale ridge skeletonization method is shown in Fig. 7.

5   Conclusion

The main contribution of this paper is to propose a fingerprint ridge skeletonization methodology that works directly on gray intensity fingerprint images. Parallel thinning conditions modified to work on gray scale images and refinement procedures have been combined to obtain good quality gray intensity skeleton. Performance analysis and results demonstrate that the proposed method exhibit ideal characteristics in terms of connectivity, unitary thickness and superior parallel computational speed. The ridge skeletons are useful for extracting minutiae for fingerprint matching.

References

1. Maltoni, D., Maio, D., Jain, A.K., Prabhakar, S.: Handbook of Fingerprint Recognition. Springer, Heidelberg (2009)
2. Dyre, S., Sumathi, C.P.: Hybrid approach to enhancing fingerprint images using filters in the frequency domain. In: IEEE International Conference on Computational Intelligence and Computing Research (ICCIC), pp. 1–6 (2014)
3. Dacheng, X., Li, B., Nijholt, A.: A novel approach based on PCNNs template for fingerprint image thinning. In: Eighth IEEE/ACIS International Conference on Computer and Information Science, pp. 115–119 (2009)
4. Fang, B., Wen, H., Liu, R.-Z., Tang, Y.Y.: A new fingerprint thinning algorithm. In: 2010 Chinese Conference on Pattern Recognition (CCPR). IEEE (2010)
5. Ablameyko, S., Uchida, S., Nedzved, A.: Gray-scale thinning by using a pseudo-distance map. In: 18th International Conference on Pattern Recognition, Hong Kong, vol. 2, pp. 239–242 (2006)
6. Guo, Z., Hall, R.: Parallel thinning with two sub iteration algorithms. Commun. ACM **32**, 359–373 (1989)
7. Zhang, Y.Y., Wang, P.S.P.: A modified parallel thinning algorithm. In: 9th International Conference on Pattern Recognition, Rome (1988)
8. Kwon, J.: Improved parallel thinning algorithm to obtain unit - width skeleton. Int. J. Multimedia Appl. (IJMA) **5**(2), 1–14 (2013)
9. Saleh, A.M., Bahaa Eldin, A.M., Wahdan, A.-M.A.: A modified thinning algorithm for fingerprint identification systems. In: International Conference on Computer Engineering and Systems, Cairo, pp. 371–376 (2009)
10. Rockett, P.I.: An improved rotation-invariant thinning algorithm. IEEE Trans. Pattern Anal. Mach. Intell. **27**(10), 1671–1674 (2005)
11. Tariq, A., Akram, M.U., Nasir, S., Arshad, R.: Fingerprint image postprocessing using windowing technique. In: Campilho, A., Kamel, M. (eds.) ICIAR 2008. LNCS, vol. 5112, pp. 915–924. Springer, Heidelberg (2008). doi:10.1007/978-3-540-69812-8_91
12. Jang, B.K., Chin, R.T.: One pass parallel thinning, analysis, properties and quantitative evaluation. IEEE Trans. Pattern Anal. Mach. Intell. **14**(11), 1129–1140 (1992)
13. Zhang, T.Y., Suen, C.Y.: A fast thinning algorithm for thinning digital patterns. Commun. ACM **27**(3), 236–239 (1984)
14. Peter, T.: Performance measurements of thinning algorithms. J. Inf. Control Manag. Syst. **6**(2), 125–132 (2008)
15. Farina, A., Kovacs-Vajna, Z.M., Leone, A.: Fingerprint minutiae extraction from skeletonized binary images. Pattern Recogn. **32**, 877–889 (1999)

Author Index